Lecture Notes in Computer Science 13331

More information about this series at https://link.springer.com/bookseries/558

Qin Gao · Jia Zhou (Eds.)

Human Aspects of IT for the Aged Population

Technology in Everyday Living

8th International Conference, ITAP 2022
Held as Part of the 24th HCI International Conference, HCII 2022
Virtual Event, June 26 – July 1, 2022
Proceedings, Part II

Editors
Qin Gao
Tsinghua University
Beijing, China

Jia Zhou
Chongqing University
Chongqing, China

ISSN 0302-9743 ISSN 1611-3349 (electronic)
Lecture Notes in Computer Science
ISBN 978-3-031-05653-6 ISBN 978-3-031-05654-3 (eBook)
https://doi.org/10.1007/978-3-031-05654-3

This Springer imprint is published by the registered company Springer Nature Switzerland AG
The registered company address is: Gewerbestrasse 11, 6330 Cham, Switzerland

Foreword

Human-computer interaction (HCI) is acquiring an ever-increasing scientific and industrial importance, as well as having more impact on people's everyday life, as an ever-growing number of human activities are progressively moving from the physical to the digital world. This process, which has been ongoing for some time now, has been dramatically accelerated by the COVID-19 pandemic. The HCI International (HCII) conference series, held yearly, aims to respond to the compelling need to advance the exchange of knowledge and research and development efforts on the human aspects of design and use of computing systems.

The 24th International Conference on Human-Computer Interaction, HCI International 2022 (HCII 2022), was planned to be held at the Gothia Towers Hotel and Swedish Exhibition & Congress Centre, Göteborg, Sweden, during June 26 to July 1, 2022. Due to the COVID-19 pandemic and with everyone's health and safety in mind, HCII 2022 was organized and run as a virtual conference. It incorporated the 21 thematic areas and affiliated conferences listed on the following page.

A total of 5583 individuals from academia, research institutes, industry, and governmental agencies from 88 countries submitted contributions, and 1276 papers and 275 posters were included in the proceedings to appear just before the start of the conference. The contributions thoroughly cover the entire field of human-computer interaction, addressing major advances in knowledge and effective use of computers in a variety of application areas. These papers provide academics, researchers, engineers, scientists, practitioners, and students with state-of-the-art information on the most recent advances in HCI. The volumes constituting the set of proceedings to appear before the start of the conference are listed in the following pages.

The HCI International (HCII) conference also offers the option of 'Late Breaking Work' which applies both for papers and posters, and the corresponding volume(s) of the proceedings will appear after the conference. Full papers will be included in the 'HCII 2022 - Late Breaking Papers' volumes of the proceedings to be published in the Springer LNCS series, while 'Poster Extended Abstracts' will be included as short research papers in the 'HCII 2022 - Late Breaking Posters' volumes to be published in the Springer CCIS series.

I would like to thank the Program Board Chairs and the members of the Program Boards of all thematic areas and affiliated conferences for their contribution and support towards the highest scientific quality and overall success of the HCI International 2022 conference; they have helped in so many ways, including session organization, paper reviewing (single-blind review process, with a minimum of two reviews per submission) and, more generally, acting as goodwill ambassadors for the HCII conference.

This conference would not have been possible without the continuous and unwavering support and advice of Gavriel Salvendy, founder, General Chair Emeritus, and Scientific Advisor. For his outstanding efforts, I would like to express my appreciation to Abbas Moallem, Communications Chair and Editor of HCI International News.

June 2022 Constantine Stephanidis

HCI International 2022 Thematic Areas and Affiliated Conferences

Thematic Areas

- HCI: Human-Computer Interaction
- HIMI: Human Interface and the Management of Information

Affiliated Conferences

- EPCE: 19th International Conference on Engineering Psychology and Cognitive Ergonomics
- AC: 16th International Conference on Augmented Cognition
- UAHCI: 16th International Conference on Universal Access in Human-Computer Interaction
- CCD: 14th International Conference on Cross-Cultural Design
- SCSM: 14th International Conference on Social Computing and Social Media
- VAMR: 14th International Conference on Virtual, Augmented and Mixed Reality
- DHM: 13th International Conference on Digital Human Modeling and Applications in Health, Safety, Ergonomics and Risk Management
- DUXU: 11th International Conference on Design, User Experience and Usability
- C&C: 10th International Conference on Culture and Computing
- DAPI: 10th International Conference on Distributed, Ambient and Pervasive Interactions
- HCIBGO: 9th International Conference on HCI in Business, Government and Organizations
- LCT: 9th International Conference on Learning and Collaboration Technologies
- ITAP: 8th International Conference on Human Aspects of IT for the Aged Population
- AIS: 4th International Conference on Adaptive Instructional Systems
- HCI-CPT: 4th International Conference on HCI for Cybersecurity, Privacy and Trust
- HCI-Games: 4th International Conference on HCI in Games
- MobiTAS: 4th International Conference on HCI in Mobility, Transport and Automotive Systems
- AI-HCI: 3rd International Conference on Artificial Intelligence in HCI
- MOBILE: 3rd International Conference on Design, Operation and Evaluation of Mobile Communications

List of Conference Proceedings Volumes Appearing Before the Conference

1. LNCS 13302, Human-Computer Interaction: Theoretical Approaches and Design Methods (Part I), edited by Masaaki Kurosu
2. LNCS 13303, Human-Computer Interaction: Technological Innovation (Part II), edited by Masaaki Kurosu
3. LNCS 13304, Human-Computer Interaction: User Experience and Behavior (Part III), edited by Masaaki Kurosu
4. LNCS 13305, Human Interface and the Management of Information: Visual and Information Design (Part I), edited by Sakae Yamamoto and Hirohiko Mori
5. LNCS 13306, Human Interface and the Management of Information: Applications in Complex Technological Environments (Part II), edited by Sakae Yamamoto and Hirohiko Mori
6. LNAI 13307, Engineering Psychology and Cognitive Ergonomics, edited by Don Harris and Wen-Chin Li
7. LNCS 13308, Universal Access in Human-Computer Interaction: Novel Design Approaches and Technologies (Part I), edited by Margherita Antona and Constantine Stephanidis
8. LNCS 13309, Universal Access in Human-Computer Interaction: User and Context Diversity (Part II), edited by Margherita Antona and Constantine Stephanidis
9. LNAI 13310, Augmented Cognition, edited by Dylan D. Schmorrow and Cali M. Fidopiastis
10. LNCS 13311, Cross-Cultural Design: Interaction Design Across Cultures (Part I), edited by Pei-Luen Patrick Rau
11. LNCS 13312, Cross-Cultural Design: Applications in Learning, Arts, Cultural Heritage, Creative Industries, and Virtual Reality (Part II), edited by Pei-Luen Patrick Rau
12. LNCS 13313, Cross-Cultural Design: Applications in Business, Communication, Health, Well-being, and Inclusiveness (Part III), edited by Pei-Luen Patrick Rau
13. LNCS 13314, Cross-Cultural Design: Product and Service Design, Mobility and Automotive Design, Cities, Urban Areas, and Intelligent Environments Design (Part IV), edited by Pei-Luen Patrick Rau
14. LNCS 13315, Social Computing and Social Media: Design, User Experience and Impact (Part I), edited by Gabriele Meiselwitz
15. LNCS 13316, Social Computing and Social Media: Applications in Education and Commerce (Part II), edited by Gabriele Meiselwitz
16. LNCS 13317, Virtual, Augmented and Mixed Reality: Design and Development (Part I), edited by Jessie Y. C. Chen and Gino Fragomeni
17. LNCS 13318, Virtual, Augmented and Mixed Reality: Applications in Education, Aviation and Industry (Part II), edited by Jessie Y. C. Chen and Gino Fragomeni

18. LNCS 13319, Digital Human Modeling and Applications in Health, Safety, Ergonomics and Risk Management: Anthropometry, Human Behavior, and Communication (Part I), edited by Vincent G. Duffy
19. LNCS 13320, Digital Human Modeling and Applications in Health, Safety, Ergonomics and Risk Management: Health, Operations Management, and Design (Part II), edited by Vincent G. Duffy
20. LNCS 13321, Design, User Experience, and Usability: UX Research, Design, and Assessment (Part I), edited by Marcelo M. Soares, Elizabeth Rosenzweig and Aaron Marcus
21. LNCS 13322, Design, User Experience, and Usability: Design for Emotion, Well-being and Health, Learning, and Culture (Part II), edited by Marcelo M. Soares, Elizabeth Rosenzweig and Aaron Marcus
22. LNCS 13323, Design, User Experience, and Usability: Design Thinking and Practice in Contemporary and Emerging Technologies (Part III), edited by Marcelo M. Soares, Elizabeth Rosenzweig and Aaron Marcus
23. LNCS 13324, Culture and Computing, edited by Matthias Rauterberg
24. LNCS 13325, Distributed, Ambient and Pervasive Interactions: Smart Environments, Ecosystems, and Cities (Part I), edited by Norbert A. Streitz and Shin'ichi Konomi
25. LNCS 13326, Distributed, Ambient and Pervasive Interactions: Smart Living, Learning, Well-being and Health, Art and Creativity (Part II), edited by Norbert A. Streitz and Shin'ichi Konomi
26. LNCS 13327, HCI in Business, Government and Organizations, edited by Fiona Fui-Hoon Nah and Keng Siau
27. LNCS 13328, Learning and Collaboration Technologies: Designing the Learner and Teacher Experience (Part I), edited by Panayiotis Zaphiris and Andri Ioannou
28. LNCS 13329, Learning and Collaboration Technologies: Novel Technological Environments (Part II), edited by Panayiotis Zaphiris and Andri Ioannou
29. LNCS 13330, Human Aspects of IT for the Aged Population: Design, Interaction and Technology Acceptance (Part I), edited by Qin Gao and Jia Zhou
30. LNCS 13331, Human Aspects of IT for the Aged Population: Technology in Everyday Living (Part II), edited by Qin Gao and Jia Zhou
31. LNCS 13332, Adaptive Instructional Systems, edited by Robert A. Sottilare and Jessica Schwarz
32. LNCS 13333, HCI for Cybersecurity, Privacy and Trust, edited by Abbas Moallem
33. LNCS 13334, HCI in Games, edited by Xiaowen Fang
34. LNCS 13335, HCI in Mobility, Transport and Automotive Systems, edited by Heidi Krömker
35. LNAI 13336, Artificial Intelligence in HCI, edited by Helmut Degen and Stavroula Ntoa
36. LNCS 13337, Design, Operation and Evaluation of Mobile Communications, edited by Gavriel Salvendy and June Wei
37. CCIS 1580, HCI International 2022 Posters - Part I, edited by Constantine Stephanidis, Margherita Antona and Stavroula Ntoa
38. CCIS 1581, HCI International 2022 Posters - Part II, edited by Constantine Stephanidis, Margherita Antona and Stavroula Ntoa

39. CCIS 1582, HCI International 2022 Posters - Part III, edited by Constantine Stephanidis, Margherita Antona and Stavroula Ntoa
40. CCIS 1583, HCI International 2022 Posters - Part IV, edited by Constantine Stephanidis, Margherita Antona and Stavroula Ntoa

http://2022.hci.international/proceedings

Preface

The 8th International Conference on Human Aspects of IT for the Aged Population (ITAP 2022) was part of HCI International 2022. The ITAP conference addresses the design, adaptation, and use of IT technologies targeted to older people in order to counterbalance ability changes due to age, support cognitive, physical, and social activities, and maintain independent living and quality of life.

A strong and unique theme of this year's proceedings is the role and impact of information technologies in older people's life during the COVID-19 pandemic. Researchers from all over the world shared their findings on how older people accepted new technologies, including those applications specific to this special period, how they used new technologies to stay informed and connected during lockdown, and what the experience of this intense term reveals for the design and development of technologies to provide more reliable and resilient support for older people. Another emerging research area concerns innovative ways to involve older people in the design process to ensure that their needs and requirements are adequately elicited and properly addressed. Researchers continue to experiment on innovation and design of smart homes, robots, and VR/AR applications for older people, and the design of voice-based AI has received notable research attention. In addition to supporting older people's health and safety, enhancing social connections, and facilitating daily life activities, this years' proceedings also discuss how technologies can help older people to expand their life experience by bridging the gap between virtual and physical worlds, and how the wide adoption of information technologies has influenced intergenerational dynamics, which brings about further cultural and societal impact.

Two volumes of the HCII 2022 proceedings are dedicated to this year's edition of the ITAP conference, entitled Human Aspects of IT for the Aged Population: Design, Interaction, and Technology Acceptance (Part I) and Human Aspects of IT for the Aged Population: Technology in Everyday Living (Part II). The first focuses on topics related to design and gamification for aging; mobile, wearable and multimodal interaction for aging; and social media use and digital literacy of the elderly, as well as technology acceptance and adoption and related barriers and facilitators for older adults, while the second focuses on topics related to intelligent environments for daily activities support, health and wellbeing technologies for the elderly, and communication and social interaction for older adults.

Papers of these volumes are included for publication after a minimum of two single-blind reviews from the members of the ITAP Program Board or, in some cases, from members of the Program Boards of other affiliated conferences. We would like to thank all of them for their invaluable contribution, support, and efforts.

June 2022

Qin Gao
Jia Zhou

8th International Conference on Human Aspects of IT for the Aged Population (ITAP 2022)

Program Board Chairs: **Qin Gao**, Tsinghua University, China and **Jia Zhou**, Chongqing University, China

- Inês Amaral, University of Coimbra, Portugal
- Ning An, Hefei University of Technology, China
- Maria José Brites, Lusófona University, Portugal
- Alan H. S. Chan, City University of Hong Kong, Hong Kong
- Honglin Chen, Eastern Finland University, Finland
- Hongtu Chen, Harvard Medical School, USA
- Loredana Ivan, National University of Political Studies and Public Administration, Romania
- Chaiwoo Lee, MIT, USA
- Hai-Ning Liang, Xi'an Jiaotong-Liverpool University, China
- Chi-Hung Lo, Tunghai University, Taiwan
- Eugene Loos, Utrecht University, The Netherlands
- Xinggang Luo, Hangzhou Dianzi University, China
- Yan Luximon, Hong Kong Polytechnic University, Hong Kong
- Lourdes Moreno Lopez, Universidad Carlos III de Madrid, Spain
- Simone Mulargia, Lumsa University, Italy
- Karen Renaud, University of Strathclyde, UK
- Wang-Chin Tsai, National Yunlin University of Science and Technology, Taiwan
- Ana Isabel Veloso, University of Aveiro, Portugal
- Nadine Vigouroux, University of Toulouse, France
- Konstantinos Votis, CERTH/ITI, Greece
- Yuxiang (Chris) Zhao, Nanjing University of Science and Technology, China

The full list with the Program Board Chairs and the members of the Program Boards of all thematic areas and affiliated conferences is available online at

http://www.hci.international/board-members-2022.php

HCI International 2023

The 25th International Conference on Human-Computer Interaction, HCI International 2023, will be held jointly with the affiliated conferences at the AC Bella Sky Hotel and Bella Center, Copenhagen, Denmark, 23–28 July 2023. It will cover a broad spectrum of themes related to human-computer interaction, including theoretical issues, methods, tools, processes, and case studies in HCI design, as well as novel interaction techniques, interfaces, and applications. The proceedings will be published by Springer. More information will be available on the conference website: http://2023.hci.international/.

General Chair
Constantine Stephanidis
University of Crete and ICS-FORTH
Heraklion, Crete, Greece
Email: general_chair@hcii2023.org

http://2023.hci.international/

Contents – Part II

Intelligent Environment for Daily Activities Support

Design Changes to a Synthetic Elderly Companion Based on an Intrusiveness Survey 3
Ron Fulbright, Nariman Abushanab, and Elizabeth Sullivan

Iterative User Centered Design of Robot-Mediated Paired Activities for Older Adults with Mild Cognitive Impairment (MCI) 14
Ritam Ghosh, Nibraas Khan, Miroslava Migovich, Devon Wilson, Emily Latshaw, Judith A. Tate, Lorraine C. Mion, and Nilanjan Sarkar

Nadine Robot in Elderly Care Simulation Recreational Activity: Using Computer Vision and Observations for Analysis 29
Nidhi Mishra, Gauri Tulsulkar, and Nadia Magnenat Thalmann

Encouraging Elderly Self-care by Integrating Speech Dialogue Agent and Wearable Device 52
Hayato Ozono, Sinan Chen, and Masahide Nakamura

To Dot or Not to Dot: The Effect of Instruction Design on Smart Home Device Set-Up for Older Adults 71
Shivani Patel, Elaine Choy, Paige Lawton, Jade Lovell, Barbara Chaparro, and Alex Chaparro

Robots as Welfare Technologies to Reduce Falls Amongst Older Adults: An Explorative Study from Norway 88
Diana Saplacan and Jim Tørresen

Smart Home for the Elderly - A Survey of Desires, Needs, and Problems 107
Monika Schak, Rainer Blum, and Birgit Bomsdorf

Knowledge-Based Dialogue System for the Ageing Support on Daily Activities 122
Julio Vizcarra and Kristiina Jokinen

Design and Verification of a Smart Home Management System for Making a Smart Home Composable and Adjustable by the Elderly 134
Reina Yoshizaki, SooIn Kang, Hiroki Kogami, Kenichiro Ito, Daisuke Yoshioka, Koki Nakano, Yuriki Sakurai, Takahiro Miura, Mahiro Fujisaki-Sueda-Sakai, Ken-ichiro Yabu, Hiroshige Matsumoto, Ikuko Sugawara, Misato Nihei, Hiroko Akiyama, and Tohru Ifukube

LIGHT: A Smart Lamp Design for the Sleep Disorders and Sundown Syndrome of Alzheimer's Patients ... 154
Jingchun Zeng, Bingjian Liu, Xu Sun, Jiang Wu, and Xinwei Wang

System Design of Smart Banking Based on Service Design Thinking ... 170
Zhaorui Zhang, Xi Cheng, Shengtai Zhang, and Na Liu

Health and Wellbeing Technologies for the Elderly

Exploration and Practice of Service Design Intervention for the Elderly with Mild Cognitive Impairment ... 183
Xiatong Chen and Zhang Zhang

Integration Analysis of Heterogeneous Data on Mind Externalization of Elderly People at Home ... 197
Sinan Chen, Hayato Ozono, and Masahide Nakamura

Development of an Electronic Healthcare Tool to Elicit Patient Preferences in Older Adults Diagnosed with Hematologic Malignancies ... 210
Amy Cole, Amro Khasawneh, Karthik Adapa, Lukasz Mazur, and Daniel R. Richardson

Analysis of the Influencing Factors of the Elderly User's Somatosensory Game Themes Preferences – Based on the DEMATEL Method ... 229
Yi Ding, Ting Han, Chunrong Liu, Yahui Zhang, and Shuyu Zhao

Hazard Identification for a Virtual Coaching System for Active Healthy Ageing ... 243
Keiko Homma and Yoshio Matsumoto

FEEL2: An Interactive Device for Older Adults to Experience Synesthesia and Age Creatively ... 255
Liang-Ming Jia and Fang-Wu Tung

Improving Self-diet Management of Chronic Kidney Disease Patients Through Chatbots ... 268
Wang-Chin Tsai, Wen-Yi Li, Jen-Yu Tsai, and Jieng-Sheng Yang

A Preliminary Study on Application of Tangible User Interface and Augmented Reality Technology with Table Game and Hand-Eye Coordination Operation Tasks in the Fields of Memory and Visuospatial Perception for the Elderly ... 277
Li-Lan Wang and I.-Jui Lee

Feasibility Study of Portable Simulated Pet 'KEDAMA' for Relieving Depression 290
Jiang Wu, Yuan Yuan, and Yihang Dai

Design of Somatosensory Interactive Balance Training Exergame for the Elderly Based on Tai Chi 305
Yahui Zhang, Ting Han, Yi Ding, and Shuyu Zhao

Analysis on Influencing Factors of Medical Seeking Behavior of the Elderly Under COVID-19–Based on the DEMATEL Method 320
Shuyu Zhao, Ting Han, Chunrong Liu, Yahui Zhang, and Yi Ding

Aging, Communication and Social Interaction

Intergenerational Digitally Mediated Relationships: How Portuguese Young Adults Interact with Family Members Over 65+ 335
Inês Amaral, Ana Marta Flores, Eduardo Antunes, and Maria José Brites

Cognitive Difference of Generations in the 1970s and 1990s Towards Ancestor Worship Culture 349
Chia-Ling Chang

Prototype Development of an Interpretative Game with Location-Based AR for Ecomuseum 360
Chun-Wen Chen and Ya Hsin Chen

Intergenerational Contacts During the COVID-19 Pandemic: Personal or Electronic? 371
Mihaela Hărăguș

Virtual Museum Visits in a Pandemic: Older Adults Discuss Experiences of Art, Culture and Social Connection 383
Constance Lafontaine and Kim Sawchuk

Designing an Innovative Intergenerational Educational Program to Bridge the Digital Divide: The Cyber School for Grandparents Initiative 398
Elena Rolandi, Emanuela Sala, Mauro Colombo, Roberta Vaccaro, and Antonio Guaita

Applying Asymmetrical VR Collaborative Games to the Enhancement of Peer Collaboration and Oral Communication in Children with Autism 413
Wan-Chen Yang and I.-Jui Lee

Older Women Images and Technologies to Increase Gender Peace in Crisis and COVID-19 Times 427
Vanessa Zorrilla-Muñoz, María Silveria Agulló-Tomás, Mônica Donio Bellegarde, Maria João Forjaz, Eduardo Fernandez, Carmen Rodriguez-Blazquez, Alba Ayala, and Gloria Fernandez-Mayoralas

Author Index 441

Contents – Part I

Aging, Design and Gamification

Contribution Participatory Methodologies and Generational Research 3
Maria José Brites, Teresa Sofia Castro, Ana Filipa Oliveira, and Inês Amaral

Safety and Ethical Considerations When Designing a Virtual Reality Study with Older Adult Participants 12
Julie A. Brown, An T. Dinh, and Chorong Oh

A Study on the Recognition and Memory of Shapes for the Elderly 27
Ku-Hsi Chu, Jui-Che Tu, and Chang-Franw Lee

E-Focus Groups as a Conceptual Tool for Co-creation of Products and Services for the Elderly 40
Maria Lilian de Araújo Barbosa and Maria Lucia Leite Ribeiro Okimoto

The Role of Information and Communication Technologies in Researching Older People During the Covid-19 Pandemic: The Case of the Italian Longitudinal Study on Older People's Quality of Life During the Covid-19 Pandemic (ILQA-19) 53
Giulia Melis, Emanuela Sala, and Daniele Zaccaria

Senior Citizens as Storytellers: Contribution to Gamified Contexts 69
Cláudia Ortet, Ana Isabel Veloso, and Liliana Vale Costa

Senior-Centered Gamification: An Approach for Cyclotourism 80
Cláudia Ortet, Liliana Vale Costa, and Ana Isabel Veloso

A Study of the Effects of Interactive AI Image Processing Functions on Children's Painting Education 93
Jie Sun, Chao Gu, Jiangjie Chen, Wei Wei, Chun Yang, and Qianling Jiang

Environmental Boundaries and Road Regularity in Virtual Reality: Examining Their Effects on Navigation Performance and Spatial Cognition 109
Liu Tang, Yanling Zuo, and Jia Zhou

A Pilot Study on Synesthesia Between Color Senses and Musical Scales in Chinese Musical Instrument "Guqin" 127
Cheng-Min Tsai, Ya-Ting Chang, and Wang-Chin Tsai

Mobile, Wearable and Multimodal Interaction for Aging

Pandemic-Driven Mobile Technology in Saudi Arabia: Experience of the Elderly Pilgrims and Visitors During COVID-19 139
Asmaa S. Alayed

The Impact of the Interface on the Perception of Trust of Older Adults Users When Using the Smartphone 151
Mayckel Barbosa de Oliveira Camargo, Marcelo Valério Rino, Paula da Cruz Landim, and Antônio Carlos Sementille

Research on Wearable Smart Products for Elderly Users Based on Kano Model 160
Xin Chen and Shuyuan Li

Voice Controlled Devices and Older Adults – A Systematic Literature Review 175
Dietmar Jakob

A Data Collection and Annotation Tool for Asynchronous Multimodal Data During Human-Computer Interactions 201
Nibraas Khan, Ritam Ghosh, Miroslava Migovich, Andrew Johnson, Austin Witherow, Curtis Taylor, Matt Schroder, Tyler Vongpanya, Medha Sarkar, and Nilanjan Sarkar

Why It is Easier to Slay a Dragon Than to Kill a Myth About Older People's Smartphone Use 212
Eugène Loos, Mireia Fernández-Ardèvol, Andrea Rosales, and Alexander Peine

3D QR Cube for Elderly Information System Design 224
Ameersing Luximon, Ravindra S. Goonetilleke, and Yan Luximon

Willingness to Participate in Smartphone-Based Mobile Data Collection Studies 237
Alexander Seifert

Research on the Age-Appropriate Design of Mobile Phone APPs Based on the Experience of Using Smartphones for Chinese Young-Old 248
Yuxuan Xiao, Yanghao Ye, and Yi Liu

Aging, Social Media and Digital Literacy

Challenges of the Intergenerational Feminist Movement(s): Some Reflections 265
Carla Cerqueira and Célia Taborda Silva

Why the Elderly Indulges in Live Shopping: Optimization of Interaction Mechanism Under the Live E-commerce Scenario? 276
Xinyi Ding, Cong Cao, and Dan Li

A Generational Approach to Fight Fake News: In Search of Effective Media Literacy Training and Interventions 291
Elena-Alexandra Dumitru, Loredana Ivan, and Eugène Loos

Missing Voices and Gendered Ageism –Patterns of Invisibility in Global News Media 311
Maria Edström

An Interface Design of Chat Application for the Elderly Based on Color Cognition and User Demand 321
Linlin Feng and Jing Luo

Digital Literacy of Older People and the Role of Intergenerational Approach in Supporting Their Competencies in Times of COVID-19 Pandemic 335
Igor Kanižaj and Maria José Brites

A Social-Media Study of the Older Adults Coping with the COVID-19 Stress by Information and Communication Technologies 346
Najmeh Khalili-Mahani, Kim Sawchuk, Sasha Elbaz, Shannon Hebblethwaite, and Janis Timm-Bottos

Older Adults and Communication Technologies During the Lockdown in Romania 365
Luminiţa-Anda Mandache and Loredana Ivan

Digital Campaigning: Challenges for Older Bulgarian Electorate 381
Lilia Raycheva, Andreana Eftimova, Neli Velinova, and Lora Metanova

"Online Gameable Communities": Social Digital Games in the Infocommunication Ageing Society 398
Francisco Regalado and Ana Isabel Veloso

Tech Mentors, Warm Experts and Digital Care Work: Pandemic Lessons from a Remote Digital Literacy Training Program for Older Adults 411
Kim Sawchuk and Constance Lafontaine

Understanding Older Adults' Stickiness Intention of Health Information on Social Media: A Time and Gratification Perspective 432
Xindi Wang and Yuxiang Chris Zhao

Technology Acceptance and Adoption: Barriers and Facilitators for Older Adults

Work, Digital Devices and Later Life: A Quanti-qualitative Research 451
Simone Carlo and Giulia Buscicchio

Barriers and Facilitators to Technology Among Older Adults During COVID-19 Pandemic: A Systematic Review Using Thematic Analysis 466
Susann Keohane, Caroline Swarbrick, and Sumi Helal

Virtual Cardiac Rehabilitation in a Pandemic Scenario: A Review of HCI Design Features, User Acceptance and Barriers 485
Irina Kondratova and Helene Fournier

Evolution of Applied Variables in the Research on Technology Acceptance of the Elderly 500
Ruisi Liu, Xueai Li, and Junjie Chu

Exploring Older Adults' Adoption of WeChat Pay: A Cognitive Lock-In Perspective 521
Tianchang Liu and Xinyue Li

Attitude to Use Information and Communication Technology in Older Adults Under "Stay Home" to Prevent COVID-19 Infection 541
Takahiro Miura, Ryoko Yoshida, Ikuko Sugawara, Mahiro Fujisaki-Sueda-Sakai, Kenichiro Ito, Ken-ichiro Yabu, Tohru Ifukube, and Hiroko Akiyama

Internet-Able Older Adults: Text Notifications and Satisfaction with Online Questionnaires 555
Elizabeth Nichols, Shelley Feuer, Erica Olmsted-Hawala, and Rachel Gliozzi

Older Icelanders' Experience of Barriers to Health Information: Association with Age, Sex, and Education 567
Ágústa Pálsdóttir

Internet Use of Older Caregivers and Their Sociodemographic Characteristics 584
Javiera Rosell, Josefa Guerra, and Felipe Bustamante

Non-use of Digital Services Among Older Adults During the Second Wave of COVID-19 Pandemic in Finland: Population-Based Survey Study 596
Petra Saukkonen, Emma Kainiemi, Lotta Virtanen, Anu-Marja Kaihlanen, Seppo Koskinen, Päivi Sainio, Päivikki Koponen, Sari Kehusmaa, and Tarja Heponiemi

Adoption of a COVID-19 Contact Tracing App Among Older Internet Users in Finland 614
Sakari Taipale and Tomi Oinas

Prediction and Analysis of Acceptance of the Elderly for Bus Interior Space Layout Based on Visual Search 625
Hao Yang, Quanxin Jin, Xinrui Zhang, Yueran Wang, and Ying Zhao

Age and Gender Differences in Mobile Game Acceptance Amongst Older Adults 641
Rita W. L. Yu, Alan H. S. Chan, and T. H. Ko

Older Adults' Actual Use and Adoption Intention of Smart Health Care Technologies in Hong Kong 658
Jiaxin Zhang, Hailiang Wang, Brian Y. H. Lee, Marco Y. C. Pang, and Yan Luximon

Author Index 671

Intelligent Environment for Daily Activities Support

Design Changes to a Synthetic Elderly Companion Based on an Intrusiveness Survey

Ron Fulbright(✉), Nariman Abushanab, and Elizabeth Sullivan

University of South Carolina Upstate, 800 University Way, Spartanburg, SC 29303, USA
fulbrigh@uscupstate.edu, beebokie@bellsouth.net

Abstract. Lois is envisioned to be a synthetic elderly companion able to tend to an elderly person's needs, monitor overall well-being, detect decline and signs of further medical problems, and in general, 'be there' for an elder. Lois is a cognitive system comprised of computer displays, cameras, speakers, microphones, and various sensors placed throughout the home turning the elder's home into a 'smart home' with services designed specifically for the needs of the elderly. Therefore, by definition, Lois is an intrusive technology. The question is, how much intrusion into their lives will an elderly person permit? To find out, we conducted a survey asking elderly and their caregivers about different levels of intrusiveness. The result was they want the technology, but they want it to be "invisible" and non-intrusive and they want to have ultimate control over the technology. Elders do not want their homes to turn into hospital rooms nor do they want to be nagged or overlorded by a computer. The survey results indicate the need to make design changes to Lois to minimize the profile in the elder's home and life.

Keywords: Cognitive systems · Synthetic companions · Obtrusiveness · Intrusiveness · Elderly care · Independent living

1 Introduction

As people age, they naturally encounter cognitive and physical degradation often requiring the assistance of a caregiver, moving into the home on younger family members, or moving to a nursing home/assisted living facility. All of these options mean the end of independence for the elderly person. Previously, we have described the architecture and design of a synthetic elderly companion named Lois (short for Loved One's Information System) intended to extend an elderly person's independence [1, 11]. Lois is envisioned as an intelligent "smart home" requiring installation of various cameras, microphones, sensors, screens, and other devices throughout the home [21–24]. Lois monitors the elder's activities throughout the day continually building a dossier of information about the elder's well-being, eating/sleeping/exercising habits, medication, social interaction, etc. noticing anything a human caregiver would notice. Lois also detects the onset of new, or worsening of existing, symptoms possibly indicating degradation of the elder's condition. When needed, Lois can assist the elder in performance of daily activities and can alert family members and first responders in the case of emergencies.

Q. Gao and J. Zhou (Eds.): HCII 2022, LNCS 13331, pp. 3–13, 2022.
https://doi.org/10.1007/978-3-031-05654-3_1

We have always envisioned Lois to be an "artificial caregiver" Therefore, we sought to imbue Lois with all of the capabilities a human caregiver would have including monitoring the elder's overall well-being, detecting departures from normal, assisting the elder with routine daily tasks, and being a friend and confidant. To perform these tasks Lois and its technology must necessarily be intrusive into the elder's home and life to some degree. However, elders may not favor medicalization of their home and elders may not be comfortable with intrusion into their personal and private space [21–23].

An open question is how much intrusion will the elder allow? If we make Lois too intrusive, it will not be welcomed into the home and adoption of this new technology will be limited. If we make Lois completely unintrusive, we run the risk of Lois not being able to perform its functions. If Lois does not detect important events, or collect enough information, the utility and reputation of the new technology will suffer also limiting adoption. There must be some intermediate value at which Lois is intrusive enough but not so much as to turn away potential users. As a result of our own discussions within the research group and ad-hoc conversations with others, we constructed the following hypotheses:

- **H1:** Elders want Lois to continually monitor their well-being, warn them, and interact/intervene in case of an emergency, including notifying family members.
- **H2:** Elders will feel safer knowing their health and well-being is being monitored continuously.
- **H3:** Elders want Lois to converse with them when required but also interact with them casually, socially, and informally much as they would with a human caretaker.
- **H4:** Elders want the ability to "throttle" the level of interaction overall and on a daily basis. Elders will want the ability to "turn Lois off" at their convenience. However, even when "off" Lois will continue to monitor the elder but just not interact with the elder needlessly.
- **H5:** Lois can be more intrusive than the current setting if the value of the interaction is perceived as high.
- **H6:** Elders will not mind wearing a ring, necklace, bracelet, pendant, watch, or some other kind of jewelry providing a link to Lois at all times.
- **H7:** Elders will react more positively to Lois if it uses a human-realistic face as an avatar of their choosing.
- **H8:** Elders will accept a smart-mirror as a primary interface if it appears only in the bathroom and not in every room in the house but will accept other interface devices throughout the house.

To test these hypotheses, we created a survey with questions exploring each hypothesis. We then had elderly people and caregivers living and working in independent living situations and assisted living situations complete the survey (N = 62). Respondents were asked to rate their comfort level with each situation explained in the question by selecting one of five answers ranging from "very comfortable" to "very uncomfortable."

This paper first describes previous work related to Lois and cognitive systems in general. The paper then provides detail about the survey itself, the responses received, and the disposition of each hypothesis, either "confirmed" or "refuted." The paper then discusses design changes to Lois made obvious by our new understanding of the elderly's feelings about intrusiveness.

2 Literature

Many robotic/semi-robotic assistants for the elderly are currently available. Some of these are desktop units such as Catalia Health's Mabu (http://www.cataliahealth.com) [2, 3], JIBO (https://jibo.com), Intuition Robotics' ElliQ [4], Pillo Health's Pria (https://www.okpria.com). Some are artificial pets such as Blue Frog Robotics' Buddy (https://buddytherobot.com/en/buddy-the-emotional-robot/), offerings by Ageless Innovations, a spinoff of Hasbro (https://joyforall.com), and PARO the Therapeutic robot (http://www.parorobots.com). Others are semi-humanoid robots such as Pepper by SoftBank Robotics (https://www.softbankrobotics.com/emea/en/pepper), Lynx, by UB Tech (https://ubtrobot.com/products/lynx-with-amazon-alexa?ls=en), and Aido by InGen Dynamics (http://aidorobot.com). Some are full-sized robots such as Asia Robotics' Dinsow (https://www.dinsow.com) [5], and Riken's Robobear (https://www.riken.com) [6]. Unlike these devices, Lois is not encased in a single physical unit. Rather, Lois sensors and interface devices are distributed throughout every room in the elder's home and therefore is considered to be more of a "smart home" solution with more similarities to Amazon's Alexa (www.amazon.com/alexa) and Google's Connected Home (store.google.com/category/connected_home) [21, 22].

In software agent terminology, Lois is a smart hybrid interface agent capable of and acting on behalf of the elder as well as collaborating with humans and other software agents [7]. While we don't consider Lois to be artificially intelligent, Lois is capable of human-level information processing, thus making Lois a cognitive system (a "cog" for short) [8]. Cognitive systems must interact with one or more humans in a *human/cog ensemble* [9]. As shown in Fig. 1, by working together, Lois, the elder, the elder's family members, and the elder's medical professionals form a human/cog ensemble collectively capable of performance exceeding that of a human caregiver—a synthetic elderly companion [1, 9–11].

The adoption of smart home technology is underway. An estimated 258 million homes worldwide will employ smart home technology by the end of 2021 and is projected to increase to over 400 million homes by 2025 [12]. Issues such as *usability* (usefulness, complexity, and reliability), *intrusiveness* (presenteeism, anonymity), and *dynamism* (pace of change) contribute to unease among the adopters of this technology [13]. The survey reported on in this paper involves intrusiveness. The presenteeism aspect of intrusiveness involves how accessible Lois is to the elder and vice versa [14]. We think Lois should always be accessible via voice command and also by detection of an abnormal situation or event. The anonymity aspect of intrusiveness involves how visible Lois and its associated devices are in the home of the elder. Other work has studied how using anthropomorphic design features mitigates the perceived intrusiveness of smart home technology [15].

The less invasive Lois is, the more likely the elderly are to adopt the technology. The results from the survey reported on in this paper confirmed most people want Lois to be there all the time (present) but invisible (anonymous).

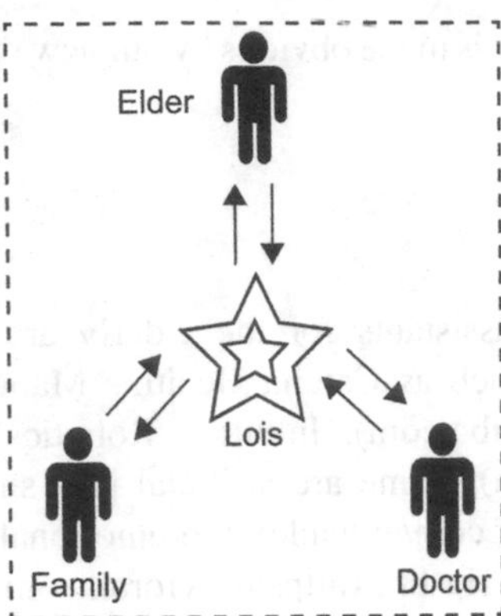

Fig. 1. The synthetic elderly companion human/cog ensemble

3 The Survey and the Respondents

Prior to completing the survey, each respondent was shown a brief presentation describing Lois, the kind of technology Lois uses, the purpose of Lois, and the purpose of the survey. The presentation explained how Lois is embedded throughout the elder's home and is able to communicate directly with the elder on a daily basis via spoken natural language and various display screens. It was further explained how Lois compiled a dossier of information about the elder by continually receiving data from numerous cameras, microphones, and other sensors placed throughout the home. The overall purpose of Lois was explained to assist the elder and monitor the elder's overall well-being regarding various aspects of the elder's life, as shown in Fig. 2.

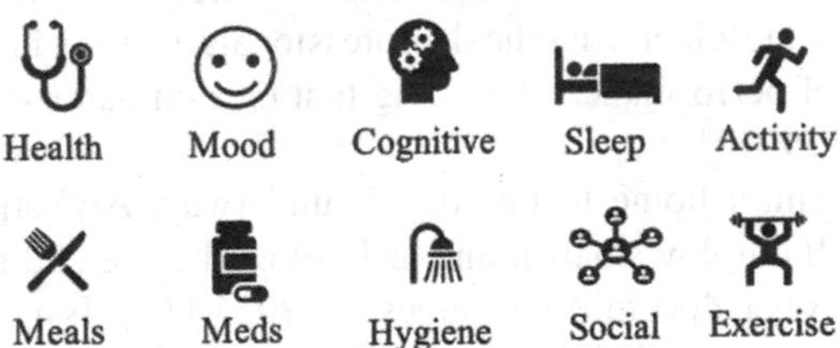

Fig. 2. Areas of the elder's life Lois monitors

Following the presentation, each respondent was asked to complete the survey consisting of 26 questions designed to explore each of the eight hypotheses listed earlier. Four questions relate to H1, three questions relate to H2, four questions relate to H3, two questions relate to H4, three questions relate to H5, four questions relate to H6, three questions relate to H7, and three questions relate to H8. Each question describes a feature of Lois and requires the selection of one of five different choices with the choices depicting the range of comfort the respondent has with the subject matter of the question. Figure 3 shows a typical question on the survey.

How comfortable are you with Lois continually monitoring your well-being? For example, Lois continually monitoring your heart rate, blood pressure, and blood sugar level?

1. Very Comfortable
2. Comfortable
3. Neither comfortable/uncomfortable
4. Uncomfortable
5. Very uncomfortable

Fig. 3. Typical question on the survey

The survey was completed by 62 respondents. We sought to query elderly who were living independently, elderly living in assisted living situations, and also elderly caregivers. Of the respondents, 9 (14.5%) were employed as elderly caregivers. As a result, most of the respondents were over the age of 55 currently living in their own home as shown in Fig. 4.

Age	N	Percent
55 or under	11	17.7
56-65	29	46.8
66-75	14	22.6
76-85	5	8.1
Over 85	3	4.8

Living Arrangements	N	Percent
Own Home with Someone	46	74.2
Own Home Alone	10	16.1
Someone Else's Home	5	8.1
No Answer	1	1.6

Fig. 4. Distribution of respondents by age and living arrangement

We were also interested in how comfortable the respondents were to using existing technology such as: a smartphone, a smart home device, and one of the existing elderly care robots. As shown in Fig. 5, almost all use smartphones, about one-half have a smart home device, but no respondents use an elderly care robot like those described earlier.

Of the respondents, 37 (59.7%) are female and 25 (40.3%) are male, 39 (63%) are not yet retired while 23 (37%) are retired.

4 The Results

Each of the five choices respondents could select was assigned a numerical value 1–5 with 1 corresponding to "very comfortable" and 5 corresponding to "very uncomfortable." Therefore, a lower average score on a question indicates the respondents are more comfortable with the subject matter in the question. A higher average score indicates the respondents were more uncomfortable with the subject matter. The lowest possible average score is 1 (if all respondents answered "very comfortable") and the highest possible average score is 5 (if all respondents answered "very uncomfortable").

Smartphone	N	Percent
Yes	56	90.3
No	6	9.7

Smart Home	N	Percent
Yes	29	46.8
No	33	53.2

Elder Robot	N	Percen
Yes	0	0
No	62	100

Fig. 5. Respondents' use of existing technology

The average score for each question was tabulated and then an average of all questions pertaining to a hypothesis was computed. The average score for each hypothesis is shown in Fig. 6.

H1	1.98	**H5**	2.72
H2	1.97	**H6**	2.48
H3	2.73	**H7**	2.64
H4	1.45	**H8**	3.24

Fig. 6. Average score for each hypothesis

The results of the survey resoundingly confirm three of the eight hypotheses:

- **H1:** Elders want Lois to continually monitor their well-being, warn them, and interact/intervene in case of an emergency, including notifying family members (score: 2.10).
- **H2:** Elders will feel safer knowing their health and well-being is being monitored continuously (score: 1.97).
- **H4:** Elders want the ability to "throttle" the level of interaction overall and on a daily basis. Elders will want the ability to "turn Lois off" at their convenience. However, even when "off" Lois will continue to monitor the elder but just not interact with the elder needlessly (score: 1.45).

The survey shows respondents are comfortable with Lois continually monitoring their well-being and feel safer knowing Lois is watching out for them. Respondents were somewhat comfortable with wearing a device allowing Lois to monitor their vital signs:

- **H6:** Elders will not mind wearing a ring, necklace, bracelet, pendant, watch, or some other kind of jewelry providing a link to Lois at all times (score: 2.48).

An interpretation of these results might be elders are willing to put up with wearing a monitoring device if absolutely necessary because they value Lois' ability to monitor their vital signs. However, they would rather not have to wear such a device. It is obvious respondents want to be able to control how intrusive Lois is. In fact, the questions pertaining to H4 received the lowest score of all questions. These questions asked respondents if they would like to the ability to turn Lois' speech off and the ability to put Lois "to sleep" for a period of time. The survey convincingly *refuted:*

- **H8:** Elders will accept a smart-mirror as a primary interface if it appears only in the bathroom and not in every room in the house but will accept other interface devices throughout the house (score: 3.24).

One of the questions pertaining to H8 involved using a mirror in the elder's bathroom as a smart mirror user interface for Lois. The score of this question, 3.79, was the most negative score of any question on the survey indicating respondents definitely do not want Lois appearing in their bathroom mirrors. Similarly, respondents seemed ambivalent about the style of Lois' user interface:

- **H7:** Elders will react more positively to Lois if it uses a human-realistic face as an avatar of their choosing (score: 2.64).

Hypotheses H3 and H5 involved questions exploring the level of intrusiveness allowed into the elder's personal life. The question asking about Lois continuously monitoring the elder's vital signs and alerting the elder if an out-of-bounds reading is detected received a favorable score of 2.06 corresponding to "comfortable."

- **H3:** Elders want Lois to converse with them when required but also interact with them casually, socially, and informally much as they would with a human caretaker (score: 2.73).
- **H5:** Lois can be more intrusive than the current setting if the value of the interaction is perceived as high (score: 2.72).

However, two other questions involving Lois engaging in unsolicited "small talk" and randomly commenting on the elder's likes and dislikes received scores of 3.00 and 3.10 respectively. Questions involving Lois keeping with the elder's social media and giving updates in an unsolicited manner scored 2.95. These scores correspond to the "neither comfortable or uncomfortable" response. So, while not totally negative, respondents did not seem to particularly like this more intrusive behavior by Lois.

Overall, respondents like the idea of Lois monitoring their well-being however, they want the technology to be as invisible and unintrusive as possible and they want to be able to control how present and intrusive Lois is.

5 Design Changes

We have long imagined a smart mirror user interface for Lois. This would involve a two-way mirror with a computer displaying information from behind the mirror so as to superimpose the computer-generated information on top of the image reflected in the mirror as shown in Fig. 7.

Fig. 7. Smart mirror user interface for Lois.

Furthermore, we thought the bathroom would be an ideal place for the smart mirror user interface since the bathroom is a natural place to have a mirror and the elder is likely to use the mirror in the bathroom every day. We also imagined a realistic human facial image presented as the "face" of Lois. We thought this would anthropomorphize Lois making the technology more desirable as indicated in other research [15]. However, the score of the question describing this user interface received the most unfavorable score on the survey (3.79). Perhaps respondents view the bathroom as their private space so interpret the presence of Lois in the bathroom as an invasion of their privacy. Therefore, going forward, we will not plan on employing the smart bathroom mirror concept.

We have always thought of Lois as being a companion to the elder able to communicate in natural language much as a human friend, loved one, or human caretaker would. Furthermore, using machine learning technology, we envisioned Lois learning the likes, dislikes, motivations, concerns, and worries of the elder and using the information to customize dialog-based interaction with the elder. We have thought Lois would then become a trusted confidant and friendly voice in the life of the elder. However, the survey indicates respondents are uncomfortable with this type of intrusion into their personal lives. Respondents like the idea of Lois keeping an eye on them and monitoring their well-being, but they do not like the idea of Lois becoming their friend. It seems this crosses a line and becomes intrusive in the view of the respondents [23]. Therefore, going forward, we will focus on Lois' well-being monitoring functions and not the "friend and confidant" functions.

This is an interesting and concerning result for us. Every day, tens of millions of people are using "intelligent" companion chatbot technology, based on XioAce, in China, Japan, India, and Indonesia [19]. XioAce is designed to be an empathetic companion able to satisfy an emotional connection with the user. Although not yet a success in the United States, mass adoption by millions of people elsewhere certainly indicates humans can, and will, form emotionally significant relationship with such technology. Since most of XioAce users are teenagers, it may be this is something a future generation of Lois users will desire.

A primary function for Lois is monitoring the elder's vital signs. Since the respondents are telling us they desire this ability but want the enabling technology to be invisible, we must look for emerging sensor technology able to work from a distance and be built into normal objects in the household. One such device, announced at CES 2022, is the Sengled Smart Health Monitoring Light, a WiFi/Bluetooth enabled lightbulb with built-in radar technology able to track sleep, heart rate, body temperature, and other vital signs [16]. These could replace existing lightbulbs in the home without having to change the lighting fixtures themselves and could provide coverage in every room. Any such ubiquitous technology will be of interest to us in the future.

Also emerging are low-impact sensors like Onera Health's Biomedical Lab-on-a-Chip technology announced at CES 2022 [17]. Embodied as a patch worn by the elder, this technology replaces bulky sensors and is able to monitor sleep disorders and perform other medical-grade experiments. Such patches do represent an intrusion but once applied, the patch would be forgotten about. In fact, medicinal patches are used by many patients already. We feel, this form of technology will be tolerated easier than technology requiring conscious and deliberative interaction on the part of the elder.

Sensory technology designed for use in hospital beds already exists [20]. This technology consists of a large number of undetectable sensors locate in an overlay for the mattress. Ideas like this are promising for Lois, however, such technology will have to be designed for in-home use.

There are many devices in development and in early-market stages involving medical diagnosis from analyzing a person's breath [18]. Lois could use devices like this innocuously in the elder's bedroom, bathroom, living room, or smartphone. For example, we can envision breath-sniffing technology mounted invisibly near the elder's bed providing many hours of sensing time without the elder ever knowing it is being done.

6 Conclusion and Future Work

Presented are results of a survey exploring how intrusive a cognitive system, named Lois, can be when tasked with monitoring the well-being of an elderly person. The idea is by using such a system as a smart home technology, an elder can remain living independently in their own home longer. We have always envisioned Lois to be an "artificial caregiver." Therefore, we sought to imbue Lois with all of the capabilities a human caregiver would have including monitoring the elder's overall well-being, detecting departures from normal, assisting the elder with routine daily tasks, and being a friend and confidant. However, we have worried about how accepting the elderly will be of such technology and incursion of the technology into their homes and lives.

There is recent evidence the elderly are becoming more accepting of technology in general with over 50% owning a tablet and 69% using them on a daily basis and spending on technology almost tripling in the last two years. [25]. This agrees with the results of our survey finding 90% currently own a smartphone and almost 50% owning some type of smart-home device.

The survey consisted of 26 questions investigating eight hypotheses posited by the research team before the survey and listed earlier. Respondents (N = 62) answered the questions by rating their level of comfort to the subject matter in each question on a scale of very comfortable to very uncomfortable. Most respondents (56) currently live independently and the majority of the respondents are of an age where dependent/independent living decisions are likely 10–15 years in the future.

In general, respondents were comfortable with Lois monitoring their overall well-being and their vital signs, even if this meant wearing a device facilitating the sensing and monitoring. Furthermore, respondents were comfortable about Lois being able to detect emergency situations and notifying family members and first responders.

However, it was clear, respondents want the technology to be invisible and unintrusive as possible. Respondents seem to want Lois to be there when needed but they feel less comfortable about Lois being there as an interactive entity like a friend, family member, or human caregiver would. Therefore, going forward, we will focus on Lois' well-being monitoring functions and technology and not the "friend and confidant" functions and technology.

Respondents rejected the idea of Lois having a presence in the form of a smart mirror interface in the bathroom. Combining this with the cool response to the "friend and confidant" functionality, leads us to think going forward, we will seek to minimize any overt user interface or obvious presence of Lois in the home of the elder.

The immediate future for our work is clear: make Lois as invisible as possible in the homes and lives of the elderly people Lois is watching out for. Our next task will be to revisit each function we envision for Lois and ask ourselves how we can achieve the result with minimally invasive technology.

References

1. Fulbright, R.: A synthetic elderly companion named Lois. In: Gao, Q., Zhou, J. (eds.) HCII 2021. LNCS, vol. 12787, pp. 403–417. Springer, Cham (2021). https://doi.org/10.1007/978-3-030-78111-8_27
2. Catalia Health: How Mabu Works, Catalia Health (2019). http://www.cataliahealth.com/how-it-works/. Accessed Dec 2019. Video. https://www.youtube.com/watch?v=A3XwzlvOW7k. Accessed Jan 2021
3. Kidd, C.: Introducing the Mabu Personal Healthcare Companion, Catalia Health (2015). http://www.cataliahealth.com/introducing-the-mabu-personal-healthcare-companion/. Accessed Jan 2021
4. ElliQ: Hi, I'm ElliQ, Intuition Robotics (2019). https://elliq.com. Accessed Jan 2021
5. Dinsow: CT Asia Robotics (2019). https://www.dinsow.com. Accessed Jan 2021
6. Riken: The strong robot with the gentle touch, Riken (2015). https://www.riken.jp/en/news_pubs/research_news/2015/20150223_2/. Accessed Jan 2021
7. Nwana, H.S.: Intelligent tutoring systems: an overview. Artif. Intell. Rev. **4**(4), 251–277 (1990)
8. Kelly, J.E., Hamm, S.: Smart Machines: IBMs Watson and the Era of Cognitive Computing. Columbia Business School Publishing, Columbia University Press, New York (2013)
9. Fulbright, R., Walters, G.: Synthetic expertise. In: Schmorrow, D.D., Fidopiastis, C.M. (eds.) HCII 2020. LNCS (LNAI), vol. 12197, pp. 27–48. Springer, Cham (2020). https://doi.org/10.1007/978-3-030-50439-7_3
10. Fulbright, R.: The expertise level. In: Schmorrow, D.D., Fidopiastis, C.M. (eds.) HCII 2020. LNCS (LNAI), vol. 12197, pp. 49–68. Springer, Cham (2020). https://doi.org/10.1007/978-3-030-50439-7_4

11. Fulbright, R.: Democratization of Expertise: How Cognitive Systems Will Revolutionize Your Life. CRC Press, Boca Raton (2020)
12. Holst, A.: Smart Home – Statistics & Facts, Statista (2021). https://www.statista.com/topics/2430/smart-homes/#dossierKeyfigures. Accessed Jan 2022
13. Ayyagari, R., Grover, V., Purvis, R.: Technostress: technological antecedents and implications. MIS Q. **35**(4), 831–858 (2011)
14. Luoma, R., Penttinen, E., Rinta-Kahila, T.: How to enforce presenteeism with ICT while mitigating technostress- a case study. In: Proceedings of the 53rd Hawaii International Conference on Systems Sciences (2020)
15. Benlian, A., Klumpe, J., Hinz, O.: Mitigating the intrusive effects of smart home assistants by using anthropomorphic design features: a mulit-method investigation. Inf. Syst. J. **30**, 1010–1042 (2019)
16. Yuohy, J.T.: Sengled's newest smart bulb can track your heart rate, The Verge (2022). https://www.theverge.com/2022/1/3/22864783/sengled-smart-health-monitoring-smart-bulb-ces 2022. Accessed Jan 2022
17. Kirsh, D.: CES 2022: Medical technologies you need to know, Medical Design and Outsourcing (2022). https://www.medicaldesignandoutsourcing.com/ces-2022-medical-technologies-you-need-to-know/6/. Accessed Jan 2022
18. SniffPhone: SniffPhone wins 2018 Innovation Award, SniffPhone (2022). https://www.sniffphone.eu/. Accessed Jan 2022
19. Zhou, L., Gao, J., Li, D., Shum, H.-Y.: The design and implementation of XiaoIce, an empathetic social chatbot. Comput. Linguist. **46**(1), 53–93 (2020)
20. XSensor: Patient Bed Monotoring, XSensor (2022). https://www.xsensor.com/solutions-and-platform/csm/patient-bed-monitoring. Accessed Jan 2022
21. Demiris, G., Hensel, B.: Smart homes for patients at the end of life. J. Hous. Elder. **23**(1–2), 106–115 (2009)
22. Arras, J.D., Neveloff-Dubler, N.: Ethical and social implications of high-tech home care. In: Arras, J.D. (ed.) Bringing the Hospital Home, pp. 1–31. Johns Hopkins University Press, Baltimore (1995)
23. Hensel, B.K., Demiris, G., Courtney, K.L.: Defining obtrusiveness in home telehealth technologies: a conceptual framework. J. Am. Med. Inform. Assoc. **13**, 428–431 (2006)
24. Sanchez, V.G., Pfeiffer, C.F., Skeie, N.O.: A review of smart house analysis methods for assisting older people living alone. J. Sens. Actuator Netw. **6**, 11 (2017)
25. Kakuula, B.: Personal Tech and the Pandemic: Older Adults are Upgrading for a Better Online Experience, AARP Research, September 2021. https://www.aarp.org/research/topics/technology/info-2021/2021-technology-trends-older-americans.html. Accessed Feb 2022

Iterative User Centered Design of Robot-Mediated Paired Activities for Older Adults with Mild Cognitive Impairment (MCI)

Ritam Ghosh[1](✉), Nibraas Khan[1], Miroslava Migovich[1], Devon Wilson[1], Emily Latshaw[2], Judith A. Tate[2], Lorraine C. Mion[2], and Nilanjan Sarkar[1]

[1] Vanderbilt University, Nashville, TN 37212, USA
ritam.ghosh@Vanderbilt.Edu

[2] Ohio State University, Columbus, OH 42310, USA

Abstract. This paper describes the design and implementation of a human-computer interaction (HCI) and human-robot interaction (HRI) based activity designed to foster human-human interaction (HHI) in older adults with cognitive impairment who reside in long term care (LTC) facilities. Apathy is a major condition among this population; apathy is associated with social isolation, cognitive decline, and a reduced quality of life. Few options exist in the treatment of apathy; multi-modal activities addressing cognitive, physical, and social domains hold the most promise but are the most resource intensive. Given the shortage of caregivers, use of technology such as social robots and virtual reality may be useful to complement activity programs. In this paper, we present the iterative design process of a virtual dog training activity using Unity game engine, the humanoid robot Nao, and the puppy robot Aibo. We solicited inputs from expert stakeholders (physicians, nurses, activity directors, and occupational therapists) and residents living in LTC facilities during each step of the design process. We describe their feedback and corresponding changes to the activity. Initial participant testing data in a LTC community, participants' final thoughts, and approval rating of the various components of the system are also presented. The participants rated the system on six categories on a scale of one to five; the mean rating per category increased by 0.58 after the second session.

Keywords: User centered design · Human-Computer interaction · Human-Robot interaction · Human-Human interaction · Social robots · Virtual reality · Mixed reality · Older adults · Cognitive impairment · Dementia

1 Introduction

Approximately 6.2 million Americans ages 65 and older live with Alzheimer's disease and related dementia (ADRD). By 2060, this number is expected to rise to 13.9 million, representing 3.3% of the U.S. population [1, 2]. Official death certificates recorded 121,499 deaths from ADRD in 2019, making ADRD the sixth leading cause of death in the United States and the fifth leading cause for those 65 and older [3]. Many individuals

Q. Gao and J. Zhou (Eds.): HCII 2022, LNCS 13331, pp. 14–28, 2022.
https://doi.org/10.1007/978-3-031-05654-3_2

with ADRD experience difficulties with memory retention, problem solving, communication, and other everyday activities. One of the main symptoms exhibited by people with dementia is apathy; it leads to indifference, lack of initiative, aversion towards social interaction, lack of interest in daily life activities, and reduced quality of life. Apathy results in loneliness, social isolation, and further decline in mental and physical health [4].

Apathy is difficult to address and very few pharmacologic options are available. Common interventions include guided physical exercise sessions, group activities, cognitive games [5, 6], music, art, and reminiscence therapy [7, 8]. Multimodal intervention techniques that combine physical and cognitive stimulus and encourage social interaction are most effective [7]. Physical activities slow the decline in voluntary motor skills and cognitive activities and social interactions boost attention, mood, and overall cognitive function [9, 10].

These multi-modal activities are resource intensive. Unfortunately, nurses and activity personnel who provide activities to older adult residents in long term care settings are in short supply [11]. To address manpower issues in long term care, various technological interventions using Virtual Reality (VR) and Socially Assistive Robots (SAR) have been explored [12–14]. A brief background on existing VR and SAR intervention techniques for older adults in long term care (LTC) settings are presented in the next section.

2 Background

Investigators have explored robotic fitness coaches to lead group physical activities or provide feedback and encouragement [15–17]. Brian 2.1, a humanoid robot, was designed to encourage older adults to eat meals [18]. Nao, a widely used SAR, has been used to perform memory training activities with older adults [19]. These systems were designed to be used by only one user at a time and provided only a single mode of stimulation. They were also open loop systems, hence could not adapt to the participants' individual capabilities and performance.

Paro, a therapeutic baby seal robot, has been one of the most widely used SARs in LTCs, primarily to improve mood and initiate social interaction [20, 21]. Paro has been used at the individual level where the older adult held and petted it, and at the group level where it was passed around among a group of older adults to initiate conversation. While Paro can engage multiple users at the same time and initiate social interaction, it is limited in nature and dependent on the care givers and their expertise in motivating the older adults to participate in the activity.

Several LTC SAR systems used the Wizard of Oz (WoZ) paradigm [22, 23]. In WoZ-based systems, a human operator controls the system remotely but is not visible to the participants, who are under the impression that they are interacting with an autonomous agent. This enables the system to be adaptive to individual performance but requires a trained operator to manually control the system.

Though the above studies are promising, the range of activities provided solely by SARs is limited. To expand SAR capabilities, virtual reality systems and other game environments have been used in conjunction with SARs. A guided exercise program [24] used the Oculus rift head mounted display and touch controllers. The robot Tangy was used to facilitate a Bingo game with seven residents at a LTC facility [25].

These studies demonstrate the potential of SARs paired with VR or other game environments to engage older adults. However, the majority of these studies provided only a single mode of stimulation with open loop control or required operators to deliver the intervention. Research shows that multimodal interventions that involve physical, cognitive, and social stimuli are more effective than single mode intervention techniques [26, 27]. Research also shows that participants are likely to respond better to instructions from physically embodied robots than from a virtual environment on a computer [28, 29]. Last, the system should be able to adapt to each individual's capabilities with minimal input from the operator.

To combine the benefits of all of the above methods and address the limitations, we designed a virtual dog training activity using the Unity game engine (www.unity.com), the humanoid robot Nao (SoftBank robotics) as instructor, the puppy robot Aibo (Sony) (Fig. 1) and a custom-built human computer interaction (HCI) device, as described in [13]. We followed the principles of user centered design [30] to ensure the acceptability and usability of the activity by our target population.

Fig. 1. NAO humanoid robot (left), Aibo puppy robot (right)

3 Robot-Mediated Activity Design

3.1 Activity Objectives

The objectives of the activity are to provide physical and cognitive challenges to older adults and to promote human-human interaction (HHI). To fulfill these objectives the activity needs to have components that require physical movement, cognitive components that require the participant to recognize, memorize, synchronize, sort, or compute, and social stimuli that require multiple participants to cooperate or coordinate to achieve a common goal. The activity should also have metrics to measure progress of each participant and provide rewards or positive re-enforcement to encourage greater effort and increase engagement. The participant should also be able to perform the activity alone for practice. To accommodate participants of different abilities, the activities should provide different levels of physical and cognitive challenges. Most importantly, the activity should be engaging and fun for the older adults. After a series of discussions with long term care (LTC) activity directors about activities that residents of their facilities enjoy the most, and consulting with geriatric researchers and occupational therapists specializing in dementia intervention, a virtual dog training activity was selected.

3.2 Robot Acceptance by Target Population

To determine if older adults would find the two robots fun and engaging, we first met with two residents of a long-term care facility via teleconferencing (due to COVID protocols) and showed them videos of the two robots. Nao was programmed to introduce itself and do a dance, Aibo was programmed to walk around and perform some tricks. Both residents responded positively to the robots and indicated they would like to interact with the robots.

3.3 Activity Prototype 1

The first prototype of the activity required the participants to move their "wands" in a sequence as instructed by Nao to make Aibo do a trick. The wands are a custom-built human computer interaction device as described in [13]. There were six possible motions: up, down, left, right, rotate clockwise and rotate counterclockwise. A random sequence of these movements was generated and shown on a computer screen (Fig. 2). The number of sequential movements depended on the chosen difficulty level based on the older adult's level of cognition. Nao demonstrated the movements and provided encouragement and feedback based on the participants' performance. Once the sequence was completed, Aibo performed a trick, such as sitting, dancing etc. This activity focused on gross motor movements of the arm and required comprehending instructions from Nao. We tested this activity with two pairs of nursing faculty to get their opinion on the ability of this activity to engage older adults. They were of the opinion that the randomized arm motions did not correspond to the tricks that Aibo performed and was counter intuitive. In addition, the gross arm motions may not be feasible for all members of our target population; instead, an activity that focused more on reduced arm motions and cognitive abilities would be a better strategy.

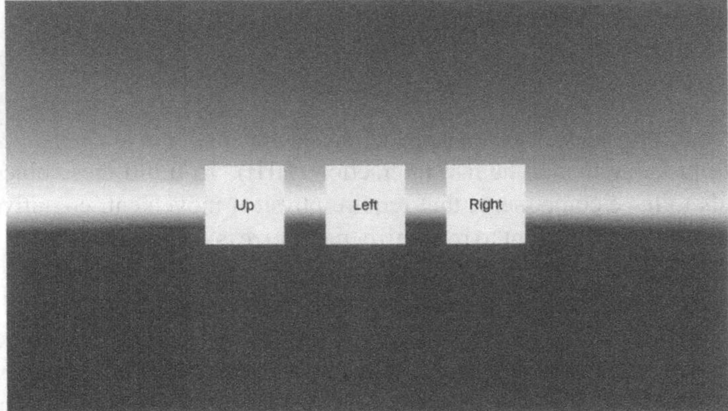

Fig. 2. Example movement sequence for Dog training activity prototype 1: The user has to move their arm up, then left and then right to complete the sequence

3.4 Activity Prototype 2

The second prototype of the activity required pairs of participants to spell out a word on the virtual environment. Figure 3 shows the user interface of this activity prototype. Each participant used a wand to interact with the system. The twenty-six randomly colored red and blue letters of the alphabet were displayed on the screen. Each participant was designated one color and could only pick letters of that color. Nao acted as the instructor for the activity. He would state a word, e.g., 'dance', and the participants had to spell the word by picking their correctly colored letters through use of the wand-controlled cursor. Once the word was completed, the puppy robot Aibo performed the corresponding trick. Nao also provided hints or encouragement as needed. The wand movements provided the physical component of the activity, memorization of the word and its spelling provided

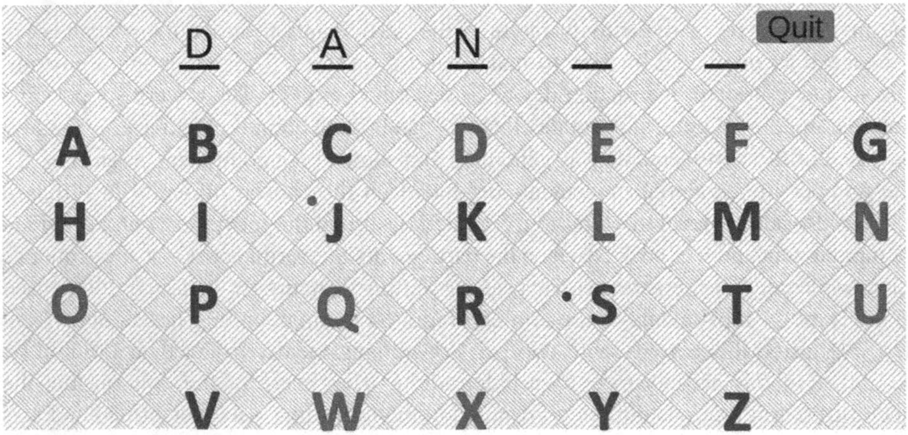

Fig. 3. Dog training activity prototype 2: The assigned word is 'DANCE', the red player has to pick the red letters and the blue player has to pick the blue letters

the cognitive stimulus. Since the participants could only choose letters of one color, they had to cooperate with each other to complete the activity, providing the social component. The activity had three difficulty levels: 1) all the letters were static; 2) letters bounced up and down from their mean position, and 3) letters changed their positions horizontally, which required the participants to track their position in order to select them. We started preliminary participant testing with this prototype.

4 Experiment

4.1 Recruitment Process

Researchers contacted the administrator and medical officer at a local LTC to explain the study and gain permission to approach older adult residents. At a time specified by LTC staff, researchers presented the robots and explained the study to interested residents. Potential participants were screened for study eligibility: age 70+, residing in the LTC facility for at least three months, able to hear, speak and understand English, sit comfortably, and move both arms. During the screening process, participants were seated in front of the computer screen at a similar distance that they would be while performing the activities and asked if they could see the text on the screen. Nao was also programmed to introduce himself and state his favorite color, and the participants were asked to repeat his name and favorite color to determine if they could hear and understand Nao. Multiple voices were generated for Nao using an online AI speech synthesizer (play.ht) and the participants were asked which pitch and pace they preferred. Eligible participants provided informed consent. This study was reviewed and approved by the Vanderbilt University Institutional Review Board.

4.2 Participant Testing

Six participants were screened and consented of whom two dropped out of the study. Four participants each performed the activity twice in pairs. There was a total of five sessions, three sessions where the participants paired up with each other and two sessions where one participant paired with a researcher due to scheduling conflicts with other participants. Sessions lasted approximately 30 min. The sessions were conducted once a week and feedback from each session was used to modify the activity and the next iteration was used in the following session. All sessions were video-taped. Figure 4 shows a session in progress. After each session, the participants completed a questionnaire about their comfort level and confidence level with the various components of the system and answered several open-ended questions.

4.3 Problems Observed

Over the course of the five sessions, through our observations and participant feedback, we identified the following issues:

1. Participants had difficulty understanding the instructions of the activity and the researchers had to provide additional instructions and reminders in addition to the instructions Nao was programmed to provide.

Fig. 4. Participant testing of the dog training activity at an LTC: footage showing participants' movements (left), footage showing robot behavior (right)

2. Some participants had difficulty finding the correct letters. They mentioned that the high number of animated letters were often overwhelming.
3. We observed that occasionally the participants did not pay attention to the feedback Nao was providing and had difficulty understanding which feedback was meant for which participant.
4. We also observed that occasionally the participants were too focused on the animations on the screen and ignored Nao's feedback.

5 Activity Redesign

5.1 Architecture

The system consists of three major blocks: Human-Computer Interaction (HCI), Human-Robot Interaction (HRI), and Human-Human interaction (HHI) (Fig. 5). The VR system is run on a Windows desktop computer. It consists of the Interaction Layer that accepts input from the wands and translates it into the corresponding movements in the game environment; the Communications Layer that facilitates the communication of commands from the state machine to NAO and Aibo; and the Finite State Machine (FSM) that controls the logic of the activity, adapts the difficulty level based on participant performance, generates appropriate feedback and encouragement, and calculates the score. The participants interact with the system using the wands. A static infrared (IR) LED marker is used as a reference; the wands calculate the position of the on-screen cursor based on the relative movement with respect to this IR marker. The VR system together with the wands constitute the HCI block. The details of the wand design and communications layer can be found in [13].

HRI is controlled by the state machine described in the next section. NAO provides instructions, feedback, and encouragement, and also demonstrates the movements required for the activity. The movements and feedback messages are programmed into blocks called 'behaviors' using the 'Choregraphe' software developed by Aldebaran robotics (now SoftBank robotics). Aibo is programmed to perform tricks once each level of the task is completed. The FSM triggers the appropriate behaviors and tricks depending on the state of the task.

HHI is measured using participants' head pose data from a Kinect sensor and speech and is verified from video. Multimodal physiological data are collected using the Empatica E4 sensor (Empatica.com). The audio, video, and data from all the sensors are synchronized using time stamps.

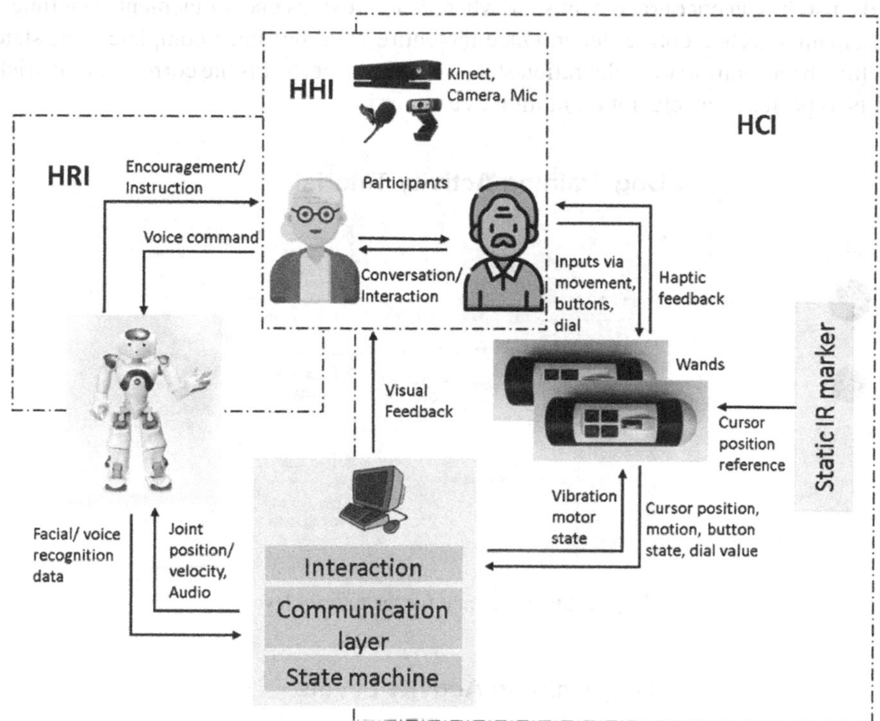

Fig. 5. Architecture of the system

5.2 State Machine

The interaction among the various components of the architecture is governed by the state machine. We designed two state machines, one for the interactive tutorial level and another for the three main levels of the activity. The tutorial level was designed to familiarize the participants with the task. Figure 6 shows the state machine that controls the tutorial level and Fig. 7 shows the state machine for the main levels. Both perform a system check on start to verify all components are connected and properly functioning before proceeding to the activity in the stable state. For the tutorial level, there is an introduction state before the stable state where Nao introduces himself and states the rules of the activity followed by a demonstration. Nao also points out the reference IR LED towards which the participants have to point their wands. He then assigns a color to each of the two participants and encourages them to pick the letter corresponding to their color. The state machine then transitions to the stable state where it monitors the performance of the participants. The system is capable of detecting if the participant is not pointing the wand towards the reference IR LED, if the participant is taking too long to pick their letter, or if they are trying to pick the letter designated to their partner. If any of the above situations arise, the state machine transitions to the corresponding state where Nao addresses the particular player by name and provides individualized feedback, then the system returns to the stable state. The state machine for the main levels also has an encouragement state where Nao provides encouragement each time a participant selects a correct letter. Once the entire word has been completed, the state machine transitions to the celebration state where Aibo performs the corresponding trick and Nao performs a celebration motion as a reward.

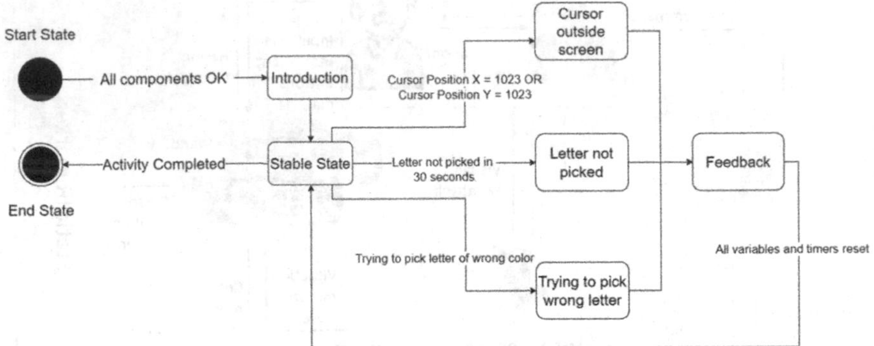

Fig. 6. State machine for the tutorial level

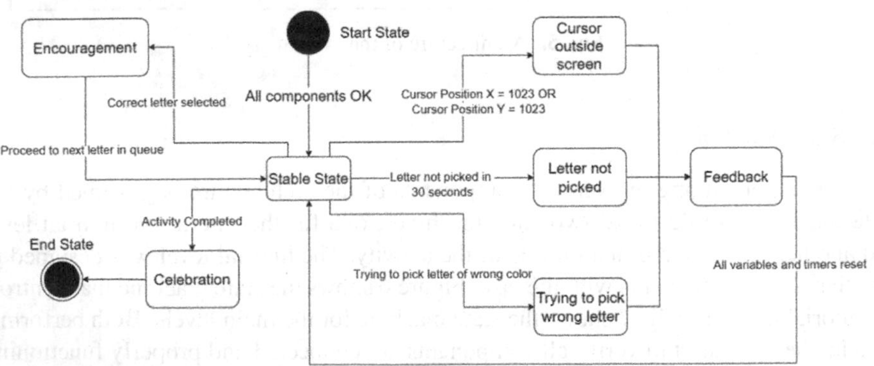

Fig. 7. State machine for the main levels

5.3 Changes to Address the Observed Problems

The following changes were made to address the issues noted in Sect. 4.3.

1. An interactive tutorial level was created where Nao provided step by step instructions and waited for the participants to complete each step. Every step had instructions and reminders after a set interval of time. A flowchart of the control logic of the tutorial is shown in Fig. 6.
2. A slider was created in the graphical user interface to control the number of extra letters that are presented on the activity screen. This was done to reduce excessive visual stimuli that led to participants being unable to find the correct letters. The slider allows the difficulty level to be determined for each pair of participants based on their cognitive function level.
3. Nao was programmed to address participants by name before giving them individualized feedback to draw their attention and avoid confusion.
4. The animations of the activity were suspended when Nao delivered instructions or feedback to reduce the number of simultaneous stimuli.

6 User Centered Design Principles

We solicited inputs from expert stakeholders (physicians, nurses, activity directors, and occupational therapists) and residents living in long term care facilities during each step of the design process. Research shows that involving target users from an early design stage results in products that are better suited to the needs of the stakeholders and better received [30–33]. The following principles of user centered design were followed:

1. Prototyping: We began the design process by creating prototypes and consulting with experts in the field as well as target users to get opinions on the concept.
2. Contextual validity: Once a prototype was selected for further development, all testing was done ‘in the wild’. We conducted our testing sessions in a long-term care facility, using a similar setup that will be used for the final product, to enhance the discovery of potential obstacles.
3. Active user participation: We involved the end user from the very early stages of development starting with activity selection and prototyping to ensure the final product is acceptable and enjoyable.
4. Iterative design: After each testing session, we noted the feedback and the issues faced and addressed them in subsequent iterations.
5. Multidisciplinary design team: Our research team is comprised of engineers of various disciplines, nurses specializing in geriatrics and advised by physicians, nurses, occupational therapists, and activity directors who are all experienced in working with older adults with cognitive impairment.
6. Research flexibility: Since the testing took place outside of the laboratory, we designed the system to be modular and flexible to accommodate the many unexpected variables in the real world.

7 Data Collection

7.1 Kinect Data

We collected head pose data using the Kinect sensor to detect non-verbal communication between the participants. We assumed that if the yaw angle of the head exceeded 45° towards their partner's sitting direction, then the participant was looking at their partner. We logged the head rotation about the X, Y, and Z axis with timestamps and then isolated the instances with head yaw angle more than 45° for the left participant and less than −45° for the right participant. We verified the accuracy of the head pose detection manually from time stamped video. We also recorded audio from the sessions to detect verbal communication. This data will be later used to automatically detect participant interaction.

7.2 Physiological Data

We collected physiological data using the Empatica E4 wrist mounted sensors. E4 contains a Photoplethysmography (PPG) sensor to measure Blood Volume Pulse (BVP) from which heart rate variability can be derived, an Electrodermal Activity (EDA) sensor that measures the fluctuating electrical properties of the skin, an infrared thermopile to measure skin temperature, and a three-axis accelerometer to measure motion. We also used a similar sensor, Emotibit (emotibit.com), on one of the participants to compare its data with the E4 data to validate Emotibit as a potential alternative. The physiological data will be later used to detect stress and engagement and inform the state machine to further adapt the activity for the individual.

7.3 Activity Approval

After each session, participants completed a questionnaire and rated their comfort and confidence levels with the wand, the robot, and the VR system on a scale of 1 (least) to 5 (greatest). Each participant had performed the activity twice; their responses after the first and second sessions are summarized in the Tables 1 and 2. While the ratings are subjective and dependent on the participants' mood and well-being on that particular day, we can see an increase in the total individual scores after the second session for three out of four participants. The individual total score increased by an average of 3.5. The mean category-wise ratings also increased for five out of the six categories after the second session, with the mean increase being 0.58. After their second session, participant A1005 mentioned that while they liked the robot addressing them by name, the amount of feedback was overwhelming. They also mentioned that they had difficulty seeing the screen on that day. To address these issues, we are adjusting the feedback timing and considering other colors to improve the visibility and contrast on the screen.

Table 1. Participant ratings after first session

Participant	Wand		Robot		VR system		Total
	Comfort	Confidence	Comfort	Confidence	Comfort	Confidence	
A1001	4	4	4	4	3	4	**23**
A1002	3	2	2	3	5	5	**20**
A1004	3	2	2	3	4	5	**19**
A1005	2	2	3	4	1	3	**15**
Total	12	10	11	14	13	17	
Mean	**3**	**2.5**	**2.75**	**3.5**	**3.25**	**4.25**	

Table 2. Participant ratings after second session

Participant	Wand		Robot		VR system		Total
	Comfort	Confidence	Comfort	Confidence	Comfort	Confidence	
A1001	4	4	5	5	5	4	**27**
A1002	4	3	5	5	5	4	**26**
A1004	4	4	5	4	4	4	**25**
A1005	3	2	2	2	2	2	**13**
Total	15	13	17	16	16	14	
Mean	**3.75**	**3.25**	**4.25**	**4**	**4**	**3.5**	

8 Participant Final Thoughts

After each session, the participants were asked open-ended question: what they liked about the task, if they would like to do the task again, what changes, if any, they would like to see, and if the difficulty level of the activity was appropriate. All the participants mentioned that they liked the dog training activity and enjoyed seeing Aibo perform the tricks that they spelled out by picking the letters. Some of them wanted to play with Aibo and pet him after the session. They mentioned that they liked the moving letters and finding the correct ones. When asked if the instructions they received from Nao were clear and adequate, they said some instructions required further clarification. We made the necessary changes to Nao's instructions and when asked the same question again after their second session, they said that they were satisfied with the instructions. After their first session, one of the participants commented that having too many letters on the screen was overwhelming and they faced difficulty finding the correct ones. We implemented a slider that can regulate the number of excess letters visible on the screen. After the second session, the participants mentioned that they liked the task with reduced number of letters and did not feel overwhelmed. All of them indicated that they would like to do this activity again in the future.

9 Discussion and Conclusion

We designed this activity to keep the older adults engaged, provide physical and cognitive stimulation, and initiate social interaction. We followed the principles of participant centered design and involved the stakeholders in every step of the design process. We consulted with our panel of experts consisting of physicians, nurses, activity directors, and occupational therapists to brainstorm ideas for appropriate activities and gain an insight into the unique challenges faced by our target population. We tested our prototype activity design with two pairs of nursing faculty and incorporated the suggested changes. We consulted with older adults residing in long term care facilities to see if they would enjoy interacting with the robots and ensured that the voice of the robot and the pace of instructions was acceptable. The activity was designed to be easily modifiable and with a variety of difficulty levels to accommodate the abilities of a wide range of individuals.

A participant study involving four older adults residing in a long-term care facility showed that the activity is well received by our target population. They liked the task and the robots, especially the puppy robot Aibo. We made changes iteratively to address the problems that they faced, and the approval rating increased after their second sessions.

A limitation of this study is the small sample size. The initial aim was to conduct the study with twelve participants but due to difficulty in recruitment due to COVID-19, the number of participants had to be reduced to four. A larger sample size will enable us to test the activity on subjects with a wider range of physical and cognitive abilities and make the activity design more robust and better adapted for our target population.

Future work includes testing the system on a larger sample size, include more ways of customizing the task to make it more accommodating to a wider range of population, and using the physiological data for online stress detection to enable the system to adapt dynamically to the individual participant's abilities. We are also working on incorporating natural language processing to better identify and classify participant interaction.

Acknowledgements. Research reported in this publication was supported by the National Institute on Aging of the National Institutes of Health under award number R01AG062685. The content is solely the responsibility of the authors and does not necessarily represent the official views of the National Institutes of Health. One author was also supported by the National Science Foundation Research Traineeship DGE 19-22697. The authors would like to thank the participants for their time and feedback.

References

1. 2021 Alzheimer's disease facts and figures: Alzheimers Dement. **17**(3):327–406 (2021). https://doi.org/10.1002/alz.12328. Epub 23 March 2021. PMID: 33756057
2. https://www.usnews.com/news/health-news/articles/2021-07-21/1-in-20-cases-of-dementia-occurs-in-people-under-65
3. https://www.cdc.gov/nchs/fastats/leading-causes-of-death.htm
4. Volicer, L.: Behavioral problems and dementia. Clin. Geriatr. Med. **34**(4), 637–651 (2018). W.B. Saundershttps://doi.org/10.1016/j.cger.2018.06.009.

5. Lanctôt, K.L., et al.: Apathy associated with neurocognitive disorders: recent progress and future directions. Alzheimer's Dement. **13**(1), 84–100 (2017). https://doi.org/10.1016/j.jalz.2016.05.008. Elsevier Inc.
6. Brodaty, H., Burns, K.: Nonpharmacological management of apathy in dementia: a systematic review. Am. J. Geriatr. Psychiatry **20**(7), 549–564 (2012). https://doi.org/10.1097/JGP.0b013e31822be242
7. Cohen-Mansfield, J., Marx, M.S., Dakheel-Ali, M., Thein, K.: The use and utility of specific nonpharmacological interventions for behavioral symptoms in dementia: an exploratory study. Am. J. Geriatr. Psychiatry **23**(2), 160–170 (2015). https://doi.org/10.1016/j.jagp.2014.06.006
8. Woods, B., O'Philbin, L., Farrell, E.M., Spector, A.E., Orrell, M.: Reminiscence therapy for dementia. Cochrane Database Syst. Rev. **3** (2018)
9. McCallum, S., Boletsis, C.: Dementia games: a literature review of dementia-related serious games. In: Ma, M., Oliveira, M.F., Petersen, S., Hauge, J.B. (eds.) SGDA 2013. LNCS, vol. 8101, pp. 15–27. Springer, Heidelberg (2013). https://doi.org/10.1007/978-3-642-40790-1_2
10. Krueger, K.R., Wilson, R.S., Kamenetsky, J.M., Barnes, L.L., Bienias, J.L., Bennett, D.A.: Social engagement and cognitive function in old age. Exp. Aging Res. **35**(1), 45–60 (2009). https://doi.org/10.1080/03610730802545028
11. Long-Term Services and Supports: Nursing Workforce Demand Projections About the National Center for Health Workforce Analysis (2015). http://bhw.hrsa.gov/healthworkforce/index.html
12. Moyle, W., et al.: Exploring the effect of companion robots on emotional expression in older adults with dementia: a pilot randomized controlled trial. J. Gerontol. Nurs. **39**(5), 46–53 (2013)
13. Migovich, M., Ghosh, R., Khan, N., Tate, J.A., Mion, L.C., Sarkar, N.: System architecture and user interface design for a human-machine interaction system for dementia intervention. In: Gao, Q., Zhou, J. (eds.) HCII 2021. LNCS, vol. 12787, pp. 277–292. Springer, Cham (2021). https://doi.org/10.1007/978-3-030-78111-8_19
14. Lihui Pu, M.S.N., Moyle, W., Jones, C., Todorovic, M.: The effectiveness of social robots for older adults: a systematic review and meta-analysis of randomized controlled studies. Gerontologist **59**(1), e37–e51 (2019)
15. Görer, B., Salah, A.A., Akın, H.L.: A robotic fitness coach for the elderly. In: Augusto, J.C., Wichert, R., Collier, R., Keyson, D., Salah, A.A., Tan, A.-H. (eds.) AmI. LNCS, vol. 8309, pp. 124–139. Springer, Cham (2013). https://doi.org/10.1007/978-3-319-03647-2_9
16. Fasola, J., Mataric, M.: A socially assistive robot exercise coach for the elderly. J. Hum.-Robot Interact. **2**(2), 3–32 (2013). https://doi.org/10.5898/jhri.2.2.fasola
17. Matsusaka, Y., Fujii, H., Okano, T., Hara, I.: Health exercise demonstration robot TAIZO and effects of using voice command in robot-human collaborative demonstration. In: Proceedings - IEEE International Workshop on Robot and Human Interactive Communication, pp. 472–477 (2009). https://doi.org/10.1109/ROMAN.2009.5326042
18. McColl, D., Louie, W.Y.G., Nejat, G.: Brian 2.1: a socially assistive robot for the elderly and cognitively impaired. IEEE Robot. Autom. Mag. **20**(1), 74–83 (2013). https://doi.org/10.1109/MRA.2012.2229939
19. Pino, O., Palestra, G., Trevino, R., De Carolis, B.: The humanoid robot NAO as trainer in a memory program for elderly people with mild cognitive impairment. Int. J. Soc. Robot. **12**(1), 21–33 (2019). https://doi.org/10.1007/s12369-019-00533-y
20. Yu, R., et al.: Use of a therapeutic, socially assistive Pet Robot (PARO) in improving mood and stimulating social interaction and communication for people with dementia: study protocol for a randomized controlled trial. JMIR Res. Protoc. **4**(2), e45 (2015). https://doi.org/10.2196/resprot.4189

21. Šabanovic, S., Bennett, C.C., Chang, W.L., Huber, L.: PARO robot affects diverse interaction modalities in group sensory therapy for older adults with dementia (2013). https://doi.org/10.1109/ICORR.2013.6650427
22. Thunberg, S., et al.: A wizard of Oz approach to robotic therapy for older adults with depressive symptoms. In: Companion of the 2021 ACM/IEEE International Conference on Human-Robot Interaction, pp. 294–297, March 2021
23. Schiavo, G., et al.: Wizard of Oz studies with older adults: a methodological note. Int. Rep. Socio-Inf. **13**(3), 93–100 (2016)
24. Eisapour, M., Cao, S., Domenicucci, L., Boger, J.: Virtual reality exergames for people living with dementia based on exercise therapy best practices. In: Proceedings of the Human Factors and Ergonomics Society, vol. 1, pp. 528–532 (2018). https://doi.org/10.1177/1541931218621120
25. Li, J., Louie, W.-Y.G., Mohamed, S., Despond, F., Nejat, G.: A user-study with tangy the bingo facilitating robot and long-term care residents. In: 2016 IEEE International Symposium on Robotics and Intelligent Sensors (IRIS), pp. 109–115 (2016)
26. Burgener, S.C., Yang, Y., Gilbert, R., Marsh-Yant, S.: The effects of a multimodal intervention on outcomes of persons with early-stage dementia. Am. J. Alzheimer's Dis. Other Dementias® 382–394 (2008). https://doi.org/10.1177/1533317508317527
27. Olanrewaju, O., Clare, L., Barnes, L., Brayne, C.: A multimodal approach to dementia prevention: a report from the Cambridge Institute of Public Health. Alzheimer's Dementia Transl. Res. Clin. Interv. **1**(3), 151–156 (2015). https://doi.org/10.1016/j.trci.2015.08.003. ISSN 2352-8737
28. Mann, J.A., Macdonald, B.A., Kuo, I.H., Li, X., Broadbent, E.: People respond better to robots than computer tablets delivering healthcare instructions. Comput. Hum. Behav. **43**, 112–117 (2015). https://doi.org/10.1016/j.chb.2014.10.029
29. Bainbridge, W.A., Hart, J.W., Kim, E.S., Scassellati, B.: The benefits of interactions with physically present robots over video-displayed agents. Int. J. Soc. Robot. **3**(1), 41–52 (2011). https://doi.org/10.1007/s12369-010-0082-7
30. Fischer, B., Peine, A., Östlund, B.: The importance of user involvement: a systematic review of involving older users in technology design. Gerontologist **60**(7), e513–e523 (2020)
31. Björling, E.A., Rose, E.: Participatory research principles in human-centered design: engaging teens in the co-design of a social robot. Multimodal Technol. Interact. **3**(1), 8 (2019)
32. Gould, J.D., Lewis, C.: Designing for usability: key principles and what designers think. Commun. ACM **28**(3), 300–311 (1985)
33. Gulliksen, J., Göransson, B., Boivie, I., Blomkvist, S., Persson, J., Cajander, Å.: Key principles for user-centred systems design. Behav. Inf. Technol. **22**(6), 397–409 (2003)

Nadine Robot in Elderly Care Simulation Recreational Activity: Using Computer Vision and Observations for Analysis

Nidhi Mishra[1(✉)], Gauri Tulsulkar[1], and Nadia Magnenat Thalmann[1,2]

[1] Nanyang Technological University, Singapore, Singapore
nidhimishra2906@gmail.com

[2] Miralab, University of Geneva, Geneva, Switzerland

Abstract. Many elderly residing in nursing homes have age-prevalent cognitive impairment and would benefit from regular social and cognitive engagements to maintain their well-being. However, manpower and resources to cater for both healthy elderly and their cognitively impaired co-inhabitants effectively are often inadequate in elderly care settings; therefore, other measures must be considered. Here, we subjectively and objectively evaluated the feasibility and impact of Nadine, our humanoid social robot, conducting Bingo games for a group of cognitively impaired elderly at a nursing home, compared to Staff-led sessions. The elderly engaged more and sought less attention from staff during Nadine-led Bingo games than during Staff-championed sessions. They were also calmer, happier, more at ease, and more communicative during Nadine-led games. These findings can guide future designs of humanoid robots that could be extended to become mobile robots to engage with the elderly of various functional and cognitive abilities and provide more manpower.

Keywords: Human-computer interaction · Human robot interaction · User studies · Usability testing · Nadine social robot · Social assistive robotics (SAR) · Robot companions · Social robots · Social intelligence for robots · Human-humanoid interaction · Computer vision · Observational scales

1 Introduction

The rising global ageing population has seen the incidence of cognitive impairment in seniors rise. According to the World Health Organization's (WHO) predictions, 82 million seniors will suffer from these conditions by 2030 and 152 million by 2050[1]. This progressively deteriorating condition affects the daily activities and lifestyle of cognitively impaired persons who suffer from loss of memory, language, problem-solving, and other thinking abilities. In addition to the cognitive decline, a cognitively impaired individual also experiences psychological changes, including personality disorders, depression, agitation, and hallucinations.

[1] https://alz.org.sg/dementia/singapore/.

Q. Gao and J. Zhou (Eds.): HCII 2022, LNCS 13331, pp. 29–51, 2022.
https://doi.org/10.1007/978-3-031-05654-3_3

Because there is no cure for cognitive impairment at the moment, emphasized care interventions and efforts must be invested in promoting well-being and improving a cognitively impaired person's quality of life [1]. Caregiving aims to maintain the safety and holistic well-being of cognitively impaired people through pharmacological and non-pharmacological interventions, which often require significant manpower and resources. Non-pharmacological approaches include interventions that promote physical, cognitive, emotional, and social well-being, for instance, art and music therapy, socialization activities, or simulated presence therapy. Such activities can stimulate cognitively impaired elderly at nursing homes, promote active engagement among them, and significantly improve their quality of life [5], and they may also provide further benefits, like reduced agitation and depression, improved mood, pleasure, and interest among this group of elderly [6].

The demand for more staff power at nursing homes has led to considerations and tests of other forms of support, such as the use of robots in various capacities. With the impetus to explore the feasibility of a robot as a non-pharmacological intervention, our study focused on leveraging Nadine, our humanoid social robot, in activities as a way to improve the stimulation and engagement of the elderly with age-related cognitive impairment in a nursing home setting. Care staff at nursing homes are often overwhelmed by behavioural challenges, such as agitation, non-compliance to care, aggression, wandering, and persistent calling out, from inhabitants with cognitive impairments [33]. Therefore, we also aimed to determine the impact of using Nadine and her kind as a productivity measure to augment manpower resources during care and support services commonly plagued by manpower shortage, expertise, and resource limitations.

To understand the impact of humanoid-led activities on the cognitively impaired elderly and staff at a nursing home, we observed the responses and behaviours of this group of elderly and staff during Nadine-steered Bingo games and compared findings from her sessions with those of Staff-conducted games. To establish her comprehensive influence at the nursing home when hosting Bingo games, we used objective and subjective tools for validation; objective tools are based on computer vision techniques, while subjective tools are based on observational tools. We used the Deep Neural Networks (DNNs) and Person-centred Interactions Observational Tool (PCIO) to capture and evaluate cognitively impaired elderly's emotional states and quality of engagement. With our primary aim to stimulate the cognitively impaired elderly of a nursing home through a recreational activity, like Bingo games, and keep them engaged, we deployed Nadine to host Bingo games for nursing home elderly with cognitive impairment and used the human-robot interaction (HRI) technology to answer the following questions (Fig. 1):

- What is the impact of a humanoid-led Bingo game on the emotional and engagement states of a cognitively impaired elderly in a nursing home?
- How can a humanoid-led Bingo game be used to augment the current manpower resource?

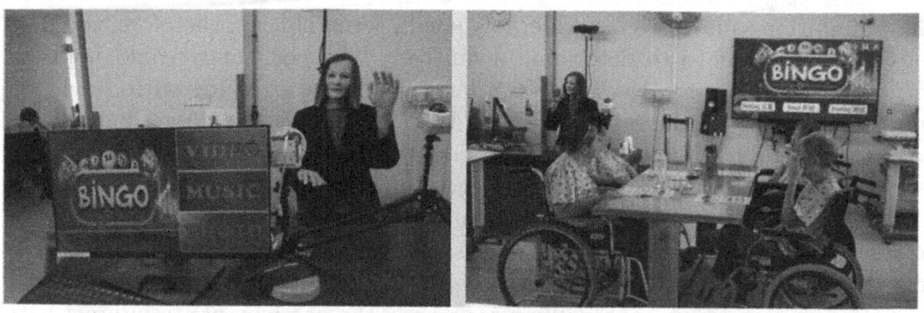

Fig. 1. Nadine hosting bingo for elderly.

The rest of the paper is organized as follows: we review existing literature on humanoid robots assisting in nursing homes in Sect. 2, explain the experimental setup and adaptation technique of Nadine at the nursing home in Sect. 3, provide details of our data collection methods and framework to analyze the data collected in Sect. 4, present and discuss experimental results in Sect. 5, and conclude in Sect. 6.

2 Literature Survey

Socially Assistive Robot systems have been used to provide interventions and companionship for older adults; these offer physical and cognitive assistance. Social assistive-robot-based systems capable of performing activities, playing cognitive games, and socializing can be used to stimulate the physical, cognitive, and social conditions of older adults and arrest the deterioration of their cognitive state [28]. The potential use of these robots to provide assistance or services through personalizing the robots to individual participants could enable users to live independently in their own homes and communities [19]. Research has shown that different types of stimuli, including moderate sound levels, small group activities, animals, tasks, puzzles, engaging music and videos, and even robotic animals and robots have enabled participants in nursing homes to engage more frequently and avoid agitation [12,13].

Mario, a social robot deployed in an elderly home to lead various recreational games, such as the painting game Scopa, which is an Italian card game, and Bingo, enhanced the quality of life of the elderly with cognitive impairments and reduced their depression and perceived social support [3,9,27].

Tangy the robot used in a long-term care (LTC) facility to lead a multi-player Bingo game [22,24,25,41] autonomously announced Bingo numbers, helped check players' cards individually, verified winnings, and alerted winners. Tangy's facilitation of the game was highly effective with high significantly improved levels of compliance and engagement from participants noted during the sessions. Although Tangy was humanlike, his appearance was not realistically humanoid. Moreover, the duration of the study was short with about six 1 h sessions, and the population sample was considerably small, seven elderly; therefore, the findings were inadequate to determine definitively whether Tangy could hold the interest over a longer period and for a larger audience. A study with Stevie the robot showed he cognitively stimulated the elderly when playing Bingo games with them, and he did so while largely entertaining participants [39].

Research with Paro, a seal robot placed in nursery homes [10], and everyday elderly care [37] revealed that the extended use of the robot led to an increase in sociability within groups of elderly, as well as other social benefits [36]. Also observed were a steady increase in the physical interaction between the elderly and the robot and a growing willingness among the participants to interact with it. Paro even positively influenced mood change, reduced loneliness, and instigated a statistically significant increase in interactions in group activities. The use of Matilda the robot in three care facilities with 70 elderly participants in Australia to improve their emotional wellbeing [17] resulted in her engaging the elderly and elevating their social interaction levels during games with demonstrable efficiency. Participants' emotional, visual, and behavioural engagement also increased, and Matilda rewarded winners by singing and dancing due to which some participants wanted her to participate in all the group activities.

In a two-year investigation with Silbot the robot in an elderly care facility in Denmark [7], during which the robot hosted Bingo games as part of a brain fitness instructor, results were hard to come by because the study was blighted by many hardware and software problems undoubtedly associated with the length of the research. Battery, usability, and multiple other issues were also reported. We used the complications encountered in the Danish study as the reference point for our test (Fig. 2).

Based on similar studies with robots conducting a recreational activity, we classified the available state-of-the-art robots in Table 1. '✓' indicates the presence and 'X' indicates the absence of certain characteristics.

In most studies, the robots used are not as realistic as Nadine. Nadine can emote natural human communication with her humanlike features, as reported in [2]. She can produce facial expressions, respond with gestures, make eye contact with the elderly, and we compare these with the capabilities of other robots. Interactions with the face and arm movements are stimulating and could arouse curiosity and interest [19]. We have also classified robots' ability to speak and understand speech; if yes, are they multilingual? For functionalities, we have addressed different aspects of the vision-based capabilities of Robots. We examined robots' ability to understand the environment and stare at the elderly and understand their facial emotions. We look at previously studied robots' ability to control and interact with devices (such as TV, speakers, temperature control, etc.) to facilitate recreational activities. Furthermore, our classification builds on the analysis method used for the statistical results in previous studies; specifically, if they were AI- or ML-enabled.

The above parameters are deduced from the Table 1 that has not been taken into account in the literature so far. We believe firmly that our study could

Fig. 2. Robots used for recreational activities for elderly

provide a step forward towards teaching Nadine, with her humanlike characteristics in appearance and ability, to mimic human behaviour.

To evaluate the effectiveness and the impact of Nadine in conducting stimulating activities, we used the PCIO observational tool (a subjective tool) and the Deep Learning-Based methods, (objective tools) to capture the engagement between care staff/Nadine humanoid robot and the cognitively impaired elderly during the scrutinized Bingo games. Our study is undoubtedly a step forward in the research and development of a humanoid social robot with a humanlike appearance, characteristics, emotion recognition, and gesture synthesis that mimic human behaviour at an elderly home. Our combined technique using the deep learning-based model and PCIO tool to verify and validate results obtained in data analysis can help understand the impact of a humanoid robot on users

Table 1. Summary of the robots for recreational activity for elderly care where (a) Humanoid realistic appearance, (b) Cognitively impaired elderly's information, (c) Empathy, (d) Facial expressions, (e) Gestures, (f) Multilingual, (g) Computer Vision-based analysis, (h) Observational tools based analysis, (i) Internet of Things and (j) Gazing

Paper	(a)	(b)	(c)	(d)	(e)	(f)	(g)	(h)	(i)	(j)
Mario [3]	X	✓	✓	X	✓	✓	X	X	✓	✓
Mario [27]	X	✓	✓	X	✓	✓	X	✓	✓	✓
Pepper [22]	X	X	✓	✓	✓	✓	X	X	✓	✓
Zora [29]	X	X	✓	N/A	✓	N/A	X	X	✓	✓
Tangy [21]	X	X	✓	✓	✓	N/A	X	X	✓	✓
Silbot [7]	X	✓	✓	✓	✓	N/A	X	X	✓	✓
Zora [16]	X	X	✓	✓	✓	X	X	X	✓	✓
Zora [42]	X	X	✓	✓	✓	X	X	X	✓	✓
Stevie [39]	X	✓	✓	X	✓	X	X	X	✓	✓
Matilda [17]	X	✓	✓	X	✓	N/A	X	X	X	✓
Nadine	✓	✓	✓	✓	✓	✓	✓	✓	✓	✓

and is the first of its kind. Our evaluation method incorporates video analysis and the use of the observational tool PCIO to determine the holistic effect of Nadine-led Bingo sessions on the cognitively impaired elderly.

Our study is undoubtedly a step forward in the research and development of a humanoid social robot with a human-like appearance, characteristics, emotion recognition, and gesture synthesis that mimic human behaviour at an elderly home. Our combined technique using the deep learning-based model and PCIO tool to verify and validate results obtained in data analysis can help understand the impact of a humanoid robot on users and it's the first of its kind. Our evaluation method incorporates video analysis and the use of the observational tool PCIO to determine the holistic effect of Nadine-led Bingo sessions on the elderly.

3 Experimental Setup

Nadine is a socially intelligent, realistic humanoid robot with natural skin, hair, and appearance. She has 27 DOF, enabling her to make facial movements and gesticulate effectively, as documented in [44] and [4]. In this research, we seated Nadine in the activity area of a ward of the nursing home, where she hosted Bingo games and interacted with the elderly.

3.1 Architecture

Nadine's architecture as per Fig. 3 is described in [35]; it consists of three layers: perception, processing, and interaction. She receives audio and visual stimuli from microphones, 3D cameras, and web cameras to perceive user characteristics and her environment sent to the processing layer. The processing layer is her core module that receives all the information about the environment from the perception layer and acts upon them. This processing layer includes various submodules, such as dialogue processing (chatbot), affective system (emotions, personality, mood), and Nadine's memory of previous encounters with users. The action/interaction layer consists of a dedicated robot controller for actions, like emotion expression, lip synchronization, and gaze generation.

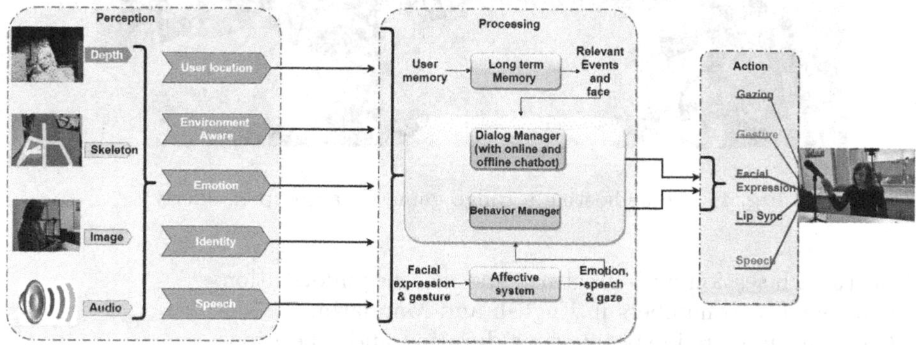

Fig. 3. Nadine's architecture

Nadine can recognise people she has met before and engage in a flowing conversation. She can be considered a part of human-assistive technology [26], as she is capable of assisting people over a continuous period without breaks; she has previously been deployed in different places that required her to work for long hours [30].

3.2 Adaptation

According to [32] and [20], most robots designed for the elderly do not fulfil the needs and requirements for optimal performance. For Nadine to be at her best in nursing homes, we updated some previous models and developed new modules recommended previously [11] (Fig. 4).

Bingo Game. Before deploying Nadine to the nursing home, the care staff was tasked with hosting Bingo sessions for the elderly. They announced numbers and used a small whiteboard to display these numbers for the elderly with hearing impairment. The new module we developed to help Nadine perform optimally when hosting Bingo games enabled her to do the following:

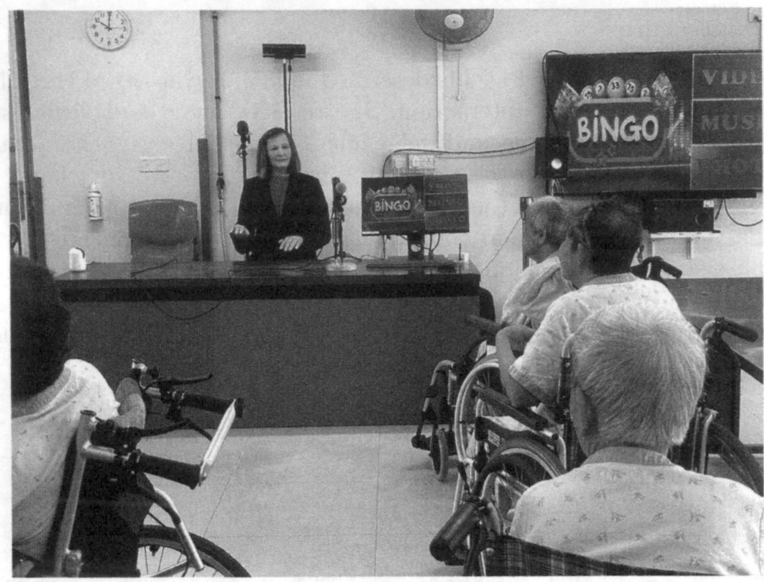

Fig. 4. Nadine hosting a Bingo game for a group of elderly

- Start each session with greetings and weather information.
- Call out Bingo numbers in English and Mandarin.
- Call out numbers in specific time duration and repetitions.
- Display the current number and four previous numbers on the TV screen.
- Accompany called out numbers with hand gestures, facial expressions, gaze, and background music.
- Allow care staff to control and customize her Bingo sessions using an attached touch screen.
- Verify winning players and applaud them.

Participating elderly were provided fabricated in-house buzzers to press upon realizing they had won a game, and Nadine played a cheering sound upon confirming Bingo calls from the elderly.

Update in Nadine's Existing Module. As a social humanoid robot, Nadine has an emotion engine that controls her emotions, personality, and mood during an interaction, enabling her to perceive the situation (user and environment) and adjust her emotions and behaviour accordingly. As a result, she can generate different emotions, including pleasure, arousal, and dominance. For Nadine function optimally in nursing homes, she must appear patient and show no negativity or anger; she must exhibit only a positive temperament. Therefore, we set a configuration file to different parameters that allowed her to stay positive and behave accordingly, even when an elderly is frustrated, angry, or upset with her. Also crucial is endowing Nadine's speech synthesis output with positive emotions. This mainly relates to changing the pitch, tone, and speed modulations.

We modified the speech synthesizer to adapt speech output allowing Nadine to speak slower, louder, and in a low tone to make it easier for the elderly to understand her.

3.3 Ethical Protocol and Participants

Our research was reviewed by the Research Integrity & Ethics office and approved by the Institutional Review Board. Participation in our study was entirely voluntary, with each participant choosing whether to participate or not; they had the right to refuse to partake in or withdraw from the study, even if they had agreed to take part in it earlier. All participants were given pertinent information (according to their level of understanding and in the language they understood) to make an informed decision about participating in the study. Those who agreed to be involved signed a consent form. For non-English speaking participants, an interpreter fluent in both English and the participant's spoken language assisted in the consent process.

Twenty-nine participants participated in the research and were never left unattended during sessions. The nursing Home took responsibility for the safety of the elderly who were monitored by the care staff during interactions with Nadine. The participating elderly did not engage in any form of physical interaction with her, only verbal and staring interactions. Overall, we recorded 24 Nadine-hosted Bingo sessions and 2 Staff-led games.

In our consideration of the ethical issues in deploying Nadine in elderly care, we observed and emphatically implemented safety protocols and safe distancing measures for Covid-19.

4 Data Analysis

In order to fully comprehend the impact of Nadine's presence conducting Bingo games at the nursing home, we used objective tools (based on computer vision techniques, such as Deep Neural Networks (DNNs)) and subjective tools (such as a PCIO observational tool) to scrutinize our data. Using the analytical procedures detailed below, we obtained the data for every video of Nadine-hosted Bingo versus Staff-led games and comparatively analysed them using statistical methods.

4.1 Computer Vision Method as an Objective Tool

We used deep neural networks (DNNs) to evaluate the emotional and physical states of the elderly automatically focusing on the following three evaluation metrics:

- *Happiness*, (the satisfaction level of elderly during Nadine-steered Bingo games).
- *Movement*, (Nadine's effect on the physical movement of the elderly during games she championed).

- *Activity*, (the overall physical movement of the care staff during Nadine-hosted Bingo games).

To quantitatively analyse these three metrics, we exploited DNNs' advantages in processing videos efficiently. Specifically, we used four different networks for this study: a face detector[2], an expression recognizer, an action detector[3] and an optical flow estimator [40].

The face detector, which estimates the locations of faces in a given frame (see Fig. 5), was particularly useful, given that all participating elderly were in wheelchairs; their relative locations were inferred based on the location of their faces. Additionally, the nursing care staff were all wearing medical masks throughout their intervention in Nadine's Bingo sessions, and their faces were, therefore, not detected. We adopted the Dlib library with its pre-trained convolutional neural network (CNN) to implement the face detector.

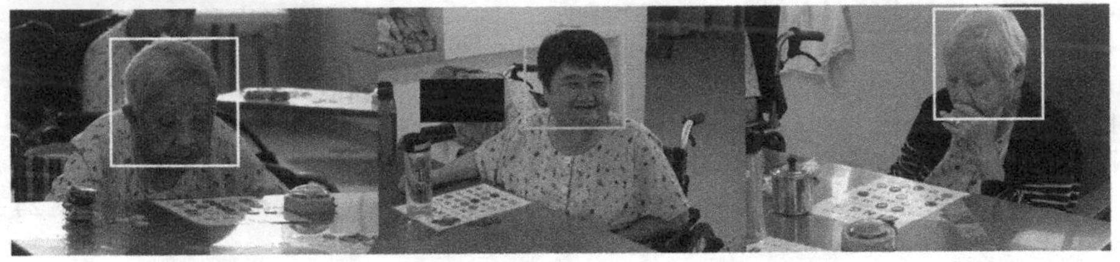

Fig. 5. Examples of the face detector output

The expression recognizer categorizes the expression of a detected face and is trained on the CelebA dataset [23] until convergence. We considered two classes of expression in our case, i.e., smiling and neutral, and constructed a CNN with ResNet-50 [15] as the backbone.

The action detector measures the motions and actions of a detected face, generating action proposals, which are the locations and confidences of detecting an action. We implemented the action detector based on the pre-trained temporal segment network [43] provided in the MMAction2 library; it detected the movement of the elderly during Nadine's run Bingo game sessions, as the face detector detected only faces.

The optical flow estimator determines moving targets (see Fig. 6). We recommend estimating dense optical flow via the recurrent all-pairs field transformation network. At this moment, for an arbitrary region in each frame, the average magnitude of the estimated optical flow in the region can be used to measure the intensity of movement of care staff during the Bingo game sessions.

Using these DNNs, we defined the quantitative measures of *Happiness*, *Movement* and *Activity*.

[2] http://dlib.net/.

[3] https://github.com/open-mmlab/mmaction2.

Fig. 6. Staff movement in the patch using optical flow estimator

Happiness is closely associated with smiling and laughing expressions. Hence, given a target video of L frames, we defined group happiness h as:

$$h = \frac{1}{L} \sum_{l=1}^{L} \frac{1}{n_l} \sum_{t=1}^{n_l} p_t, \tag{1}$$

where $p_t \in [0, 1]$ denotes the probability of the t-th detected face in the l-th frame belonging to the smiling class, which is estimated by the expression recognizer.

We defined the *Movement* of the elderly using the action detector in the following equation, where d_t is the confidence of detecting an action:

$$b = \frac{1}{L} \sum_{l=1}^{L} \frac{1}{n_l} \sum_{l=1}^{n_l} d_t \tag{2}$$

For the *Activity* of the care staff, we used the optical flow estimator in the following equation where o_l is the magnitude of optical flow per frame:

$$f = \frac{1}{L} \sum_{l=1}^{L} o_l \tag{3}$$

Using these analyses (example shown in Fig. 6), we obtained the data for every video across all sessions and scrutinized them further using statistical methods to obtain meaningful comparisons.

4.2 An Observational Method as a Subjective Tool

The PCIO tool measures the quality of a "task" conducted and the responses provided by the cognitively impaired elderly. Other tools can also be used to assess these interactions. Such person-centred assessments and further necessary care planning must be the focus in providing persons with cognitive impairments with unique requirements, support, and characteristics [14]. The Quality of Interactions Schedule (QuIS) [8,34], the CARES ® observational tool [14,38], the Greater Cincinnati Chapter Well-Being Observation Tool© [18], and Dementia Mapping Tool [38], are such valid measures that use independent observers to assess the quality of social interactions between staff and patients in a care setting where the patients cannot self-report. These tools can help understand, address, and provide better emotional and healthcare facilities [31].

Cognitive impairment primarily causes memory loss and affects the thinking process and communication. With this in mind, we selected the PCIO observation tool to gain insight into the experiences of the elderly during Nadine's run of Bingo games and determine her influence during the activity.

The PCIO Tool has 2 components: the Staff Interaction Code (SIC) and Client Reaction Code (CRC). The SIC measures the quality of the care activity conducted and the CRC evaluates the engagement state of the elderly. We used the CRC to determine the state of engagement and participation during the Bingo session. CRC is coded in one of 5 states, namely, Connected state, Collaborative state, Compliant state, Alerting state, and Assertive state. The Connected state denotes the elderly's happiness, optimal and spontaneous participation in tasks, and engagement in positive communications. The Collaborative state refers to the elderly's relaxed state, which enables them to attempt to participate in tasks, show some signs of happiness, comfort, and occasional engagement in positive communications. The Compliant state is a state at which the elderly routinely accepts care to avoid negative consequences, displays no notable emotion, and engages in minimal communication. In the Alerting State, the elderly attempts to avoid and reject care delivery and shows signs of displeasure, discomfort, and negative communication. During the Assertive state, the elderly strongly refuses and rejects the provision of care, are unhappy, distressed, aggressive, angry, and communicates negatively most of the time.

Nadine's performance when leading Bingo sessions was also of significance in determining her potential to augment productivity. Therefore, we collected data for the study based on 2 key observations of the elderly and staff:

- **For cognitively impaired elderly:** Observations of their engagement responses during Nadine-led Bingo games versus Staff-conducted sessions.
- **For staff:** Observations of their work during Nadine-led Bingo games versus their sessions.

The elderly's level of engagement was observed through their emotional expressions, e.g., showing signs of happiness, sadness, or flat affect and the demonstrated behaviour, such as initiating action, communication, and cooperation. The observation of the elderly's responses and behaviours were coded with the PCIO Tool using the following client reaction codes (CRC) as the metrics of evaluation:

- **Connected state:** The elderly are happy and participate optimally and spontaneously: shows happiness; participates in tasks as much as they can; consistent positive communication.

- **Collaborative state:** The elderly are at ease and attempt to participate when prompted: shows some signs of happiness, comfort; attempt to participate in tasks; occasional positive communication.
- **Compliant state:** The elderly accept assistance routinely to avoid negativity: no obvious display of emotions; minimal communication.
- **Alerting state:** The elderly attempt to avoid and reject assistance: shows signs of unhappiness and discomfort; attempts to avoid or refuse care delivery; some signs of negative communication.
- **Assertive state:** The elderly strongly refuse and reject assistance: shows unhappiness, distress, aggression, frustration, anger; forcefully stop or refuse assistance; obvious signs of negative communication.

Staff responses and behaviours were observed using the same videos that captured Nadine-led Bingo sessions versus Staff-conducted sessions and evaluated through observations of the following:

- **Tasks:** The types and number of tasks performed during Bingo games.
- **Interaction approach:** The approach they adopted as they interacted with and assisted the elderly during Bingo games.

Twenty-four sessions with 29 participants were recorded, and the engagement responses of 15 elderly and 2 staff were observed and analysed over 12 Bingo sessions.

5 Results

5.1 Computer Vision Method as an Objective Tool

To determine Nadine's impact on the elderly when hosting Bingo games, we analysed the video material we obtained. We compared four aspects of the video material (smile, neutral, body score, and optical flow) between Nadine-hosted sessions and those hosted by staff. After cleaning the footage, we identified 24 sessions hosted by Nadine with 29 participating elderly in each game and 2 sessions hosted by the caretakers. For each session, multiple camera angles generated the footage. We compared all the footage from each of the available cameras without compressing them into single averages for the sessions.

For comparisons of the scores between Nadine's hosting and the caretakers' hosting, we performed an independent samples t-test; results are shown in Table 2. The means and standard deviations of the four variables in the two situations are presented in Fig. 7. Before conducting the t-tests, Levene's test of equality of variance was performed to check for the assumption of homoscedasticity. We determined that two of the variables had unequal variance (variables smile and body score); therefore, we analysed these two variables using modified degrees of freedom.

Table 2. Results of the t-tests during Nadine-led sessions.

Variable	t	df	Sig. (2-tailed)	Mean difference
Smile	3.341	23.122	0.003	0.009
Neutral	−0.678	63	0.500	−0.043
Body score	−2.123	38.275	0.040	−0.019
Optical flow	−2.211	63	0.031	−0.107

Variable	Std. error difference	95% confidence interval of the difference	
		Lower	Upper
Smile	0.003	0.004	0.015
Neutral	0.064	−0.171	0.084
Body score	0.009	−0.036	−0.001
Optical flow	0.049	−0.204	−0.010

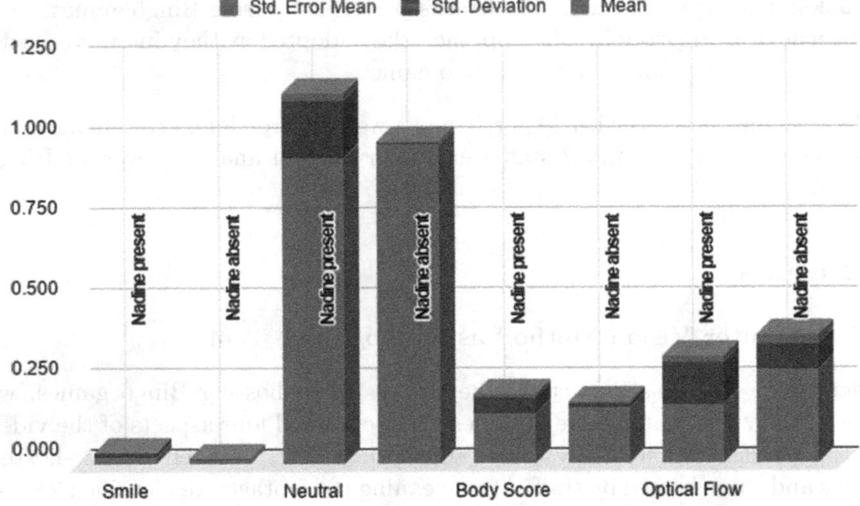

Fig. 7. Means and 95% CI of measurements.

As shown in Fig. 7, three of the variables demonstrated significant differences between the two circumstances: the smile variable was considerably higher during Nadine's sessions, while the body score and the optical flow variables were markedly higher in the Staff-led games. No differences were recorded in neutral measurements between the two groups.

Table 3. Bivariate correlations the between serial numbers of sessions and the four variables.

Variable	Pearson correlation	Significance
Smile	0.249	0.062
Neutral	−0.241	0.071
Body score	−0.069	0.609
Optical flow	0.113	0.403

To determine whether or not the reactions of the elderly changed with time, we looked for bivariate correlations between the four variables and the serial numbers of the sessions; the higher a serial number, the later the session; therefore, a correlation would imply a linear change in the variables with time. The results of the correlational analysis are presented in Table 3.

None of the variables had a significant correlation with the serial number. Smile and neutral did have a marginally significant correlation and perhaps could show more significance with a larger sample of data.

5.2 Observational Methods as a Subjective Tool

Based on the PCIO Tool, our observational findings on the cognitively impaired elderly showed positive changes in the engagement levels between Nadine-led Bingo sessions and Staff-orchestrated games. The elderly's engagement levels improved significantly during Nadine-led Bingo sessions: 22% were positively engaged during the Staff-conducted Bingo games compared to 91% during Nadine's sessions (Fig. 8).

That positive engagement is further exhibited in Fig. 9, with elderly being significantly more in the Collaborative state (positive engagement) during Nadine-hosted sessions and considerably more in the Compliance state (neutral engagement) during Staff-conducted games.

Similarly, the elderly were more positively engaged (person-focused and care-focused) during Nadine's sessions (at 99.7% versus 25% during Staff-championed sessions) and more neutrally engaged (task-focused) during Staff-led sessions (at 75% versus 0.3% during Nadine-championed sessions), as Fig. 10 shows.

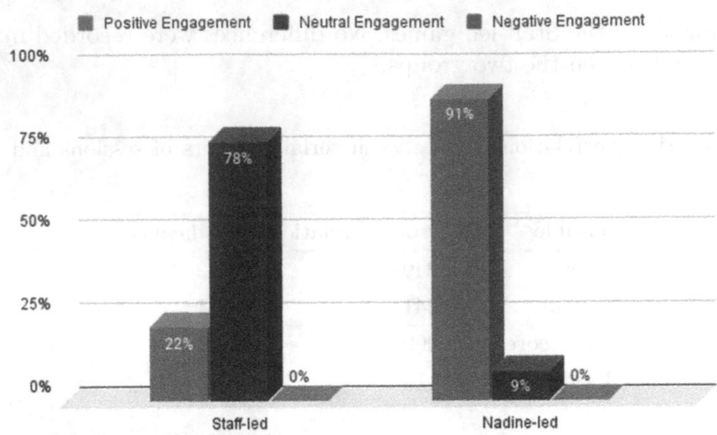

Fig. 8. Elderly's engagement level during Nadine-led versus Staff-led Bingo games, where Positive Engagement is Connected & Collaborative, Neutral Engagement is Compliance and Negative Engagement is Alerting & Assertive

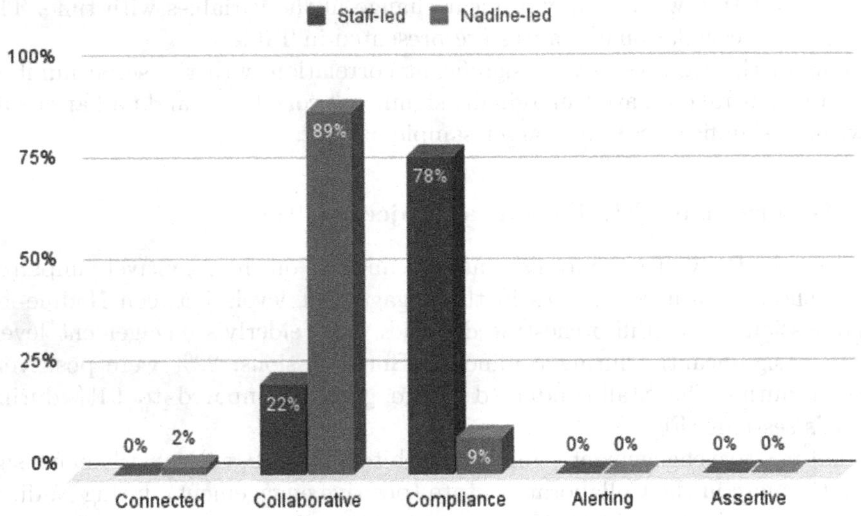

Fig. 9. Elderly's CRC during Bingo games (Nadine-led versus Staff-led). 15 cognitively impaired elderly/5 min/20 min interval over 40 min for 12 Bingo sessions

Nadine's impact during Bingo games was evident in the staff members' interaction approach and the changes in tasks performed (Table 4). The key findings in comparing Staff-conducted Bingo games to Nadine-led Bingo games suggest the following:

Table 4. Key impact on staff during Nadine and staff conducted Bingo games

	Conducted by staff	Conducted by Nadine
Staff task	Staff run around juggling multiple tasks – Calling out loudly the numbers in English, Mandarin, and dialects – Writing numbers on white board and showing all the elderly – Reminding elderly to pay attention after number has been called (E.g., Hard of hearing, poor vision, forgetful) – Checking all elderly to encourage participation and assist to play game – Check elderly if they "win" and shout "Bingo" to get "prizes"	Staff walks around calmly to – Assist elderly who need help to check Bingo card and play – Prompt elderly to hit buzzer when they "Bingo" – Present prizes to elderly when they hit buzzer after the "Bingo" Nadine calls the numbers – Numbers are projected on TV screen and monitor for easy viewing – All elderly (e.g., poor vision, hard of hearing and forgetful) are conditioned to look to TV screen and monitor to look out for number
Staff interaction approach	Staff tends to be – Rushing and doing things quickly when assisting elderly – Giving instructions that are short and lacks clarity – Doing for tasks for elderly Refer to Fig. 10 Coding the SIC of the staff with and without Nadine assisted Bingo sessions	Staff observed to be – Calm and patient when assisting elderly – Direct elderly to visual cues – Enabling and encouraging elderly to do more for themselves Refer to Fig. 10 Coding the SIC of the staff with and without Nadine assisted Bingo sessions
Set up	– Elderly seated around table with 50% of them back facing staff	– TV screen and monitor to flash the numbers – Elderly seated all facing the Nadine and TV screen and monitor
Key outcomes	– Staff are busy running around juggling multiple tasks – Bingo sessions can be chaotic and noisy, affecting elderly' engagement. As a result, some elderly are disengaged or "switched" off during the session. This results in staff spending a lot of effort to encourage elderly to participate	–Staff provide assistance only when elderly require therefore encouraging greater resident's involvement and autonomy – Bingo sessions are calm and organised. elderly despite their impairments are engaged throughout whole session with very minimal prompting from staff

– Nadine-led Bingo sessions are more organized and structured enabling elderly to be more attentive and participative throughout the sessions and
– Nadine-led Bingo sessions require lesser staff effort and involvement to encourage resident participation and to provide assistance

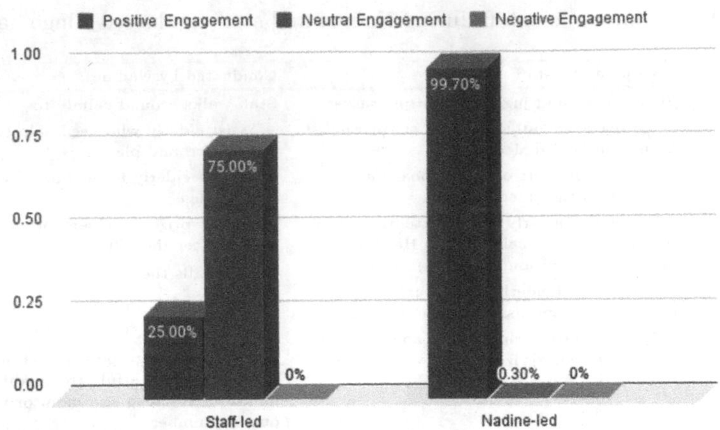

Fig. 10. Staff's Interaction approach with the elderly during Nadine-led versus Staff-led Bingo sessions. Positive Engagement is Person-focused & Care-focused, Neutral Engagement is Task-focused and Negative Engagement is Risk-focused & Discipline-focused

6 Conclusion and Discussion

In this study, we deployed Nadine to assist in Bingo games and assessed her impact on the engagement of cognitively impaired elderly and her potential to augment the productivity of the staff in a nursing home setting. Our results show that using a humanoid robot, like Nadine, as a non-pharmacological intervention that enhances conventional activities, like Bingo, to promote emotional and engagement benefits for cognitively impaired persons was efficient. Bingo is a widely popular activity in all nursing homes in Singapore. Because it is often conducted in large group sizes, many elderly, particularly those with cognitive impairment tend to be overlooked or left behind due to their difficulty participating without extensive support. Conducting such group activities requires significant manpower, a luxury that all nursing homes do not have, given the manpower and resource constraints.

Our finding with objective tools revealed three significant differences between the Nadine-led Bingo sessions and the Staff-conducted games. The elderly smiled more, moved around less, and the optical flow, which primarily relates to how much movement nursing home care staff have to make, was also lower during Nadine-led sessions. It was apparent that the situation in the nursing home was better during Nadine-steered games: elderly were also calmer and happier, and the staff had less work to do. Past studies produced similar findings, all showing the potential benefits of employing robotic assistance in nursing homes. With Nadine's humanoid appearance and her ability to communicate, read, and make facial expressions associated with emotions, it is logical to assume that her presence can and will simultaneously improved elderly's state of being in nursing homes and relieve the burden on the nursing home staff. This supposition is factual if we go by our findings, given that all the changes in the measured variables between the two circumstances (Nadine-led versus Staff-led games) point in that direction.

On the other hand, these variables did not change significantly over time, possibly due to the nature of them: given that Nadine renders the elderly more focused, happier, and less needy (seen through the fewer movements of the staff – Fig. 7), it is plausible that these effects remained constant over time. Hence, Nadine provided a significant degree of content, which would mean she was efficient in maintaining a high degree of interest from the elderly. Furthermore, this means Nadine's positive impact is felt very early on, with no period of adaptation required. Therefore, a humanoid robot's presence can bear an immediate positive impact in nursing homes or similar facilities.

Observational tool analyses also yielded promising results that can be used to address these common challenges in nursing homes where there is limited support for engagement during activity due to manpower shortage. The cognitively impaired elderly generally showed positivity, denoted by signs of happiness, comfort, ease, occasional positive communications, and attempts at autonomously doing things for themselves, as shown by their significant occupation of the collaborative state (Fig. 8, Fig. 9, and Fig. 10). While both the connected and collaborative states represent positive engagement, there is a temptation to wonder why the highest level of positivity (connected state) was not met. It is safe to hypothetically explain this phenomenon using human elements. Perhaps, fatigue, monotony, boredom, and memory loss, a component of cognitive impairment, can account for this. The elderly in nursing homes are senior citizens who, unlike younger people, do not have the same level of enthusiasm that would trigger the degree of willingness associated with the connected state. These are citizens who if they suffer memory loss might have to reacquaint themselves with the environment and everything else around them. Fatigue, something these elderly also experience frequently, can also impact their positivity, as can boredom from monotony. Therefore, that these cognitively impaired elderly did not attain the connected state should not deter from the fact that they retained a significant level of positive performance during Nadine-led Bingo sessions, which is a testament of how effective her present was and can be in nursing homes and similar institutions.

Given these findings and that humanoid robot-assisted interventions for persons with cognitive impairment have shown encouraging results to benefit both persons living with these conditions, care staff, and care organizations, we came to the following conclusions with regards to using Nadine to lead Bingo games:

– The significant improvement in the engagement level of the elderly with cognitive impairment associated with enhanced cognitive abilities, like increased alertness and attention span, and psychosocial responses, such as improved mood, autonomy, and sociability is a strong argument for the use of humanoid robots in more interventions provide more autonomous, interactive, and engaging modes of interactions with elderly.

- Nadine's support of the care home staff also improved their interaction approach with the elderly, providing strong evidence that the staff can adopt a more supportive and enabling approach during humanoid-led activities, like Bingo sessions, resulting in improved the elderly participation levels. Therefore, a boost in the staff's role by a humanoid's presence results in them devoting more time and effort to encourage and support the elderly to use their remaining cognitive abilities, which further translates into optimising the therapeutic benefits of such activities as the Bingo session on the cognitive abilities of impaired elderly.
- Also, in relation to the Nadine-provided boost to care staff, which enabled them to invest more time and effort to enable and encourage the elderly's use of their remaining abilities, particularly those with cognitive impairment, streamlining the activity sessions to review activity-related tasks that can be simplified or automated should significantly reduce the manpower resources required to conduct these activities. This benefit can be further expanded if the humanoid is mobile; a mobile humanoid could engage the elderly who require higher care support when they are predominantly in bed or isolated in care. Such a mobile humanoid robot can address the manpower gap by augmenting manpower resources while providing attention and assisting elderly of different functional abilities with their engagements.

We believe these findings to be useful for the future design of humanoids robots that could be extended to become mobile robots and engage with the elderly of various functional and cognitive abilities. We aim to further study the use of such humanoid robots to potentially address current manpower challenges in a variety of sectors.

References

1. Algar, K., Woods, R.T., Windle, G.: Measuring the quality of life and well-being of people with dementia: a review of observational measures. Dementia **15**(4), 832–857 (2016)
2. Baka, E., Vishwanath, A., Mishra, N., Vleioras, G., Thalmann, N.M.: "Am i talking to a human or a robot?": a preliminary study of human's perception in human-humanoid interaction and its effects in cognitive and emotional states. In: Gavrilova, M., Chang, J., Thalmann, N.M., Hitzer, E., Ishikawa, H. (eds.) CGI 2019. LNCS, vol. 11542, pp. 240–252. Springer, Cham (2019). https://doi.org/10.1007/978-3-030-22514-8_20
3. Barrett, E., et al.: Evaluation of a companion robot for individuals with dementia: quantitative findings of the MARIO project in an Irish residential care setting. J. Gerontol. Nurs. **45**(7), 36–45 (2019)
4. Beck, A., Zhijun, Z., Magnenat-Thalmann, N.: Motion control for social behaviors. In: Magnenat-Thalmann, N., Yuan, J., Thalmann, D., You, B.-J. (eds.) Context Aware Human-Robot and Human-Agent Interaction. HIS, pp. 237–256. Springer, Cham (2016). https://doi.org/10.1007/978-3-319-19947-4_11
5. Beerens, H.C., et al.: The association between aspects of daily life and quality of life of people with dementia living in long-term care facilities: a momentary assessment study. Int. Psychogeriatr. **28**(8), 1323–1331 (2016)

6. Beerens, H.C., et al.: The relation between mood, activity, and interaction in long-term dementia care. Aging Mental Health **22**(1), 26–32 (2018)
7. Blond, L.: Studying robots outside the lab: HRI as ethnography. Paladyn J. Behav. Robot. **10**(1), 117–127 (2019). https://doi.org/10.1515/pjbr-2019-0007
8. Bridges, J., Gould, L., Hope, J., Schoonhoven, L., Griffiths, P.: The quality of interactions schedule (QuIS) and person-centred care: concurrent validity in acute hospital settings. Int. J. Nurs. Stud. Adv. **1**, 100001 (2019)
9. Casey, D., et al.: What people with dementia want: designing MARIO an acceptable robot companion. In: Miesenberger, K., Bühler, C., Penaz, P. (eds.) ICCHP 2016. LNCS, vol. 9758, pp. 318–325. Springer, Cham (2016). https://doi.org/10.1007/978-3-319-41264-1_44
10. Chang, W., Šabanovic, S., Huber, L.: Use of seal-like robot PARO in sensory group therapy for older adults with dementia. In: 2013 8th ACM/IEEE International Conference on Human-Robot Interaction (HRI), pp. 101–102 (2013)
11. Chang, W.L., Šabanović, S.: Exploring Taiwanese nursing homes as product ecologies for assistive robots. In: 2014 IEEE International Workshop on Advanced Robotics and its Social Impacts, pp. 32–37. IEEE (2014)
12. Cohen-Mansfield, J., Dakheel-Ali, M., Marx, M.S.: Engagement in persons with dementia: the concept and its measurement. Am. J. Geriatr. Psychiatry **17**(4), 299–307 (2009)
13. Cohen-Mansfield, J., Marx, M.S., Dakheel-Ali, M., Regier, N.G., Thein, K., Freedman, L.: Can agitated behavior of nursing home residents with dementia be prevented with the use of standardized stimuli? J. Am. Geriatr. Soc. **58**(8), 1459–1464 (2010)
14. Gaugler, J.E., Hobday, J.V., Savik, K.: The cares® observational tool: a valid and reliable instrument to assess person-centered dementia care. Geriatr. Nurs. **34**(3), 194–198 (2013)
15. He, K., Zhang, X., Ren, S., Sun, J.: Deep residual learning for image recognition. In: Proceedings of European Conference on Computer Vision, pp. 770–778 (2016)
16. Huisman, C., Kort, H.: Two-year use of care robot Zora in Dutch nursing homes: an evaluation study. In: Healthcare, vol. 7, p. 31. Multidisciplinary Digital Publishing Institute (2019)
17. Khosla, R., Chu, M.T.: Embodying care in matilda: an affective communication robot for emotional wellbeing of older people in Australian residential care facilities. ACM Trans. Manag. Inf. Syst. (TMIS) **4**(4), 1–33 (2013)
18. Kinney, J.M., Rentz, C.A.: Observed well-being among individuals with dementia: memories in the making, an art program, versus other structured activity. Am. J. Alzheimer's Disease Other Dementias® **20**(4), 220–227 (2005)
19. Law, M., et al.: Developing assistive robots for people with mild cognitive impairment and mild dementia: a qualitative study with older adults and experts in aged care. BMJ Open **9**(9), e031937 (2019)
20. Lee, H.R., Tan, H., Šabanović, S.: That robot is not for me: addressing stereotypes of aging in assistive robot design. In: 2016 25th IEEE International Symposium on Robot and Human Interactive Communication (RO-MAN), pp. 312–317. IEEE (2016)
21. Li, J., Louie, W.G., Mohamed, S., Despond, F., Nejat, G.: A user-study with tangy the bingo facilitating robot and long-term care residents. In: 2016 IEEE International Symposium on Robotics and Intelligent Sensors (IRIS), pp. 109–115 (2016)

22. Li, J., Louie, W.Y.G., Mohamed, S., Despond, F., Nejat, G.: A user-study with tangy the bingo facilitating robot and long-term care residents. In: 2016 IEEE International Symposium on Robotics and Intelligent Sensors (IRIS), pp. 109–115. IEEE (2016)
23. Liu, Z., Luo, P., Wang, X., Tang, X.: Large-scale CelebFaces attributes (CelebA) dataset (2018). Accessed 15 Aug 2018
24. Louie, W.Y.G., Li, J., Mohamed, C., Despond, F., Lee, V., Nejat, G.: Tangy the robot bingo facilitator: a performance review. J. Med. Dev. **9**(2) (2015)
25. Louie, W.Y.G., Nejat, G.: A social robot learning to facilitate an assistive group-based activity from non-expert caregivers. Int. J. Soc. Robot. **12**, 1–18 (2020)
26. Magnenat Thalmann, N., Zhang, Z.: Social robots and virtual humans as assistive tools for improving our quality of life. In: 2014 5th International Conference on Digital Home, pp. 1–7. IEEE (2014)
27. Mannion, A., et al.: Introducing the social robot MARIO to people living with dementia in long term residential care: reflections. Int. J. Soc. Robot. **12**, 1–13 (2019)
28. Martinez-Martin, E., Escalona, F., Cazorla, M.: Socially assistive robots for older adults and people with autism: an overview. Electronics **9**(2), 367 (2020)
29. Melkas, H., Hennala, L., Pekkarinen, S., Kyrki, V.: Impacts of robot implementation on care personnel and clients in elderly-care institutions. Int. J. Med. Inform. **134**, 104041 (2020)
30. Mishra, N., Ramanathan, M., Satapathy, R., Cambria, E., Magnenat Thalmann, N.: Can a humanoid robot be part of the organizational workforce? A user study leveraging sentiment analysis. In: 2019 28th IEEE International Conference on Robot and Human Interactive Communication (RO-MAN), pp. 1–7. IEEE (2019)
31. Molinari, V., et al.: Impact of serious mental illness online training for certified nursing assistants in long term care. Gerontol. Geriatr. Educ. **38**(4), 359–374 (2017)
32. Neven, L.: 'But obviously not for me': robots, laboratories and the defiant identity of elder test users. Sociol. Health Illn. **32**(2), 335–347 (2010)
33. Norman, R.: Observations of the experiences of people with dementia on general hospital wards. J. Res. Nurs. **11**(5), 453–465 (2006)
34. Paudel, A., Resnick, B., Galik, E.: The quality of interactions between staff and residents with cognitive impairment in nursing homes. Am. J. Alzheimer's Disease Other Dementias® **35**, 1533317519863259 (2020)
35. Ramanathan, M., Mishra, N., Thalmann, N.M.: Nadine humanoid social robotics platform. In: Gavrilova, M., Chang, J., Thalmann, N.M., Hitzer, E., Ishikawa, H. (eds.) CGI 2019. LNCS, vol. 11542, pp. 490–496. Springer, Cham (2019). https://doi.org/10.1007/978-3-030-22514-8_49
36. Šabanović, S., Bennett, C.C., Chang, W.L., Huber, L.: Paro robot affects diverse interaction modalities in group sensory therapy for older adults with dementia. In: 2013 IEEE 13th International Conference on Rehabilitation Robotics (ICORR), pp. 1–6. IEEE (2013)
37. Šabanović, S., Chang, W.L.: Socializing robots: constructing robotic sociality in the design and use of the assistive robot PARO. AI Soc. **31**(4), 537–551 (2016)
38. Alzheimer's Society: Observation as an evaluation tool for people with advanced dementia. https://www.alzheimers.org.uk/dementia-professionals/dementia-experience-toolkit/real-life-examples/strategy-evaluation/observation-evaluation-tool-people-advanced-dementia
39. Business Case Studies: Meet stevie the social robot that holds bingo lessons in a care home (2020). https://businesscasestudies.co.uk/meet-stevie-the-social-robot-that-holds-bingo-lessons-in-a-care-home/

40. Teed, Z., Deng, J.: RAFT: recurrent all-pairs field transforms for optical flow. In: Vedaldi, A., Bischof, H., Brox, T., Frahm, J.-M. (eds.) ECCV 2020. LNCS, vol. 12347, pp. 402–419. Springer, Cham (2020). https://doi.org/10.1007/978-3-030-58536-5_24
41. Thompson, C., Mohamed, S., Louie, W.Y.G., He, J.C., Li, J., Nejat, G.: The robot tangy facilitating trivia games: a team-based user-study with long-term care residents. In: 2017 IEEE International Symposium on Robotics and Intelligent Sensors (IRIS), pp. 173–178. IEEE (2017)
42. Tuisku, O., Pekkarinen, S., Hennala, L., Melkas, H.: Robots do not replace a nurse with a beating heart. Inf. Technol. People (2019)
43. Wang, L., et al.: Temporal segment networks for action recognition in videos. IEEE Trans. Pattern Anal. Mach. Intell. **41**(11), 2740–2755 (2018)
44. Xiao, Y., Zhang, Z., Beck, A., Yuan, J., Thalmann, D.: Human-robot interaction by understanding upper body gestures. Presence: Teleoperators Virtual Environ. **23**(2), 133–154 (2014)

Encouraging Elderly Self-care by Integrating Speech Dialogue Agent and Wearable Device

Hayato Ozono[1(✉)], Sinan Chen[1], and Masahide Nakamura[1,2]

[1] Graduate School of System Informatics, Kobe University, 1-1 Rokkodai-cho, Nada, Kobe 657-8501, Japan
ozono@ws.cs.kobe-u.ac.jp, chensinan@ws.cs.kobe-u.ac.jp, masa-n@cs.kobe-u.ac.jp
[2] RIKEN Center for Advanced Intelligence Project, 1-4-1 Nihonbashi, Chuo-ku, Tokyo 103-0027, Japan

Abstract. Currently, the world's population has been aging. Especially, Japan has entered a super-aging society. We develop a listening service using a spoken dialogue agent as a system to support self-help for the in-home elderly in our research group. However, it is impossible to promote self-care for physical and mental illnesses that the elderly are not aware of. The purpose of this paper is to encourage more self-care among the elderly. The key idea is to make the elderly aware of the need for care by adding health data to the agent's topics of conversation, not just the content of past utterances. As an approach, we link wearable devices with interactive agents. The proposed system is expected to make the elderly aware of their physical and mental discomforts, which they are not aware of themselves, and to promote self-care.

Keywords: Spoken dialogue agent · Wearable device · Self-care · Elderly support · Smart healthcare

1 Introduction

Currently, the world's population has been aging. In particular, Japan has entered a super-aging society, and the number of elderly people and the aging rate are expected to continue to increase. As a result, the shortage of nursing care facilities and human resources has become a social problem. Under such circumstances, the government is planning to shift from conventional institutional care to home care [11]. However, many people live alone, and even if they have family members, they often lack the skills and time to provide such care. Therefore, there are high expectations for technology support [14].

One of the assistive technologies is **wearable device**. A wearable device is a general term for a computer device worn on the wrist, arm, or head. In recent years, there has been a lot of progress in the development of these devices, and they can be worn to easily acquire health data. It is used for smart healthcare in various areas such as medical care, nursing care, and activity recording.

Q. Gao and J. Zhou (Eds.): HCII 2022, LNCS 13331, pp. 52–70, 2022.
https://doi.org/10.1007/978-3-031-05654-3_4

Our research group has been studying and developing a system to support self-help and mutual-help for the elderly at home. As one of them, we are developing **listening service** using a spoken dialogue agent [2–4,10]. This listening service is a "mind sensing" service in which an agent listens to the elderly and records and analyzes their speech to obtain information about their minds that cannot be observed by sensors. However, since the conventional listening service for psychosensing is based on the contents of past speech, **it is impossible to analyze matters that the patient is not aware of or has not talked about**. So it is impossible to provide sufficient self-care.

The purpose of this paper is to promote self-care for what the elderly themselves are not aware of. Our key idea is to make the agent aware of the need for care by adding health data as well as past speech content to the agent's topics of conversation. To achieve this, there are two technical challenges.

- **C1: Acquisition of health data via wearable devices**
- **C2: Realization of personalized self-care**

As an approach, we link a spoken dialogue agent with a wearable device. In order to link them together, five steps must be taken.

- **Step 1: Acquisition and storage of health data**
- **Step 2: Generating dialogue scenarios based on health data**
- **Step 3: Executing dialogue with agents**
- **Step 4: Obtaining and storing health status through dialogue**
- **Step 5: Suggesting coping strategies based on health conditions**

We then implemented a system that generates and executes dialogue scenarios based on health data using Steps 1 through 4 of the proposed method. By obtaining health data from wearable devices and generating and executing corresponding dialogue scenarios, we were able to obtain data through dialogue to explain the need for care and analyze the causes of discomfort. This shows that the proposed method can be used to link a spoken dialogue agent with a wearable device. On the other hand, some issues remained, such as the fact that the acquired health status was not being used and that real-time response was not yet implemented.

In order to verify whether the system really promotes self-care, we consider the following four research questions.

- **RQ1: Is it possible to generate and execute dialogue scenario based on health data?**
- **RQ2: Is it possible to obtain health status through dialogue?**
- **RQ3: Is it possible to make users aware of physical and mental illnesses that they are not aware of?**
- **RQ4: Is it possible to encourage self-care?**

Then, as a preliminary experiment for the evaluation of the proposed system, we conducted a usage experiment with five subjects. As a result, the proposed system was able to promote self-care of the in this experiment. On the other hand, there were still some issues to be solved in terms of how to execute the scenarios and how to acquire raw health data.

2 Preliminaries

In this section, we describe the background of this research as preparation. First, the current situation in Japan regarding the aging of the population is described. We also describe wearable devices as one of the assistive technologies. Then, we describe previous studies and their issues.

2.1 Current Situation in Japan

Currently, Japan is entering a **super-aging society**. The number of people aged 65 years or older is approximately 36 million, and the proportion of the total population (aging rate) is 28.8%. Furthermore, the aging rate is expected to exceed 30% in 2025 and 35% in 2040, and continue to increase thereafter [7]. In addition, the shortage of nursing care facilities and human resources has become a social problem. In light of this situation, the government is planning a shift from conventional institutional care to in-home care. **Community-based comprehensive care system**[1] to support this shift is based on the four "aids" of self-help, mutual aid, mutual assistance, and deduction. Given the declining birthrate, aging population, and financial constraints, it will be difficult to expand mutual aid and public assistance, making it even more important to focus on self-help and mutual aid. However, self-help and mutual aid in home care is not an easy task. There is a limit to the amount of care that can be provided by hand, due to the burden of care placed on family members, as well as the problems of caring for the elderly, caring for a single person, and living alone. In such a situation, there are high expectations for **support by technology**.

2.2 Assistive Technology: Wearable Devices

One of the assistive technologies is a **wearable device**. A wearable device is a general term for a computer device worn on the wrist, arm, or head. In recent years, wearable devices have been developed to measure and record heartbeat, stress, and sleep time. These devices are often used for health management and behavioral recording because they can easily acquire data. By utilizing these devices, smart healthcare technology can be deployed in various areas such as exercise, sleep, medical care, and nursing care.

Garmin[2] is one of the wearable devices. Garmin is a wristwatch-type activity tracker. We can obtain health data such as heart rate, stress, sleep quality, and body battery by wearing the device. Then, the health data stored on the device is sent to the cloud by using a mobile app called **Garmin Connect** [5].

2.3 Previous Research: Listening Services

Our research group is developing a method to support self-help and mutual-help in home life for elderly people and dementia patients at home, and is working to

---

[1] https://www.mhlw.go.jp/stf/seisakunitsuite/bunya/hukushi_kaigo/kaigo_koureisha/chiiki-houkatsu/.

[2] https://www.garmin.com/en-US/.

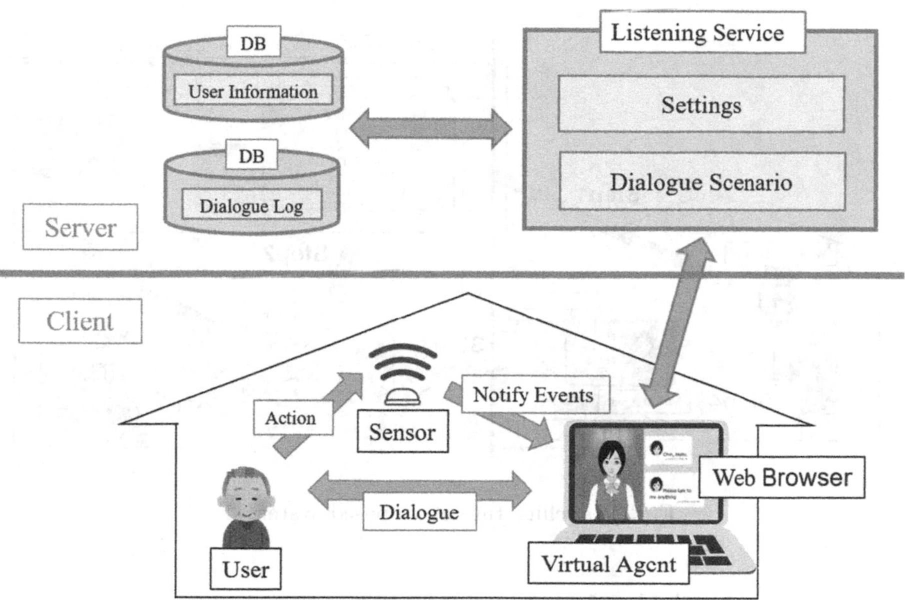

Fig. 1. Architecture of listening service

build a system that can be introduced to general households. As one of them, we are developing a **listening service** using a spoken dialogue agent (MMDAgent [9]: Mei-chan). In this service, the agent listens to the elderly and records and analyzes their speech in a log to obtain information about their minds that cannot be observed by sensors. Figure 1 shows the architecture of the listening service. A web browser, MMDAgent, and IoT sensor are placed on the client side, and user information, dialogue scenarios, and logs of past utterances are placed on the server side. When the sensor responds, the agent executes the corresponding scenario, listens to the elderly person, and asks the elderly person about his or her current situation. It then stores the obtained speech in a database. In addition, we are also developing a service that not only listens to speech, but also helps the elderly to help themselves by executing microservices through spoken dialogue [12]. However, because this listening service provides care based on the content of speech, **it is not possible to provide care for content that the elderly themselves do not recognize.**

3 Proposed Method

In this section, we first describe the objectives and key ideas of this paper, as well as the technical challenges and approaches needed to achieve them. Then, we propose a method for linking a spoken dialogue agent with a wearable device.

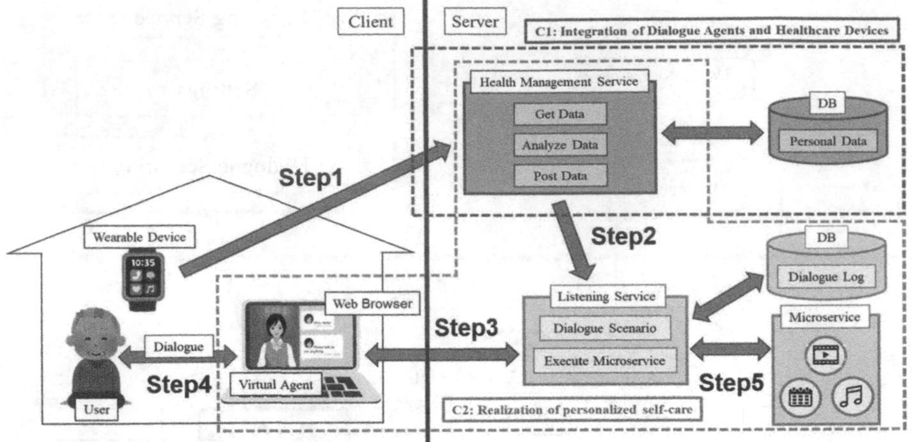

Fig. 2. Architecture of proposed system

3.1 Purposes and Key Ideas

The purpose of this paper is to promote self-care for the elderly regarding things they themselves are not aware of. The key idea is to add health data as well as past speech content to the agent's topics of conversation, so that the agent can recognize physical and mental illnesses and realize the need for care. The technical challenges addressed in this paper are as follows.

- **C1: Acquisition of health data via wearable devices**
- **C2: Realization of personalized self-care**

As an approach, we link a spoken dialogue agent with a wearable device.

3.2 Proposed Method and Architecture

In order to integrate a speech dialogue agent and an wearable device, we need to take five steps.

- **Step 1: Acquisition and storage of health data**
- **Step 2: Generating dialogue scenarios based on health data**
- **Step 3: Executing dialogue with agents**
- **Step 4: Obtaining and storing health status through dialogue**
- **Step 5: Suggesting coping strategies based on health conditions**

Then, Fig. 2 shows the overall architecture of the proposed system. Compared with the conventional listening service, we added a wearable device on the client side and a database to store health data obtained from the wearable device and a service to manage it on the server side. The yellow dotted line corresponds to C1, and the green dotted line corresponds to C2.

3.3 Flow of Proposed Method

In this section, we describe the five steps of the proposed method.

Step 1: Acquisition and storage of health data
In Step 1, we acquire and store health data of the elderly from wearable devices. For this purpose, we need to implement **Health Data Management Service**. This service has the following four main functions.

- **Acquisition of raw health data**
  Many wearable devices have services and Application Programming Interface (API) to acquire data. We use them to acquire data.
- **Analysis of health data**
  The average and range of change of each data vary depending on the user. Therefore, it is necessary to analyze and manage them.
- **Formatting and storage of health data**
  Save the health data, including the analyzed data in a database. At this time, the acquired data should not be saved as is, but should be formatted for future use.
- **Retrieval of health data**
  Retrieve the health data stored in the database. The data can be searched by user, date and time, and type of data.

Step 2: Generating dialogue scenarios based on health data
In Step 2, we generate dialogue scenarios based on the health data acquired and stored in Step 1. The scenarios to be generated can be divided into two categories: "**Praise**" and "**Warning**".

- **Praise**
  In case of the health data being normal, tell elderly people about it, and reassure or praise. And improve the motivation for self-care.
- **Warning**
  In case of the health data being abnormal, tell elderly people about the malfunction. And make them aware of the need for care.

A threshold value is set for each data in advance. The system decides which scenario to generate by comparing the threshold values with the acquired health data.

Step 3: Executing dialogue with agents
In Step 3, we have the agent execute the dialogue scenario generated in Step 2. The timing of the scenario execution can be divided into two categories. One is **real-time execution**, which is executed when new data is sent. To use the latest data, we can achieve timely dialogue. The other is **on-time execution**, which is executed at a fixed time. To execute at a fixed time, we can achieve calm dialogue. The timing of execution is determined by the type of wearable device and data.

Table 1. Settings of implementation environment

Items	Technology
Virtual Agent	MMDAgent
Web Browser	Google Chrome
Wearable Device	Garmin vívosmart 4
Data Base	MongoDB
Health Management Service・API	JavaScript, Node.js

Step 4: Obtaining and storing health status through dialogue
In Step 4, we elicit the **health status** through dialogue after executing the scenario in Step 3, and store the contents. Here, health status refers to the actual situation of the elderly, including the actions they took and the feelings they had. The agent asks the elderly person questions about his or her health status and stores the responses in a database. Then, we use the acquired health status to analyze the causes of health problems or to propose solutions.

Step 5: Suggesting coping strategies based on health conditions
In Step 5, the agent proposes a coping strategy based on the health status obtained in Step 4. Therefore, it is necessary to set up a coping strategy that is linked to the health situation. There are two ways to set it up. One is for the developer to prepare solutions for each case in advance. This method is good if we know how to deal with a certain problem. The other is to set up solutions based on the contents of past dialogues. This method is good if different individuals have different coping requirements.

4 Implementation

In this section, we implement a system that generates and executes scenarios corresponding to health data using the proposed method shown in the previous section. However, since this paper focuses on the integration of a spoken dialogue agent and a wearable device, we will implement Step 1 to Step 4 and not Step 5.

4.1 Implementation Environment

The implementation environment for this paper is summarized in Table 1. As in the conventional listening service, we use **MMDAgent** as the spoken dialogue agent and **Google Chrome** as the web browser. As a wearable device, we use a **Garmin vívosmart 4** (Hereafter referred to as "garmin device".) a type of Garmin. We use **MongoDB** to store the health data obtained from the Garmin device. The health management service and its API were developed using **JavaScript** and **Node.js**.

4.2 Implementation Flow

In this section, we describe the implementation details for each step of the proposed method shown in the previous section.

```
{
    "id" : "urn:ngsi-ld:stress:1638370800000",
    "type" : "stress",
    "user" : {
        "type" : "String",
        "value" : "ozono8810@gmail.com"
    },
    "datetime" : {
        "type" : "String",
        "value" : "2021-12-01 00:00:00"
    },
    "data_value" : {
        "type" : "Integer",
        "value" : 58
    }
}
```


Fig. 3. Health data (stress)

Table 2. APIs of Garmin data management service

Operation	API
Get Garmin raw data	GET /garmin-api/eml={eml}/pwd={pwd}/date={date}/data={category}
Get health data	GET /garmin2mongo-api/eml={eml}/date={date}/data={category}
Post health data	POST /garmin2mongo-api/post body : Formatted data (JSON)

Step 1

In this implementation, we obtain **heart rate**, **stress**, **sleep**, and **steps** from the Garmin device. Then, we implement the **Garmin Data Management Service** as a health data management service. First, the acquisition of raw data from the garmin device is implemented using **garmin-connect**[3] in Node Package Manager. Next, the mean, maximum, and total values are analyzed, and comprehensive data for the day is created for each data. Then, the acquired health data is formatted and stored in a database with comprehensive data. An example of health data being stored is shown in Fig. 3. Then, the user can retrieve health data from the database by specifying the email address, date, and type of data. And finally, we will create APIs for these functions so that they can be called from the listening service. The API we created is shown in Table 2.

Step 2

We will generate a dialogue scenario based on the data of garmin device retrieved from MongoDB by executing the API. In the following, we will explain how to determine whether to praise or warn, and the contents of the dialogue scenario to be generated, for each category.

[3] https://www.npmjs.com/package/garmin-connect.

- **heart rate**
  Praise and warning in heart rate is determined by whether the heart rate exceeds 120 beats per minute. This is because the heart rate of an average adult is considered to be 60–80, and a heart rate exceeding 120 is suspected to be tachycardia due to illness [1]. When the maximum daily heart rate is less than 120, the patient should be praised for having a normal and calm heart rate, and the elderly person should be reassured. On the other hand, when the maximum heart rate is over 120, the patient should be warned that the heart rate was high and the time of the high heart rate. However, there is a possibility that the cause of tachycardia may be other than illness, such as exercise, so be careful about the content of the scenario, as too much anxiety may have a negative impact.
- **stress**
  Praise and warning in stress is determined by whether the stress level exceeds 75 or not. This is based on the index used by Garmin. When the maximum daily stress level is less than 75, the elderly person is praised for being calm and not too stressed, which gives them peace of mind. On the other hand, when the maximum stress level is 75 or higher, the system warns the elderly that they are under a lot of stress and tells them how long it took to recover.
- **sleep**
  Praise and warning in sleep is based on whether or not the duration of sleep exceeds 6 h. This is because it is generally believed that the ideal amount of sleep for an adult is 6 to 8 h [6]. When the daily sleep time is more than 6 h, it is said that the patient slept well. If the amount of time spent in deep sleep is more than one hour, we tell them that their body was well rested. On the other hand, if the sleep time was less than 6 h, we tell them that they did not sleep well as a warning and tell them to rest well if possible. If they are awake for more than one hour during sleep, they are additionally told that they did not get much rest.
- **steps**
  Praise or warning in terms of the number of steps taken is based on whether or not the number of steps taken in a day exceeds 7,000. This is because it is said that 8,000 steps or more is necessary for men and 7,000 steps or more is necessary for women in order to prevent muscle mass loss, muscle weakness, and physical function decline that occur with aging [13]. When the number of steps taken in a day is 7,000 or more, the total number of steps taken is given as praise to maintain motivation. On the other hand, when the number of steps is less than 7,000, the total number of steps and how many more steps are needed are given as a warning, and motivation is improved by cheering.

Step 3
In order to use the data from the garmin device, we need to start Garmin Connect and send the data to the cloud. Therefore, it is difficult to execute the scenario in real time, so we decided to execute it on time. In other words, the scenario is executed once a day for each category at a fixed time. The sleep scenario is executed after waking up (6:00–11:00), and the heart rate, stress, and steps

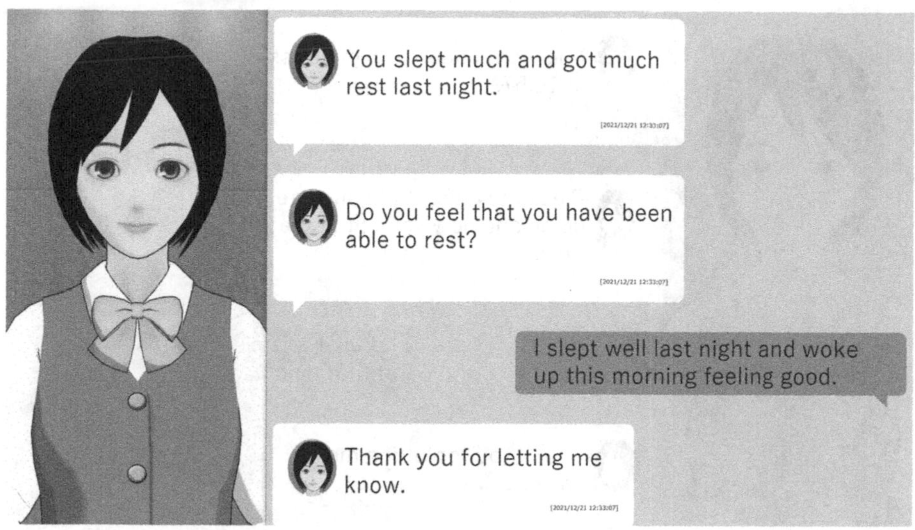

Fig. 4. Sleep scenarios (Praise) Copyright 2009–2018 Nagoya Institute of Technology (MMDAgent Model "Mei")

scenarios are executed when the sensors respond before bedtime (21:00–23:00). The agent asks the user to start Garmin Connect before each execution.

Step 4
An agent asks a question to obtain the health status of an elderly person. In the case of a heart rate, if it is a warning, find out the cause. In the case of stress, if it is praise, ask the person what he or she did that day; if it is a warning, ask the person what caused it. In the case of sleep, ask how you felt at the time (refreshed, sleepy, etc.) and why you slept the way you did. In the case of steps, ask the reason for the number of steps. Then we add the user's name, date and time, data type, praise and warning information to the reply content, and store it in a database.

4.3 Implementation Results

An example of a dialogue scenario when implemented as described in the previous section is shown below. Figure 4 shows a praise scenario when there is no abnormality in the sleep data. Figure 5 shows a warning scenario when there is an abnormality in the stress data.

4.4 Implementation Considerations

In this section, we describe the findings and the remaining issues from the implementation.

Fig. 5. Stress scenarios (Warning) Copyright 2009–2018 Nagoya Institute of Technology (MMDAgent Model "Mei")

Findings. Through the implementation, we were able to obtain health data from the wearable device and generate and execute dialogue scenarios accordingly. In addition, we were able to obtain health status through dialogue. This shows that the proposed method can integrate a spoken dialogue agent with a wearable device.

Remaining Issues. In this implementation, two issues remain. One is to suggest coping strategies based on the health situation. Although we were able to obtain health status through the dialogue, we have not yet implemented the function to propose a coping strategy based on health status, which corresponds to Step 5. The other is to respond in real time. In order to use Garmin data, it is necessary to send it from Garmin Connect to the cloud, so it is difficult to realize real-time response.

5 Experiment

In this section, we describe the preliminary experiments for the evaluation of the proposed system.

5.1 Experiment Purpose

The purpose of this experiment is to evaluate whether the proposed system can function properly and improve the users' awareness of self-care. Therefore, we set the following four research questions.

Table 3. List of questions in the questionnaire

Q1	Do you think you are aware of your own health problems?
Q2	Why did you answer that in Q1?
Q3	Do you think your awareness of self-care has increased?
Q4	Why did you answer that in Q3?
Q5	Do you think it was hard to wear Garmin all the time?
Q6	Do you think it was difficult to have health dialogues morning and evening?
Q7	Do you think that the health dialogue has helped you in your self care?
Q8	Would you like to use this service in the future?
Q9	Do you think you can trust the Garmin data?
Q10	Do you think you can trust health dialogue with Mei-chan?
Q11	Do you think it's nice to be complimented by Mei-chan?
Q12	Do you think it makes you happy that Mei-chan is worried about you?
Q13	Do you think it makes you happy that Mei-chan is worried about you?
Q14	Do you think you were able to reflect on your health easily?
Q15	Do you think you could have easily told Mei-chan about your health status?
Q16	Do you think there was a risk to your health or safety?
Q17	Do you think you could have a dialogue every morning and evening?
Q18	Do you think you could have worn your Garmin all the time?
Q19	Do you think that real-time execution is better than on-time execution?
Q20	Do you think it is better to have a health dialogue whenever you want?

- **RQ1: Is it possible to generate and execute dialogue scenario based on health data?**
- **RQ2: Is it possible to obtain health status through dialogue?**
- **RQ3: Is it possible to make users aware of physical and mental illnesses that they are not aware of?**
- **RQ4: Is it possible to encourage self-care?**

5.2 Experiment Description

In this experiment, we set up a laptop with a voice dialogue agent and sensors in the subject's house, and let the subject live with a Garmin device. Then, we have her have two conversations about health, one in the morning and one at night. The period is one week, from 26 January, 2022 to 1 February, 2022. The subjects were five members of the same research group. After the experiment, a questionnaire on this experiment is given. The questionnaire was developed based on the international standard **SQuaRE** (Systems and software Quality Requirements and Evaluation) [8]. The questions in the questionnaire are shown in Table 3.

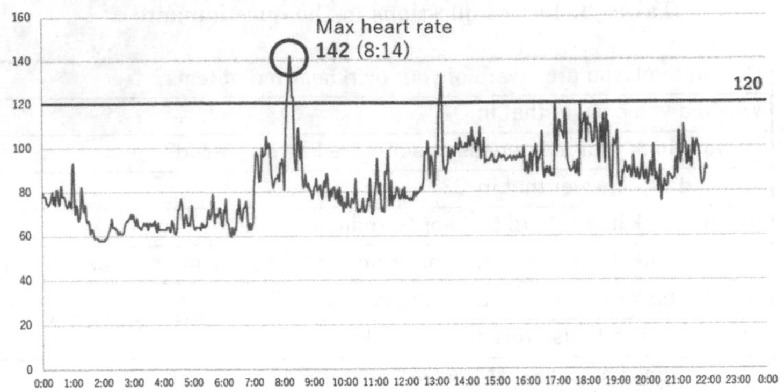

Fig. 6. Heart rate of subject 1 (27 January)

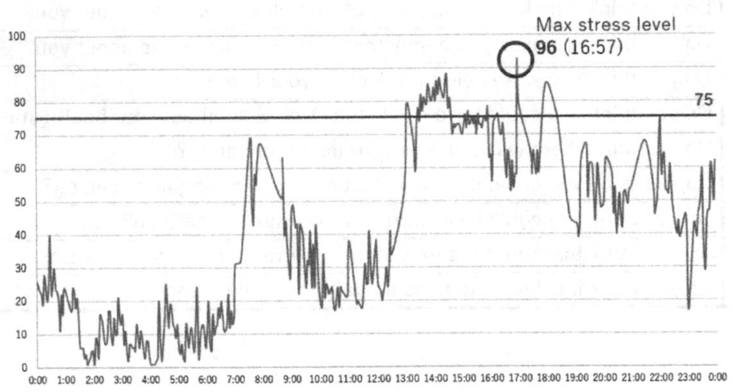

Fig. 7. Stress level of subject 1 (27 January)

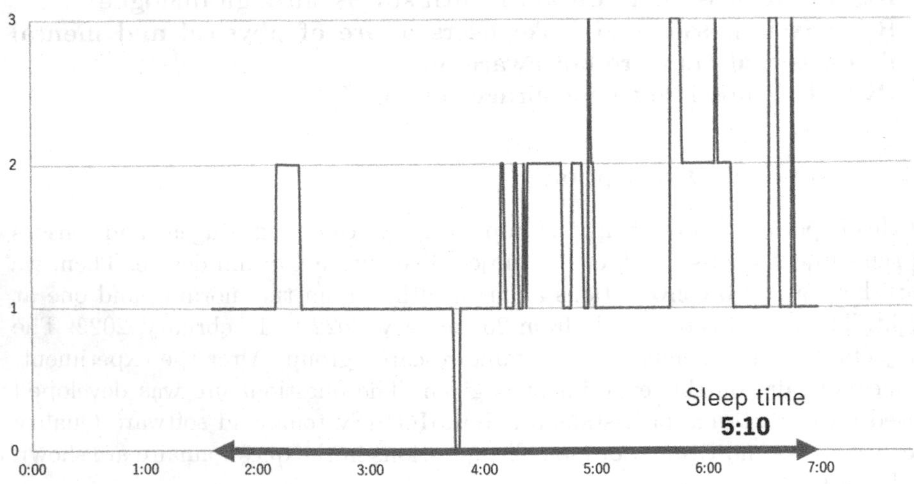

Fig. 8. Sleep level of subject 1 (27 January)

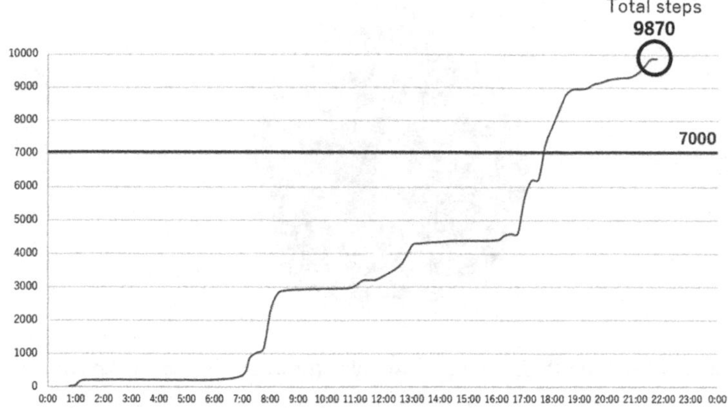

Fig. 9. Total steps of subject 1 (27 January)

Table 4. Example of dialoge log of subject 1 (27 January)

Speaker	Speech content
Mei-chan	Good morning. Could you please open the Garmin app on your smartphone to transmit sleep data? (Yes / No)
Subject 1	Yes.
Mei-chan	Please wait a minute while I check the status. You didn't sleep much and didn't get much rest last night. Do you feel that you have been able to rest?
Subject 1	No, I'm quite sleepy.
Mei-chan	Thank you for letting me know.
⋮	⋮
Mei-chan	Good evening. Could you please open the Garmin app on your smartphone to transmit healthdata? (Yes / No)
Subject 1	Yes.
Mei-chan	Please wait a minute while I check the status. You were under a lot of stress at 16:57. Please tell me what you were doing and how you felt at that time.
Subject 1	At that time, I was supervising Mr. Horie's thesis.
Mei-chan	Thank you for letting me know. Your heart rate was elevated at 8:14. Please tell me what you were doing and how you felt at that time.
Subject 1	At that time, I was looking for the remote control for the TV. I was in a great hurry because I couldn't find it easily.
Mei-chan	Thank you for letting me know. You walked 9,870 steps. That's great!

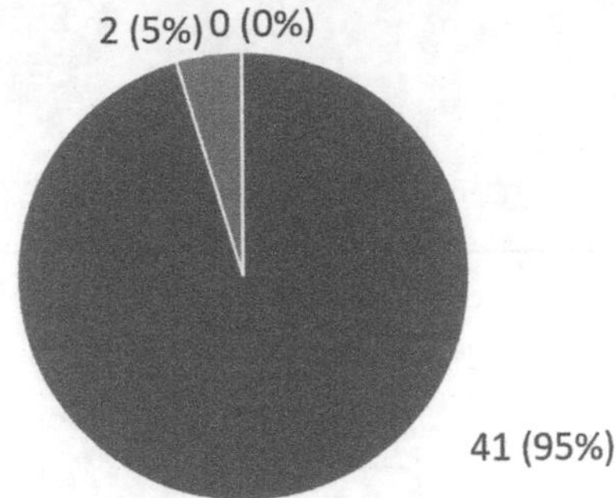

Fig. 10. Response rate for questions about health status

Table 5. Example of representative dialogue logs (Subject 1)

	Heart rate	Stress level	Sleep level	Total steps
26 January	I was on the train.	I was on the train.	It's hard to get up these days, and I think I should be reminded of that.	※2
27 January	At that time, I was looking for the remote control for the TV. I was in a great hurry because I couldn't find it easily.	At that time, I was supervising Mr. Horie's thesis.	No, I'm quite sleepy.	※2
28 January	At that time, I had just arrived at the lab.	Well, I think I was on the train at the time.	No, not at all. I feel that the quality of my sleep is not good these days.	※2
29 January	※2	At that time, I was about to prepare for a meeting with Mr. Nakata.	※1	※2
30 January	※1	※1	※1	※1
31 January	At that time, I had just arrived at the lab.	I had a meeting with Mr. Nakata around 15:00 this afternoon.	※1	※2
1 February	※1	※1	Yes, I slept well last night.	※1

※1：No scenario execution ※2：No questions

5.3 Experiment Results

In this section, we describe the results obtained in this experiment. Figure 6, 7, 8 and 9 respectively show the data of heart rate, stress, sleep, and steps of subject 1 on 27 January. The maximum value of the heart rate is 142 at 8:14. Stress was at a maximum of 96 at 16:57. The total duration of sleep is 5 h and 10 min, including 3 min of deep sleep. The total number of steps is 9870. Table 4 shows a part of

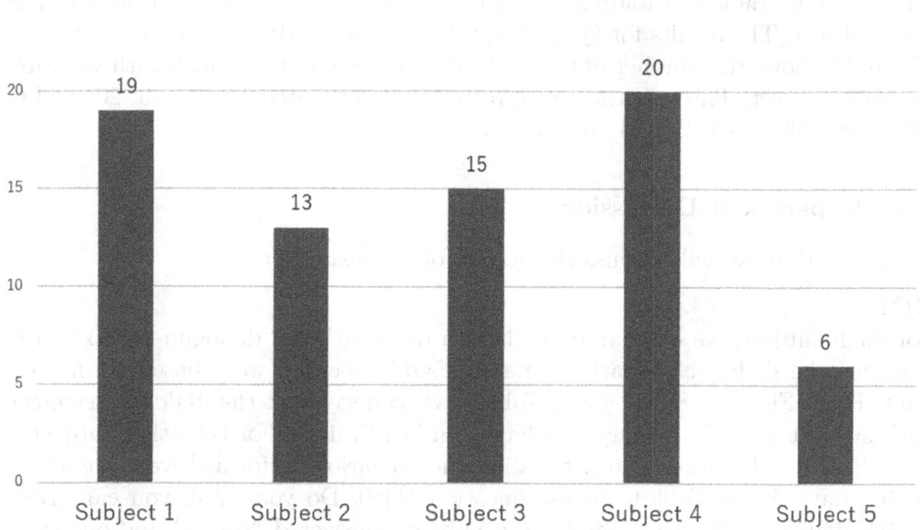

Fig. 11. Scenario execution count

Table 6. Example of survey results

	Q1	Q2	Q3	Q4	Q7	Q10
Subject 1	Disagree	Because I didn't feel it even though the agent pointed out my health problems.	Agree	Because I was happy that the agent cared about my health.	Agree	Agree
Subject 2	Agree	Because Mei-chan told me about sleep, which I usually don't pay attention to.	Agree	Because it informs us about my own health.	Agree	Agree
Subject 3	Agree	Because I felt that I was able to clarify what I had been feeling somehow by thinking back on the day and verbalizing it.	Strongly agree	Because I felt that I had more opportunities to think about my health by reflecting on my day.	Agree	Strongly agree
Subject 4	Agree	Because the agent told me that I was not sleeping well.	Agree	Because I started to have trouble falling asleep and waking up.	Agree	Agree
Subject 5	Disagree	Because sometimes, I couldn't think of the cause when the agent warned me.	Agree	Because Mei-chan can tell me about our stress and sleep status.	Agree	Agree

the dialogue log of 27 January for Subject 1. The agent tells the subject that he did not sleep much and did not feel physically rested. The agent tells the subject that the stress was high at 8:14. The agent tells the subject that the heart rate was high at 16:57. The agent tells the subject that he has walked 9,870 steps and praises him. Figure 10 shows the response rate to questions about health status. All subjects responded to all questions. In addition, there were only two responses such as "I don't know." or "I don't remember." and all the rest were about health conditions. As an example, the health status answered by subject

1 is shown in Table 5. Table 6 shows some of the results of the questionnaire for each subject. The results for Q1, Q2, Q3, Q4, Q7, and Q10 in Table 3 are shown. Figure 11 shows the number of times the dialogue scenario about health was run for each subject. The scenarios were respectively executed 19, 13, 15, 20, and 6 times for subjects 1, 2, 3, 4, and 5.

5.4 Experiment Discussion

In this section, we will discuss the results of this experiment.

RQ1
For each subject, we compared the health data with the dialogue log to verify whether the dialogue scenarios generated and executed were based on health data. From Fig. 6, 7, 8 and 9 and Table 4, we can say that the dialogue scenario with subject 1 on 27 January was based on health data. For the other subjects, as well as for the other dates, the dialogue scenarios performed were based on health data. From Table 6, to the question "Q10. Do you think you can trust health dialogue with Mei-chan?", four subjects answered "Agree" and one subject "Strongly agree". This results show that the subjects themselves felt that the dialogue was based on health data. Therefore, we were able to generate and execute dialogues based on health data in this experiment.

RQ2
From Fig. 10, we can see that all the questions asking about health status were answered this time. In two of these cases, the health status could not be obtained due to "I don't remember" or other reasons. Other than that, health conditions were spoken. Then, from Table 5, we can see that we were able to obtain the spoken health status. Therefore, we were able to obtain health status through dialogue in this experiment.

RQ3
From Table 6, to the question, "Q1. Do you think you are aware of your own health problems?", three subjects answered "Agree", and two subjects answered "Disagree". Even if we exclude subject 5 who did not run the scenario as many times, one subject answered "Disagree". The main reason for answering "Agree" is "When I looked back on my day, there were a few things that came to mind.". The main reason for answering "Disagree" is "When I looked back on my day, there were few things that came to mind.". Therefore, we could not say that we were able to make the subjects aware of their physical and mental discomfort that they were not aware of. However, it did provide an opportunity for the subjects to reflect on their daily lives.

RQ4
From Table 6, to the question, "Q3. Do you think your awareness of self-care has increased?", four subjects answered "Agree" and one subject "Strongly agree". As a result of the increased awareness of self-care, the participants mentioned that they reviewed their sleeping hours and methods, and began to exercise more than usual. In addition, to the question "Q7. Do you think that the health

dialogue has helped you in your self care?", all the subjects answered "Agree". Therefore, it can be said that the awareness of self-care was improved by the proposed system in this experiment.

Remaining Issues

In this section, we describe the challenges that we have encountered through this experiment. The most important issue we found in this experiment is the reliable execution of the dialogue scenario. Originally, the scenario would be run 28 times, once a day for each of the four health data. However, the number of executions is low with a maximum of 20 and a minimum of 6 looking at Fig. 11. This could be due to the fact that the sensor did not respond at that time, or due to limitations in the API being used. Since the scenario is set to run at a certain fixed time, the scenario may not run properly depending on the location of the sensor or the user's lifestyle. In addition, npm's garmin-connect, which is used for the API, will generate an error and fail to retrieve data if it is executed multiple times in a certain period of time. Therefore, in the future, we will review the timing and method of executing the scenario, and consider how to get the raw Garmin data using methods other than garmin-connect.

6 Conclusion

In this paper, we proposed a method of integrating a spoken dialogue agent and a wearable device in order to promote self-care for elderly people by incorporating health data into the agent's topic of conversation. We also implemented a system that generates and executes scenarios corresponding to the health data obtained from the wearable device using the proposed method. The results show that the proposed method can be used to integrate a spoken dialogue agent with a wearable device. Furthermore, we conducted an evaluation experiment of the system implemented based on the proposed method with five subjects. As a result, the proposed system was able to promote self-care of the in this experiment. On the other hand, there were still some issues to be solved in terms of how to execute the scenarios and how to acquire raw health data. Due to the effects of the new coronavirus, we were not able to conduct the experiment with the in-home elderly that we had originally planned. Therefore, it has not yet been verified whether the proposed system is also effective for the elderly. In the future, we plan to improve the issues left over from this preliminary experiment. And we will conduct evaluation experiments with in-home elderly as soon as the spread of the infection calms down.

Acknowledgements. This research was partially supported by JSPS KAKENHI Grant Numbers JP19H01138, JP18H03242, JP18H03342, JP19H04154, JP19K02973, JP20K11059, JP20H04014, JP20H05706 and Tateishi Science and Technology Foundation (C) (No. 2207004).

References

1. Bleyer, A.J., et al.: Longitudinal analysis of one million vital signs in patients in an academic medical center. Resuscitation **82**(11), 1387–1392 (2011)
2. Chen, S., Nakamura, M.: Designing an elderly virtual caregiver using dialogue agents and WebRTC. In: 2021 4th International Conference on Signal Processing and Information Security (ICSPIS), pp. 53–56. IEEE (2021)
3. Chen, S., Nakamura, M.: Generating personalized dialogues based on conversation log summarization and sentiment analysis. In: The 23rd International Conference on Information Integration and Web Intelligence, pp. 217–222 (2021)
4. Chen, S., Nakamura, M., Saiki, S.: Developing a platform of personalized conversation scenarios for in-home care assistance. In: 2021 IEEE International Conference on Industry 4.0, Artificial Intelligence, and Communications Technology (IAICT), pp. 148–153. IEEE (2021)
5. Connect, G.: Garmin connect (2020)
6. Hirshkowitz, M., et al.: National sleep foundation's sleep time duration recommendations: methodology and results summary. Sleep health **1**(1), 40–43 (2015)
7. Inagaki, S.: A microsimulation model for projections of Japanese socioeconomic structure. Rev. Socionetwork Strat. **2**(1), 25–41 (2008). https://doi.org/10.1007/s12626-008-0003-5
8. International Organization for Standardization: Systems and software quality requirements and evaluation (square), March 2011. https://www.iso.org/standard/35733.html/
9. Lee, A., Oura, K., Tokuda, K.: MMDAgent-a fully open-source toolkit for voice interaction systems. In: 2013 IEEE International Conference on Acoustics, Speech and Signal Processing, pp. 8382–8385. IEEE (2013)
10. Maeda, H., Saiki, S., Nakamura, M., Yasuda, K.: Memory aid service using mind sensing and daily retrospective by virtual agent. In: Duffy, V.G. (ed.) HCII 2019, Part II. LNCS, vol. 11582, pp. 353–364. Springer, Cham (2019). https://doi.org/10.1007/978-3-030-22219-2_27
11. Murashima, S., Nagata, S., Magilvy, J.K., Fukui, S., Kayama, M.: Home care nursing in Japan: a challenge for providing good care at home. Public Health Nurs. **19**(2), 94–103 (2002)
12. Ozono, H., Chen, S., Nakamura, M.: Study of microservice execution framework using spoken dialogue agents. In: 22th IEEE-ACIS International Conference on Software Engineering, Artificial Intelligence, Networking and Parallel Distributed Computing (SNPD2021), pp. 273–278, November 2021
13. Shibutani, T.: Utility of the number of steps walked daily as a health promotion parameter in community-dwelling elderly persons. Nihon Ronen Igakkai zasshi. Jpn. J. Geriatr. **44**(6), 726–733 (2007)
14. Song, P., Tang, W.: The community-based integrated care system in Japan: health care and nursing care challenges posed by super-aged society. Biosci. Trends **13**(3), 279–281 (2019)

To Dot or Not to Dot: The Effect of Instruction Design on Smart Home Device Set-Up for Older Adults

Shivani Patel(✉), Elaine Choy, Paige Lawton, Jade Lovell, Barbara Chaparro, and Alex Chaparro

Embry-Riddle Aeronautical University, Daytona Beach, FL 32114, USA
{patels37,choye,lawtonp,lovellj3}@my.erau.edu, {chaparb1, chapara3}@erau.edu

Abstract. Smart home devices, like Amazon Echo Dot, allow users to connect and control in-home technologies (e.g., lights, Wi-Fi, TV) by voice control or through a smartphone application. These devices are primarily marketed toward young adults, yet many of the device set-up instructions can be difficult to follow, even for digital natives. Poor instructions may represent a greater barrier to older adults who often have less experience with the new technologies, but may also benefit the most from using them. Smart home devices are perceived to positively impact the quality of life of older adults that have visual impairment or restricted mobility; it also promotes virtual connectivity with friends and family [1]. The utility of smart home devices is diminished by the challenges of setting up and connecting them. This presents a barrier to the adoption and use of the technologies across multiple generations. The goal of this study was to evaluate the set-up process for two connected smart home devices: an Amazon Echo Dot and an Amazon Smart Plug with older adults using either the original equipment manufacturer (OEM) instructions or a set of the instructions redesigned to accommodate older adults. The results from this study suggest that there is opportunity to improve instructions of smart home devices for older adult populations.

Keywords: Out-of-box experience · Older adult · Smart home devices · Instruction design

1 Introduction

The use of technology is becoming more common with older adults, ranging from smartphones to smart home devices. In a 2017 Pew Research Center study [2], approximately 42% of survey respondents aged 65 or older reported owning a smartphone and 32% reported owning a tablet, up from 1% in 2010. Additionally, in less than 20 years, 67% of older adults use the internet and 51% now have a home broadband connection. The same study [2] also showed that 58% of adults 65 years of age or older say "technology has had a mostly positive impact on society." In a survey by Harris, Blocker, and Rogers [3], older adult respondents reported that their smartphones and smart home devices were

Q. Gao and J. Zhou (Eds.): HCII 2022, LNCS 13331, pp. 71–87, 2022.
https://doi.org/10.1007/978-3-031-05654-3_5

easy to use and entertaining. Given that technology is becoming more popular among older adults, it is important to understand how they learn about use, and how accepting they are of new technologies.

The Pew Research Center study [2] provides data on older adults' ability to learn about new technology. In this study, just 26% of those aged 65 or older who reported using the internet felt confident when they used technology such as computers, smartphones, or other devices to complete tasks online. Approximately one third of those 65 or older said they felt "only a little" (23%) or "not at all" (11%) confident when using devices for online activities [2]. Those 65 and older also reported that the statement, "When I get a new electronic device, I usually need someone to set it up or show me how to use it," characterizes them very (48%) or somewhat (25%) well [2]. These findings are further supported by Harris and colleagues [3], where half (*35 people*) of older adult survey respondents found initial set-up of smartphones "difficult" and that the instructions were confusing.

In addition, a Pew Research Center report [4] stated that, when compared to those under 65, older adults represent a larger proportion of those considered "digitally unprepared." Given that older adults did not grow up with these devices and may have only recently been introduced to technologies like the internet or smartphones, their familiarity with the devices is most likely lower than that of younger age groups. Older adults may also have age-related physical or cognitive difficulties, making acclimation to new devices more challenging. Taken together, the results suggest these age differences manifested in the way older adults use technology, as well as, their own confidence in their ability to use technology. This may affect an older adult's attitudes toward technology, especially depending upon how positive or negative their experience was with it.

Regarding perceptions and attitudes older adults have toward smart home technologies, a pilot study reported an overall positive attitude toward devices in their homes [1]. This study used focus group sessions to ask 15 older adults their perceptions of technology and how they think technology could help them in their daily lives. The group sessions discussed topics such as usefulness, health-related sensors, improving mobility, reducing isolation, managing medications, and monitoring physiological markers. Across all topics, older adults had a favorable view of technology and could see how it might benefit them. Similar findings were reported in a survey of older adults in 2020, over half (*35 people*) of survey respondents found smartphones and smart home devices useful in daily lives [3]. However, older adults consistently preferred the assistance of family and friends without attempting on their own with instructions for set-up [3]. Effective instructions may also guide older adults and help them think creatively about how smart devices, for example, could assist them in their daily lives.

1.1 Out-of-Box Experience

Out-of-box experience (OOBE) is a method that assesses the unpacking, the configuration, and the first use of a new product. OOBE plays an important role in the adoption and utilization of a product because it should be fairly intuitive for users. A good OOBE creates an enjoyable and productive first experience [5].

During the unpacking stage, it is very important to clarify what the user needs to do at each step and ensure the packaging is easy to open and minimizes waste.

During configuration or set-up, the importance shifts to clear instructions, managing transitions between mediums, and time. This phase should be direct and simple. The need to troubleshoot an installation or set-up can result in a negative OOBE. Lastly, the user's first use of the new product should be engaging with an appropriate balance of structure and flexibility. It is crucial to guide the user through the capabilities in an intuitive and enjoyable manner.

The OOBE is important for all users of a product, but it may be even more critical for older adults. Technology, like smart home devices, have become prevalent in the past decade, so it is critical to consider the needs of potential users that are not as familiar with this technology.

There is an interesting dilemma when it comes to the use of technology among older adults. Many developers of smart devices do not always consider the needs of older adults, yet older adults may benefit the most from the use of smart devices. Research has shown that older adults are less likely to use technology due to "complexity and jargon, rather than physical difficulties" [6].

It is common for most older adults, even those reporting "high computer anxiety and low self-efficacy," to adopt new technology because of recommendation and motivation by younger family and friends [5]. Less than a third of older adults that owned computers actually chose the specific product and model themselves [7].

When it comes to the OOBE of newer technologies, it is common for older adults to avoid it entirely. Burrows [6] found that 14 out of 24 participants preferred to have someone else complete the set-up for them because it would be faster and more effective. If an older adult was left to learn to use a new technology on their own, it is common for them to report that the product functions were not clear and could not use it to the full potential [6].

It is in a developer and manufacturer's interest to ensure a positive OOBE for older adults as they are the users that can benefit from smart home devices, whether it is for productivity or socialization. As a first step, it is extremely important to simplify OOBE instructions for the older adult and include them into the target market.

1.2 Instruction Effectiveness

While most products or devices come with some form of instructions for set-up or device manual, it has been determined that older adults usually take a different approach to learning a device than younger adults. Though it may be assumed that younger or middle-aged individuals will be a device's primary users, older adults represent a growing portion of smart device users.

With device instructions, it is important to outline the main functions of a device in a manner that most users can understand. With an aging population, it is becoming even more important to ensure that older adults are able to effectively set up and use various devices. The usability of instructions for a device also may significantly impact the user's first impression of the device as well as their mental model of the device's functions.

It has been found that younger users tend to employ a "trial and error" method for learning a device and prefer to figure out device functions themselves; however, older adults tend to prefer using a device's instruction manual but report difficulty using it [8].

In addition, when troubleshooting due to trial and error, younger and middle-aged users may seek additional information from the internet or someone of their own generation, whereas, older users tend to seek help through the device manual or someone in a younger generation, such as a child or grandchild. Leung and colleagues [8] observed that younger users prefer to use the internet to learn a device's functions, whereas older adults prefer to use the device's "help" feature. Older adults also prefer demonstrations and having the chance to practice using a device, through device assistance, before moving to unassisted use [8].

It is also important to account for users who may not previously have accounts set-up with the various brands and devices. Instructions should be informative even for the most novice users. While many younger users may have accounts set-up with various companies like Amazon and Google, older adults may not have these established accounts and device instructions may need to make it clear when such accounts are necessary in order to set up a device.

With an aging population, it is important to ensure that older adults feel confident using a technological product and being able to understand the instructions without significant intervention from outside sources. Understanding instructions is important since older adults rely on instructions to familiarize themselves with products but find them overwhelming and filled with jargon [9].

1.3 Purpose

The goal of this study was to evaluate the set-up process for two connected smart home devices: an Echo Dot (*Echo Dot*) and a Smart Plug (*Smart Plug*) with older adults using either the original equipment manufacturer (OEM) instructions or a set of the instructions redesigned to accommodate older adults.

2 Method

2.1 Participants

The participants for this study consisted of 11 subjects (*6 male and 5 female*) ranging from the ages of 53–65 years of age ($M = 59$, SD $= 2.72$). The predominant ethnicity of participants was Caucasian. Seven out of 10 participants worked full-time, three were retired, and one was unemployed. Majority of the participants (*7/10*) rated their daily technology use either 4–5 or 6+ h each day, and the majority (*6/10*) own or have owned smart home devices. No participants in this study had previous experience with Echo Dot or Smart Plug.

2.2 Experimental Design

Participants were asked to conduct an OOBE, including unpacking, configuration, and first use of the Echo Dot and the Smart Plug. They were asked to think aloud throughout the OOBE process. This study used a between-subjects design; five participants completed the OOBE using the OEM instructions, while six performed the OOBE using the revised instructions made by the researchers.

2.3 Measures

During the think-aloud, participants' positive and negative perceptions of the device were recorded. To assess product usability, the Microsoft Product- Relation Cards (MPRC) and the Post-Study System Usability Questionnaire (PSSUQ) were used. The MPRC measures the participants' attitudes towards the device using a controlled vocabulary test from the researchers [10]. The PSSUQ is a 16-item standardized questionnaire that was used to measure the users' perceived satisfaction with the devices at the end of the study. Each item is a positive statement which participants are asked to rate on a scale of 1–7 (*1 being strongly agree and 7 being strongly disagree*). The questionnaire addressed three overarching usability metrics: system usefulness, information quality, and interface quality. Ease of use rating measured how the participants were to rate their perceived level of ease when using the device and was based on a scale of 1–10 (*1 being very difficult and 10 being very easy*) [11]. Lastly, points of delight and frustration were assessed, and a demographics survey was given to the participants in the beginning of the study.

2.4 Materials

The materials used in this study were the Echo Dot, Smart Plug, and a smartphone (see Fig. 1). An electric fan was also provided to be used with the Smart Plug once configured. The participant was given either the OEM instructions or the redesigned instructions.

Amazon Echo Dot

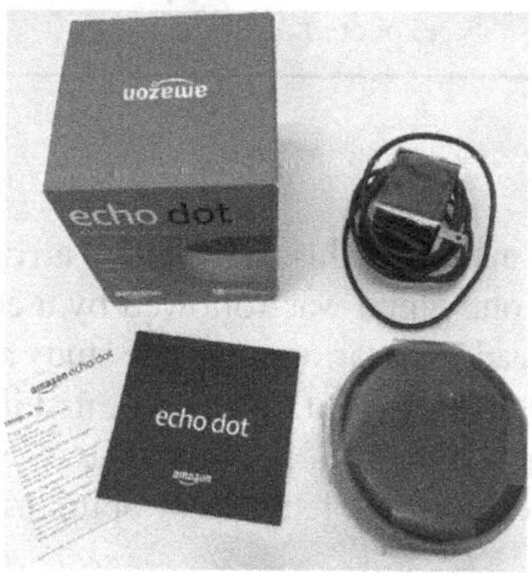

Amazon Smart Plug

Fig. 1. OOBE device packaging and documentation

2.5 Instruction Design

The researchers conducted an expert review of the OEM instructions taking into account older adult design heuristics involving visual, auditory, and cognitive capabilities. This resulted in the creation of a new instructional set with changes to text size, clarity/contrast of images, clarification of steps, and inclusion of smartphone mobile application (or simply, app) images (see Table 1).

Table 1. OEM Instructions vs redesigned instructions.

	OEM Instructions	Redesign Instructions
Text Size/Font	8 pt. Ember	11 pt. Arial
Images	• Included 2 Images (per device) • Black and White Images • Incorrect icon location in one image	• Included 5 Images (per device) • Colored Images • Added callouts highlighting icons to tap per set-up task
Contrast/Clarity	• Higher contrast (black/white images) • Low clarity • Thin diagram labels and outlines	• Lower contrast (color images because it matches real world • Higher clarity • Thicker diagram labels and outlines
Clarification of Steps	• Short and vague steps • Lacked information to troubleshoot issues	• Added descriptive hierarchical steps • Included troubleshooting steps if device doesn't perform as expected

2.6 Procedure

Participants were recruited via email and word of mouth for this study. Upon arrival, the participant was given a brief welcome introduction, which was followed by a consent form. Upon consent, the facilitator proceeded to read a scenario to start the study and the Echo Dot packaging would be placed in front of the participant. A series of first impression questions were asked regarding the outer appearances of the box. The researcher then asked the participant to open the box and vocalize any feelings or opinions about the initial layout of the interior of the box.

The participant was then asked to unpack the Echo Dot fully, answer post-unpacking questions, and provide five adjectives from the MPRC about their impressions of the device. Afterward, information was given to the participant, which included the smartphone passcode and Amazon login information. Then, the participant was asked to set up the Echo Dot using either the instructions provided by Amazon or the redesigned instructions created by the researchers. Once the device was set-up, they were asked a series of questions about their experience setting up the Echo Dot. Participants were asked to complete three tasks using verbal commands with the Echo Dot: (1) find the nearest restaurant, (2) set a timer for five minutes, and (3) turn off the timer. After completing all tasks, participants were asked about their impressions and answered the PSSUQ.

The participant repeated the same procedure for the Smart Plug set-up. Once the Smart Plug was set-up with the electric fan plugged into it, the participant was tasked to turn on and off a fan using voice controls with the Echo Dot (see Fig. 2). The participants completed a demographic survey at the end of the study.

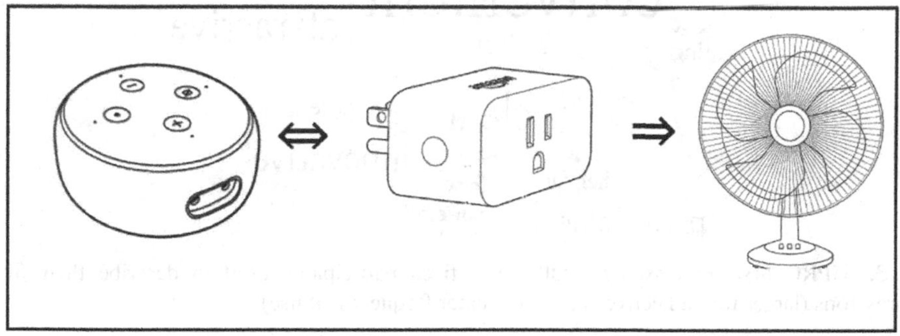

Fig. 2. Schematic of Echo Dot to desk fan functionality

3 Results

3.1 Packaging and First Impressions

First impressions of the packaging and unboxing process were very similar for both the Echo Dot and the Smart Plug. When asked to choose words from the MPRC that best described their first impression of the products, participants most often described the products as convenient, clean, and attractive (see Fig. 3). There was consensus amongst all participants that the packaging for both devices were of good quality, well-constructed, and organized. The product was also easy to unbox because no special tools were required. However, participants were surprised by the large size of the Smart Plug and expected it to be smaller. Some had concerns about the amount of space it required when plugged into an outlet. Additionally, participants expressed that the devices' target audience were younger to middle-aged adults or those who are "more tech-savvy" and not targeted to their age group.

Fig. 3. MPRC first impressions results; adjectives participants used to describe their first impressions (larger font adjectives indicate greater frequency of use)

3.2 Set-Up Configuration

Four key barriers (see Table 2) were identified that impacted the usability of smart home device set-up and usage in both instruction conditions. These included assumed technology literacy, poor information placement, insufficient time allotted by the device programming to accomplish tasks during the setup process, and lack of feedback.

- Assumed technology literacy: set-up instructions lacked sufficient detail for users novice to understand
- Information placement: key information was in locations that were difficult to find
- Insufficient time: several steps of the process required participants to complete them in a time frame smaller than the device is programmed to wait
- Lack of feedback: little to no feedback was provided upon user error or task completion

Assumed Technology Literacy

Echo Dot. Frustrations occurred with the Echo Dot OEM instructions due to unclear terminology during the lengthy set-up process. The design of the set-up process and the OEM instructions function under the assumption that all users of the device have a certain base level of technology literacy. This was not the case for the older adults. Participants did not have a general understanding of the processes needed to set-up a smart home device, including tasks, such as downloading an app, connecting devices to Wi-Fi, and using voice commands. For example, frustrations arose when participants needed to download an app on the smartphone. Many of the participants did not know how to download an app, or that an app is a requirement in the set-up process and tried to proceed without it. With the redesigned instructions, participants found the images, shown for each step, beneficial to reference when completing actions they were unfamiliar with but some technical jargon sill needed to be simplified for better understanding.

Table 2. Four key barriers impacting smart home device usability.

Barriers	Recurring Issues
Assumed Technology Literacy	Downloading Apps Scanning QR Codes Connecting to Wi-Fi
Information Placement	Back-tracking Steps Device Switching
Insufficient Time	Underlying Time Restrictions Restarting Steps
Lack of Feedback	Vague/No Error Messages

Smart Plug. During the set-up of the Smart Plug, participants who did not have prior knowledge or experience of scanning QR codes and bluetooth pairing, found the OEM instructions lacking in information to aid them through the set-up process. Steps on the OEM instruction pamphlet ended after users opened the mobile app and did not provide any aid when participants referred back when in need of help completing the in-app set-up. The redesigned instructions, which included all steps from start to end of set-up and troubleshooting tips, lessened the frustration during events of confusion.

Information Placement

Echo Dot. Using the OEM instructions, participants reported points of frustration when they were unable to find detailed information regarding the steps to complete. With the OEM instructions, participants saw the two-step instruction pamphlet and expected the set-up to be simple, whereas participants who received the redesigned instructions expected the set-up to be harder due to the number of steps. But after the set-up process was complete, those who received the redesigned instructions perceived the set-up to be easier than expected (see Fig. 4).

Within the PSSUQ, participants are asked to state their level of agreement with this statement: "It was easy to find the information I needed." Five out of six participants reported that it was easy to find the information they needed in the redesigned in-structions, while only two out of five participants reported the same for the OEM instructions. Overall, participants reported higher satisfaction with information quality for the redesigned instructions than for the OEM instruction as seen in Fig. 6 (lower scores indicate a higher level of satisfaction). Scores associated with poor information quality were related to switching attention between the paper instructions, the smartphone app, and the auditory information from the smart home device. Some participants with OEM instructions stated that they expected the whole process to be outlined on paper instructions so that they could refer to one location during the entire set-up process.

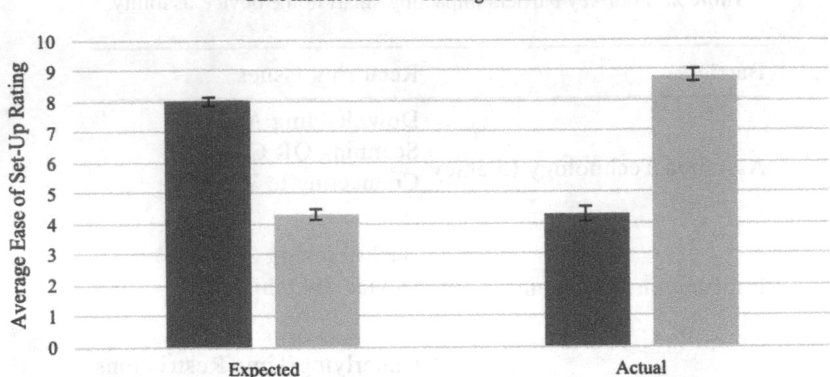

Fig. 4. Echo Dot Ease of Set-Up ($n_{OEM} = 5$; $n_{Redesign} = 6$). Error bars represent ±1 standard error. (*1 being very difficult and 10 being very easy;* higher score indicates higher levels of perceived ease of set-up)

Smart Plug. Overall, after setting up the Echo Dot, participants expected the set-up process for the Smart Plug would be easier in comparison to the Echo Dot. Participants who received the OEM instructions, which included two steps, rated the set-up more difficult than expected. However, participants who received the redesigned instructions found the set-up process to be easier than their initial expectation (see Fig. 5).

Within the PSSUQ, when participants were asked to state their level of agreement with this statement: "It was easy to find the information I needed." All six participants reported that it was easy to find the information they needed in the redesigned instructions, while only two out of five participants reported the same for the OEM instructions. Overall, participants reported higher satisfaction with information quality with the redesigned instructions than with the OEM instructions as seen in Fig. 7.

Participants with the OEM instructions indicated that the QR code was placed inconveniently on the OEM instructions. The QR code was located on the back of the instruction booklet and caused many participants to scan the wrong item (e.g., universal product code). The QR code placement within the instruction steps of the redesign mitigated these issues. Participants reported no frustration with the set-up process using the redesigned instructions and were delighted by how quickly and easy it was to set up the Smart Plug.

Insufficient Time

Echo Dot. A prevalent issue for the users was that the amount of time they needed to complete the steps in the set-up process exceeded the time allotted by the device. Participants would often take longer to download, open the mobile app, and connect to a network than the smart home device would allow in set-up mode. By the time these steps were completed, the device would have disengaged from set-up mode, and the participant would have to restart the process resulting in additional confusion.

Smart Plug. Time constraints were not a barrier for Smart Plug set-up.

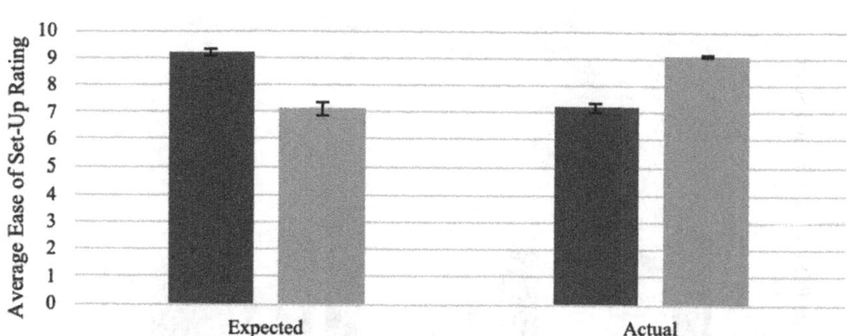

Fig. 5. Smart Plug Ease of Set-Up ($n_{OEM} = 5$; $n_{Redesign} = 6$). Error bars represent ±1 standard error. (*1 being very difficult and 10 being very easy;* higher score indicates higher levels of perceived ease of set-up)

Lack of Feedback

Echo Dot. The lack of feedback during the Echo Dot set-up process was a barrier regardless of instruction. For instance, when participants were unable to complete set-up steps in the allotted amount of time, the Echo Dot would disengage set-up mode due to inactivity. The device does not give feedback (e.g., auditory prompts) to notify the user that it will be turning off set-up mode. This caused frustration when participants finished downloading and setting up the app because they were unaware Echo Dot disengaged. Participants were unable to move forward in the set-up since the OEM instructions do not provide any information on how to re-engage set-up mode. This required the researcher to intervene to complete the re-engage step to allow participants to continue the study.

Smart Plug. Participants expressed frustration with the feedback from the Smart Plug. The LED light on the Smart Plug that indicates the status of the device (e.g., device on, pairing mode). Both instruction sets provided information on the meaning of the indicator light, but were too small to see or interpret.

3.3 First Use of Device

Echo Dot. Participants reported higher satisfaction with usability on the PSSUQ for the redesigned instructions than for the OEM instructions, across all dimensions, as seen in Fig. 6 (lower scores indicate a higher level of satisfaction).

Although the Echo Dot provided a few practice commands during part of the set-up process, participants had some difficulty adapting to the command phrasing required to interact with the Echo Dot when completing tasks. Participants would commonly forget to say "Alexa" at the start of each command, or often state incorrect name variations, such as "Alexis" or "Alex," in which the device would not respond. But once participants were able to successfully carry out tasks using the Echo Dot, they were immediately delighted with using the device.

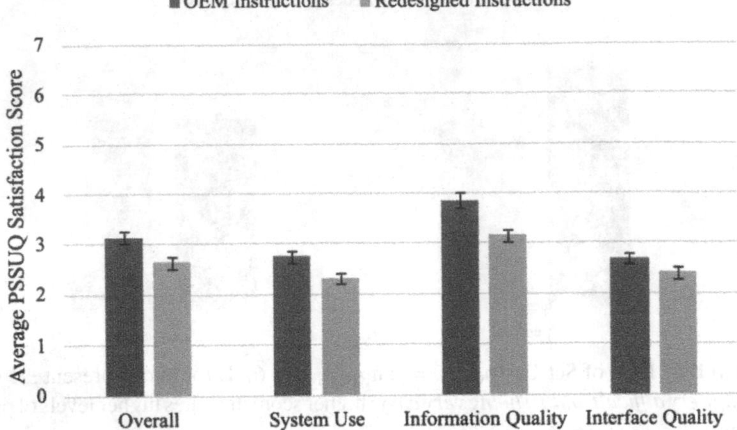

Fig. 6. PSSUQ Satisfaction Scores for Echo Dot ($n_{OEM} = 5$; $n_{Redesign} = 6$). Error bars represent ±1 standard error. *(1 being strongly agree and 7 being strongly disagreeing with positive statements;* lower scores indicate a higher level of satisfaction)

Smart Plug. Participants were pleasantly surprised with how easy the Smart Plug was to use to turn on the small fan, once set-up was complete. Most participants reported marginally higher overall satisfaction with usability for the redesigned instructions than for the OEM instructions (see Fig. 7). None of the participants reported points of frustration or confusion when using the Smart Plug.

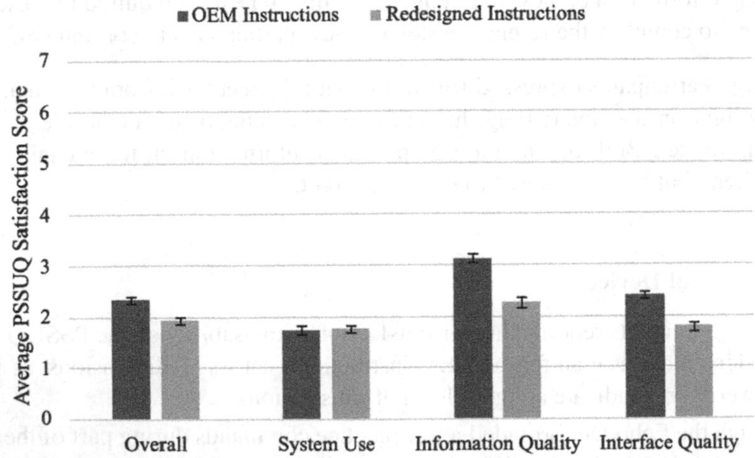

Fig. 7. PSSUQ Satisfaction Scores: Smart Plug ($n_{OEM} = 5$; $n_{Redesign} = 6$). Error bars represent ±1 standard error. *(1 being strongly agree and 7 being strongly disagreeing with positive statements;* lower scores indicate a higher level of satisfaction)

4 Discussion

Smart home devices can be a useful aid to many older adults. Older adults are a growing consumer group of technology, such as smart home devices. However, this realm of technology presents a number of barriers to adoption by older adults as evidenced by our findings.

4.1 Packaging and First Impressions

The packaging for both the Echo Dot and the Smart Plug were found to be organized and easy to unbox by all of the participants in this study. Using the MPRC, adjectives such as convenient, clean, attractive were frequently used to describe the packaging of both devices. The minimal packaging and no additional tools necessary to set up the devices were rated positively by the participants. However, many perceived that these devices were marketed toward the younger generation due to the perception that younger digital natives are more comfortable with technology, speaking to devices, and enjoy wireless connectivity.

4.2 Set-Up Configuration

There are many instances of how the four key barriers overlap during the completion of a single set-up task (see Table 2).

Assumed Technological Literacy, Poor Information Placement, and Lack of Feedback

OEM Instructions. As instructed by the Smart Plug OEM instructions, scanning a QR code was one task that encompassed three out of the four key barriers for the participants: assumed technological literacy, poor information placement, and lack of feedback.

First, the on-screen mobile app instruction asks the user to "Scan barcode." This primed participants to look for a universal product code (UPC) rather than a QR code and frustrated participants when scanning did not work. Users need enough technological literacy to associate the message with scanning a QR code and feedback to notify them when they are performing an incorrect action. Second, participants were unfamiliar with QR codes and were unaware of what to look for and how to scan it. Third, the QR code was located on the back of the OEM instruction pamphlet. This is an example of poor information placement which caused frustration for the user when trying to locate what to scan.

Redesigned Instructions. The participants using the redesigned instructions did not have frustrations with locating or scanning the QR code due to its placement within the instructions. The improved information placement also helped with technological literacy because participants who were unfamiliar with QR codes knew to scan it based on the context of when it appeared in the instruction steps. Though feedback through the mobile app when an incorrect code is scanned is beneficial regardless of instruction design.

Insufficient Time

OEM Instructions and Redesigned Instructions. Insufficient time was an overarching issue regardless of the set of instructions that were given to the participant. For a user to successfully connect their smartphone to the Echo Dot they must download a mobile app, login to their Amazon account, verify personal information, go through permissions (i.e., allowing notifications, locations, etc.), and set up a voice profile. All these steps are required prior to even setting up the Echo Dot itself. While the participant is completing this in the mobile app, the Echo Dot is plugged in and waiting in set-up mode for an unknown amount of time before ultimately disengaging set-up mode. Importantly, neither the instructions nor the device alerts the user to the existence of an input time constraint. This left participants either confused as to why the Echo Dot was not responding or frustrated in trying to re-engage set-up mode when they unknowingly surpassed the underlying time limit. This also required participants to restart parts of the set-up process. When asked if they would use external resources, such as Google, Youtube, or friends and family to help in solving the issue, many participants state they would not. Some went on to state that the set-up was so frustrating that they would return the item entirely.

It is important to note that participants in this study were readily provided information, such as Amazon account login and W-Fi information. Therefore, this study did not take into account the additional time necessary for users needing to either make a new Amazon account or recall their account or Wi-Fi credentials. This further exemplifies the insufficient time duration programmed for the Echo Dot set-up mode.

OEM Instructions vs. Redesigned Instructions

Did the redesigned instructions make a difference? Per our results, participants provided with the redesigned instructions rated set-up easier than those who received the OEM instructions for both the Echo Dot and Smart Plug (Fig. 4, Fig. 5) Additionally, after use of the redesigned instructions, participants' satisfaction scores (Fig. 6, Fig. 7) with device set-up improved across all dimensions detailed by the PSSUQ (e.g., overall, system usefulness, information quality, interface quality).

What was learned?

- The redesigned instructions can be further improved to simplify technical jargon that may be unfamiliar to novice users
- Older adults rely on instructions when they confront problems with technology and are less likely to seek information elsewhere
- Participants would rather return a device at the first sign of confusion than troubleshoot
- Users refer to instructions to gauge where they are in the set-up process

4.3 First Use

Echo Dot. Once set-up was complete, participants went through three tasks using the Echo Dot. Participants found it difficult to alter their natural speech to effectively communicate the device. The word choice for commands and necessary speech rate did not feel natural to the older adults. Many felt the need to slow their speech rate for the device to acknowledge and reply to the command. Participants also often had difficulty remembering to use the command, "Alexa" or "Hey Alexa," before each use.

Smart Plug. After successfully connecting the Smart Plug to the Echo Dot, all participants found it simple to command the smart home devices to toggle an electric fan on/off. Participants, who initially felt frustrated after the set-up processes of the Amazon devices, were delighted when using the Smart Plug and Echo Dot was "smooth and easy" to use to control the fan. Participants valued the capabilities the Echo Dot and Smart Plug can provide after using the devices, but it is important to note that many of them would have returned the devices before experiencing the use of the products due to a complicated set-up process without referring to other external sources for help.

4.4 Recommendations to Improve Instruction

Based on the findings of this study, Table 1 highlights the key barriers that should be avoided when designing set-up instructions. Below are our recommendations to combat each barrier.

1. Assumed technology literacy

- Provide sufficient information that allows novice technology users to successfully set-up the device
  - Downloading mobile apps, connecting devices to Wi-Fi, and scanning QR codes are examples of technology literacy novice users often lack

2. Poor Information Placement

- Avoid placing instructions in multiple formats (visual, auditory) and multiple locations (e.g. pamphlet, smartphone app)
  - This prevents the user from having to switch attention between physical instructions, on-screen mobile app instructions, and auditory device instructions

3. Lack of Feedback

- Feedback should be provided to inform users of their status in the set-up process, along with successes or errors when moving through steps
- Feedback should also be descriptive to aid users in the event of errors and troubleshooting
- Modality of feedback (e.g., visual, auditory) should be designed to accommodate older adults

4. Time Outs

- Underlying time constraints for user input should reflect consideration of older adults who may take longer to accomplish the tasks.

4.5 Limitations and Future Research

This study was limited to 11 participants between 53–65 years of age. Researching a wider age range of older adults could encompass other difficulties that may appear with people over 65. Another limitation of this study were the frequent updates that would change the mobile app interface. These updates made it difficult to keep the redesigned instructions up-to-date and consistent with the latest software. Some of the updates changed the order of the actions the user had to complete. This study did not address problems associated with updates to the mobile app interface.

Future research should investigate the set-up and use of smart home devices such as Echo Dot in conjunction with other smart home devices (e.g., smart lights, smart TVs). Also, further research is needed to better understand the timing and duration of user input that are typically found for a broader range of users including older adults and other special populations. Finally, it is important to understand how older adults adapt to the use of technology over time and understand the learning curve for this form of knowledge.

5 Conclusion

Current instructions for the Echo Dot, Smart Plug, and other smart home devices need to take into account limitations and abilities of older adult users. These instructions can be improved to aid older adults to set up and use the devices independently. The perceived ease of set-up can make or break the OOBE for many older adults. If they perceive the device will be difficult to set-up, they might not purchase the device from a store shelf or order it online. Also, it is important to note that if the actual set-up becomes difficult or frustrating and requires the user to troubleshoot, some older adults are not likely to look for outside information, such as Google or YouTube, or call customer support. Instead, they would simply return the device. Smart home device instructions and set-up processes should not deter older adults from using the products. The results from this study indicate that there is much room to improve in adapting set-up instructions.

References

1. Demiris, G., et al.: Older adults' attitude towards and perceptions of "smart home" technologies: a pilot study. Med. Inf. Internet Med. **29**(2), 87–94 (2004). https://doi.org/10.1080/14639230410001684387
2. Anderson, M., Perrin, A.: Tech Adoption Climbs Among Older Adults, pp. 1–23. Pew Research Center (2017)
3. Harris, M.T., Blocker, K.A., Rogers, W.A.: Smartphone and digital home assistant use among older adults: Understanding adoption and learning preferences. In: Proceedings of 2021 HFES 65th International Annual Meeting, pp. 742–746 (2021). https://doi.org/10.1177/1071181321651316
4. Horrigan, J.B.: Digital Readiness Gaps, pp. 1–29. Pew Research Center (2016)
5. Burrows, A., Mitchell, V., Nicolle, C.: Let's spend some time together: exploring the out-of-box experience of technology for older adults. Int. J. Mob. Hum. Comput. Interact. **8**(2), 69–82 (2016)
6. Burrows, A.: Designing Out-of-Box Experiences for Older Adults: Exploring the Boundaries of Inclusive Design, pp. 1–282. Loughborough's Research Repository (2019)
7. Eisma, R., Dickenson, A., Goodman-Deane, J., Syme, A. J., Tiwari, L., Newell, A.: Early user involvement in the development of information technology-related products for older people (2004)

8. Leung, R., Tang, C., Haddad, S., McGrenere, J., Graf, P., Ingriany, V.: How older adults learn to use mobile devices: survey and field investigations. ACM Trans. Access. Comput. **4**(3), 1–33 (2012)
9. Tsai, W., Rogers, W., Lee, C.: Older adults' motivations, patterns, and improvised strategies of using product manuals. Int. J. Des. **6**(2), 55–65 (2012)
10. Benedek, J., Miner, T.: Product reaction cards. Microsoft (2002)
11. Lewis, J. R.: Psychometric evaluation of the post-study system usability questionnaire: the PSSUQ. In: Proceedings of the Human Factors Society Annual Meeting, vol. 36, issue number 16, pp. 1259–1260. Sage Publications, Los Angeles (1992)

Robots as Welfare Technologies to Reduce Falls Amongst Older Adults: An Explorative Study from Norway

Diana Saplacan[1(✉)] and Jim Tørresen[1,2]

[1] Robotics and Intelligent Systems Research Group (ROBIN), Department of Informatics, Faculty of Mathematics and Natural Sciences, University of Oslo, 0373 Oslo, Norway
{diana.saplacan,dianasa,jim.torresen,jimtoer}@ifi.uio.no

[2] RITMO Centre of Interdisciplinary Studies in Rhythm, Time, and Motion, Centre of Excellence in Research, Research Council of Norway, University of Oslo, 0373 Oslo, Norway

Abstract. This paper investigates robots as Welfare Technologies (WT), in Norway. Previous studies show that Norway follows the demographic trends around the world regarding the aging of the population, the shortage of nurses, and thus, increased costs due to co-morbidity and multiple chronic diseases. The research question addressed is: *Is the notion of WT challenged by the adoption of intelligent robots within home care, and if yes, how?* To explore robots as WT, we focused specifically on the case of robots as safety alarms for fall prevention, detection, and prediction as part of the Vulnerability in Robot Society research project, and by drawing on the previous research project, namely Multimodal Elderly Care Systems project. At the basis of our theoretical framework, the paper is anchored into the Scandinavian notion of welfare technology. To achieve this, we analyzed data from different research activities ($n = 10$, $hs = 25$) through thematic analysis. Findings show that current WT for fall detection has design and technical limitations, whereas robots as advanced Artificial Intelligence (AI) systems could potentially be a solution. We then discuss the findings in the light of the welfare concept. Finally, we conclude that robots as WT does not differ from other technologies, with one exception: they differ from the traditional way of providing (home-)care, bringing in both challenges related to privacy and safety, but also opportunities for reduced costs, personalized, adapted, and higher quality care in the heart of the home.

Keywords: Welfare Technology (WT) · Robots · Robot as WT · Elderly care · Home care · Fall · Norway

1 Introduction

The increasing aging population across the world [1, 2] seems to be a key aspect in the development and adoption of robots [3]. Thus, many countries recognize a demographic change in terms of an increased life expectancy but also societal needs due to an increased prevalence of co-morbidity, multiple chronic conditions, and the patient in focus [4]. This

Q. Gao and J. Zhou (Eds.): HCII 2022, LNCS 13331, pp. 88–106, 2022.
https://doi.org/10.1007/978-3-031-05654-3_6

also implies increased expenses on healthcare services [4]. Therefore, robotics seems to be a potential means for reducing healthcare costs, but not at the cost of a decreased healthcare service quality.

However, many studies regarding Human-Robot Interaction for the aged population in supporting their Activities of Daily Living (ADL) are currently available, but not often under the umbrella term of WT. For instance, the study from [5] reviews recent literature regarding the tasks that the robots are able to carry out and the elderly's views, needs, acceptance, and values regarding robots. Similarly, [6–8] present the elderly's views on the use of robots in the home, the articulation work needed to be performed by the human users in order to make the domestic robot work, and the division of work tasks between humans and robots. Other studies focused on the concept of care and which activities should be delegated to robots and which should not [9, 10, 11]. In addition, others have focused on identifying potential challenges with so-called care robots and opportunities with such robots [12].

Similarly, [13] points out future ethical perspectives of robotics and Artificial Intelligence (AI). However, fewer studies on robots seen through the lens of WT as a Nordic or Scandinavian concept are available. For example, we found only one study from [4], which presents the case of using robots in the Danish health service. The authors argue that "the welfare, and health sector will undergo significant changes in the coming 20 years and the robots will play an important role in that change" [4] (p. 198). At the same time, there are some barriers in using robots, such as "adaptation to user needs and lacking evident on the effect of applying robots" [4] (pp. 197–198). This indicates that there is a current need for more research with in this area.

Thus, the notion of WT might be challenged. This occurs when advanced technology, such as social assistive care robots, is introduced as a part of the home- and healthcare services due to the advancements of the technical equipment (e.g., sensors, cameras of the robot) that may afford advanced AI and Machine Learning (ML) techniques for collecting, predicting, and detecting different states or health condition of the care receiver. Thus, this may compromise the privacy, safety, and security of the elderly but may also bring in some new opportunities.

Hence, this paper aims to investigate the concept of WT, a well-established concept within the Nordic countries, in relation to social assistive care robots used within home care. Thus, our research question that we explore in this paper is: *Is the notion of WT challenged by the adoption of intelligent robots within home care, and if yes, how?*

In order to explore our question, we draw on our findings from two different research projects, Multimodal Elderly Care Systems (MECS) and Vulnerability in Robot Society (VIROS). MECS (2015–2021, 16MNOK) and VIROS (2019–2024, 25.1 MNOK) are two research projects funded by the Research Council of Norway (RCN), by the IKTPluss Program (MECS grant agreement #247697, VIROS grant agreement #288285). Finally, to explore the research question, we continue first by presenting the background to this paper and then the theoretical concept. Thereafter, we briefly present our method, followed by our findings. Finally, we end with a discussion, followed by the conclusions.

2 Background

To investigate robots as WT, we look at the case of robots as safety alarms for falls. Falls are defined as an event that results "in a person coming to rest inadvertently on the ground or floor or other lower level." [14], or as "an unexpected event in which the participants come to rest on the ground, floor, or lower level." [15]. It seems that the meaning of a fall varies across cultures, e.g., there is no literal translation of the English term "fall" in German [15]. However, in the Norwegian Patient Safety Program, a fall is defined as "an unintended event that causes a person to end up on the ground, floor or another lower level, regardless of the cause and whether there is damage as a result of the fall." [16]. At the same time, falls can be lethal or non-lethal [14]. It seems that 37.3 million non-lethal falls per year occur every year across the whole population, whereas almost 700 000 lethal falls occur almost every year [14]. This makes falls placing second after road traffic accidents [14]. However, regardless of their outcome, falls are a significant public health issue, which results in major financial and non-financial costs for the states.

Special attention with regard to falls is placed on the aging population, which present different risk factors related to falls. An older person suffering a fall may result in hip fracture, head traumas, or bruises, which may have, in worst cases, fatal consequences, or long-term consequences, contributing to a decreased quality of life [14]. Similarly, the elderly that have experienced falls are also often afraid of falling again, limiting their physical activity and isolating themselves. Thus, falls also have a psychological consequence [15]. In Norway, there are over 170 000 falls per year [17], with 70% of those who fall hurting themselves. Hip fractures, neck fractures, head injuries, long-term disability, and fear of falling again and lost independence occur following a fall. There are around 9000 hip fractures per year in Norway due to falls [18]. 9000 hip fractures cost the Norwegian state around 1.5 billion NOK. One hip fracture cost the state around 500 000 NOK within health and rehabilitation during the first year of recovery, in 2014 [19], but since then, the costs have increased. So, it is also a question of economic consequences on the welfare state. At the same time, around 80% of all injuries and accidents amongst the elderly are due to falls, while 10% of all falls lead to serious injuries. Further, according to Statistics Norway [17], in 2020, 29% of all elderly over 80 years old use homecare services. Specifically, 197 738 people are currently using the home care services in Norway, whereas almost 90 000 are over 80 years old. Each year, half of those over 80 years old fall, and one-third over 65 years old fall. Of those who fall, around 50% are likely to fall again. Moreover, 80% of the falls occur when elderlies are alone.

Falls are, therefore, an interesting research area to be addressed when it comes to intelligent robots because current technologies for detecting falls still have some shortcomings.

3 Theoretical Framework: The Notion of Welfare Technology (WT)

The concept of Welfare Technology (WT) originates from Denmark (2007) as a term describing technology that supports the everyday life of the users, often used in welfare societies [20]. It can either compensate due to a disability or support it [21]. It is anchored within the notion of "welfare," which means that something is doing or being well [22]. [23] defines it as "the common Nordic term for technology used for environmental control, safety and well-being in particular for elderly and disabled people." (p. 335), whereas in other countries outside of Scandinavia, it is mostly known as Ambient Assisted Living (AAL).

Studies show that the concept of WT has several application areas, such as: 1) communication support, such as monitoring applications for elderly people, or telecommunication solutions; 2) assistive technology, sometimes known as compensatory technology, such as safety alarm systems, fall detectors, advanced wheelchairs or staircases, exoskeletons, or GPS; 3) consumer services or products, such as practical help with everyday tasks, such as vacuum cleaning robots, automatic pill dispenser, or washing automates; 4) disease monitoring, such as monitoring of vital signs and alarms; 5) remote treatment, such as check-ups, robot technology, VR, and telepresence; 6) rehabilitation technology, such as exercise guidance, actuation of movement, or electromechanical training; 7) entertainment applications for leisure and pleasure; and 8) social and emotional support and stimulation, such as robot companions, or conversational agents [24].

WT has often been seen as single entity devices, such as smart- or connected systems, and as simple technologies used in isolation (e.g., sensors, wheelchairs, lifts). However, the notion of WT is challenged with the development and integration of intelligent robots as part of the home- and healthcare services. A robot is defined by the International Standard Organization (ISO) as an "actuated mechanism programmable in two or more axes with a degree of autonomy, moving within its environment to perform intended tasks." However, a service robot is defined as a "robot that performs useful tasks for humans or equipment excluding industrial automation application." In this paper, we refer to robots as part of professional and personal service robots, as defined by [25]. The service, in our case, refers to homecare. Further, robots as WT are intelligent care robots, i.e., complex systems often equipped with a series of other simple WT that should work well and in symbiosis with the rest of the systems. However, robots as WT should not make the users, e.g., elderly or other care receivers, even more, vulnerable by compromising in any way their privacy, dignity, security, or safety.

Thus, if intelligent robots were earlier considered as the WT of the future [6], it is time to explore whether robots as WT challenge the notion of WT or offer opportunities for development and whether these kinds of intelligent WT may raise fundamental questions about what is "the good life" and "being human" [24].

4 Method

A summary of the data collection is presented in this section. The data collection can be summarized in two phases.

In Phase I, we have collected qualitative and quantitative data on behalf of the MECS research project (Fig. 1 and Fig. 2). In phase II, part of the VIROS research project, we have conducted interviews with legal experts, HRI experts, and user group representatives. We have also participated in and organized several activities complementary to our data collection. In this paper, we draw upon our findings from Phase I. We are currently in the progress of analyzing the data from Phase II. The current data collected in Phase II are presented elsewhere [26].

In this paper, we, therefore, limit our focus on presenting some of the findings from Phase I to better understand the problem investigated, along with the complementary activities, in Phase II, as part of a sense-making stage. Data collection and analysis from Phase I was presented in several publications [6–8, 27–36]. In terms of complementary activities within the frame of Phase II, more than 25 h were spent in these field activities. The complementary activities or sources (n = 10) were documented through the researchers' log reports acting as researchers' diary or ethnographic notes, other official or non-official documents, and photos (n = 347). The data generated from these various activities were analyzed using thematic analysis [37]. The analysis was done in several steps. First, we have familiarized ourselves with the data. Second, initial codes were generated (n > 500). These were then transferred to the *miro* software tool based on their source. In the third step, we searched for collating the codes, i.e., the codes were organized in sub-categories (n = 63) illustrated through an affinity diagram in *miro software.* These sub-categories were then organized into categories (n = 10). The categories included: robots, WT, methods, innovation, rehabilitation, user groups, other technologies, problem definition/gap. The initial themes (n = 5) were reviewed a couple of times. At the end, we arrived at the main theme: *about safety alarms as WT in the elderly's home.* Finally, the last step, was to produce the report of the findings. This is presented in the next section.

Fig. 1. Images from data collection with the elderly (Permission to use the images was obtained) [6, 51, 52]

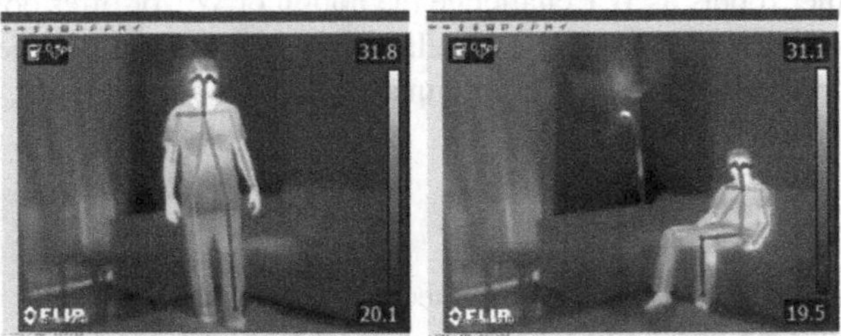

Fig. 2. Images from MECS experiments using Depth Camera Images and OpenPose (Permission was obtained to use these images) [31]

Both MECS and VIROS projects were approved by the Norwegian Center for Research Data (NSD) (MECS ref. nr. 50689, VIROS ref. nr. 381736). For each of the projects, the data was stored safely on the Services for Sensitive Data (Tjenster for Sensitive Data) at the University of Oslo, provided by the IT Department, USIT (MECS TSD #p260 and p400, VIROS TSD #p1582). The data reported in this paper does not contain any personal or sensitive data.

5 Findings: About Safety Alarms as Welfare Technologies in Elderly's Homes

It seems that a lot of focus has been put until now on wearable technologies, such as safety alarms for fall detection. However, less focus has been on fall prevention and prediction. There are several issues with WT, such as wearables for fall detection, e.g., bracelets or necklaces safety alarms. We describe some of them that have been emphasized during the activities carried out and how the elderly see robots as WT.

5.1 How Today's Fall Safety Alarms as WT Work in Practice

Elderly Encountering Falls. The elderly are exposed to serious injuries due to falls as they age. The experts mentioned that the elderly encountering a fall often remain on the floor for a long time after a fall, while 4 out of 5 elderlies usually need assistance to get up. In addition, after a fall, the elderly usually get a reduced quality of life, at least for a while. Moreover, it seems, according to the experts, that there is a high mortality rate within the first year after a fall. At the same time, as a person ages, s/he is more exposed to falls due to problems with balance, intake of medications that affect their balance, lowered sensing perception, impairment from previous falls, other diagnoses such as epilepsy, but also due to the arrangement of the physical environment such as carpets or cables. Also, many elderly sleep badly during the night because they are afraid of falling. This leads, in its turn to that they are usually tired during the day, and they do not have the energy to eat. Thus, they often get nutrition problems and are more exposed to falling again.

In MECS, our partner organization, an accommodation facility for the independent living elderly, called Omsorg Kampen+ (OK+), there were experienced 305 falls amongst the elderly between 2015–2017 [6], while many of those interviewed as part of the MECS project experienced balance problems [6].

Safety WT for Fall Detection Gives False Impression of Safety. The focus within the VIROS projects is on assistive home- and healthcare robots and not necessarily on *falls*. However, during our complementary research activities within VIROS, we found out that safety in relation to falls needs to be further investigated. Safety is also a central notion within the VIROS project.

Some of our findings show that the Norwegian municipalities responsible for distributing and following-up users that receive fall alarms wish to deliver "safety," but, as the experts mentioned in one of the activities, "today's technology does not live up to the requirements.", as it was also explained in the earlier subsections. Further, their concern is that they cannot distribute "safety alarms that do not work in practice." The experts mentioned that the technology does not work in practice, often giving the false impression of safety, although this type of technology has been used for more than ten years now.

One of the issues is that the technology is hypersensitive, being triggered when it is not the case of a fall, hence resulting in false-positive alarms. Another issue is that it does not detect different types of falls. Similarly, another problem is that the technology uses sensors that seem to do not always work in practice or have low accuracy. For instance, many fall alarms use acceleration sensors for falls, but they cannot detect when the person falls from a sitting state, for instance, while sitting on a chair. For instance, a usual situation that was described as when the technology triggers and gives false positive when a nurse comes in during the morning round and helps out an elder person with compression socks: the technology often detects it is one body and is a fall; thus, resulting in a false alarm.

Another issue is that a fall situation can be illustrated in different ways, such as *soft falls, falls where the user collapses, controlled falls where the user falls towards a wall or chair,* etc. However, the current fall technology does not allow analysis and interpretation of different types of falls. Similarly, a constellation of sensors that work in symbiosis shall be used for detecting: if the person has fallen, if the person has left the bed, if s/he was too long in the bathroom if s/he is sitting upraised in the bed, if leaving a chair, leaving or entering a room, if s/he makes high noises due to a fall, or if there is any lack of movement in bed.

5.2 Shortcomings of Today's Fall Safety Alarms as WT: Cost, Design, and Technical Aspects

Costs Related to the WT for Fall Detection. Our study shows that there are currently huge expenses with regard to fall detection technology. According to the informants, there is a need for "both cheap technology and technology that works; [this] did not happen yet." Similarly, testbeds are needed where the technology is tested in real-life use. Some suggested that the data collected should be open source, and the software use should help the researchers to advance and innovate fall technology, e.g., technology that both works in practice and is cheap.

Limitations in Terms of Design of the WT for Falls. Amongst the issues with the current wearable technology for fall detection are: its aesthetics, elderly considering it as a stigmatizing technology showing that "they are old and vulnerable," according to the elderly themselves. Similarly, another limitation is the number of false-positive alarms it gives. Many elderly think that the wearable fall alarms are not user-friendly, uncomfortable to wear and that their battery does not last for long.

Moreover, the elderly argued that they should be able to press the alarm button when a fall occurs – which often is not the case. For example, when a person falls, if the alarm is a necklace-type of fall alarm, it may end up on the side or the back of the person, s/he not being able to reach the alarm button after the fall. Wearables are also often misplaced or forgotten, according to the participants. In addition, at the alarm response center, the responders cannot see the user, only hear him or her, since this type of WT is often not provided with a camera. Also, while cameras would help the responders get a better overview of the fall and eventual injuries of the elderly, the elderly do not wish camera technologies in their homes since they perceive it as too intrusive. Finally, when using this type of technology, the user/patient often gets irritated over the many questions asked by the responders at the alarm center after a fall. Overall, the experts concluded that there is a need for mass research on safety alarms – a solution that may collect data over the years, and that small studies investigating safety alarms in isolation are no anymore interesting.

Another aspect that emerged from these different activities was the personalization and customization of the WT. The technology should be designed to give personalized recommendations for that specific user. In addition, the interaction of the technology should be likewise personalized and adapted to the specific user. The technology should learn over time by monitoring the user's activities and recommending a personalized behavior specific to that user. This means that the current technology used for fall detection is not adapted for the specific needs of each older individual using it. Similarly, not all wearable fall alarms can be used with people with reduced cognitive abilities, or some users may not understand how to use them. According to the experts, the design and aesthetics should also be customizable, accessible, and usable for different types of users. Similarly, many fall alarms do not allow the user to use the WT outside of the home.

In addition, some agreed that the technology should be camera-based, whereas others agreed that it should not include any camera-based techniques due to privacy issues. At the same time, a consensus was made that it is important to detect what happened *before* the fall.

Finally, to create a future WT for falls, advanced technical capacities of the technology are needed. This is indicated in the next sub-section.

Technical Limitations of the Current WT for Falls that can be Further Improved. There are currently several technical solutions for detecting falls, but these do not satisfy today's needs. This type of technology currently presents some weaknesses. For instance, one aspect discussed was the different standard procedures for fall alarms calls and its limitation. One such example is when the response center has to follow the standard pre-determined procedures when they receive an alarm: if the person can breathe, how is the circulation, whether he or she is warm or cold; whether the person has any injuries, and, if yes, where and what kind of injury has occurred; whether the person has any fracture, whether it is an opened or closed oned, and where the person is located (indoor or outdoor). Next, it is also important to know the cause of the fall: what happened, why did the person fall, whether it's about the person fainting, stumbling in something, or losing the balance. They also need to know how many persons the elderly need to go there and help her/him. Moreover, after the fall, they will look at whether the person has been able to get up him or herself and whether there is a need for following up for additional injuries or fractures.

However, this kind of information is hard to be retrieved when the older adult encountering a fall is highly injured. This information could be retrieved and provided instead by more advanced technology. For instance, the experts indicated that Artificial Intelligence (AI) and Machine Learning (ML) techniques should be used to improve the current technology or create new innovative solutions for *preventing and predicting falls rather than detecting falls.* In this way, the probability, risk, and consequences of falls will be reduced, detecting and predicting potentially dangerous situations. These techniques should be applied to improve the accuracy of falls prevention and prediction and should be implemented in combination with different types of sensor data, including vital signs monitoring and fall risk prediction.

Amongst the aspects to be improved with the fall alarms are: for instance, the embedding of fall alarm technology into assistive and companion robots, technology that can also be used outside of the home (e.g., shoes or sensors on shoes, foot bend, sensors that are connected to an indoor robot system), or something that is not directly body-worn or attached to the body and can be used while showering, e.g., robots. This leads us to the next type of welfare technology, namely robots.

5.3 Future Fall Safety Alarms: Robots as WT and the Need for New Standards, Regulations, and Legislation

Robots as WT for Fall Detection, Prevention, and Prediction: Elderly Expect that the Robots as WT also Have Social and Assistive Properties or Affordances. Within the framework of the MECS project, while researchers wished to talk about robots as potential safety alarms that shall be used by the elderly, the elderly had a hard time understanding the concept of a robot. Instead, they were familiar with industrial robots, or robots that have been seen on TV, such as AV1 telerobot from NoIsolation, lawnmowers, or vacuum cleaner robots [6].

However, they seemed to do not wish robots that monitor and surveil their health state, often not wishing to see themselves as *vulnerable*. Instead, they wished for robots that could assist them in everyday tasks or chores, such as picking up items and bringing those to them, cleaning the home, or as companions, interacting with them through speech [6]. In other words, our main findings from the MECS project showed that the elderly were interested in social and assistive or servant robots rather than in safety alarm robots for detecting, predicting, and preventing falls. They were also often not using their alarm wearable, either because they forgot to wear it or did not wish to use it while showering, because they did not want the wearable safety alarm to get broken.

Similarly, the elderly were also concerned about the ethical aspects of the robot as a safety alarm, such as privacy, e.g., whether the robot "could see through walls" [7], what kind of data it was collecting, or safety issues, i.e., they were afraid of getting stumble into the robot while it was navigating their indoor environment. In addition, the elderly indicated challenges in interacting with the robot through visual display, preferring that the robot interacts through speech. Specifically, the elderly wished the robot to interact through their mother tongue. They also expressed that they were very afraid of"doing something wrong." On the positive side, they developed social relationships with the robot, giving it names and talking to it, such as Frida or Robot King [7].

The Need of Standards, Regulations and Policy Work Around WT for Elderly Home Care. The elderly in MECS was concerned about the regulations not being adapted to the current technological advancements, arguing that the laws are not ready yet, and that "the authorities do not allow for their retirement and resignation [6] (p. 264). Similarly, some additional aspects that emerged from the activities carried out within the frame of the VIROS research project show that policy work, such as health policy, health legislation, and social legislation needs to be taken into consideration. These policies and legislations should be updated and allow researchers, municipalities, and the public sector to undergo agreements for developing the technology further and collecting health data. Lack of national standards and routines on how to procure technology, along with different agreements that sometimes the municipality does not have with those on the market and therefore cannot buy it, makes it difficult for the municipalities to take those WT into use. In addition, the legislation should both provide opportunities and facilitate more partnerships among the various organizations so that these technologies can be tested safely and securely.

6 Discussion

Robots as Welfare Technologies (WT) are introduced in the elderly's homes in order to increase their Quality of Life (QoL) and prolong their independent living [38] as part of the home- and healthcare services. For instance, until now, several studies focused on different Information Communication Technologies (ICT) as WTs (see [39–44]. On the other hand, only a few studies focused on robots seen through the conceptual lens of WT [4].

However, the notion of welfare is challenged with the integration of care robots in the home. Thus, in this paper, we address the following research question: *Is the notion of WT challenged by the adoption of intelligent robots within home care, and if yes, how?* Our findings are twofold. First, municipalities delivering home care services and user representatives receiving home care argue that current wearable technologies used as safety alarms do not perform at a good level, even after more than ten years of use. For instance, these do not detect all types of falls, often give false-positive alarms, and are inaesthetic and stigmatizing. They recommend more powerful solutions that include AI and ML techniques. In this case, robots could be considered as WT. However, these solutions might be costly if not designed and integrated well within the home care service. Second, our research in MECS shows that the elderly were not interested in robots as safety alarms but wished for safety alarm robots as WT that also embed social and assistive properties. In other words, the elderly wished the robots as WT to help them with house chores and be social companions. However, the elderly still did not actively use other kinds of safety alarms, such as wearables.

At the same time, in Sect. 3, we defined our theoretical lens, namely the concept of WT. [24] has structured WT into eight (8) categories, earlier described in Sect. 3. Thus, our findings seen through the lens of the WT as the theoretical framework gives us a multi-folded answer to the initial stated research question. First, different stakeholders have different needs to be addressed. For instance, elderly as care receivers understand robots as WT for fall detection through the lenses of WT consumer services (#3 in [24]), as a form of entertainment used for leisure and pleasure (#7 in [24]), and as social and emotional support or stimulation (#8 in [24]). However, caregivers have seen the WT for fall detection rather as assistive or compensatory technology (#2 in [24]) in case of elder's falls, as a monitoring device (#4 in [24]), and as a remote form of monitoring the elderlies' falls (#5 in [24]).

In other words, our findings show that the elderly do not see themselves as vulnerable users and would rather prefer social and assistive robots than safety alarm robots. However, they agree that the current safety alarm solutions are not extensively used. At the same time, municipalities need better solutions for preventing, detecting, and predicting falls – advanced solutions that also involve AI and ML techniques. Since robots as WT may be regarded from many angles by different stakeholders, we choose to limit our discussion next to the elderly's attitudes towards WT for falls and to some ethical robots as WT for fall prevention, detection, and prediction, and to the eventual ethical challenges and opportunities that may arise with robots as WT.

6.1 From Wearables to Robots as WT for Fall Prevention, Detection and, Prediction

Elderly's Attitudes Towards WT for Falls. It seems that WT is a means in addressing the challenge of the increased elderly population [24]. WT can facilitate sustainable healthcare that is able to respond to societal demands and changes with regard to a shortage of healthcare personnel and an increased elderly population [45]. A white paper from the Ministry of Health and Care Services in Norway confirms that the most common problems encountered in the healthcare services were: falls, loneliness, and cognitive decline (ibid, p. 11). Falls may lead to fear of falling again, withdrawal and social isolation, and (physical) inactivity [45] (p. 28). "Experiencing a fall may, however, impede safe and active living." [40] (p. 11). Similarly, one of the critical factors in falls is its severity and the time spent on the ground right after the fall, where one hour or more spent lying on the floor correlates with higher mortality rates and hospitalization due to severe injuries [40]. This is also confirmed in our findings.

Similarly, [40] confirms our findings that a high number of WT for fall detection amongst older people were adopted so far. However, it seems that many of these WTs are either improperly or infrequently used [40]. For instance, the elderly take them off when showering or sleeping. Some of these are also not used because they require manual activation after a fall, which sometimes is difficult to do right after a fall, i.e., because the device is worn on an arm that cannot be moved after the fall. Our study also confirmed these findings, as shown in Sect. 5.

In addition, other studies confirm that the elderly prefer not to use these devices due to the elderly's preferences not being considered when designing and developing such devices [40]. Similarly, our study shows that the design of WT for falls is often lacking in terms of aesthetics and how they are worn, leading to feelings of stigmatization amongst the elderly.

Elderly's Attitudes Towards Robots as WT. In our study, the elderly's attitudes towards robots as WT acting as safety alarms were less positive, being oriented towards robots as servants rather than robots as safety alarms. It seems, however, that in general, the attitudes amongst the elderly people towards the use of WT in their homes is positive, with regard to changes in their behavior and detection of their daily routine [41] (p. 846). At the same time, many of our participants were afraid of falling while showering but preferred robots as WT to do not enter their bathrooms, considering these as private and intimate rooms. Similar findings are also confirmed in other studies, but in those cases elderly had "replaced their bath tubes with shower stalls" to reduce the fall risk instead [41] (p. 846). In addition, in other studies, the elderly indicated various design solutions for wearing a wearable safety alarm while showering, such as: expressing that a waterproof fall alarm would be preferred or that the safety alarm should be attached to the body, a small and comfortable device, that can be worn as a bracelet, watch, or jewellery, and that it will also indicate the GPS location, so their exact location can easily be sent to the emergency response center (ibid). However, in our study, the elderly stated that they did not wish to use wearables as safety alarms while showering because they wished to protect the WT from getting wet and broken. Our argument is that elderly should actively be involved in the design process of the robot as WT for the elderly to use these WT. Similarly, Thilo and colleagues involved the elderly in designing and developing WT for fall detection, although in that case, the WT was wearable [40]. The color, size and shape, weight, material, body location, duration of wearing, fixation on the body, and use from feasible and practical aspects of the WT for fall detection are essential to design properties to be taken into account [40]. Also, the study shows that some of the elderly preferred the WT to be transparent, while others wished for strong colors that easily make the WT detectable in case of loss. The shape of the WT was preferred to be "round, oval or the shape of a blossom" [40] (p. 16). The prototypes presented were waterproof, weighed only 10 g, and could be bendable and rigid. Furthermore, the prototypes' materials were considered to be compatible with sensitive skin. Thus, the prototypes were tested with the elderly from a visual and tactile point of view. Similarly, these design properties are also important in designing a robot as WT. We, therefore, suggest that Universal Design's principles could act as guidelines or ethical charter for the future design of social and assistive care robots, robots as WT, to be used within the home- and healthcare [46].

From Wearables to Robots as WT for Fall Detection, Prevention, and Prediction. In general, it seems that the elderly's attitudes towards WT and robots as WT need to be considered when developing advanced AI and ML technologies, with the elderly as target users. Therefore, the elderly should actively be involved in the design, development, and testing process of WT through, for instance, participatory design [47]. This will ensure avoiding ageism and the risk of bias in the development of advanced technology, but will also ensure an inclusive design considering the elderly as a diverse user group, with all their differences, health conditions, and abilities, as indicated by [47]. This leads us to our next point of discussion, namely addressing eventual ethical challenges but also opportunities with robots as WT.

6.2 Some Ethical Challenges and Opportunities with Robots as WT

The robot technology is among the identified WT for falls and remote treatment [24]. Robots as WT bring in new advantages but also challenges. WT can improve the care-receiver's daily life, but it can also introduce new ethical questions and risks and change their practices and relationships [41] (p. 842).

The Challenge of Responsibility with Robots as WT. Another issue is the problem of responsibility – who is responsible for the elderly's care – is that responsibility delegated to the robot? In other words, the notion of *care* is challenged when introducing intelligent robots as part of the care services [9, 11] When new stakeholders or third parties responsible for the technical infrastructure maintenance of the WT or service come into place, confidentiality and privacy of the user are challenged [24]. For instance, some WT turns out to be more useful for the care provider and the society than the individual care receiver, e.g., the end-user, the elder [24]. Moreover, trust and relationships between the end-user, the elder, and different professions, such as healthcare and technical professionals, are challenged [24]. Healthcare services are no longer independent professions, but they depend on technical competence. According to [24], the delimitation of responsibility amongst different professions may be ethically and legally challenging. This might raise ethical challenges and a social dilemma, whether technical professionals should be licensed professions, such that the developers are better equipped with ethical competencies relevant to the care domains [48]. A question is also addressed whether developers should have a similar oath to the Hippocrates one from the medical field.

Robots as WT May Challenge the Notion of Home as a Safe and Private Environment. Home is an intimate, private, safe, and secure place that should be treated as such. However, introducing advanced technologies in this setting may challenge the core concepts of what a home means with a privacy-invading technology. It may also make the user feel vulnerable and monitored in its own home. In a way, technology redirects the attention from human values, such as vulnerability and dignity, thus welfare, towards instrumental values, such as functionality, efficiency, and productivity [24]. Thus, with so many challenges around the penetration of advanced technologies such as robots in private homes, the notion of welfare is also challenged.

Privacy, Safety, and Security Aspects Regarding Robots as WT to be Used in the Home. By moving some of the treatment to the home, some other challenges may arise: physical safety of using the robot in a private environment, or privacy aspects that may arise with the integration of the robot in the home [24], or psycho-social aspects that may arise with long-term use of a robot in the home, while being isolated from other social contacts. Our study showed that the elderly were concerned about their privacy, if "the robot can see through walls," but not about sharing their data. Amongst the challenges of using robots as WT within healthcare services, the issue of safety is indicated, not only as physical safety but also as eventual safety risks due to long cognitive interaction [4] (p. 198).

The Elderly's Understanding of Robots as a Complex WT. Another challenge could be that the elderly decline to use the robot. They might fear that they have a limited understanding of the technology, avoid using the robot from the fear of "doing something wrong" due to their unfamiliarity or lack of experience with the advanced technology [49], or the fear of stumbling on it. At the same time, robots may not be as stigmatizing as wearables and provide additional features, such as companionship and help with various assistive tasks in the home.

Robots as WT and the Basic Rights, such as the Right to Healthcare Services, Autonomy, and Dignity. At the same time, WT can also challenge the Right to Health [50], creating inequalities amongst the care receivers. WT can be discriminating, increase differences in the access to healthcare and the WT, or enhance other inequalities [24]. For instance, WT may contribute to discrimination based on who is prioritized receiving a service containing a WT. It can also create discrimination based on age or gender and may also create a burden for the relatives of the care receiver [24]. Both the right to health and eventual inequalities across a wide span of the diversity of users will be seen in the future of healthcare if robots as welfare technologies are not treated with care. This also applies to robots as WT.

In addition, WT used for tracking daily habits and routines, monitoring, detecting, preventing, and predicting events, such as falls, may challenge basic rights such as autonomy, confidentiality, and privacy [24]. Therefore, balancing the risks and benefits of such WT is challenging [24]. One example given is diabetes which requires continuous monitoring, indicating an increase in self-care and the individual's (lack of) self-control [24]. However, with the integration of robots as part of healthcare services, this becomes even more challenging.

Another concern covered aspects of loss of personal autonomy and who will control the WT [41]. At the same time, simple WT is easier for the elderly to comprehend compared to robots as WT and to give their consent for using it, but with more advanced technologies, such as robots, the issue of consent is raised [24]. When the elderly do not understand the technology they are going to use, this can also decrease their autonomy and dis-empower them [24]. In addition, when intelligent robots shall be used in the home, other people may also be around (grandchildren, other family members, acquaintances, etc.) who may not have given their consent to the intelligent robot to collect data about them. A similar view is presented in another study, where WT in the form of sensor monitoring in the homes of the older people as a preventive healthcare measure and as a watchdog, i.e., to monitor their daily activities [42]. The authors argue that although WT can provide increased safety for elderly people, this type of technology may also introduce new privacy and security issues. This type of WT acted as a safety measure and allowed elderly people to live independently and longer in their homes. Neither in this study did the elderly participants' present concerns regarding their privacy. For them, safety was more important than privacy. Although the elderly did not feel "watched," they were concerned about sharing their daily activities and routines with others – however, they were willing to use the welfare technology anyway [42] (p. 489). However, it seems that the majority of the elderly were not concerned about the privacy challenges that the welfare technology may introduce. In general, they were willing to share private information with doctors and family members. However, some were concerned about their privacy and did not know how to address it. Feelings of being surveilled, use of cameras and video recordings, were OK if this were shared only with their healthcare providers, and the aim was to get help when falling and keep living in their own homes [41]. This is in line with the findings from our study.

The Cost and Ownership of the Robot as WT. Other concerns regarding the WT for fall detection regarded its cost, its ownership, and whether the elderly themselves have to purchase it or the healthcare services providers can provide it. Similarly, the elderly in our study were concerned about who will pay for the WT. Potentially, a robot as WT for fall detection, prevention, and prediction, can come at a much higher cost than other wearables technologies, and this may lead to questions of who will be able to have access to this type of technology.

Development of Policies and Regulations of Robots as WT. Older people need to be actively involved in formulating regulatory guidelines for advanced technologies such as WT robots using AI or ML techniques to ensure that these are designed, implemented, and deployed appropriately on their behalf [47].

Opportunities with Robots as WT. At the same time, robots as WT may also bring in a set of opportunities with each challenge they present. They may also free up resources, as seen in this study. Other studies confirm this finding. It is said that WT can both be able to free resources while reducing the state's healthcare costs and providing help to those in need [24]. At the same time, a WT for fall detection may provide peace of mind for the elderly themselves, but also their family members [41]. In addition, robots as WT may provide social interaction, remote telecommunication, access to remote health care services, better health monitoring, and in general, increased quality of life. Similarly, WT is said to both rehabilitate and enhance people's autonomy, empowering them [24]. The authors also argue that, for instance, autonomy, safety, and independence were important aspects for the elderly (Sánchez et al. 2019). They also saw WT as an empowerment tool for achieving autonomy, independence and keeping their dignity. Nevertheless, the current assessment of a clinical fall risk evaluation is very long and time-consuming. The elderly often have to be referred by a General Practitioner (GP) to a specialized fall clinique to be assessed. The process often takes several months, while the elderly's health state can worsen and encounter several falls during this time. With new innovative technical solutions, using AI/ML techniques, a fall or the risk for falling could be easily evaluated, prevented, predicted, and detected in the heart of the elderly's home. This could be done either through an already existing WT robot, such as a off-the-shelf consumer product, that the elderly have already in their homes, by attaching more advanced sensors to these, or through other technical solutions.

Limitations of the Study. In terms of limitations of this study, the current study does not look at how robots as WT look in other countries in general, nor other Scandinavian countries, besides the Norwegian context. For instance, institutional, social, or political factors might impact how robots as WT are adopted within elderly home care. At the same time, in less developed countries, robots such as WT are far from being adopted, e.g., countries in the Global South, where technology, in general, and gerontechnology are not yet highly adopted.

7 Conclusion

This paper discusses the concept of a robot as a WT focusing on the case of fall technology. The paper shows that although a range of WT is available for falls as wearables technologies, they do not work in practice due to their technical and design limitations. However, falls are a great problem in public health in Norway, following trends worldwide. Therefore, advanced WT for falls should focus on prevention and prediction, rather than only detection as previous technologies did. This may have a huge potential in preventing falls, improving access to healthcare right from the heart of the home, and highly reducing financial costs associated with falls, enabling the elderly to live in their homes longer. In addition, robot as WT, and WT in general, does not differ from other technologies, with one exception: they differ from the traditional way of providing healthcare (Hofmann 2013), may provide great opportunities, but it may also have some ethical and legal implications. This, of course, raises a series of ethical questions, but likewise lots of opportunities with every challenge. Finally, the paper concludes that more studies are needed shedding light on robots as WT, especially in the welfare countries.

Future studies should address how advanced technology, including robots as WT, shall be accessible and inclusive and do not create a greater digital divide and focus on the long-term study interaction with these types of AI and ML technologies, including intelligent robots [47]. Similarly, future studies should actively involve elderly people in the design, testing, and use of robots as WT, or in general gerontechnology, technology destined to be used by the elderly people as the main target group [47]. This is, in other words, designed *for* and *with* elderly people, rather than focusing only on designing them *for* elderly people [47].

Acknowledgments. This work is partially supported by The Research Council of Norway (RCN) as a part of the projects: Vulnerability in the Robot Society (VIROS) under Grant Agreement No. 288285, Predictive and Intuitive Robot Companion (PIRC) under Grant Agreement No. 312333 and through its Centres of Excellence scheme, RITMO with Project No. 262762.

References

1. Beer, J.M., et al.: The domesticated robot: design guidelines for assisting older adults to age in place. In: Proceedings of the Seventh Annual ACM/IEEE International Conference on Human-Robot Interaction, pp. 335–342. New York, NY, USA (2012). https://doi.org/10.1145/2157689.2157806
2. Unbehaun, D., Aal, K., Carros, F., Wieching, R., Wulf, V.: Creative and cognitive activities in social assistive robots and older adults: results from an exploratory field study with pepper. In: ECSCW 2019 Proceedings of 17th European Conference on. Computer-Supported Cooperative Work ECSCW 2019 Demos Posters Panels (2019). https://doi.org/10.18420/ecscw2019_p07
3. Doelling, K., Shin, J., Popa, D.O.: Service robotics for the home: a state of the art review. In: Proceedings of the 7th International Conference on PErvasive Technologies Related to Assistive Environments, pp. 35:1–35:8. New York, NY, USA (2014). https://doi.org/10.1145/2674396.2674459
4. Bodenhagen, L., Suvei, S.-D., Juel, W.K., Brander, E., Krüger, N.: Robot technology for future welfare: meeting upcoming societal challenges – an outlook with offset in the development in Scandinavia. Heal. Technol. **9**(3), 197–218 (2019). https://doi.org/10.1007/s12553-019-00302-x
5. Petrie, H., Darzentas, J.: Older people and robotic technologies in the home: perspectives from recent research literature. In: Proceedings of the 10th International Conference on PErvasive Technologies Related to Assistive Environments, pp. 29–36. New York, NY, USA (2017). https://doi.org/10.1145/3056540.3056553

6. Saplacan, D., Herstad, J., Pajalic, Z.: An analysis of independent living elderly's views on robots - a descriptive study from the Norwegian context. In: Proceedings of the International Conference on Advances in Computer-Human Interactions (ACHI). IARIA Conferences, Valencia, Spain (2020)
7. Saplacan, D., Herstad, J.: An explorative study on motion as feedback: using semi-autonomous robots in domestic settings. Int. J. Adv. Softw. **12**(1 & 2), 23 (2019)
8. Saplacan, D., Herstad, J., Tørresen, J., Pajalic, Z.: Division of work tasks between humans and robots: an instrumental analytical study from the home. Multimodal Technol. Interact. J. **4**(3), 44 (2020)
9. van Wynsberghe, A.: Designing robots for care: care centered value-sensitive design. Sci. Eng. Ethics **19**(2), 407–433 (2013). https://doi.org/10.1007/s11948-011-9343-6
10. Santoni de Sio, F., van Wynsberghe, A.: When should we use care robots? the nature-of-activities approach. Sci. Eng. Ethics **22**(6), 1745–1760 (2015). https://doi.org/10.1007/s11948-015-9715-4
11. van Wynsberghe, A.: To delegate or not to delegate: care robots, moral agency and moral responsibility (2014)
12. Saplacan, D., Khaksar, W., Torresen, J.: On ethical challenges raised by care robots: a review of the existing regulatory-, theoretical-, and research gaps. In: Proceedings of the 20th International Conference on Advanced Robotics and its Social Impacts, Japan/Virtual, p. 8 (2021). https://doi.org/10.1109/ARSO51874.2021.9542844
13. Torresen, J.: A review of future and ethical perspectives of robotics and AI. Front. Robot. AI **4** (2018). https://doi.org/10.3389/frobt.2017.00075
14. World Health Organization, Falls (2021). https://www.who.int/news-room/fact-sheets/detail/falls. Accessed 26 Jan 2022
15. Lamb, S.E., Jørstad-Stein, E.C., Hauer, K., Becker, C.: Prevention of Falls Network Europe and Outcomes Consensus Group, Development of a common outcome data set for fall injury prevention trials: the Prevention of Falls Network Europe consensus. J. Am. Geriatr. Soc. **53**(9), 1618–1622 (2005). https://doi.org/10.1111/j.1532-5415.2005.53455.x
16. Holte, H.H., Underland, V., Haftstad, E.: Review of systematic reviews on prevention of falls in institutions (Norwegian title: oppsummering av systematiske oversikter om forebygging av fall i institusjone), Knowledge Department, Norwegian Institute of Public Health, Systematic overview 13–2015 (2015). https://www.fhi.no/publ/2015/oppsummering-av-systematiske-oversikter-om-forebygging-av-fall-i-institusjo/. Accessed 24 Nov 2021
17. Statistics Norway, Care services, SSB (2021). https://www.ssb.no/en/helse/helsetjenester/statistikk/sjukeheimar-heimetenester-og-andre-omsorgstenester. Accessed 23 Nov 2021
18. Gjertsen, J.-E., Fevang, J., Vinje, T., Engesæter, L.B., Steindal, K., Furnes, O.: The norwegian hip fracture register/Nasjonalt Hoftebruddregister. Nor. Epidemiol. **16**(2)(Art. no. 2) (2006). https://doi.org/10.5324/nje.v16i2.190
19. Hektoen, L.F.: Kostnader ved hoftebrudd hos elder. Skriftserien (2014). https://www.skriftserien.oslomet.no/index.php/skriftserien/article/view/18. Accessed 14 Feb 2022
20. Søndergård, D.: Velferdsteknologi: Verktøykasse (2017). http://urn.kb.se/resolve?urn=urn:nbn:se:norden:org:diva-4779. Accessed 20 Oct 2021
21. Nordic Centre for Welfare and Social Issues, Welfare technology. Nordic Centre for Welfare and Social Issues. http://www.nordicwelfare.org/PageFiles/5488/Velferdsteknologi_eng.pdf. Accessed 10 Dec 2017
22. OED: welfare, n., OED Online. Oxford University Press (2017). http://www.oed.com/view/Entry/226968
23. Brynn, R.: Universal design and welfare technology. Stud. Health Technol. Inform. **229**, 335–344 (2016)
24. Hofmann, B.: Ethical challenges with welfare technology: a review of the literature. Sci. Eng. Ethics **19**(2), 389–406 (2013). https://doi.org/10.1007/s11948-011-9348-1

25. Thrun, S.: Toward a framework for human-robot interaction. Hum-Comput Interact **19**(1), 9–24 (2004). https://doi.org/10.1207/s15327051hci1901&2_2
26. Saplacan, D., Torresen, J.: Design, legal, and ethical aspects on intelligent social and care robots: a critical and integrative perspective on the human right to health (care) seen through the lenses of universal design principles. In: Cambridge Handbook on Law, Regulation, and Policy for Human-Robot Interaction, Cambridge University Press (in progress)
27. Schulz, T., Herstad, J., Torresen, J.: Moving with Style: Classifying Human and Robot Movement at Home, pp. 188–193 (2018). https://www.thinkmind.org/index.php?view=article&articleid=achi_2018_10_20_20053. Accessed 24 Mar 2018
28. Schulz, T., Holthaus, P., Amirabdollahian, F., Koay, K.L.: Humans' perception of a robot moving using a slow in and slow out velocity profile. In: Proceedings of the 14th ACM/IEEE International Conference on Human-Robot Interaction, pp. 594–595. Daegu, Republic of Korea (2019)
29. Schulz, T., Herstad, J.: Walking away from the robot: negotiating privacy with a robot. Presented at the HCI 2017. Sunderland, UK (2018). https://doi.org/10.14236/ewic/HCI2017.83
30. Schulz, T., Herstad, J., Holone, H.: Privacy at home: an inquiry into sensors and robots for the stay at home elderly. In: Zhou, J., Salvendy, G. (eds.) ITAP 2018. LNCS, vol. 10927, pp. 377–394. Springer, Cham (2018). https://doi.org/10.1007/978-3-319-92037-5_28
31. Tørresen, J.: Undertaking research with humans within artificial intelligence and robotics: multimodal elderly care systems. Technol. Des. **5**(2), 141–145 (2021). https://doi.org/10.1080/24751448.2021.1967052
32. Uddin, M.Z., Khaksar, W., Torresen, J.: Ambient sensors for elderly care and independent living: a survey. Sensors **18**(7)(Art. no. 7) (2018). https://doi.org/10.3390/s18072027
33. Noori, F.M., Riegler, M., Uddin, M.Z., Torresen, J.: Human activity recognition from multiple sensors data using multi-fusion representations and CNNs ACM Trans. Multimed. Comput. Commun. Appl. **16**(2), 45:1–45:19 (2020). https://doi.org/10.1145/3377882
34. Zia Uddin, Md., Khaksar, W., Torresen, J.: A thermal camera-based activity recognition using discriminant skeleton features and RNN. In: 2019 IEEE 17th International Conference on Industrial Informatics (INDIN), vol. 1, pp. 777–782 (2019). https://doi.org/10.1109/INDIN41052.2019.8972082
35. Uddin, Md. Z., Noori, F.M., Torresen, J.: In-home emergency detection using an ambient ultra-wideband radar sensor and deep learning. In: 2020 IEEE Ukrainian Microwave Week (UkrMW), pp. 1089–1093. (2020). https://doi.org/10.1109/UkrMW49653.2020.9252708
36. Khaksar, W., Uddin, M.Z., Torresen, J.: Learning from virtual experience: mapless navigation with neuro-fuzzy intelligence. In: 2018 International Conference on Intelligent Systems (IS), pp. 117–124 (2018). https://doi.org/10.1109/IS.2018.8710525
37. Braun, V., Clarke, V.: Using thematic analysis in psychology. Qual. Res. Psychol. **3**(2), 77–101 (2006). https://doi.org/10.1191/1478088706qp063oa
38. Bedaf, S., de Witte, L.: Robots for elderly care: their level of social interactions and the targeted end user. Stud. Health Technol. Inform. **242**, 472–478 (2017)
39. Shulver, W., Killington, M., Morris, C., Crotty, M.: 'Well, if the kids can do it, I can do it': older rehabilitation patients' experiences of telerehabilitation. Health Expect. Int. J. Public Particip. Health Care Health Policy **20**(1), 120–129 (2017). https://doi.org/10.1111/hex.12443
40. Thilo, F.J., Bilger, S., Halfens, R.J., Schols, J.M., Hahn, S.: Involvement of the end user: exploration of older people's needs and preferences for a wearable fall detection device – a qualitative descriptive study. Patient Prefer. Adherence **11**, 11–22 (2016). https://doi.org/10.2147/PPA.S119177
41. Sánchez, V.G., Anker-Hansen, C., Taylor, I., Eilertsen, G.: Older people's attitudes and perspectives of welfare technology in Norway. J. Multidiscip. Health. **12**, 841–853 (2019). https://doi.org/10.2147/JMDH.S219458

42. Pol, M., van Nes, F., van Hartingsveldt, M., Buurman, B., de Rooij, S., Kröse, B.: Older people's perspectives regarding the use of sensor monitoring in their home. Gerontologist **56**(3), 485–493 (2016). https://doi.org/10.1093/geront/gnu104
43. Mortenson, W.B., Sixsmith, A., Beringer, R.: No place like home? Surveillance and what home means in old age. Can. J. Aging Rev. Can. Vieil. **35**(1), 103–114 (2016). https://doi.org/10.1017/S0714980815000549
44. Kärki, A., Sallinen, M., Kuusinen, J.: How to live independently with or without technology? Stud. Health Technol. Inform. **217**, 306–310 (2015)
45. Ministry of Health and Care Services: Innovation in the Care Services, NOU 2011: 11. Ministry of Health and Care Services (2011). https://www.regjeringen.no/en/dokumenter/nou-2011-11/id646812/Accessed 2 Feb 2022
46. Saplacan, D., Martinez, S., Bygrave, L.A., Torresen, J.: Universal design principles: an ethical charter for care robots' design and regulation. Presented at the Sixth International Conference on Universal Design - Transforming our World through Universal Design for Human Development S, Brescia, Italy (2022)
47. WHO: Ageism in Artificial Intelligence for Health, Global Campaign to combat ageism ISBN 978-92-4-004079-3 (2022). https://www.who.int/publications/i/item/9789240040793. Accessed 14 Feb 2022
48. Strümke, I., Slavkovik, M., Madai, V.I.: The social dilemma in AI development and why we have to solve it (2021). http://arxiv.org/abs/2107.12977. Accessed 6 Sep 2021
49. Saplacan, D., Herstad, J.: Fear, Feedback, Familiarity... How are These Connected? - Can familiarity as a design concept applied to digital feedback reduce fear? Proceedings of the Eleventh International Conference on Advances in Computer-Human Interactions (ACHI) (2018)
50. WHO: The Right to Health, Office of the United Nations High Commissioner for Human Rights, Fact Sheet No. 31. https://www.ohchr.org/documents/publications/factsheet31.pdf
51. Saplacan, D.: Situated abilities: Understanding everyday use of ICTs. Ph.D. Thesis. Department of Informatics, University of Oslo. Reprosentralen (2020). https://www.duo.uio.no/handle/10852/81852
52. Khaksar, W., Neggers, M., Barakova, E., Torresen, J.: Generation differences in perception of the elderly care robot. In: 2021 30th IEEE International Conference on Robot & Human Interactive Communication (RO-MAN), pp. 551–558 (2021). https://doi.org/10.1109/RO-MAN50785.2021.9515534. https://ieeexplore-ieee-org.ezproxy.uio.no/abstract/document/9515534/figures#figures

Smart Home for the Elderly - A Survey of Desires, Needs, and Problems

Monika Schak(✉), Rainer Blum, and Birgit Bomsdorf

Fulda University of Applied Sciences, Fulda, Germany
{monika.schak,rainer.blum,birgit.bomsdorf}@cs.hs-fulda.de

Abstract. We present the results of a survey with 87 senior citizens aged 62 to 90 years to gain insight into their use of technological devices such as smartphones and smart home devices, into common issues they encounter when using such devices, and into their preferences when interacting with a smart home system, e.g., the form of control such as touch control, voice control, gesture control or activity control. We found that a big part of the target group uses smartphones daily and regularly uses other touch devices such as tablets and navigation systems. We also detected that the use of smart home devices is less common. Although most of the respondents have heard about smart homes, only a very small part has devices in their homes.

The results show that senior citizens are open to receiving support from technical systems if help from other people can not be sufficiently provided. They show great interest but also require help in how to select, set up and use devices. The survey showed that the elderly are worried about their privacy, initial and running costs and the actual benefits provided by smart home systems. We noticed that respondents with limitations in vision, hearing, or mobility seem to be more open about technical support in general and more intuitive forms of interaction in particular.

Keywords: Human aspects of IT for the aged population · Accommodations for aging-in-place · Daily living activity support · Generational differences in IT use · Smart home and IoT

1 Introduction

It is a widespread assumption that the elderly can highly benefit from smart home devices, e.g. to pursue a self-determined life at home instead of having to move to an assisted living facility. But currently, mostly younger men are the main adopters of smart home technology. About one-third of all smart home users are between the age of 25 and 34 years old, while only 10% are above 55 years old [24]. It can be assumed that senior citizens with an age above 65 years are even less commonly using smart home devices.

Therefore, we conducted a survey with senior citizens to gain insight into the following questions: To what extent do senior citizens already know and

Q. Gao and J. Zhou (Eds.): HCII 2022, LNCS 13331, pp. 107–121, 2022.
https://doi.org/10.1007/978-3-031-05654-3_7

use technological devices such as smartphones or smart home devices? What are common issues when using such devices, especially regarding limitations in vision, hearing, or mobility? How do they want to interact with a smart home system and how high or low is the acceptance of such systems, with the main focus on the interaction techniques touch control, voice control, gesture control, and activity control? Why do the elderly not use technical devices, especially smart home systems, more frequently although a lot of research is done on how to develop technical systems adapted to the needs of senior citizens? Another goal of the survey is to gain an insight into the status quo of the usage of technical devices and smart home systems by senior citizens in the rural area around the university.

Touch control describes the very common way of interacting with a touch device, e.g. a smartphone or tablet, by touching the display with one or more fingers at predefined interactive areas (graphical control elements) or performing predefined gestures on the screen.

Voice control means interacting with a device by spoken voice commands. Examples are smart assistants like Siri or Cortana, or smart speakers like Amazon Echo or Google Assistant.

Gesture control relies on freehand gestures to interact with a device without direct physical contact. Today, this technique is, e.g., used in cars to allow interaction with the cars infotainment system without having to touch any buttons or a screen, therefore supporting the driver to keep their focus on the road. An example is BMW Gesture Control [2].

Activity control describes a system consisting of multiple sensors installed in a smart home environment that monitor daily living activities, classify and predict them to trigger actions accordingly, e.g. turning on the lights if the resident is going to read. Such a system is available only in research yet, and not on the market. Similar functionality can be observed in smartwatches, which can recognize and record activities like Sleep or Workout.

2 Related Work

Smart home systems for the elderly are a growing subject of academic and industrial research and thus play an important role in the area of human-computer interaction. A thorough overview of this research field was given by D. Marikyan et al. [16]. Related areas of our research project are smart homes for the elderly, as well as different forms of human-computer interaction, e.g. touch control, voice control, gesture control, and activity control, with a focus on senior citizens.

The survey conducted by Chernbumroong et al. [1] explores the perception of smart home technologies such as an automatic lighting system, activity monitoring, or oven safety control to assist elderly people. Their approach is based on the fact that the elderly population has increased dramatically. Thus, costs for healthcare and assistance for the elderly will rise significantly. To face these issues, they propose that smart home technologies can be used in elderly care, but therefore the needs and concerns of the elderly must be thoroughly assessed and understood, which is also explored by Visutsak and Daoudi [25]. They find that smart home technologies have to be adapted specifically for the elderly. The stakeholders raised the concerns that the devices have to be easy-to-use and the need for learning how to use the new technology has to be low, which is why we research intuitive forms of interaction that do not require extensive training.

The research conducted by Bejanaro et al. [7] goes even further by focusing on what the home can do automatically rather than expecting the user to control it. Besides examining the technology itself they assess user interfaces, especially the key factor of intuitiveness. They state that "as long as mobile devices are required [...], they will continue to be the preferred interface by many users". This is the starting point for our research as we intend to prove this hypothesis to be correct and that senior citizens would rather adopt other forms of interaction if they were broadly available.

According to Pal et al. [17] there is a lack of research that focuses on the intention and needs of senior citizens to use smart homes that assist them in their daily life, which to our knowledge still holds true to this day. They assert that most of today's research concentrates on the underlying technology and services rather than the acceptance by the elderly population, which is also confirmed by Alaa et al. [3]. Besides using an acceptance-based approach, like we also do in our work, it is possible to identify the main barriers by using a negative perception-based approach [18]. Holzinger et al. [12] also state that older adults actually are motivated to use touch devices when they are aware of the resulting benefits, but a lack of understanding and reluctance or fear to learn something new can alleviate their motivation.

A major part of the elderly prefers to live at their home instead of having to move into institutional care [8]. Although some of the senior citizens already use smart technologies, the lack of adaption to people with impairments is preventing a larger group from adopting such devices into their daily life [21]. As stated by Williams et al. [28], useful human-computer interfaces need to take into account the abilities of the user and adapt to the difficulties the user may face, which can be clustered into the following categories: cognition, auditory, haptic, visual and motor-based troubles. Touch devices are prone to causing difficulties in multiple of the aforementioned categories, and therefore other forms of interaction might be better suited.

Most research regarding human-computer interaction tailored to the elderly has been conducted in the area of touch control. Kobayashi et al. [14] evaluate how the elderly interact with a touch device and which problems they face. They found that basic gestures such as taps, drags and pinching motions are generally easy to use for the elderly, but that they need experience and repetitions to fully master them. They did not take possible impairments into account, such as limitations in vision or motion, which certainly reduce the acceptance of touch devices. This issue has been only partially addressed by Bara et al. [6], who suggest user interaction concepts in smart homes specially designed for the elderly with chronic conditions, but they focus more on how to notify the user in case of events than on how the user can interact with the system and control the devices. The special needs of users with impairments are not addressed here, which leaves room for further research including our own work.

There has also been extensive research on voice control for the elderly. Jakob et al. [13] state that over a third of the elderly do not use touch devices because they experience difficulties in operating them. They suggest using speech to interact with devices since it is more natural and familiar, as also stated by Sahlab et al. [19]. They surveyed elderly people to assess the reservations senior citizens might have about using voice-controlled devices. Their respondents mentioned reservations such as no known benefit, safety and security concerns, and insecurities about how to use such devices. This indicates that voice control might not be the desired form of interaction for the elderly despite the benefits it has over touch control.

Also, a widely researched area is gesture control for senior citizens. Most work is done on the technical aspect, e.g. Vorwerg et al. [26] as well as Ayubi et al. [5] who suggest an intuitive form of interaction using a gesture-controlled device that can be used to control smart home devices. They assessed the requirements of elderly people with and without impairments in mobility. Using an interview as well as a questionnaire, they found that seniors see a benefit for themselves and voiced clear expectations regarding the needed functionality. They also prove that it is technically possible to design a gesture control interface in such a way that it can be used by people with mobility impairments without major limitations in the user experience. The same conclusion is drawn by Wang et al. [27]. Their developed gesture-controlled smart home system can effectively be operated by people with impairments in motion, hearing, or speaking.

Recent publications show that human activity recognition, abnormal behavior detection, and activity control – which are all related areas – are of increasing interest in the scientific community, as shown by Lentzas and Vrakas [15]. Compared to the other forms of interaction it is not yet as present, although it holds many advantages over other forms of interaction. Thakur and Han [23] state that their suggested system can analyze and predict the behavior of the elderly in their homes and can therefore improve the user experience of senior citizens in smart homes by anticipating activities to assist with everyday tasks and to adapt to the users' current needs, without the need of conscious interaction. The focus of activity control in current research is on fall detection for the elderly, for example as presented in Alazrai et al. [4]. They propose a system for effective fall detection to provide immediate support by notifying health care services or relatives, thus reducing the risks for the life and health of the elderly person. Sucerquia et al. [22] suggest a similar approach for fall detection for the elderly by using an accelerometer and conducting real-life validations with senior citizens in their everyday life. Another benefit of activity control is the constant monitoring of the users' activity pattern, as stated by Chernbumroong et al. [9], which can be used to detect behavioral changes that can be an early sign of long-term health damage.

Our approach fills gaps in current research by addressing the wishes and needs of senior citizens as the future user group. We do not present a system with predefined functionality for them to assess, but rather focus on how they prefer to interact with such a system to support them in their everyday life, as well as determining their openness towards such a system in general and what functionality they see as useful and helpful. We follow the methodology of a vast majority of other recent studies by utilizing a survey.

3 Methodology

We sent a postal survey to 425 people aged 62 years or older stemming from a senior citizens panel from a rural German region (including a smaller city with approximately 70,000 residents). All of them had signed up for the panel to participate in research about health, nutrition, and care for the elderly [11] and we selected our participants solely on their age without any further knowledge about their living situation or experiences with technical devices.

Questions prompted their demographic data, their experiences and knowledge with technical devices, and how to interact with them. We asked about their experiences with touch control, voice control, gesture control, and activity control, and how they feel about them. To make the questions understandable for the elderly, we used easy-to-understand language and avoided technical terms whenever possible. All other terms were thoroughly explained in the survey, e.g. smart home, activity control, and the difference between touch control and gesture control.

Overall, the questionnaire featured 18 questions, with five of them being single choice questions, four open-ended, and the remaining nine questions constituting a mixture of single choice combined with a request for further explanation.

To evaluate the responses we accumulated all given responses. The responses on the open-ended question were clustered into different categories depending on the main message of the response. The single choice questions as well as the mixed questions were quantitatively evaluated. For the single choice and mixed questions, we calculated if differences between people with and without impairments as well as people of different age groups are statistically significant using the chi-square test.

3.1 Demographic Data

The first part of the survey prompted the participants for their demographic data to enable us to find out if conclusions can be drawn about relation between demographic data and certain opinions or experiences.

At first, we asked for their age and sex to determine if there is a difference between age groups or males and females. Then, we asked if there are any existing impairments in their vision, hearing, or mobility. Participants were able to indicate if they have an impairment in vision, hearing, or mobility separately and we asked them to describe their limitations if present. Our motivation for these questions was the hypothesis that impairments influence the user experience more than age does.

3.2 Technical Devices

In the next section of the questionnaire, we asked about the participants' knowledge and usage of technical devices. In the first question, their level of experience with technical devices such as PCs, laptops, or smartphones had to be assessed. The participants were given five possible options to pick from, ranging from very high to very low:

- **Very high.** The respondent is familiar with basic and advanced functionality and does not need help when using technical devices.
- **High.** The respondent is familiar with basic and advanced functionality, but sometimes needs help when using technical devices.
- **Intermediate.** The respondent is familiar with basic functionality but often needs help with advanced functionality.
- **Low.** The respondent is familiar with some basic functionality but always needs help with advanced functionality.
- **Very low.** The respondent always needs help when using technical devices.

Basic functionality means for example sending and receiving emails or visiting websites. Advanced functionality means editing documents, changing settings, or setting up new devices.

The second question of this section prompted how often the participants use certain devices. They had to rate their usage habits between daily, weekly, monthly, less often, or never. The devices asked about were smartphones, tablet computers, other devices with touch control like navigation systems, smart speakers or voice assistants like Google Alexa, Siri or Cortana, video game consoles using gesture control like Microsoft Kinect, Nintendo Wii or PS Move, and other devices using gesture control.

3.3 Smart Home and Forms of Interaction

In the last section of the survey, we asked the participants for their opinion on and experience with smart home devices and the four given basic forms of interaction.

The first question of this section explained the term activity control and asked if the respondents have heard of it before. Secondly, we asked the participants to rate their level of experience with smart home devices, e.g. smart temperature control devices, roller shutter control devices, or smart light control. They were given the following five options:

- The participant has not heard of smart homes before.
- The participant has heard of smart homes before but has not seen or used any smart home device.
- The participant knows someone who owns smart home devices and has observed how to use them.

- The participant owns smart home devices but barely uses them or does not use them at all.
- The participant owns smart home devices and uses them regularly.

If the respondents indicated that they own smart home devices, we also asked them to list them.

In the next question, we asked the respondents to imagine themselves in a specific situation and then tell us how they feel about it. The given scenario was their neighbor showing them a new smart home device that automatically controls the lights in the living room depending on what daily living activity the system recognizes. E.g. when the person is reading, the light is bright, when he is watching TV, it reduces the brightness, and if no one is present, the light is turned off.

Afterward, we asked the participants about their opinion on touch control, voice control, gesture control, and activity control. To classify their stance on the given forms of interaction, participants were supposed to rate their position on an inacceptance-acceptance-scale. The original scale proposed by Sauer et al. [20] consists of eight levels. To reduce complexity and due to resemblance in content, we combined the original levels three (Indifference) and four (Ignorance) to our level three (Indifference/Ignorance) and the original levels five (Compulsion) and six (Conditional Acceptance) to our level four (Compulsion/Conditional Acceptance). Therefore, the inacceptance-acceptance scale we use differentiates between the six levels shown in Fig. 1:

- **Active opposition.** The respondent consequently rejects the given form of interaction and actively advises others against it.
- **Rejection.** The respondent rejects the given form of interaction, but only shares their opinion if asked about it.
- **Indifference/Ignorance.** The respondent does not know or care enough about the given form of interaction to have an opinion.
- **Compulsion/Conditional Acceptance.** The respondent only uses the given form of interaction if they have to or if there is no alternative.
- **Approval.** The respondent is in favor of the given form of interaction, but only shares their opinion if asked about it.
- **Commitment.** The respondent is committed to the given form of interaction and tries to persuade others to use it too.

We also asked the participants to justify their selection.

Afterward, we asked the participants to share problems they have encountered when using technical devices irrespective of the form of interaction. Also, we asked them to prioritize the four forms of interaction from 1 to 4, with 1 being the option they prefer the most and 4 being the option they prefer the least.

Lastly, the survey allowed some space for the respondents to make suggestions on how else smart home devices could be controlled or to add anything they wanted that was not part of the survey.

Level 1	Level 2	Level 3	Level 4	Level 5	Level 6
Active Opposition	Rejection	Indifference/ Ignorance	Compulsion/ Conditional Acceptance	Approval	Commitment

Inacceptance Acceptance

Fig. 1. Inacceptance-Acceptance scale based on [20] used to rate the respondents stance on the four given forms of interaction.

4 Findings

In total, we received 87 surveys of 47 men (54%) and 40 women (46%) aged 62 to 90 years with an average age of 75.2 years. Figure 2(a) shows the age distribution for men and women respectively, while Fig. 2(b) shows the number of people with and without impairments of vision, hearing, and mobility.

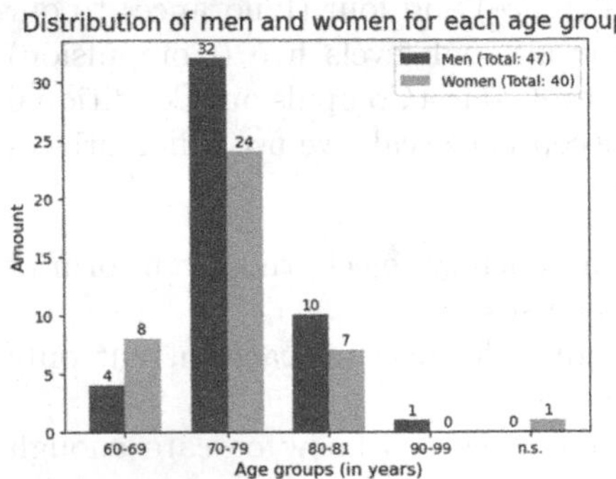

(a) Age distribution of the participants for men and women.

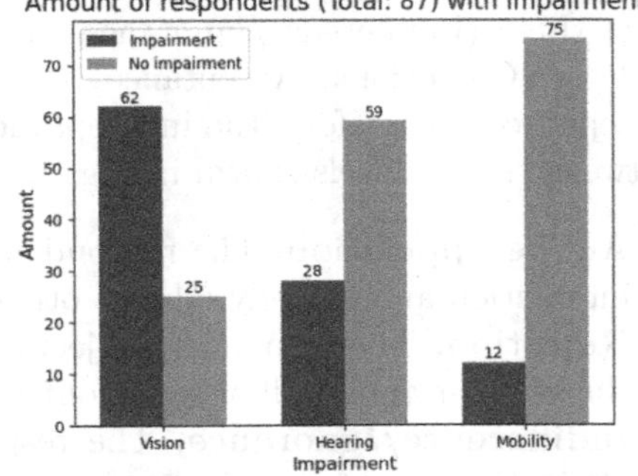

(b) Occurence of impairments among the participants.

Fig. 2. Demographic data (a) and occurence of impairments (b) in the group of participants.

Due to the COVID pandemic, the last contact with the members of the utilized senior citizens panel was over a year before we conducted our survey. Therefore, since then, part of the recipients possibly lost interest in participating, moved, passed away or was not able to respond anymore for other reasons, which could explain the small share of senior citizens who responded to our survey.

4.1 Technical Devices

As shown in Fig. 3, over a third of the respondents (37.93%) indicate a high or very high level of experience with technical devices. Only 22.99% of the respondents ranked their level of experience low or very low. Section 3.2 describes

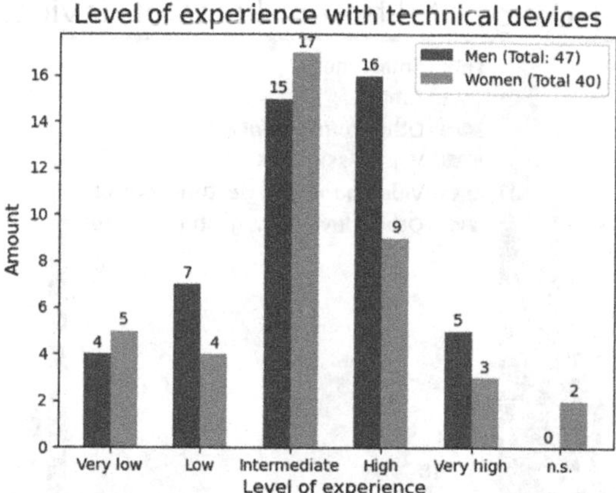

Fig. 3. Level of experience with technical devices as reported by the participants.

how each level of experience is defined and was explained to the participants. There was no statistically significant difference between people with and without hearing impairments. Respondents with vision impairments expressed that they rather use voice control than touch control. People without mobility impairments stated more often that they had a high level of experience with technical devices than people with mobility impairments. Men usually assess their abilities higher than women. The latter more often indicate an intermediate level of experience. Meanwhile, there are no statistically significant differences between both genders at low and very low levels.

Only 14 participants (16%) stated that they do not use smartphones, while 66 participants (76%) use their smartphones daily. Regular or occasional use of tablets (54%), other devices with touch control like navigation systems or car multimedia systems (59%), or voice assistants (28%) is also not unusual in our target group. Figure 4 shows an overview of the usage of various devices and forms of interaction as indicated by the participants.

4.2 Smart Home and Forms of Interaction

Smart home devices, on the other hand, showed to be far less common. Although 93% of the respondents stated that they had already heard about smart homes, only 8% own smart home devices of their own. The devices that the participants listed as having them installed in their homes are e.g. vacuum or lawn mowing robots, smart plugs, smart smoke detectors, security systems as well as roller shutter and light control devices.

In general, the consensus among the respondents is that required support in everyday life should primarily be provided by other people and not technical systems. However, where this is not possible, a large part of the participants agreed that technology can be a good way of receiving support. For example, if they have disabilities or restrictions that no longer allow for a self-determined

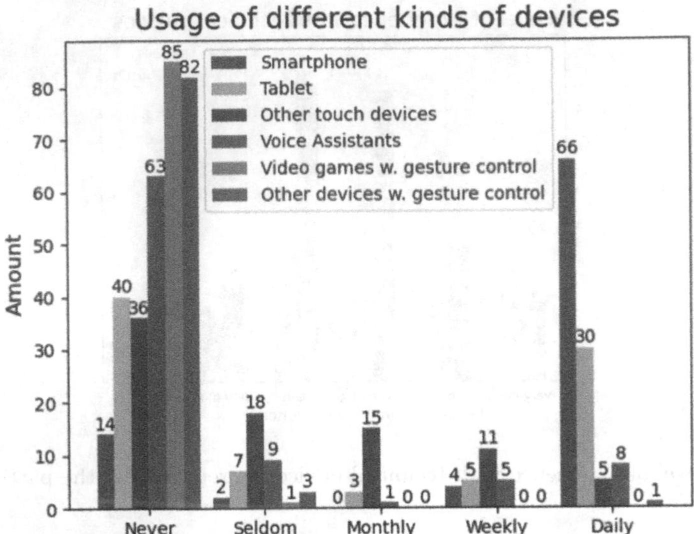

Fig. 4. Shows the usage of smartphones, tablet computers, other touch devices, voice assistants or smart speakers, video games using gesture control, and other devices with gesture control as indicated by the participants.

life at home and moving to a nursing home or assisted living facility would be necessary, they would prefer and accept technical support. Although many senior citizens acknowledge the benefit of technical systems in a smart home, the responses given in open-ended questions show that their openness is mainly directed towards other – older, more limited or disabled – people using such devices, not themselves. They do not want to see themselves as limited or in need of help. (cf. [10]).

The participants showed great interest in the topic. However, it is obvious that proper education, easy-to-use devices, and support in how to select and set up certain devices are necessary but currently not available. Also, some respondents were not able to see the benefit technical devices can add to their daily life and reported to fear losing their self-determination.

In addition, the participants critically questioned technology. Many of them asked about the actual benefits for their situation, about initial costs as well as running costs for maintenance and repairs. Further questions were asked about the life span of devices, the effects on the environment, and who can offer support in case of an emergency. Some of them questioned whether the cost of learning how to use such devices outweighs the benefit of additional support provided by technical devices.

It can be stated that people with impaired vision are reluctant to use devices with touch control, such as smartphones or tablets, or only use them if there are no alternatives. This is probably because a specific area on the screen has to be touched to trigger an action, and therefore, people who cannot recognize this area easily face difficulties when using touch control. We noticed, that, in general, senior citizens with limitations seem to be more open to learning about more "innate" forms of interaction like activity control.

Figure 5 shows how the respondents classified their stance on the given forms of interaction on the inacceptance-acceptance scale described in Sect. 3.3. Unsurprisingly, a great part of them chose level 3 (Indifference or Ignorance) for gesture control and activity control since those two forms of interaction are not commonly used yet.

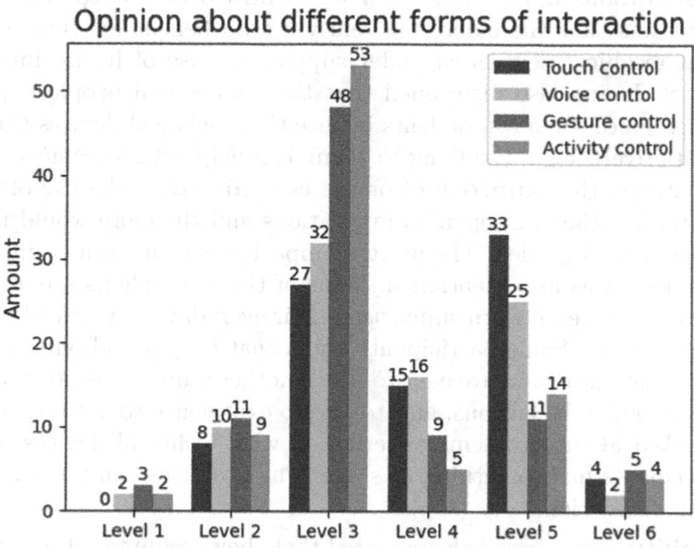

Fig. 5. The respondents stance on the four given forms of interaction according to the inacceptance-acceptance scale. Level 1 = Active opposition, Level 2 = Rejection, Level 3 = Indifference or Ignorance, Level 4 = Compulsion or Conditional Acceptance, Level 5 = Approval, Level 6 = Commitment.

The reasons given for **active opposition** were fear of hackers or excessive surveillance, but also a lack of trust in the technical devices. Especially with gesture control, some respondents noted that the rate of recognition is currently still very imprecise, and using these devices can therefore be complicated and frustrating. Other participants who showed active opposition indicated that they feel disturbed by being overly observed by technical devices.

Various reasons were given as justification for the **rejection** of the given forms of interaction. First, the respondents noted that increased exposure to radiation results from using these technical devices, since many of today's devices need to be connected to the internet to function properly. Furthermore, the fear of misuse of data or the devices themselves was mentioned by several participants. Others brought up that they disapprove of the usage of technical devices in their homes for themselves, but realize the positive impact it can have on people with impairments or disabilities. It was also mentioned that the elderly find it difficult to learn how to use unknown and new forms of interaction at their age and that they, therefore, would rather stick to what they already know and use.

Participants who showed **indifference or ignorance** often mentioned that technology is too complicated and that they do not know what advantages the technical devices can offer them. It was also noted that the respondents have lived the past sixty to eighty years without the support of technical devices and therefore see no personal benefit in using them now.

The justifications most often given for **conditional acceptance** of technical devices was that the elderly currently see no benefit for themselves, but believe that technical devices can offer support in case of future impairments or disabilities. It was also mentioned that the help of real people is preferred. On the other hand, some respondents believe that technical devices that can be operated intuitively, e.g. by talking to them, can help with loneliness.

Senior citizens that **approve** of or are **committed** to the use of technical devices state that they are open to innovations and therefore would not reject anything before having tried. The positive impact of learning something new and solving problems was also mentioned. Some of the respondents see a benefit in using technical devices, e.g., in supporting their everyday life task or by reducing energy consumption. Some participants noted that they would only use devices that function flawlessly and are easy to use. Another group of respondents stated to enjoy learning, to be curious, and to like to experience something new.

When asked about problems experienced with technical devices almost all of the participants had something to share. The problems can be clustered into five different categories:

- **Readability.** Some respondents stated that they encountered problems with the readability of the text displayed on technical devices. Either the text was too small so they could not read it properly or when text was readable they had difficulties understanding the meaning.
- **Malfunction.** Many participants described situations in which technical devices do not work as expected. Examples are voice control that does not properly understand voice commands when several people are present or there is a lot of background noise, or if the user expects different functionality behind buttons than what is actually the case.
- **Security concerns.** Some of the respondents are worried about being spied on, for example by their vacuum robot which uploads images and the floor plan of their apartment to the Internet, or by voice assistants that listen to every conversation.
- **Insecurities.** Some senior citizens describe that they feel insecure when using technical devices because they do not know exactly what consequences an action can have or they are not sufficiently familiar with their devices. They mention that they often need help with using or setting up devices or when they encounter new functionality.
- **Technical problems.** Another problem, which has been mentioned several times, was incomprehensible problems with technical devices, e.g. if the

connection to the Internet is lost or if the device freezes and needs to be restarted, for no apparent reason.

When participants were asked to prioritize the given forms of interaction, touch control was chosen as the most favorable form of interaction by many respondents. Voice control was chosen as the second option, while gesture control and activity control share the third place. We think this result can be explained by the fact that both touch and voice control are commonly used, while there are only a few devices with which you can interact via gesture control or activity control. We believe that these two more intuitive forms of interaction would be chosen more often if the senior citizens could try them out and get to know them. Therefore, in further research, we plan to present all forms of interaction to a group of participants and let them try out for themselves. We hypothesize that the prioritization will then be different and plan to verify this through further research.

5 Conclusion and Future Work

In summary, our gathered data shows that the elderly can benefit from smart home devices and are open-minded towards this topic. But, it is necessary to educate and support senior citizens accordingly. In addition, it still holds true that devices for the elderly must become easier and more intuitive to use.

The technical devices must be easy-to-use and must not offer too much functionality to not unnecessarily complicate the learning process. It is important that the elderly get support, both in choosing the right equipment and setting it up, as well as offering support for the case of problems arising.

Many participants are curious and would be willing to get support from technical devices in their households. For some, however, it was important to mention that they can currently still live independently and are afraid of losing that independence through the increased use of technical devices. The participants agree that in the event of physical limitations like impairments of vision, hearing, and mobility, and if adequate help from other people cannot be guaranteed, support from smart home devices could help to be able to live independently at home for an extended period of time.

Our further research will focus primarily on gesture control and activity control. The following aspects are particularly important to us: Are these more intuitive forms of interaction easier to learn for the elderly? What role do limitations of vision, hearing, or mobility play? Is our assumption correct that gesture control and activity control would be preferred by the target group if they were available in the same way as touch control and voice control?

Acknowledgement. The authors acknowledge the financial support by the Federal Ministry of Education and Research of Germany (BMBF) in the framework of "Innovative Hochschule" (project number 03IHS052, Regionales Innovationszentrum Gesundheit und Lebensqualität Fulda (RIGL), Umsetzungsprojekt GetAll - Gesundheitstechnik für die Alltagsbewältigung).

References

1. Perception of Smart Home Technologies to Assist Elderly People (2010)
2. Dorofte, A.: OPINION: BMW gesture control really improves in-car operation. https://www.bmwblog.com/2019/11/08/opinion-bmw-gesture-control-really-improves-in-car-operation/. Accessed 7 Feb 2022
3. Alaa, M., Zaidan, A., Zaidan, B., Talal, M., Kiah, M.: A review of smart home applications based on internet of things. J. Netw. Comput. Appl. **97**, 48–65 (2017). https://doi.org/10.1016/j.jnca.2017.08.017, https://www.sciencedirect.com/science/article/pii/1084804517302801
4. Alazrai, R., Zmily, A., Mowafi, Y.: Fall detection for elderly using anatomical-plane-based representation. In: 2014 36th Annual International Conference of the IEEE Engineering in Medicine and Biology Society, pp. 5916–5919 (2014). https://doi.org/10.1109/EMBC.2014.6944975
5. Ayubi, S.A., Sudiharto, D.W., Jadied, E.M., Aryanto, E.: The prototype of hand gesture recognition for elderly people to control connected home devices. J. Phys. Conf. Ser. **1201**(1), 012042 (2019). https://doi.org/10.1088/1742-6596/1201/1/012042
6. Bara, C.D., Cabrita, M., op den Akker, H., Hermens, H.J.: User interaction concepts in smart caring homes for elderly with chronic conditions. In: Geissbühler, A., Demongeot, J., Mokhtari, M., Abdulrazak, B., Aloulou, H. (eds.) Inclusive Smart Cities and e-Health. pp. 38–49. Springer, Cham (2015). https://doi.org/10.1007/978-3-319-19312-0
7. Bejarano, A., Fernández, A., Jimeno, M., Salazar, A., Wightman, P.: Towards the evolution of smart home environments: a survey. Int. J. Autom. Smart Technol. **6**, 105–136 (2016). https://doi.org/10.5875/ausmt.v6i3.1039
8. Cheek, P., Nikpour, L., Nowlin, H.: Aging well with smart technology. Nurs. Adm. Q. **29**, 329–338 (2005). https://doi.org/10.1097/00006216-200510000-00007
9. Chernbumroong, S., Cang, S., Atkins, A., Yu, H.: Elderly activities recognition and classification for applications in assisted living. Exp. Syst. Appl. **40**(5), 1662–1674 (2013). https://doi.org/10.1016/j.eswa.2012.09.004
10. Courtney, K., Demiris, G., Rantz, M., Skubic, M.: Needing smart home technologies: the perspectives of older adults in continuing care retirement communities. Inform. Primary Care **16**, 195–201 (2008). https://doi.org/10.14236/jhi.v16i3.694
11. Hochschule Fulda: Das GEViA-Panel. https://www.hs-fulda.de/forschen/forschungseinrichtungen/wissenschaftliche-zentren-und-forschungsverbuende/elve/forschen/das-gevia-panel. Accessed 11 Jan 2022
12. Holzinger, A., Searle, G., Nischelwitzer, A.: On some aspects of improving mobile applications for the elderly. In: Stephanidis, C. (ed.) Universal Access in Human Computer Interaction. Coping with Diversity. pp. 923–932. Springer, Berlin (2007). https://doi.org/10.1007/978-3-540-73279-2
13. Jakob, D., Wilhelm, S., Gerl, A., Ahrens, D.: A quantitative study on awareness, usage and reservations of voice control interfaces by elderly people. In: Stephanidis, C., et al. (eds.) HCI International 2021 - Late Breaking Papers: Cognition, Inclusion, Learning, and Culture, pp. 237–257. Springer, Cham (2021). https://doi.org/10.1007/978-3-030-90328-2
14. Kobayashi, M., Hiyama, A., Miura, T., Asakawa, C., Hirose, M., Ifukube, T.: Elderly user evaluation of mobile touchscreen interactions. In: Campos, P., Graham, N., Jorge, J., Nunes, N., Palanque, P., Winckler, M. (eds.) INTERACT 2011. LNCS, vol. 6946, pp. 83–99. Springer, Heidelberg (2011). https://doi.org/10.1007/978-3-642-23774-4_9

15. Lentzas, A., Vrakas, D.: Non-intrusive human activity recognition and abnormal behavior detection on elderly people: a review. Arti. Intelli. Rev. **53**(3), 1975–2021 (2019). https://doi.org/10.1007/s10462-019-09724-5
16. Marikyan, D., Papagiannidis, S., Alamanos, E.: A systematic review of the smart home literature: a user perspective. Technol. Forecast. Soc. Change **138**, 139–154 (2019). https://doi.org/10.1016/j.techfore.2018.08.015, https://www.sciencedirect.com/science/article/pii/S0040162517315676
17. Pal, D., Funilkul, S., Vanijja, V., Papasratorn, B.: Analyzing the elderly users' adoption of smart-home services. IEEE Access **6**, 51238–51252 (2018). https://doi.org/10.1109/ACCESS.2018.2869599
18. Pal, D., Papasratorn, B., Chutimaskul, W., Funilkul, S.: Embracing the smart-home revolution in Asia by the elderly: an end-user negative perception modeling. IEEE Access **7**, 38535–38549 (2019). https://doi.org/10.1109/ACCESS.2019.2906346
19. Sahlab, N., Sailer, C., Jazdi, N., Weyrich, M.: Designing an elderly-appropriate voice control for a pill dispenser. In: Proceedings on Automation in Medical Engineering, February 2020. https://doi.org/10.18416/AUTOMED.2020
20. Sauer, A., Luz, F., Suda, M., Weiland, U.: Steigerung der Akzeptanz von FFH-Gebieten. BfN-Skripten (144) (2005)
21. Sharma, R., Nah, F.F.H., Sharma, K., Katta, T.S.S.S., Pang, N., Yong, A.: Smart living for elderly: Design and human-computer interaction considerations. In: Zhou, J., Salvendy, G. (eds.) Human Aspects of IT for the Aged Population. Healthy and Active Aging. pp. 112–122. Springer, Cham (2016). https://doi.org/10.1007/978-3-319-39949-2
22. Sucerquia, A., López, J.D., Vargas-Bonilla, J.F.: Real-life/real-time elderly fall detection with a triaxial accelerometer. Sensors **18**(4) (2018). https://doi.org/10.3390/s18041101
23. Thakur, N., Han, C.Y.: Framework for an intelligent affect aware smart home environment for elderly people. CoRR abs/2106.15599 (2021), https://arxiv.org/abs/2106.15599
24. Uptodate: Smart Home Deutschland 2020 - Potenziale und Hemmnisse smarter Wohnwelten in Deutschland (Whitepaper). https://www.uptodate.de/pages/expertenbei-trag-smarthome. Accessed 8 Oct 2021
25. Visutsak, P., Daoudi, M.: The smart home for the elderly: perceptions, technologies and psychological accessibilities: the requirements analysis for the elderly in Thailand. In: 2017 XXVI International Conference on Information, Communication and Automation Technologies (ICAT), pp. 1–6 (2017). https://doi.org/10.1109/ICAT.2017.8171625
26. Vorwerg, S., Eicher, C., Ruser, H., Piela, F., Obée, F., Kaltenbach, A., Mechold, L.: Requirements for Gesture-controlled remote operation to facilitate human-technology interaction in the living environment of elderly people. In: Zhou, J., Salvendy, G. (eds.) HCII 2019. LNCS, vol. 11592, pp. 551–569. Springer, Cham (2019). https://doi.org/10.1007/978-3-030-22012-9_39
27. Wang, R.J., Lai, S.C., Jhuang, J.Y., Ho, M.C., Shiau, Y.C.: Development of smart home gesture-based control system. Sensors Mater. **33**, 3459 (2021). https://doi.org/10.18494/SAM.2021.3522
28. Williams, D., Ul Alam, M.A., Ahamed, S.I., Chu, W.: Considerations in designing human-computer interfaces for elderly people. In: 2013 13th International Conference on Quality Software, pp. 372–377 (2013). https://doi.org/10.1109/QSIC.2013.36

Knowledge-Based Dialogue System for the Ageing Support on Daily Activities

Julio Vizcarra(✉) and Kristiina Jokinen

National Institute of Advanced Industrial Science and Technology (AIST), Tokyo, Japan
{julio.vizcarra,kristiina.jokinen}@aist.go.jp

Abstract. With the increasing digitalization of society, we need to use a wide range of digitalized services in our daily activities such as searching for events in a calendar, checking the weather forecast, receiving guidance for completing certain tasks or recommendations for certain topics. Assistance for digital services is often needed, and particularly in the ageing stages, support for these tasks from a coach can become valuable. We introduce our work on a dialogue system that is part of a digital coach providing interactive support for elder adults in their daily activities. The work centers on using knowledge graphs to improve coaching interventions and is part of a larger project that focuses on supporting elder people and their healthy active living. Knowledge graphs are models of the domain content, defined by the domain experts, and they are used in the dialogue system to understand the content of the user utterances and to generate appropriate system responses. The dialogue coach can thus personalize conversations with the elder users and provide empathic and informative responses.

Keywords: Dialogue system · Knowledge graph · Machine learning · Natural language processing

1 Introduction

In daily life, with the increasing digitalization of society, we need to use a wide range of digitalized services such as searching for events in a calendar, checking the weather forecast, receiving guidance for completing certain tasks or recommendations for certain topics. Assistance for digital services is often needed, and particularly in the ageing stages, support for these tasks from a coach can become valuable. A digital coach can provide the needed help by enabling natural interaction and thus support elder adults in their daily activities. By analysing the conversations, it is also possible to learn more about the user concerns and needs, and offer more personalized support.

However, current conversational AI systems often ignore the semantic knowledge underlying the utterance content, or they use domain knowledge hardcoded in the system's conversational flow. Consequently, porting of the system to new task-specific domains or customizing dialogue interactions to different users can be difficult. If the expert knowledge can be modelled for the processing of the conversations, it is possible

Q. Gao and J. Zhou (Eds.): HCII 2022, LNCS 13331, pp. 122–133, 2022.
https://doi.org/10.1007/978-3-031-05654-3_8

to improve the system's capability to understand what the user needs, which can result in better assistance, recommendations, and flow in the conversations in general.

Knowledge Graph (KG) [1] has become an effective mechanism of representation that provides explainability, explicit definition of entities and relations, semantic interpretation, and it can contain fine-grained descriptions of the domain. Big advances in AI, NLP, and database technologies have enabled development of knowledge graphs and databases on multiple domains [2]. We have especially explored knowledge graphs as labeled property graphs (LPG) in the Neo4j graph database system [3].

In this paper, we propose a knowledge-based approach that tackles the acquisition of expert knowledge and its integration in KG, to be used in dialogue processing. The work centers the work on a semantic approach and exploitation of large knowledge bases, and their integration in conversational AI aiming to provide coaching for the users in daily living tasks. In the implementation, we can personalize the conversation considering the domain knowledge located in knowledge graphs related to the user profiles as well as the content in the sentences. We use the Rasa Open-Source Conversational AI framework [4] for dialogue modelling and present a dialogue system that supports elderly people in several tasks related to their daily living.

The novelty of the presented work is the conceptual-semantic handling of user utterances and conversations using knowledge graphs. An advantage of our approach is that the design of dialogue systems allows different domains to be included as knowledge graphs, which also adds on the flexibility of the system over hardcoded dialogue strategies by updates of the knowledge base.

The paper is structured as follows. We first give a short overview of the background and related research in Sect. 2. We then briefly describe the system and use cases in Sect. 3, while Sect. 4 focuses on knowledge graph and dialogue modelling, and the integration of the two in the dialogue system. Section 5 provides examples of the system function and finally Sect. 6 provides conclusions and future work.

2 Related Work

Many significant improvements have been achieved recently in dialogue systems using knowledge graphs. The inclusion of prior knowledge in the conversation has led to a better user response and interaction. The most promising use of KG has been in language generation. For instance, Yi-Lin Tuan et al. [5] implemented dynamic knowledge graphs in knowledge-grounded dialogue generation. The goal was to facilitate neural conversation models to learn zero-shot adaptation to updated, unseen knowledge graphs, by exploiting user data related to dialogues, speakers, and scenes. For this task, they presented a TV series conversation corpus (DyKgChat) with facts of the fictitious life of characters, and corresponding knowledge graphs including explicit information such as the relations *friend-of*, *enemy-of*, and *residence-of* as well as the linked entities.

Similarly, Houyu Zhang et al. [6] presented a conversation generation model ConceptFlow (Conversation generation with Concept Flow), that leverages commonsense knowledge graphs to explicitly model conversation flows. The model could generate semantically appropriate and informative responses. while using graph attention mechanism with few parameters. The work experimented with Reddit conversations.

In spoken dialogue understanding, Yi Ma et al. [7] proposed an inference knowledge graph that used semantic knowledge graphs and remapping using Markov Random Fields to create user goal tracking models that could form part of a spoken dialogue system. In their experiments, the authors demonstrated that their model could return more relevant entities to the user than the database lookup baseline. In dialogue generation, Sixing Wu et al. [8] proposed a method that uses a knowledge graph to alleviate the issue of generating boring responses. The commonsense knowledge-aware dialogue generation model (ConKADI) focuses on the knowledge facts that are highly relevant to the context. The main contribution was the use of knowledge graphs in learning models to add context and generate dialogues.

Tackling conversational context, Jaehun Jung et al. [9] proposed a dialogue-conditioned path traversal model called AttnIO that uses knowledge graphs based on attention flows. The authors claimed that they implemented a full use of structural information in the KG. Their method is capable of exploring a broad range of multi-hop knowledge paths, and also flexibly adjusting the varying range of plausible nodes and edges to attend depending on the dialogue context. Moreover, the system can intuitively model knowledge exploration depending on the dialogue characteristics.

In the area of human-robot interaction, Wilcock and Jokinen [10] describe an integration of Neo4j KGs with the Rasa dialogue framework and demonstrate it on the Furhat robot [11]. The generic framework aims to support a variety of social robots to provide high-quality information to users by accessing semantically rich knowledge about multiple different domains.

3 System Overview and Use Cases

We focus on using the knowledge graph to enable a coaching dialogue system that could provide useful information and empathic responses to the user. The research is conducted in the context of the project e-VITA (https://www.e-vita.coach/) a large collaboration project between EU and Japan, which aims to develop a virtual coaching system to support older adult's wellbeing in a smart living environment, promote their active healthy living, and provide personalized recommendations and trustworthy interaction (see background and more details in [12]). Some inspiration is found in Diogo Martinho et al. [13] who proposed a conceptual approach for improving the well-being of elderly people which used social networks to analyze user preferences, detected affective states, and evaluated cognitive capabilities. Similarly, Paulo Menezes et al. [14] proposed a multi-agent system designed to promote physical activity in elderly users.

The general overview of the system is depicted in Fig. 1. In the diagram, our contribution is marked in green dashes. The red dash box represents the Rasa [4] conversational AI framework. The process starts when the user shares a sentence and the module of natural language understanding (NLU) tries to interpret the user intention and extract relevant entities. The dialogue management module (DM) interacts with the action server to interpret the user input with respect to domain knowledge, provided by the domain experts and stored in the knowledge graphs. This process is referred to as "semantic processing" in Fig. 1, and it is carried out by computing queries on a knowledge graph. The result of the KG query is used as the basis of the system response, and the DM module enables interaction by generating a corresponding natural language sentence and sending it to the user.

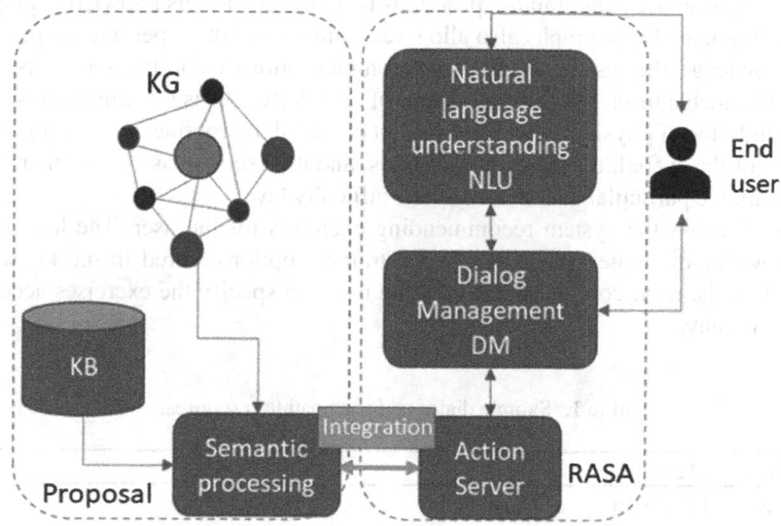

Fig. 1. Overview of the system.

3.1 Examples of Use Cases and Dialogue Design

The full e-VITA coach is envisaged to provide support in a wide variety of use cases ranging from exercise recommendations to daily reminders, providing information on news and weather reports, and emotional support in stressful situations. We have chosen two cases to exemplify the system functionality: the user experiences certain emotion and the user asks for information about exercises. The dialogues were designed in collaboration with the domain experts.

In the first case, the system is expected to take the user's affective state into account when providing its responses. For instance, if the user expresses sadness, the coach aims to provide empathic and consoling companionship. The action is triggered if the user explicitly informs about their emotional state, or if the system infers such a state from the user's voice. In the current version of the system, the emotion recognition is not fully integrated, so the example focuses on conversations where the users explicit express certain sentiment in their verbal utterances. Recognizing the user's intent to convey their mood, the system then responds by providing an appropriate feedback or suggestion that accords with the user's feelings. In the example case, the user's sad mood causes the system to accompany its message by a song that is assumed to improve the mood (Sakura-Sakura is a popular song in Japan), while in a happy case, the system joins the user's experience by providing an encouraging message and a happy song.

Table 1 shows an example dialogue when the user expresses sadness. The coach asks the reason and provides a song that may help. Finally, the coach confirms if the song improved the user's mood, and two paths, depending on the user response, are shown.

In the second case, the system enables factual information providing dialogues, and provides the user with relevant information. For instance, if the system recognizes the user's intention to find out more about exercises and physical training, the system will tell about the exercises and training programs that are stored in its knowledge graphs.

Since the knowledge graphs also allow reasoning about the types and properties of stored knowledge, the system can provide recommendations according to user specifications and available information. If the intent of an elderly user is recognized to solicit a recommendation of physical exercises as a part of their daily routine, the system provide examples of the available training possibilities, and the user can ask for further details or filter suitable particular exercises by their difficulty level.

Table 2 shows the system recommending exercises for the user. The left column shows how the dialogue system lists some training options stored in the knowledge graph, while the right column shows how the user can specify the exercises according to their difficulty.

Table 1. Sample dialogue for empathic responses.

Actor	Message	
User	I feel sad	
Coach	are you OK?. what is the reason you are sad?	
User	I feel lonely	
Coach	You look sad, would you like me to put on your favorite music?	
User	ok	
Coach	I'll go to play a song that can make you to feel better. Please let me know when to stop the music. [plays the song Sakura Sakura]	
User	please stop	
Coach	Do you feel a bit better now?	
User	Yes	No
Coach	I wish you keep feeling alright ... Is there anything else I can help you with?	I am sorry, I hope I could help you. Is there anything else I can help you with?

4 Modeling

4.1 Knowledge Graph Models

Figure 2 presents a knowledge graph for the actions that the system can perform when it recognizes that the user experiences a certain emotion. The emotion is linked to a particular countermeasure, which can have a property describing recommendation as text or URL. Similarly, Fig. 3 presents an excerpt of a knowledge graph that represents

Table 2. Dialogues for exercises recommendations.

	Story listing all exercises	Story filtering exercises by difficulty
Actor	Message	Message
User	can you recommend me an exercise	can you recommend me an easy exercise
Coach	I know three exercises. According to my knowledge, you can practice Walking, Dancing, or Yoga.	Sure, an exercise with easy difficulty is: Walking

exercises, their level of difficulty, recommended poses, and other indicators that a user can perform. The knowledge graphs are modelled as Neo4j type labeled property graphs [3] and they can be queried using the Cypher query language [19].

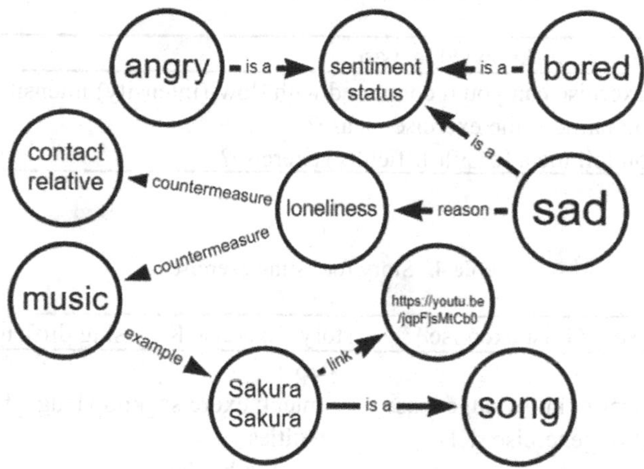

Fig. 2. Excerpt of a LPG representing emotional states and possible countermeasures.

4.2 Dialogue Model

The Rasa-based dialogue modelling [4] requires that example utterances representing the user intents are designed, together with the suitable system responses. Also sample dialogue flows, called stories can be defined. These are used in the training of Rasa's dialogue policy to decide on the suitable dialogue action after the recognition of the user intent.

Table 3 shows some user sentences corresponding to the user intent related to asking for exercises. The examples sentences are also labeled with respect to the important entities that describe the content of the intents. For instance, the word "easy" is labeled as a type of entity "difficulty". Labels are used for Name Entity Extraction (NER).

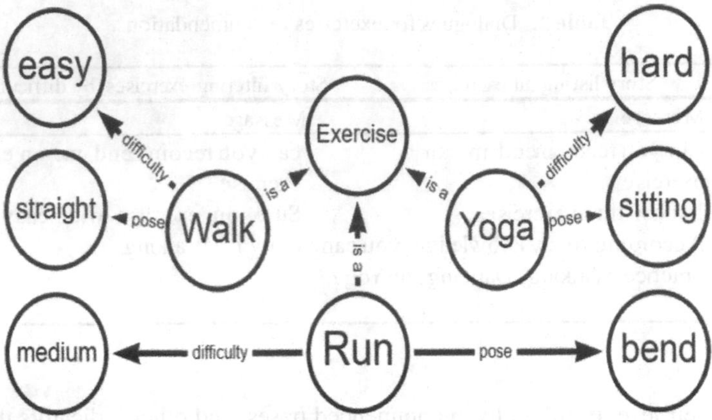

Fig. 3. Excerpt of a LPG representing physical exercises and their properties.

Table 3. Intent classification and entities.

intent: exercise_knowledge_base
-what exercise can you recommend with [low](intensity) intensity? -can you name some exercise please? -can you tell me a [easy](difficulty) exercise?

Table 4. Story for listing exercises.

story: Exercise KG list exercise	story: Exercise KG using difficulty
steps: - intent: exercise_knowledge_base - action: action_exercise_KB	steps: - intent: exercise_knowledge_base entities: - difficulty: hard - slot_was_set: - difficulty: hard - action: action_exercise_KB_difficulty

The story that the dialogue can follow deals with the 'happy path' case where the system successfully lists all the exercises (Table 4 left column) or the case when the user wants exercises filtered by a level of difficulty (Table 4 right column). The story is defined as a dialogue flow of user intents and system actions, and it also specifies the entities required to complete the path. The system actions are the so called knowledgebaseActions, which retrieve data from the KG referred to by its name.

4.3 Knowledge Graph Integration in the Dialogue System

The overall view of the dialogue system modules is presented in Fig. 4. The modules are based on the Rasa architecture and modified according to the project needs. The user interacts with the coach through the coaching device (in our case Nao robot [21]). The user's utterances will be analyzed by the speech recognizer (not shown in Fig. 4), and the text transcription will be the input to Natural Language Understanding (NLU) pipeline which consists of a series of modules that are needed for the preprocessing, entity extraction, and intent classification, and transforms the user input into a vector format. The user input then goes through the "knowledge processing" where the content is analysed with respect to the system's domain knowledge, and semantic inferences are performed. The important part concerns querying the knowledgebase, which in our case uses Cypher queries based on the extracted entities in the graph database. The query results are inserted in the suitable system response form, which is determined by the dialogue model using the learnt state tracking policy. The text sentence thus augmented is sent further to the text-to-speech synthesizer by the dialogue manager, to be ultimately uttered by the coaching agent to the user.

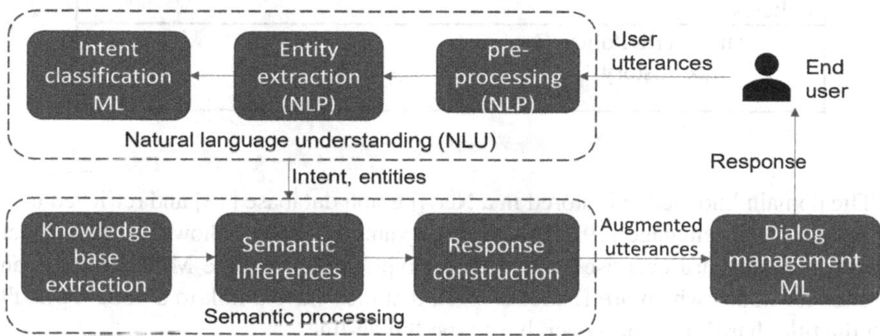

Fig. 4. Content-based processing of user utterances.

We use the Rasa Open-Source Conversational AI [4] to enable the above dialogue processing. We customised Rasa's NLU pipeline by the spaCy [15] tokenizer, entity extractor (NER), and featurizer, together with other featurizers available in Rasa. To extract the intent and relevant entities from the user message, Rasa's Dual Intent and Entity Transformer (DIET) [16] is used. Table 5 shows the NLU pipeline.

To determine the system response, the dialogue manager predicts the best next action using a dialogue policy. We used the Transformer Embedding Dialogue (TED) policy implemented in Rasa [17] (Table 6). The max history was set to 3. We experimented with different context lengths for the policy performance, and the length 3 produced the best performance for our example conversations.

Table 5. The NLU Pipeline used in the study.

pipeline:
- name: SpacyNLP   model: "en_core_web_md" - name: SpacyTokenizer - name: "SpacyEntityExtractor" - name: SpacyFeaturizer - name: RegexEntityExtractor - name: LexicalSyntacticFeaturizer - name: CountVectorsFeaturizer - name: DIETClassifier

Table 6. Rasa's dialogue policy for best next action in the study.

policies:
- name: TEDPolicy   max_history: 3

The domain knowledge is stored in a Neo4j graph database [18] and retrieved using Cypher querying language [19]. As a simple example, Table 7 shows a Cypher query that retrieves all hard exercises which are of type guideline. The MATCH command searches for nodes which are Exercises such that they have a link to a node Difficulty with the title 'hard', and moreover, have type 'guide-line'.

Table 7. Example Cypher query.

Query that retrieves hard exercises
MATCH (e:Exercise) WHERE exists ((e)-[*..3]->(:Difficulty{title: 'hard'})) and e.type = 'guide_line' RETURN e.title

5 Rasa X Examples

Some examples of the interaction between a user and the e-VITA coach are shown in the screenshots below. The dialogues are conducted through text on a web-based extension Rasa X [20].

Figure 5 depicts a dialogue where the system gives recommendations to the user according to a level of difficulty. Figure 6 presents the case when the user experiences sadness, and receives consolation with a song.

Fig. 5. A dialogue that recommends an exercise by difficulty.

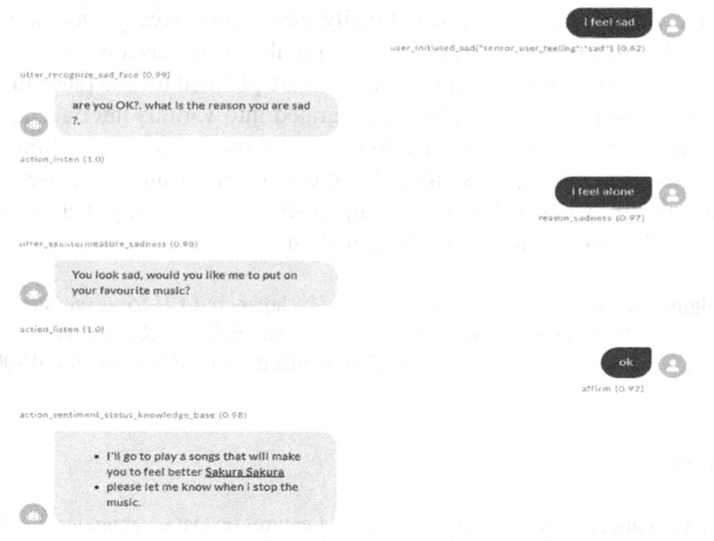

Fig. 6. A fragment of conversation that alleviates sadness.

6 Conclusions and Future Work

In this paper, we discussed a knowledgebase approach that integrates domain knowledge stored in knowledge graphs into system responses and actions. The work constructs knowledge graphs that describe the domain and use cases selected for the e-VITA project which aims to develop a coach to support elder people's active healthy living and daily activities. The system integrates content from the KG to process user utterances and to provide suitable recommendations and information to the user based on the domain knowledge, and the dialogues can be conducted using a web-based interface or by interacting with an embodied coach, the NAO robot. The e-VITA coach aims to cover several use cases, and we exemplified two example scenarios in this paper: first, the coach tries to provide a sympathetic response when it recognizes the user experiencing an emotional state, and the second one, where the coach provides information and recommendation to the user when it recognized the user wants to receive particular training recommendations.

The future work deals with sophisticating and extending knowledge graphs and their content with respect to the demands for natural and trustworthy dialogues. In particular, we will study solutions related to graph embedding to integrate knowledge graph reasoning into dialogue management. Important aspects also concern dialogue strategies and dialogue management so as to support friendly, contextually appropriate dialogues between the user and the coach. Subtle issues in emotional and empathic interaction need to be studied and discussed further for appropriate interaction design, and in order to take cultural and individual differences into account. Moreover, integration of several other domains in the system is important in order to increase the system functionality. We will also closely look at the technical of knowledge base construction and integration of heterogenous sensor data in the system, given availability of various environmental sensors in the smart home environment. Finally, ethical and privacy issues are important, and they will be studied and taken into account in the project as a whole.

Extensive user studies in living lab condition are planned to take place in the project context, with the dialogue system being integrated into various interface agents. Such evaluations have been problematic due to the Covid pandemic, but preliminary experiments with the first system version could be conducted, resulting in useful feedback on the dialogue strategies and technical implementation, showing that the system has potential to be developed into a useful application.

Acknowledgments. We thank our project partners in Japan and EU for discussions. This work was supported by the Strategic Information and Communications R&D Promotion Programme (SCOPE) of Ministry of Internal Affairs and Communications (MIC), Grant no. JPJ000595.

References

1. Hogan, A., et al.: Knowledge graphs. Synthesis Lectures on Data, Semantics, and Knowledge, vol. 12, pp. 1–257. Morgan & Claypool Publishers (2021)
2. Ji, S., Pan, S., Cambria, E., Marttinen, P., Philip, S.Y.: A survey on knowledge graphs: representation, acquisition, and applications. IEEE Trans. Neural Networks Learn. Syst. IEEE **33**(2), 494–514 (2021)
3. Robinson, I., Webber, J., Eifrem, E.: Graph DataBases, 2nd edn. O'Reilly Media (2015)
4. Bocklisch, T., Faulkner, J., Pawlowski, N., Nichol, A.: Rasa: open source language understanding and dialogue management. arXiv:1712.05181 (2017)
5. Tuan, Y.-L., Chen, Y.-N., Lee, H.-Y.: DyKgChat: benchmarking dialogue generation grounding on dynamic knowledge graphs. arXiv:1910.00610 (2019)

6. Zhang, H., Liu, Z., Xiong, C., Liu, Z.: Grounded conversation generation as guided traverses in commonsense knowledge graphs. arXiv:1911.02707 (2019)
7. Ma, Y., Crook, P.A., Sarikaya, R., Fosler-Lussier, E.: Knowledge graph inference for spoken dialog systems. In: IEEE International Conference on Acoustics, Speech and Signal Processing (ICASSP), pp. 5346–5350 (2015)
8. Wu, S., Li, Y., Zhang, D., Zhou, Y., Wu, Z.: Diverse and informative dialogue generation with context-specific commonsense knowledge awareness. In: Proceedings of the 58th Annual Meeting of the Association for Computational Linguistics, pp. 5811–5820 (2020)
9. Jung, J., Son, B., Lyu, S.: Attnio: knowledge graph exploration with in-and-out attention flow for knowledge-grounded dialogue. In: Proceedings of the 2020 Conference on Empirical Methods in Natural Language Processing (EMNLP), pp. 3484–3497 (2020)
10. Wilcock, G., Jokinen, K.: Conversational AI and knowledge graphs for social robot interaction. late-breaking reports. In: The 17th ACM/IEEE International Conference on Human-Robot Interaction (HRI-2022) (2022)
11. Furhat Robotics Homepage. https://furhatrobotics.com//. Accessed 07 Feb 2022
12. Katsutoshi, Y., et al. (eds.): JSAI 2020. AISC, vol. 1357. Springer, Cham (2021). https://doi.org/10.1007/978-3-030-73113-7
13. Martinho, D., Carneiro, J., Novais, P., Neves, J., Corchado, J., Marreiros, G.: A conceptual approach to enhance the well-being of elderly people. In: Moura Oliveira, P., Novais, P., Reis, L. P. (eds.) EPIA 2019. LNCS (LNAI), vol. 11805, pp. 50–61. Springer, Cham (2019). https://doi.org/10.1007/978-3-030-30244-3_5
14. Menezes, P., Rocha, R.P.: Promotion of active ageing through interactive artificial agents in a smart environment. SN Appl. Sci. **3**(5), 1–15 (2021). https://doi.org/10.1007/s42452-021-04567-8
15. spaCy Homepage. https://spacy.io/. Accessed 04 Feb 2022
16. Bunk, T., Varshneya, D., Vlasov, V., Nichol, A.: Diet: lightweight language understanding for dialogue systems. arXiv:2004.09936 (2020)
17. Vlasov, V., Mosig, J. E., Nichol, A.: Dialogue transformers. arXiv:1910.00486 (2019)
18. Neo4j Homepage. https://neo4j.com/. Accessed 7 Feb 2022
19. Francis, N., et al.: Cypher: an evolving query language for property graphs. In: Proceedings of the 2018 International Conference on Management of Data, pp. 1433–1445 (2018)
20. RASA X Homepage. https://rasa.com/docs/rasa-x/. Accessed 7 Feb 2022
21. NAO Homepage. https://www.softbankrobotics.com/emea/en/nao. Accessed 7 Feb 2022

Design and Verification of a Smart Home Management System for Making a Smart Home Composable and Adjustable by the Elderly

Reina Yoshizaki[1(✉)], SooIn Kang[2], Hiroki Kogami[1], Kenichiro Ito[3], Daisuke Yoshioka[4], Koki Nakano[5], Yuriki Sakurai[4], Takahiro Miura[6], Mahiro Fujisaki-Sueda-Sakai[7], Ken-ichiro Yabu[8], Hiroshige Matsumoto[9], Ikuko Sugawara[10,11], Misato Nihei[4], Hiroko Akiyama[12], and Tohru Ifukube[8]

[1] Graduate School of Engineering, The University of Tokyo, Tokyo, Japan
r.yoshizaki@mfg.t.u-tokyo.ac.jp
[2] Graduate School of Interdisciplinary Information Studies, The University of Tokyo, Tokyo, Japan
[3] Virtual Reality Educational Research Center, The University of Tokyo, Tokyo, Japan
[4] Graduate School of Frontier Sciences, The University of Tokyo, Tokyo, Japan
[5] Graduate School of Humanities and Sociology, The University of Tokyo, Tokyo, Japan
[6] Human Augmentation Research Center, National Institute of Advanced Industrial Science and Technology (AIST), Kashiwa, Japan
[7] School of Medicine, Tohoku University, Sendai, Japan
[8] Research Center for Advanced Science and Technology, The University of Tokyo, Tokyo, Japan
[9] Graduate School of Medicine, The University of Tokyo, Tokyo, Japan
[10] Institute of Gerontology, The University of Tokyo, Tokyo, Japan
[11] Bunri University of Hospitality, Sayama, Japan
[12] Institute for Future Initiatives, The University of Tokyo, 7-3-1 Hongo, Bunkyo-ku, Tokyo 113-8656, Japan

Abstract. As the aging population continues to increase globally, the development of methods to support the independent living of the elderly is becoming increasingly essential. Although smart home technology is expected to be used to support independent living in the homes of the elderly, the barriers to introducing this technology into the homes of elderly people are high. To support the continuation of independent living tailored to each elderly person, we aim to realize a system that can be composed and adjusted by the elderly themselves to turn their homes into smart homes using an easy-to-understand framework and an age-friendly interface that visualizes the framework. In this study, we developed a simple system described by a combination of trigger and action and a straightforward iPad configuration application. To evaluate the usability of the developed system, we performed an experiment in which young people experienced the configuration and adjustment of the system in a simulated environment. The results showed that the average time required for setting up the system was approximately 2 min, and the average of the system usability scale to evaluate the configuration system was 78.5, which was sufficiently high, indicating that the system was acceptable. In the future, we will verify whether this system can be accepted by the elderly as well.

Q. Gao and J. Zhou (Eds.): HCII 2022, LNCS 13331, pp. 134–153, 2022.
https://doi.org/10.1007/978-3-031-05654-3_9

Keywords: Smart home · Internet of things · End-user development · Independent living and usability evaluation

1 Introduction

As the aging population continues to increase globally, methods to support the lives of the elderly become paramount. In Japan, where the aging rate and average life expectancy are particularly high [1], support for independent living by the elderly is attracting attention, not only because of the shortage of nursing staff but also due to the desire of the elderly to continue living at home [2]. Although smart home technology (SHT) [3] using various sensors and Internet of things (IoT) devices are expected to be used to support independent living in the homes of the elderly [4–6], barriers to introducing SHT into the homes of elderly people who are unfamiliar with information technology and devices such as smartphones are high [7–9]; thus, in many cases, SHT is introduced and operated by caregivers when nursing care becomes necessary, and their practical applications are limited. In addition, the elderly who have established their lifestyles prefer to be supported in various manners, and it is necessary to change the support according to the changes in the state of aging, thereby making it difficult to support the elderly with SHT.

Because of the above expectations and difficulties, there have been many studies on how to support the lives of the elderly using SHT. However, in previous research, the target elderly is generally very old or dementia patients with high care needs, and they are always monitored and assisted by SHT, which are managed and operated by caregivers, mainly to detect emergencies or manage physical conditions [4–6]. Moreover, SHT is useful for elderly people who need a little physical care and patients with mild dementia to enhance convenience in their life [3, 10, 11].

End-user development (EUD) approaches are ideally suited to the necessity of allowing users to customize their environments to support personal situational needs [12]. Therefore, the EUD of smart homes (SHs) or DIY (do it yourself) SHs is researched extensively, and it has been shown that nontechnical end users can compose and customize their environment using well-designed systems and user interfaces (UIs) [13–17]. These results suggested that the improvement of EUD makes more people able to customize their smart environment. The further improvement for the EUD will allow the younger elderly who need a little physical care and patients with mild dementia to manage and operate systems themselves, in addition to being monitored and supported. If the younger elderly can customize a smart environment for their life as the young in ref. [17], it is expected that they can tailor their environment to fit their state of aging.

Therefore, to support the continuation of independent living and individualize the support for each elderly person, we aim to realize a system that can be composed and adjusted by the elderly themselves, turning their homes into SHs, using an easy framework and an age-friendly interface. In this system, the elderly is assisted by themselves. In this study, we have three working hypotheses.

- Elderly people with no programming experience can learn and understand sensor-feedback systems and implement the functions necessary for their own lives.

- With an age-friendly interface, elderly people with little experience in using IoT devices can manage and operate an SH system (SHS).
- Through the operation of the SHS by the elderly themselves, new techniques of using the system will be discovered, and it will become possible to support the continuation of independent living for each elderly person.

Regarding the first point, we reported in a previous study [18] that a sensor feedback system described as a simple trigger–action rule is easy for the elderly to understand, and they can devise a system with functions necessary for their own lives. In this study, we present a system developed to verify the second point and the evaluation by young people. This study aims to develop an SHS that can be operated by elderly people with little experience in using IoT devices, but it can also be used by elderly people with adequate experience, middle-aged people who will become elderly, and family members of the elderly. In other words, the design should be universal. Therefore, we performed a preliminary verification against young people, although it does not have to be optimal.

2 Related Works

2.1 SH Environment and Components for the Elderly

Owing to the aging of the global population, various approaches for SH have been developed for elderly people's quality of life [19]. The aspects of managing healthcare quality led to a focus on the SHs for health monitoring as elderly people need continuous care and medical services at home [20]. Advanced data analytic technology in health monitoring could provide an alerting system by gathering data from various sensors in homes and hospitals [21]. Further, considering the user's independent lifestyle with various activities, wireless technology is adopted to IoT system architecture [22]. Not only medical services but also other support systems have tried helping the elderly living, such as encouraging social interaction [23]. However, satisfying the needs of the elderly is challenging, and considering the subjects and environments is necessary [4, 19].

To meet the personal requirement in IoT products, efforts for a user-center design that integrates a specific user's need with the process of designing IoT products have been made [24]. Designing a house with consideration for the specific users using various sensors and platforms brought satisfaction for people, such as self-sufficient elderly and non-self-sufficient elderly with their respective caregivers [25].

The person-specific setting is crucial to satisfy personal needs, assistance dynamics, and care solutions, indicating the necessity of giving control of such systems to end-users, allowing them to specify how their SH interacts with the elderly [26]. The idea about accessing data and selecting the personal essential parameter by the elderly themselves could bring a better health-related quality of life [6, 27]. Self-engagement in IoT systems can bring more interaction between users and medical services than only using alerting systems [28]. A method for IoT setting needs to be more user-friendly to be adopted by elderly people. Because of the difference with young users who are used to using the devices and controlling the data process, a system for automated data processing is required to date for the elderly [29]. Providing IoT systems that can improve end-users' acceptability in IoT is crucial for elderlies' self-engagement [30]. However, further studies are required to discover the techniques to enrich the elderlies' acceptance of IoT and encourage them to build a do-it-yourself IoT environment.

2.2 Self-engagement in SH and IoT Setting Methods

IoT systems have difficulty in heterogeneous distribution due to the various systems from different brands and products [31]. Thus, integrating into a single platform and providing user access efficiently has been considered [32]. Based on this platform, a previous study confirmed the users' demand toward IoT data visualization by providing participants with customizable IoT data visualization systems [33]. The Trigger-action programming has shown easiness for learning programming in automated house [34]. The installation of an IoT system using several wireless products by users has been examined, and the study confirmed that application for device connections is required for easy DIY by measuring latency [16]. Previous research has pointed out that the trigger-action programming is only sufficient for simple automated tasks and users might desire relatively complex automated system by using process-oriented configuration [17]. Thus, confirming the user's usability in IoT system for self-engagement is important for every age group to prevent the restricted feeling.

To provide a flexible and easier device connection, providing a programming method for the end-users has been discussed extensively [35, 36]. Various UIs that could enhance the end-users' acceptability have been developed based on trigger–action programming [37]. The trigger–action programming has shown easiness for simple tasks in automated houses compared with other methods such as process-oriented notation [38]. Friendly visualization methods for trigger–action programming have also been developed to encourage the user's self-engagement [39, 40]. In addition, a supporting method for self-engagement in IoT systems has been developed by providing attachable and detachable sensors and actuators [13]. Further, the users' guideline of reflecting their lifestyle into IoT systems has been presented [41].

3 Methods

In this section, we introduce the developed SH environment, SHS, and UI design for user evaluation of SHS management and construction systems.

3.1 Concept of the SHS

Figure 1 shows the concept of the proposed system for elderly people to turn their homes into SHs by themselves. Residents themselves place wireless sensor devices in their houses, and by combining them, they can add arbitrary functions to their houses. Elderly people often do not have internet equipment; however, in urban areas, it is possible to easily install the equipment using a mobile router. We constructed a system that makes a home smart by simply placing and setting a set of connected sensors, devices, local servers, and mobile routers. We named this system the "Shitara-suru system."

The SH environment was implemented in a residence simulating an elderly person's house (Fig. 2(a)). In our evaluation experiment, the subjects who became residents were

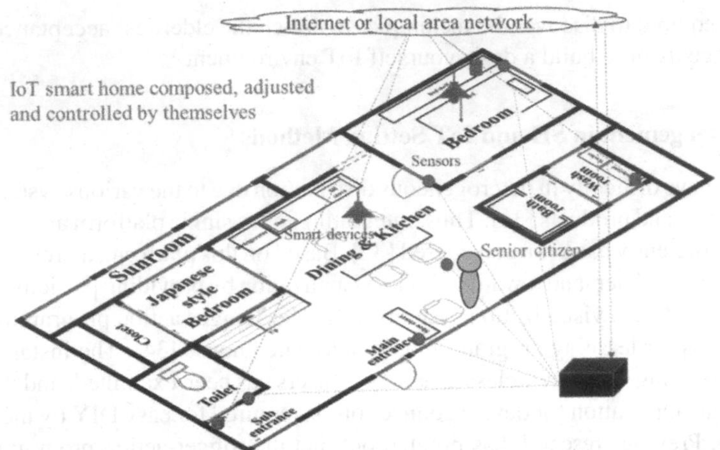

Fig. 1. Conceptional image of DIY SHS for the elderly, "Shitara-suru system".

asked to place and set the connected sensors and devices (Fig. 2(b)), and the simulated residence was made into an SH. Intel NUC (BOXNUC7i7BNH, Intel) was employed as the local server, and the router (GL-MT1300, GL-iNET) was used because the optical internet could be used for the simulated residence. The sensors and devices will be described in later sections.

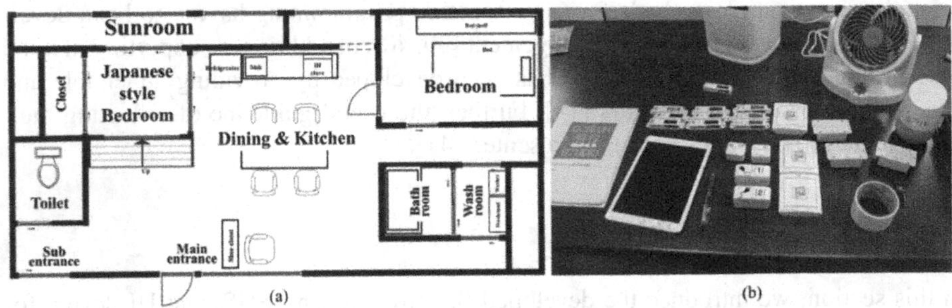

Fig. 2. (a) Simulated residence for the elderly. (b) Sensors, devices, a tablet PC, and a manual for the experiment.

Figure 3(a) shows the configuration of the proposed system. The system comprises a tablet PC operated by the user and a local server that communicates with the sensors and devices related to IoT. The user registers and manages the settings from the web application running on the tablet. The sequence diagram for registering a new setting on the web application is shown in Fig. 3(b). The setting information in the web application is input to the sheet (Google spreadsheet) on the cloud. When the sheet on the cloud is updated, a notification arrives at the local server via the MQTT (Message Queueing Telemetry Transport) server (Beebotte). The notification triggers the local server to acquire the setting information on the cloud. As such, the setting information in the local server is always updated to the latest one.

The SH application using Node-RED (IBM Inc.) is running in the local server, and each IoT device is operated according to the input settings. The local server and sensors communicate directly, and the SH application judges the sent sensor information according to the settings and makes a request. By sending a request to the external application programming interface of each IoT device, the devices are operated. Apart from the abovementioned operation as the SH application, the sensor data are overwritten and saved in the sheet on the cloud, and the current sensor status can be confirmed from the web application on the tablet.

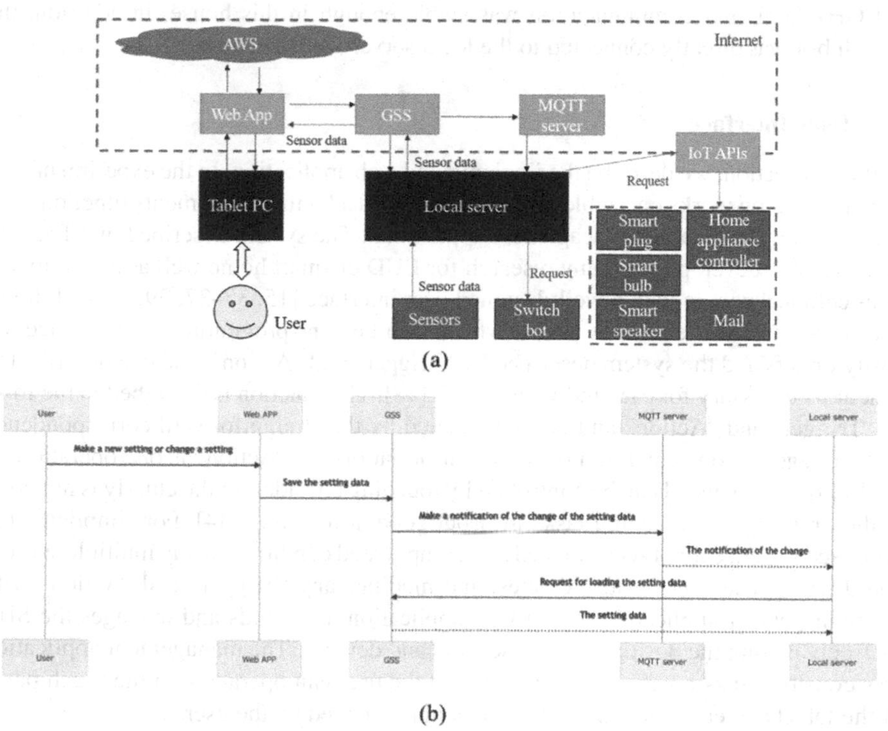

Fig. 3. (a) System configuration diagram. (b) Sequence diagram of registering a new setting.

3.2 System Components

Now, we describe the sensors and devices in Fig. 3(a). Five types of sensors were used: button switches (PTM210J, ROHM co.), passive infrared motion sensors (ETC-PIR, iTec co.), door open/close sensors (ETB-OCS, iTec co.), temperature/humidity sensors (ETB-RHT, iTec co.), brightness sensors (ETB-ILL, iTec co.). All sensors sent data to the local server located approximately in the center of the house by EnOcean in the 928.35-MHz frequency band. No matter where the sensor was placed in the living environment assuming living alone, the local server received the data sufficiently stably.

As the IoT devices, smart light bulbs (Kasa Smart Light Bulb KL110, TP-Link Inc.), smart plugs (Plug, SwitchBot Inc.), switch-pushing machines, switch bots (Bot, SwitchBot Inc.), smart speaker (Google Home, Google Inc.), a tablet PC (A1893 32 GB Gold, Apple Inc.) for receiving emails, and a home appliance controller (Nature Remo mini 2, Nature Inc.) were employed. In the residence simulating an elderly person's house shown in Fig. 2(a), there is a refrigerator, microwave oven, washing machine, circulator, air purifier, air conditioner, ventilation fan, and various types of lighting; switch bots and smart plugs were able to be placed anywhere.

However, because the only machine that could be controlled by infrared signals was the air conditioner, the home appliance controller was used only to control the air conditioner. All devices other than the switch bot were connected to the router via 2.4-GHz Wifi, and communication was stable enough in this house. In addition, the switch bot was directly connected to the local server via Bluetooth.

3.3 User Interface

In this subsection, we describe the implemented web application. In the experiment, this web application works on a tablet PC. We developed a UI that implements functions that users want through an SH management application. The system described by "Trigger" and "Action" developed in many research for EUD of smart home well accepted by the non-technical people with a well-designed user interface [15, 35–37, 39, 40, 42]. It has been reported that even elderly people who have little or no programming experience can easily understand the system described by "Trigger" and "Action," and can describe the functions necessary for each individual's life [18]. The function is described in the form of "Trigger" and "Action" and is implemented by the straightforward correspondence that "Trigger" is one condition by sensor information and "Action" is one operation by the IoT device. This UI can be controlled by touching considering the elderly is not good at the dragging and pinching tasks [43] but good at touching [44]. For simplicity, the proposed system cannot set advanced and complicated conditions using multiple sensors and devices. The user creates, deletes, and modifies any "Trigger" and "Action" with the management application on the web application and builds and manages the SHS by freely putting the positions of the sensors and devices. The management application was constructed as a web application so that the user can operate it on the touch panel of the tablet and easily identify all settings implemented by the user.

Figure 4(a) shows the initial screen of the setting application on the web application. When the user adds a new setting, i.e., when implementing a new "Trigger" and "Action" setting, the user goes to the setting screen (Fig. 4(b)). The user selects the sensor and condition settings as "Trigger" and the device and operation as "Action." First, when setting "Trigger," touch the empty square on the upper left of Fig. 4(b) to proceed to the sensor setting screen. On the sensor selection screen (Fig. 4(c)), a list of sensor types is displayed by icon and name and can be selected. The icon corresponds to the sticker attached to the actual sensor (Fig. 4(l)). After deciding the type of sensor, the page for selecting the number of the sensor is displayed. When there are multiple sensors of the same type, the sensors are numbered serially (Fig. 4(l)), and the sensor used is selected by the number (Fig. 4(d)). The icon and number can also be identified by a sticker on the device (Fig. 4(m)). After selecting which sensor and number to use, the screen transitions to a different condition setting screen for each sensor type, and the conditions are set (Fig. 4(e)). When the last setting of the sensor for "Trigger" is completed, the screen returns to the setting screen in which what type of "Trigger" was set is entered (Fig. 4(f)). If you touch the empty square at the top right of the screen (Fig. 4(f)), the user can set the device type (Fig. 4(g)), number, and operation type similarly as for "Trigger." When the user finishes inputting "Action" to the end, the user will get a setting screen in which both "Trigger" and "Action" are input (Fig. 4(h)). Notably, it does not matter which of "Trigger" or "Action" is set first. Table 1 shows a list of condition setting types for each sensor as "Trigger" and a list of operation types for each device as "Action." After making the final confirmation on this screen, by pressing the enter button at the bottom right, this setting is read into the local server through the flow shown in Fig. 3(b), and the setting is implemented (Fig. 4(i)). As shown above, this web application is straightforward and makes it easy to grasp which type of setting a user will make.

When the user confirms or corrects the setting contents, he/she can go to confirm the setting list from the initial screen (Fig. 4(a)). The setting list is displayed as shown in Fig. 4(j), and it is possible to temporarily turn it off and delete the settings. If the user wants to modify the settings, he/she can move to the detail confirmation screen (Fig. 4(k)) from the detail button and modify it.

After putting the local server in the residence, the user basically touches only the tablet, sensors, devices, and manuals that operate the setting application. Because this system aims to be age-friendly, the manual is printed and details the functions of each sensor and device, so that the user can check it freely.

3.4 Evaluation Experiment

To evaluate the developed management web application and the entire SHS, a 120-min hands-on workshop was conducted for 10 subjects [5 men and 5 women, average age 26.6 ± 2.1 (SD)]. The workshop comprised greetings and introduction (15 min), scenario experience (10 min), questionnaire 1 (5 min), room tour (5 min), freely experience the developed system (45 min), questionnaire 2 (10 min), and interview (30 min). The subjects participated individually.

First, the experimenter ("facilitator") explained the outline of the SHS in about 15 min (Fig. 5(a)) for the subjects, and then the implementation experiences of two to three prepared scenarios were performed in 10 min. For example, after the subjects added new settings for "when you press a button" and "the smart light bulb turns on," they actually pressed the specified button to experience the smart light bulb turning on. This scenario experience was performed not only for the subjects to become accustomed to the setting UI but also for evaluating the usability of the setting of the SHS. Therefore, to evaluate the setting system itself without considering whether the functions required by the user can be implemented, questionnaire 1 using the system usability scale (SUS) was conducted after the scenario experience.

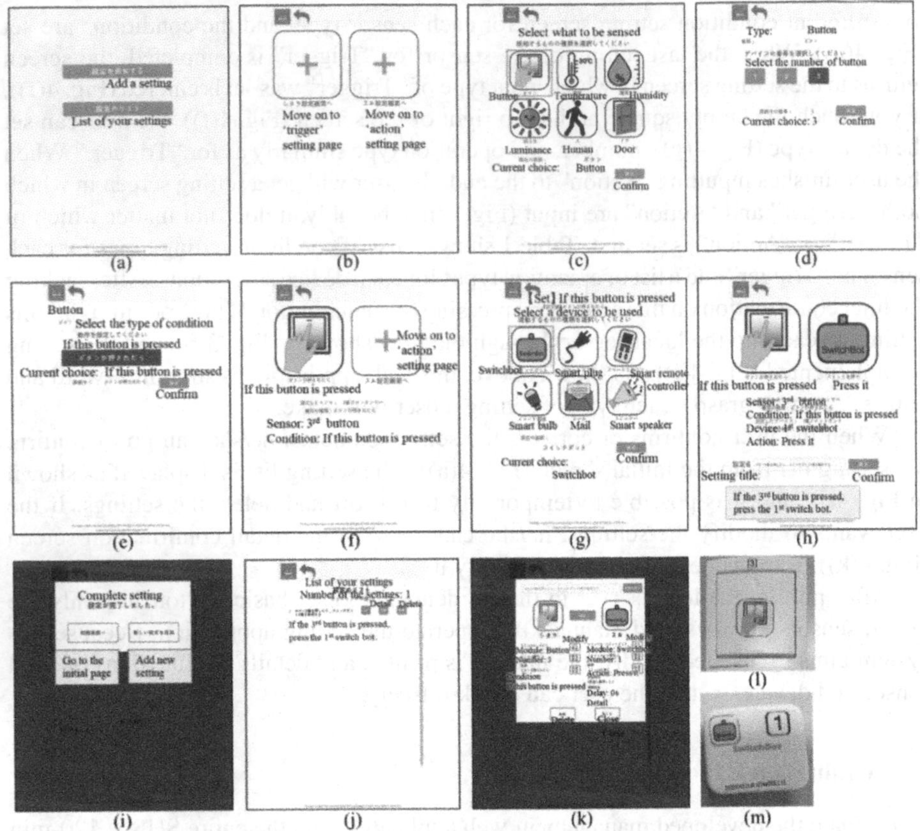

Fig. 4. (a)–(k) Screens in the web application. (l) Button switch. (m) Switch bot.

After experiencing the scenario, the subjects were asked to assume that they lived in this residence and to experience the implementation of functions they wanted. First, the facilitator took a room tour with the subjects to introduce the floor plan for about 5 min so that they could assume living in this house. The subjects were asked to imagine life in the simulated residence by having them walk along the flow lines from when they got up to when they went out, and when they came back from outsides.

Based on the situations, the subjects engaged in a 45-min implementation experience (Fig. 5(b)). The facilitator who conducted the room tour observed the implementation experience of the subjects and helped with the installation of the sensors at the request of the subjects. Because this system aims to allow elderly people to operate on their own, the facilitator encouraged the subject to refer to the manual when asking questions about the manual contents and tried minimizing the assistance to the subject. The subjects were free to place sensors and devices in a simulated residence using double-sided tapes, tapes, and power extension cables (Figs. 5(c) and (d)).

Table 1. Lists of sensors and triggers, and devices and actions.

Sensor	Trigger
Button	If this button is pressed
Motion sensor	If this sensor detect a motion
Door sensor	If this sensor detect a door opening
	If this sensor detect a door closing
	If this sensor detect a door moving
Thermometer	If temperature measured by this sensor is higher than the threshold you set
	If temperature measured by this sensor is lower than the threshold you set
	If temperature measured by this sensor is lower than the lower threshold or higher than the higher one
	If temperature measured by this sensor is higher than the lower threshold and lower than the higher one
Hygrometer	If humidity measured by this sensor is higher than the threshold you set
	If humidity measured by this sensor is lower than the threshold you set
	If humidity measured by this sensor is lower than the lower threshold or higher than the higher one
	If humidity measured by this sensor is higher than the lower threshold and lower than the higher one
Illuminance meter	If illuminance measured by this sensor is higher than the threshold you set
	If illuminance measured by this sensor is lower than the threshold you set
	If illuminance measured by this sensor is lower than the lower threshold or higher than the higher one
	If illuminance measured by this sensor is higher than the lower threshold and lower than the higher one

Devices	Action
Smart bulb	Turn it on
	Turn it off
Smart plug	Turn it on
	Turn it off
Switch bot	Press it
Smart speaker	Read out the text you set
Mail	Send a text mail to the address you set
Home appliance controller	Turn it on in ventilation mode
	Turn it on in cooling mode
	Turn it on in dehumidification mode
	Turn it off

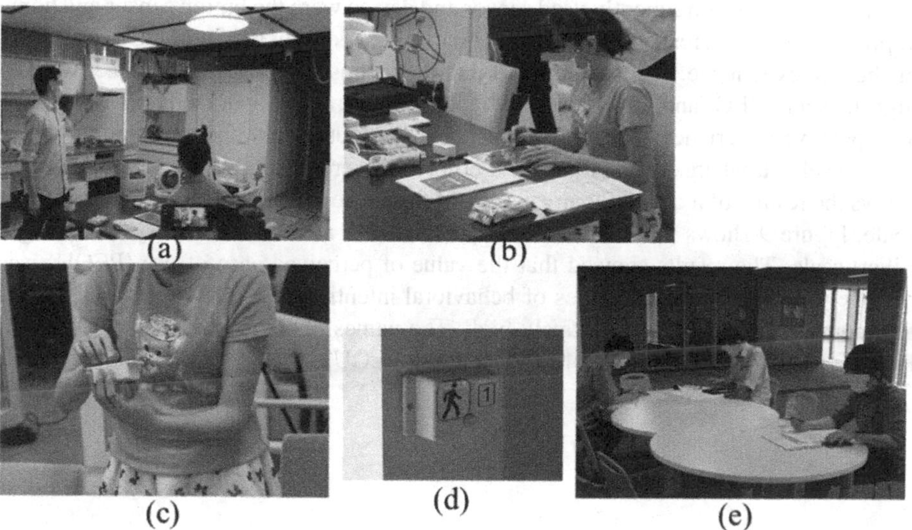

Fig. 5. Sceneries of the evaluation experiment.

After the 45-min experience, the subjects changed places and responded to questionnaire 2 (10 min) and a 30-min interview. In the questionnaire, the subjects evaluated the SHS using SUS and the experience in the workshop using the short user experience questionnaire (Short UEQ) based on the 45-min implementation experience.

4 Results

The SUS scores after the scenario and free experiences are shown in Fig. 6 as SUS1 and SUS2, respectively. The mean $\pm$ SD of the SUS scores are 78.5 $\pm$ 18.4 and 72.3 $\pm$ 16.4, respectively, indicating that the system is sufficiently acceptable. In particular, the SUS score after the scenario experience was large enough to exceed 75, indicating that the usability of this smart management system was good. Figure 7 shows the average setting time for each subject during the free experience. Although there was a large variation in the time taken to complete a new setting, it took an average of 115 s. However, there was one case in which the subject took more than 20 min from the start of the setting to complete it due to reexamination of the setting during the setting process. This setting time was excluded from the statistics as an outlier. In one case, the measurement of the setting time failed, so that value was also excluded. The average number of new settings was 8.8, and the average number of modifications was 2.2 during the 45 min of free time per person. Table 2 shows the combinations of sensors and devices set by all subjects. The total number of combinations is 92, which is larger than the total number of new settings because when the type of sensor or device was changed by modification, the modified settings were also recorded as different combinations. The results showed that the combination of the temperature sensor as a trigger to control the home appliance controller was tested the most, followed by the button switch and smart plug, the door sensor and smart bulb, and the humidity sensor and home appliance controller. The most frequently used sensor and device were the button sensor and home appliance controller, respectively. Figure 8 shows the results of the Short UEQ evaluation of the free experience. It was confirmed that the inconsistency of each subject was not high in Short UEQ, and the data are reliable. In general, the workshop was evaluated as a positive experience. The individual items—attractiveness and stimulation—were rated excellent, whereas perspicuity and efficiency were rated above average. Figure 9 shows the results of a questionnaire survey of the entire system (Table 3) using a Likert scale. Figure 9 shows the results of the questionnaire about the entire system using a Likert scale. The results showed that the value of perceived ease of use (PEOU) was relatively low, whereas the values of behavioral intention to use (BIU) and likelihood to recommend (LTR) were relatively high. The names of scores are listed in Table 3; PEOU2 represents the average of PEOU2-1 and PEOU2-2.

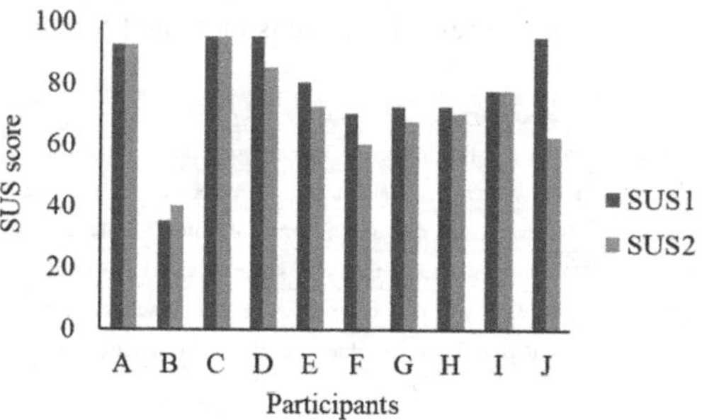

Fig. 6. SUS scores of each participant.

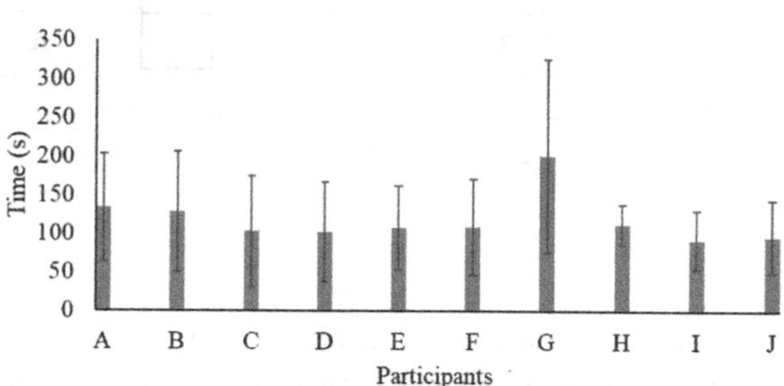

Fig. 7. Setting time in the web application of each participant (error bar means SD).

Table 2. Implemented setting in the free experience of the system.

	Smart bulb	Smart plug	Switch bot	Smart speaker	Mail	Home appliance controller	Total
Button	4	7	5	2	2	1	21
PIR motion sensor	3	1	4	4	4	2	18
Door sensor	6	2	4	1	0	3	16
Thermometer	1	0	0	4	0	14	19
Hygrometer	0	0	1	0	0	6	7
Illuminance meter	2	1	4	3	0	1	11
Total	16	11	18	14	6	27	92

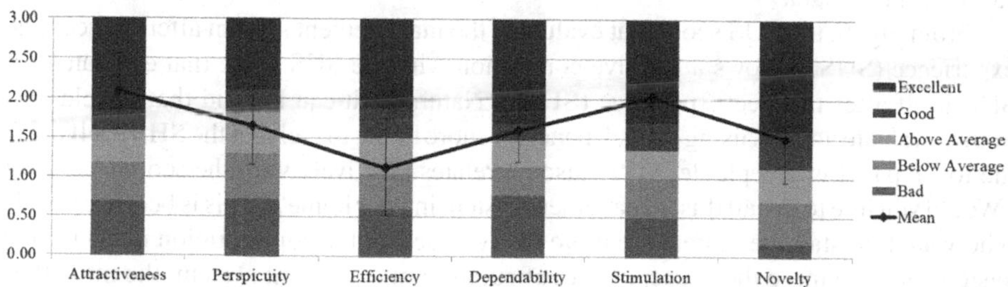

Fig. 8. Short UEQ result (error bar means 95% confidence interval).

Table 3. List of questionnaires. The score is measured 5-point Likert scale.

Label	Timing	Questionnaire
BIU1	After the senario experience	Would you like to use this system using the touch panel in your home?
PEOU2-1	After the free experience	It is easy to make adjustments and corrections to "Sitara-suru system".
PEOU2-2	After the free experience	The time required to use "Sitara-suru system" is short enough.
PU2	After the free experience	Do you think that "Sitara-suru system" provide you with the functions you need?
LTR2	After the free experience	How likely will you recommend this 'Sitara-suru'system to a friend or colleague?
BIU2	After the free experience	Would you like to introduce the 'Sitara-suru system' into your home?

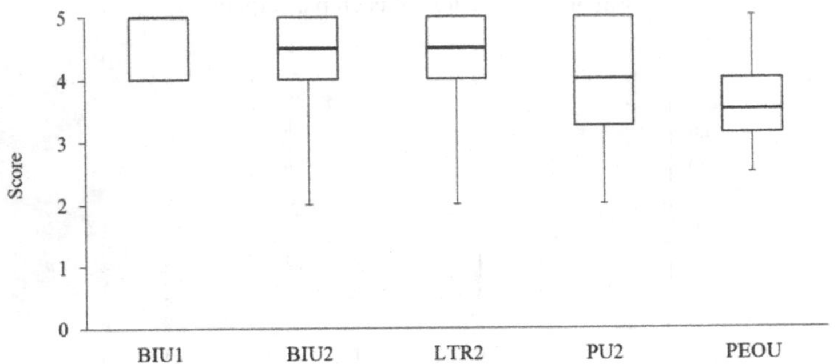

Fig. 9. Box-and-whisker diagram of the scores of questionnaires.

5 Discussion

Correlation coefficients are shown in Table 4 for SUS scores (SUS1, SUS2), an average setting time during the free experience, Short UEQ, BIU after the scenario experience (BIU1), PEU (PEU2), perceived usefulness (PU) (PU2), LTR (LTR2), and BIU (BIU2) after the free experience. For the SUS scores, the correlation coefficient calculated by excluding the score of one subject who rated very low is shown in parentheses in the table. As shown in Fig. 9, the distribution of scores of the questionnaires does not follow a normal distribution because of the small numbers of participants and scales. The analysis was performed assuming that the distribution followed a normal distribution when the number of people was increased. However, the scale should be increased for better analysis. The correlation coefficients of the score of the questionnaires are supplementary data.

From Fig. 6, the SUS score that evaluated the management system after the scenario experience (SUS1) shows a positive correlation with the SUS score that evaluated the SHS itself after the free experience (SUS2). Naturally, it can be said that people who highly evaluate an SHS using a touch panel are more likely to feel that the SHS itself using the touch panel is acceptable. SUS1 also correlates positively with the score (BIU1) of "Would you like to install this management system in your home?" This is because people who want to install the system are more likely to accept the configuration management system, and the more they accept the configuration management system, the more they intend to use the system. In previous studies of acceptance models examined in SHs [45–48], the perceived value, PU and PEOU increase the attitude toward using and thus the intention to use. Notably, the technology acceptance model (TAM) model assumed in these previous studies does not evaluate the actual use of the systems, but rather evaluates how subjects' expectations, such as PU and PEOU, affect their intention to use the systems. However, with the actual use, the tendency is expected to be similar, and it can be thought that the perceived control increases the PU and finally affect the intention to use. Pal and Vanijja [49] attempted to use SUS for postusage evaluation of an actual system and reported that the structure of PU and especially PEOU in the SUS and TAM models are similar and can be substituted when explaining other evaluation criteria, such as LTR. Therefore, it is natural that the higher the SUS score of the setting management system, the higher the BIU score tended to be. When introducing this system to the elderly, they need to accept the setting management system before moving on to the actual verification of its practicality. An input method using a touch panel similar to our UI was accepted by the elderly as an IoT setting method [50], but whether it will be accepted as an SH management system in combination with actual sensors and devices needs to be verified in the future.

The SUS evaluation of the entire system after the free experience showed strong positive correlations with the perspicuity and dependability in the Short UEQ evaluation of the free experience as well as the SUS1 score, and some positive correlations with the efficiency of the experience. Although there was a difference between SUS and Short UEQ in that SUS evaluated the system, whereas Short UEQ evaluated the experience of the system, the perspicuity and dependability of the experience meant that the system was easy to understand and trust. Of course, SUS evaluates overall usability and not only perspicuity and dependability, but perspicuity and dependability are important in system evaluation, and this is reflected in the SUS score. There is also a relatively weak correlation between the effectiveness of the experience and the SUS score, but this is because people who were more familiar with the system felt that the experience was more efficient. As mentioned above, SUS2 shows a correlation with SUS2, but they are not the same. Although the correlation between SUS1 and Short UEQ ratings is not meaningful, SUS2 has a higher correlation with three Short UEQ scores compared with SUS1. This result supports that the dependability and ease of understanding of the SHS, which were not measured by the usability of the setting system itself, appeared in the evaluation of SUS2. In fact, in the interviews, we received comments such as "The motion sensor did not work properly," "The sensor did not respond (as expected) and the number of errors is large," and "There was a time lag (in operation)." We believe that the failure of the SHS to operate as expected at the time of setup reduced the reliability of the SHS and lowered the SUS rating of the SHS as a whole.

An interesting result in terms of whether the system worked as expected was the correlation between the response score (PU2) to the question of whether they thought the necessary functions would be implemented and the attractiveness of the experience and the number of revisions. It is easy to understand that the more necessary functions are implemented, the more attractive the experience of the system is. From the results of the questionnaire and interview, we can conclude that the score of the question whether the required function was implemented depends on whether the required function worked as expected by setting and adjusting the sensors and devices, whether there was a device

Table 4. The heatmap of the correlations.

	SUS1	SUS2	Setting time	NoS	NoM	Attractiveness	Perspicuity	Efficiency	Dependability	Stimulation	Novelty	BIU1	PEU2	PU2	LTR2
SUS2	[illegible] (0.93)														
Setting time	-0.28 (-0.38)	-0.16 (-0.08)													
NoS	0.43 (0.59)	0.63 (*0.75)	-0.35												
NoM	0.26 (*0.70)	0.08 (0.26)	-0.38	0.50											
Attractiveness	0.23 (0.35)	0.58 (*0.76)	0.22	0.56	0.35										
Perspicuity	*0.59 (0.41)	[illegible] (**0.82)	0.09	0.41	0.03	0.63									
Efficiency	0.42 (0.16)	*0.67 (0.60)	0.08	0.41	0.23	**0.64	*0.76								
Dependability	*0.71 (*0.67)	**0.85 (**0.85)	-0.31	*0.76	0.53	*0.76	*0.76	**0.80							
Stimulation	0.29 (0.15)	0.57 (0.57)	0.49	0.38	0.02	**0.82	0.53	*0.66	0.55						
Novelty	-0.12 (-0.07)	0.32 (0.54)	-0.03	0.37	-0.05	0.55	0.22	0.55	0.38	0.48					
BIU1	*0.69 (*0.69)	0.54 (0.40)	0.22	0.31	0.55	0.51	0.63	0.50	0.63	0.47	-0.18				
PEU2	0.32 (0.51)	0.17 (0.19)	*-0.65	0.29	0.50	-0.01	0.02	-0.18	0.32	-0.26	-0.25	0.11			
PU2	0.14 (*0.78)	0.24 (*0.67)	-0.05	0.50	*0.79	*0.67	0.13	0.32	0.55	0.48	0.31	0.47	0.36		
LTR2	0.38 (0.52)	0.54 (0.64)	0.27	0.56	0.46	*0.70	0.56	0.47	0.62	*0.67	0.29	*0.73	0.10	0.62	
BIU2	0.09 (0.57)	0.31 (*0.70)	0.35	0.46	0.34	0.60	0.30	0.17	0.35	0.50	0.26	0.50	0.10	*0.73	**0.88

that could achieve the required function, and whether there was a system to implement the required function. As for the first point, because the necessary functions were implemented by making adjustments and modifications, it is thought that there was a correlation between the PU2 score and number of modifications. Regarding the second point, in the interviews, there were requests for additional types and functions of sensors and devices, such as a pressure sensor, a device to open curtains, and a function to play music. Regarding the third point, in the interview survey, there were four major requests: intelligent judgment of condition settings, multiple conditions and actions, the addition of the day of the week and time to condition settings, and the ability to check a list of sensor information and event logs. The second and third requirements were basically to implement the first requirement, so the first requirement was essential. Notably, there were also opinions such as "It would be convenient if AI (artificial Intelligence) (etc.) could do everything (understanding my intentions), but it would be scary" and "Conditioning (by oneself) might be a little inconvenient (but preferable)." To satisfy the first requirement, function of context awareness [50] is necessary. This is also important for the elderly [51]. Context awareness technology in home has been developed rapidly [52, 53] and some researchers developed context awareness home application for EUD to some degree to each extent [15, 54, 55]. These contexts are installed by the experts and set by the users in these researches.

In an experiment of the Living Lab of an actual SH [17], it was essential to visualize changes in sensor data over a time range in which repetitive patterns could be observed to understand the context of daily life in relation to sensor timeseries data. They also reported that it was necessary to provide sensor data as events. That is context awareness in EUD of SHS. From this, it can be said that it is necessary to add three functions in accordance with the previous study [17] when introducing this system into actual living. The first is the ability to display a timeseries of sensor or event data and the system's behavior on various time scales. The second is to cluster multiple sensor responses as a single event and set it as a trigger, and the third is to set multiple device actions as a single action. In this experiment, we used a straightforward configuration system and obtained a relatively high SUS evaluation because the experiment was performed in a simulated residence for a short time. Moreover, if the second and third functions were simply implemented, the configuration UI would become more complicated, which is undesirable when considering the application to elderly people. Therefore, it is necessary to study a method to realize complex settings while maintaining the simplicity of the input method, which is a future issue. In this experiment, we installed the sensors after the subjects had decided what they would be used for, but in real life, it is necessary to place the sensors first and have the users understand the connection between the sensors and their own lives. However, it is difficult to combine flexible sensor placement with the ability to link sensor data to daily life. Therefore, to save data as different data when sensor placement is changed, it is necessary to allow users to change sensor names and manage data by sensor name.

This also confirms the challenges in implementing an SH. To use the sensor data as conveniently as possible, it is necessary to install sensors and connect sensor data with our own lives, meaning that the economic and time costs of installing sensors will be required before the maximum benefits of the SH are expected by the user. In this experiment, the BIU and LTR of a simple SHS were high, and the experience was evaluated as favorable. Therefore, it can be said that this system will play a role as an entrance for people to implement more advanced functions in their daily lives. It is necessary to build a system and a learning method to enable the use of advanced sensor information sequentially to implement a smarter life at home using this system, especially when the system is used by the elderly. First, it is necessary to verify whether a simple system can be accepted by the elderly as an introduction to an SHS, and what steps are necessary to expand the system to a more advanced SHS. As the next step, we will examine whether the elderly can construct a simple system with sensor feedback in the same experiment, how to evaluate usability, and how to evaluate the experience.

Now, we describe the limitation of this research. In this experiment, the subjects who pretended to be the resident of the simulated house and imagined their life in the house had 50 min to implement and check the operation of the SHS. As an SH is used for a long period, it becomes a part of the living environment, and continuous use makes their main interest errors and maintenance [17]. Therefore, although the configuration is only the first step in an actual SHS, in this experiment, the evaluation focuses on the configuration of the SHS. Of course, the participant goes through a series of experiences, such as setting, checking the operation, adjusting, and checking the operation, but the setting part is evaluated as a factor that occupies a larger part than the actual one. Because the configuration part is a task that users must perform at an early stage in DIY SH, having sufficiently high usability of this part is a prerequisite for SH DIY; thus, the evaluation in this study is relevant. Moreover, if the usability of the configuration system shown in the SUS is high enough (not the highest), there will be no problem with the subsequent SH use. The scores of BIU2 do not show a correlation with SUS or Short UEQ. We cannot conclude from this study whether any SUS or Short UEQ scores can be used as a guide for the adoption of SHSs. In addition, it is imperative to tailor more advanced settings and adjustments to make better use of SHSs, and this requires continuous use and adjustment. Therefore, it is necessary to continue to investigate not only the initial introduction but also what factors encourage continuous use and whether there is a standard value that can be used as a guide for the young and elderly.

6 Conclusion

In this study, we developed a DIY SHS for the elderly with a simple framework described by a combination of trigger and action and a straightforward iPad configuration application. To first evaluate the usability of the developed system, we implemented the system in a simulated dwelling and performed an experiment in which young people experienced the configuration and adjustment of the system. The results showed that the average SUS score to evaluate the configuration system was 78.5 and the SUS score to evaluate the entire SHS was 72.3, which was sufficiently high to indicate that the system was acceptable. In addition, Short UEQ showed that our conducted workshop was evaluated as a positive experience. These results imply that the proposed simple system will play a sufficient role as an entrance for people to implement more advanced SH tailored to their daily living. In the future, we will verify whether this system can be accepted by the elderly as well.

Acknowledgments. The research was partially supported from the following funds: JSPS Program for Leading Graduate Schools (Graduate Program in Gerontology, Global Leadership Initiative for an Age Friendly Society, The University of Tokyo), Foundation of Support Center for Advanced Telecommunications Technology Research (SCAT), JSPS KAKENHI Grant Numbers JP19K14028, JP20H01753, and JP20K20494.

References

1. Ministry of Health, Labor and Welfare: Overview of Reiwa 2nd year simple life table. https://www.mhlw.go.jp/toukei/saikin/hw/life/life20/. Accessed 22 Feb 2022
2. Ministry of Health, Labor and Welfare: Annual health, labour and welfare report 2016. https://www.mhlw.go.jp/wp/hakusyo/kousei/16/. Accessed 22 Feb 2022
3. Alam, M.R., Reaz, M.B.I., Ali, M.A.M.: A review of smart homes-past, present, and future. IEEE Trans. Syst. Man Cybern. Part C (Appl. Rev.) **42**(6), 1190–1203 (2012)
4. Scanaill, C.N., et al.: A review of approaches to mobility telemonitoring of the elderly in their living environment. Ann. Biomed. Eng. **34**(4), 547–563 (2006)
5. Peetoom, K.K., Lexis, M.A., Joore, M., Dirksen, C.D., De Witte, L.P.: Literature review on monitoring technologies and their outcomes in independently living elderly people. Disabil. Rehabil. Assist. Technol. **10**(4), 271–294 (2015)
6. Azimi, I., Rahmani, A.M., Liljeberg, P., Tenhunen, H.: Internet of things for remote elderly monitoring: a study from user-centered perspective. J. Ambient. Intell. Humaniz. Comput. , 1–17 (2016). https://doi.org/10.1007/s12652-016-0387-y
7. Balta-Ozkan, N., Davidson, R., Bicket, M., Whitmarsh, L.: Social barriers to the adoption of smart homes. Energy Policy **63**, 363–374 (2013)
8. Pal, D., Funilkul, S., Vanijja, V., Papasratorn, B.: Analyzing the elderly users' adoption of smart-home services. IEEE Access **6**, 51238–51252 (2018)
9. Alzahrani, T., Michelle, H., Dick, W.: Barriers and facilitators to using smart home technologies to support older adults: perspectives of three stakeholder groups. Int. J. Healthcare Inf. Syst. Inf. **16**(4), 1–14 (2021)

10. Haigh, K.Z., Kiff, L.M., Ho, G.: The independent lifestyle assistant: lessons learned. Assist. Technol. **18**(1), 87–106 (2006)
11. Kleinberger, T., Becker, M., Ras, E., Holzinger, A., Müller, P.: Ambient intelligence in assisted living: Enable elderly people to handle future interfaces. In: Stephanidis, C. (ed.) UAHCI 2007. LNCS, vol. 4555, pp. 103–112. Springer, Heidelberg (2007). https://doi.org/10.1007/978-3-540-73281-5_11
12. Fischer, G.: End-user development and meta-design: foundations for cultures of participation. In: Pipek, V., Rosson, M.B., de Ruyter, B., Wulf, V. (eds.) IS-EUD 2009. LNCS, vol. 5435, pp. 3–14. Springer, Heidelberg (2009). https://doi.org/10.1007/978-3-642-00427-8_1
13. Woo, J., Lim, Y.: User experience in do-it-yourself-style smart homes. In: Proceedings of the 2015 ACM International Joint Conference on Pervasive and Ubiquitous Computing, pp. 779–790. ACM, New York (2015)
14. Desolda, G., Ardito, C., Matera, M.: Empowering end users to customize their smart environments: model, composition paradigms, and domain-specific tools. ACM Trans. Comput. Hum. Interact. **24**(2), 1–52 (2017)
15. Ghiani, G., Manca, M., Paternò, F., Santoro, C.: Personalization of context-dependent applications through trigger-action rules. ACM Trans. Comput. Hum. Interact. **24**(2), 1–33 (2017)
16. Abdallah, R., Xu, L., Shi, W.: Lessons and experiences of a DIY smart home. In: Proceedings of the Workshop on Smart Internet of Things, pp. 1–6. ACM, New York (2017)
17. Jakobi, T., et al.: Evolving needs in IoT control and accountability: a longitudinal study on smart home intelligibility. In: Proceedings of the ACM on Interactive, Mobile, Wearable and Ubiquitous Technologies, pp. 1–28. ACM, New York (2018)
18. Kang, S., et al. : Design and implementation of age-friendly activity for supporting elderly's daily life by IoT. In: Jia, Z., Gavriel, S. (eds.) HCII 2019. LNCS, vol. 11593, pp. 353–368. Springer, Cham (2019). https://doi.org/10.1007/978-3-030-22015-0_28
19. Maswadi, K., Ghani, N.B.A., Hamid, S.B.: Systematic literature review of smart home monitoring technologies based on IoT for the elderly. IEEE Access **8**, 92244–92261 (2020)
20. Stavropoulos, T.G., Papastergiou, A., Mpaltadoros, L., Nikolopoulos, S., Kompatsiaris, I.: IoT wearable sensors and devices in elderly care: a literature review. Sensors **20**(10), 2826 (2020)
21. Almeida, A., et al.: A critical analysis of an IoT-aware AAL system for elderly monitoring. Futur. Gener. Comput. Syst. **97**, 598–619 (2019)
22. Pinto, S., Cabral, J., Gomes, T.: We-care: an IoT-based health care system for elderly people. In: 2017 IEEE International Conference on Industrial Technology, pp. 1378–1383. IEEE (2017)
23. Coradeschi, S., et al.: GiraffPlus: a system for monitoring activities and physiological parameters and promoting social interaction for elderly. In: Hippe, Z.S., Kulikowski, J.L., Mroczek, T., Wtorek, J. (eds.) Human-Computer Systems Interaction: Backgrounds and Applications 3. AISC, vol. 300, pp. 261–271. Springer, Cham (2014). https://doi.org/10.1007/978-3-319-08491-6_22
24. ISO: Ergonomics of human-system interaction - part 210: human centred design for interactive systems. ISO 9241-210:2010. ISO, Geneva (2010)
25. Borelli, E., et al.: HABITAT: an IoT solution for independent elderly. Sensors **19**(5), 1258 (2019)
26. Hwang, A.S., Hoey, J.: Smart home, the next generation: closing the gap between users and technology. In: AAAI Fall Symposium: Artificial Intelligence for Gerontechnology, pp. 14–21. Association for the Advancement of Artificial Intelligence, Palo Alto (2012)

27. Coughlin, J., D'Ambrosio, L.A., Reimer, B., Pratt, M.R.: Older adult perceptions of smart home technologies: implications for research, policy and market innovations in healthcare. In: 2007 29th Annual International Conference of the IEEE Engineering in Medicine and Biology Society, pp. 1810–1815. IEEE (2007)
28. Davis, S., Roudsari, A., Raworth, R., Courtney, K.L., Mackay, L.: Shared decision-making using personal health record technology: a scoping review at the crossroads. J. Am. Med. Inform. Assoc. **24**(4), 857–866 (2017)
29. Chan, M., Estève, D., Escriba, C., Campo, E.: A review of smart homes – present state and future challenges. Comput. Methods Programs Biomed. **91**(1), 55–81 (2008)
30. Baig, M.M., Afifi, S., GholamHosseini, H., Mirza, F.: A systematic review of wearable sensors and IoT-based monitoring applications for older adults – a focus on ageing population and independent living. J. Med. Syst. **43**(8), 233 (2019)
31. Perumal, T., Datta, S.K., Bonnet, C.: IoT device management framework for smart home scenarios. In: 2015 IEEE 4th Global Conference on Consumer Electronics, pp. 54–55. IEEE (2016)
32. Sovacool, B.K., Furszyfer Del Rio, D.D.: Smart home technologies in Europe: a critical review of concepts, benefits, risks and policies. Renew. Sustain. Energy Rev. **120**, 109663 (2020)
33. Castelli, N., et al.: What happened in my home?: an end-user development approach for smart home data visualization. In: Proceedings of the 2017 CHI Conference on Human Factors in Computing Systems, pp. 853–866. ACM, New York (2017)
34. Blase, U., McManus, E., Ho, M.P.Y., Littman, M.L.: Practical trigger-action programming in the smart home. In: Proceedings of the SIGCHI conference on human factors in computing systems, pp. 803–812. ACM, New York (2014)
35. Dahl, Y., Reidar-Martin, S.: End-user composition interfaces for smart environments: a preliminary study of usability factors. In: Aaron, M. (ed.) DUXU 2011. LNCS, vol. 6770, pp. 118–127. Springer, Heidelberg (2011). https://doi.org/10.1007/978-3-642-21708-1_14
36. Litvinova, E., Vuorimaa, P.: Engaging end users in real smart space programming. In: Proceedings of the 2012 ACM Conference on Ubiquitous Computing, pp. 1090–1095. ACM, New York (2012)
37. Caivano, D., Fogli, D., Lanzilotti, R., Piccinno, A., Cassano, F.: Supporting end users to control their smart home: design implications from a literature review and an empirical investigation. J. Syst. Softw. **144**, 295–313 (2018)
38. Brich, J., Walch, M., Rietzler, M., Weber, M., Schaub, F.: Exploring end user programming needs in home automation. ACM Trans. Comput. Hum. Interact. **24**(2), 1–35 (2017)
39. Serna, M.A., Sreenan, C.J., Fedor, S.: A visual programming framework for wireless sensor networks in smart home applications. In: 2015 IEEE Tenth International Conference on Intelligent Sensors, Sensor Networks and Information Processing 2015, pp. 1–6. IEEE (2015)
40. Manca, M., Paternò, F., Santoro, C., Corcella, L.: Supporting end-user debugging of trigger-action rules for IoT applications. Int. J. Hum Comput Stud. **123**, 56–69 (2019)
41. Woo, J., Lim, Y.: Routinoscope: collaborative routine reflection for routine-driven do-it-yourself smart homes. Int. J. Des. **14**(3), 19–36 (2020)
42. Chang, H., Tsai, T., Chang, Y., Chang, Y.: Touch panel usability of elderly and children. Comput. Hum. Behav. **37**(C), 258–269 (2014)
43. Murata, A., Iwase, H.: Usability of touch-panel interfaces for older adults. Hum. Factors **47**(4), 767–776 (2005)
44. Park, E., Cho, Y., Han, J., Kwon, S.J.: Comprehensive approaches to user acceptance of Internet of Things in a smart home environment. IEEE Internet Things J. **4**(6), 2342–2350 (2017)
45. Shin, J., Park, Y., Lee, D.: Who will be smart home users? An analysis of adoption and diffusion of smart homes. Technol. Forecast. Soc. Chang. **134**, 246–253 (2018)

46. Park, E., Kim, S., Kim, Y., Kwon, S.J.: Smart home services as the next mainstream of the ICT industry: determinants of the adoption of smart home services. Univ. Access Inf. Soc. **17**, 175–190 (2018)
47. Hubert, M., et al.: The influence of acceptance and adoption drivers on smart home usage. Eur. J. Mark. **53**(6), 1073–1098 (2019)
48. Pal, D., Vanijja, V.: Perceived usability evaluation of Microsoft Teams as an online learning platform during COVID-19 using system usability scale and technology acceptance model in India. Child Youth Serv. Rev. **119**, 105535 (2020)
49. Yoshioka, D., et al.: Evaluation of IoT-setting method among senior citizens in Japan. In: Qin, G., Jia, Z. (eds.) HCII 2021. LNCS, vol. 12786, pp. 278–292. Springer, Cham (2021). https://doi.org/10.1007/978-3-030-78108-8_21
50. Dey, A.K., Abowd, G.D., Salber, D.: A conceptual framework and a toolkit for supporting the rapid prototyping of context-aware applications. Hum. Comput. Interact. **16**(2), 97–166 (2001)
51. Mynatt, E.D., Essa, I., Rogers, W.: Increasing the opportunities for aging in place. In: Proceedings on the 2000 Conference on Universal Usability, pp. 65–71. ACM, New York (2000)
52. Meyer, S., Rakotonirainy, A.: A survey of research on context-aware homes. In: Proceedings of the Australasian information security workshop conference on ACSW frontiers 2003, vol. 21, pp. 159–168. Australian Computer Society, Sydney (2003)
53. Benmansour, A., Bouchachia, A., Feham, M.: Multioccupant activity recognition in pervasive smart home environments. ACM Comput. Surv. **48**(3), 1–36 (2015)
54. Kawsar, F., Nakajima, T., Fujinami, K.: Deploy spontaneously: supporting end-users in building and enhancing a smart home. In: Proceedings of the 10th International Conference on Ubiquitous Computing, pp. 282–291. ACM, New York (2008)
55. Coutaz, J., Crowley, J.L.: A first-person experience with end-user development for smart homes. IEEE Pervasive Comput. **15**(2), 26–39 (2016)

LIGHT: A Smart Lamp Design for the Sleep Disorders and Sundown Syndrome of Alzheimer's Patients

Jingchun Zeng[1], Bingjian Liu[1,2](✉), Xu Sun[1,2], Jiang Wu[1,2], and Xinwei Wang[1,2]

[1] University of Nottingham Ningbo China, Ningbo, China
[2] Nottingham Ningbo China Beacons of Excellence Research and Innovation Institute, Ningbo, China
bingjian.liu@nottingam.edu.cn

Abstract. Many family caregivers and Alzheimer's patients suffer from the lack of appropriate dementia management products. In this study, to explore the situation of Alzheimer's patients and find potential solutions to improve the issue of sleep disturbances, this project attached great importance to the user research. The main barriers for managing Alzheimer's disease were analyzed by observing and interviewing a number of Alzheimer's patients and family caregivers. In addition, a workshop was organized with doctors and experts to explore design solutions for solving the issues. Furthermore, the market research was conducted to compare the different current products, and then predict the potential trend and solutions. Based on the results of the research and the feedback from the interviewee and the experts, a design concept of a smart lamp employing a light treatment has been proposed to offer assistance and support for Alzheimer's patients.

Keywords: Product design · Interaction design · Alzheimer's disease · Wellbeing

1 Introduction

Nowadays, the number of Alzheimer's patients increased dramatically around the world. According to Dowling et al. [1], Alzheimer's disease is the most common factor to cause dementia among the elderly. It is also reported by Prince et al. [2], because of the increasing ageing population, the predicted number of people with dementia will be more than 132 million by 2050. For the country with a big population, such as China, a large number of Alzheimer's patients can bring a significant burden on their families and society. According to Zhang, Li and Ma [3], China has the largest population of Alzheimer's patients, but the rates of diagnosis and treatment remains low level. As a result of it, the number of Alzheimer's patients in China would increase dramatically, and the economy and development of the society would face a huge challenge.

In this study, the main issues of Alzheimer's patients living with family caregivers will be defined as sleep disturbances and sundown syndrome according to UCLA Health's categories [4] and results of user studies. Based on the interview with two doctors

Q. Gao and J. Zhou (Eds.): HCII 2022, LNCS 13331, pp. 154–169, 2022.
https://doi.org/10.1007/978-3-031-05654-3_10

and literature review, light treatment could be a possible solution to these two issues. Therefore, a smart lamp design is proposed to provide light treatment in the morning, the hint of the current time during a day and a dim light at night to improve these issues for Alzheimer's patients and an APP to help caregivers take care of patients and themselves. Based on the observation of target users, the size of the final design could be more personalized according to patients' different heights and habits. Although this concept received doctors' and users' positive feedback, due to the limit of time and technology, the ease of implementation needs to be further tested.

2 Problem Definition

To further investigate and classify the issues related to Alzheimer's patients, the UCLA Health's classifications [4] was used as a reference and, over 333 family caregivers on a public platform (a WeChat group) were observed to define their problems with Alzheimer's patients.

Methods: UCLA Health [4] classified the common issues of Alzheimer's patients into 14 categories (see Fig. 1). To find the most common issues the patients' families have, the authors joined a WeChat public platform, which is for the family caregivers to discuss the problems they have in taking care of Alzheimer's patients. By observing 333 family caregivers for a month, the authors anonymously recorded the issues raised and a number of frequencies discussed (see Fig. 2).

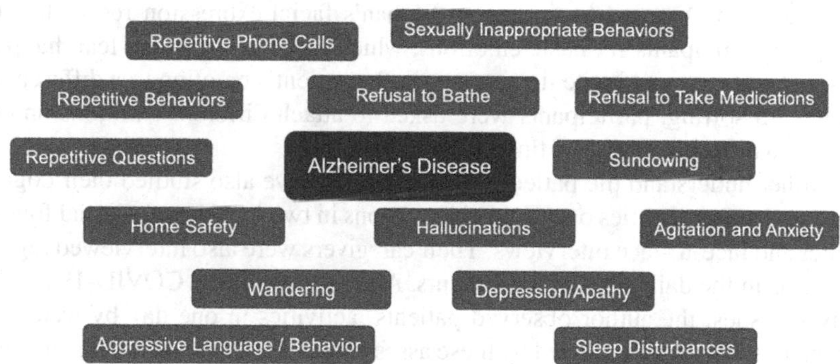

Fig. 1. The main issues of Alzheimer's patients

Findings: According to Fig. 2, the result shows that most of patients are suffering from the issue of sleep disturbances and sundown syndrome. This result is also supported by McCurry et al. [5] that 44% of Alzheimer's patients are affected by sleep disorders. They state that the sleep disturbances of the patients not only make their physical condition worse but also will bring huge physical and psychological pressure on the family caregivers. For family caregivers of Alzheimer's patients, because they need to take care of the patients at night, sleep disturbances, anxiety and depression are their main issues [6]. Therefore, improving the issue of sleep disturbances of Alzheimer's patients living at home become the focus of this design project.

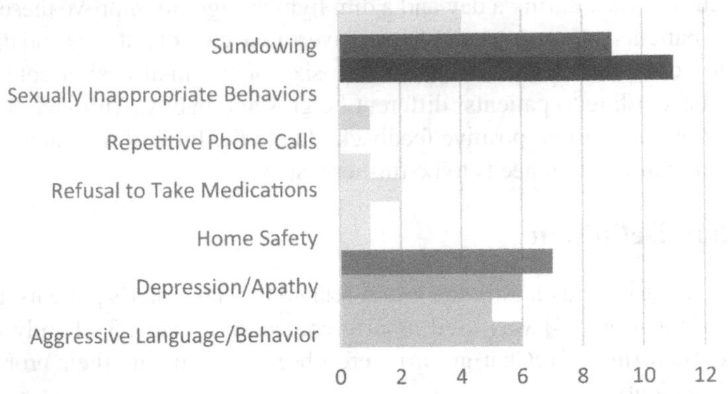

Fig. 2. The number of times different questions were asked by family caregivers

3 User Studies

Methods: To gain an initial understanding of the patients and explore potential solutions, field studies were conducted with four Alzheimer's patients who live at home with their family and caregivers and four family members living with normal elderly who do not have Alzheimer's Disease. According to Ekman's facial-expression research [7], the authors gave participants six basic emotions, which are anger, disgust, fear, happiness, sadness and surprise, and invite them to attach the patient's emotion to a different time. By using card sorting, participants were asked to attach different emotions and daily activities to a different period of time.

To further understand the patients' needs in-depth, we also studied their cognitive, self-care, and motor abilities over field observations in two local hospitals and four nursing homes and face-to-face interviews. Their caregivers were also interviewed regarding the problems in the daily care of the patients. And because of the COVID-19 pandemic and private issues, the author observed patients' activities in one day by watching 10 documentaries. The data collected by these assessments were analyzed with an empathy map (see Fig. 3).

Findings: Through these empathy maps, authors found the common behaviours of patients when they wake up at midnight. They tended to walk at home at a fast speed or sit in the living room in a dark environment, which was dangerous for them and easy to fall. The authors also noticed that when patients woke up, they needed caregivers to come to calm them down and tell them it was the time to sleep so that they would go back to sleep. The results from the user study further proved that many Alzheimer's patients have sleep disturbances and sundown syndrome. Figures 4 and 5 show the mood changes of four Alzheimer's patients and four normal elderly people in a day. Compared with normal elderly people, the results show the moodiness of four Alzheimer's patients. It can be seen from the graph that three patients are in the bad mood at night, especially from time 18:00 to 24:00. According to the questionnaires, there are several factors

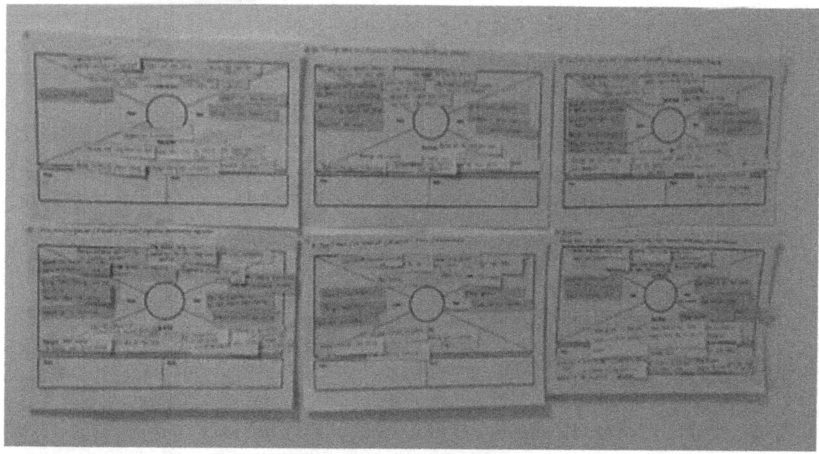

Fig. 3. The empathy maps

leading to this change. The first reason is that the patients do not go to sleep and they feel nervous and unsafe at home. According to the family caregivers, sometimes the patients will repeat going to bed and getting up for a walk. The second possible factor is sundown syndrome. The interviewees mentioned that patients are easy to feel anxious when the sun goes down. And this issue will get worse in Spring and Winter. This finding was supported by Figueiro et al. [8], because there is less daylight availability in Winter, the circadian disruption is more pronounced.

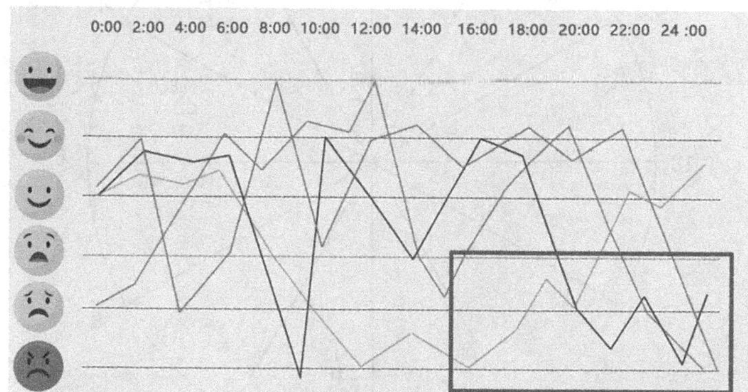

Fig. 4. The mood of Alzheimer's patients in a day

By summarizing the data from the questionnaire, the following graph (Fig. 6) introduces the daily activities of an Alzheimer's patient. Compared with the normal elderly's routines, the daily activities of Alzheimer's patients are simple and unitary. The first finding is that compared with normal elderly, the Alzheimer's patients seldom go out. Because they would forget the way back home, family caregivers tend to let them stay

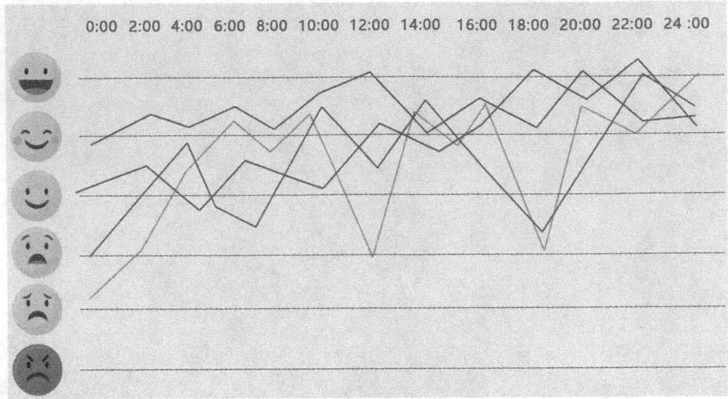

Fig. 5. The mood of normal elderly in a day

at home. The second finding is that most of the patients mainly spend their time in the living room and bedroom. In addition, the results also show that the patients who have sleep disturbances always have excessive napping in the daytime.

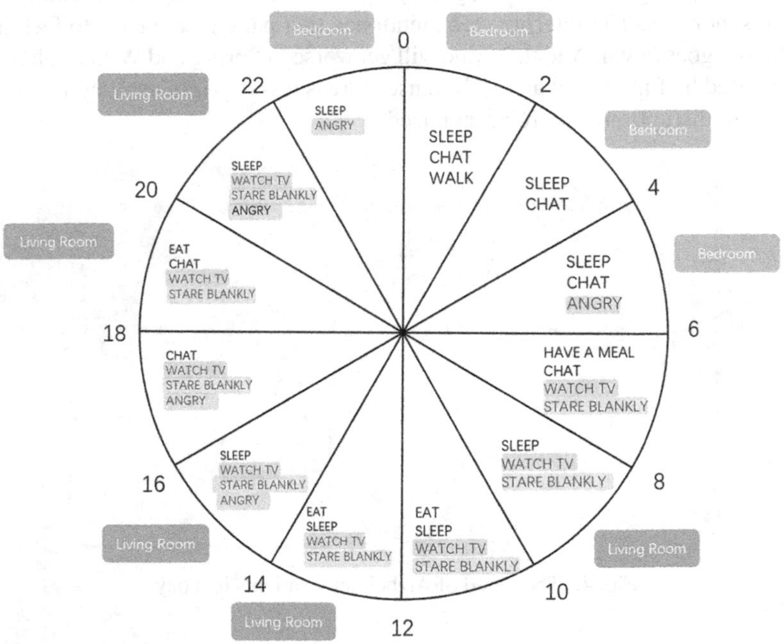

Fig. 6. The timetable of an Alzheimer's patient

According to the observation of patients and feedback from caregivers, patients tend to feel confused, anxious or become aggressive in the time of sunset, in the evening or at night which was described as the characteristics of sundown syndrome. And at night, they are energetic. It seems that they do not know it is the time to sleep. They will repeat getting up and going to bed many times, and the dark environment is dangerous for them to walk. The behaviours and moods of patients varied at different times slots were described in a user journey map (see Fig. 7).

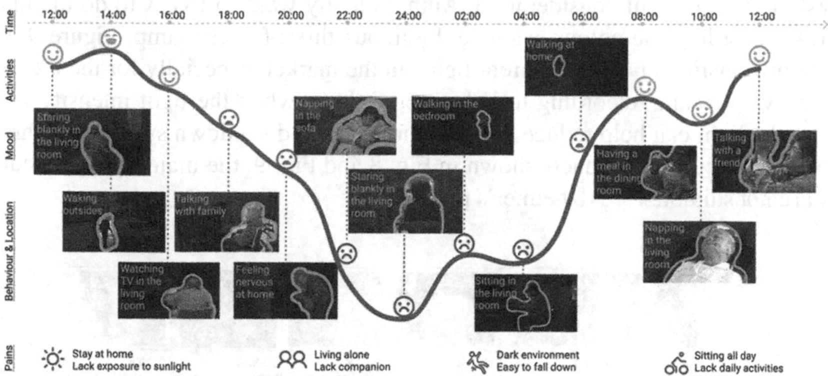

Fig. 7. The user journey map of the Alzheimer's patients in China

4 Current Solutions

Sleep disturbances of Alzheimer's patients include sleep-wake alteration, nocturnal sleep fragmentation, decrease in nocturnal sleep duration, diurnal napping and sundown syndrome [9]. And the characteristic of sundown syndrome is that the patients will more easily feel confused, anxious or become aggressive in the time of sunset, in the evening or at night [10].

The current solutions with a physical product to the sleep disturbances include light treatment, encouraging the patients to do some exercise, joining some activities, and not having medicines or coffee at night. According to Hanford and Figueiro [11], the 24-h light/dark pattern incident on the retina is a powerful non-pharmacological method to improve sleep quality. Being exposed in a morning bright light can make the circadian rhythms more robust [12]. It was improved by Fetveit et al. [14] that bright light exposure (>1000 lx) in the morning can increase the daytime wakefulness and reduce the evening agitation behavior. In addition, UCLA Health [4] also points out that the lack of daytime activities, excessive napping, no exposure to sunlight and caffeine can disrupt the sleep/wake cycles. And according to the interview with two doctors, having light treatment was further proved that it would help reduce sundown syndrome and sleep disturbances.

5 Market Research

Taking the various psychological and physical difficulties into consideration, when designing products or built environment for the eldering is an important and future trend. Like normal elderly, most Alzheimer's patients are also suffering from visual diseases, like cataracts and glaucoma, which cause a reduction in visual performance [13]. Chronic disease, mental decline, restricted mobility and ultimately loss of independence are the crucial issues that badly influence the elderly's quality of life. Therefore, when designing lighting systems for the elderly, physiological changes in their eyes and optical system need careful consideration. Authors firstly went to IKEA to do the market research, recording the colour, wattage, luminous flux of every lamp. Figure 9 is the table of information about the current lights in the market, especially for the nightlight and the living room. According to Fetveit et al. [14], when the light intensity is over 1000 lx, the light can help reduce sleep disturbances and sundown syndrome. Through analysis of the current products shown in Fig. 8 and Fig. 9, the majority of the current lights are not suitable for Alzheimer's patients.

Lamp						
Color	2700 K	2700 K	2700 K	3500 K	2700 K	2700 K
Wattage	1.4 W	5.3 W	22 W	34 W	22 W	7 W
Luminous Flux	65 Lm	400 Lm	400 Lm	3000 Lm	400 Lm	200 Lm
Lamp						
Color	2700 K	2700 K	2700 K	2700 K	2700 K	2700 K
Wattage	8 W	75 W	4.5 W	60 W	70 W	8.6 W
Luminous Flux	230 Lm	1055 Lm	470 Lm	806 Lm	1000 Lm	400 Lm

Fig. 8. The research of the lamps in IKEA

Fig. 9. The evaluation of different kinds of lamps in the market

The current mainstream of the market is the desk lamp with different lighting modes, the light uses the magnet to fix on the wall and the light which can be moved along the trails. The following figure shows the comparison between the two popular kinds of lights in the market. Among these products, because the lamps using the magnet is wireless, which has small volume and can be moved along the trails, they are popular in indoor lighting. Therefore, when designing a lamp for Alzheimer's patients, the advantages of the mainstream products were taken into consideration (see Fig. 10).

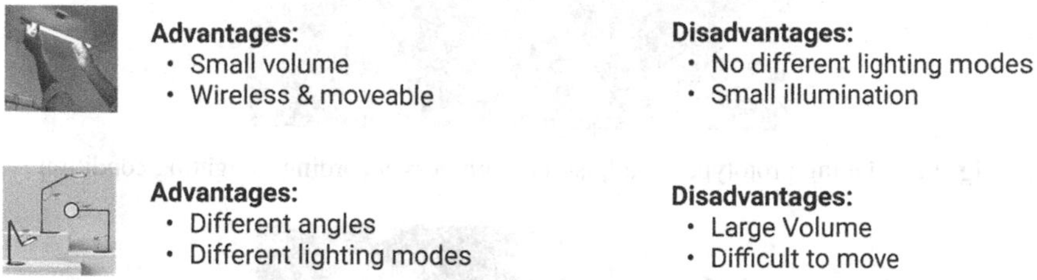

Advantages:
- Small volume
- Wireless & moveable

Disadvantages:
- No different lighting modes
- Small illumination

Advantages:
- Different angles
- Different lighting modes

Disadvantages:
- Large Volume
- Difficult to move

Fig. 10. The advantages and disadvantages of mainstream products

6 Proposed Design Solution

Context of Use. According to the findings in user research, Alzheimer's patients spend most of their time in the bedroom and living room, which are the places the design can be used. The product is designed to be placed by the family caregivers according to their needs. It has two light sources. Because many patients with sleep disturbances do not sleep at night, the nightlight is for the patients who will wake up and walk around at midnight, to make sure of their safety. The other light is for the Alzheimer's patients to have enough daily light. And according to the solutions of sundown syndrome, when the sun goes down, the lamp will also increase automatically to make sure there is enough light indoors.

Designing the Light Control System. Because the lamp will offer light to make sure the indoor environment is bright enough for the patients at dusk or on a cloudy day. The photoconductive resistance was used to make the lamp adjust its brightness according to the lighting condition (see Fig. 11). And the night-light needs to offer light when detecting people's movement in a dark environment, the photosensitive resistor elements and infrared sensor were used (see Fig. 12). To achieve these functions, Arduino was applied to the product prototypes andthe Fig. 13 show the code to control the LED (see Fig. 11).

Size Restrictions. According to the literature review and the feedback from a doctor, the current methods to receive the daily light are having a ceiling light or having the light in front of the patients, which need to make the light go into the patient's eyes. Because the product is supposed to be used in the living room, when the patients are sitting in the sofa and watching TV, this lamp is designed to be put on the side table near the sofa. According to Fetveit et al. [14], the light treatment is currently improved to have no bad effect. However, when having the light treatment, the bright light should prevent from going into the users' eyes straightly. To design for the majority of elderly people, the 95th percentile of users should be considered. To make sure the light is working, the sitting eye height (see Fig. 14) should be attached with great importance.

Fig. 11. Making prototypes to adjust its brightness according to lighting condition

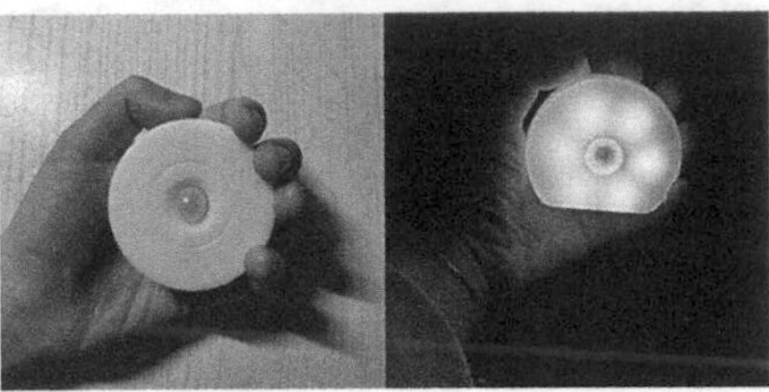

Fig. 12. Making prototypes to offer a dim light when detecting movement in a dark environment

light | Arduino 1.8.15 (Windows Store 1.8.49.0)
文件 编辑 项目 工具 帮助

light

```
/*
  AutoLed
  通过光敏电阻检测环境光，逆向控制LED灯亮度
*/

int ledPin = 10;

int sensorValue = 0; //保存读到的传感器模拟值
int ledValue = 0;  //保存LED灯占空比

void setup()
{
  pinMode(ledPin, OUTPUT);      //数字口要选择带~号的具有pwm功能的输出口
}

void loop()
{
  sensorValue = analogRead(A0);      //读取A0模拟口的数值
  ledValue = map(sensorValue, 550, 500, 0, 200); //将400到600之间的数据映射成0到200之间的数据
  analogWrite(ledPin, ledValue);   //PWM控制LED灯亮度
  delay(100);
  Serial.begin(9600);
  Serial.println(ledValue);
Serial.println(sensorValue);
delay(100);
}
```

sketch_may22a | Arduino 1.8.15 (Windows Store 1.8.49.0)
文件 编辑 项目 工具 帮助

sketch_may22a §

```
int irSensor = 2;

void setup() {
  // 初始化 串口通讯
  Serial.begin(9600);
  pinMode(LED_BUILTIN, OUTPUT); //连接内置LED的引脚设置为输出模式
  pinMode(irSensor, INPUT);     //连接人体红外感应模块的OUT引脚设置为输入模式
}

//
void loop() {
  bool sensorReading = digitalRead(irSensor);  //建立变量存储感应模块的输出信号

  if ( sensorReading ) {
    digitalWrite(LED_BUILTIN, HIGH);   // 模块感应到人,输出高电平,点亮LED
  }
  else {
    digitalWrite(LED_BUILTIN, LOW);   //  无人状态保持LED关闭
  }
    Serial.println(sensorReading);  //将模块输出信号通过串口监视器显示
}
```

Fig. 13. The code for the night-light design

The 36 anthropometric data and gender differences for Singapore elderly.

Dimensions	Male (n = 50)				Female (n = 50)				Difference	p-value
	5th	95th	Mean	SD	5th	95th	Mean	SD		
Standing measurements										
1. Stature	153.0	171.7	163.5	4.9	144.2	169.5	157.8	6.4	5.7	***
2. Eye height	142.8	160.5	152.4	4.9	136.8	157.6	147.7	5.2	4.7	***
3. Shoulder height	123.9	142.3	134.9	5.0	121.1	138.5	130.7	4.5	4.2	***
4. Elbow height	96.5	113.5	106.0	4.8	93.0	104.6	99.8	3.2	6.2	***
5. Hip height	87.5	102.6	96.2	4.2	84.0	93.6	90.2	2.8	6.0	***
6. Knuckle height	70.0	83.6	77.6	3.7	67.8	75.4	71.6	2.3	6.0	***
7. Fingertip height	60.4	73.5	67.2	3.7	59.2	67.2	62.7	2.3	4.5	***
8. Vertical grip reach	179.6	204.4	191.7	7.5	173.9	199.0	187.8	6.9	3.9	**
9. Forward grip reach	54.9	69.5	61.2	4.2	50.7	62.6	56.3	3.6	4.9	***
10. Span	152.4	179.2	165.0	7.6	151.2	176.1	161.3	6.2	3.7	**
11. Elbow span	80.3	96.2	89.5	4.4	64.4	97.2	79.8	9.1	9.7	***
Sitting measurements										
12. Sitting height	80.7	87.2	83.2	2.0	73.4	86.6	80.4	4.0	2.8	***
13. Sitting eye height	69.3	77.8	72.1	2.4	65.5	75.4	70.3	3.1	1.8	**
14. Sitting shoulder height	50.9	60.1	54.6	2.7	48.8	57.7	53.3	2.7	1.3	*
15. Sitting elbow height	20.9	30.3	25.6	2.8	17.5	26.6	22.4	2.7	3.2	***
16. Sitting thigh height	9.7	12.6	11.0	0.9	8.4	12.5	10.4	1.3	0.6	**
17. Sitting knee height	44.1	50.4	47.5	1.7	43.1	49.8	46.6	1.7	0.9	*
18. Sitting popliteal height	36.5	42.4	39.4	1.7	36.2	41.4	38.6	1.5	0.8	**
19. Sitting vertical grip reach	104.8	118.1	110.7	4.4	101.5	118.3	110.6	4.7	0.1	NS
20. Abdominal depth	18.1	29.8	22.8	3.6	15.9	24.6	20.0	2.5	2.8	***
21. Buttock-knee depth	54.3	59.7	57.1	1.5	49.8	60.5	55.2	3.1	1.9	***
22. Buttock-popliteal depth	44.2	48.2	46.2	1.3	40.0	50.4	45.2	3.1	1.0	*
23. Hip breadth	27.2	32.5	30.0	1.6	27.7	33.5	30.2	1.9	−0.2	NS
24. Shoulder-elbow length	29.9	35.2	32.0	1.5	28.4	34.3	31.4	1.7	0.6	NS
25. Elbow-fingertip length	39.7	49.6	45.9	2.9	38.2	45.5	41.9	2.2	4.0	***
26. Upper limb length	62.1	79.8	73.4	4.9	66.9	78.3	71.6	3.0	1.8	*
27. Shoulder-grip length	54.0	71.6	63.6	4.8	59.2	68.5	64.5	2.6	−0.9	NS
28. Chest depth	18.6	23.6	20.6	1.4	16.8	23.2	19.9	1.9	0.7	NS
29. Shoulder breadth biacromial	34.7	41.0	32.7	1.8	26.8	33.9	29.8	1.8	2.9	***
30. Shoulder breadth bideltoid	39.3	45.8	42.1	1.9	30.7	39.0	34.3	2.2	7.8	***
31. Head length	17.5	19.2	18.3	0.5	16.3	18.4	17.4	0.7	0.9	***
32. Head breadth	12.8	14.3	13.4	0.5	11.8	13.7	12.6	0.5	0.8	***
33. Hand length	16.8	19.2	18.1	0.7	15.6	17.9	16.7	0.7	1.4	***
34. Hand breadth	7.4	8.6	8.0	0.4	6.8	8.2	7.4	0.4	0.6	***
35. Foot length	24.2	27.7	26.1	1.0	23.2	27.2	25.4	1.1	0.7	**
36. Foot breadth	9.1	10.9	10.0	0.6	8.3	11.1	9.5	0.8	0.5	*

Notes: All dimensions are in cm; *: $p < 0.05$; **: $p < 0.01$; ***: $p < 0.001$; NS: non-significant; Singapore population in this study refers to the Chinese residents in Singapore.

Fig. 14. The ergonomic data of elderly people [15]

Iteration Through Sketches and Prototypes in Product Development. The initial concept idea is using the changeable shapes and structures to interact with target users when changing the brightness, to attract their attention to avoid being nervous or anxious. However, the doctor held an adverse opinion and suggested that using the simple shape is better. Because the patients are sensitive and are very easy to feel nervous and unsafe, the dramatic changes in the structure might have bad influences. After the first round of ideation through sketches (Fig. 15), according to the feedback from the doctor, the structure of the product needs not be much creative and changed quickly, because the patients are very easy to feel nervous. Therefore, the second round of sketching is to find the shape and material which can make people feel safe and comfortable.

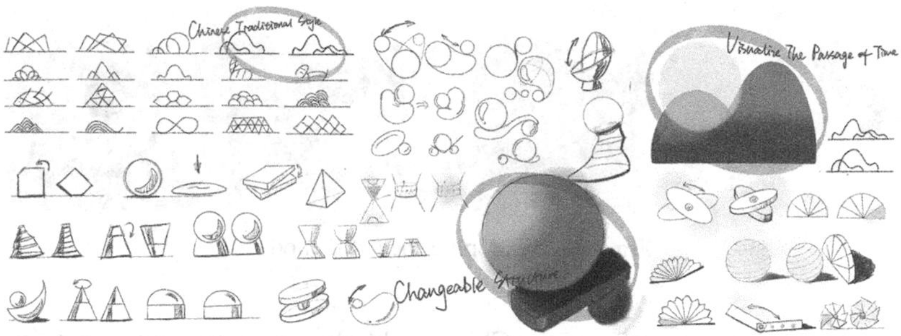

Fig. 15. Ideation through sketches

To get an intuitive sense of changing structures, many physical models were made by using hard cardboard, laser cutting and disassembling existing products. After making these physical models, the author had a deeper understanding of the way to interact with users. However, due to the difficulty of finding a proper material to meet the need of changing shapes and the structures that are not suggested by the doctors, more prototypes need to be explored. Then the author tried the round shape and more structures. Because the author designed to use the LED bulb in the initial stage, the round shape needs to cover the bulb. To simulate the real size of the bulb and the material, paper lanterns and insulation material were used to test the strength of the light and the user's feeling. After doing these 1:1 physical models, the author found the real size is not suitable for the side table. The size is much bigger than a normal lamp, because of the round shapes and the big bulb. Therefore, to decrease the size of the design, the cylinder shape was used. What's more, to make the whole design look more balanced, the basement changed from a simple cylinder to a set of irregular shapes. And to make the basement, the CAD file was converted into the AI files to do the laser cutting (see Fig. 16).

Thinking about the function and the lights, this initial idea wanted to use the situation of two round shapes and a straight line to imply about the current time, and the big one was for the daily light and improving the sundown syndrome, the small one was for the night light. The round shape was a soft design language, and it is could also be the symbol of the sun and moon. However, doctors and tutors thought this structure was unbalanced, which need to be considered. Therefore, based on the trend of modern Chinese style and

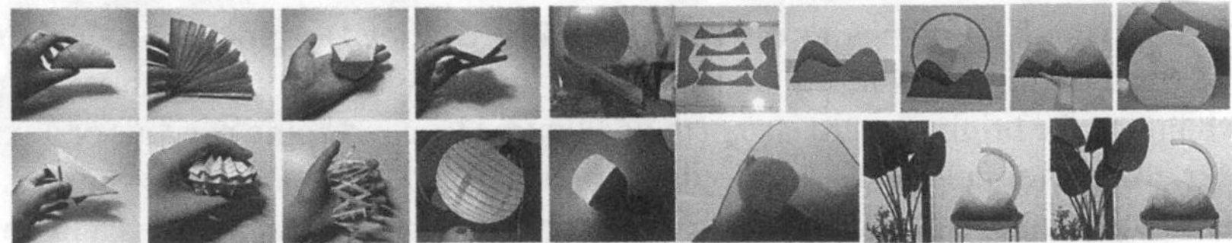

Fig. 16. Making prototypes to explore the interactive structure

the Chinese elderly target users, the author considered to add Chinese elements to the basement. What's more, considering the height and the width of this lamp, the sphere shape changed into the cylinder (see Fig. 17).

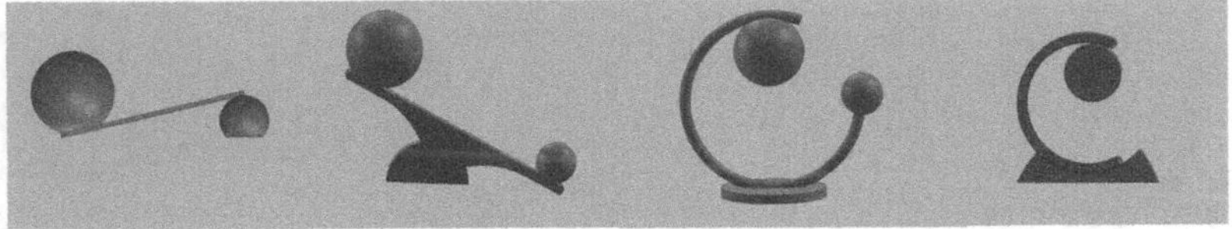

Fig. 17. Developing the CAD model

Considering the preference of the Chinese elderly, the author got inspiration from traditional Chinese paintings. And to visualize the passage of time, different physical structures and patterns were tested. The round shape and mountain shape were chosen because they combined the elderly's preference and visualized the passage of time best.

The Movement of the Light. Because the idea of this design is to simulate the sunrise and the sunset, to make the light move along the trail, the mechanical construction inside need to be designed. In the initial stage, gears, bearings and belts were taken into consideration. However, the shape of the lamp is a big circle, if the cogs do not mesh correctly, the gears will keep slipping. Due to the big curve of the structure and the accurate back and forth movement, it is difficult to use the gears or belt.

Through the market research, considering the structure of magnetic led track lights, which can be moved along the track freely, the magnet is tried to be used in the solution.

The Fig. 18 shows the principle of the propulsion, levitation, and guidance of the Maglev train. According to Song and Fujino [16], when the electrical current is generated in the coils installed in the trails, the electrical fields of pole-N and pole-S are formed in the coils. The maglev train uses the attractive and repulsive force between different poles to do the movement. Because the trails of the lamp will warp the LED's basement, which is as same as the structure of the maglev train, the principle of propulsion and guidance can be used to guide the movement of the lamp. What's more, the principle of the maglev train has been used in the design of electric toothbrushes, clock and the production line, which proves the feasibility of this idea.

Therefore, the movement of the lamp is designed to be controlled by the principle of maglev, because of the small volume, low noise, and suitable for complex movement. In addition, because magnetic charging is easy to recharge, all of the chargers are designed

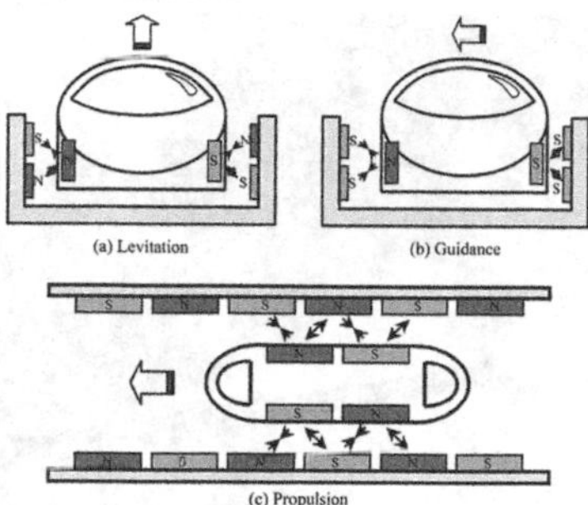

Fig. 18. The principle of the maglev train [16]

to use the magnet, considering the elderly's bad eyesight and bad ability to grab objects (see Fig. 19).

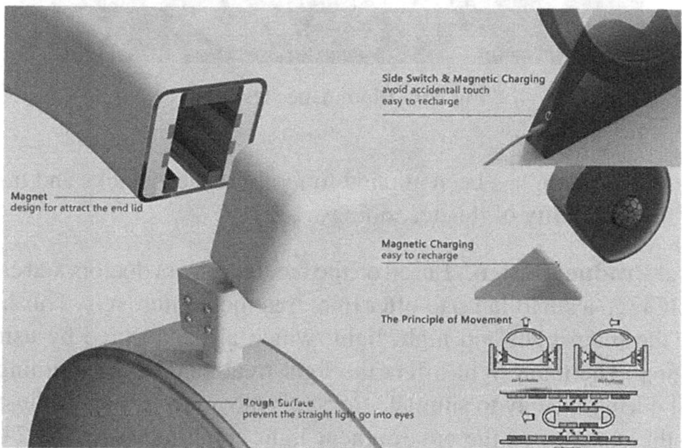

Fig. 19. The details of the 'LIGHT' design

Prototype Evaluation. Because this product needs to simulate the sunlight, the illuminance detector and user testing (Fig. 20) were used to ensure that this design meets the need of the light and the light is friendly to users' eyes.

Based on the market research, the common height of desk lamps are around 40 cm. According to the testing of illuminance with different heights, the need for illuminance and the market research, the height of the design was decided to be 440 cm. And to make the strong light gentler, the surface of the cover is rough, which can effectively prevent the straight light.

To conclude, the prototypes make sure that the design can gradually offer a gentle light when detecting the surroundings is dark. And the function of the nightlight was also proved to be feasible. Because of the limited time and materials, the application of the working principle of electromagnetic induction has no prototypes. However, because

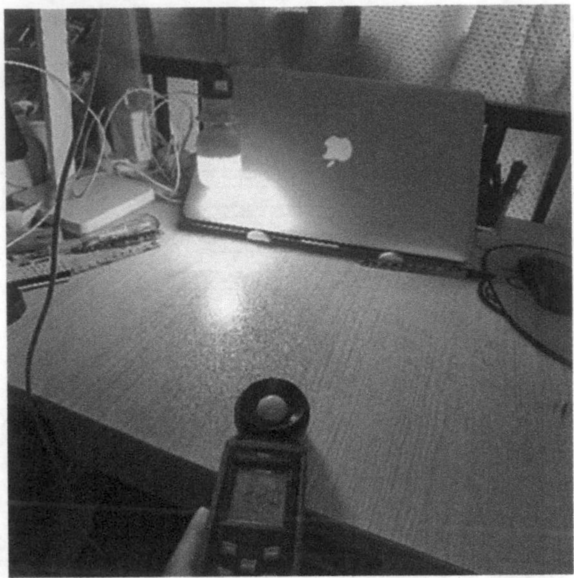

Fig. 20. Illuminance testing

electromagnetic induction has been applied to toothbrushes, clocks and transportation, which shows the feasibility of this technology.

Finalization of Product Design. Based on the feedback from doctors and caregivers, we developed 'LIGHT,' a smart lamp to offer light treatment intuitively. This lamp consists of two parts, the main light and night light, which are connected by using magnetic suction charging. The main light offers the light treatment in the morning and moves along the trail during the day to simulate the sun's movement. It also adjusts brightness according to the changes of the environment light condition (see Fig. 21). The night light offers comfortable dim light when detecting the patients waking up at midnight and sending a notification to the caregivers through an APP.

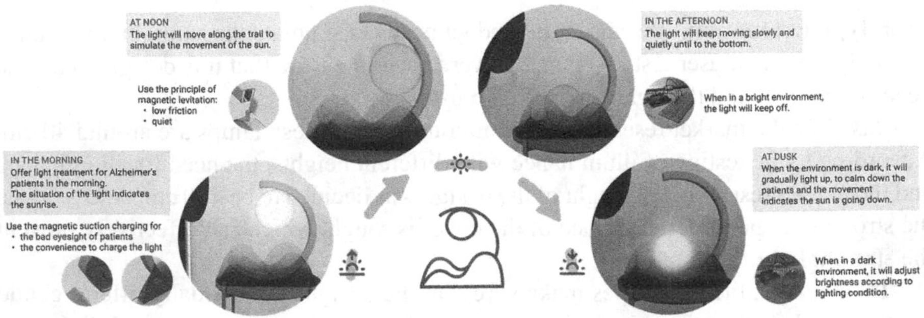

Fig. 21. Concept visualizations of the 'LIGHT'

For the design of the nightlight, through user research, target users are likely to spend their time in two places, so the nightlight is portable. The round shape uses the same design language as the big lamp. And Considering the bad eyesight of elderly people and the weak ability to grab objects the way to turn on/off the nightlight is sliding a big button with a rough surface. To make the difference between "ON" and "OFF", the bright orange and blue are used to show the situation of the switch (see Fig. 22).

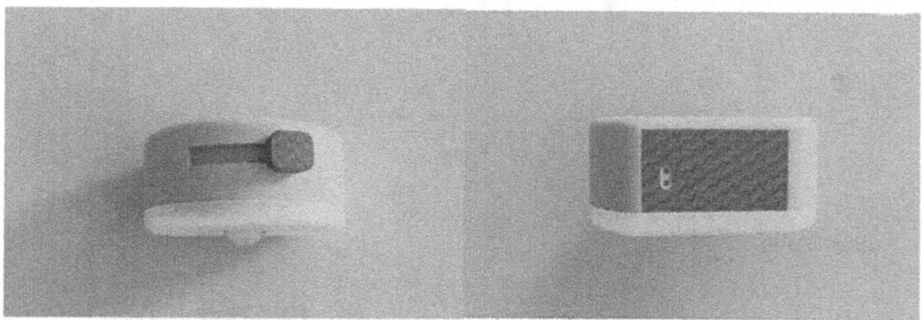

Fig. 22. The details of the night-light design

APP Design. Because the night-light can detect the patient's time in bed, it is designed to be connected to an APP to offer family caregivers notifications when detecting the patient is waking up and reports of patient's and caregiver's sleep quality.

To make the information architecture, the author ranked the information that caregivers want to see on the APP after interviewing 4 caregivers. Based on the feedback from caregivers, it was surprised to find that they also want to see their sleep quality. They find themselves lacking sleep because they need to take care of patients at night and work in the daytime. They also mentioned that if there would be a platform for them to discuss their issues or share their experiences with other caregivers, the APP might be more helpful. After talking with a doctor and 4 caregivers, the author iterated the information architecture (see Fig. 23) and designed five crucial user flows (see Fig. 24) to do the user testing (see Fig. 25).

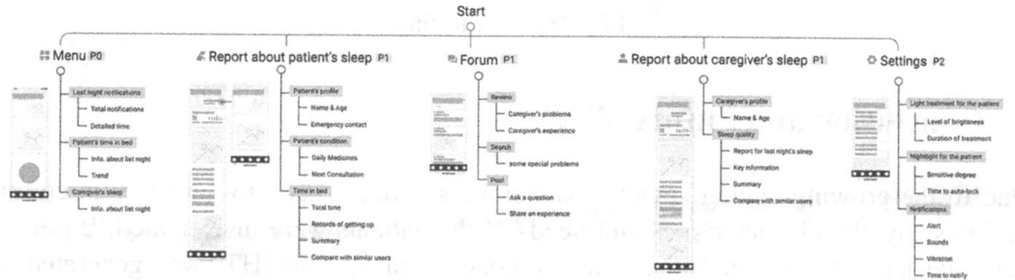

Fig. 23. The information architecture of the APP design

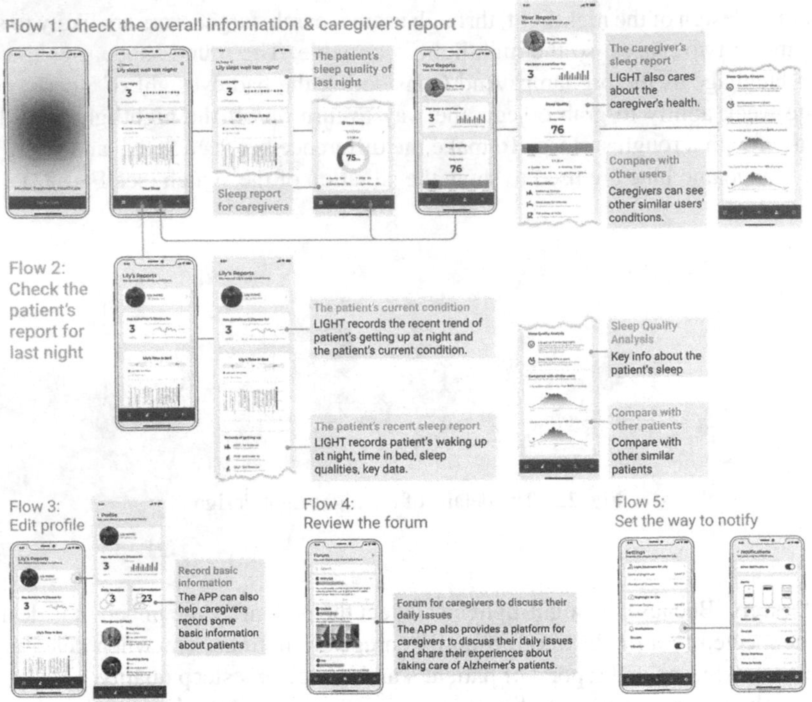

Fig. 24. The crucial user flow of the APP design

Fig. 25. User testing

7 Conclusion and Future Work

Due to the growing ageing society, Alzheimer's patients need to get more attention. In this study, the characteristics and needs of the patients were investigated. Based on the collected data and analysis, a design concept named 'LIGHT' was generated. A prototype of the 'LIGHT' using, 3D printing, laser cutting and Arduino techniques was built to gain insights from experts. Two neurologists and three industrial design experts were invited for the preliminary evaluation study. Based on their feedback, the shape and function of 'LIGHT' were reviewed and iterated. The early-stage study indicated that the smart lamp design could provide a promising solution for the sleep disturbances and sundown syndrome of Alzheimer's patients. However, though electromagnetic induction has been applied to many existing products, the feasibility and implementation of this technology need further experiment. In addition, the size of the design can be more personalized due to the different hobbies of patients and living environment.

References

1. Dowling, G.A., Hubbard, E.M., Mastick, J., Luxenberg, J.S., Burr, R.L., Van Someren, E.J.: Effect of morning bright light treatment for rest–activity disruption in institutionalized patients with severe Alzheimer's disease. Int. Psychogeriatrics/IPA **17**(2), 221 (2005)
2. Prince, M., Albanese, E., Guerchet, M., et al.: World Alzheimer Report 2014: Dementia and Risk Reduction an Analysis of Protective and Modifiable Factors (2014)
3. Zhang, Y., Li, Y., Ma, L.: Recent advances in research on Alzheimer's disease in China. J. Clin. Neurosci. **81**, 43–46 (2020)
4. UCLA Health: Caregiver Training Videos. https://www.uclahealth.org/dementia/caregiver-education-videos. Accessed 2 Nov 2021
5. McCurry, S.M., Reynolds, C.F., III., Ancoli-Israel, S., Teri, L., Vitiello, M.V.: Treatment of sleep disturbance in Alzheimer's disease. Sleep Med. Rev. **4**(6), 603–628 (2000)
6. Liu, S., et al.: Caregiver burden and prevalence of depression, anxiety and sleep disturbances in Alzheimer's disease caregivers in China. J. Clin. Nurs. **26**(9–10), 1291–1300 (2017)
7. Shiota, M.N.: Ekman's theory of basic emotions. In: Thousand Oaks, C.A. (ed.) The Sage encyclopedia of theory in psychology, pp. 248–250. Sage Publications (2016)
8. Figueiro, M.G., Hamner, R., Higgins, P., Hornick, T., Rea, M.S.: Field measurements of light exposures and circadian disruption in two populations of older adults. J. Alzheimers Dis. **31**(4), 711–715 (2012)
9. Peter-Derex, L., et al.: Sleep and Alzheimer's disease. Sleep Med. Rev. **19**, 29–38 (2014)
10. Khachiyants, N., Trinkle, D., Son, S.J., Kim, K.Y.: Sundown syndrome in persons with dementia: an update. Psychiatry Investig. **8**(4), 275 (2011)
11. Hanford, N., Figueiro, M.: Light therapy and Alzheimer's disease and related dementia: past, present, and future. J. Alzheimers Dis. **33**(4), 913–922 (2013)
12. Ancoli-Israel, S., Martin, J.L., Kripke, D.F., Marler, M., Klauber, M.R.: Effect of light treatment on sleep and circadian rhythms in demented nursing home patients. J. Am. Geriatr. Soc. **50**(2), 282–289 (2002)
13. Shikder, S., Mourshed, M., Price, A.: Therapeutic lighting design for the elderly: a review. Perspect. Public Health **132**(6), 282–291 (2012)
14. Fetveit, A., Skjerve, A., Bjorvatn, B.: Bright light treatment improves sleep in institutionalised elderly—an open trial. Int. J. Geriatr. Psychiatry **18**(6), 520–526 (2003)
15. Lee, Y.C., Chen, C.H., Lee, C.H.: Body anthropometric measurements of Singaporean adult and elderly population. Measurement **148**, 106949 (2019)
16. Song, M.K., Fujino, Y.: Dynamic analysis of guideway structures by considering ultra high-speed Maglev train-guideway interaction. Struct. Eng. Mech. **29**(4), 355–380 (2008)

System Design of Smart Banking Based on Service Design Thinking

Zhaorui Zhang[1], Xi Cheng[2], Shengtai Zhang[1], and Na Liu[1](✉)

[1] School of Economics and Management, Beijing University of Posts and Telecommunications, Beijing, China
{2021111487,liuna18}@bupt.edu.cn

[2] School of Digital Media and Design Arts, Beijing University of Posts and Telecommunications, Beijing, China

Abstract. Branches provide bank services and play an essential role in maintaining the normal operation of banks. Emerging technology impacts the design of branches. This study designed a smart banking system based on the systematic thinking of *Service Design*. The smart banking design reformed the smart branch space distribution, improved the business process, designed the self-service section, queuing section, and information-displaying section. In addition, this study adds the business-auxiliary section and evaluation-lottery section targeted at smart banking. The design plan can effectively improve customers' business experience in the smart branch, and provide a reference for the branch facing transformation. This study encourages the intelligent transformation of the traditional branch, and thus promotes the construction and development of "Smart City".

Keywords: Smart branch · Service system · Service design · Systematic thinking

1 Introduction

Bank is an important social tool to realize the coordinated development of the economy and society. As important supporters for banks to provide business services, branches have a complete business system and manual services, which play an important role in finance. The service in traditional branches is mainly manual, focusing on the standardization of business and the qualification of service facilities. However, with the change of people's lifestyle brought by the development of technology, people are looking forward to convenient, efficient, and intelligent business management mode. As a result, the service mode of traditional branches cannot fully meet the needs of customers, showing a series of problems such as long queuing time, low efficiency of business handling, and great pressure of staff. The smart service mode makes up for the deficiency of traditional service mode, relying on artificial intelligence, the Internet of Things, and other technologies. It not only satisfies the new requirements of costumers under the new social background but also reduces the working pressure of staff. At present, the traditional bank branch has entered the stage of smart transformation. The research of smart banking takes extensive attention. Banks began to focus on the construction of smart banking to retain offline users.

Q. Gao and J. Zhou (Eds.): HCII 2022, LNCS 13331, pp. 170–180, 2022.
https://doi.org/10.1007/978-3-031-05654-3_11

Smart banking is the advanced stage of traditional banking and e-banking. With the cohesion of products, services, and processes, it helps banks build a new generation of full-function and full-intelligent financial intelligent service systems through some innovative technology like Internet, big data, AI, and IoT. Smart branches provide financial services at anytime, anywhere, which satisfies or even exceeds customers' demands and creates the best experience [1, 2]. In recent years, branches have transformed from traditional counter mode to customer self-service mode mainly by adding intelligent devices. However, due to the lack of intelligence, the information architecture is complex, the interface is unfriendly, and the actual self-service handling has not been fully realized. It is limited in improving the efficiency and eliminating the working pressure of staff [3]. This "intelligence" is superficially, and the service orientation and business model of branches have not changed fundamentally. Some banks took the lead in building smart branches and started trial operations, but the feedback from customers was unexpected. In general, there are two problems in existing smart branches: (1) scattered intelligent services with few customers, lacking systematism; (2) the form is more like an exhibition, displaying but impractical.

Service design systematically solves problems and innovates by designing service touchpoints between service providers and recipients [4]. Service design focuses on customers' behaviors and situations and integrates key factors such as products, processes, and so on. The basic process is divided into seven steps: insight, definition, design, prototype, test, iteration, implementation. The bank has a huge organizational system. The business types are complex, involving a wide range of customer groups. Branches integrate business and services. Using service design to build the smart branches will help the traditional branches to better transform and fully satisfy the new needs of customers in the intelligent scenario.

Product-Service System (*PSS*) covers tangible products and intangible services. There are three key elements in the PSS: product (designing tangible products that are sold and satisfy the needs of customers); service (activities that provide economic benefit to others in the business); system (set of all related elements and relationships) [5]. System thinking considers a system by understanding each entity element in the system and the relationship and interaction between each element. Branches are equipped with business products, hardware, information, interpersonal interaction, and other elements of the service system. Using PSS and system thinking to analyze each element as a whole can guarantee the integrity of the branch and improve the service comprehensively.

Based on the systematic thinking of service design, this study focuses on services in smart branches and aims to design an integrated product-service system of smart branches that enables customers to complete business transactions clearly, efficiently and joyfully. Through preliminary investigation and analysis, the research summarized the pain points and expectations of service providers and service recipients. And then, the study designed the smart branches from three aspects: space distribution, business process, and part of products. Finally, this study shows the smart branch of an overall 3D model. Specifically. This study focuses on five areas involving *the Business-Auxiliary Area, Leisure-Entertainment Area_(queueing section), Self-Service Area, Information-Displaying Area, and Evaluation-Lottery Area* in the smart branch. A comprehensive smart coffee table that can be used for leisure and entertainment is designed to reduce the customer's perception of waiting time. In addition, this study added the evaluation-lottery section, and developed the queue number bar, aiming to enrich customers' processing journey and obtain effective feedback to provide references for future improvement of the smart branch. The results of this study provide a case reference for the transformation from traditional branch to smart branch and promote the intelligent transformation of traditional banking, thus promoting the development of the smart city.

2 What Kind of Smart Branch Should Be Designed?

User-centered is the basic requirement of service design [6]. First, this study conducted multi-layered customer research.

2.1 Customer Research

This study selected four nearby traditional bank branches for field observation research. The spatial layout of traditional branches is mainly divided into *Advisory Area, Counter Management Area, Customer Waiting Area, Self-Service Area, Electronic Banking Area, Financial Services Area, VIP Center,* and *Officing area.* The main process of customer business is service classification, number pick-up, queuing, waiting, business processing. The field observation found three major problems for traditional branches, namely serious queuing, unfriendly service facilities, and inefficient bank information displaying.

To further understand customers' opinions, this study performed an online questionnaire survey. People with bank accounts were selected, including students (n = 134), office workers (n = 55), freelancers (n = 7), retired workers (n = 2), and other occupations (n = 3). A total of 216 questionnaires were distributed and 201 valid answers were collected. 79.85% of the customers said that the long queuing time is a serious problem for the bank branch. A lot of customers hoped that the business management could be more convenient and reduce the waiting time in line. If the queuing is inevitable, people expect to get feedback on the queue situation, know in advance that how many people there are in front of them and have a certain estimate of their queue time; second, they hope to open more counters to refine the needs of customers so as to reduce the queuing time. In addition, some participants hope to strengthen the addition of auxiliary facilities as much as possible. And some hope that branches can provide personalized services.

Finally, this study performed a small-scale customer interview. The questions in this interview mainly involve customers' experiences in dealing with business in the branches, problems related to queuing and their expectations for dealing with business in the future. Eight interviewees were interviewed, including six customers (service recipients) who had been to branches for business and two staff of banks (service providers). In the interview, customers showed their acceptance and expectation of intelligent services. The bank staff expressed that they had work pressure due to marketing tasks and social pressure in daily communication with customers. In the previous questionnaire survey, some participants also reported that they would be distressed because of financial products being recommended when they handle business at the branches. It can be seen that the improper promotion of financial products has caused pressure to both service recipients and service providers.

In summary, the main findings of the customer research on traditional bank branches are as follows:

(1) Long waiting time in queues.
(2) Unfriendly service facilities.
(3) Poor promotion effect of information and financial products.
(4) Low usage of intelligent service.

2.2 Design Objectives

The design objective of the current study are as follows:

(1) *Redesign space distribution.* The rational distribution of space can improve the environment of the whole branch, and enhance customers' service experience. The study aimed to rearrange *the Self-Service Area, Business Auxiliary Area, Advisory Area, Financial Services Area and Customer Waiting Area.*
(2) *Fit the business and enrich the process.* A rich business process can give customers a pleasant experience and enhance the competitiveness of banks in the industry. This study decided to optimize the business management process. Attention should be taken to the design to fit the business processing process.
(3) *Develop key products.* Service design is mainly carried out by designing *Service Touchpoints* in the system. Service touchpoints are the points where service parties substantially interact, including interpersonal touchpoints, physical touchpoints, and information touchpoints. Products, as physical touchpoints in the service system, have an important role in influencing the overall service experience of customers. This study plans to select several key products to design.

3 Systematic Design of Service System for Smart Bank Branches

According to the field survey of traditional branches, the main functional areas in the branches include the Advisory Area, Counter Management Area, Customer Waiting Area, Self-Service Area, Electronic Banking Area, Financial Services Area, VIP Center, and Officing Area. Due to the professionalism and complexity of banking business, this study mainly focuses on the design of additional services of smart branches. Therefore, the study retains the basic areas of the traditional branch and adds the Business-Auxiliary Area, Evaluation-Lottery Area, and Information-Display Area based on the preliminary research.

Finally, the main areas of the smart branch designed in this study include *Advisory Area* (Entrance), *Business-Auxiliary Area, Self-Service Area, Leisure-Entertainment Area, Electronic Banking Area, Countering Area, Financial Service Area, VIP Center, Evaluation-Lottery Area,* and *Information-Displaying Area* (combined with Exit). Depending on the branch space area, this study systematically optimizes the business processing and draws the service blueprint (Fig. 1). The main steps of customers from entering the branch to leaving are welcoming (Q&A diversion), preparation, leisure (queuing), business management, service evaluation, and information acquisition. The main touchpoints between customers and the branch service system include staff, queuing number bar, forms, auxiliary tools, leisure service facilities, intelligent device, lottery machine and information interaction screen. The systems supporting the service of the whole smart branch are the Ranking System, Auxiliary System, Information Management System, Business System, and Lottery System.

The following is the description of key areas for design:

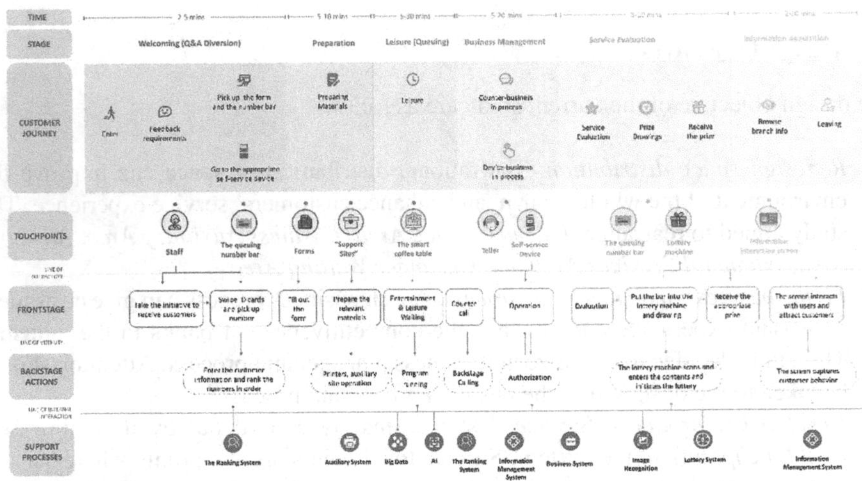

Fig. 1. The service blueprint

3.1 Business-Auxiliary Area

The provision of business auxiliary services can greatly facilitate customers. This area provides customers with office equipment such as printers, copiers, shredders, and also sets up "Support Sites". This machine is similar to a locker, with some assistive tools placed in the compartment (Fig. 2). Customers can click on the small screen on the cabinet to select, swipe the ID card to get the tools. After use, customers need to return to the corresponding compartment of the cabinet. The filling desk and consultation desk were combined and placed in the Business-Auxiliary Area to reduce the work pressure of lobby managers. The effect of this area is shown in Fig. 3.

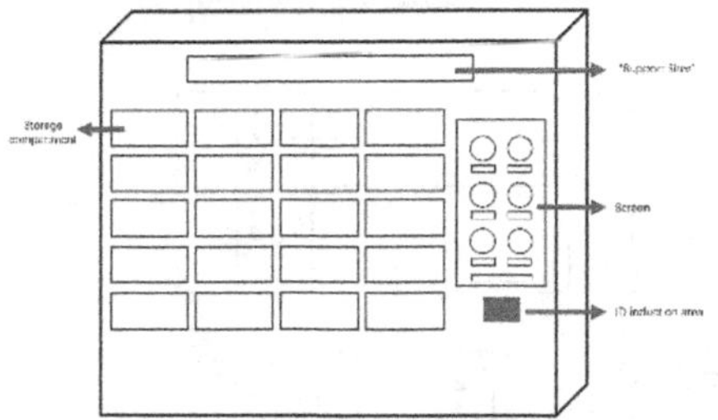

Fig. 2. Support Sites

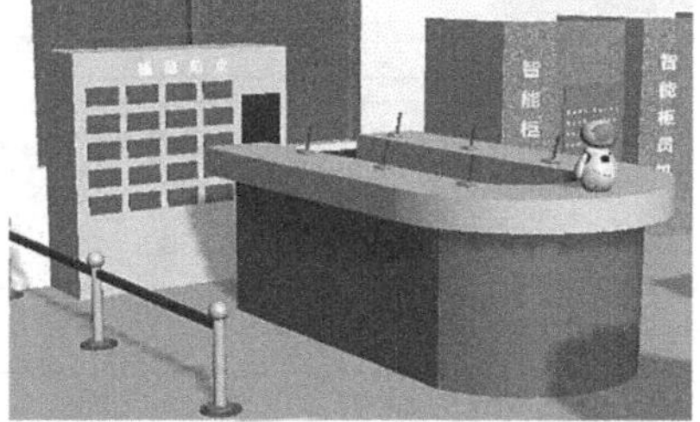

Fig. 3. Business-Auxiliary Area

3.2 Leisure-entertainment Area

At the present stage, the service facilities in the customer waiting area are conventional, monotonous, and boring. The existing smart branches set various seats in the waiting area, and add leisure and entertainment facilities such as health experience machines and game interactive screens. But the effect is not satisfactory. The main reason is that the function distribution is too scattered and lacks systematicness.

Donald A. Norman mentions: in addition to the most basic fairness, (1) uncertainty and anxiety should be eliminated when queueing; (2) meet or even exceed customers' expectations, give the expected length of the queue, which is usually higher than the actual waiting time; (3) keep customers busy and reduce their perceived waiting time; (4) start and end on a positive note [8]. In this study, the Customer Waiting Area is designed as *the Leisure-Entertainment Area*, customers can have some leisure and entertainment activities while waiting, so as to reduce the perceived waiting time to improve the experience. A comprehensive smart coffee table is designed to improve the scattered distribution with three main functions: (1) Providing drinking water at two temperatures by the two storage bins on both sides of the coffee table. Customers can open or close the storage bins to take water by touching the sensing areas on the side (Fig. 4). The two side storage bins are supported by lifting rod support, both can be lifted independently. (2) Providing power supply to charge mobile devices by sliding power track; (3) setting leisure and entertainment items around the smart table screen, which includes financial recommendation, announcement information, queuing process, peak prompt, some entertainment items (games, shopping, reading). The screen can be tilted to facilitate customer operation and browsing. Tap the screen anywhere with knuckles twice to activate the screen tilt (Fig. 5). Based on the needs of financial recommendation, shopping and other functions, cameras are provided on both sides to Face Recognition in certification. The dimensions of the comprehensive smart coffee table are shown in Fig. 6.

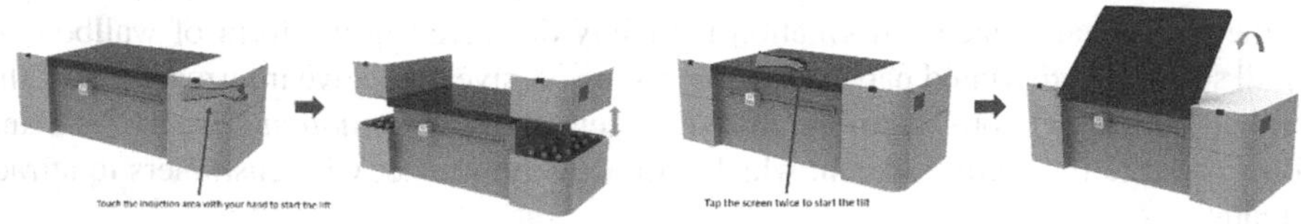

Fig. 4. Switching water storage bins

Fig. 5. Screen tilting

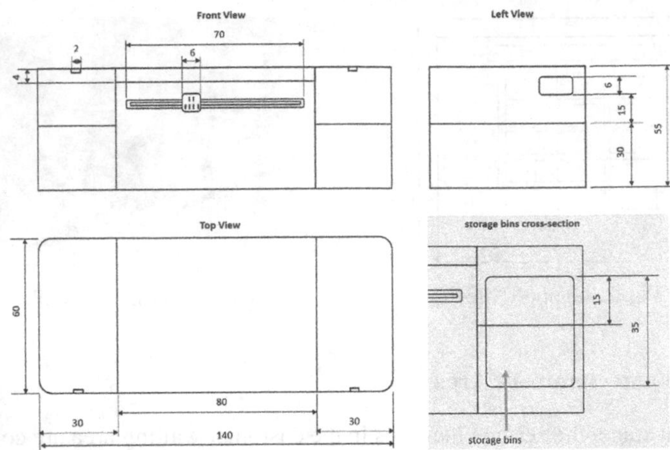

Fig. 6. The comprehensive smart coffee table three views (unit: centimeters)

3.3 Self-service Area

Since the design of self-service devices depends on the professional banking business, this study mainly carries out regional design for the Self-Service Area. Customers' privacy and information security are involved when operating the intelligent device, the study sets partitions for each intelligent self-service device to separate semi-private spaces (Fig. 7). At the same time, aiming at the problem that there are various types of devices and customers are not clear about the scope of each device, the names and the business scope of each machine are displayed on the partition board. The effect of the Self-Service Area is shown in Fig. 8.

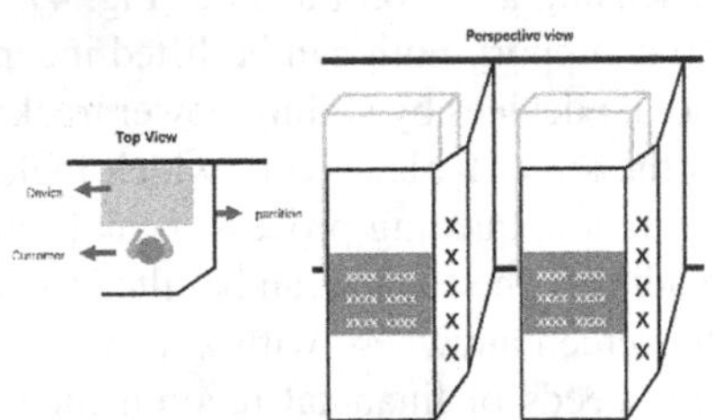

Fig. 7. Partition

Fig. 8. Self-Service Area

3.4 Information-Displaying Area

In the traditional branch, information is mainly displayed in the form of wallboards, small screens, and printed papers. Customers are passive to receive information, and the publicity effect is poor. Therefore, this study sets up *the Information-Display Area* and adopts a large interactive screen, which will actively interact with customers to attract attention.

The information to be displayed in the smart branch includes publicity information, recommendation information and notification information. *Publicity information*, including bank brand and image, is mainly aimed at showing and popularizing, so it can be displayed scrolling through two interactive screens in the Leisure-Entertainment Area and the exit. *Recommendation information*, including part of the marketing tasks of the staff, is displayed on the two interactive screens on the one hand. On the other hand, as a leisure project, the smart coffee table is used to recommend customers when they are waiting to improve the purchase rate of products. *Notification information* is about some recent matters about banks needing attention, which may generally have an impact on customers' business management. Customers need to be informed earlier in the whole process, so this type of information is mainly displayed on the screen in the Leisure-Entertainment Area.

3.5 Evaluation-Lottery Area

Donald A. Norman, in *Living with Complexity* [8], refers to the "Serial Position Effect": when everything is relatively consistent, feelings in memory rank in order of importance as end > beginning > intermediate. If some pleasant elements are added at the end of the process, even though the whole process is still unpleasant, the user's overall experience of the process will even become more positive [8]. Based on this theory, this study relies on the queuing number bar to set up an evaluation-lottery section at the end of the bank business process. Customers can take a prize by evaluating the service in the queue number bar, which can not only enrich customers' business journey but also enable the branch to obtain effective service feedback from customers. Therefore, this study set up the Evaluation-Lottery Area close to the exit in the smart branch. The area is composed of two lottery machines. The combination of service evaluation and queuing number bar can make effective use of the queuing number bar.

In traditional branches, the queuing number bar is simple in form, which only contains the bank name, the customer's queuing number, and warm tips. Its function is limited to maintaining the order of queuing. After completing the business, customers generally throw it away unconcernedly. However, the number bar is the item that the customer will always carry and keep before handling the business, so it has great use-value. Therefore, in addition to combining it with service evaluation, the number bar can also be used for product promotion. The form of the number bar is based on tickets. On the front side, product advertising is placed on the left side, and queuing information is placed on the right side. Queuing information includes the queue number, number of people waiting, the number taking time, and warm tips. The service evaluation content is set on the back, customers can score various aspects of the branch service. Set the barcode on the top, the lottery machine will scan this barcode to identify the customer information and automatically enter the evaluation content. When entering the smart branch, the lobby manager will swipe the customer's ID card to get the queue number bar, so each customer has a bar code corresponding to his identity to ensure that the evaluation content matches with the evaluator (Fig. 9).

In addition, a simple design of the lottery machine was carried out, and its appearance was similar to that of Autonomous Vending Machines (see Fig. 10). When evaluators fill in the queue number bar with the evaluation, the lottery machine will input the content by the barcode and start drawing. The prize will pop out from under the machine.

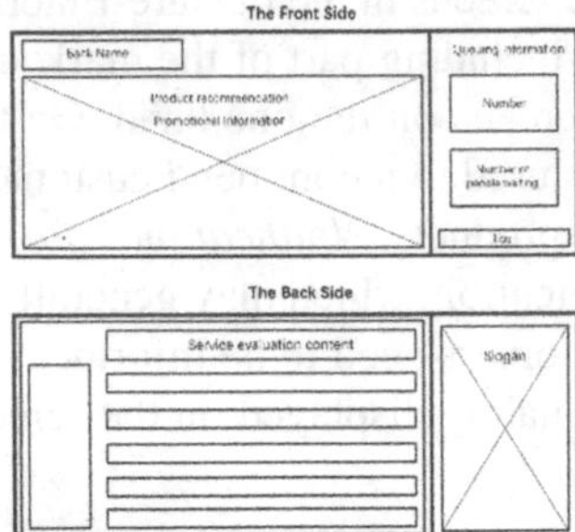

Fig. 9. The queuing number bar

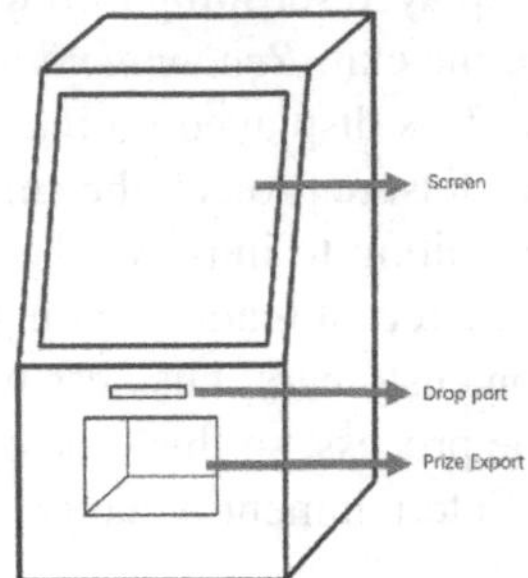

Fig. 10. The lottery machine

The software Autodesk 3dMax2016 is finally used to conduct 3D modeling for the designed smart branch, and the overall effect is shown in Fig. 11.

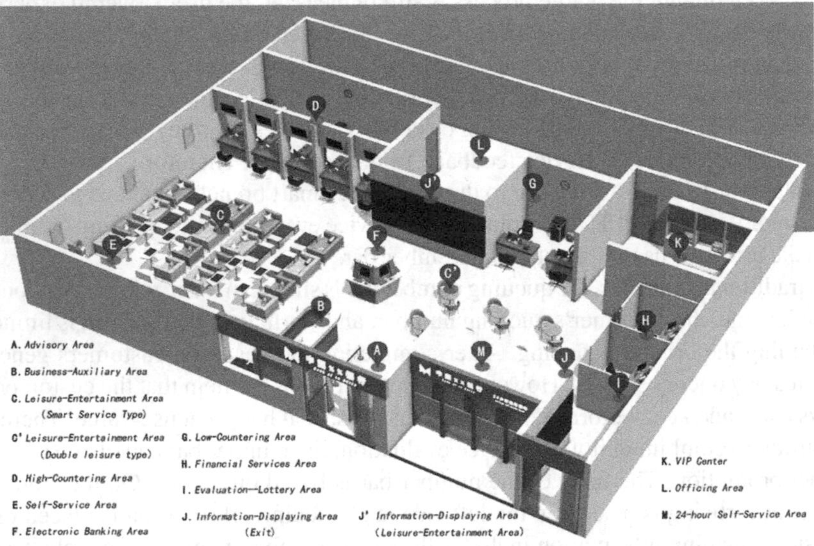

Fig. 11. The overall effect of the smart branch (3D model)

4 Discussion

Based on the systematic thinking of service design, this study analyzes the stakeholders of the smart branch, focuses on the needs and expectations of both service recipients and service providers, and designs the service system of the smart branch from three aspects: space distribution, business process optimization, and products design. The final result of this study is a 3D model of the smart branch that can effectively enhance the customer experience.

In the intelligent scenario, convenience and efficiency are the basic requirements of smart devices. Customers further expect a better service experience. Therefore, it is necessary to put customer experience in the first place in the construction of a smart branch. In the context of big data, customers' behavioral data is easier to collect, but customers' private data is also exposed to the risk [9]. Information insecurity incidents have been common. In the smart bank branch, although the bank itself is a security organization psychologically, many people still have doubts about the intelligent self-service device. Funds are the part that people are highly concerned about. Consequently, the protection of customers' funds and information security is an important topic in the construction of smart branches. In the customer survey conducted in this study, some participants indicated that they were more inclined to go to manual counters compared with self-service devices. On the one hand, the business is complex, they don't operate on the intelligent machine, on the other hand, they feel that the teller will be safer and more assured. This phenomenon is particularly notable among the elderly, who are very concerned about the security of their funds and often prefer to handle their business at manual counters. Even some elderly people will show extreme distrust of self-service machines, and although the staff says they will assist them, the elderly will still refuse. Therefore, the manual counter should be retained in the smart branch. Bank staff can guide elderly customers to experience smart devices to improve their trust in intelligent business processing.

Compared with young people, older adults' cognitive ability has declined, and their acceptance of intelligence is generally low. The elderly will encounter more difficulties in operating smart devices. Therefore, when building smart branches, there should be dedicated staff to provide timely assistance to the elderly. In addition, banks should simplify the operation interface of smart devices, set the elderly mode as much as possible, and provide clear operating guidelines. The elderly generally has a more fixed source of funds (social security payments, retirement wages, etc.), the time to visit the branch is more regular. At the same time, the elderly usually has more time and will accept waiting. In this regard, the smart branch can set up the "green channel" for the elderly and open a special service area during a certain period of time. Smart bank branches can build caring service stations for the elderly in the Leisure-Entertainment Area by using intelligent technologies.

At the present stage, intelligent self-service devices in branches are directly placed in the hall, and there is no independent business handling space. Considering the particularity of banks, in order to ensure safety in banks, branches should not set up completely closed spaces for customers. Although t this study only aims at the additional services in the branch, the construction of the security environment in the branch is also considered in the physical layer. For example, the partition board of the Self-Service Area is set up to construct a semi-private space, which not only ensures the security of the bank environment but also ensures the security of the customer's information.

In this study, there is no in-depth design for areas involving specific businesses, such as the High or Low Countering Area, Financial Service Area, Intelligent Self-Service Machine, and the related processes are not optimized. Therefore, the final results of this study can only provide a reference for the design of additional services in the transition from traditional branch to smart branch. In the future, it is necessary to systematically improve the overall business system of banks. In addition, this study did not make focused exploration of related technologies, such as Artificial Intelligence and Internet of Things, and did not set too many application scenarios in this study, but reserved design space for these technologies. The lack of in-depth study of the elderly as a special group has also limited the construction of this smart branch. Nevertheless, the results of this study have important implications. (1) The results are based on real customer data, which can effectively improve the business processing experience. (2) it is conducive to maintaining the competitiveness of banks and getting better development in the new era. (3) It can also provide a pleasant working environment for branch staff, reduce work pressure and increase their enthusiasm. (4) It can also provide a reference for branches that are transforming, and the study promotes the smart change of traditional branches, thus promoting the development of smart cities.

Acknowledgements. This work was supported by grants from Natural Science Foundation of China (Project No. 71901033).

References

1. Tianchi Rongsheng Intelligent Financial: The six state-owned banks' intelligent outlets are gorgeous and stunning times [Online e-bulletin] (2019). https://baijiahao.baidu.com/s?id=1625783347299188715&wfr=spider&for=pc
2. Yuxiang. L.: Research on China construction bank smarter banking development strategy. Hunan University (2016)
3. Xiaoke, R., Jie, H.: Exploring the wisdom transformation path of commercial bank branches: based on the practical perspective of grassroots banks. China Bank. **12**, 60–62 (2020)
4. Qiang, Y., Yizi, C.:: Research on the design of campus catering unmanned delivery system based on service design. Ind. Des. **2**, 26–27 (2021)
5. Xi, C.: Review of research on product service system and service design, J. Beijing Univ. Posts Telecommun. (Social Sciences Edition). **22**(05), 61–73 (2020)
6. Editorial board of design: user experience design. Design **34**(03), 7 (2021)
7. Chengxiang, Y., Mingchen, C., Cheng. Z.: Research on the design of bank space based on service concept, West. Leather **42**(04), 76–77 (2020)
8. Norman, D.A.: Living with Complexity. MIT Press. Cambridge (2010). ISBN: 978-0262014861
9. Ruxia, H.: Research on Internet user behavior under the background of big data. Inf. Comput. (Theory Edition), **32**(04), 155–157 (2020)

Health and Wellbeing Technologies for the Elderly

Exploration and Practice of Service Design Intervention for the Elderly with Mild Cognitive Impairment

Xiatong Chen and Zhang Zhang(✉)

East China University of Science and Technology, Shanghai 200237, People's Republic of China
15618746761@qq.com

Abstract. To serve the elderly population with mild cognitive impairment, this study applied a service design approach to enhance the friendliness and effectiveness of training activities in cognitive intervention service organizations, practicing four processes of exploration, definition, development, and implementation. Based on the desktop study, a field visit was made to the Shanghai cognitive disorder charity for in-depth research. To understand the agency's profile and analyze its environment, a semi-structured interview was conducted to derive a user profile and preliminary pain point needs of elderly with mild cognitive impairment. The user journey was mapped through non-participant observation to summarize the hierarchy of advanced needs, define key issues, and guide the design practice. The final output is a service system map, service blueprint and product contact point wall module design for cognitive intervention organizations in implementing training activities, and summarizes the service design strategies for mild cognitive impairment in terms of environmental and physical contact content, stakeholder services and emotional care to explore more possibilities for design interventions in mild cognitive impairment training interventions.

Keywords: Service design · Mild cognitive impairment · Alzheimer's disease (AD) · Cognitive intervention · Design for the elderly

1 Introduction

The World Alzheimer's Disease Report released by the International Alzheimer's Association (ADI) in 2018 shows that the number of people with dementia (Dementia) worldwide is about 50 million, and according to the World Health Organization (WHO), the number of patients is expected to reach 152 million in 30 years [1]. China accounts for a quarter of these patients, and is the country with the largest number of patients [2]. Along with the trend of deep aging of China's population and the increased pressure of life, work and health of the younger generation [3], the prevalence of dementia is increasing significantly with age on the one hand, and the trend of younger people suffering from dementia is also on the rise.

According to global statistics, one person develops the disease every three seconds. In the face of this major chronic disease, which is the only disease that cannot be cured

Q. Gao and J. Zhou (Eds.): HCII 2022, LNCS 13331, pp. 183–196, 2022.
https://doi.org/10.1007/978-3-031-05654-3_12

and is the fifth leading cause of death in the world [4], society has a long way to go in understanding and preventing Cognitive Disorder (CD), the most serious manifestation of Alzheimer's Disease (AD). Early screening and assessment and preventive interventions for high-risk groups are the best means to control and delay the onset of the disease. Among the seven stages of cognitive impairment proposed by Dr. Barry Reisberg et al. [5], Mild Cognitive Impairment (MCI) and previous stages, i.e., pre-dementia, are the most valuable interventions [6], and cognitive intervention training for MCI patients can largely reduce the probability of conversion to AD [7].

In its World Alzheimer's Report 2020, ADI emphasized design as a crucial non-pharmacological intervention [8], and looked at design cases in architecture and environment, also pointed out that cognitive impairment design lags behind physical impairment design by 30 years, and called for social change. At the same time, domestic and international research in the field of design has been conducted on the topic of cognitive impairment care, especially overseas has made many useful practices on the use of participatory design methods in the pre-design stage [9], however, there is less research on service design for cognitive intervention activities in the MCI stage.

2 Research Background and Methodology

2.1 Current Status of Mild Cognitive Impairment and Cognitive Intervention

Cognitive impairment is a collective term for symptoms of impairment of cognitive functions such as perception, memory, thinking or reasoning due to localized tissue lesions or damage to the brain, and there are no uniform criteria for patients' symptoms, triggers, therapies and development. The vast majority of cognitive disorders typified by AD are irreversible progressive brain disorders that progressively disrupt memory and thinking abilities, resulting in a decrease or even loss of the patient's ability to perform actions of daily living. Mild cognitive impairment belongs to the high-risk group of Alzheimer's disease, which has not yet developed abnormal effects, but has shown some degree of detectable cognitive decline. Research statistics show that the annual conversion rate of MCI patients developing AD is about 7.5 to 10 times higher than that of normal people [10].

According to the scholars' combing of existing domestic and international research findings on non-pharmacological interventions for MCI, interventions such as reaching a certain intensity of aerobic exercise, multi-domain combined cognitive function training, diet and emotional psychotherapy can produce significant improvements [11–13]. Specific cognitive training methods include language, memory, computation, perceptual attention, time, and orientation [14]. The common recommendation of research scholars for future cognitive intervention training is to tailor systematic and individualized intervention programs based on different states and performance of patients with MCI through in-depth and detailed observation, interview and continuous evaluation of the training process, forming assessment-oriented training approaches and levels, and then judging the match between the programs and patients during the training process, so as to continuously update more suitable The interventions are then judged to be a good match for the patient during the training process, so that more appropriate interventions can be updated.

2.2 Feasibility and Positive Implications of Service Design Interventions for MCI Cognition

With the increased attention of the state and society, international experience has been gradually introduced across the country to establish cognitive disorder-related services in community-based nodes, which provides a very favorable basis for service design interventions for mild cognitive impairment.

Using the service design approach, the design process can be made more comprehensive and ultimately more friendly and effective by focusing on the elderly MCI patients, taking into account the experience of the organizations and other stakeholders and the overall environment of the service, researching the needs in real-life scenarios, discussing with the service providers and service recipients, and systematically planning and designing tangible products and intangible services during the process, iterating until implementation. For example, Taiwan's social design platform 5% Design Action uses design thinking as a tool to solve social problems and drive social innovation through design interventions. In its "Positive Aging" project, it uses the strategy of "design activism" to enable designers to communicate with senior citizens, communities and other stakeholders to create solutions [15].

A cognitive disorder charity in Shanghai is a 4A-level social organization focusing on brain health education and risk management, and is committed to the "2030 Brain Health Plan" in 2020, building a three-level (prevention, intervention and care) service system for cognitive disorders in the community and promoting a full service model and project-based management. In this study, we conducted research and practice on the service design of this public service organization as an example.

2.3 MCI Cognitive Intervention Activity Service Design Research Process

Service design is an approach that helps organizations review services from the customer's perspective, using research and visualization design tools to reshape problem thinking and propose appropriate solutions to meet stakeholder needs. The process of service design is based on the double diamond model, which contains four stages: exploration, definition, development and implementation [16]. And the specific type of double diamond process used is determined by the focused goals of the project, including four different focuses on constructing the problem, solving the problem, functionality and usability, and aesthetics [17]. This study focuses on the real problems that exist in the MCI cognitive intervention activities, and therefore focuses on the exploration and definition phases.

The research starts from the topics of "inclusive design" and "design for aging", and narrows down the topics to cognitive barriers through background research.

In the exploratory research phase, firstly, a systematic literature study on cognitive impairment was done to confirm the importance of design in the MCI stage and the existing non-pharmacological treatment solutions; secondly, field research was conducted in public welfare organizations to understand the organization and its environment profile, focus on MCI activity service scenarios, conduct semi-structured interviews with the organization, users and other stakeholders to derive user profiles and preliminary needs, and through non-participatory observation of activity scenarios to derive user journey maps and advanced needs. The user journey map and advanced needs were derived from non-participatory observation of the activity scenarios, and finally the hierarchy of needs was summarized.

In the definition and integration phase, key issues are identified based on the research results.

Service design and interior space product design practice in the conceptualization phase of development. Produce service systems and service blueprints focusing on "MCI cognitive intervention" scenarios, as well as wall module designs for demand-driven service scenarios.

During the delivery implementation phase, the prototype is designed to obtain user and institutional feedback, validate the requirements hierarchy, and iterate accordingly. The process is iteratively optimized in the actual landing output, which will be implemented in subsequent studies, leading to the final design results (see Fig. 1).

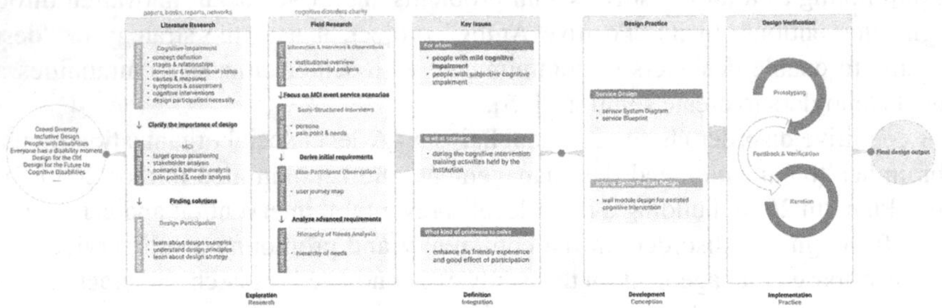

Fig. 1. MCI cognitive intervention activity service design research process and methodological framework

3 Research Exploration and Integration Definition - Focus on Scenarios and Needs

3.1 Institutional Overview

The study targeted the second level of the institutional service system, the intervention module, by visiting the elderly body-brain activation center in the cognitive-friendly community program, observing and interviewing the participants of the program's body-brain activation course activities while inviting them to participate in the discussion of needs and design opinions together. The participants included 14 elderly people with MCI/SCI (subjective cognitive impairment) (aged 66–84, 10 females and 4 males), 2 institutional program managers, 1 brain-body activation and emotional counselor, 2 trainees, 2 social workers, and 2 volunteers.

The facility is located in a service center at the entrance of the community, with meal service points and day care centers nearby, and the interior of the facility is designed in a warm "living room at home" style. The main activity area is heated, so there are physical activities touching the ground in winter to ensure a clean environment. To the left of the entrance is the front office area with a seat to observe the whole interior; to the right is the living room sofa area; to the left of the center is the kitchen, equipped with Mediterranean diet therapy, and the activity time is used as an observation area; to the right is the largest area, the main activity area; to the upper left is the office area and temporary storage area, and the innermost is a meditation room (see Fig. 2).

The main activity area as the target scene, due to the overall environment is not spacious, during and after the activity period, often according to the need to maneuver to configure tables and chairs or vacate the site, when switching institutional staff and the elderly will take the initiative to help carry, resulting in a certain degree of crowding inconvenience and safety risks.

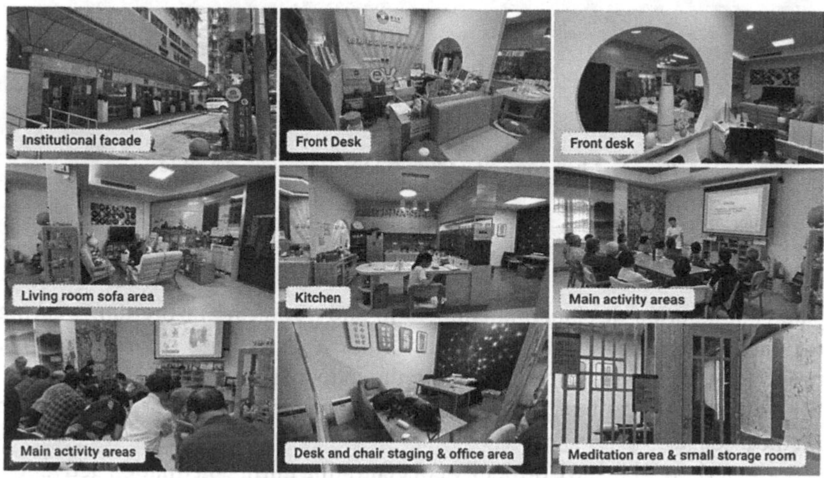

Fig. 2. Institutional environment

3.2 User Research in Activity Scenarios

After combing one-on-one interviews with the elderly and preliminary literature research, a typical user profile of MCI seniors was derived. The physiological status was some stumbling of speech, some slow reaction and movement, in retirement status, living in a community near the institution, and core demands were training intervention and companionship socialization (Fig. 3).

A research-based, product-oriented, and detailed user journey map of the service process of cognitive training activities was developed based on user characteristics and through non-participant observation. The content of the institutional training activities was divided into two parts, namely, homework intervention and somatic brain activation. The homework intervention included Boone guitar music therapy, cognitive games (e.g., "you tell me, I guess", associative memory, Schulte table, reading words and saying colors, etc.) therapy; the somatic brain activation was based on motor exercises assisted by apparatus such as Dantian ring, elastic rope, and induction ball.

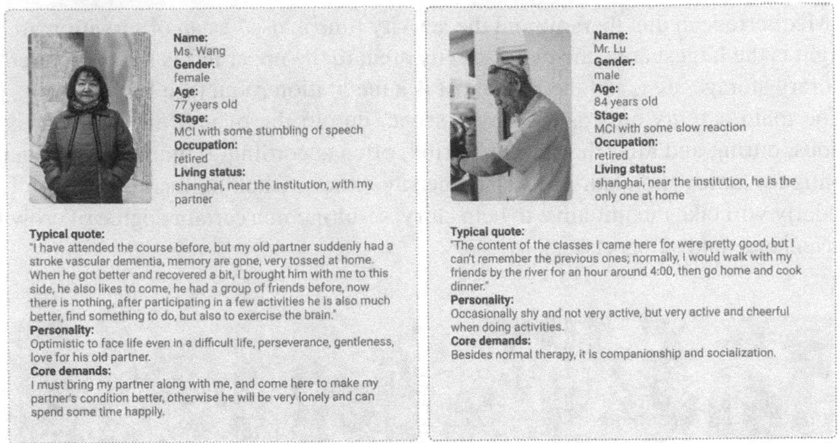

Fig. 3. Mild cognitive impairment elderly user profile

The problems and needs reflected are: (see Fig. 4)

1. The contradiction of changing slippers in and out of the institution, wearing the original shoes when exercising did not achieve the purpose of neatness, can be prepared for the elderly sports shoes in the indoor special.
2. Slight psychological burden when measuring blood pressure, need to weaken the medical sense.
3. Some elderly people have difficulty concentrating during meditation activation and need to improve the sustained attraction of the activity.
4. Some restraint in completing single person tasks for homework intervention, training needs to be more targeted and pay attention to the self-esteem of the elderly.
5. The frequency of the same activity in a course is low, which affects the effectiveness of training, and the content and frequency of activities can be adjusted through observation and feedback.
6. Carry items placed in space is variable, need to move in the middle, can set a fixed storage space.
7. Moving tables and chairs during the event causes crowding and potential hazards and can be avoided or made more spacious.
8. The scale interview needs to pay attention to the words, try to keep the elderly relaxed and happy in a chatty way, and hide the form of recording.
9. Social participation needs, more activities can be created for the elderly to participate together.
10. Older people's rejection of cognitive disorders and lack of confidence in the effectiveness of activities, the need to improve persuasion and emotional care, timely communication and guidance to service providers.
11. Post-activity continuity is weak, social attention needs to be enhanced, and the institution tries to maintain long-term case visits and training services.

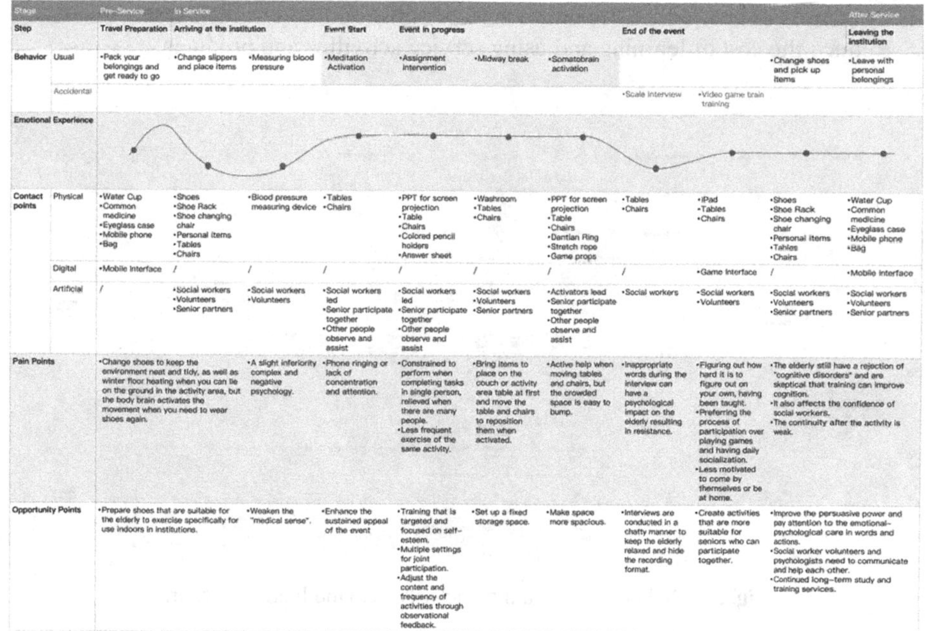

Fig. 4. Cognitive training course activity user journey map

3.3 Hierarchy of Needs

Comprehensive literature research section of MCI cognitive training and senior product needs [18–20], universal design requirements [21], and field research results, including interviews with stakeholders for service enhancement co-creation, with key issues as the target layer to derive the hierarchy of needs [22]. The sub-criteria layer of user needs is divided into user and institutional needs, and the sub-criteria layer of user needs is divided into physiological, safety, social, respect, cognitive, aesthetic and self-actualization needs using Maslow's hierarchy of needs as a framework [23]; the sub-criteria layer of institutional needs is divided into promotion and service needs, and the sub-criteria layer corresponds to the corresponding solution layer. The product and service needs are thus summarized, and provisions are made for the size, material, shape, color, vocalization, functional ease of use, fair and flexible use, methodological science, safety, cooperative completion, autonomy, no right and wrong criteria as much as possible, beauty, accomplishment and portability of the training products.

The improvement strategies for the service are: (see Fig. 5)

1. Moderate length of training.
2. Training methods and effects vary from person to person.
3. Promote trust and persuasion.
4. A sense of surprise and attraction.
5. Increasing the number of people and their effectiveness.
6. Continuity of service.

7. Content is as comprehensive and rich as possible, tailored to each case.
8. Reduce the cost of learning and using service activities and products.

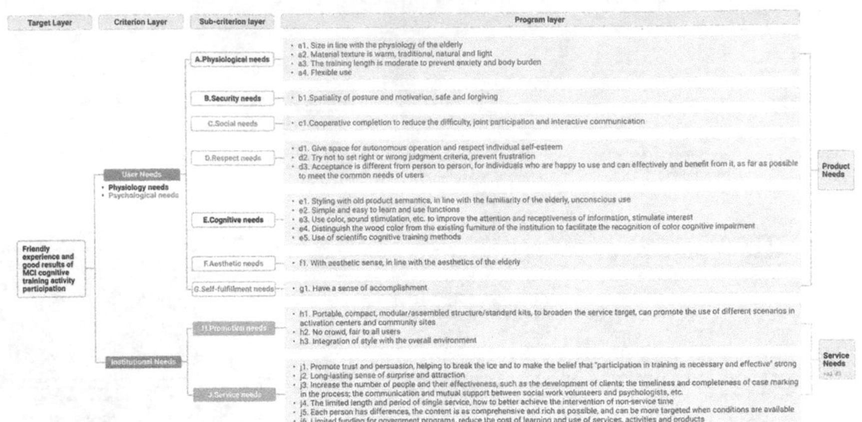

Fig. 5. MCI cognitive training activity demand hierarchy chart

3.4 Defining Key Issues

In summary, the problem and the goal of the solution were identified as "to design a friendly experience and good results for elderly people with mild cognitive impairment to participate in cognitive intervention training activities". In the process of arriving at the requirement, it was analyzed that the training products are the key link to the elderly, and the small space of the institution has a greater impact on the safety of the elderly and the efficiency of the training, so the large wall in the main activity area can be used to place some of the products. Therefore, the practical part was developed from the service blueprint, and the wall module products were selected to improve the physical contact point design.

4 Service Design Practice - An Example of a Cognitive Disorder Charity in Shanghai

4.1 Service System and Service Blueprint

In the service system, the value network diagram is divided into three layers, from inside to outside: MCI users, internal stakeholders and external stakeholders. Internal stakeholders include family members and service organization-focused staff, social workers, volunteers, and senior partners who are also involved in training. External stakeholders include government agencies, communities, hospitals and other members of the community. Agencies, social workers and volunteers provide comprehensive services, training products and emotional care to users, information about their condition is recorded and evaluated, and they become emotionally attached to service staff. Government, service agencies, communities, hospitals, and users are the aggregators of funding, services, and information delivery. Agencies need to put effort into attracting the attention of the community, and stakeholders are critical to the emotional help of MCI (see Fig. 6).

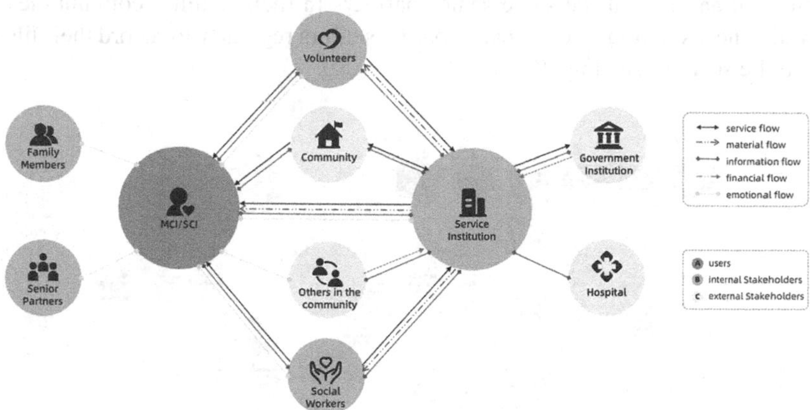

Fig. 6. Stakeholder value network diagram of MCI cognitive training activities in service system

The service blueprint optimizes the front and back-end processes of the institution's existing MCI cognitive intervention activity service, and the effectiveness of the service design is demonstrated by comparing the evaluation of the before and after experience curves.

Pre-services: Government funding and support to guide the implementation of the agency's program, the user or his family detects a cognitive problem, the community assessor does a brain health assessment for him using the simplified MoCA-B scale at the time of the physical examination and collects preliminary information, and then goes to the hospital for professional scale and medical (blood draw, MRI, use of some of the PET/CT free testing slots supported by state funding, etc.) examinations The assessment is determined to be a service recipient and information is collected.

In service: The agency does scientific and ideological work with MCI seniors and the community, prepares supplies, recruits service users, joins the intervention team, and prepares social workers and volunteers as well as pilot tests of the activity products beforehand. At each activity, the agency turns on soothing background music in advance, users arrive at the agency, change into special sneakers and place their personal belongings in lockers, and weaken medical traces in products or behaviors when measuring blood pressure. At the beginning of the activity, the social worker leads the homework intervention. Because the number of props needed for training is large and different for each session, in order to improve the social interaction of joint participation, the change of table and chair space is reduced and the wall of the institution space is used to add modular product design to assist the activity intervention. During the whole process of service, social workers or volunteers are dedicated to observe, mark and assist MCI elderly. After the activity, staff review, analyze and summarize, make timely adjustments and arrange the next work content, and strengthen the communication and guidance between counselors and service users to find better ways to dissipate their confusion, frustration and powerlessness and maintain their motivation.

After the service: In addition to participating in other activities organized by the agency, seniors with less severe symptoms of MCI or SCI can apply to join the volunteers on their own and recruit the same senior partners in their familiar communities. The agency also needs to return to the participating seniors regularly to record their files and continue the service (see Fig. 7).

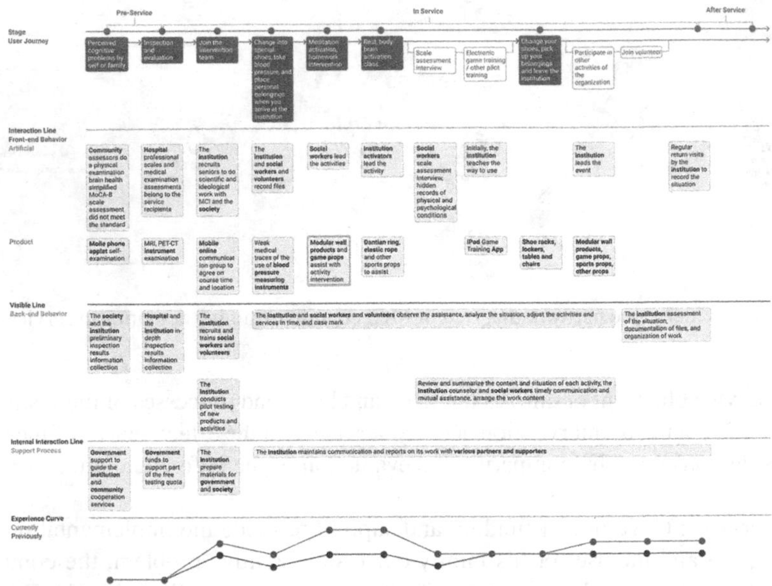

Fig. 7. MCI cognitive intervention services blueprint

4.2 Wall Module Design

Due to the constraint of the activity space plane, the opportunity point of using the wall to place training products was explored, and the modular hole board wall design was conceived according to the demand hierarchy diagram, which helps to meet the needs of MCI elderly for physiology, safety, socialization, respect, cognitive training and self-actualization: the size, material, color and shape are suitable for the elderly; the training length is moderate; it can be used flexibly; only agency personnel are needed when switching activities The training can be done cooperatively to achieve the purpose of social interaction; the functions are simple and easy to learn and use. Each functional module can be installed and disassembled as needed, and this form can also be used in small spaces in community activation centers, and can also meet the needs of institutional outreach services.

During the product design practice phase, we also co-creatively worked with agency staff and the elderly to obtain feedback and iterate during the program conceptualization, and finally produced a wall module design plan, which received good evaluations from the agency and the elderly about the service and product (see Fig. 8).

Examples of the modules shown in the design rendering are: Schulte Scale physical training blocks, which can be cycled through moving numerical positions to exercise attention; darts and flying chess games, which exercise executive, attention, orientation, and calculation skills, and serve as entertaining interactive icebreakers; colorful music pipes, with simple music scores, which exercise executive, attention, and memory skills, and serve as music therapy and emotional relief; blackboard and puzzles, free interactive creation, can also be used as institutional teaching activities content prompts; and shelf space, etc., subsequent to the need to add different modules (see Fig. 9).

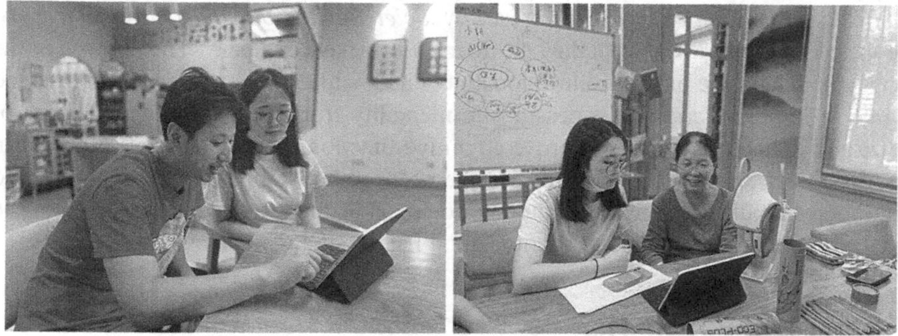

Fig. 8. Exploring co-creation with institutions and the elderly

Fig. 9. MCI cognitive intervention wall module design

4.3 Design Summary

To summarize the service design strategies for MCI cognitive intervention activities are as follows:

The physical contact content of the activity environment and products meet the needs of MCI elderly. In the intervention context, the physiology, safety and cognition of the elderly are fully taken care of, warm feelings are given, and danger is avoided.

To improve the precision and information symmetry of stakeholders. The MCI cognitive intervention scenario involves the government, hospitals, communities and institutions, and involves important information sharing and determination in the early stage of active search and testing to identify service recipients, the middle stage of communication and optimization of the service process, and the later stage of follow-up.

Enhance the emotional care of patients by society, institutions and family and friends. For the elderly with MCI, what they desire most is to have company. The purpose of the service is to help the elderly relieve loneliness and helplessness, correctly under-stand cognitive disorders and adjust pessimistic mentality from the psychological point of view; and to help the elderly improve cognitive functions and reduce transitions from the physiological point of view. The service needs to be well publicized and appealed to the general public as an important emotional connection to expand the scope of the service and lead more people to become good friends of cognitive disorders.

5 Concluding Remarks

In mild cognitive impairment intervention contexts, research has found that for MCI seniors, the greatest needs are socialization and training. For institutional services, the most important thing is to enhance the psycho-emotional care for MCI people, which needs to be done in an appropriate way to make the elderly accept the intervention and have a good state of mind and trust. To enhance the effectiveness of training on this basis, careful observation and case marking, paying attention to each elderly person and adjusting accordingly, has practical implications for the role of intervention. At the same time, working with stakeholders and emotional adjustment is also essential.

The article focuses on qualitative research, and the field research section requires longer-term research on the breadth and depth of sample selection, the foresight of design output results, and the verification of design feasibility in the implementation phase. The social concern for cognitively impaired groups is gradually increasing, and the study hopes to provide a kind of help for them in the field of service design. With the development of information technology and the progress of humanistic care, it is believed that in the future, more humane services will be created for the disadvantaged groups and for us in the future.

Acknowledgments. This research was supported by the project of "Social Innovation and Green Design Research" supported by shanghai summit discipline in design 2022, 2020 Shanghai Pujiang Program (2020PJC026). Special Fund for Research Base of Institute of Art and Design, East China University of Science and Technology, Shanghai Dream Foundation in 2022.

References

1. Alzheimer's Disease International: World Alzheimer Report 2018-The state of the art of dementia research: New frontiers. 7. Alzheimer's Disease International (ADI), London (2018)
2. Alzheimer's Disease Branch of Chinese Geriatric Health Care Association (ADC): Research report on the living conditions of Families with Alzheimer's disease in China in 2019. 1. Health Times, Beijing (2020). 国老年保健协会阿尔茨海默病分会 (ADC):2019中国阿尔茨海默病患者家庭生存状况调研报告. 1. 健康时报, 北京 (2020)
3. Liu, J-y.: Research on educational toys for prevention of Senile dementia. 19. Hubei University of Technology, Hubei (2020). 刘靖贻: 预防老年痴呆症的益智玩具研究. 19. 湖北工业大学, 湖北 (2020)
4. Alzheimer's Disease International: World Alzheimer Report 2019-Attitudes to dementia. 13. Alzheimer's Disease International (ADI), London (2019)
5. Reisberg, B., Ferris, S.H., De Leon, M.J., et al: The global deterioration scale for assessment of primary degenerative dementia. Am. J. Psychiatry **139**(9), 1136–1139 (1982)
6. Li, B.-y., Tang, H.-d.: Research progress of cognitive training in mild cognitive impairment. Shanghai Med. **38**(17), 19–22 (2017).李彬寅, 汤荟冬: 认知功能训练改善轻度认知功能障碍的研究进展. 上海医药 38(17), 19–22 (2017)
7. Wan, M.-x.: Research on product design for elderly patients with mild cognitive impairment. 9. Tianjin Academy of Fine Arts, Tianjin (2019) 万梦雪: 针对轻度认知障碍老年患者的产品设计研究. 9. 天津美术学院,天津 (2019)
8. Alzheimer's Disease International: World Alzheimer Report 2020-Design, Dignity, Dementia: Dementia-related design and the built environment. 247. Alzheimer's Disease International (ADI), London (2020)
9. Hendriks, N., Huybrechts, L., Slegers, K., et al.: Valuing implicit decision-making in participatory design: a relational approach in design with people with dementia. Des. Stud. **59**, 58–76 (2018)
10. Shigemizu, D., AkiyamA, S., Higaki, S., et al.: Prognosis prediction model for conversion from mild cognitive impairment to Alzheimer's disease created by integrative analysis of multi-omics data. Alzheimer's Res. Therapy **12**(1), 1–12 (2020)
11. Li, N., Liang, W.-d., Zhang, S.-h., et al: Research progress in non-drug intervention of mild cognitive impairment in the elderly. Chin. J. Nurs. Manag. **18**(5), 688–692 (2018). 梁炜东, 张善红, 等: 老年人轻度认知障碍非药物干预研究进展. 中国护理管理 18(5), 688–692 (2018)
12. Liu, L.-l., Zhang, Y.-q., Yang, D., et al: Research progress of non-drug intervention in elderly patients with mild cognitive impairment. Nurs. Res. **33**(22), 3910–3914 (2019) 刘莱莱, 张勇勤, 杨丹, 等: 老年轻度认知障碍病人非药物干预的研究进展. 护理研究 33(22), 3910–3914 (2019)
13. Zhang, J.-x., Xu, X.-q., Ding, Z.-h., et al: Application of hospital-community-home nursing intervention model in patients with mild cognitive impairment. China Nurs. Manag. **18**(9), 1230–1235 (2018). 张菊霞, 徐晓琴, 丁兆红, 等: 医院—社区—家庭护理干预模式在轻度认知功能障碍患者中的应用. 中国护理管理 18(9), 1230–1235 (2018)
14. Yang, M.-q., Weng, Y.-l., Bai, Y.-m., et al: Research progress in nursing of patients with comorbidities with mild cognitive impairment. J. Nurs. Educ. **35**(10), 895–899 (2020). 杨梦琴, 翁艳翎, 柏亚妹, 等: 轻度认知障碍共病患者护理的研究进展. 护士进修杂志 35 (10), 895–899 (2020)
15. Zhu, W.-t., Wen, X.: A study on the design activism strategy of healthy aging in Taiwan – a case study of the "Old-school Life Necessity" community design action. Decoration 1, 92–94 (2019). 朱文涛, 文昕: 台湾健康老龄化的设计行动主义策略研究——以"老派人生之必要"社区设计行动为例. 装饰 1, 92–94 (2019)

16. Stickdorn, M., Lawrence, A., Hormess, M., et al: This is Service Design Doing. O'Reilly Media, Sebastopol (2018)
17. How to Mash-Up and Benefit from PM and the Design Thinking Process, https://marvelapp.com/blog/mash-benefit-pm-design-thinking-process/. Accessed 27 Jan 2021
18. Tu, H.-l.: Research on the design of educational products for early Alzheimer's patients based on universal design concept, pp. 35–45. Wuhan University of Technology, Wuhan (2018). 涂寒露: 通用设计理念下早期阿尔茨海默患者益智产品设计研究. 35–45. 武汉理工大学,武汉 (2018)
19. Zeng, S.-W., Zeng, W.Y.: Research on the cognitive impairment of time orientation in the elderly with dementia by service experience. J. Well-being Technol. Serv. Manag. **6**(1), 29–40 (2018). 曾谁我, 曾琬懿: 以服务体验洞察失智长者时间定向感认知障碍需求之研究. 福祉科技与服务管理学刊 6(1), 29–40 (2018)
20. Miao, W.: Research on product Design for elderly with Mild cognitive Impairment, pp. 32–40. Beijing Institute of Technology, Beijing (2015). 苗薇: 轻度认知障碍老年群体产品设计研究. 32–40. 北京理工大学,北京 (2015)
21. Huang, Q.: Barrier-Free · Universal Design. China Machine Press, Beijing (2009). 黄群. 无障碍·通用设计. 机械工业出版社, 北京 (2009)
22. Deng, X., Li, J.-m., Zeng, H.-j., et al: Research on weight calculation method of Ahp and its application. Math. Pract. Theory **42**(7), 93–100 (2012). 邓雪, 李家铭, 曾浩健, 等. 层次分析法权重计算方法分析及其应用研究. 数学的实践与认识 42(7), 93–100 (2012)
23. Wang, Y.: Analysis on problems and countermeasures of community elderly service in Chengdu – based on Maslow's demand theory. Sci. Theory **3**, 49–51 (2021). 王玥: 成都市社区养老服务问题及对策分析——基于马斯洛需求理论视角. 学理论 3, 49–51 (2021)

Integration Analysis of Heterogeneous Data on Mind Externalization of Elderly People at Home

Sinan Chen[1(✉)], Hayato Ozono[1], and Masahide Nakamura[1,2]

[1] Graduate School of System Informatics, Kobe University, 1-1 Rokkodai-cho, Nada, Kobe 657-8501, Japan
{chensinan,ozono}@ws.cs.kobe-u.ac.jp, masa-n@cs.kobe-u.ac.jp

[2] RIKEN Center for Advanced Intelligence Project, 1-4-1 Nihonbashi, Chuo-ku, Tokyo 103-0027, Japan

Abstract. As the aging population around the world, figuring out the reason for changes in the health status of elderly adults at home is pressing. In our research group, to comprehend the scientific self-care of elderly adults at home, a core concept called "mind externalization" that retrieves the elders' thoughts as much as possible using spoken dialogue agent technology has developed swiftly. The purpose of this paper is to consider an approach to elucidating reasons for health changes in the elderly at home. Our key idea is to merge the results of health status, dialogue logs, and emotional values (recognized from images and audio during the spoken dialogue) into a time series. More specifically, we describe an approach for extracting the features of changes in health data (i.e., heart rate, stress, sleep quality, step, and activity level from the wearable device). It intends to add health data retrieved from a wearable device and unite heterogeneous data (i.e., health data and dialogue data). Based on the integration between health data and dialogue data (i.e., text logs, audio, and images), we discuss an approach to estimating the reasoning context before and after the period. In this way, assisting elderly adults at home by grasping their daily living in detail can be appreciated. Meanwhile, executing personalized self-management is promising.

Keywords: Elderly at home · Mind externalization · Spoken dialogue · Wearable device · Smart healthcare

1 Introduction

Population aging is currently a big issue in Japan, Germany, and Italy. Specifically, the number of people aged 65 years has reached 28.4% in Japan. It exceeds 21% of the national total, and the country is confronting a **super-aging society**[1]. As the population and disease structure change, the demand for nursing

[1] https://www8.cao.go.jp/kourei/english/annualreport/2020/pdf/2020.pdf.

Q. Gao and J. Zhou (Eds.): HCII 2022, LNCS 13331, pp. 197–209, 2022.
https://doi.org/10.1007/978-3-031-05654-3_13

care is expanding year by year. In particular, many chronic diseases (e.g., mild cognitive impairment, disease syndrome) require long-term care. However, the shortage of facilities and humans for medical welfare and nursing care is becoming more severe. As the trend toward conversion from **institutional care to home care** continues, the number of elderly adults (requiring nursing care) at home is expanding more swiftly. Furthermore, the number of individual cases is also expanding, such as one elderly adult caring for another, and elder adults living alone.

Encouraging **self-care** among elderly adults within differences between households is a big challenge. For example, the degree of completion of *activities of daily living (ADL)*, the degree of achieving a regular rhythm of life, and the degree of physical and mental health are important indicators. In recent years, research on *assistive technology* applying engineering technology to support the lives of the elderly has been spreading around the world. A representative technology is to monitor elderly adults at home. It mainly utilizes the *internet of things (IoT)* and *information and communication technology (ICT)*. A machine monitors the situation (called *context*) of the elderly adult instead of the family caregiver and communicates with the family caregiver **only when required**. In this way, enhancing the *quality of life (QoL)* of the elderly and decreasing the burden on their families is promising.

Our research group is studying various systems and services from two perspectives: the "environment" and "humans" in houses. Related research from the perspective of the environment includes environmental sensing [20], behavior estimation [21], and context recognition [5]. On the other hand, related research from the perspective of the elderly includes facial expression recognition [10], health monitoring [19], and mental externalization through a virtual agent (VA) listening service [14]. However, in the VA listening service conducted in previous research, various kinds of heterogeneous data (e.g., text, image, and voice data in a time series) that acquired and accumulated remain. We have not yet been able to conduct an **integrated analysis of the health status (e.g., heart rate, stress) and the "mental state" of the elderly**.

The purpose of this paper is to consider a method to elucidate the reasons for causing changes in the health status of elderly adults at home. Figure 2 shows an image diagram of integration analysis of health data and dialogue data for elderly people at home. As an approach, we add health data retrieved from a **wearable health device** (i.e., an activity meter worn on the arm) and consider an integrated analysis of heterogeneous data (health data and dialogue data) in a time series. Our key idea is to merge the results of health status, dialogue logs, and emotional values in a time series. In our approach, we consider the following five concrete steps:

- **Step 1:** VA Listening Service and Wearable Health Installation
- **Step 2:** Acquisition and Storage of Heterogeneous Data
- **Step 3:** Extraction of Health Feature Changes in Time Series
- **Step 4:** Analysis of Interrelationships Among Changing Features
- **Step 5:** Context Estimation Based on Past Feature Analysis

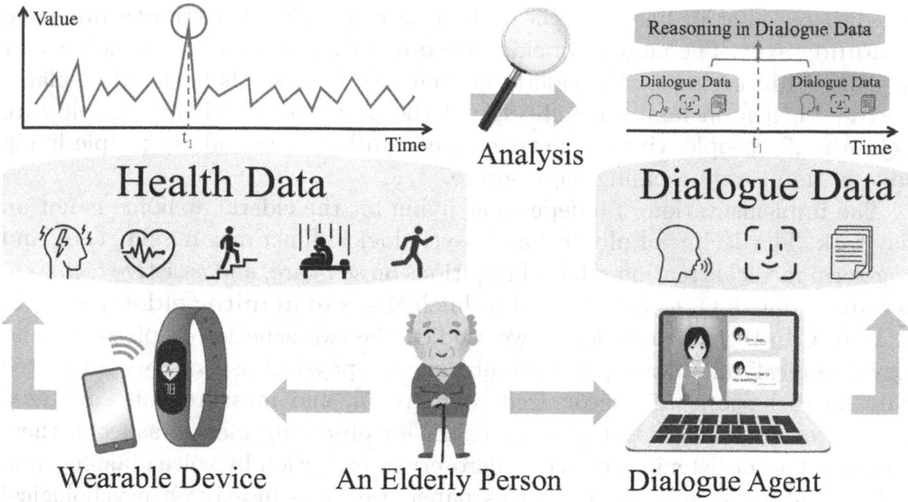

Fig. 1. Integration analysis of health data and dialogue data for elderly people at home.

In the discussion, the advantage of the research approach is that it provides a more multifaceted analysis of the elderly at home by utilizing heterogeneous data. The abundance of available data has likewise improved, allowing for a more granular understanding of the daily living conditions of the elderly at home. As for a limitation of the research approach, we have not yet resolved the problem of dealing with missing data in time series. Furthermore, we anticipate the interrelationships among different types of data. They have not evaluated for individual elderly adults. In particular, the correctness of the acquired data requires investigation. It also requires checking the effects of these data in case studies.

2 Previous Study: Monitoring Assistance for Elderly People at Home

This section depicts the background surrounding the current situation of the elderly at home. It presents previous studies aimed at understanding the mind of elderly adults.

2.1 Mental Externalization of the Elderly at Home

The "externalization of the mind" of the elderly refers to the act of blurting out to the outside world as much as possible of what is on the "mind" of the elderly. In recent years, with the aging of the world's population, **the shortage of nursing care facilities and human resources** [16] has become a social problem. In Japan, which is confronting a super-aging society, the number of elderly people at home is expanding every year as the structure of the population and diseases alter in line with the shift from conventional **institutional care to home care**[2]. The number of elderly people living at home is expanding year by year. While caring for the elderly in their own homes is habituated, it places a heavy burden on family members, and the problems of "elderly couple care each other," "people with dementia care each other," and elderly people living alone at home are becoming more severe.

The implementation of independent living for the elderly at home is not an easy task. The decline of physical and psychological functions, nursing care, and long-term medical treatment have limitations on self-care, and assistive technologies are required. One of the typical technologies is to **monitor elderly people at home**. In the previous study, we studied the two aspects of "physical" and "psychological" monitoring. For monitoring the physical aspects, we estimated daily life behaviors [21], recognized contexts [5], and measured and analyzed physical activities [6]. On the other hand, for observing mental aspects, there are virtual agent listening services, microservice execution by voice dialogue, and multimodal diary services [4]. In this paper, we focus mostly on psychological monitoring and support technologies.

2.2 Virtual Agent Listening Service

Virtual Agent (VA) technology refers to a technology that is equipped with a software (i.e., virtual) interface. It acts as an intermediary to promote smooth interactions between machines and humans. In our previous study, we proposed a VA listening service with voice interaction function to listen to the "feelings" of elderly people in their daily lives. Figure 2 shows the components of the VA listening service in the edge and cloud environments.

In the VA listening service, the components are described in detail from two aspects: hardware and software. The hardware component consists of IoT sensors (i.e., *Phidgets*[3] motion and pressure sensor modules) and a general-purpose computer (i.e., including built-in speakers, cameras, and microphones). On the other hand, we explain the details of the software components from two perspectives: local and cloud. First, the local component consists of a sensor driver, a VA (i.e., *MMDAgent* [13]: including speech synthesis and character materials), a local server (i.e., *Apache Tomcat* [15]), and a Web browser (i.e., including speech recognition by *Web Speech API* [1] and display of dialogue contents by *Web user interface*). Next, the cloud-side component consists of a cloud server (i.e., *WebSocket* and *Pub/Sub* [12]) and a database (i.e., dialogue scenarios (including gestures, time periods, and questions) and dialogue logs).

By linking the IoT sensor with a general-purpose computer, it is possible to drive the VA Listening Service in two modes: "passive mode" and "active mode". In the "passive mode," the VA listening service is automatically activated when an elderly person at home approaches the motion sensor. Based on the user-defined time of day and the questions to be asked, the VA listening service can

[2] https://www.mhlw.go.jp/english/policy/care-welfare/care-welfare-elderly/dl/establish_e.pdf.

[3] https://www.phidgets.com/?tier=0&catid=3&pcid=8.

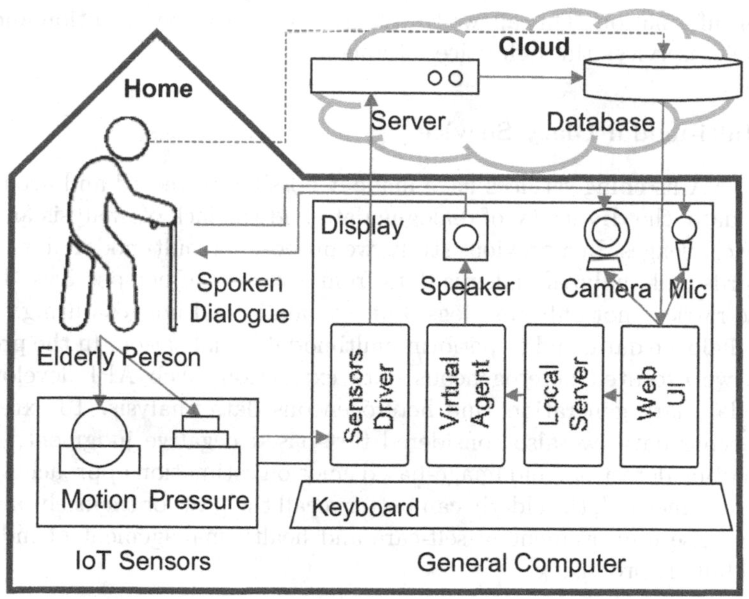

Fig. 2. Component structure of virtual agent listening service

ask about the person's mood, physical condition, eating and drinking status, etc. In the "active mode," the VA listening service is automatically activated when the elderly person at home presses the pressure sensor. When the elderly person tells the VA any tale by voice, the VA can give a random response (e.g., "Is that so?", "Yes", etc.) by voice. Through interaction between the VA listening service and the elderly person at home, thoughts and concepts in daily life, as well as answers to specific questions, can be extracted, recorded, and stored externally (i.e., externalization of the elderly adult at home).

2.3 Microservice Execution Through Voice Interaction

The use of various **microservices**, such as contents and services on the Web, as well as the externalization of the mind through voice dialogue between elderly people at home and VA is also promising. In our previous study, we aimed to help elderly people who are not accustomed to operating smart devices (e.g., computers, smartphones, etc.) to smoothly use Web services and information based on the spoken dialogue function described in Sect. 2.2. The key idea is to apply the application programming interface (API) to microservices in Web services (e.g., calendar, video watching, to-do management, etc.) and incorporate the appropriate content into the VA dialogue scenario. The approach includes two parts: (1) User information and microservice management. (2) Configuring VA behavior at API runtime. To demonstrate the effectiveness of the proposed framework, we linked the "ToDo management service" and the "YouTube watching service" with user information. This allows the elderly to control the execution and stopping of microservices through voice interaction.

2.4 Multi-modal Diary Service

Although VA listening services have made it possible to record and accumulate dialogue data, the **diversity** of dialogue data and the lack of analysis and reuse still pose challenges. In a previous study, we proposed a multimodal diary service that records and analyzes dialogue data from a variety of perspectives. The key idea is to retrieve not only text logs, but also audio and images during the dialogue as dialogue data, and to perform multimodal visualization. In the proposed method, we executed heterogeneous data extraction, Web API development, multimodal diary generation, and heterogeneous data analysis. To extend the heterogeneous data, we also considered text-based negative judgment, speech-based emotion detection, and image-based emotion estimation approaches. Using the proposed method, the elderly can better recall the past for themselves. Hence, a more precise improvement in self-care and health management of individual elderly adults is promising.

3 Development of Advancing Technology: Wearable Health

This section describes the challenges and measurement items for wearable health devices for the elderly at home, based on smart healthcare technology.

3.1 Smart Healthcare of Elderly People at Home

The use of information and communication technology (ICT), internet of things (IoT), and artificial intelligence (AI) technologies to support the traditional **healthcare** of the elderly at home (e.g., visiting hospitals, managing health, receiving care from family members, etc.) has been accelerating. The introduction of smart sensors (i.e., environmental sensors, opening/closing sensors, etc.), smart speakers, and 360-degree cameras to make the homes of the elderly into an environment similar to that of a facility has enabled safety confirmation [11], status confirmation [17], and automatic operation of home appliances [2]. However, these smart devices and approaches are only capable of sensing external environmental conditions, including the externalization of the elderly as described in Secti. 2, and are not capable of **monitoring the health** of individual elderly people, including changes in heart rate and stress, distance traveled, and number of steps taken.

3.2 Emergence of Wearable Health Devices

Wearable health devices are emerging to monitor the health of the elderly at home. Smart apparel (i.e., clothing-type devices) include Xenoma[4] and Hamon[5]. On the other hand, arm-worn smart watches (i.e., activity meters) include Garmin[6] and Fitbit[7]. Through the use of these devices, smart healthcare technology can be deployed in various areas such as fitness, sleep, and nursing care. By collaborating with local facilities and hospitals, it is possible to provide preventive medicine or telemedicine by utilizing health data. However, wearable health devices may not be suitable for bedridden elderly people and may be **invasive to their daily lives.** In the case of clothing-type devices, the user has to change and wash the related clothing regularly, which increases the **burden of daily life.**

3.3 Collection of Health Data by Activity Tracker

In order to **minimize the existing challenges**, we focus on the collection of health data by arm-worn activity tracker. Specifically, here is an example of handling health data from the following six items:

- **Number of Steps:** Measuring the number of steps and the intensity of exercise leads to the prevention of lifestyle-related diseases and the extension of healthy life span.
- **Sleep Quality:** The quality of sleep (i.e., REM/non-REM sleep) is expressed by analyzing heart rate, heart rate variability (i.e., HRV, the change in the length of the heartbeat with each beat), and activity level data.
- **Stress:** Estimates the factors that influence stress, such as training and physical activity, by measuring heart rate variability.
- **Heart Rate:** The heart rate is measured continuously for 24 hours using an optical heart rate monitor.
- **Calories burned:** The total number of calories burned during exercise/rest.
- **Body Battery:** This unique Garmin feature measures remaining physical energy by analyzing heart rate variability, stress levels, sleep quality, and activity levels.

4 Considering Approach: Integration Analysis of Heterogeneous Data

4.1 Technical Challenges

We are considering the following two technical challenges to elucidate the factors that cause changes in the health status of the elderly at home.

[4] https://xenoma.com/products/eskin-sleep-lounge/.
[5] https://www.mitsufuji.co.jp/en/service/.
[6] https://www.garmin.co.jp/minisite/health/guide/ (in Japanese).
[7] https://healthsolutions.fitbit.com/.

The first is the **lack of richness** in data types. In our research on support systems for elderly people living at home, we have studied the extraction of biometric data (e.g., heart rate, blood pressure, amount of activity, etc.) using sensor devices and dedicated devices, the collection of multimedia data (e.g., text, voice, images, etc.) using IoT devices, and the collection of environmental data (e.g., temperature, illumination, humidity, etc.). Sensing of environmental data (e.g., temperature, illumination, humidity). However, many studies have been conducted using each of these methods independently, and there have been few studies using different types of data together.

Second, there is a **lack of integration analysis** among the data used. In order to elucidate the factors that contribute to changes in the health of the elderly at home, it is not enough to collect and analyze each piece of data, but an integrated analysis (meta-analysis) among the data is necessary. Integration analysis refers to the integration of the results of multiple studies and analysis from a higher perspective, or methods and statistical analysis for this purpose[8]. In particular, by supplementing and verifying the results obtained from heterogeneous data, multifaceted relationships can be clarified. For example, heart rate variability in the elderly may be related to temperature.

4.2 Goal and Key Idea

The purpose of this study is to examine methods to elucidate the factors that cause changes in the health status of elderly people at home, based on the previous studies described in Sect. 2. The key idea is to integrate and analyze health data, dialogue data, and the results of further analysis of dialogue data in a time series.

4.3 Overall Architecture

Figure 3 shows the overall architecture of the study approach, which consists of five steps: In Step 1, the elderly person wears a wearable health device and the VA listening service with voice interaction is set up. In Step 2, health data and interaction data are acquired and stored through the wearable health device and the VA listening service. In Step 3, we extract the typical changes in health data over time. In Step 4, we focus on dialogue data during health changes and analyze the interrelationships among different features. In Step 5, we search for personal rhythms from the previous feature analysis and consider context estimation from the latest data. More specifically, each step is described below.

4.4 Flows of Considering Approach

Step 1: VA Listening Service and Wearable Health Installation
In Step 1, we first deploy the VA listening service to the homes of the elderly based on previous studies. In addition, the elderly will wear a wearable health

[8] https://en.wikipedia.org/wiki/Meta-analysis.

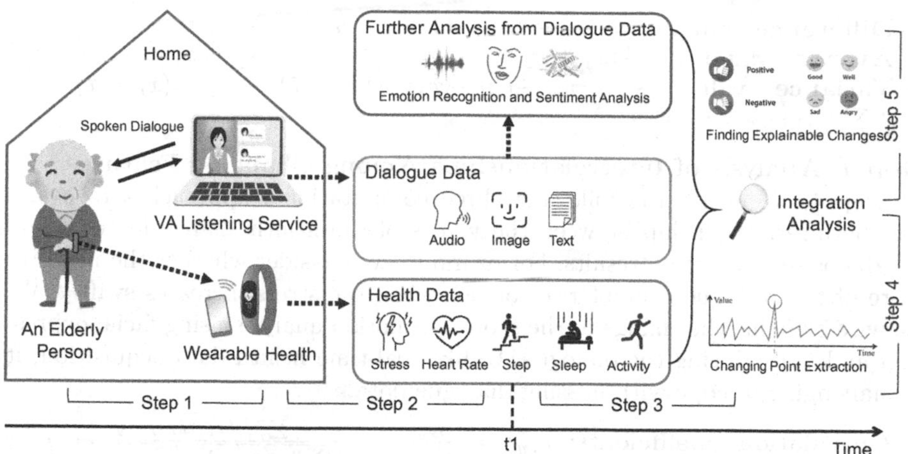

Fig. 3. Overall architecture of considering approach.

device on their arms. In this research, we chiefly focus on arm-worn activity meters (e.g., Garmin vivosmart 4[9]).

Step 2: Acquisition and Storage of Heterogeneous Data
In Step 2, we first acquire voice data, text data recognized from the voice, and image data taken at one-second intervals during the voice dialogue process between the elderly person and the agent based on the VA Listening Service, and send them to the cloud database. AI techniques such as emotion analysis are applied to these data, and the recognized results are also sent to the cloud database. With regard to health data, activity meters are generally linked to a dedicated smartphone application via *Bluetooth*, and by manually opening the dedicated application, health data is transmitted and sent to a cloud database. In order to transmit health data to the cloud database on a regular basis, we also introduce a dialogue scenario that reminds the user to open the dedicated application, and the agent asks the user to do so once a day.

Step 3: Extraction of Health Feature Changes in Time Series
In Step 3, we first develop a *Web Application Programming Interface (API)* that can retrieve health data for each item (see Sect. 3.3) to the computer local (edge). `GET` or `POST/date={yyyy-MM-dd}/data={data}` in the format of REST API [3] to retrieve the relevant health data by specifying the date and data item. Although each health data has a different measurement interval, the following five measures of feature change are defined to create a feature extraction program from past health data.

- **Maximum value**: $m_1 = max\{x_1, x_2, \cdots, x_n\}$ $(n = count(x_i))$
- **Minimum value**: $m_2 = min\{x_1, x_2, \cdots, x_n\}$

[9] https://www.garmin.co.jp/products/wearables/vivosmart-4-gray-r/.

- **Difference value:** $d_i = |(x_i - x_{i+1})|\ (1 \leq i \leq n)$
- **Average value:** $\bar{x} = \frac{1}{n}(x_1 + x_2 + x_3 + \cdots + x_n) = \frac{1}{n}\sum_{i=1}^{n} x_i$
- **Variance value:** $s^2 = \frac{1}{n}(x_1 - \bar{x})^2 + (x_2 - \bar{x})^2 + \cdots + (x_n - \bar{x})^2 = \frac{1}{n}\sum_{i=1}^{n}(x_i - \bar{x})^2$

Step 4: Analysis of Interrelationships Among Changing Features
In Step 4, we utilize the following three computational approaches to evaluate the interrelationship between the values of the health change features and the dialogue recognition results. For example, we consider whether the negative score of the dialogue content rises or not when the stress increases swiftly. We likewise examine the change in the score of emotion analysis using facial expression and voice during the dialogue. Unlike real-time health data acquisition, it is challenging to cope with missing dialogue data.

- **Correlation coefficients:** $r_{xy} = \frac{s_{xy}}{s_x s_y} = \frac{\sum_{i=1}^{n}(x_i - \bar{x})(y_i - \bar{y})}{\sqrt{\sum_{i=1}^{n}(x_i - \bar{x})^2}\sqrt{\sum_{i=1}^{n}(y_i - \bar{y})^2}} = \frac{1}{n}\sum_{i=1}^{n}\frac{x_i - \bar{x}}{s_x} \cdot \frac{y_i - \bar{y}}{s_y}$
- **Partial correlation coefficient:** $r_{xy \cdot z} = \frac{r_{xy} - r_{xz} r_{yz}}{\sqrt{1 - r_{xz}^2}\sqrt{1 - r_{yz}^2}}$
- **Covariance:** $s_{xy} = \frac{1}{n}\sum_{i=1}^{n}(x_i - \bar{x})(y_i - \bar{y})$

Step 5: Context Estimation Based on Past Feature Analysis
In Step 5, we first consider the interrelated feature data from the past as training data. Next, we estimate the context by applying lightweight machine learning (e.g., supervised learning) to them. Context refers to an individual's emotional state and negative/positive changes. Through context estimation, we expect to understand the individual's emotional state and negative/positive changes by analyzing and estimating the health change characteristics obtained from the wearable health device even during the time when the VA listening service is not used.

5 Discussion

This section summarizes each of the main points regarding the advantages and limitations of the approaches considered in Sect. 4, and discusses the specifics.

5.1 Advantage

The following two advantages of the research approach are considered:

- **Utilization of heterogeneous data**: Unlike previous related research, we will utilize different devices and approaches to collect and warehouse data. This allows us to enhance the richness of the data types utilized. It can also be used to enhance the scalability of existing systems.
- **Expansion of multifaceted analysis**: In addition to the utilization of heterogeneous data, the analysis of interrelationships can be anticipated to infer the factors behind changes in the health status of the elderly at home from a more multifaceted perspective. Furthermore, it can promote and enhance the implementation of self-care for the elderly at home.

5.2 Limitation

We examine the following two limitations of the research approach:

- **Trouble in dealing with missing data**: There are times when the wearer is not wearing the wearable health device (e.g., recharging, taking a bath, etc.), and there are times when the wearer is not utilizing the VA listening service. During these times, data acquisition is not feasible, and it is hard to deal with missing data.
- **Problems with data acquisition accuracy**: Depending on the tightness of the wearable health device's belt, there are subtle differences in the data values such as heart rate attained. There are also occasional problems with mis-recognition of dialogue text gained by speech recognition, negative judgments, and emotion analysis.

6 Related Work

Two researches related to the approach considered in this study are described below. Research [7] proposed a web-based medical data integration and management platform that collects heterogeneous types of health-related medical records and real-time lifelog data. Unlike the wearable health used in this study, the proposed platform in this study provides the ability to manage real-time data such as heart rate, blood pressure, and activity information extracted from medical devices and send them to a server. It also applies machine learning tools to analyze risks based on domain knowledge and individual differences, and dynamically visualizes the results to patients and doctors based on how the information is simplified.

Research [8] described all these important aspects of smart healthcare wearable sensors, body domain sensors, advanced pervasive healthcare systems, and new IoT technologies for big data analytics. Unlike the focus of this work on integrated analysis in heterogeneous data, we identify new perspectives and focus on issues such as scalability, interoperability, device-network-human interface, and security. We also present the results of an evaluation of the applicability of knowledge in the field of *CAD*, such as large-scale analysis and optimization methods, to key *eHealth* problems.

7 Conclusion

In this paper, we focused on the self-help of the elderly at home in the super-aged society, and we organized and discussed the flow of considering the approach of integrating and analyzing heterogeneous data in order to elucidate the factors of health status change.

However, in order to obtain health data, the wearable health device to be used still has the challenge of being invasive to daily life. The wearable **remote** health monitoring device [9] is expected to provide a portable health care system and facilitate the provision of decentralized health care, as opposed to the traditional centralized clinical care. The correlation between non-verbal data (e.g., facial expression, posture, etc.) and health status of the elderly also needs to be verified in evaluation experiments. In research [18], facial features that convey a sense of familiarity were associated with a decrease in patients' pain perception.

As future work, we will conduct case studies and evaluation experiments using the study approach to clarify the correlation between actual interaction data and health data of elderly people at home. In addition, we will utilize data on daily behavior, daily rhythms, and environmental conditions to examine the correlation with changes in health status.

Acknowledgements. This research was partially supported by JSPS KAKENHI Grant Numbers JP19H01138, JP18H03242, JP18H03342, JP19H04154, JP19K02973, JP20K11059, JP20H04014, JP20H05706 and Tateishi Science and Technology Foundation (C) (No. 2207004).

References

1. Adorf, J.: Web speech API. KTH Royal Institute of Technology (2013)
2. Arun Francis, G., Lexmitha, S., Aruna Devi, N., Swathika, C.: Embedded system based smart automation for elderly and disabled people. Ann. Roman. Soc. Cell Biol. **25**, 9909–9917 (2021)
3. Atlidakis, V., Godefroid, P., Polishchuk, M.: Checking security properties of cloud service rest APIs. In: 2020 IEEE 13th International Conference on Software Testing, Validation and Verification (ICST), pp. 387–397. IEEE (2020)
4. Chen, S., Nakamura, M.: Generating personalized dialogues based on conversation log summarization and sentiment analysis. In: The 23nd International Conference on Information Integration and Web-based Applications & Services (iiWAS2021), pp. 221–226, November 2021
5. Chen, S., Saiki, S., Nakamura, M.: Recognizing fine-grained home contexts using multiple cognitive APIs. In: 2019 International Conference on Cyber-Enabled Distributed Computing and Knowledge Discovery (CyberC), pp. 360–366. IEEE (2019)
6. Chen, S., Saiki, S., Nakamura, M.: Nonintrusive fine-grained home care monitoring: characterizing quality of in-home postural changes using bone-based human sensing. Sensors **20**(20), 5894 (2020)
7. Choi, A., Shin, H.: Longitudinal healthcare data management platform of healthcare IoT devices for personalized services. J. Univers. Comput. Sci. **24**(9), 1153–1169 (2018)
8. Firouzi, F., Farahani, B., Ibrahim, M., Chakrabarty, K.: Keynote paper: from EDA to IoT eHealth: promises, challenges, and solutions. IEEE Trans. Comput. Aid. Desi. Integr. Circ. Syst. **37**(12), 2965–2978 (2018)
9. Ghosh, R., et al.: Micro/nanofiber-based noninvasive devices for health monitoring diagnosis and rehabilitation. Appl. Phys. Rev. **7**(4), 041309 (2020)
10. Hirayama, K., Chen, S., Saiki, S., Nakamura, M.: Toward capturing scientific evidence in elderly care: Efficient extraction of changing facial feature points. Sensors **21**(20), 6726 (2021)

11. Jan, H., Yar, H., Iqbal, J., Farman, H., Khan, Z., Koubaa, A.: Raspberry PI assisted safety system for elderly people: an application of smart home. In: 2020 First International Conference of Smart Systems and Emerging Technologies (SMARTTECH), pp. 155–160. IEEE (2020)
12. Kul, S., Sayar, A.: A survey of publish/subscribe middleware systems for microservice communication. In: 2021 5th International Symposium on Multidisciplinary Studies and Innovative Technologies (ISMSIT), pp. 781–785. IEEE (2021)
13. Lee, A., Oura, K., Tokuda, K.: MMDAgent-a fully open-source toolkit for voice interaction systems. In: 2013 IEEE International Conference on Acoustics, Speech and Signal Processing, pp. 8382–8385. IEEE (2013)
14. Maeda, H., Saiki, S., Nakamura, M., Yasuda, K.: Rule-based inquiry service to elderly at home for efficient mind sensing. In: Proceedings of the 21st International Conference on Information Integration and Web-Based Applications & Services, pp. 664–668 (2019)
15. Manelli, L., Zambon, G.: Introducing JSP and Tomcat. In: Beginning Jakarta EE Web Development, pp. 1–53. Apress, Berkeley (2020). https://doi.org/10.1007/978-1-4842-5866-8_1
16. Marć, M., Bartosiewicz, A., Burzyńska, J., Chmiel, Z., Januszewicz, P.: A nursing shortage-a prospect of global and local policies. Int. Nurs. Rev. **66**(1), 9–16 (2019)
17. Martins, H., Gupta, N., Reis, M.J.C.S.: A non-intrusive IoT-based real-time alert system for elderly people monitoring. In: Paiva, S., Lopes, S.I., Zitouni, R., Gupta, N., Lopes, S.F., Yonezawa, T. (eds.) SmartCity360 2020. LNICST, vol. 372, pp. 339–357. Springer, Cham (2021). https://doi.org/10.1007/978-3-030-76063-2_24
18. Mattarozzi, K., et al.: Pain and satisfaction: healthcare providers' facial appearance matters. Psychol. Res. **85**, 1706–1712 (2021)
19. Miura, C., Saiki, S., Nakamura, M., Yasuda, K.: Implementing and evaluating feedback feature of mind monitoring service for elderly people at home. In: Proceedings of the 22nd International Conference on Information Integration and Web-based Applications & Services, pp. 390–395 (2020)
20. Sakakibara, S., Saiki, S., Nakamura, M., Matsumoto, S.: Implementing autonomous environmental sensing in smart city with IoT based sensor box and cloud services. Inform. Eng. Express **4**(1), 1–10 (2018)
21. Tamamizu, K., Sakakibara, S., Saiki, S., Nakamura, M., Yasuda, K.: Capturing activities of daily living for elderly at home based on environment change and speech dialog. In: Duffy, V.G. (ed.) DHM 2017. LNCS, vol. 10287, pp. 183–194. Springer, Cham (2017). https://doi.org/10.1007/978-3-319-58466-9_18

Development of an Electronic Healthcare Tool to Elicit Patient Preferences in Older Adults Diagnosed with Hematologic Malignancies

Amy Cole[1(✉)], Amro Khasawneh[2], Karthik Adapa[1], Lukasz Mazur[1,2], and Daniel R. Richardson[3]

[1] Carolina Health Informatics Program, University of North Carolina, Chapel Hill, NC, USA
amy_cole@med.unc.edu

[2] Department of Radiation Oncology, University of North Carolina, Chapel Hill, NC, USA

[3] UNC Lineberger Comprehensive Cancer Center, University of North Carolina, Chapel Hill, NC, USA

Abstract. The objective of this study was to develop and evaluate iterative prototypes for an electronic healthcare tool (EHT) using three versions of a discrete choice experiment (DCE) designed to elicit the treatment preferences of older adults with hematologic malignancies. We used a mixed-methods approach including qualitative assessments (think-aloud sessions and semi-structured interviews) to develop an affinity diagram for thematic analysis, and questionnaires (Post-Study System Usability and the National Aeronautical and Space administration's Task Load Index [NASA-TLX]) to evaluate human-computer interaction, human factors and ergonomics standards on the perceived usability of, and the cognitive workload (CWL) required to perform tasks within the prototypes. DCEs included object case, profile case and multi-profile case. Iterative changes to the prototype were planned after each 5 participants. Overall, 15 healthy volunteers completed all assessments with 3 prototypes. Participants reported the prototypes were easy to complete and straightforward but usability issues around definitions, instructions, information overload, and navigation were revealed. Participants also reported feeling overwhelmed at the information presented in the DCEs and having difficulty understanding definitions. Usability and CWL levels were acceptable for all prototypes. The profile case DCE had higher frustration scores than the other versions (NASA-TLX subscale, $p = 0.04$). Iterative improvements were guided by usability principles and included easier access to definitions, the addition of instructive videos and the inclusion of a more straightforward DCE (object case). This process should improve the validity of results from the DCE and the feasibility of clinical implementation of the EHT.

Keywords: Cognitive workload · Electronic healthcare tools · Shared decision-making · Oncology

Q. Gao and J. Zhou (Eds.): HCII 2022, LNCS 13331, pp. 210–228, 2022.
https://doi.org/10.1007/978-3-031-05654-3_14

1 Introduction

1.1 Background

Hematologic malignancies, including leukemia, lymphoma, and myeloma, account for approximately 10% of cancer cases each year and nearly 57,000 deaths [1]. These cancers predominantly affect older adults over the age of 60. Treatment decision-making is complex for many patients. Chemotherapy causes substantial side effects and offers uncertain benefits. Oncologists and patients can engage in shared decision-making to clarify patient values and preferences to guide chemotherapy decisions. Multiple stakeholders have called for using validated methods to elicit patients' values and preferences to inform shared decision-making [2–7].

Quantitative methods using conjoint analysis to elicit patient preferences and values are increasingly used in healthcare to elicit patient preferences for treatment outcomes [8]. A recent systematic review and meta-analysis demonstrated that the use of these methods can improve values-congruent care [9]. We previously developed two distinct versions of a discrete choice experiment (DCE) (a multi-profile case and an object case) to elicit the preferences of patients with acute myeloid leukemia [10–12]. An electronic health tool (EHT) may facilitate the use of these instruments to improve shared decision-making and allow for real-time reporting of results to patients and clinicians. To the best of our knowledge, DCEs have not been designed and developed as electronic health tools for older patients with hematologic malignancies.

The utilization of EHTs has been shown to increase knowledge of treatment options, improve risk perception, and improve communication between providers and patients, including those diagnosed with hematologic malignancies [13, 14]. Some older adults lack confidence in using technology or have diminished physical abilities, which may present challenges when they try to utilize EHTs in which their specific needs are not considered in the design [15]. A recent systematic review found that older adults recommend that EHTs are designed with detailed instructions, intuitive user interfaces, and attention to the accessibility of the text and layout [15]. Further, for an EHT to be beneficial for newly-diagnosed older patients with hematologic malignancies, it must be understandable, usable, functional and optimize the cognitive workload (CWL) associated with treatment decisions.

2 Methods

2.1 Participants

We recruited healthy volunteers, aged 21 years of age and older, between August and September 2021. This development study enrolled 15 healthy volunteers, chosen both for ease of recruitment, and for the potential to identify approximately 90% of usability issues before testing with our target patient population (older adults with hematologic malignancies) [16]. Before enrollment, each participant was asked to review and sign an online consent form. Participants received a $25 gift card upon completion of the study. We obtained approval from the Institutional Review Board at the University of North Carolina for this study.

2.2 Baseline Characteristics of Participants

After being enrolled in the study, participants self-reported demographics including gender, race, ethnicity, education level, employment status, and comfort level with technology through REDCap, a secure online database.

2.3 Study Design

We designed a mixed-methods study using an iterative co-design approach [17, 18] including 3 cohorts of participants (total n = 15) in the evaluation of medium-fidelity prototypes (developed in AdobeXD-v.40.0.22). Participants were scheduled to attend a usability session, which was held in the Human Factors Laboratory housed within the Department of Radiation Oncology at the University of North Carolina at Chapel Hill. Recruitment efforts stopped after we reached a point of thematic saturation, in which our final testing sessions were not producing new data to evaluate [19].

Discrete Choice Experiments. Patients were asked to complete choice tasks within DCEs to elicit their preferences for treatment outcomes. Prototypes of an EHT containing three alternative DCEs were used: object case, profile case, and multi-profile case. Each EHT prototype contained two DCE versions. Cohort 1 completed the profile case and multi-profile case and cohorts 2–3 completed the object case and multi-profile case. The order of cases presented to each participant was randomly assigned to account for the effect of order and to ensure information from one case type was not transferred across cases [20].

Object Case: The choice tasks within this version of the DCE, also referred to as a best-worst scaling instrument, were adapted from our prior study to identify which outcomes are most important and least important to participants (see Fig. 1). Our initial study used an object case DCE to identify which outcomes patients with leukemia were most worried about. We altered the object case in order to allow for direct comparison between DCEs and to better inform shared decision-making. The following seven attributes were included: maintain day-to-day activities, avoid long-term side effects, avoid short-term side effects, living longer, avoid hospitalizations, avoid becoming dependent on others, and avoid high financial costs. These attributes are condensed from the prior study that included 10 attributes. Each choice task included 4 of the 7 attributes. Participants completed 7 choice tasks.

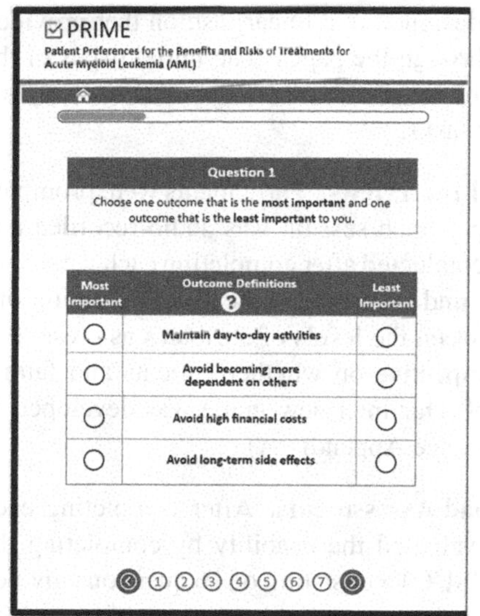

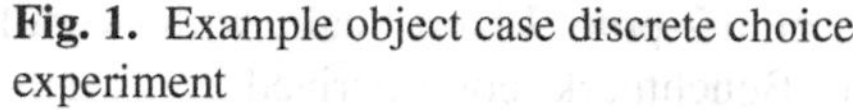

Fig. 1. Example object case discrete choice experiment

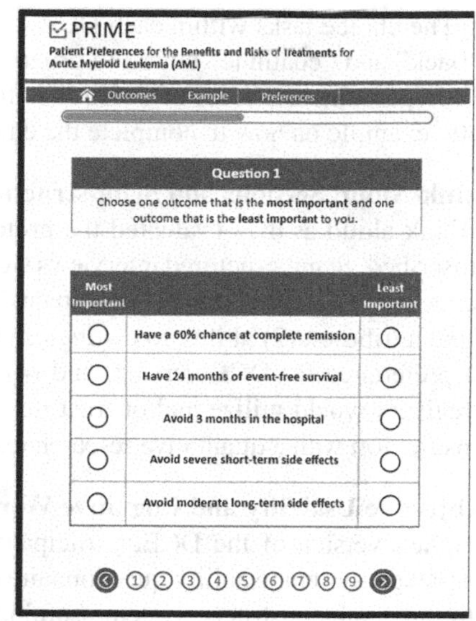

Fig. 2. Example profile case discrete choice experiment

Profile Case: The choice tasks within this version of the DCE followed the same logic as the object case where participants chose the most important and least important items among a series of options (see Fig. 2). In this version, however, participants were presented with an attribute at a specific level that varied throughout the choice tasks (e.g., avoid mild short-term side effects, avoid moderate short-term side effects, or avoid severe short-term side effects). Each choice task in this DCE included 5 attributes, with each attribute represented at 3 distinct levels. Participants completed 10 choice tasks. Attributes and levels were identical to those in the multi-profile case.

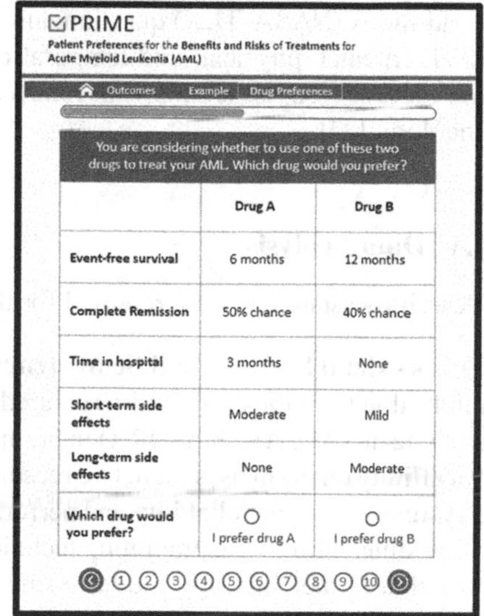

Fig. 3. Example multi-profile case discrete choice experiment

Multi-Profile Case: The choice tasks in this DCE differ from the object case and the profile case. Each choice task required participants to choose which of two profiles they preferred each with 5 attributes at varying levels (see Fig. 3).

This DCE is unchanged from our prior work [11]. Each choice task included 5 attributes (event-free survival, complete remission, time in hospital, short-term side effects, and long-term side effects) each with three levels. Participants completed 10 choice tasks.

The choice tasks within each DCE were designed in a linear fashion that provided a "back" and "continue" button to progress through the pages. The initial pages of the prototype contained a set of definitions for the terms that would be used as well as a static example on how to complete the choice tasks.

Think-Aloud Sessions and Semi-structured Interviews. Participants were prompted to think aloud as they evaluated the prototype. Each session was audio-recorded and transcribed. Semi-structured interviews were conducted after completing each version of the DCE to elicit feedback on participants' (1) understanding of the provided definitions of the attributes, (2) ability to distinguish between the levels of attributes as presented, (3) preference for DCE version, and (4) perspective on whether patients and family caregivers would utilize and/or trust this tool. Our interview guide was developed in consultation with a qualitative research expert (see Appendix A).

Subjective Usability and Cognitive Workload Assessments. After completing each assigned version of the DCE, participants evaluated the usability by completing the post-study system usability questionnaire (PSSUQ), consisting of 16 questions divided into three sub-constructs: system usefulness, information quality, and interface quality [21]. Each question within the PSSUQ is rated on a 7-point Likert Scale, with overall scores calculated by averaging all sub-constructs. Benchmark scores derived from Sauro and Lewis provide the means depicted in Table 2 to interpret overall and subconstruct PSSUQ scores, with better performance and satisfaction reflected in a lower PSSUQ score [22].

Following completion of each assigned DCE, participants also assessed the CWL, quantified subjectively using the National Aeronautical and Space administration's Task Load Index (NASA-TLX) questionnaire. The NASA-TLX measures six dimensions of CWL (mental, physical, and temporal demands, frustration, effort, and performance) with scores $\geq$55 associated with reduced performance in numerous settings including oncology [23].

2.4 Data Analysis

Descriptive statistics were reported for the demographic information.

Think-Aloud Sessions and Semi-structured Interviews. Qualitative data from both think-aloud sessions and semi-structured interviews were coded by four members of our study team (AC, AK, KA, DRR) in brainstorming sessions to create an affinity diagram. An affinity diagram uses inductive reasoning to gain insight into the key requirements of a system, including reliability and performance [24]. A recent analysis described the use of modified affinity diagramming techniques that were originally developed from from Holtzblatt's methodology and have since been used for prototype evaluation in Human Computer Interaction and interaction design [25]. Holtzblatt's classic approach to affinity diagramming is intended to gain insight during the discovery stages of design and focuses on contextual inquiries, work modeling, consolidation and affinity diagram building, storyboarding and paper prototyping. Lucero's analysis suggests that once interactive prototypes are established, contextual inquiries, work modeling and paper prototyping are no longer relevant [25]. As we had created medium-fidelity prototypes based on paper versions from previous studies, we chose to use a modified approach that uses affinity diagramming for prototype evaluations. This approach includes four stages, including creating notes, clustering notes, walking the wall, and documentation. Data gathered during usability testing was consolidated, and team members were invited to group the user feedback into themes. Team members began placing their suggested themes on the wall, inviting others to "walk the wall", by creating additional subgroups and relocating cards, until all final themes had emerged. Upon completion, the diagramming was converted into an electronic format. We evaluated these findings by selecting relevant quotes within the themes and translated them into specific design recommendations.

Subjective Usability and Workload Assessments. Descriptive statistics for subjective assessments of usability and CWL were calculated using Microsoft Excel. Descriptive statistics established for the subjective assessments (PSSUQ and NASA-TLX) were broken down by case type and cohort.

We compared the obtained usability to existing standards to assess if each case type met acceptable usability levels. PSSUQ scores recorded from each cohort, by assigned case type, were compared to existing standards to assess overall usability, system usefulness, information quality, and interface quality. Paired t-tests were performed, using JMP 15 Pro, to examine differences in overall usability scores between assigned case types within cohorts, and between case types across cohorts. We considered P values of less than .05 to have statistical significance.

We compared the obtained CWL scores to existing CWL standards to assess if the cases met acceptable levels of user interactions with EHTs. The six dimensions of CWL (mental, physical, and temporal demands, frustration, effort, and performance) were compared for each case type and broken down by cohort. Paired t-tests were performed, using JMP 15 Pro, to examine differences between versions of the DCE.

3 Results

3.1 Participant Characteristics

15 participants divided into 3 cohorts were enrolled in the study and completed all assessments. Table 1 summarizes demographic information and comfort level with technology assessments. The median age of all participants was 29 years (range: 21–50). Most participants were female (78.6%) (Table 1). Participants identified as Caucasian (53.3%), Asian (26.7%), African American (13.3%), and Black/White (6.7%). Most participants identified as not Hispanic/Latino (86.7%). All participants were college-educated, with most having completed a bachelor's degree or higher (93.3%). The median household income was \$50,000 to \$74,999. Most participants indicated they are very comfortable with technology (93.3%).

3.2 Participant Preference for Version of the DCE

When asked to specify the preferred version of the DCE, 80% (n = 4) of participants in cohort 1 preferred the multi-profile case, with 20% (n = 1) equally preferring the profile

Table 1. Baseline characteristics of participants

Characteristic	Cohort 1(n = 5)	Cohort 2 (n = 5)	Cohort 3 (n = 5)
Age, y			
Mean (SD)	29.8 (11.4)	25.4 (2.9)	30.8 (11.6)
Range	23–50	23–30	21–50
Sex			
Male	2	1	0
Female	3	4	4
Chose not to specify			1
Race			
Caucasian	2	3	3
African American	1	1	
Asian	1	1	2
Other	1 (Black/white)		
Ethnicity			
Hispanic/Latino			2
Not Hispanic/Latino	5	5	3
Education			
Some college, no degree	1		
Bachelor's degree	3	4	2
Graduate or professional degree	1	1	3
Household income			
Less than $25,000	1	2	2
$25,000 to $34,999	1		
$35,000 to $49,999	2		1
$50,000 to $74,999	2	2	2
Prefer to not answer		1	
Employment status			
35 h a week or more	3	3	1
Less than 35 h a week			3
Unemployed	2		
Other (please specify)		2 (Student)	1 (Student)
Comfort level with technology			
I am very comfortable using technology with little or no help from others	5	5	4

(*continued*)

Table 1. *(continued)*

Characteristic	Cohort 1(n = 5)	Cohort 2 (n = 5)	Cohort 3 (n = 5)
I am somewhat comfortable using technology, but need help getting started			1

case and multi-profile case. In cohort 2, 80% (n = 4) preferred the multi-profile case, with 20% (n = 1) equally preferring the object case and multi-profile case. In cohort 3, 60% (n = 3) preferred the multi-profile case, with 40% (n = 2) preferring the object case.

3.3 Thematic Analysis

Overall, 14 themes emerged during our affinity diagramming sessions (Fig. 4). The themes and subgroupings associated with usability and CWL, and that led to specific design improvements are presented in (Fig. 5). Additional themes emerged that focused on trust for using the tool and appropriate settings (e.g., clinical setting with assistance from a provider) for completing the prototypes. Data from these additional themes will be analyzed when evaluating this tool for clinical implementation.

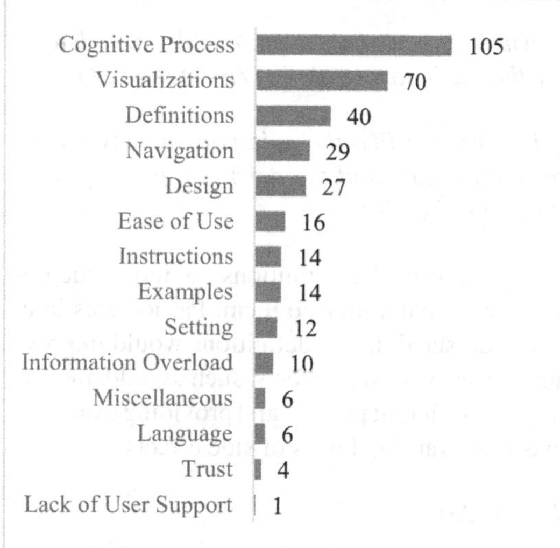

Fig. 4. Affinity diagramming themes

All participants indicated that the prototypes were not challenging to complete. Some participants indicated that while the user interface made it easy to select their answers, cognitive challenges arose when asked to complete the DCEs. These challenges were most often reported with the profile cases, especially the single profile case.

Overall, 4 of the 14 themes that emerged, led to most of the key design change decisions, and are focused on definitions, instructions, information overload, and navigation.

Theme 1: Definitions. All participants (n = 15) reported understanding the attribute definitions well enough to complete the choice tasks, however, 33% needed to reference the definitions. Many participants commented on the need for clarity and having easy access to definitions of the attributes and levels. Study participants mentioned that having the definitions presented before answering the questions was helpful, however, by

Cognitive Process
Preference Clarity
Equipoise between attributes
General (Heuristic)
Clarity of Attributes
Money
Attribute (no subheading)
Levels
One-offs

Definitions
Clear/Helpful
Suggested Improvements

Design
Font
Color
Labels
Layout

Navigation
Straightforward
Navigating between questions
Progress
Dislikes

Examples
Clear
Not Clear

Ease of Use
Ease of Use

Instructions
Clear
Not Clear

Information Overload
Information Overload

Fig. 5. Affinity diagram

the time they were asked to complete the questions, many were uncertain they could accurately recall how a term was defined. Participants suggested adding the ability to review the definitions while answering the questions.

> *"If there is a way to add a feature where if you could click on like complete remission or something, it could show that definition again" (Female, Age 31)*

> *"Maybe when they start actually going through like the quiz part, having like you know how you can like hover over something and the definition pops up, a reminder of maybe what it means." (Female, Age 26)*

Participants also emphasized the need to clarify the definitions, as terms such as event-free survival and complete remission were unfamiliar to them. Participants indicated that emphasizing the importance of understanding the definitions would improve the prototype. Many suggested that the terms used with side effects, such as mild, moderate, and severe, can have different meanings for different people, and providing examples would make it easier to distinguish between the varying levels of side effects.

> *"What is event free survival?" (Male, Age 23).*

> *"People without medical background may not know what this meant." (Female, Age 25)*

> *"It's like after reading the top paragraph, I think I understand event free survival, but yeah, I don't know, I've never heard that term before. At first, I was like oh, remission, and then it says it does not mean you are in remission. And I feel like understanding what event free survival is important for the next questions I'm going to have to respond to, and like I understand the definition, but it's just not really intuitive what event free survival means." (Female, Age 31)*

> *"What is moderate, what is severe, that was the lingering question." (Female, Age 30)*

A disease related event, could that also be any other health thing such as acute respiratory disease or some other complication from the drug? Does that count as an event? I need clarification. (Female, Age 50)

"What does a moderate long term side effect mean right? Does that mean? Oh, I may not be able to have kids." (Female, age 27)

Design Changes: After completing user testing sessions with cohort 1, we added an "information icon" to each choice task page. Within the object case, the icon was located above the attributes and provided definitions of all attributes when selected. For the multi-profile case, the information icon ("i") was located on the left side of each attribute. Cohort 2 noted the icon resembled a bullet point, and that its function was unclear. In response, it was changed to a question mark, relocated to the right side of the attribute, and enlarged by 50% to make it more visible. Text was added to the multi-profile case to state users can "click on any word to display the definition."

With the support of a health literacy expert, we modified the terminology used to define each attribute by removing medical jargon to not exceed a sixth-grade reading level as recommended by the American Medical Association and the Agency for Healthcare Research and Quality [26, 27].

We also simplified the language for attribute levels and incorporated graphs for visual representation. For example, we utilized anthropomorphic representations to indicate the chance of achieving complete remission, and we utilized bullet charts to indicate differences between mild, moderate, and severe (as shown in Figs. 6 and 7 respectively).

We also removed the static "text-based" definition pages and replaced these with audio/video overviews of the simplified definition. Participants can pause or replay the videos if desired.

Theme 2: Instructions. One common preference among participants was the need to have clearer instructions at the onset of the prototype. Participants indicated that providing an overview page or table of contents for the surveys would improve the prototype.

"An overview to see everything that is available on the prototype on one page first might be good because it's when you start going through those continued questions it is not immediately clear what is going to come next. So, it's not clear how much information you are missing. For example, the page that said benefits and risks, it would have been nice to know this would be elaborated on a different page." (Female, Age 25)

"It would be nice if there were a Table of Contents. Let them know the number of questions at the beginning." (Male, Age 23)

"Maybe in the beginning, more of a title to the slides because the title was kind of small up there and I had to sometimes say, like, what am I doing again?" (Female, Age 50)

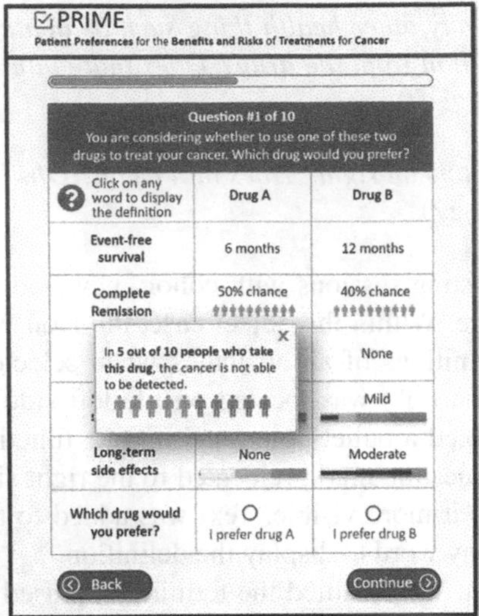

Fig. 6. Multi-profile case with 50% chance of complete remission selected to show pop-up definition.

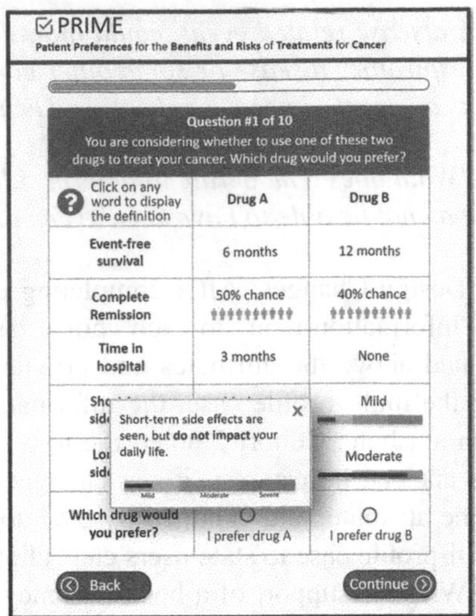

Fig. 7. Multi-profile case with mild short term side effects select to show pop-up definition.

Many felt that the instructions did not provide a clear direction on what they were expected to do, nor how many questions were included. Participants commented that the instructions did not make them aware of the importance of thoroughly understanding the definitions.

> *"Maybe the survey should reference earlier on, I didn't know this is like a survey. It might have been a little confusing." (Female, Age 27)*

> *"It's kind of the way that the mind works if I know this is something that I have to retain until the very end of all of this stuff, then my mind is going to process it differently." (Female, Age 50)*

> *"I don't really understand those directions. I couldn't imagine like older person doing that like that was kind of confusing." (Female, Age 26)*

Participants felt examples of the DCE choice tasks were very helpful. However, for many participants, the static examples contained too much text and caused confusion rather than clarification.

> *"The first example is very confusing. I didn't know what it was asking me to do." (Male, Age 23)*

> *"Oh, this is his choice, not my choice in this example. I did not read that properly." (Male, Age 23)*

Design Changes: We added a welcome video that provided an overview of each prototype for participants to view before interacting with the prototypes. A title page was added to each prototype, as well as an introductory page that provides information about the assigned prototype. The welcome video includes a statement about the importance of understanding the definitions for completing the prototypes.

We also replaced the "text-based" examples with short example videos that walk the participant through the choice tasks and provide them information about how to access definitions, if needed.

Theme 3: Information Overload. Participants stated they felt a sense of information overload and noted that there was too much content on each page. Recommendations were made to simplify the information presented. Although these statements referred to the appearance of the prototype generally, participants noted that the information overload made understanding definitions and answering choice tasks within the DCE difficult. Many participants found it challenging to comprehend and retain the information due to the amount of text and the terminology used.

> *"A lot of information, it was an overload. That made it hard especially when it is something difficult to think about. It was so much. People have different ways of taking in information. There was a lot of text." (Female, Age 27)*

> *"A couple of the screens were a bit too wordy. There was just too much information on the screen and they just needed to be broken up so I can process. I think fit into multiple pages." (Female, Age 50)*

> *"It felt long and time consuming. It felt like it was a lot for one sitting." (Male, Age 24)*

> *"OK, now I got to read all this. I thought it was just going to be pictures." (Female, Age 30)*

> *"I think this could be streamlined into more like one or two sentences. This page looks complicated on first glance." (Female, Age 32)*

Design Changes: We simplified the terminology, focusing primarily on improving the attribute definitions. This resulted in a reduced word count on each page, thereby reducing the clutter and improving the overall appearance.

Theme 4: Navigation. Some parts of the initial prototype contained a navigation bar at the top of the screen. Many commented it was not necessary and oftentimes caused confusion as to its purpose.

> *"I like that there's not the thing on the top there because I was wondering if I need to do something up there." (Reference to the navigation bar) (Female, Age 50)*

> *"I noticed this survey doesn't have the buttons on top, which I think makes it look cleaner because I didn't really need it for them in the last one." (Reference to the navigation bar) (Male, Age 24)*

Each prototype was initially designed with an overall progress bar, located at the top of the screen, and an additional numerical bar located at the bottom of each choice task page to indicate which choice task they were on, as seen displayed in (Figs. 1, 2 and 3). Participants indicated that having two progress bars was confusing.

> *"So the progress bar thing or the advancement thing has changed and that's maybe a little bit jarring." (Referencing the addition of the numerical choice task progress bar) (Female, Age 31)*

> *"When I see this, I feel like I can like choose which question." (Referencing the numerical choice task progress bar) (Age 23)*

Design Changes: We removed the top navigation bar. We also removed the choice task progress bar located at bottom of all DCEs. We added text to the top of each choice task page indicating which question participants were on (e.g. Question 1 of 10).

3.4 Usability

Usability was reported as acceptable for all DCEs, with mean PSSUQ scores below the validated mean scores presented by Sauro and Lewis. [22] Table 2 includes detailed PSSUQ results broken down by DCE type and cohort. When examining the subscales by case type, the best subscale scores for all case types were system usefulness. There was no difference in overall PSSUQ scores between assigned case types within cohorts. When evaluating between case types across cohorts, cohort 1 reported lower mean usability scores for the multi-profile case compared to cohort 2 (−2.8, $p = 0.02$). The multi-profile case was the only case presented to each cohort, of which we saw an improved overall mean score from 2.13 (SD 0.59) to 1.66 (SD 0.30) as well as improved scores in each subscale.

3.5 Cognitive Workload

Global NASA-TLX scores for each DCE case type were all below 55, indicating acceptable cognitive workload. Table 3 includes detailed NASA-TLX results broken down by case type and cohort. There was no difference in global NASA-TLX scores between assigned case types within cohorts. There was a significant difference in the frustration rating between the profile case and object case (cohort 2) (−2.23, $p = 0.04$) and the profile case and object case (cohort 3) (−2.33, $p = 0.04$).

Table 2. Usability scores

Type of DCE (Cohort)	System Usefulness (SYSUSE)	Information Quality (INFOQUAL)	Interface Quality (INTERQUAL)	Overall PSSUQ
Multi-Profile	Mean (SD)			
Cohort 1	1.57 (0.40)	2.35 (0.81)	2.05 (0.51)	2.13 (0.59)
Cohort 2	1.10 (0.08)	1.28 (0.47)	1.25 (0.32)	1.25 (0.39)
Cohort 3	1.49 (0.44)	1.46 (0.43)	1.85 (0.30)	1.66 (0.30)
Profile				
Cohort 1	1.63 (0.53)	2.43 (0.98)	2.25 (0.47)	2.26 (0.60)
Object				
Cohort 2	1.27 (0.53)	1.32 (0.64)	1.20 (0.40)	1.30 (0.60)
Cohort 3	1.24 (0.31)	1.45 (0.39)	1.50 (0.57)	1.45 (0.44)
*Sauro & Lewis **[22]**	2.80	3.02	2.49	2.82

*Recommended means provided by Sauro and Lewis to interpret PSSUQ scores. Better performance and satisfaction are reflected in lower PSSUQ scores [22].

Table 3. Cognitive workload scores

Type of DCE	Global	Mental	Physical	Temporal	Performance	Effort	Frustration
Multi-Profile	Mean (SD)						
Cohort 1	12.32 (3.93)	55.00 (18.71)	0.00 (0.00)	9.00 (13.57)	48.00 (40.82)	40.00 (17.61)	16.00 (11.58)
Cohort 2	6.03 (3.93)	22.00 (25.81)	2.00 (4.00)	2.00 (4.00)	42.00 (47.39)	5.00 (7.75)	2.00 (4.00)
Cohort 3	14.73 (4.83)	69.00 (22.23)	0.00 (0.00)	7.00 (7.48)	85.00 14.14	35.00 (32.71)	10.00 (20.00)
Profile							
Cohort 1	16.13 (6.21)	58.0 (17.94)	2.0 (2.24)	31.0 (21.29)	50.0 (32.53)	37.0 (25.43)	49.0 (29.50)
Object							
Cohort 2	7.27 (2.91)	26.00 (10.20)	2.00 (2.45)	1.00 (2.00)	41.00 (48.21)	13.00 (12.08)	11.00 (22.00)
Cohort 3	14.67 (5.82)	67.00 (26.94)	0.00 (0.00)	14.00 (15.94)	78.00 (34.29)	36.00 (32.77)	10.00 (12.65)

* Global Scores ≥ 55 are associated with reduced performance [23].

4 Discussion

4.1 Principal Findings

The objective of this study was to evaluate and compare standards on the perceived usability and cognitive workload of healthy volunteers interacting with a prototype EHT containing three distinct versions of a DCE: multi-profile case, profile case, and object case. We found similarities between case types, mainly from the results of the PSSUQ and NASA-TLX assessments that suggest usability and the mental workload levels were acceptable. Overall, the qualitative feedback received was positive, with most participants indicating the EHT prototypes containing the DCEs were straightforward, user-friendly, and easy to use.

Utilizing a modified affinity diagramming process for evaluating our prototypes was an effective approach to gain insight from usability testing. Consolidating the qualitative data and creating groupings led to the discovery of usability issues as common themes began to emerge during the diagramming process, including definitions, instructions, information overload, and navigation. Specific design improvements were made to the prototypes based on the discovery of these usability issues. This is consistent with previous studies that indicated this modified approach helped the study team prioritize the issues that needed to be addressed and ultimately led to improved prototypes [25, 28, 29].

Data from DCEs are derived from individual choice tasks where participants indicate their preference for one attribute over another. Poor understanding of attributes fundamentally undermines the validity of results from DCEs. Participants in our study had difficulty recalling the definitions of the attribute terms used in the DCEs. We found that participants desired the option to reference definitions in real-time. Similar to other studies evaluating EHTs, we also found that the terminology used to define each attribute included some medical jargon that was challenging for participants to comprehend [30–32]. We simplified definitions, eliminated medical jargon, and added an information icon to allow for easy reference to definitions. These changes were essential to maintain the validity of the choice tasks by ensuring that participants clearly understood each attribute.

We saw high levels of frustration (NASA-TLX subscale) with the profile case DCE. Participants also reported that they disregarded several attributes in this DCE in order to simplify the process. Previous studies have demonstrated that this strategy, termed attribute non-attendance, is frequently employed by participants in complex DCE choice tasks and may undermine the validity of results [33]. Therefore, we decided to remove the profile case from the prototype and replace it with the object case. This change resulted in decreased levels of frustration and should result in higher levels of confidence about the validity of future results.

Although prototypes were not directly compared by individual participants, usability improved for the multi-profile case in each prototype suggesting that prototypes were progressively more usable. These findings are supported by interviews with participants who indicated that improvements, such as adding the ability to review definitions made the tool more usable.

Published recommendations for developing DCEs for use in healthcare do not currently include a recommendation to evaluate CWL, nor is it a standard practice to evaluate the usability of DCEs embedded in EHTs [34, 35]. This study demonstrates that these methods are useful at identifying potential challenges to the validity of DCE results. Participants universally reported on questionnaires that the DCEs were easy to understand; however, it was clear that many participants did not understand the definitions of attributes and felt frustrated completing choice tasks. These findings suggest that subjective reporting may not be a reliable metric of participant understanding. As we intend to use this EHT to inform shared decision-making regarding chemotherapy, ensuring participant understanding of attributes is critical.

4.2 Limitations

Participants in this study were all healthy volunteers. These participants were younger and likely have different life-experience to our target population of older adults with hematologic malignancies. Our target population will likely experience the EHT differently than these volunteers. Although we attempted to make versions of the DCE similar by containing similar attributes, our study was not designed to directly compare versions of the DCE. For example, the number of choice tasks varied for each DCE. Also, the profile case was only presented to one cohort of patients and was replaced by the object case due to high levels of frustration and subjective report. This reduced the number of participants that completed the profile case. In addition to our small sample size, these considerations make definitive conclusions regarding preference for DCE versions impossible. While our sample size was small, this was adequate for informing the design recommendation of the prototypes, as we were able to identify common themes and achieve thematic saturation. Previous studies using healthy volunteers, and similar sample sizes have shown to be an effective method to resolving usability problems prior to definitive work in our target population [32, 36].

4.3 Conclusion

Shared decision-making in oncology requires a clear understanding of what matters most to each patient. Methods to reliably capture patient preferences at the point-of-care have not been fully developed. We used an innovative approach with healthy volunteers to design efforts that would leverage insights on completing choice tasks within iteratively refined prototypes and improve the processes involved in capturing patient preferences. When implemented, an EHT to elicit patient preferences has the potential to improve shared decision-making and patient-centered care across oncology.

Acknowledgments. We would like to thank UNC Health for their ongoing support devoted to our research efforts. We thank Paul Mihas for his help in preparing an interview guide for use in soliciting participants' comments and feedback about the prototypes. We thank Terri Ottosen for assisting with assessing and providing reports on the terminology used within the prototypes.

Appendix A

Semi-structured Interview Guide (asked after completing each prototype):

1. What is your overall impression of the prototype?
   a. What did you like about the prototype?

   b. What did you not like about it?
   c. What additional features would you like?

2. Did you find the prototype challenging to complete?

   a. Can you tell me more about that?

3. [Multi-Profile Case] You were presented with 10 questions that asked you to choose between drug a and drug b. Can you walk me through how you made a decision regarding treatment preferences in the prototype?
4. [Profile Case/Object Case] You were asked to think about what was most important and least important. Can you walk me through how you made a decision regarding treatment preferences in this prototype.

Semi-structured Interview Guide (asked after completing both prototypes):

5. Did the definitions of the attributes make sense to you as they were presented?
6. Did you feel that you understood the definitions of the attributes well enough to complete the prototype?
7. Could you distinguish between the levels of each attribute as they were presented in the prototype? For example, the levels presented for remission were 40%, 50%, or 60%.

   a. Can you tell me more about that?

8. When you read the words mild, moderate, and severe, what kinds of things came to mind?
9. You were asked 10 questions about drug a and drug b. You were also asked 7 questions about what was most important and least important.

   a. Which of these question series, if either, would help you have a more informed discussion with your providers?

10. Do you think patients with newly diagnosed cancer and their family caregivers will use this? If they do use this, do you think they will trust it?

    a. Can you tell me more about that? (What are the barriers and facilitators?)

References

1. Lymphoma Survival Rate | Blood Cancer Survival Rates | LLS. https://www.lls.org/facts-and-statistics/facts-and-statistics-overview. Accessed 09 Oct 2021
2. Smith, M.Y., et al.: Patient engagement at a tipping point-the need for cultural change across patient, sponsor, and regulator stakeholders: insights from the DIA conference, 'patient engagement in benefit risk assessment throughout the life cycle of medical products.' Ther. Innov. Regul. Sci. **50**(5), 546–553 (2016)
3. Sekeres, M.A., et al.: American society of hematology 2020 guidelines for treating newly diagnosed acute myeloid Leukemia in older adults. Blood Adv. **4**(15), 3528–3549 (2020)

4. Hunter, N.L., O'Callaghan, K.M., Califf, R.M.: Engaging patients across the spectrum of medical product development: view from the US food and drug administration. JAMA **314**(23), 2499–2500 (2015)
5. Rocque, G., et al.: Engaging multidisciplinary stakeholders to drive shared decision-making in oncology. J. Palliat. Care **34**(1), 29–31 (2019)
6. Text - S.1597 - 114th Congress (2015–2016): Patient-Focused Impact Assessment Act of 2016 | Congress.gov | Library of Congress. https://www.congress.gov/bill/114th-congress/senate-bill/1597/text. Accessed 21 Oct 2021
7. Text - H.R.34 - 114th Congress (2015–2016): 21st Century Cures Act | Congress.gov | Library of Congress. https://www.congress.gov/bill/114th-congress/house-bill/34/text. Accessed 21 Oct 2021
8. Cheung, K.L., et al.: Using best-worst scaling to investigate preferences in health care. Pharmacoeconomics **34**(12), 1195–1209 (2016)
9. Witteman, H.O., et al.: Clarifying values: an updated and expanded systematic review and meta-analysis. Med. Decis. Making. **41**, 801–820 (2021)
10. Seo, J., Smith, B.D., Estey, E., Voyard, E., O'Donoghue, B., Bridges, J.F.P.: Developing an instrument to assess patient preferences for benefits and risks of treating acute myeloid leukemia to promote patient-focused drug development. Curr. Med. Res. Opin. **34**(12), 2031–2039 (2018)
11. Richardson, D.R., et al.: Age at diagnosis and patient preferences for treatment outcomes in AML: a discrete choice experiment to explore meaningful benefits. Cancer Epidemiol. Biomark. Prev. **29**(5), 942–948 (2020)
12. Bridges, J.F., Oakes, A.H., Reinhart, C.A., Voyard, E., O'Donoghue, B.: Developing and piloting an instrument to prioritize the worries of patients with acute myeloid leukemia. Patient Prefer. Adher. **12**, 647–655 (2018)
13. Stacey, D., et al.: Decision aids for people facing health treatment or screening decisions. Cochrane Database Syst. Rev. **4**, CD001431 (2017)
14. Walker, J.G., Licqurish, S., Chiang, P.P.C., Pirotta, M., Emery, J.D.: Cancer risk assessment tools in primary care: a systematic review of randomized controlled trials. Ann. Fam. Med. **13**(5), 480–489 (2015)
15. McLean, B., et al.: Providing medical information to older adults in a web-based environment: systematic review. JMIR Aging **4**(1), e24092 (2021)
16. Faulkner, L.: Beyond the five-user assumption: benefits of increased sample sizes in usability testing. Behav. Res. Methods. Instrum. Comput. **35**(3), 379–383 (2003)
17. Sumner, J., Chong, L.S., Bundele, A., Lim, Y.W.: Co-designing technology for ageing in place: a systematic review. Gerontologist. **61**, e395-409 (2020)
18. Vandekerckhove, P., de Mul, M., Bramer, W.M., de Bont, A.A.: Generative participatory design methodology to develop electronic health interventions: systematic literature review. J. Med. Internet Res. **22**(4), e13780 (2020)
19. Watling, C.J., Lingard, L.: Grounded theory in medical education research: AMEE guide No. 70. Med. Teach. **34**(10), 850–861 (2012)
20. Between-Subjects vs. Within-Subjects Study Design. https://www.nngroup.com/articles/between-within-subjects/. Accessed 09 Oct 2021
21. PSSUQ (Post-Study System Usability Questionnaire) - UIUX Trend. https://uiuxtrend.com/pssuq-post-study-system-usability-questionnaire/. Accessed 31 May 2021
22. Sauro, J., Lewis, J.R.: Standardized usability questionnaires. In: Quantifying the User Experience: Practical Statistics for User Research, Waltham, MA 02451, pp. 185–240. Elsevier, USA (2012)
23. Mazur, L.M., et al.: Positive effects of neurofeedback intervention on radiation oncology physicians' workload during go/no-go performance test. Trav. Hum. **80**(1), 113 (2017)

24. Holtzblatt, K., Beyer, H.: The affinity diagram. In: Contextual Design, pp. 127–146. Elsevier (2017)
25. Lucero, A.: Using affinity diagrams to evaluate interactive prototypes. In: Abascal, J., Barbosa, S., Fetter, M., Gross, T., Palanque, P., Winckler, M. (eds.) INTERACT 2015. LNCS, vol. 9297, pp. 231–248. Springer, Cham (2015). https://doi.org/10.1007/978-3-319-22668-2_19
26. Weiss, B.D.: Health Literacy - A Manual for Clinicians. American Medical Association Foundation and American Medical Association Chicago, IL (2006)
27. Health Literacy | PSNet. https://psnet.ahrq.gov/primer/health-literacy. Accessed 29 Jan 2022
28. Buur, J., Soendergaard, A.: Video card game: an augmented environment for user centred design discussions. In: Proceedings of DARE 2000 on Designing Augmented Reality Environments - DARE 2000, New York, New York, USA, pp. 63–69 (2000)
29. Cox, D., Greenberg, S.: Supporting collaborative interpretation in distributed Groupware. In: Proceedings of the 2000 ACM Conference on Computer Supported Cooperative Work - CSCW 2000, New York, New York, USA, pp. 289–298 (2000)
30. De Clercq, P.A., Hasman, A., Wolffenbuttel, B.H.R.: A consumer health record for supporting the patient-centered management of chronic diseases. Med. Inform. Internet Med. **28**(2), 117–127 (2003)
31. Pyper, C., Amery, J., Watson, M., Crook, C.: Patients' experiences when accessing their on-line electronic patient records in primary care. Br J Gen Pract **54**(498), 38–43 (2004)
32. Britto, M.T., Jimison, H.B., Munafo, J.K., Wissman, J., Rogers, M.L., Hersh, W.: Usability testing finds problems for novice users of pediatric portals. J. Am. Med. Inform. Assoc. **16**(5), 660–669 (2009)
33. Lew, D.K., Whitehead, J.C.: Attribute non-attendance as an information processing strategy in stated preference choice experiments: origins, current practices, and future directions. Mar. Resour. Econ. **35**(3), 285–317 (2020)
34. Bridges, J.F.P., et al.: Conjoint analysis applications in health–a checklist: a report of the ISPOR good research practices for conjoint analysis task force. Value Health **14**(4), 403–413 (2011)
35. Reed Johnson, F., et al.: Constructing experimental designs for discrete-choice experiments: report of the ISPOR conjoint analysis experimental design good research practices task force. Value Health. **16**(1), 3–13 (2013)
36. Bansback, N., Li, L.C., Lynd, L., Bryan, S.: Development and preliminary user testing of the DCIDA (dynamic computer interactive decision application) for 'nudging' patients towards high quality decisions. BMC Med. Inform. Decis. Making **14**, 62 (2014)

Analysis of the Influencing Factors of the Elderly User's Somatosensory Game Themes Preferences – Based on the DEMATEL Method

Yi Ding, Ting Han(✉), Chunrong Liu, Yahui Zhang, and Shuyu Zhao

School of Design, Shanghai Jiao Tong University, 800 Dongchuan Road, Minhang District, Shanghai 200240, China
hanting@sjtu.edu.cn

Abstract. This research aims to investigate the main factors that affect the selection of different somatosensory games for the elderly. The research uses literature research, questionnaire survey and interview method to summarize ten main influencing factors, then combines the Decision-Making Trial and Evaluation Laboratory method (DEMATEL) to evaluate the interaction and degree of interaction among the main influencing factors.

The result shows that the factors of 'Happiness perception', 'Exercise behavior' and 'Self-worth' are the three core factors that affect the somatosensory game theme preference among the elderly. 'Exercise behavior', 'Health status' and 'Altruistic behavior' have the greatest influence on other factors, as well as 'Happiness perception', 'Self-worth' and 'Friendly relations' are more likely to be affected by other factors. The purpose of this research is to analyze the interaction of factors which influencing the somatosensory game preferences among the elderly. It is hoped that this research can provide theoretical references for the design of somatosensory games for the elderly in the future, to improve the elderly's exercise experience, and to promote the application of emerging technologies in the elderly.

Keywords: The elderly · Somatosensory games preferences · User decision-making · Decision-making Trial and Evaluation Laboratory (DEMATEL)

1 Introduction

1.1 Background

According to the World Health Organization (WHO) [1], the proportion of the global population over the age of 60 will increase from 12% to 22% from 2015 to 2050. With the development of the global aging trend, the quality of life and medical care of the elderly has become one of the most important global issues [2]. Faced with substantial social and economic problems produced by population aging, the concept of "Active Aging" has received more widespread recognition and attention. A large number of domestic and foreign studies have shown that exercise is a key factor in achieving 'Active Aging'

Q. Gao and J. Zhou (Eds.): HCII 2022, LNCS 13331, pp. 229–242, 2022.
https://doi.org/10.1007/978-3-031-05654-3_15

goals. Regular exercise has positive effect on the healthy development of both the brain system and nervous system [3].

With the improvement of technology and people's consumption level, the forms of fitness activities are constantly being updated. Compared with traditional sports, somatosensory games have received more and more widespread recognition and attention due to their entertainment, freedom and interactivity.

In addition to its application in daily exercise, somatosensory games have gradually become an emerging medical method, allowing users to penetrate from the young to the elderly. Some studies also have shown that exercise can be used to encourage physical and mental activity in the elderly and delay their disease attack.

However, although regular exercise has many benefits for the elderly, their actual participation in exercise is still low due to their limitations of movement and accustomed living habits [4]. Meanwhile, although somatosensory games have become more and more widely accepted, most of them are not designed for the elderly, which makes them unable to enjoy the benefits. Facing the huge market of products suitable for the elderly, it is necessary to combine their special physical and psychological conditions to design somatosensory games which can make them more willing to exercise.

1.2 Literature Review

The literature research is conducted through databases and search engines, primarily initiated through the Web of Science, CNKI, Google Scholar, and ScienceDirect. This research starts from the database collection research, based on the keywords 'Exercise suitable for aging', 'Somatosensory games', 'Exercise willingness', 'User experience', etc., and the publication year ranges from 2000 to 2021. The authors sort out and the research on the aging of somatosensory games and the factors influencing the exercise decision-making of the elderly.

Scholars Mandryk [5] and others have summarized the factors obstructing movement from three aspects, including psychological barriers, physical barriers, and time barriers. Psychological barriers include lack of exercise awareness and exercise interest, lack of confidence, etc. Physical barriers include weather conditions and site restrictions. Amado [6] pointed out that the aging process of the elderly will be accompanied with the decline of physical function, which will result in the decline of exercise ability and self-control ability. Further, it will result in negative emotions and weakened willingness to exercise. On the other hand, the characteristics of exercise (such as boring, single-person participation, etc.), will also lead to the decrease in the exercise willingness and the reduction in the exercise duration.

Some research [7] show that, compared with traditional video games, somatosensory games have higher intensity and can induce more energy consumption. Therefore, somatosensory games can be used as an effective daily exercise tool. A three-year-long study [8] have showed that the elderly in the case of somatosensory game intervention showed higher willingness and participation than those under traditional exercise intervention. The study by Kappen [9] et al. also reached the same conclusion.

Somatosensory games can also provide positive emotional experience for the elderly. Li X et al. [10] found that somatosensory games have significant relieving effect on anxiety in the elderly. The experiments of Chao [11] et al. also verified this point of view, and further pointed out that such positive effects may originate from the cooperation and interaction of peers during games. The research of Bandura [12] et al. showed that the goal setting, progress display, role building, support and encouragement during the somatosensory games can improve the participation willingness and completion of the elderly. Also, the research by Jung [11] and others showed that the loneliness of the elderly in the experimental group using Nintendo Wii was much lower than that in the control group using traditional board games, which indicating that somatosensory games can effectively reduce the negative emotions of the elderly.

Research by Skjæret et al. [13] showed that the quality of somatosensory games is determined by both the action features and the game design. They studied the game elements and the movement characteristics of the elderly in the step-by-step movement. The game elements include game graphics, sound, game mechanics, game narrative, etc. The movement characteristics include step change, movement direction, and center of gravity movement. In terms of promoting exercise motivation, somatosensory games which support multiplayer modes are becoming more and more widely used. 'Competition' and 'cooperation' are the most common multiplayer interaction mode. The research of Woohyeok [14] et al. integrated the competition mechanism and cooperation mechanism into swimming sports games. In the competition mode, the players' respective points are determined by the ranking of the stroke frequency of all players in the team; In the cooperation mode, all the players are in the same lane and need to control their frequency to avoid collisions with each other and deduct points. The study showed that besides achieving group goals, this game also effectively promoted group friendly relations. It introduced a rich social experience, and enhanced user experience. Seungmin Lee [15] pointed out that social interaction and feedback (including visual and sound) in somatosensory games will have an impact on players' psychology. At the same time, the study also pointed out that there is a relationship between energy consumption and psychological emotions during the games. Scholar Zhao [16] pointed out that personalized game content and gradually unlocking & releasing game mechanics can effectively improve players' participation and completion, then improve the user experience during the game.

However, most studies only analyze from one certain perspective, which cannot comprehensively analyze the users' decision-making. Therefore, this research aimes to use the DEMATEL method to conduct a comprehensive analysis of the influencing factors of elderly users' somatosensory game themes preference.

1.3 Research Purposes

This study focuses on the somatosensory games for the elderly, explores the factors that affect their preferences and the interrelationships between the factors. Through literature search and questionnaire survey, ten main factors affecting users' choice behavior were summarized. It is hoped that by using the Decision-making and Evaluation Laboratory method (DEMATEL), the research can evaluate these influencing factors to determine the correlation between them. Furthermore, providing theoretical models and scientific references for the somatosensory games design for the elderly, so as to improve their user experience, investigate the direction of related products and service systems to promote the application of emerging technologies among the elderly.

2 Analysis of Factors Influencing the Theme Preferences of Somatosensory Games Among the Elderly

2.1 Summary of Factors Influencing the Theme Preferences of Somatosensory Games Among the Elderly

Based on literature search, 50 high-frequency keywords related to 'Aging exercise', 'Somatosensory game experience' and 'Exercise willingness' in relevant literature were extracted, as shown in Table 1.

Table 1. Topics related high frequency keywords.

Number	Keywords	Number	Keywords
1	Age	26	Keep a clear mind
2	Gender	27	Self-achievement
3	Educational level	28	Future hope
4	Monthly income	29	Decision making
5	Medical insurance	30	Depend on
6	Living habit	31	Interest in life
7	Diet	32	Emotional management
8	Medication	33	Degree of fatigue
9	Sleep quality and duration	34	Depressive condition
10	Urinating and defecation	35	Hearing & vision
11	Living environment	36	Age perception
12	Family company	37	Quality of life
13	Peer communication	38	Independence
14	Privacy respect	39	Confidence
15	Self-determination	40	Chronic disease severity
16	Verbal respect	41	Family and friends contact
17	Self-management	42	Personality growth
18	Act respectfully	43	Psychological well-being
19	Hobby	44	Self-worth
20	Learning attitude	45	Altruistic behavior
21	Specialty	46	Vitality
22	Social support	47	Friendly relations
23	Family support	48	Family structure
24	Health status	49	Memory capacity
25	Self-care ability	50	Balance ability

2.2 Classify the Factors Influencing the Theme Preferences of Somatosensory Games Among the Elderly

Since the excessive number of keywords (50) and some duplication of internal factors will lead to the difficulty of subsequent data collection and low accuracy, this research adopts qualitative analysis and further literature review. The elements are extracted, classified and summarized, as the main influencing factors (MIF). The specific contents are shown in Table 2.

Table 2. Main factors influencing the elderly to choose somatosensory games with different themes.

Number	Influencing factors	Specific items
1	Health status	Balance ability, muscle strength, disease prevention, disease treatment, psychological condition
2	Nutritional behavior	Eating habits, nutritional science, dietary taboos, dietary recommendations
3	Living habit	Vitality, hobbies, medication habits
4	Exercise behavior	Energy expenditure, strength training, desire to exercise, fatigue level
5	Self-domination	Self-care ability, daily independence, activity restriction, learning attitude, self-determination
6	Happiness perception	Life quality, vitality, hope of life, source of income, medical security, living environment, social support, family support, teamwork, familiarity
7	Self-worth	Education level, self-management, age perception, personality growth, specialty
8	Altruistic behavior	Family decision-making, degree of dependence, self-influence on others
9	Friendly relations	Marital status, family structure, family accompaniment, privacy and verbal respect, social relations
10	Stress management	Health distress, emotional management, depression, and heart-to-heart talks

2.3 DEMATEL Procedure

The Decision-Making Trial and Evaluation Laboratory (DEMATEL) technique was first employed by Fontela between 1972 and 1976 by the Scientific and Human Affairs Program of the Battle Memorial Institute in Geneva [17]. DEMATEL is a structural modeling method that helps to analyze the relationship between system components, confirm whether there is a relationship or interdependence between components, and can also reflect the relative relationship between components level [18]. It has been widely used in many fields such as hospital management [19], car sharing services [20], as well as intelligent product service system [21] and management system for Small and medium-sized enterprises [22].

The DEMATEL procedure in this research is carried out according to the following steps (see Fig. 1.). (1) Determine the 10 main influencing factors that affect the selection of somatosensory games of different themes for the elderly users; (2) Design a DeMATEL scale to establish the relationship between each factor. Go to the community to collect the target users' opinions through face-to-face interviews and questionnaires. Then sort the data and establish the direct relationship matrix Z; (3) Normalize the original relationship matrix to obtain the normalized direct influence matrix; (4) Calculate the direct/indirect relationship matrix T, and obtain the influence degree (D), influenced degree (R), the corresponding Prominence value (D + R), and Relation value (D − R) of each factor, and observe the relationship structure among the factors; (5) Draw the Influential Relation Diagram (IRD); (6) Determine the interaction degree among the factors and provide scientific references and suggestions for the design of somatosensory games for the elderly.

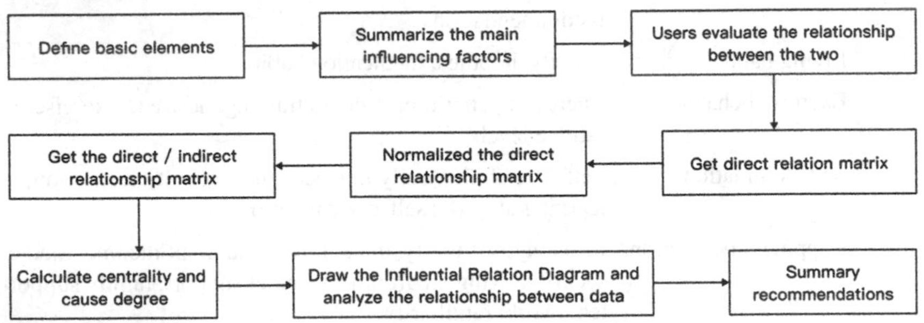

Fig. 1. Research process of Decision-Making Trial and Evaluation Laboratory method (DEMATEL)

Questionnaire Distribution and Data Analysis. The above 10 main influencing factors (MIF) are made into a 10 * 10 matrix of rows and columns, as shown in Table 3. The author went to Hongqi Community, Minhang District, Shanghai to collect questionnaire data (the interview scene is shown in Fig. 2), and explored the influence relationship between each two factors through the DEMATEL questionnaire. The users can score the influence degree by their own subjective judgment. The degree is divided into four levels, where "0" represents "No influence", "1" represents "Very low influence", and "2" represents "Low influence", "3" stands for "High influence".

After selected according to the restriction of age (65 ± 5 years old), a total of 31 questionnaire data were obtained, and the 31 data were calculated according to the following Eq. (1).

$$Z = \frac{1}{n}\sum\nolimits_{m=1}^{n}\left[Z_{ij}^{m}\right],\ ij = 1,\ 2,\ 3,\ \ldots,\ k. \tag{1}$$

Table 3. DEMATEL questionnaire.

	Health status	Nutritional behavior	Living habit	Exercise behavior	Self-domination	Happiness perception	Self-worth	Altruistic behavior	Friendly relations	Stress management
Health status	0									
Nutritional behavior		0								
Living habit			0							
Exercise behavior				0						
Self-domination					0					
Happiness perception						0				
Self-worth							0			
Altruistic behavior								0		
Friendly relations									0	
Stress management										0

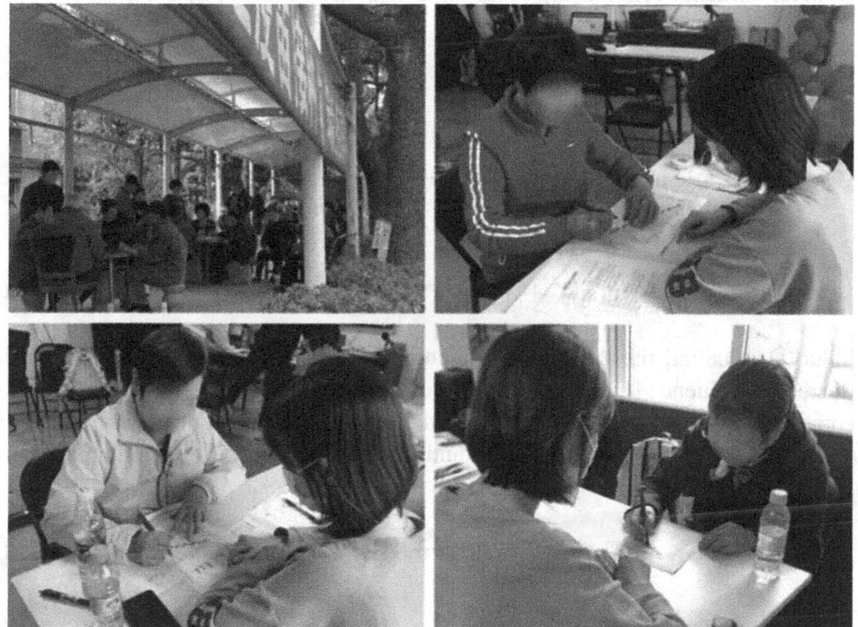

Fig. 2. DEMATEL questionnaire collection site (Hongqi Community, Minhang District, Shanghai)

The averaged Direct-relation matrix Z was obtained, such as shown in Table 4.

Table 4. The averaged Direct-relation matrix Z.

	F1	F2	F3	F4	F5	F6	F7	F8	F9	F10
F1	0.000	1.839	1.935	2.226	2.194	2.323	1.903	1.548	1.742	2.065
F2	2.129	0.000	1.742	1.355	1.484	1.677	1.355	0.903	1.290	1.548
F3	2.065	1.806	0.000	1.903	1.645	1.968	1.742	1.419	1.548	1.419
F4	2.194	1.871	2.226	0.000	2.355	1.935	2.194	1.935	1.935	2.219
F5	1.645	1.194	1.645	2.129	0.000	2.484	2.323	1.290	1.355	1.710
F6	1.935	1.000	1.774	1.903	1.839	0.000	1.935	1.935	2.032	2.290
F7	1.452	0.774	1.677	1.871	1.839	2.129	0.000	1.968	1.839	2.226
F8	1.419	1.000	1.452	1.452	1.355	2.355	2.677	0.000	2.194	1.613
F9	1.484	1.000	1.516	1.710	1.194	2.323	2.290	2.032	0.000	1.774
F10	2.355	1.645	1.581	1.839	1.613	2.516	2.129	1.613	1.806	0.000

Next, standardize the averaged direct relationship matrix, and calculate the direct and indirect influence relationship matrix T as shown in Table 5, by using Eqs. (2)–(4).

$$\mathrm{X} = [x_{ij}]_{k\times k} = \mathrm{sZ} \tag{2}$$

$$\mathrm{s} = \min\left(\frac{1}{\underset{1 \leqq j \leqq k}{max} \sum_{i=1}^{k} z_{ij}}, \frac{1}{\underset{1 \leqq j \leqq k}{max} \sum_{i=1}^{k} z_{ij}}\right) \tag{3}$$

$$\mathrm{T} = \lim_{m\to\infty}(X + X^2 + \ldots + X^m) = \mathrm{X}(1 - X)^{-1} \tag{4}$$

Value D is called the degree of influential impact, as well as Value R is called the degree of influenced impact. Value D_i of each factor is the sum of the values of the corresponding row, and the value R_i is the sum of the values of the corresponding columns of each factor. Calculate the D and R values of each of the ten factors, using Eqs. (5)–(6).

$$D_i = \sum\nolimits_{j=1}^{n} t_{ij}, \ (\mathrm{i} = 1, 2, 3, \ldots, \mathrm{n}) \tag{5}$$

$$R_i = \sum\nolimits_{j=1}^{n} t_{ij}, \ (\mathrm{i} = 1, 2, 3, \ldots, \mathrm{n}) \tag{6}$$

Calculate the quartile in the matrix, and get the threshold value of 0.698. Delete the factor 'Nutrition behavio' in the matrix whose D_i value and R_i value are both lower than the threshold value. This factor will not be analyzed and discussed in this research.

Table 5. The direct/indirect relation matrix T.

	F1	F2	F3	F4	F5	F6	F7	F8	F9	F10
F1	0.629	~~0.556~~	0.685	***0.731***	***0.700***	****0.845***	****0.788***	0.644	0.687	***0.740***
F2	~~0.591~~	~~0.364~~	~~0.545~~	~~0.553~~	~~0.535~~	~~0.652~~	~~0.606~~	~~0.487~~	~~0.531~~	~~0.574~~
F3	0.654	~~0.500~~	0.522	0.643	0.606	***0.743***	***0.698***	0.571	0.607	0.636
F4	***0.763***	~~0.580~~	***0.726***	0.655	***0.734***	****0.864***	****0.834***	0.688	***0.724***	****0.773***
F5	0.647	~~0.480~~	0.614	0.666	0.537	****0.780***	***0.738***	0.578	0.611	0.663
F6	0.687	~~0.492~~	0.645	0.683	0.651	0.696	***0.753***	0.632	0.668	***0.715***
F7	0.637	~~0.460~~	0.614	0.653	0.624	****0.765***	0.629	0.608	0.633	0.684
F8	0.622	~~0.459~~	0.592	0.622	0.590	***0.760***	***0.741***	0.503	0.638	0.645
F9	0.622	~~0.457~~	0.592	0.629	0.580	***0.754***	***0.719***	0.597	0.529	0.648
F10	***0.719***	~~0.531~~	0.650	0.693	0.654	****0.829***	****0.774***	0.629	0.670	0.620

~~Underline~~represents all values in the row and the column that correspond to a factor in the matrix T are below the threshold value of 0.698

Bold italics type represents general influences, which is above the threshold of 0.698

*represents strong influences, which is above 0.764

Taking 2/3 of the value greater than the threshold value in the matrix, the result is 0.764. This value will be used as the criterion for distinguishing the influence strength between factors. Greater than 0.764 means strong influence.

Calculate the Prominence (D + R), which represents the importance, and the Net effect (D – R), which represents the influence degree of this factor or the affected degree of other factors (see Table 6).

Table 6. Prominence (D + R) and Net effect (D – R) values.

		D + R			D – R
F6	Happiness perception	14.310	F4	Exercise behavior	0.812
F4	Exercise behavior	13.869	F1	Health status	0.434
F7	Self-worth	13.587	F8	Altruistic behavior	0.237
F1	Health status	13.576	F5	Self-domination	0.102
F10	Stress management	13.468	F10	Stress management	0.072
F5	Self-domination	12.524	F3	Living habit	−0.005
F9	Friendly relations	12.424	F9	Friendly relations	−0.173
F3	Living habit	12.366	F7	Self-worth	−0.970
F8	Altruistic behavior	12.111	F6	Happiness perception	−1.068
	Average value	13.137			

The larger the (D + R) value, the higher the importance of the influencing factor in the overall evaluation system. In this research, factors with higher (D + R) value than the average level are 'Happiness perception', 'Exercise behavior', 'Self-worth', 'Health status' and 'stress management'. These above factors are the core factors which affect the preferences of different somatosensory games for elderly users.

When (D − R) is positive, it indicates that the factor can directly affect other factors. The larger the value is, the stronger it can influence; when (D − R) is negative, it indicates that the factor is more likely to be affected by other factors, and the bigger the absolute value is, the easier it can be affected. The above results show that 'Exercise behavior', 'Health status', 'Altruistic behavior', 'Self-domination' and 'Stress management' have an impact on other factors (causal factors); 'Living habits', 'Friendly relations', 'Self-worth' and 'Happiness perception' were the main influenced factors (outcome factors).

The Influential Relation Diagram (IRD). The influential relation diagram can visualize the interaction between factors and quickly identify factors that have a significant impact on others or are easily affected by others. According to the data in Table 6 above, it showed the coordinate position of the 9 main influencing factors (excluding the factor T2- 'Nutritional behavior') in the diagram. The horizontal axis represents the Prominence (D + R), and the vertical axis represents the Net effect (D − R). In the Influential Relation Diagram, the solid line represents a strong influence relationship between factors (values greater than or equal to 0.764), and the dotted line represents a weak influence relationship between factors ($0.698 \leq X < 0.764$). The influencing strength value lower than 0.698 will not be drawn in the in the diagram. The arrow points from "influence" to "influenced" factors. The specific location of each factor is shown in Fig. 3.

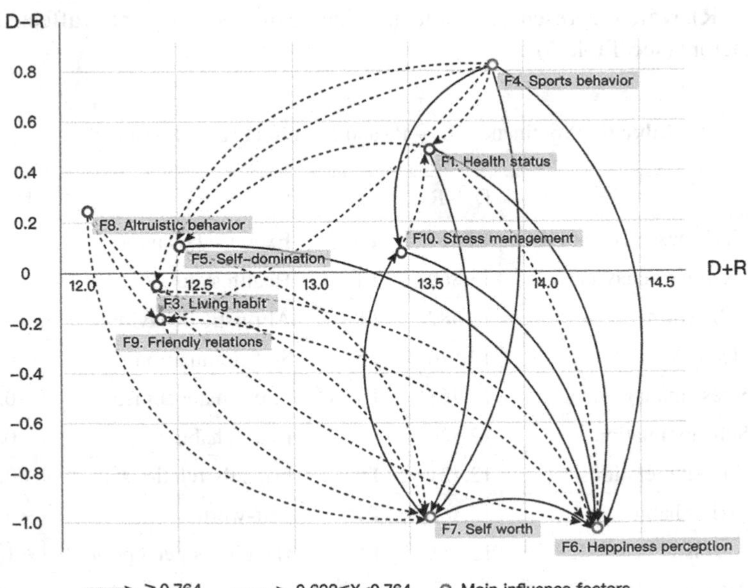

Fig. 3. DEMATEL questionnaire collection site (Hongqi Community, Minhang District, Shanghai)

2.4 Discussion

Key Factors for the Elderly Users to Choose Somatosensory Games with Different Themes. Table 7 lists the top three items and the last three items of Prominence (D + R) and Net-effect (D − R). The top three factors of (D + R) are 'Perception of happiness', 'Exercise behavior' and 'Self-worth'. These are the most critical factors that affect the theme preference of somatosensory games for elderly users. Among them, 'Happiness perception' with the highest (D + R) is the most critical factor, and it is necessary to focus on intervention. The (D + R) value of 'Friendly relationship', 'Living habits' and 'Altruistic behavior' is the smallest, which are the least influential factor. The top three of (D − R) values are 'Exercise behavior', 'Health status' and 'Altruistic behavior', which have strong impact on other factors and are the main driving factors. The last three of (D − R) values are 'Happiness perception', 'Self-worth" and 'Friendly relations', which are more susceptible to other factors (outcome factors).

Table 7. Key factors for the elderly users to choose different somatosensory games.

	The top three factors in (D + R)		The last three factors in (D + R)
F6	Happiness perception	F9	Friendly relations
F4	Exercise behavior	F3	Living habit
F7	Self-worth	F8	Altruistic behavior
	The top three factors in (D − R > 0)		The last three factors in (D − R < 0)
F4	Exercise behavior	F6	Happiness perception
F1	Health status	F7	Self-worth
F8	Altruistic behavior	F9	Friendly relations

Analysis and Discussion. The influential relation diagram (IRD) visualizes the relationship between the influencing factors of elderly users choosing different somatosensory games. As shown in the figure, 'Happiness perception' is the most critical factor affecting the preference, and it also has strong effect on others, which is a crucial intervention point. 'Exercise behavior', 'Health status' and 'Altruistic behavior' have significant influence on other factors such as 'Perception of happiness'. By improving these aspects, the preference of the elderly users for somatosensory games can be positively affected.

Based on the above, the following analysis and suggestions are put forward for the design of somatosensory games for the elderly in the future:

The elderly prefer game themes that can gain a sense of happiness, and hope to get sufficient exercise in the game. It can be seen from the influential relation diagram that 'Happiness perception' and 'Exercise behavior' have the highest (D + R) value among the nine factors. 'Exercise behavior' also has a strong impact on other factors, which plays an important role in the theme preference of somatosensory games for the elderly.

It is recommended to learn from the traditional sports that the elderly are familiar with and good at, such as Tai Chi, square dance, etc. It is a possible design scheme which integrate their core movements into the somatosensory game to effectively reduce the sense of strangeness and resistance. Also, it is recommended to give users enough positive and encouraging feedback when the goal is achieved, and avoid negative feedback with blame, so that the elderly can get enough happiness and pride.

At the same time, the visual design of the game interface can consider warm and positive colors, use the elements which the elderly are familiar to, and use soft and comfortable background music to create a warm and happy activity atmosphere.

The elderly prefer the game themes which can promote their health. It is suggested that let them get their own exercise process and physical condition to promote exercise through positive physical data. The influential relation diagram shows that 'Exercise behavior', 'Health status' and' Altruistic behavior' have strong effects on others. Promoting these three aspects can promote the improvement of other factors together.

In terms of exercise action design, the exercise intensity and duration suitable for the elderly should be carefully formulated, so that they can get sufficient exercise under the premise of ensuring safety. It is recommended to set staged game goals, record the user's exercise performance and game progress, which can help the elderly users to grasp their personal conditions, choose a suitable exercise plan, compare the data before and after exercise, and gain a sense of happiness and self-control.

Adding multiplayer cooperative/competitive mode in the Game mechanism. Competitive and cooperative are the two most common modes of multiplayer interaction. The competition mechanism can effectively motivate users' participation and completion. But it is also necessary to avoid excessive competition mode which can cause users' fear. The cooperation mechanism can effectively enrich the online social experience, promote 'Altruistic behavior' and 'Friendly relationship', thereby enhancing the elderly's degree of preference for somatosensory games, exercise actively, promoting health, and forming a positive closed loop.

3 Conclusion

This research identified ten main influencing factors of elderly users' preference for different somatosensory game themes, and used the DEMATEL method to calculate the interaction degree between the factors. Based on the influential relation diagram, the key factors were used as entry points to put forward the suggestions and references for the design of somatosensory games for the elderly in the future. It is hoped to acquire the preferences of the elderly more accurately, so as to improve their participation and completion of exercise, which can effectively improve the physical and psychological state of the elderly. And then, the elderly can really feel the benefits of emerging technologies.

References

1. Cardoso, H., Bernardino, A., Sanches, M., Loureiro, L.: Exergames and their benefits in the perception of the Quality of Life and Socialization on institutionalized older adults. In: 5th Experiment International Conference, pp. 298–304. IEEE, Funchal, Portugal (2019)

2. Chiang, I., Tsai, J., Chen, S.: Using Xbox 360 Kinect games on enhancing visual performance skills on institutionalized older adults with wheelchairs. In: 4th International Conference on Digital Game And Intelligent Toy Enhanced Learning, pp. 263–267. IEEE, Takamatsu, Japan (2012)
3. Liou, M., Chen, S.T., Fu, H.C., Chiang, I.T.: Effects of somatosensory video games on simple reactions of institutional-dwelling older adults with mild-cognitive impairments. In: 15th International Conference on Advanced Learning Technologies, pp. 428–429. IEEE, Hualien, Taiwan (2015)
4. Wu, Z., Li, J., Theng, Y.L.: Examining the influencing factors of exercise intention among older adults: a controlled study between exergame and traditional exercise. Cyberpsychol. Behav. Soc. Netw. **18**(9), 521–527 (2015)
5. Mandryk, R.L., Gerling, K.M., Stanley, K.G.: Designing games to discourage sedentary behaviour. In: Nijholt, A. (ed.) Playful User Interfaces. GMSE, pp. 253–274. Springer, Singapore (2014). https://doi.org/10.1007/978-981-4560-96-2_12
6. Velazquez, A., Martinez-Garcia, A.I., Favela, J., Hernandez, A., Ochoa, S.F.: Design of exergames with the collaborative participation of older adults. In: Proceedings of the 2013 IEEE 17th International Conference on Computer Supported Cooperative Work in Design (CSCWD), pp. 521–526. IEEE, Whistler, BC, Canada (2013)
7. Graves, L.E., Ridgers, N.D., Williams, K., Stratton, G., Atkinson, G.T.: The physiological cost and enjoyment of WII fit in adolescents, young adults, and older adults. J. Phys. Act. Health **7**(3), 393–401 (2010)
8. Taylor, L.M., Maddison, R., Pfaeffli, L.A., Rawstorn, J.C., Gant, N., Kerse, N.M.: Activity and energy expenditure in older people playing active video games. Arch. Phys. Med. Rehabil. **93**(12), 2281–2286 (2012)
9. Kappen, D., Mirza-Babaei, P., Nacke, L.: Gamification of older adults' physical activity: an eight-week study. In: Proceedings of the 51st Hawaii International Conference on System Sciences (2018)
10. Li, X., Li, R., Han, T.: Effect of gamification of exercise therapy on elderly's anxiety emotion. In: Zhou, J., Salvendy, G. (eds.) International Conference on Human-Computer Interaction 2016. LNCS, vol. 11593, pp. 533–544. Springer, Cham (2019). https://doi.org/10.1007/978-3-030-22015-0_41
11. Chao, Y.Y., Scherer, Y.K., Montgomery, C.A., Wu, Y.W., Lucke, K.T.: Physical and psychosocial effects of Wii Fit exergames use in assisted living residents: a pilot study. Clin. Nurs. Res. **24**(6), 589–603 (2015)
12. Bandura, A., Freeman, W.H., Lightsey, R.: Self-Efficacy: The Exercise of Control. Springer, New York (1999)
13. Bandura, A., Freeman, W.H., Lightsey, R.: Self-efficacy: The exercise of control. J. Cogn. Psych. **13**(2), 158–166 (1999). https://doi.org/10.1891/0889-8391.13.2.158
14. Choi, W., Oh, J., Edge, D., Kim, J., Lee, U.: SwimTrain: exploring exergame design for group fitness swimming. In: Proceedings of the 2016 CHI Conference on Human Factors in Computing Systems, pp. 1692–1704. Association for Computing Machinery, San Jose, California, USA (2016)
15. Skjæret, N., et al.: Designing for movement quality in exergames: lessons learned from observing senior citizens playing stepping games. Gerontology **61**(2), 186–194 (2015)
16. Zhao, Z.: Personalization of wearable-based exergames with continuous player modeling. Doctoral dissertation, Carleton University (2019)
17. Lee, S., Kim, W., Park, T., Peng, W.: The psychological effects of playing exergames: a systematic review. Cyberpsychol. Behav. Soc. Netw. **20**(9), 513–532 (2017)
18. Thakkar, J.J.: Decision-making trial and evaluation laboratory (DEMATEL). In: Multi-Criteria Decision Making. SSDC, vol. 336, pp. 139–159. Springer, Singapore (2021). https://doi.org/10.1007/978-981-33-4745-8_9

19. Jiang, S., Shi, H., Lin, W., Liu, H.C.: A large group linguistic Z-DEMATEL approach for identifying key performance indicators in hospital performance management. Appl. Soft Comput. **86**, 105900 (2020)
20. Xie, Y., Xiao, H., Shen, T., Han, T.: Investigating the influencing factors of user experience in car-sharing services: an application of DEMATEL method. In: Krömker, H. (ed.) HCII 2020. LNCS, vol. 12213, pp. 359–375. Springer, Cham (2020). https://doi.org/10.1007/978-3-030-50537-0_26
21. Chen, Z., Lu, M., Ming, X., Zhang, X., Zhou, T.: Explore and evaluate innovative value propositions for smart product service system: a novel graphics-based rough-fuzzy DEMATEL method. J. Clean. Prod. **243**, 118672.1–118672.17 (2020)
22. Tsai, W.H., Chou, W.C.: Selecting management systems for sustainable development in SMEs: a novel hybrid model based on DEMATEL, ANP, and ZOGP. Expert Syst. Appl. **36**(2), 1444–1458 (2009)

Hazard Identification for a Virtual Coaching System for Active Healthy Ageing

Keiko Homma(✉) and Yoshio Matsumoto

National Institute of Advanced Industrial Science and Technology (AIST), 6-2-3 Kashiwanoha, Kashiwa, Chiba 277-0882, Japan
keiko.homma@aist.go.jp

Abstract. The ageing population is a global issue. In an ageing society, it is important to support the independent living of older adults at home. Each older adult is in a different physical, mental, and environmental situation, and has different needs. Therefore, it is necessary to assess the situation of each older adult and provide personalized advice. To address this issue, the e-VITA consortium has been organized. The consortium aims to (a) build a virtual coaching system that interacts with users, assesses their situation, and provides personalized advice; (b) confirm the effectiveness of the system through demonstration tests. The target users of the system are older adults who are living independent and healthy lives in the community. The goal of the project is to slow their functional decline and extend their independent lives. Safety is always an important issue for devices that interact with people. This paper identifies and discusses safety hazards related to a virtual coaching system, based on possible-use cases.

Keywords: Virtual coaching system · Active healthy ageing · Hazard identification

1 Introduction

The ageing population is a global issue. In 2019, 9.1% of the world's population was 65 years or older, and this is expected to increase to 15.9% in 2050 [1]. In 2005, WHO adopted the resolution, "Strengthening active and healthy ageing" [2]. Although the concept of active and healthy ageing (AHA) is not clearly defined in the resolution *per se*, it is described there as "remaining in good health and maintaining their many vital contributions to the well-being of their families, communities and societies".

In an ageing society, it is important to support the independent living of older adults at home. In particular, supporting social participation is important for maintaining the well-being of such older adults, and this becomes even more important as the effects of the COVID-19 pandemic become more prolonged.

According to the "International Comparison Study on Life and Attitude of the Elderly", published by the Cabinet Office of Japan in 2020 [3], of respondents aged 60 and over, 36.9% in Japan, 24.8% in the U.S., 30.5% in Germany, and 27.9% in Sweden

Q. Gao and J. Zhou (Eds.): HCII 2022, LNCS 13331, pp. 243–254, 2022.
https://doi.org/10.1007/978-3-031-05654-3_16

answered that they have income-generating occupations; and the percentage of respondents who wanted to work (or continue to work) with an income was 40.2% in Japan, 29.9% in the U.S., 28.1% in Germany, and 26.6% in Sweden.

Regarding participation in social activities other than working, the percentage of those who participated in such activities (e.g., community events or volunteering) was 39.9% in Japan, 63.7% in the U.S., 33.1% in Germany, and 39.5% in Sweden. The most common reasons for not participating in such social activities, among those who had never participated in such activities or had participated in them in the past but not now, were "health reasons, lack of confidence in physical strength" in Japan, "lack of interest" in the U.S. and Germany, and "have other things to do" in Sweden. Those who answered, "I can't find an activity I want to do" amounted to 14.5% in Japan, 17.6% in the U.S., 17.1% in Germany, and 18.7% in Sweden; those who answered, "I can't find a suitable place nearby", accounted for 10.0% in Japan, 9.9% in the U.S., 9.3% in Germany, and 7.5% in Sweden; and those who answered, "I can't find anyone to do it with", accounted for 11.1% in Japan, 10.2% in the U.S., 4.2% in Germany, and 4.0% in Sweden. These figures suggest that providing appropriate information on social activities is useful for encouraging such people to participate in these activities.

However, each older adult is in a different physical, mental, and environmental situation, and has different needs. Thus, while it is important to provide support to active older adults living in the community, it is necessary to tailor the support to the individual, because the needs and environment of older adults are highly individualized. Therefore, it is necessary to assess the situation of each older adult and provide personalized advice.

To address this issue, an international collaboration project, the "European-Japanese Virtual Coach for Smart Ageing (e-VITA)", was launched in 2021 [4]. The e-VITA consortium, which is composed of technical, academic, industrial, and social partners from four EU countries (Germany, Belgium, France, Italy) and Japan, aims to construct a virtual coaching system that interacts with users, assesses their situation, and provides personalized advice; and to confirm the effectiveness of the system through demonstration tests. The target users of the system are older adults who are living independent and healthy lives in the community, and the goal of this project is to slow their functional decline and extend their independent lives.

The e-VITA project takes the following approaches to achieve this goal:

- Participatory design: ICT tools will be designed, together with the end-users and stakeholders, which will empower older adults in deciding how technology should support them in their daily activities.
- Development of an intercultural virtual coach: smart-living technologies, advanced AI, and tailored dialogue interaction will be integrated seamlessly to realize an advanced intercultural virtual coach.
- Provision of a new concept: a new concept will be introduced regarding wellbeing support, smart-health condition monitoring, and companionship for community-dwelling older adults in Europe and Japan.
- Improvement of QOL: the quality of life of older adults will be improved, by increasing subjective wellbeing, individual health, and social connectedness, with the aid of the virtual coach.

Safety is one of the highly important issues in this project, as the older adults will interact with robots and ICT devices on a daily basis. However, it is not clear what kinds of hazards can be identified, because the virtual coaching system is a highly complex system consisting of many components. In this paper, we assume specific-use cases involving a virtual coaching system, identify the hazards, and describe the risk reduction process based on ISO 12100 [5].

In Sect. 2, we outline the virtual coaching system that we intend to implement. In Sect. 3, we define the use cases and conduct hazard identification. In Sect. 4, the subsequent risk reduction process is discussed. Section 5 concludes the paper.

2 System Outline

The virtual coaching system which the e-VITA project is developing aims to support older adults in maintaining their intrinsic capacity. According to the "World report on ageing and health", published by WHO in 2015 [6], 'intrinsic capacity' is the composite of all the physical and mental capacities of an individual. e-VITA will address the following domains of intrinsic capacity: cognition, emotion, mobility, sensory, and vitality.

Figure 1 shows a schematic outline of the virtual coaching system under development. The system conducts speech interaction with the user through an interface device such as a communication robot (Fig. 2). The system acquires data on the status of the physical activity of the user and environmental conditions via sensors mounted on the robot or embedded in the environment. These data are analyzed using natural language processing and emotion estimation. Based on the results of the analysis, personalized advice is generated with the aid of a knowledge graph. The advice is then presented to the user through the interface device. In addition, the obtained data are accumulated as knowledge contributing to the active healthy living of older adults. As a basis for the above-mentioned processes, a platform based on FIWARE will be used. FIWARE is an open platform for data management, developed in Europe [7].

3 Hazard Identification

3.1 Purpose of Hazard Identification

In this section, we conduct hazard identification for the proposed system. The purpose of hazard identification is to evaluate the risk of each hazard and take appropriate protective measures, as well as to provide information about the risks with stakeholders such as experimental subjects, their family members, and researchers from different research areas. Since the expected system is quite complex and still under development, our present efforts are focused on hazard identification, which is the initial step in the risk reduction process.

3.2 Use Case

As explained in the previous section, the e-VITA system aims to cover several domains of intrinsic capacity [8]. In this paper, we focus on the physical exercise application (Fig. 3).

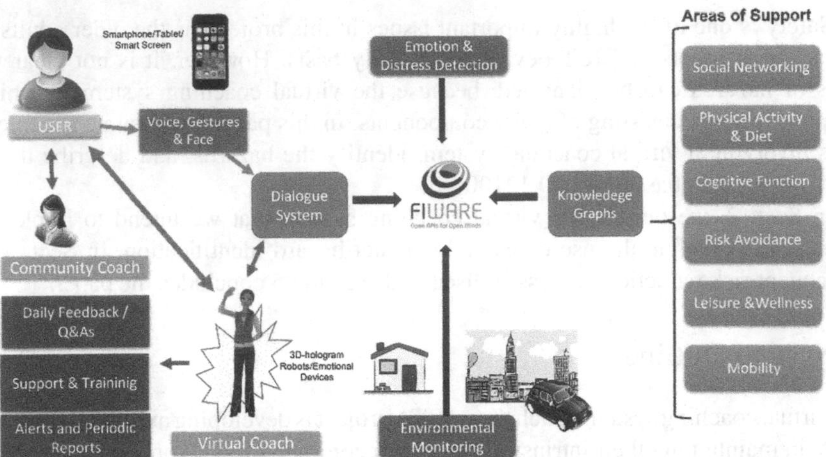

Fig. 1. Outline of the virtual coaching system.

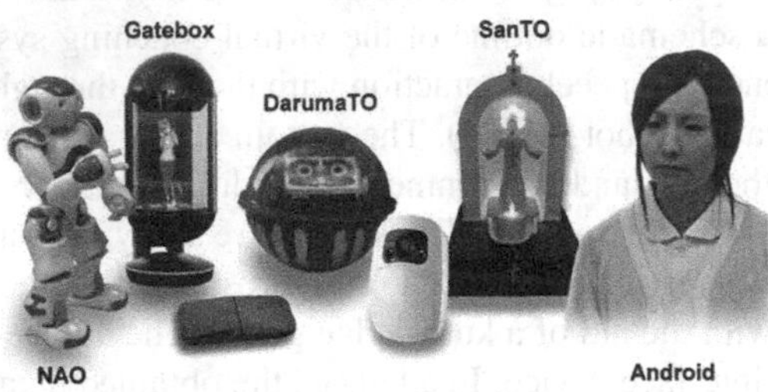

Fig. 2. Examples of interface devices.

The intended user is a healthy younger older adult who lives alone independently. To prevent physical decline and maintain mobility, an exercise program using existing video contents is provided, and the robot encourages the user to do the exercise program through speech interaction. The exercise program is personalized based on the user's preferences and the feedback from the user after each exercise.

For hazard identification, we use the following use-case scenario (Fig. 4).

Fig. 3. Use case of physical exercise coaching

1. The robot reminds the user that it is time for exercise, and asks him/her whether he/she would like to start the exercise.
2. When the user agrees to start the exercise program, the robot encourages him/her to wear the actimeter and to start the exercise video.
3. The user exercises with the video.
   (When the user completes the exercise successfully).
4. After the end of the exercise, the robot asks the user whether he/she feels satisfied with the exercise program.
5. The feedback from the user is recorded for further personalization, and the robot tells the user that the exercise program is over.
   (When the user experiences a health problem during the exercise).
6. If abnormal vital data are detected during the exercise, the robot asks the user to take a rest.
7. If the user does not recover after the rest, the robot asks the user to make an emergency call.

3.3 Methodology and Results

For the use-case scenario shown in Sect. 3.2, we extracted the hazards by brainstorming using the HAZOP guidewords [9], and classified the extracted hazards into four categories: mechanical, electrical, clinical, and information security.

Tables 1, 2, 3, 4, 5, 6 and 7 show the hazards identified for each task in the scenario. In practice, it is necessary to evaluate a series of processes, including delivery, installation, storage, and disposal of the equipment; but in this case, only the specific use-case scenario is covered.

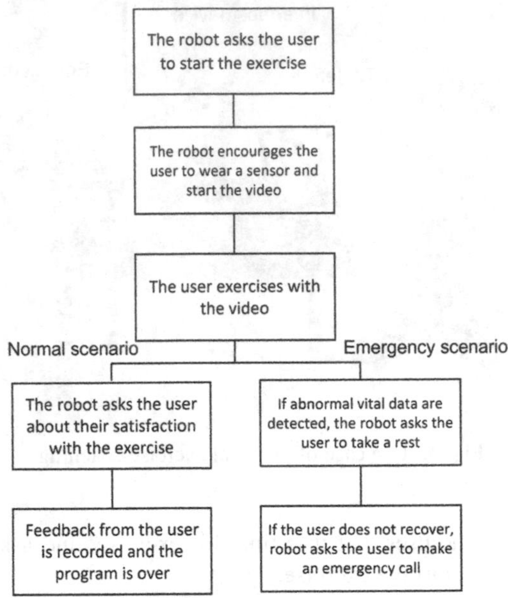

Fig. 4. Use case scenario.

4 Subsequent Steps in the Risk Reduction Process

4.1 Risk Estimation and Evaluation

According to ISO 12100, the subsequent steps in the risk reduction process are risk estimation, risk evaluation, and taking protective measures. However, since the e-VITA system is still in the process of being designed, we cannot specify every component and estimate its risk. Nevertheless, it is important to evaluate the risk. Thus, we here considered critical hazards to be those which may result in serious harm to the health of the experimental subjects. This determination was based on the severity of possible harm, not on the probability of the occurrence of harm. In Tables 1, 2, 3, 4, 5, 6 and 7, the critical hazards are marked as "◆".

Table 1. Envisaged hazards for Task 1.

Guide word		Hazard	Mechanical	Electrical	Clinical	Information
No or not	•	Robot's motion sensor does not recognize the user		X		
	•	Cannot authenticate the user				X
	•	No voice reminder		X		
More	•	Robot's voice is too loud				
Less	•	Robot's voice is too quiet		X		
	◆	User is in poor condition			X	
As well as	•	Multiple persons are in front of the robot			X	
Part of	•	User registers their health status inaccurately				X
Reverse						
Other than	•	User starts talking about an unrelated topic			X	
	◆	Robot responds based on another person's data				X
Early	•	Robot talks to the user earlier than scheduled				X
Late	•	Robot talks to the user later than scheduled				X
Before	•	User starts exercising before the robot does			X	
After						

4.2 Protective Measures

It is necessary to take protective measures that are reasonably practicable and based on the hazard categories.

1. **Mechanical hazards:** The adoption of inherently safe design measures is the first priority. In the case of the hazard of the interface device falling, for example, the device should be designed so that its center of gravity is as low as possible to minimize the risk of falling; and in the case of the hazard of injury due to contact between the inter-face device and user, the former should be designed without sharp edges, corners, or protruding parts. In addition, information for use should be provided, such as a warning not to exercise near the interface device, and a verbal warning from the device when the user is too close to the device.
2. **Electrical hazards:** In the case of electric shock hazards, the interface device should, for example, be designed to operate at extra-low voltages to minimize the risk of electric shock when the user makes contact with it.
3. **Clinical hazards:** To reduce the risk caused by clinical hazards, protective measures should be taken, such as carefully selecting the users for the system, using sensors to

Table 2. Envisaged hazards for Task 2.

Guide word		Hazard	Mechanical	Electrical	Clinical	Information
No or not	•	Robot does not talk to user		X		
	•	Video does not start		X		
	•	User does not give consent			X	
	•	User does not wear the wearable device			X	
	•	User does not play the video			X	
	•	Sensor information is not available				X
More	◆	Higher intensity exercise is selected				X
Less	•	Lower intensity exercise is selected				X
As well as	•	Sensor data is visible to a third party				X
Part of	•	Wearable device is poorly positioned			X	
Reverse						
Other than	•	User drops tablet on their foot while trying to operate it	X			
	◆	User touches the charger and is electrocuted while removing the wearable device from the charger		X		
Early	•	Video starts before the user is ready		X		
Late	•	Video does not start when the user presses a switch		X		
Before	•	User starts exercising before the video starts			X	
After						

monitor the user's physical condition and environment, and warning the user when the physical risk is increasing.

4. **Information security hazards:** In this regard, it is necessary to comply with the laws and regulations regarding the protection of personal information; specifically, the EU's General Data Protection Regulation (GDPR) and Japan's Act on the Protection of Personal Information.
5. **Other kinds of hazards:** There are also risks posed by psychological hazards such as dependence on or excessive trust in the virtual coach [10], as well as hazards related to artificial intelligence due to inappropriate machine learning.

Table 3. Envisaged hazards for Task 3.

Guide word	Hazard	Mechanical	Electrical	Clinical	Information
No or not	• Video not working		X		
	• User not exercising			X	
	• Internet connection is cut off				X
More	◆ User tries to move more than they can			X	
	• Data overflow				X
Less	• User stops exercising in the middle			X	
As well as	◆ User steps on the power cord and breaks it, causing an electric shock		X		
	• Noise in the data				
Part of	• Wearable device does not measure the biometric signal correctly			X	
	• Data is missing				X
Reverse	• Video plays backwards		X		
Other than	• User bumps into table and the robot or tablet falls on the user's feet	X			
	• User bumps into the corner of the table	X			
	◆ Rug slips and user falls	X			
	◆ User falls while in motion			X	
Early					
Late	• Data transfer is delayed				X
Before					
After					

Table 4. Envisaged hazards for Task 4A.

Guide word	Hazard	Mechanical	Electrical	Clinical	Information
No or not	• Video won't stop		X		
	• Robot does not talk to the user		X		
	• User does not stop exercising			X	
	◆ User does not report physical deterioration			X	
	• Data is not saved				X
	• Robot does not know when the exercise is finished				X
More	• Video ends and starts playing next video		X		
Less					
As well as	• User starts talking about something other than feedback			X	
Part of	• Video stops in the middle		X		
	• User feedback is inaccurate				X
Reverse	•				
Other than	◆ User's sweaty hand touches an energized part and receives an electric shock		X		
Early					
Late					
Before	• Robot calls for the end of the video before it is over				
After					

Table 5. Envisaged hazards for Task 4B.

Guide word		Hazard	Mechanical	Electrical	Clinical	Information
No or not	•	No voice for safety confirmation		X		
	◆	User does not follow the robot's instructions			X	
	◆	Data anomaly is not detected though an anomaly is occurring				X
	◆	Occurrence of an abnormality is not communicated to the robot				X
More						
Less	•	Volume of the safety confirmation is too low		X		
As well as	•	Robot responds to both abnormal and normal situations at the same time		X		
Part of						
Reverse						
Other than	◆	Robot reacts as if it were responding to a normal situation though an abnormality is detected		X		
	•	False detection of signals				
	◆	Abnormal data is judged as normal				
Early						
Late	•	Robot safety confirmation is delayed				
Before						
After						

Table 6. Envisaged hazards for Task 5A.

Guide word		Hazard	Mechanical	Electrical	Clinical	Information
No or not	•	Robot does not call for termination		X		
	•	User does not give feedback			X	
	•	Data is not saved				X
More	•	Volume of voice call is too high				
Less	•	Volume of voice call is too low				
As well as	•	Data is accessible to third parties				X
Part of						
Reverse						
Other than	◆	Data is saved as another user's data				X
Early						
Late						
Before						
After						

Table 7. Envisaged hazards for Task 5B

Guide word	Hazard	Mechanical	Electrical	Clinical	Information
No or not	◆ Button is not located where the user can press it	X			
	• Robot does not speak to the user		X		
	◆ Alarm system is not turned on		X		
	◆ User cannot press the button			X	
More					
Less	• Volume of the voice is too high		X		
As well as	• Alarm system log can be viewed by a third party				X
Part of					
Reverse					
Other than					
Early					
Late					
Before					
After	• Robot starts responding after the call button is pressed		X		

It is expected that a safe virtual coaching system will be realized by appropriately addressing the various hazards described above.

5 Conclusion

In this paper, we conducted hazard identification based on possible-use cases involving a virtual coaching device. The hazards were identified using the HAZOP guidewords, and classified into four categories. The subsequent steps in the risk reduction process were also described.

In the next phase of the study, we will conduct risk evaluation and propose appropriate protective measures for the various types of hazards with respect to the virtual coaching system and stakeholders.

Acknowledgment. This work was supported by Ministry of Internal Affairs and Communications (MIC) of Japan (Grant No. JPJ000595). The European consortium received funding from the European Union H2020 Programme under grant agreement n° 101016453.

References

1. United Nations, Department of Economic and Social Affairs, Population Division: World Population Prospects 2019, Highlights (2019), ST/ESA/SER.A/423
2. World Health Organization: WHA58.16 - Strengthening active and healthy ageing (2005). https://apps.who.int/gb/ebwha/pdf_files/WHA58/WHA58_16-en.pdf
3. Cabinet Office of Japan: 9th Comparison Study on Life and Attitude of the Elderly (2021). https://www8.cao.go.jp/kourei/ishiki/r02/zentai/pdf_index.html. (in Japanese)

4. e-VITA Consortium. e-VITA Project. https://www.e-vita.coach/
5. International Organization for Standardization: Safety of machinery—General principles for design—Risk assessment and risk reduction (ISO 12100:2010) (2010)
6. World Health Organization: World report on ageing and health (2015). https://apps.who.int/iris/handle/10665/186463
7. FIWARE Foundation: FIWARE. https://www.fiware.org/
8. Cesari, M., et al.: Evidence for the domains supporting the construct of intrinsic capacity. J. Gerontol. A. **73**, 1653–1660 (2018). https://doi.org/10.1093/gerona/gly011
9. Product Quality Research Institute: HAZOP Training Guide. https://pqri.org/wp-content/uploads/2015/08/pdf/HAZOP_Training_Guide.pdf
10. Fiske, A., Henningsen, P., Buyx, A.: Your robot therapist will see you now: ethical implications of embodied artificial intelligence in psychiatry, psychology, and psychotherapy. J. Med. Internet Res. **21**(5), e13216 (2019). https://doi.org/10.2196/13216

FEEL2: An Interactive Device for Older Adults to Experience Synesthesia and Age Creatively

Liang-Ming Jia and Fang-Wu Tung(✉)

National Taiwan University of Science and Technology, No. 43, Keelung Rd., Sec.4, Da'an Dist., Taipei City 10607, Taiwan
{D10810801,fwtung}@mail.ntust.edu.tw

Abstract. To promote creative aging, this study designed an interactive device (called FEEL2) and a complementary activity for older adults to experience the synesthesia of color and music. We implemented two iterations of a four-stage approach according to action research methodology. Through this approach, the design of FEEL2 and the accompanying activity was refined on the basis of the feedback and experiences of older adult participants. According to the participants, FEEL2 and the complementary activity enabled them to experience the synesthesia of color and music, apply new media, work both individually and in groups, in addition to being user-friendly, thus developing their potential in artistic creation. Furthermore, this activity allowed them to view their later life more positively, and increase contact with their friends and family. Accordingly, FEEL2 is a suitable tool for helping older adults to experience synesthesia and thus age creatively. Artistic activities are seen as effective ways to promote creative aging, this study provided empirical support for the intervention of the design profession in this field.

Keywords: Artistic interactive device · Artistic activity for older adults · Synesthesia of color and music · Creative aging

1 Introduction

In recent years, advancements in medical and health-care technology have engendered increases in average life expectancy and the older adult population has become the fastest-growing population group [1]. According to demographic statistics and projections presented by National Development Council [2], older adults are expected to constitute more than 20% of the Taiwanese population by 2025, placing Taiwan on the precipice of a super-aged society and engendering challenges in social development. Furthermore, older adults face unique aging-related challenges, and their needs cannot be met through the health-care system alone [3]. Therefore, addressing challenges related to an aging society is imperative. Taiwan's executive organization published the "White Paper on Aging Society" in 2015; according to the white paper, older adults should be socially engaged and lead an active lifestyle to age healthily (both mentally and physically) [4]. This is consistent with the suggestion of Cohen [5] who emphasized the need for older adults to stimulate their potential (creativity) through continual social engagement.

Q. Gao and J. Zhou (Eds.): HCII 2022, LNCS 13331, pp. 255–267, 2022.
https://doi.org/10.1007/978-3-031-05654-3_17

Moreover, the suggestions are consistent with the concept of creative aging [6]. Cohen [7] stated that artistic activities provide invaluable sensory stimulation for older adults; they could enhance their physical, mental, and social well-being [8, 9]. Furthermore, synesthesia is an emerging, multifaceted research area that has attracted increasing attention [10]. Synesthesia is a phenomenon in which the stimulation of one sense engages the other senses, which produces diverse and complex experiences [11]. Among the various synesthesia, the synesthesia of visual and aural is more common [12], which can also be referred to as color and music synesthesia [13]. Thus, artistic activities that provide older adults with synesthetic experiences (especially between color and music) are likely to be highly beneficial.

Accordingly, the objective of this study was to develop an interactive device and an accompanying activity to enable older adults to experience color and music synesthesia and to promote creative aging. This device (called FEEL2) and complementary activity were developed iteratively, where the prototype was refined through the feedback and experiences of older adult participants. This study also proposes a few design recommendations as a reference for future research.

The remainder of this paper is structured as follows. In Sect. 2, we present a review of the literature on creative aging, artistic activities for older adults, and color and music synesthesia. Section 3 details the methodology of this study. Section 4 describes how we implemented action research methodology to refine the design of our device and accompanying activity through the experiences and feedback of older adult participants. Finally, in Sect. 5, we discuss our findings and provide several recommendations.

2 Literature Review

2.1 Creative Aging and Artistic Activities

Cohen [6] introduced the concept of creative aging, which entails helping older adults to age healthily by encouraging them to participate in a variety of artistic activities. Furthermore, according to Cohen [7], the most significant factor in awakening one's potential in the second half of life is to stimulate creativity. By its creative nature, artistic activities are a crucial variable and could establish an authentic and meaningful connection between older adults and society [14]. Hanna [15] also stated that artistic activities allow older adults to share their wisdom. In addition, Hannemann [16] presented evidence for the benefits of artistic activities among older adults, including greater social engagement, lower depression and isolation, improved physical and mental health, and a keener aesthetic sense. Overall, it is shown that older adult participation in artistic activities positively impacts the aging process and social development [17].

Currently, artistic activities for older adults involve art, music, handicraft, dance, and theater, etc. Fraser et al. [18], reviewed studies on healthy aging activities for older adults during the period between 1972 and 2012 and found that 40% and 17.8% of the studies (57.8% in total) involved activities that focused on music and artistic creation, respectively. It demonstrates the increasing popularity of these two activities; this increasing popularity is particularly evinced by the fact that most of the reviewed studies were published after 2000. Additionally, Giraudeau and Bailly [19] reported an increasing focus on artistic and musical activities for older adults among researchers in Asia. Considering these trends in the literature, the present empirical study focused on Taiwan.

2.2 Activities Centered on Artistic Creation and Music

Activities that are centered on artistic creation and music are not only beneficial for the older adults but also cost-effective [20, 21]; such activities also enable older adults to share their feelings, thoughts, and meaningful life experiences through their creations [22, 23]. In a study on activities that are centered on artistic creation and music, Poulos et al. [24] conducted a quantitative analysis and demonstrated that the activities boosted creativity and encourage participation; they also performed a qualitative analysis and demonstrated that the activities promoted a sense of accomplishment and helped older adults foster meaningful social bonds. It demonstrated the benefits from an empirical perspective.

As suggested by Sandak et al. [25], activities that could combine artistic creation with musical exercises; enrich the experiences of older adults through color and music synesthesia [13], thereby increasing their interest in social engagement and guiding the development of future activities.

2.3 Synesthesia of Color and Music

Synesthesia is a conditioned reflex that automatically and continuously triggers the production of other sensations when stimulated by one particular sensation [26]. Li et al. [27] reported that stimuli in the form of light and sound could trigger people's synesthetic experiences; thus, aural stimuli (particularly music) can trigger sensations of color, texture, or shape. On the other hand, Hu [28] pointed out that the languages of color and music share some properties that can be visualized through art to produce melodic music.

Considering the findings and suggestions of the aforementioned studies, we posited that activities that incorporate color and music synesthesia would especially be beneficial for older adults. Specifically, we posited that activities centered on artistic creation and music could inspire synesthetic experiences and promote creative aging. Accordingly, we designed an interactive device and corresponding activity involving artistic creation and music to inspire color and music synesthesia among older adults and to enable them to age creatively.

3 Research Methods

This study adopted an iterative four-stage (planning–action–observation–reflection) approach according to action research methodology. It could help investigate the problems encountered in conducting the activities and find ways and strategies to solve the issues from them [29]. Specifically, we invited older adult participants to use the designed device and participate in the corresponding activity, and then provide experience and feedback; on the basis of their feedback and experiences, we then improved the device and corresponding activity. The investigation involved two iterations of the four-stage approach, as shown in Fig. 1.

Specifically, in the first iteration, in the planning stage, we understood the needs of older adults with regard to participation in artistic activities through communication with stakeholders; subsequently, we designed our interactive device and accompanying activity. In the action stage, we invited older adults in the community to use our device and participate in our activity. In the observation stage, we observed how the participants used the device and engaged in the activity, and we sought their experience and feedback. Finally, in the reflection stage, we improved the device and corresponding activity on the basis of the observation stage. In the second iteration, the steps from the previous iteration were continued and the activity was reflected on as a whole at the end.

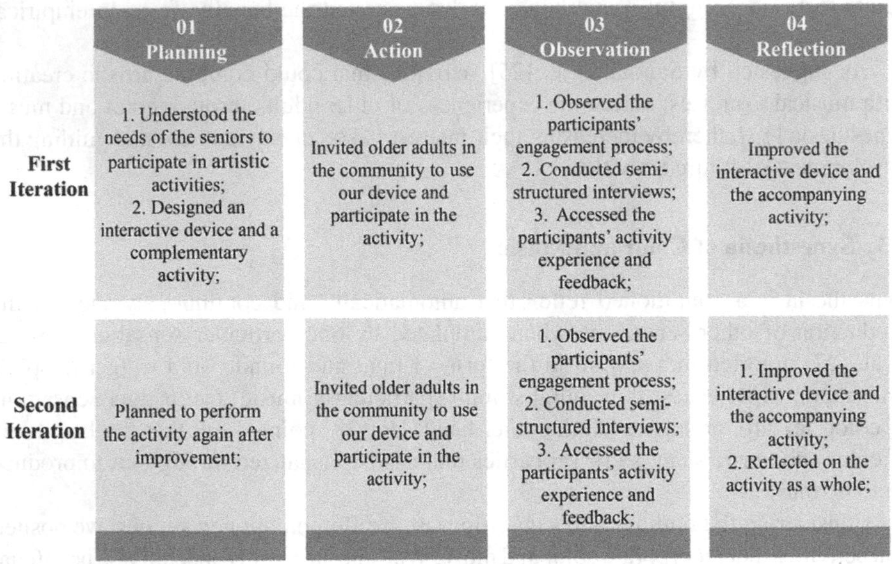

Fig. 1. Two iterations of the four-stage

4 Design and Implementation of FEEL2 and Its Corresponding Activity

4.1 First Iteration

Planning. The research team first observed the everyday activities of older adults in the community and interviewed stakeholders to understand the needs of older adults with regard to participation in artistic activities. Subsequently, group meetings were conducted. Thereafter, the research team designed FEEL2 interactive device (Fig. 2.), which allows the user to transform colors and musical notes for a synesthetic experience. The device resembles a vinyl record player and uses colored inserts to transform a record into a series of notes.

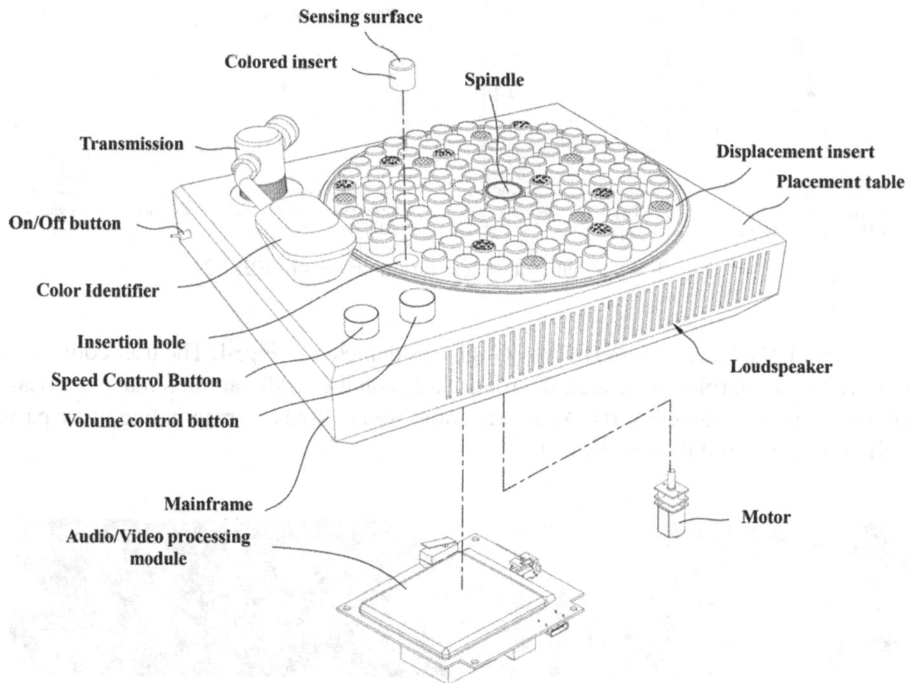

Fig. 2. Schematic of the FEEL2 interactive device

In the device, the color-to-note conversion principle (see Table 1 for details) converts the sensed color into the digital form of the target signal through the charge-coupled device (containing the RGB model) in the color identifier. Then the audio-video processing module converts the digital format of the target signal into the target note.

Table 1. Rule for color-to-note conversion.

Color	Red	Yellow	Green	Blue	Black	White
Target signal	001	002	003	004	005	006
Target note	Do/1	Re/2	Mi/3	Fa/4	So/5	La/6

The operation process is shown in Fig. 3. The user could observe everyday scenes through the round holes on a cardboard. Colored inserts corresponding to the scenes are placed into the turntable of FEEL2 to create a mosaic collage. Subsequently, the turntable is placed into the FEEL2 device. When the "play" button is pressed to activate the device, a unique melody is produced. The user could feel the synesthesia of color and music.

Finally, the research team designed the accompanying activity. We selected four masterpieces with different palettes that the user could choose from. These masterpieces were *The Kiss* (by Klimt), *Haystacks* (by Monet), *A Sunday on La Grande Jatte* (by

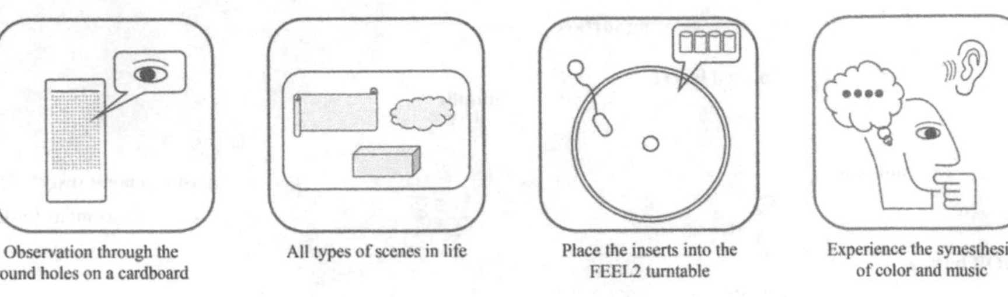

Fig. 3. Schematic of the operation process of FEEL2

Seurat), and *The Starry Night* (by Van Gogh), as depicted in Fig. 4. The user could then observe the masterpieces through the round holes on the cardboard and make a mosaic collage with the colored inserts. A melody composed of notes corresponding to the parts of the collage would then be played.

Fig. 4. Four masterpieces with different palettes

Action. To ensure that a high-quality experience was provided, we invited 20 older adults—18 of whom participated—who were aged between 50 and 90 years to use the device and participate in the corresponding activity. In terms of basic statistics, for gender, females constituted the highest percentage of 83.3% ($n = 15$). In terms of age, the highest rate of participants was in the 61–80 age groups, at 77.8% ($n = 14$). Regarding educational attainment, older adults who participated in the program had a higher educational background, with 44.4% ($n = 8$) having high school/vocational high school and higher education. Living with family members was the most prevalent mode of residence at 88.9% ($n = 16$).

We conducted the activity at a community center in Xinzhuang District in New Taipei City, Taiwan, on October 7, 2020, from 1:30 to 3:30 pm. The participants were divided into four groups of four or five persons (Fig. 5), and each group chose a masterpiece. Each participant was assigned a cardboard with round holes to observe the masterpiece and select the corresponding colored inserts on the turntable; they then completed a mosaic collage as a group. Eventually, the turntable was placed into the FEEL2 device, and the participants could then listen to the corresponding melody for a synesthetic experience.

Observe the masterpiece through the cardboard with round holes and select the corresponding colored inserts on the turntable
Complete a mosaic collage as a group
Place the turntable into the FEEL2 interactive device, and listen to the corresponding melody for a synesthetic experience

Fig. 5. Participants in the activity stage

Observation. Observations of and interviews with the participants indicated the following. First, we noted the need for a warm-up activity. Because a warm-up activity was absent, and the shape and size of the cardboard did not match the shape and size of the FEEL2 turntable. This hindered the participants' understanding of the concept of extracting the colors from the masterpiece. The participants confused during the collage creation process. Therefore, several participants were unable to select the corresponding colored inserts. Second, we noted that the participants were less receptive of masterpieces with a cool palette (e.g., *The Starry Night*).

Reflection. On the basis of our findings in the preceding step, we made the following changes. As shown in Fig. 6. First, we added a warm-up activity, allowing older adults to observe the masterpiece through the round holes in the card-board, and then practice extracting colors by gluing colored round stickers into the corresponding holes. Second, the cardboard with round holes was made to be of the same shape and size as the turntable. Third, we used only masterpieces with a warm palette; they were A *Sunday on La Grande Jatte* (by Seurat), *Le Chahut* (by Seurat), *The Circus* (by Seurat), and *Portrait of Félix Fénéon* (by Signac), as presented in Fig. 7.

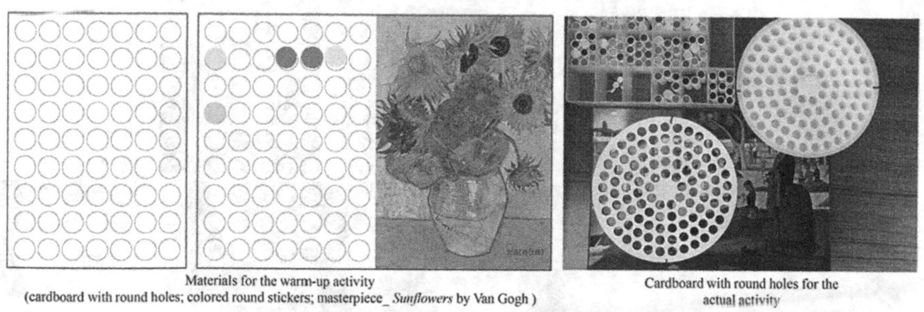
Materials for the warm-up activity
(cardboard with round holes; colored round stickers; masterpiece_ Sunflowers by Van Gogh)
Cardboard with round holes for the actual activity

Fig. 6. Materials for warm up activity and cardboard with round holes for the actual activity

Fig. 7. Masterpieces with warm colors chosen after the first iteration

4.2 Second Iteration

Planning. We planned to implement the improved activity.

Action. As mentioned in the action stage of the first iteration, sixteen older adults used the device and participated in the corresponding activity. Regarding the basic statistics, most of the participants were women (87.5%, n = 14), were aged 61–80 years (75.0%, n = 12), lived alone (50.0%, n = 8), and had high school/vocational high school education or higher (81.3%, n = 13).

We conducted the activity at a community center in Da'an District in Taipei City, Taiwan, on December 18, 2020, from 1:30 to 3:30 pm. As shown in Fig. 8. The participants undertook the aforementioned warm-up activity, in which they also completed their own collage. In the actual activity, the participants were divided into four groups of four to five persons each. They then selected a masterpiece and looked through the newly designed cardboard with round holes. They chose the corresponding colored inserts to put on the turntable for their mosaic collage. Finally, the turntable was placed into the FEEL2 interactive device, and the corresponding melody was played.

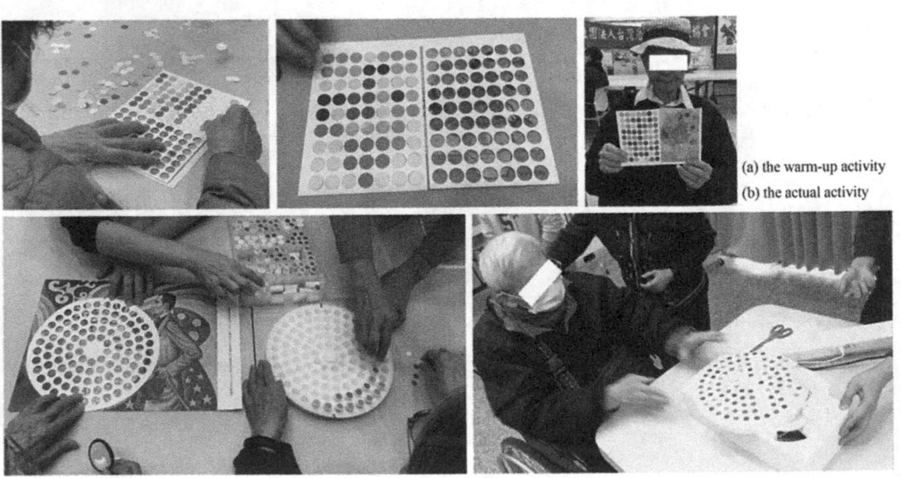

Fig. 8. Warm-up activity and actual activity

Observation. The research team observed the activity and conducted semi-structured interviews with 10 participants (voluntary participation) after the activity. Transcriptions of audio recordings and interview notes were coded and analyzed in NVivo software by two researchers (to ensure reliability). The two researchers were blinded to the identities of the interviewees. The data were coded according to the order in which the participants were interviewed; for example, "A" represents the first respondent in the interview.

In total, 58 reference points were coded. These codes were then divided into seven features, which were finally grouped into two themes, as shown in Fig. 9. The first theme was "a rich experience" (72.4%, $n = 42$), and it included the following features: experiencing creation as an individual and group (17.2%, $n = 10$), creating with ease (12.1%, $n = 7$), experiencing synesthesia of color and music (22.4%, $n = 13$), applying new media (8.6%, $n = 5$), and developing one's potential in artistic creation (12.1%, $n = 7$); The second theme was "a positive impact on one's life" (27.6%, $n = 16$), and it included the following features: developing positive thoughts about one's later life (12.1%, $n = 7$), and interacting more with others (15.5%, $n = 9$).

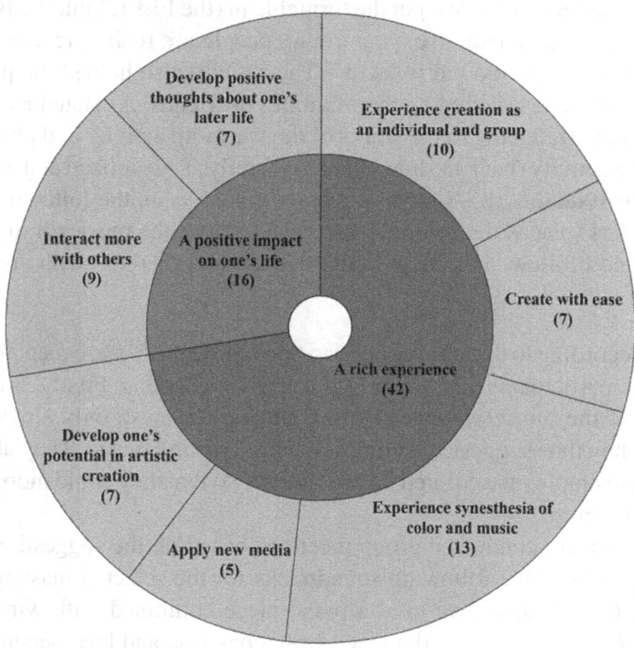

Fig. 9. Themes and features identified during coding

Regarding the first theme ("a rich experience"), the participants reported their experience of a new medium that changed their perceptions of artistic creation. According to respondent C, "I used to paint with brushes, but now I can use these things (meaning the colored round stickers and colored inserts) as my brushes to do my artwork." The use of new media also facilitated artistic creation, and the warm-up activity facilitated the creative process, allowed them to create with ease. Respondent A noted the following:

"After the teachers' explanation (referring to the warm-up activity), it was so easy to complete a piece of artwork." The user-friendliness of the device and activity fostered the development of participants' potential in artistic creation. As described by respondent I, "I've never studied how to create art before, and I was wondering what to do before I joined this activity. However, the teachers just gave me some suggestions, and we were able to produce such good work." Furthermore, the presence of both group and individual activities enabled the participants to express their individuality while interacting with others. Respondent H stated the following: "Individual creation lets me enjoy the personal joy of creating something on my own, while group creation lets me learn from others." The activity also allowed the older adults to experience synesthesia by converting a collage into a melody. As respondent B stated, "I found that after this activity, I could create a piece of music this way and that the darker and lighter colors reflect different musical styles."

Regarding the second theme ("a positive impact on one's life"), the activity helped the participants to expand their horizons and perceive their later life more positively. Respondent D stated the following: "Now the technology has advanced to the point where we don't understand it. We put the turntable in (the FEEL2 interactive device) for listening, and wow, so imaginative, your young people are really great, now we finally feel like we can never be too old to learn." The activity also helped the participants to interact more with others, including their families or friends. As stated by respondent I, "I would take them (referring to the works of the warm-up activity and photos or videos taken during the activity) back to show off to my family. They looked at it and said 'wow, mom you can still do these!'" Similarly, respondent A stated the following: "When we lined up the colors (placed the colored inserts) and played the music through the device, it felt terrific, and I followed the steps of our activity and shared it with my friends from another club."

Reflection. According to the activity observations and interviews, except for the activity experience, the participants also expressed a few suggestions. Firstly, the participants pointed out that the music was bland (monophonic) because only single notes were played back. They thus suggested adding some background music. They also suggested allowing users to employ the colored inserts directly so that they could more freely create their collage and music.

The research team conducted group meetings based on the suggestions of the participants and produced the following soundtracks for the selected masterpieces. For *A Sunday on La Grande Jatte*, we used a piano piece combined with wind sounds and bird calls. For *Le Chahut*, we used a piece with a bassoon and bass accompaniment on a 24-beat swing rhythm. For *The Circus*, we used a piece with a Tuba bassline combined with trombone and euphonium harmonies. For the *Portrait of Félix Fénéon*, we used psychedelic electronic music that heavily featured a metallic-sounding synthesizer patch.

In addition, rather than associating colors with notes, we associated colors (with their representation) with instruments or songs, as shown in Fig. 10. Brown (BR) was used in depictions of earth, rock, or the evening sunset; it corresponded to a steady bassline or atmospheric soundscape. Yellow (Y) was used in depictions of flowers and ornaments and to signify arrogance or exuberance; it corresponded to woodwind instruments (e.g., the flute, piccolo, and clarinet) or to cymbals. Orange (Y) was used in depictions of accessories, clothing, and color of hair and to signify richness; it corresponded to the French horn, saxophone, and bass piccolo. Red (R) was used in depictions of theaters and dresses and to signify focus; it corresponded to soprano string instruments. Purple (P) was used to signify elegance, mystery, and romance; it corresponded to the strumming of bass strings. Wine (PR) was used to signify ambience and fantasy; it corresponded to brass instruments (e.g., the trumpet). Blue (BL) was used to signify melancholy and imagination; it corresponded to mellow PAD music. Blue–green (BG) was used to depict oceans, green mountains, and plants; it corresponded to idiophonic instruments. Cyan (T) was used to depict nobility, bashfulness, and modernity; it corresponded to the piano or synthesizer. Forest green (DG) was used for urban backgrounds and to signify impurity and chaos; it corresponded to ambient music. Green (G) was used to depict buds and to signify novelty and growth; it corresponded to the xylophone, fiddle, or mallet. Finally, black, white, and gray corresponded to the sound of bass drum or snare drum.

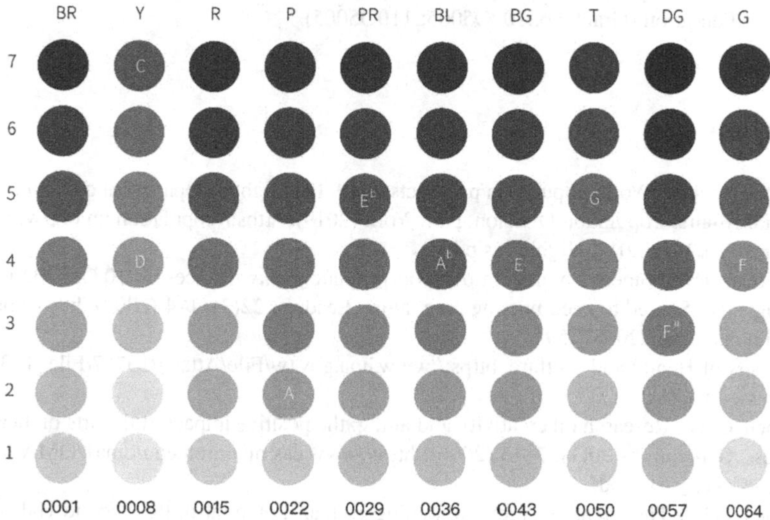

Fig. 10. Colors in final iteration of FEEL2 (Color figure online)

5 Discussion and Recommendations

To promote creative aging, we developed an interactive device (called FEEL2) with an accompanying activity that allows older adult users to experience color and music synesthesia. We applied two iterations of a four-stage approach according to action research methodology. Thus, where we refined the design on the basis of the feedback and experiences of older adult participants.

The participants reported that this activity provided them with a rich experience; they also noted that the FEEL2 device and the accompanying activity were user-friendly, developed their potential, enabled them to be creative through the use of new media and to create both individually and with others. Moreover, the participants reported gaining a new perspective of artistic activities and being more positive toward their later life. They also noted this activity's usefulness in helping them interact with friends and family. These findings indicate that the FEEL2 device and the accompanying activity are consistent with a few of the factors for promoting creative aging [6, 7, 16, 17].

Future studies could combine the FEEL2 device with other artistic or musical activities to broaden the program's impact on the aging elderly. In addition, since this activity was launched in New Taipei and Taipei, the results are limited to these two areas. Accordingly, future studies can also apply our device and activity to populations outside of Taipei City and New Taipei City to extend the findings.

Acknowledgments. We would like to thank our research team members Chen-Ling Hung, Wei-Ju Chiu, Chia-En Chen, Wei-Zhe Tzeng, Ryo-Wei Liu, and Chia-Hsuan Ku for their contribution to this study. We are also grateful to the staff of the Suang Line Social Welfare Foundation and the He Ping Station of the Taiwan Cuo Bian Caring Association for their tremendous support. This work was supported by a grant from the University Social Responsibility (USR) Program, Taiwan Ministry of Education (Grant No.:109O5005; 110O5005).

References

1. United Nations: World population prospects 2019: Highlights. Department of Economic and Social Affairs, Population Division, New York (2019). https://population.un.org/wpp/Publications/Files/WPP2019_Highlights.pdf
2. National Development Council. https://pop-proj.ndc.gov.tw/. Accessed 10 Oct 2020
3. Pringle, D.: Scared to need nursing care. Nurs. Leaders. **22**(3), 1–4 (2009). https://pubmed.ncbi.nlm.nih.gov/20057259/
4. Ministry of Health and Welfare. https://www.hpa.gov.tw/File/Attach/10767/File_12355.pdf. Accessed 10 Dec 2020
5. Cohen, G. D.: Research on creativity and aging: the positive impact of the arts on health and illness. Generations **30**(1), 7–15 (2006). http://www.cas.miamioh.edu/oma1/OMARoot/Research/Cohen_2006.pdf
6. Cohen, G.D.: The Creative Age: Awakening Human Potential in the Second Half of Life. Harper & Collins, New York (2001)
7. Cohen, G.D.: In The Mature Mind: The Positive Power of the Aging Brain. Basic Books, New York (2005)
8. Schweitzer, M., Gilpin, L., Frampton, S.: Healing spaces: elements of environmental design that make an impact on health. J. Altern. Complement. Med. **10**(Supplement 1), S71–S83 (2004). https://doi.org/10.1089/acm.2004.10.S-71
9. Torres, A., Venâncio, J.: Effects of an innovative group program of multisensory stimulation of older adults. In: 2nd icH&Hpsy International Conference on Health and Health Psychology (icH&Hpsy 2016), pp. 387–396 (2016). http://hdl.handle.net/10400.26/23079
10. Simner, J.: Defining synaesthesia. Br. J. Psychol. **103**(1), 1–15 (2012). https://doi.org/10.1348/000712610X528305
11. Nomura, J.: The Secret of Color-An Introduction to the Latest Color Science. Literary Arts, Tokyo (1996)
12. Ward, J., Thompson-Lake, D., Ely, R., Kaminski, F.: Synaesthesia, creativity and art: what is the link? Br. J. Psychol. **99**(1), 127–141 (2008). https://doi.org/10.1348/000712607X204164

13. Curwen, C.: Music-colour synaesthesia: concept, context and qualia. Conscious. Cogn. **61**, 94–106 (2018). https://doi.org/10.1016/j.concog.2018.04.005
14. Hanna, G., Perlstein, S.: Creativity matters: Arts and aging in America. Americans for the Arts, Washington (2008). https://www.creativeworkers.net/sites/default/files/Monograph%20Sept%202008.pdf
15. Hanna, G.: Focus on creativity and aging in the United States. Generations **30**(1), 47–49 (2006). https://scholar.google.com/scholar_lookup?title=Focus+on+creativity+and+aging+in+the+United+States&author=Hanna+G&publication+year=2006&journal=Generations&volume=30&pages=47-49
16. Hannemann, B.T.: Creativity with dementia patients. Gerontology **52**(1), 59–65 (2006). https://doi.org/10.1159/000089827
17. Cohen, G.: New theories and research findings on the positive influence of music and art on health with ageing. Arts Health **1**(1), 48–62 (2009). https://doi.org/10.1080/17533010802528033
18. Fraser, K.D., O'Rourke, H.M., Wiens, H., Lai, J., Howell, C., Brett-MacLean, P.: A scoping review of research on the arts, aging, and quality of life. Gerontologist **55**(4), 719–729 (2015). https://doi.org/10.1016/S0890-4065(99)00021-3
19. Giraudeau, C., Bailly, N.: Intergenerational programs: what can school-age children and older people expect from them? A systematic review. Eur. J. Ageing **16**(3), 363–376 (2019). https://doi.org/10.1007/s10433-018-00497-4
20. Fisher, B.J., Specht, D.K.: Successful aging and creativity in later life. J. Aging Stud. **13**(4), 457–472 (1999). https://doi.org/10.1016/S0890-4065(99)00021-3
21. Hanna, G. P.: The central role of creative aging. J. Art Life **4**(1), 1–15 (2013). https://journals.flvc.org/jafl/article/view/84239
22. Kim, S.K.: A randomized, controlled study of the effects of art therapy on older Korean-Americans' healthy aging. Arts Psychother. **40**(1), 158–164 (2013). https://doi.org/10.1016/j.aip.2012.11.002
23. Reynolds, F.: 'Colour and communion': exploring the influences of visual art-making as a leisure activity on older women's subjective well-being. J. Aging Stud. **24**(2), 135–143 (2010). https://doi.org/10.1016/j.jaging.2008.10.004
24. Poulos, R.G., et al.: Arts on prescription for community-dwelling older people with a range of health and wellness needs. Health Soc. Care Community **27**(2), 483–492 (2019). https://doi.org/10.1111/hsc.12669
25. Sandak, B., Gilboa, A., Harel, D.: Computational paradigm to elucidate the effects of arts-based approaches: art and music studies and implications for research and therapy. Front. Psychol. **11**, 1–20 (2020). https://doi.org/10.3389/fpsyg.2020.01200
26. Neufelda, J., et al.: The neural correlates of coloured music: a functional MRI investigation of auditory-visual synaesthesia. Neuropsychologia **50**(1), 85–89 (2012). https://doi.org/10.1016/j.neuropsychologia.2011.11.001
27. Li, X., Tao, D., Maybank, S.J., Yuan, Y.: Visual music and musical vision. Neurocomputing **71**(10–12), 2023–2028 (2008). https://doi.org/10.1016/j.neucom.2008.01.025
28. Hu, G.: Art of musical color: a synesthesia-based mechanism of color art. Color. Res. Appl. **45**(5), 862–870 (2020). https://doi.org/10.1002/col.22532
29. Lewin, K.: Frontiers in group dynamics: II. Channels of group life; social planning and action research. Human Relat. **1**(2), 143–153 (1947). https://doi.org/10.1177/001872674700100201

Improving Self-diet Management of Chronic Kidney Disease Patients Through Chatbots

Wang-Chin Tsai[1(✉)], Wen-Yi Li[2,3], Jen-Yu Tsai[1], and Jieng-Sheng Yang[2,3]

[1] Department of Creative Design, National Yunlin University of Science and Technology, Douliu, Yunlin 640, Taiwan
wangwang@yuntech.edu.tw

[2] Renal Division, Department of Internal Medicine, National Taiwan University Hospital, Yunlin Branch, Yunlin, Taiwan

[3] College of Medicine, National Taiwan University, Taipei, Taiwan

Abstract. The purpose of this study is to focus on patients with chronic kidney disease mainly. Through technological services and education, the LINE APP platform is used to build a chatbot for intervention so that patients with kidney disease can use the mobile phone LINE chatbot to conduct diet management and patient education. The research results show that chatbots are not limited by any time and place, simplify the content of inquiries in a streamlined manner, improve efficiency and shorten waiting time, and do not need to install another app. Compared with other applications, chatbots are online, and it is the most familiar interface for users. The functions of blood pressure record browsing, diet query, diet record, and health education knowledge can help patients with chronic diseases reduce harmful effects caused by the disease and record blood pressure to stabilize and control the disease. Moreover, the line chatbots can cooperate with the active promotion of health care knowledge and passively allow users to inquire about dietary knowledge, help chronic disease patients improve medical care knowledge, improve lousy eating habits, and improve the quality of life.

Keywords: Self-diet management · Chronic kidney disease · Line chatbot · Health knowledge

1 Introduction

1.1 Research Background and Motives

Under the advancements of medical technology and the economy, people's eating habits and lifestyles have changed. Hence, chronic diseases are no longer limited to the elderly, and kidney disease has become the most common chronic disease. At present, there are more than 500 million people suffering from chronic kidney disease worldwide. According to the statistics of Taiwan National Health Insurance Administration, in 2018, the costs of chronic kidney disease reached NTD 51.3 billion, accounting for nearly 7% of the total national health insurance. With 364,000 patients receiving medical treatments that year, 90,000 patients received peritoneal dialysis and hemodialysis, and chronic

Q. Gao and J. Zhou (Eds.): HCII 2022, LNCS 13331, pp. 268–276, 2022.
https://doi.org/10.1007/978-3-031-05654-3_18

kidney disease ranked first in the list of national diseases. Moreover, with the aging of the population, it is estimated that the number of patients with chronic kidney disease (CKD) will continue to grow; therefore, it is important to study chronic kidney disease. Kidney disease requires long-term control, and patients have different adaptations to the disease, thus, how to assist patients to maintain their kidneys and promote healthy behavior is an important issue to avoid progression to end-stage kidney disease (Campbell and Porter 2015; Chen et al. 2019). Therefore, improving health education knowledge is helpful for patients to learn how to coexist with the disease. In order to monitor the signs of disease deterioration as early as possible, patients can take the initiative to observe their own physical and symptom changes, which would allow them to perceive positive changes in their lifestyles, and thus, improve their abilities to recognize and deal with the disease (Boonstra et al. 2021; Diamantidis and Becker 2014). This study mainly focused on hospitals and patients with chronic diseases and developed a chat robot based on the dietary management and health education knowledge of patients with chronic kidney disease through a combination of scientific and technological services and education. It also used the LINE APP platform in patients' smartphones to create a chat robot for intervention, thus, patients with chronic kidney disease can improve their quality of life through the operation of the LINE chat robot, reduce the medical costs of hospitals and create a new service model, as shown in Fig. 1.

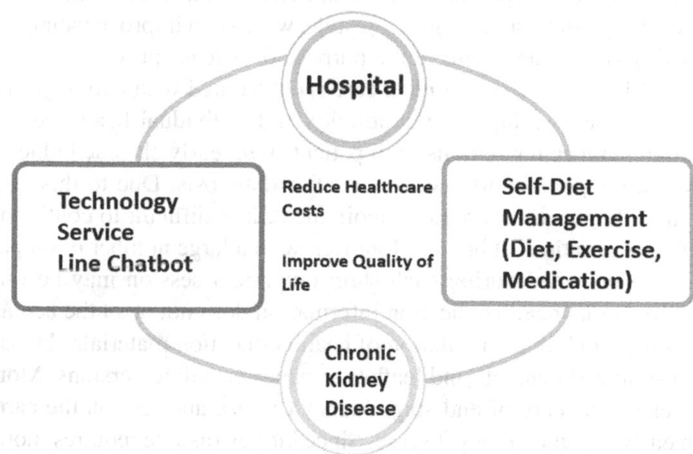

Fig. 1. Research structure

1.2 Research Field and Scope

This study selected patients with chronic kidney disease diagnosed by doctors with a glomerular filtration rate less than 60 mL/min/1.73 m^2, the course of disease over 3 months, and with experience using smartphones as subjects. Patients with chronic kidney disease in National Taiwan University Hospital Yunlin Branch were investigated, and the relevant medical staff were interviewed.

2 Literature Review

2.1 Prevention and Care of Chronic Kidney Disease

Living a healthy lifestyle can delay the progression of chronic kidney disease. The primary work of kidney disease care focuses on implementing healthy behavior in daily life, in order to reduce the incidence rate of end-stage kidney disease. However, as there are no obvious symptoms in the early stages of kidney disease, coupled with the low sense of disease awareness and low discovery rate, even when a case has been diagnosed, it is easy to ignore the implementation of a healthy lifestyle, which leads to serious deterioration from the disease. To help patients coexist with chronic kidney disease in the long-term, it is necessary to conduct regular monitoring and follow-up, and provide individualized and life-oriented care guidance, which can facilitate patients truly learning correct and effective knowledge to master their self-care skills, and then, implement further self-care, such as diet adjustment, smoking cessation, alcohol cessation, and regular exercise (Kosa et al. 2019; Li et al. 2020). Patients with chronic kidney disease require regular follow-up care, and must adjust their diet, exercise, work, and rest in daily life to avoid deterioration of renal function. Therefore, it is important for patients to understand the importance of active participation and self-care behaviors, and to be able to carry out health promotion behaviors, in order to effectively control the disease, delay deterioration, and even prevent other complications. Patients can implement kidney disease care work by establishing a good lifestyle, which can improve their overall health status and quality of life, and achieve the purpose of disease prevention and treatment (Estrella et al. 2012). At present, clinical care is confronted with two major issues. The first is a lack of case tracking, care continuity, and individual health education. The national health insurance regulations limit patients with early chronic kidney disease to making follow-up appointments six months after diagnosis. Due to this long interval between the first diagnosis and return appointment, it is difficult to continuously track patients' self-care situations at home. Moreover, with a large number of outpatients, the nursing guidance provided during each short outpatient session may be limited. The second difficulty is that health education information does not meet the actual needs. A review of the current clinical circulation of health education materials shows that most of them are formalized manuals and leaflets in paper or online versions. Moreover, the content focuses on the care of end-stage kidney disease and less on the care needs of patients with early chronic kidney disease. Since kidney disease requires more attention in care and it is difficult for most patients to obtain care information that meets their own needs, as time goes on, they may forget the contents of precautions, and such limitations in information and time may cause the risk of continuous deterioration from the disease (Boonstra et al. 2021; Chen et al. 2019). Therefore, how to assist and improve the care service model through science and technology, develop patient-centered self-care guidance programs that closely mirror life, strengthen patients' active participation in care work, and implement self-care behavior in life are important issues that require immediate attention.

2.2 Mobile Medical Treatment

The World Health Organization (WHO) put forward the concept of "smart health", which includes the expansion and technological upgrading of communication technology-related products and develops smart health innovative services with mobile devices as the medium. With the development of smart mobile devices, the technology and products of mobile applications are also growing. In addition, with the advent of an aging society, people's acceptance of education and technology is gradually increasing, and the average age of nursing staff will be relatively higher in the future, thus, the requirements for the load and quality of medical care are becoming more and more important. The acceptance degree of digital care has an increasingly important impact on caregivers, patients, and quality of care (Siddique et al. 2019; Weiner and Fink 2017), thus, if health education guidance can be provided through mobile devices, it will help to increase learning effectiveness, reduce waiting times, and save human resources (Tsai et al. 2021; Weiner and Fink 2017). Health education for chronic kidney disease is a very important link in self-care and ranges from prevention to delaying the dialysis stage, and finally, entering the dialysis period. This study suggests that mobile medical care can be used to create a new service process to reduce the expenditures of medical labor costs and improve the quality of life of patients with chronic kidney disease.

2.3 Application of Chat Robots

As chat robots help patients to reduce the inquiry time during outpatient services and waiting time outside the consulting room, they are highly accepted in medical care. As the application of medical chat robots can help improve the quality of medical care (), such online service systems are designed with the three characteristics of convenience, ease of use, and practicability (Lin et al. 2014). (1) Convenience: chat robots do not require the installation of other APPs, they operate within the original familiar interface, and can obtain information in a timely manner to facilitate information queries, which can solve the problem of repetitive consultations. (2) Ease of use: chat robots operate with a familiar interface and are designed to operate in a simple and intuitive way that users can easily understand. (3) Practicability: answers can be quickly obtained by simply inputting questions on the interface, thus, the design is more convenient to operate than a web page, and information queries can be replied to in a timely manner. In addition, general chat robots have been revised in three ways, namely, humanized dialogue mode, simple screen design, and shortened reaction time (Li et al. 2020). (1) Humanized dialogue mode: it imitates the tone of a real conversation through the humanized dialogue mode, which can enhance the feeling of a real conversation. (2) Simple screen design: chat robots present a lot of screen categories and options, which can result in a sense of visual confusion; therefore, intuitive design and reduced text options can make chat robots easy for users to operate. (3) Shortened reaction time: shortening the reaction time improves users' willingness to use by adjusting the content screen. As people are used to carrying smartphones and rely on them to provide real-time information transmission, smartphones are often used as the media in mobile devices, which is helpful for patients to obtain health-related information in real time (Klasnja and Pratt 2012).

3 Research Method

3.1 Phase 1

Phase 1 of this study mainly analyzed the existing chat robots, gathered the problems often encountered by doctors and their patients with chronic kidney disease through preliminary questionnaires and interviews, and learned their needs by interviewing patients in various stages of kidney disease, as well as experts and health educators.

1. Literature review: previous literature was discussed, and three types of medical chat robots in Taiwan were analyzed as references for function construction and interface design.
2. Structured questionnaire: this study conducted a structured questionnaire among 9 patients over 18 years old with chronic kidney disease. Among them, three were in stages 1–2, three were in stages 4–5, and the other three were left blank; five patients were aged 30–40, three aged 40–50, and one aged 50–60.
3. Case interview: this study conducted one-to-one interviews with an attending physician and a health teacher from the Department of Nephrology, Douliu Branch of National Taiwan University Hospital.

3.2 Main Research Method

This study used LINE APP to develop the system architecture of the chat robot, as shown in Fig. 2, and proposed the functions of blood pressure record browsing, dietary queries, diet records, and health education knowledge, as shown in Figs. 3 and 4, which are intended to help patients with chronic diseases reduce the harm and other negative effects caused by the disease.

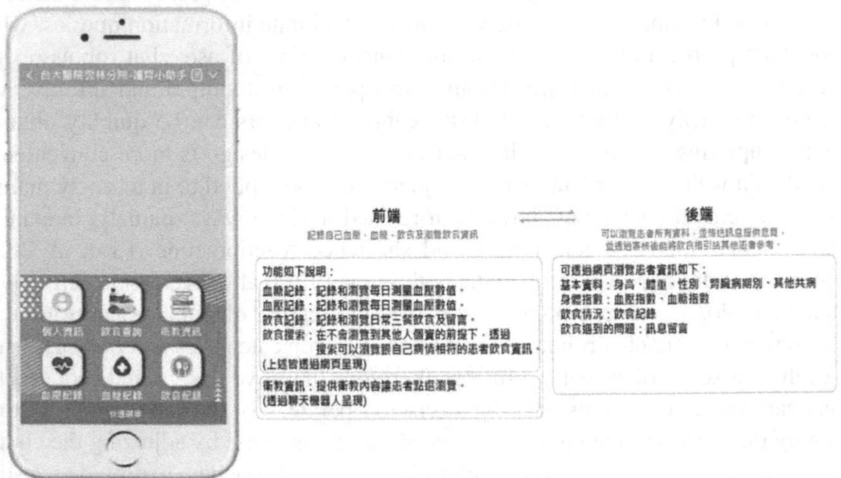

Fig. 2. System architecture

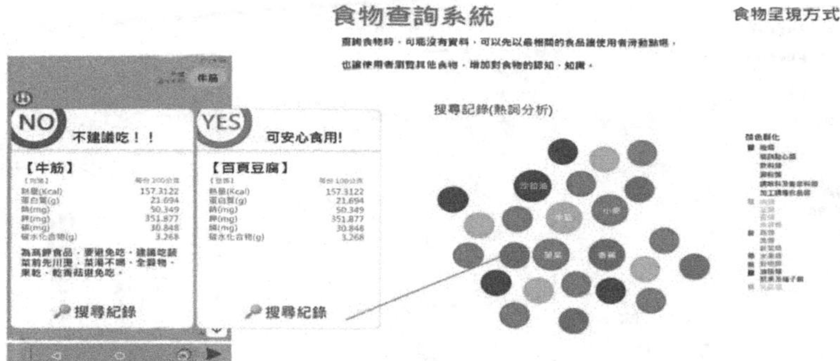

Fig. 3. Diet query

Fig. 4. Health education knowledge

Blood pressure and blood sugar records: It is known from relevant literature that high blood pressure will accelerate the deterioration of renal function and increase the risk of cardiovascular disease. Most patients with diabetes and chronic kidney disease have clinical hypertension. In order to allow patients to master their health status, the system establishes records and browse functions for blood pressure and blood sugar to help patients check the data in daily life (Fig. 5).

3.3 Phase 3

The established chat robot was tested on 15 patients over 18 years old who had never used a chat robot in the past but were experienced smartphone users. The experience and operation procedures were explained before the test, and the subjects were asked to use the chat robot randomly every day. One week later, the subjects were interviewed again to explore their needs regarding the service mode of the chat robot.

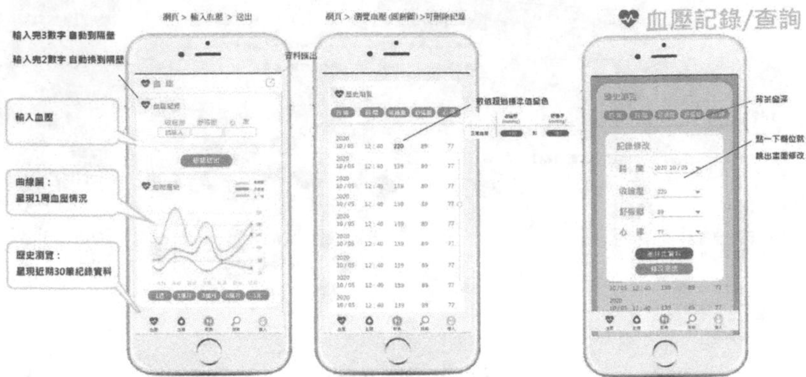

Fig. 5. Blood pressure and blood sugar records

4 Research Analysis

The survey results show that the chat robot was not limited by time or place, had improved efficiency, the waiting time was shortened by simplifying and streamlining the query mode, and usage did not require the installation of another app. Compared with other apps, the chat robot constructed by this study can be operated by users of any online platform with the most familiar interface. According to the results of this study, the ease of use, usefulness, convenience, and correctness of messages should be considered when designing a chat robot. Nonetheless, the users' trust in the chat robot is the most important, as it will affect the intention and willingness to use for middle-aged and elderly users. How to establish confidence for users to easily use chat robots is an important issue. While existing chat robots provide various functions, such as registration and query, which meet the needs of users, they seldom provide relevant health knowledge and prevention knowledge, which makes it difficult to improve patients' concept of self-health management. In addition, as patients with chronic kidney disease are mainly the elderly with poor eyesight, the design of chat robots should consider both the size of the text on the interface and simplifying the text as much as possible. Moreover, replacing text with pictures or voice messages can assist patients with chronic kidney disease to better understand the information content, hence, the correctness of operation can be improved. When the dialogue mode and screen design of chat robots imitate the tone of human conversation with the humanized dialogue mode, it can promote human-machine interaction, enhance the feeling of human conversation, and improve the willingness of users to operate. An interesting map display and the way messages are pushed can assist patients in self-management and increase the emotional level of the chat robot, while the intuitive design and reduced text options enable users to operate the chat robot conveniently. As the functions of the chat robot, as constructed in this study, can increase related disease prevention knowledge and dietary health care content, it helps patients with chronic kidney disease improve their self-health management abilities and health knowledge. When a chat robot can help patients with chronic diseases improve their exercise habits and achieve a balanced diet, it will help them to implement a healthy lifestyle, and they can have a better quality of life and health. Therefore, this study built a chat robot that can help patients with chronic diseases reduce the harm and other negative effects caused by the disease, and has the functions of blood pressure record browsing, dietary queries and diet records, and health education knowledge, which helps patients to stably maintain the disease. Furthermore, the chat robot also helps patients with chronic diseases to improve their health care knowledge by actively promoting such knowledge, and passively allowing users to query their diet knowledge. In this way, patients can break their bad habits and improve their quality of life. Based on the actual test results of patients with chronic diseases, this study explored whether the chat robot was able to meet the needs of users, and the results can provide a reference for future system construction.

5 Conclusions

In order to make the subjects trust the chat robot, it is necessary to identify the sources of the conversation and information presented by the chat robot, which must be produced and provided by professional medical personnel, thus, ensuring the correctness of the source of information. It should have a stable and good operating system that is error-free in use to build user trust in the chat robot. In addition, although users can randomly input text during the interaction, the chat robot does not require users to input their personal information, such as personal basic information or contact information, and users can decide whether or not to input such information, which facilitates personal privacy and provides improved security. As many people have the experience of receiving messages using the LINE APP, it is relatively easy for them to operate the chat robot. Moreover, the screen display is clear and easy to understand, and users can directly click on the screen text and adjust the size arbitrarily. Therefore, a chat robot should be designed in accordance with the habits and needs of users to clearly convey health information and meet the principle of practicality. The screen should be presented in a simple and intuitive manner, which is convenient for users to operate and meets the principle of ease of use, in order that users can feel that the chat robot can help them monitor their health and improve their quality of life. Users can use a chat robot to gain health care knowledge, including health and dietary information. Moreover, many hypertensive patients have the habit of recording their blood pressure, while asymptomatic patients do not need to record such information, thus, according to different usage habits and needs, the chat robot can be used for oneself or to help the elderly record their blood pressure. Therefore, the functions of the chat robot can meet all users' needs and improve their willingness to use according to their different usage habits. In terms of self-management, when users are not clear about whether certain foods can be eaten or have doubts about food, they can find relevant food information through the chat robot. By learning diet-related knowledge and health care knowledge through the chat robot, patients can cultivate their problem-solving abilities to make themselves better. In addition, the diet records are checked by dietitians, who help patients to revise their daily diet habits and develop correct diet concepts, which helps them to better understand their own health, control the disease, and stabilize their condition. With improved health awareness and active participation in health activities, users can establish a foundation of trust in the chat robot, and the operation process is in line with the principles of ease of use and practicality. Under the condition of effectively helping users to improve their health, users can perceive care and concern during the interaction process. As guidance from a chat robot can bring health, users are willing to follow the instructions and guidance of the robot and to spend time learning health knowledge. The implementation of such a knowledge system in users' daily life improves the effectiveness of self-health management.

Acknowledgements. The authors hereby extend sincere thanks to Ministry of Science and Technology (MOST) of the Republic of China (Taiwan, ROC) for their financial support of this research, whose project code is MOST 110-2410-H-224-017-. It is thanks to the generous patronage of MOST that this study has been smoothly performed.

References

Boonstra, M.D., Reijneveld, S.A., Foitzik, E.M., Westerhuis, R., Navis, G., de Winter, A.F.: How to tackle health literacy problems in chronic kidney dis-ease patients? A systematic review to identify promising intervention targets and strategies. Nephrol. Dial. Transplant. **36**(7), 1207–1221 (2021)

Campbell, J., Porter, J.: Dietary mobile apps and their effect on nutritional indicators in chronic renal disease: a systematic review. Nephrology **20**(10), 744–751 (2015)

Chen, T.K., Knicely, D.H., Grams, M.E.: Chronic kidney disease diagnosis and management: a review. JAMA **322**(13), 1294–1304 (2019)

Diamantidis, C.J., Becker, S.: Health information technology (IT) to improve the care of patients with chronic kidney disease (CKD). BMC Nephrol. **15**, 7 (2014)

Estrella, M.M., Sisson, S.D., Roth, J., Choi, M.J.: Efficacy of an internet-based tool for improving physician knowledge of chronic kidney disease: an observational study. BMC Nephrol. **13**(1) (2012). Article number: 126. https://doi.org/10.1186/1471-2369-13-126

Klasnja, P., Pratt, W.: Healthcare in the pocket: mapping the space of mobile-phone health interventions. J. Biomed. Inform. **45**(1), 184–198 (2012). https://www.sciencedirect.com/science/article/pii/S1532046411001444?via%3Dihub

Kosa, S.D., Monize, J., D'Souza, M., Joshi, A., Philip, K., Reza, S., et al.: Nutritional mobile applications for CKD patients: systematic review. Kidney Int. Rep. **4**(3), 399–407 (2019)

Li, W., Chiu, F., Zeng, J., Li, Y., Huang, S., Yeh, H., et al.: Mobile health app with social media to support self-management for patients with chronic kidney disease: prospective randomized controlled study. J. Med. Internet Res. **22**(12), e19452 (2020)

Lin, H., Wang, Y., Jing, L., Chang, P.: Mockup design of personal health diary app for patients with chronic kidney disease. In: Studies in Health Technology and Informatics, vol. 201, pp. 124–132 (2014)

Siddique, A.B., Krebs, M., Alvarez, S., Greenspan, I., Patel, A., Kinsolving, J., et al.: Mobile apps for the care management of chronic kidney and end-stage renal diseases: systematic search in app stores and evaluation. JMIR Mhealth Uhealth **7**(9), e12604 (2019)

Tsai, Y., Hsiao, P., Kuo, M., Wang, S., Chen, T., Kung, L., et al.: Mobile health, disease knowledge, and self-care behavior in chronic kidney disease: a prospective cohort study. J. Personalized Med. **11**(9), 845 (2021)

Weiner, S., Fink, J.C.: Telemedicine to promote patient safety: use of phone-based interactive voice-response system to reduce adverse safety events in pre-dialysis CKD. Adv. Chronic Kidney Dis. **24**(1), 31–38 (2017)

A Preliminary Study on Application of Tangible User Interface and Augmented Reality Technology with Table Game and Hand-Eye Coordination Operation Tasks in the Fields of Memory and Visuospatial Perception for the Elderly

Li-Lan Wang and I.-Jui Lee(✉)

Department of Industrial Design, National Taipei University of Technology, Taipei, Taiwan
t109588003@ntut.org.tw, ericlee@mail.ntut.edu.tw

Abstract. As the elderly ages, their memory, judgement and spatial orientation and cognition gradually decline. These declining abilities can result in different levels of problems in everyday life and eventually lead to a decline in the quality of life of the elderly. Therefore, this study focuses on discussing the ways to strengthen the memory and visuospatial perception skills of the elderly through simple game mechanisms.

It is known from previous works that the application of a "Tangible User Interface" combined with "Augmented Reality" (Tangible Augmented Reality, TAR) technology, together with game tasks and hand-eye coordination exercises, will help gamers to achieve better interface operability and comprehension. However, it remains to be seen whether such advantages can be equally reflected in the 'memory' and 'visuospatial perception' abilities of the elderly.

Therefore, a total of six subjects of middle-advanced age over 60 years old were recruited for this study and each of them was provided with each: (1) Tablet computer game without TAR operation (the game is operated entirely on the tablet computer), and (2) An interactive game with TAR operation (which combines virtual and physical operational objects). The participants were asked to complete six cognitive scales (mental load, game operation, cognitive load, self-expression, visuospatial perception, and memory degree) after completing the two kinds of games for the purpose of assessing whether the TAR game task was equally operative and comprehensible for the elderly in terms of "memory" and "visuospatial perception".

The results show that TAR games do have better operability and is more easily comprehensible, which is also reflected in the performance of the elderly in terms of "memory" and "visuospatial perception", with an average score of 5.55 or higher (out of 7) in memory, judgement and orientation cognition. The reason is that TAR games with physical operation is conducive to improving the spatial cognition and cognitive ability of the operator through hand-eye coordination, and this advantage is indirectly reflected by the operation and performance of games that require invoking memory, judgement and directional cognition.

Q. Gao and J. Zhou (Eds.): HCII 2022, LNCS 13331, pp. 277–289, 2022.
https://doi.org/10.1007/978-3-031-05654-3_19

Therefore, it can be concluded that TAR games have advantages over non-TAR tablet games in terms of memory, spatial cognition and perceptual judgement and processing training for middle-advanced age users. More complete data support shall be gained for such result by a larger number of case recruitment trials, which is to be promoted and fulfilled in future studies.

Keywords: Tangible Augmented Reality · Tangible user interface · Hand-eye coordination · The elderly · Cognitive ability · Memory · Visuospatial perception

1 Introduction

1.1 Impact of Cognitive Impairment on the Elderly

With the rapid socio-economic development and the improvement of medical technology, the average life expectancy of human beings has also increased significantly, leading to an aging population structure. As a result, research and design for the aging population structure has attracted increasing attention. The cognitive abilities of the elderly decline with age, especially in memory, judgement and spatial orientation cognition, including information processing speed, attention, episodic memory, visuospatial ability, executive function and other abilities [1].

Cognitive decline is a common problem in the elderly, and therefore one of the hot issues that researchers in this field are focusing on is how to slow down cognition decline in the elderly. Compared to drug therapy that brings about side effects, interventions of non-drug treatment are more important [2] as early interventions and effective preventive medicine to address cognition decline in the elderly can help to improve the quality of life of the elderly and reduce the burden on social resources.

1.2 Serious Games Applied to Trainings on Improving Cognition Impairment for the Elderly

Serious games refer to games that are not purely for entertainment and have specific purposes in themselves. It is a strategy that aims at strengthening a specific function through the process of game playing [3]. Some researchers have been conducted to solve the problem of cognitive dysfunction for the elderly.

In recent years, many clinical studies have adopted serious game or applied game to improve cognitive of the elderly. Therefore, cognition decline in the elderly can be improved by training through serious games. Compared with traditional training activities, serious games can help to improve the health condition of the elderly. At the same time, serious games are full of fun in terms of game experience to maintain the interest and learning motivation of the elderly during the training process so as to achieve specific training objectives and effects [4, 5], such as enhancing memory, judgement, spatial orientation and cognition, to name a few.

In researches, serious game can also be used in conjunction with traditional interventions to assess after-effects and conduct cognitive tests [6]. There have been many studies on the elderly who have improved their cognitive, hand-eye coordination and behavioral and psychological symptoms with good results from serious game interventions [7].

In addition, relevant studies indicate that serious games can be designed to suit different training purposes and are proved to be effective in preventing decline in cognitive function of the elderly [8]. Therefore, in this study the introduction of serious games into the training on cognitive impairment for the elderly would be quite feasible.

2 Literature Review

2.1 The Application of Augmented Reality to Cognitive Training for the Elderly

In recent years, Augmented Reality (AR) technology has been widely used in different research fields, including healthcare, education and entertainment etc. [9]. As a visualization technique that overlays virtual information on physical objects, AR has been developed rapidly due to the high maturity of visualization technology.

Furthermore, in recent studies, AR has been proved to be conducive to enhancing the sensory experience of users [10] and can effectively reduce the cognitive load of learning [11], perceptual training [12] and even maintain the social and physical abilities of the elderly through cognitive games [13]. Specific cognitive training will help to slow down the decline in memory, judgement and orientation cognition in the elderly. Thus it can be seen that there is considerable potential to apply AR technology to improve the "memory" and "visuospatial perception" of the elderly.

2.2 Augmented Reality Lacks Operational Physical Handling Cognition and Effective Haptic Feedback Mechanisms

However, the most controversial part of AR technology for the elderly is the lack of physical cognition and effective haptic feedback mechanisms. For the elderly, AR lacks a tangible user interface (TUI), which can be unintuitive in operation or intricate, making it difficult to operate.

Therefore, this study focuses on the application of "Augmented Reality" in combination with "Tangible User Interface" (Tangible Augmented Reality, TAR) [14] as a training material to explore the cognitive abilities of the elderly, in order to explore possibility of a more diverse training approach for the elderly in "memory" and "visuospatial perception".

2.3 "Tangible User Interface" Combined with "Augmented Reality" Technology for Cognitive Training of the Elderly

Based on the previous part, AR technology has been proved helpful to enhance the sensory experience of users [10] and effectively reduce the cognitive load on learning [11]. Moreover, the application of a "tangible user interface" can effectively address the feeling of illusion of AR technology due to the lack of physical operation awareness and haptic feedback, allowing AR content to be more easily and intuitively operated by the user. Furthermore, with the interactive operation of hand-eye coordination, AR will help the elderly to gain better interface operability and comprehension, thus promoting their "memory" and "visuospatial perception".

The mechanism of operation and the operational concept are mainly on linking the "operational cognition" under hand-eye coordination with the physical sense of interaction, so that this game task generates "body memory" stimulation and sensory triggering, and further enhances memory ability and body movement so as to make it a reflex action under given instructions and procedures [15].

Therefore, this study focuses on the application of a "tangible user interface" combined with "augmented reality" technology to the cognitive training for the elderly. The interface relies on physical and visual sensory stimulation through "hand-eye coordination operation" and accelerates the mental and cognitive functioning of the elderly through a game-like approach and training mechanism, thereby achieving training effects and mitigating the effects of cognitive decline at an advanced age.

2.4 Summary

Therefore, it is clear from the above literature that the use of "tangible user interface" combined with "augmented reality" technology and "tabletop gaming" tasks and "hand-eye coordination operation" for the training of "memory" and "visuospatial perception" in the elderly is possibly effective to slow down the cognition decline of the elderly.

However, this study has not been confirmed and few studies have been conducted to evaluate the operational tasks of TAR game concepts for the elderly. Therefore, this study will provide an example of a TAR game application for the elderly in order to assess whether the TAR game task is equally operational and comprehensible for the elderly in terms of "memory" and "visuospatial perception".

3 Research Methodology

3.1 Research Objects

In this study, a total of 6 elderly people aging 60 years or above (mean age of 65.2 years old) were recruited for the study, who were all female, currently living with their families. Cases were screened on the basis of subnormal elderly with a score of at least 26 on the Montreal Cognitive Assessment (MoCA) cognitive impairment scale. It is a simple scale to detect mild cognition impairment and pre-dementia covering six major cognitive measurement dimensions: attention, memory (immediate and delayed memory/computation), language, orientation, visual construction skills and executive function (abstract thinking).

3.2 Experimental Implementation and Game Playing

In this experiment, six elderly subjects were provided with two different types of games: (1) a tablet game without TAR operation and (2) an interactive game with TAR operation. The experiments were conducted with six elderly subjects playing each of the two types of games for 25 min, and the games were played for a total of 50 min, with the researcher and therapist observing during the games. After the participants had completed the two types of games, they were asked to complete a six-dimension cognitive scale. The six items in the cognitive scale were used to help the researcher understand whether the game with TAR operation was better for the elderly than the traditional tablet game interface in terms of memory, judgement and visuospatial perception.

Because of the above research topics, the games selected for the two categories of games (with TAR operation) in this study were mainly those that require combination of memory, judgement and visuospatial perception to complete the tasks. In terms of game content, the games with similar content and the same rules were selected (for example, the Simon Game and the Tangram game were chosen for this study, and the Simon Game is about memory [16] and the Tangram Game is about spatial cognition [17]). The main purpose of the study was to find out the differences in operating and comprehension of memory and visuospatial perception skills between (1) a tablet game without TAR operation and (2) an interactive game with TAR operation for the elderly.

3.3 Differences Among and Comparisons of Game Content

In this study, two games were selected for "memory" and "visuospatial perception", namely the Simon Memory Game [16] and the Tangram Game. Simon Game mainly requires users to memorize and recite the order of lighting and direction of the lights in various color, and then arrange them in order according to the prompts so as toto test their memory ability in the process.

Tangrams Game, on the other hand, is a game on shape matching and color matching for arrangement in order, which also tests the spatial and shape awareness skills of the players [17].

These two games were given the same content but with different modes of operation by the researchers (one was an interactive game with TAR operation and the other was a tablet game without TAR operation), the main difference is whether a "tangible user interface" was provided for the game players in operation.

Tablet Game Without TAR Operation
The Simon Game without TAR operation is a game published by Hasbro, Inc. and its video game version was designed by Paul Neave [18] based on its concept.

The Tangram without TAR operation is a computer game of shape collage published by ImproveMemory [19]. Both of them can be played on a tablet computer, mainly providing a no-TAR operation tablet game for elderly subjects. During the process, the elderly subjects had to use their hands to tap the interface buttons on the tablet to complete the tasks, and the game was mainly played using the tablet without gestures or hand-eye coordination (Fig. 1).

Interactive Game with TAR Operation
In contrast to the two kinds of tablet games mentioned above, the study found two other games with the same concept, and changed the content of the game to "TAR operation", which were played with OSMO (Tangible Play, Inc.) [20] and MERGE CUBE [21] respectively.

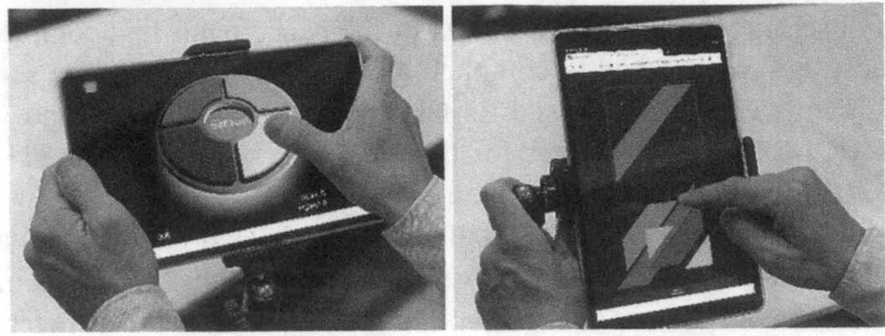

Fig. 1. Simon's memory game by Hasbro, Inc. (left), Shape collage computer game by ImproveMemory (right)

The Tangram Game uses the Tangible Play game published by OSMO for game interaction, which has physical objects that interact with the virtual interface of the tablet. In the process, users could operate on the tangram in a physical space and then receive feedback through the flat screen (Fig. 2).

OSMO Tangible Play

The tablet game is combined with a physical tangram (Fig. 2), in which the shapes of the physical objects below is reflected through the reflecting mirror on top of the tablet, and then the image recognition technology at the back end of the program is used to compare the shapes to determine whether the player has arranged the shapes in accordance with the corresponding pictures. If the arrangement is correct, the user will be given different visual animation feedback, and led to the next stage of the game.

Fig. 2. The Tangible Play game published by OSMO allows users to interact with the virtual image of the tablet using physical objects.

MERGE CUBE

Another game with TAR operation, Simon Game, uses the MERGE CUBE to operate (Elemental Order, Clevyr, Inc., Fig. 3) [22]. The game is played with a physical MERGE CUBE (the cube in Fig. 3), during which the user sees the AR technology project virtual information onto the physical object in accordance with the rotation of the cube, which is then presented on the screen of the handheld device (Fig. 3).

Game players can use their hands to turn the physical cubes to correspond to the virtual models displayed on the screen. During the process they can master game information and the interactive state of game content through hand-eye coordination. Compared to tablet games without TAR operation, the user can control the interface content directly with both hands, which is different from the sensory cognition of a simple flat screen view.

Fig. 3. Game players can pick up the physical MERGE CUBE and use the cube to play.

3.4 Assessment Methods

After the six elderly participants completed the two kinds of games, they were given a questionnaire adapted from the cognitive dimensions of the NASA-TLX (National aeronautics and space administration task load index) [23] scale to assess their subjective measurement of mental load. The scale developed for this study involves in: (1) psychological burden, (2) game operation, (3) cognitive load, (4) self-expression, (5) visuospatial perception, and (6) memory. After the game, the researchers record and interview those old people about their game operation and experience. This will be used to assess whether tangible user interfaces combined with AR technology (TAR) together with tabletop tasks and hand-eye coordination are equally operative and comprehensible for the elderly in terms of "memory" and "visuospatial perception", or whether they can reduce learning load and serve as a good medium for cognitive training (Figs. 4 and 5).

Fig. 4. Tablet Tangram Game without TAR operation (left) and interactive Tangram Game with TAR operation (right)

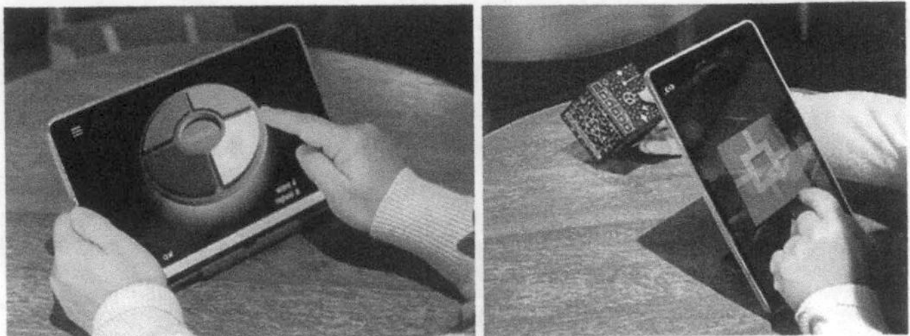

Fig. 5. Tablet Simon Game without TAR operation (left), and interactive Simon Game with TAR operation (right)

4 Results

In this study, a total of six elderly subjects (MOCA > 26) aged 60 above years old were given a test and subsequent interview. The full procedures of the experiment were recorded. The elderly subjects were provided with (1) a tablet computer game without TAR operation (which was operated entirely on the tablet) and (2) an interactive game with TAR operation (which combined virtual and physical operation objects) for sensory operation and comparison. A subjective assessment was conducted using the modified NASA-TLX cognitive scale to see if it had some impact on and advantage over "memory" and "visuospatial perception" of the elderly.

After the game, a comparison was made on a subjective scale between the game with TAR operation and the tablet game without TAR operation to see if the game had better operability and comprehension of "memory" and "visuospatial perception" and could be used in the future as a cognitive training medium to reduce learning load.

In this study game experiments and interviews were conducted, and a modified cognitive scale was used for a subjective evaluation on six dimensions (psychological burden, game operation, cognitive load, self-expression, visuospatial perception, and memory), and for assessment of the performance of the of the TAR game style with a score of 1 to 7.

After observation of the experimental games, the researcher and therapist discussed the performance and status of the elderly subjects during the game, focusing on the following six subjective aspects. Given that this study was a single game experiment, the assessment was not focused on the degree of cognitive improvement of the elderly, but on whether the TAR game was more appropriate and easier to play for the elderly in terms of operability and cognition. In addition, data from six aspects were presented to determine the extent to which the TAR game was helpful in various dimensions.

The following is the game experience of a total of six elderly subjects in playing interactive games with TAR operation compared to games without TAR operation:

1. **Psychological burden:** The interactive game with the TAR operation was relatively easy for the elderly in terms of 'psychological burden', with a score of 5.9, (1 stands for strongly disagree; 7 stands for totally agree).

2. **Game operation:** Interactive games with TAR operation is easier for the elderly to master in terms of 'game operation' with a score of 5.83, (1 stands for strongly disagree; 7 stands for totally agree).
3. **Cognitive load:** The interactive game with TAR operation was relatively easy for the elderly to understand in terms of manipulating the 'cognitive load', with a score of 5.3, (1 stands for the most difficult; 7 stands for the easiest).
4. **Self-expression:** The interactive game with the TAR operation scored 4.83 in terms of satisfaction of the elderly with 'self-expression' (1 stands for the least satisfaction with the results; 7 stands for the greatest satisfaction with the results).
5. **Visuospatial perception:** The Tangram Game with TAR operation is easier to operate for the elderly in terms of "visuospatial perception", with a score of 6.16, (1 stands for the most difficult to operate; 7 stands for the easiest to operate).
6. **Memory:** The Simon Game with TAR operation is easier to understand for the elderly in terms of "memory", with a score of 5.3, (1 stands for the most difficult to remember; 7 stands for the easiest to remember).

The data from the above six dimensions show that the six participants found the TAR-based games to be useful for comprehension and operability, and indirectly conducive to memory and spatial cognition, with an average score of 5.55. It can be seen that interactive games with TAR operation have a positive effect on the overall cognitive condition of the aged participants, and indirectly lead to better "operability" and "comprehension" in the aspect of "memory" and "visuospatial perception".

In addition, the researchers found that the Simon Game with TAR operation had more "memory points" than the non-TAR operation tablet games. It was found that the participants were more likely to enhance their memory and feelings through the "body memory" and "perceptual cognition" generated by the gestures.

In terms of visuospatial perception, the Tangram Game with TAR operation was easier to understand than the game with no TAR operation. More information feedback on such phenomena was obtained from the field observations of the participants during the game tasks and from the actual interviews.

5 Conclusion and Discussion

Based on the above, the results show that the elderly received initial positive support from the therapist when they play the interactive games with TAR operation. According to these observations and data, it is clear that the interactive game with TAR operation has advantages in the six sensory dimensions of comprehension, operation, cognitive load, cognition, memory, and visuospatial perception training through hand-eye coordination. Based on these preliminary findings, it is expected that the application of the TAR interface is generally positive in terms of delaying cognition decline of the elderly. The researcher has several explanations and suggestions for this initial performance.

5.1 TAR Games can be Helpful for the Elderly in Terms of Operation

TAR games can play combined effect of virtual visual imaging and physical object perception. In a Tangram Game with the TAR operation, the elderly can manipulate the virtual animation presented on the flat screen by actually moving the corresponding physical object. The feedback from the user's hand manipulation also makes their cognition of shape pattern and space more obvious.

In addition, such a phenomenon was also demonstrated in the Simon Game with the TAR operation concept. The subjects were stimulated by the color changes presented by the augmented reality technology while rotating the cube, and then the physical cube is operated by both hands at the same time, so that the color changes would leave a deeper impression on the subject. According to such phenomena and findings, the following three advantages are summarized through an analysis: First, previous studies on spatial cognitive training of the elderly were often done only by recognition training and comparison of spatial concepts through 2D planar graphics. This is not only more difficult for operation and lacks spatial awareness, but also less likely to arouse users' interest.

On the other hand, the Simon Game with TAR operation uses AR technology to present a 3D stereoscopic model and allows users to interact with the 3D spatial content through real physical objects. This integration of virtual and reality is also useful for spatial and memory training [24]. In addition, such outcomes are not only effective for young people, but also for the elderly, who can directly manipulate 3D objects with spatial concepts by hand and eye is much faster than converting 2D images into 3D space by imagination.

Secondly, real-time visual and physical interaction can enhance the training on hand-eye coordination. Compared to traditional tablet games with 2D interfaces or AR-only games, the use of physical models by gestures and rotating games can trigger users' associations with colors and shapes to increase their willingness to play cognitive training games [25]. Meanwhile, it can also help to improve memory and spatial cognition abilities through gesture operation.

In addition, the TAR game can also offer different contents to various kinds of games for physical objects and virtual interface operation, thus the materials introduced by games could be selected among a wide range of scope.

Finally, compared to tablet games without TAR operation, the participants remained optimistic about using new technological applications. After manipulating 3D virtual models through handheld devices such as tablets, the elderly people were clearly emotionally excited and relatively concentrated during the process of operation.

5.2 The Impact of Interactive Game Design and Usage Environment with TAR Operation

With AR technology, the virtual images are integrated with real life and the extended while TAR technology integrates physical operations into the system's operating mechanism, allowing the users to interact with virtual augmented information through physical objects, strengthening the connection between physical and 3D objects. Such state of operation would then trigger the user's body perception. The relationship between the user's hands, the handheld device and the physical operation tool shall therefore be taken into account in the design and operation of the game.

For example, in a Tangram Game with TAR operation, the players place the blocks in front of the tablet and visually see the graphics on the screen and the physical tangram blocks directly. Compared to Tangram Game without TAR operation purely operated on a tablet, TAR operation makes it easier for the elderly to recognize shapes and spatial matching relationship, and indirectly enhances their sense of interaction between operational cognition and spatial cognition.

Furthermore, according to the feedback from the test subjects, in addition to the increased memory and spatial perception when operating TAR games, the operational smoothness of environmental devices also affects the user's concentration in operation and satisfaction with the game. Considering the physical condition of the elderly, hand-held devices with TAR games that allow them to sit or stand only are easier to perform on than full-body action games, and they can also focus on hand-eye coordination tasks at the same time to achieve better operation and experience.

5.3 Future Work and Research Limitations

This study aims at enabling the elderly to engage with the game in a more intuitive and smooth manner, and to enhance memory and visuospatial perception through games actions, which can achieve better learning outcomes with more diversified interactive games and cognitive training that integrates virtual and reality as the learning medium.

Although preliminary experimental results were obtained in this study, there are still some non-negligible limitations.

First, as this experiment introduced a new technology into a traditional cognitive test and conducted in the form of game intervention, which is a new learning exercise for the elderly, the acceptance level will exert certain influence on the test results from the subjective feelings of the subjects. Moreover, the number of cases recruited for the initial experiment is quite small, so it can only be considered as a preliminary study.

Secondly, the cognitive decline of the elderly is comprehensive and varies to different degrees as the physical condition of the individual changes. This study discusses the cognition abilities such as hand-eye coordination operation, memory and visuospatial perception, and more in-depth experiments with a larger sample size are needed to ascertain the mechanism and how to master the interactive game with TAR operation in order to enhance this ability more accurately.

Finally, this study is mainly designed with the focus of whether the application of "tangible user interface" combined with "augmented reality" technology (TAR) can help memory and visuospatial perception under hand-eye coordination. In the process of the game, a virtual-real integration concept was adopted to enhance the cognitive abilities of the elderly with simple concepts and to understand and make it clear whether such a game mechanism has an effect on memory and visuospatial perception. Future research and experimental designs are needed to validate the game interventions for the elderly in reducing cognitive impairment.

References

1. Park, D.C., Lautenschlager, G., Hedden, T., Davidson, N.S., Smith, A.D., Smith, P.K.: Models of visuospatial and verbal memory across the adult life span. Psychol. Aging **17**(2), 299–320 (2002)

2. Tsolaki, M., et al.: Effectiveness of nonpharmacological approaches in patients with mild cognitive impairment. Neurodegener. Dis. **8**(3), 138–145 (2011)
3. Alvarez, J., Djaouti, D.: An introduction to Serious game Definitions and concepts. Serious Games Simul. Risks Manag. **11**(1), 11–15 (2011)
4. Wiemeyer, J., Kliem, A.: Serious games in prevention and rehabilitation—a new panacea for elderly people? Eur. Rev. Aging Phys. Act. **9**(1), 41–50 (2012)
5. Groznik, V., Sadikov, A.: Gamification in cognitive assessment and cognitive training for mild cognitive impairment. In: Geroimenko, V. (ed.) Augmented Reality Games II, pp. 179–204. Springer, Cham (2019). https://doi.org/10.1007/978-3-030-15620-6_8
6. Chicchi Giglioli, I.A., de Juan Ripoll, C., Parra, E., Alcañiz Raya, M.: EXPANSE: a novel narrative serious game for the behavioral assessment of cognitive abilities. PLoS ONE **13**(11), e0206925 (2018). https://doi.org/10.1371/journal.pone.0206925
7. Zheng, J., Chen, X., Yu, P.: Game-based interventions and their impact on dementia: a narrative review. Australas. Psychiatry **25**(6), 562–565 (2017). https://doi.org/10.1177/103985621772 6686
8. Lin, C.-W., Mao, T.-Y., Huang, C.-F.: A novel game-based intelligent test for detecting elderly cognitive function impairment. Comput. Math. Methods Med. **2021**, 10 (2021). Article ID 1698406
9. Azuma, R.T.: A survey of augmented reality. Presence Teleoperators Virtual Environ. **6**(4), 355–385 (1997)
10. Crofton, E.C., Botinestean, C., Fenelon, M., Gallagher, E.: Potential applications for virtual and augmented reality technologies in sensory science. Innov. Food Sci. Emerg. Technol. **56**, 102178 (2019)
11. Chu, H.-H.: The effect of cognitive styles, learning motivation and computer attitude on cognitive load of users in augmented reality learning system. Department of Graphic Arts Communication (2013). https://hdl.handle.net/11296/52a5j5
12. Blomqvist, S., Seipel, S., Engström, M.: Using augmented reality technology for balance training in the older adults: a feasibility pilot study. BMC Geriatr. **21**, 144 (2021). https://doi.org/10.1186/s12877-021-02061-9
13. Chen, Y., Janicki, S.: A cognitive-based board game with augmented reality for older adults: development and usability study. JMIR Serious Games **8**(4), e22007 (2020)
14. Billinghurst, M., Kato, H., Poupyrev, I.: Tangible augmented reality. ACM Siggraph Asia **7**(2), 1–10 (2008)
15. Blacker, K.J., Curby, K.M., Klobusicky, E., Chein, J.M.: Effects of action video game training on visual working memory. J. Exp. Psychol. Hum. Percept. Perform. **40**(5), 1992 (2014)
16. Kawamoto, A.L.S., Martins, V.F.: A visuospatial memory game for the elderly using gestural interface. In: Antona, M., Stephanidis, C. (eds.) UAHCI 2017. LNCS, vol. 10278, pp. 430–443. Springer, Cham (2017). https://doi.org/10.1007/978-3-319-58703-5_32
17. Desai, S., Fels, D., Astell, A.: Designing for experiences in blended reality environments for people with dementia. In: Stephanidis, C., Antona, M., Gao, Q., Zhou, J. (eds.) HCII 2020. LNCS, vol. 12426, pp. 495–509. Springer, Cham (2020). https://doi.org/10.1007/978-3-030-60149-2_38
18. The Free Video Games Project, Paul Neave. https://freesimon.org/
19. ImproveMemory, Powerblocks. https://www.improvememory.org/brain-games/block-games/powerblocks/
20. Tangible Play, Inc. https://www.playosmo.com/en/
21. Merge Labs, Inc. https://mergeedu.com/cube
22. Elemental Order, Clevyr, Inc. https://clevyr.com/games/elemental-order
23. Hart, S.G., Staveland, L.E.: Development of NASA-TLX (task load index): results of empirical and heoretical research. In: Hancock, P.A., Meshkati, N. (eds.) Human Mental Workload, North-Holland, Amsterdam, The Netherlands, pp. 139–183 (1988)

24. Juan, M.C., Mendez-Lopez, M., Perez-Hernandez, E., Albiol-Perez, S.: Augmented reality for the assessment of children's spatial memory in real settings. PLoS ONE **9**(12), e113751 (2014)
25. Bach, B., Sicat, R., Beyer, J., Cordeil, M., Pfister, H.: The hologram in my hand: how effective is interactive exploration of 3D visualizations in immersive tangible augmented reality? IEEE Trans. Vis. Comput. Graph. **24**(1), 457–467 (2017)

Feasibility Study of Portable Simulated Pet 'KEDAMA' for Relieving Depression

Jiang Wu[1,2](✉), Yuan Yuan[1], and Yihang Dai[1,3]

[1] Kakuchi Academy, Kakuchi Co., Ltd., 3-2-17 Shimoochiai, Shinjyuku-ku, Tokyo 161-0033, Japan
jiangwu@s.h.k.u-tokyo.ac.jp
[2] The University of Tokyo, 7-3-1 Hongo, Bunkyo-ku, Tokyo 113-8656, Japan
[3] Graduate School of Art and Design, Tama Art University, 2-1723 Yarimizu, Hachioji, Tokyo 192-0394, Japan

Abstract. The sudden arrival of COVID-19 has brought a lot of inconvenience to people's lives. It also has an adverse impact on people's mental health. Because COVID-19 can spread directly, aerosol and contact, this uncontrollable and rapid mode of communication restricts people's going out, and all the original party and entertainment activities are restricted, which for today's young people, is tantamount to reducing the way to vent stress, but also brings a sense of loneliness. Young people have become the biggest victims of COVID-19's restricted activities, and more and more young people suffer from mental health diseases. Keeping pets is used to improve mental health disorders, and more and more people are starting to keep pets, but on the other hand, the number of people who abandon their pets is also on the rise, and a large number of them are forced to separate from their pets for external reasons. To get rid of this situation, more and more people use virtual pets to replace real pets, but the current virtual pets are also in a state of saturation and there are many problems. Therefore, we have developed a portable simulated pet 'KEDAMA', which can be customized according to the user's personal preferences, based on the five senses, and the price is very cheap and easy to order. Not only to replace pets, but also hope that KEDAMA can improve people's mental health and prevent more young people from depression.

Keywords: Depression · Portable simulated pet · Five senses · Mental health

1 Introduction

1.1 Background

The COVID-19 virus is now known to belong to the same family as SARS and Middle East respiratory syndrome coronavirus (MERS-CoV), which are zoonotic infections thought to have originated from snakes, bats, and pangolins at the Wuhan wet markets. The virus has rapidly spread across the globe leading to many infected people and multiple deaths [1]. On March 11, 2020, the World Health Organization characterized

Q. Gao and J. Zhou (Eds.): HCII 2022, LNCS 13331, pp. 290–304, 2022.
https://doi.org/10.1007/978-3-031-05654-3_20

COVID-19 as a pandemic [2]. This pandemic has affected all aspects of human life worldwide. Due to the pandemic, many governments have imposed restrictions, of varying degrees of strictness, which have impacted people's day-to-day lives. In particular, a large proportion of young adults are facing the effects of college suspensions, teleworking, reduced income, and part-time unemployment. The government almost comprehensive restrictions such as not leaving home for any public spaces, staying home except when absolutely necessary to go out (i.e., work, in accordance with prescribed limits; buying food or medicine; receiving medical treatment; performing other essential activities), and a prohibition against congregating [3].

At the same time, restaurants and entertainment venues, shops of all kinds, malls and shopping centers, hotels, and many other businesses (excluding those defined as essential, such as grocery stores and pharmacies) were forced to close at once. Although industries considered essential maintained their activity, non-essential industries were permitted to employ only a limited number of workers [4]. When personal activity is restricted and the living environment changes, people tend to feel anxious and unsafe. In the case of infectious disease outbreaks, the state of restricting personal activities will continue when the cause or progression and outcome of COVID-19 is unclear [5]. At the SARS outbreak in 2003, anxiety levels increased significantly. In Hong Kong, for example, about 70% of people express anxiety about contracting SARS, and many say they see no hope for their life ever since [6]. The COVID-19 pandemic and resulting recession negatively impacted the mental health of many people and created new barriers for people who already suffered from mental illness and substance use disorders [7]. Such as difficulty sleeping (36%) or eating (32%), increases in alcohol consumption or substance use (12%), and worsening chronic conditions (12%), due to worry and stress over the coronavirus. Adults are one of the most affected groups in crisis. Due to the influence of COVID-19, four out of ten adults have symptoms of anxiety and depression [8]. So far, COVID-19 has not been completely resolved, and the number of psychologically impaired patients will continue to grow. According to the July 2020 KFF Health Tracking Survey [7], mental health problems among young adults account for 56.2% of the total number of people affected. It is important for adults to improve their mental health with anxiety and depression.

In recent years, pet ownership is being promoted as a way to improve mental health. Pet may become a stimulus for exercise, reduce anxiety, and provide an external focus of attention. Pets are also a source of physical contact and comfort and may decrease loneliness and depression while promoting an interesting lifestyle [9]. Pets make you walk in the morning and you have to do a lot of other activities like bathing, feeding them and so on. Pet owners will also play with their pets, these activities will keep you moving, which will eliminate all the laziness in your body, make you healthy and energetic. Some pet owners will talk to their pets when they feel lonely, and quickly make the owners laugh through the pet's pranks and lovely activities, thus alleviating the loneliness of being alone. And because some families keep pets, their houses are protected from thieves. With the development of society, the continuous growth of national economy and the continuous improvement of people's living standards, people's pursuit of spiritual life has reached a certain height while their material life is greatly enriched. On the one hand, people pay more and more attention to the cultivation of life interest and pursuit of personalized experience.

On the other hand, the change of traditional family structure and the increase of work pressure make more and more people put their emotional investment in pets, and the pet industry gradually develops from this. Due to the impact of COVID-19, 2020 was a year of profound impact and change, and the pet industry experienced its share of both. The industry exceeded over $100 billion in sales for the first time last year, according to APPA's 2020 State of the Industry Report. APPA is bullish for the coming year, projecting growth of 5.8%, well above the historical average of 3% to 4%. According to the 2021–2022 APPA National Pet Owners Survey, 70% of U.S. households own some type of pet, up from 67% in the 2019–2020 Survey. In fact, 14% of total respondents (pet owners and non-pet owners) obtained a new pet during the pandemic and at least one in four new pet owners said their recent pet acquisition was influenced by the pandemic. Millennials were also revealed to be the largest cohort of pet owners at 32%, followed closely by Boomers at 27% and Gen X at 24% [10].

Especially after COVID-19, most households now have pets, including 59% of those under 35 years old [11]. Meanwhile, pet owners tend to be younger, with those born in the 1980s and 1990s accounting for 46.3% and 20.3% respectively. Pet owners have higher income, accounting for about one-third of the monthly income above 8,000 yuan. Pet owners were highly educated, with 59.5% and 5.8% of pet owners with bachelor's and master's degrees or above [12]. More and more people keep pets. On the other hand, an increasing number of pets are being abandoned [13]. In addition to the causes of human injury, abandonment or loss, elder adults may lose the ability to keep pets as they age due to inconvenience caused by their physical condition. It is also common for people to be separated from their pets for reasons such as business trips, study trips overseas, or the death of the pet itself. Sometimes owners feel nostalgic for their former pets and wish they could be with them forever. In such cases, they cannot avoid missing their pets [14]. Although animal therapy has a certain effect on mental health, the use of live animal therapy, the burden on animals is relatively large, and animal training and feeding costs, the actual application of animal therapy cases is not many. Therefore, the use of robots instead of animals has attracted widespread attention [15]. In such cases, they cannot avoid missing their pets.

1.2 Related Works

The advancement of virtual pets is increasingly assorted, and there are more types. Like the Paro (Fig. 1(a)) in doll structure, a psychological initiation robot created by the National Institute of Advanced Modern Science and Technology (AIST) is a model for offspring of harp seals. It has been respected by Guinness World Records as the most restorative robot. Measuring 55 cm long and weighing 2.5 kg, Paro is like a stuffed toy, and equipped with five different sensors for sound, light, contact, posture, and temperature. Through continuous learning, the Paro robot can respond to external stimuli [16], and the actual contact with the patients help to evoke memories to reduce the nervousness of dementia patients. Notwithstanding, Paro's exploration objects are focused entirely on elderly, with no research on youngsters. Besides, it is hard to awaken the memory of raising pets due to the lockdown state of COVID-19 pandemic. The advancement of virtual pets is presently turning out to be diversified. In addition to the fact that it is not difficult to express, yet additionally to get a similar impact as having a pet and diminish stress [16].

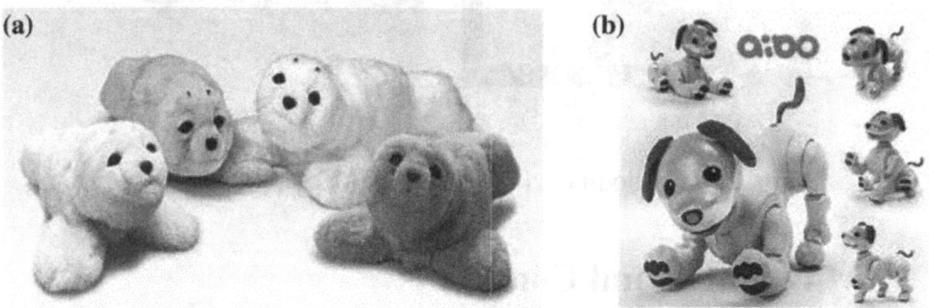

Fig. 1. (a) Paro [16], (b) Aibo [17].

There is also a well-known pet robot, Artificial Intelligence Robot (AIBO) (Fig. 1(b)), a pet robot that Sony has been selling since 1999, known as an "entertainment robots" for domestic sales. The latest model, the AIBO ERS-1000, is about the same size of a beagle and weighs under 5 lb. Its lithium particle battery lasts about 2 h, after which it needs to "rest" on a charging pad for about 3 h. It is equipped with sensors, including a camera, capacitive trackpad, motion and light sensors, and a six-axis positioning frame at the head and center. So AIBO can make a variety of appearances, along with changes in expression and body posture, as well as normal movements. AIBO's various movements include smiling, bending over, wiggling its tail, and more. Whenever its owner scratches its belly, its head and expression respond. It also remembers the voice and appearance of its owner. This is where AIBO is very unique. According to Sony's official website, the new product ERS-1000 would also be launched in Japan. The initial retail fee would be around 200,000 yen, but there are still a large number of people, including Sony employees, who think that AIBO's appearance is still too large. The price is too expensive for some consumers, and AIBO as a pet robot, its metal shell can't give a more realistic feeling, people say it doesn't look like a dog and doesn't feel like a real pet [17].

Many virtual electronic pets are also being studied. For example, there is a game similar to keeping a toy cat, named Chodji-Cat (Fig. 2(a)) that has a healing effect not only through visuals, but also by simulating the sound of the animal, it also has a therapeutic effect on the user to relieve psychological stress [18]. In addition to the visual healing effect and the advantages of interacting with the user, Chodji-Cat has a very high degree of freedom in terms of not choosing where to use it, and it can be obtained cheaply, so it can be said to be one of the healing items around. However, this virtual pet has no entity and cannot be physically touched, so the therapeutic effect may be lower compared with actual pets or pet robots.

Therefore, we have launched a portable simulated pet "KEDAMA" system through UI/UX design. As shown in Fig. 2(b), the texture of KEDAMA's fur is very similar to that of real pets, and KEDAMA can be adjusted according to the user's personal preferences and needs. The appearance, sound and many other aspects of KEDAMA can be selected and customized, which affects people's five senses [14, 19, 20]. Moreover, the price of KEDAMA is cheap, and students without income can also afford it.

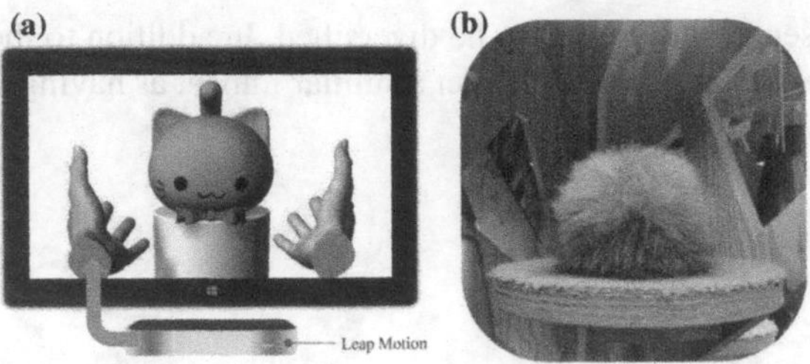

Fig. 2. (a) Chodji cat [18], (b) KEDAMA [14, 19, 20].

2 'KEDAMA' Design and Concept

The design innovation of KEDAMA is mainly in two aspects. On the one hand, it is based on the idea of different customizations from personal preferences, and design research topics according to each user's preference for raising pets, breaking the stereotype of virtual pets under traditional thinking, emphasizing that the design process should not only pay attention to the appearance of pets, but also from the perspective of personalized and customized design, it is proposed to focus on the characteristics of virtual pets from multiple perspectives such as hair length, hair color, and hair texture, as well as the selection of pet voices (Fig. 3). According to the user's experience of raising pets, the type and breed of pets, and personal characteristics.

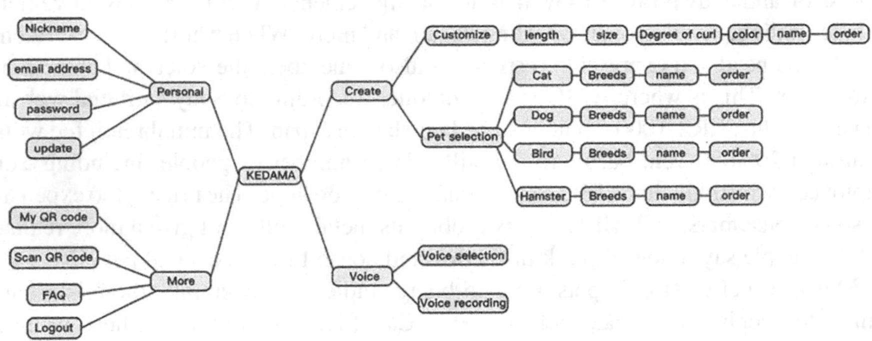

Fig. 3. KEDAMA architecture [14].

As well as the relevant context (different from the pet experience due to business trip, study abroad, travel, etc.), different KEDAMA can be customized from the aspects of color, appearance, sound, texture, etc., to meet the needs of users and promote the realization of the vision of decompression design. The system attempts to break the public's fixed perception of electronic virtual pets, revealing that not only children or the elderly have needs, but the functions of virtual pets can also help young people improve their mental health of anxiety and depression, emphasizing that using KEDAMA is not only a way to miss pets, but also a way to care for the mental health of teenagers. Therefore, this study expands a new research perspective and provides a new design framework for portable virtual pet design at the theoretical level.

Another innovation of KEDAMA is the interaction design and unique application look and feel. KEDAMA's interaction design has user engagement and interaction with any item of the product, system, or interface, and provides a good experience for the user through personalization. The key point of the detailed design of the application design is to visualize the animal selected by the user, unify it into a circle, and match it with a round KEDAMA, so that the user can see the appearance of KEDAMA more realistically (Fig. 4). In terms of application colors, the entire page is light and warm. The color palette also relaxes the user by using warm colors. Saturation selects the design style of low saturation and high brightness, and the warm colors bring users a feeling of warmth, positivity, vitality, and enthusiasm. The appearance design of the application also brings more visual comfort to the user. Relative to some focused mainly on the design research of the design strategy and theoretical perspective, this study not only put forward the related to personalized design strategy and design method, but also as far as possible to the user experience to bring comfort, soothe the mood, can better help some pressure young people better complete KEDAMA personalized design the customization process.

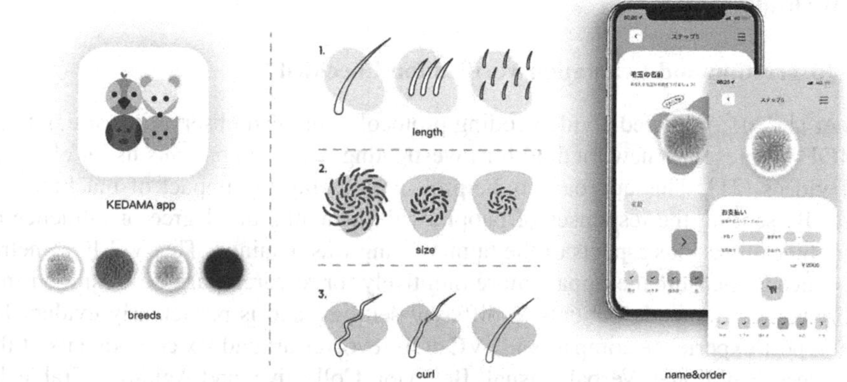

Fig. 4. KEDAMA's customization process.

Then the user input in the app users like the sound of the pet and pet name, type of pet, the size of KEDAMA from the large, medium, small three kinds of choices, the length of the hair from the long, long, short three kinds of choices, from straight, small volume, choose the hair curly hair 3 kinds of color can be customized black and white, spots, stripes, three options. If selected directly, the effect of KEDAMA is automatically generated within the application.

Finally, enter the order information into the KEDAMA system to make payment. After payment, the KEDAMA customized according to the user's personal preference will be sent to the user (Fig. 5). In the actual using of KEDAMA system, when you touch it, you can use it with lovely sound. Therefore, on the practical level, KEDAMA provides specific design strategies for the interaction design of portable virtual pets, which is of certain significance to help users' sense of experience and mental health.

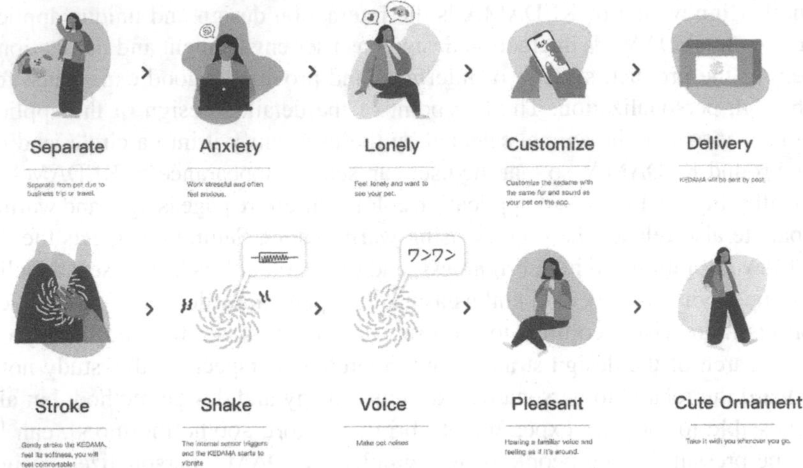

Fig. 5. KEDAMA usage scene.

3 Method

3.1 Observation and Evaluation Verification Checklist

Jones et al. (2015) utilized a video coding protocol-combined observation of emotions (VC-IOE) to present a new method for investigating dementia patients using observational videos [21]. This approach is helpful in assessing the impact of machines on people. By scoring the responses of people with dementia, the degree of influence of the machine on various aspects of the human being was obtained. This VC-IOE metric was created to measure the impact more intuitively for research purposes, using virtual pet robots with dementia patients in different settings, and is particularly evident for pre- and post-experience comparisons. VC-IOE revolves around six components of the experiencer: Emotional, Verbal, Visual, Behavior, Collective, and Agitation (Table 1). Each aspect of the experience should be evaluated independently, and then aggregated and calculated to obtain a comprehensive result.

Evaluators assessed emotional responses by observing the experiencers' facial responses in video clips and classified them into three categories: positive emotions and negative emotions, and neutral emotions. For example, anger, anxiety or fear, sadness, and neutrality. Verbal was assessed through discussions on KEDAMA. Experiencers evaluate KEDAMA for verbal praise or criticism. Vision, as a sign of the experiencer's nonverbal response, is analyzed and assessed by the point of view of the experiencer's gaze and the duration of the KEDAMA. Keeping the eye's attention on the KEDAMA while stroking the KEDAMA or moving the eye's gaze to follow the KEDAMA. Evaluation was performed according to the fitness survey of Cohen-Mansfield et al. [22] and Kolanowski et al. [23].

Behavior including touching or petting, holding, and handling the stimulus appropriately was evaluated as a positive response evaluation. Hitting, shaking, and slapping the KEDAMA, including shoving KEDAMA away are considered adverse behavioral

Table 1. Video coding checklist incorporating observed emotions.

	Engagement	Observation
Emotional	Positive emotions (Pleasure)	Smiling, laughing towards the stimulus
	Negative emotions (Anger, Anxiety or fear, Sadness)	Physical aggression, yelling, cursing, drawing eyebrows together, clenching teeth, pursing lips, narrowing eyes; voice shaking, shrieking, repetitive calling out, line between eyebrows, lines across forehead, tight facial muscles; crying, frowning, eyes drooped, moaning, sighing, eyes/head turned down
	Neutral	Relaxed or no sign of discrete facial expression
Verbal	Positive verbal engagement with stimulus or facilitator	Appreciating, praising the stimulus, making jokes, expressing happiness, fun experience, and participating and maintaining conversation, verbally responding to the stimulus
	Negative verbal engagement	Verbalizes the desire to leave, refuses to participate in the activity anymore, makes repetitive generalized somatic complaints, cursing and swearing
	No verbal engagement	Not participating and maintaining the conversation. Not responding or talking to the stimulus or facilitators
Visual	Visually engaged	Appears alerted and maintaining eye contact with the stimulus, including eyes following or looking at the stimulus
	No visual engagement	Blank stare into space. Does not make eye contact with the stimulus
Behavior	Positive behavioral engagement	Touching or attempting to touch the stimulus. Stroking, petting, holding, and handling the stimulus appropriately
	Negative behavioral engagement	Hitting, shaking, and slapping the stimulus inappropriately, including Shoving it away and pulling it out
	No behavioral engagement	No touching, physical contact and interacting with the stimulus

(*continued*)

Table 1. (*continued*)

	Engagement	Observation
Collective	Evidence of collective engagement	Encouraging others to interact with the stimulus. Introducing stimulus to others. Using stimulus as a communication channel to interact and talk with others
	No collective engagement	No sign of collective engagement
Agitation	Evidence of agitation (verbal, vocal, motor activity)	Restlessness, repeated/agitated movement, picking and fiddling with clothes; repetitive rubbing own limbs or torso; appears anxious. Repeats words or phrases, abusive or aggressive toward self or other
	No evidence of agitation	No sign of agitation as described above

reactions. Collective is divided into two parts, evidence of collective engagement or no collective engagement. For example, it would proactively recommend KEDAMA to others, or proactively communicate with others about KEDAMA's experience feedback. Agitation is coded in light of Cohen-Mansfield's exploration on tumult and fomentation practices [24], assessing "Agitation" from both verbal and non-verbal perspectives, such as non-verbal aspects of the experiencer showing fidgeting or repetitive or excited movements. Or constantly fiddling with clothes, repeatedly rubbing their limbs or shaking their body, appearing anxious. Verbally, repeating words or phrases, or abusively, attacking self or others. Table 1 above shows the nuances of various aspects of video evaluation.

3.2 User Experience Survey

First Challenge Impression. Collect experiencers' information and other data (as shown in Fig. 6). The reaction of users when they see KEDAMA for the first time is observed and recorded through video recording. It is also known whether KEDAMA can be further promoted.

Response Survey After Experiencing KEDAMA. Let users live with KEDAMA for 3 weeks. According to the users' feasible time in a week, choose 3 times in 3 weeks, touch KEDAMA for 10 min and record it, transmit the user's reaction in the video, observe the evaluation, and calculate the average value to compare the effect of the user before and after using KEDAMA for three weeks.

The evaluation standard is to perform a 5-stage evaluation (−2 poor, −1 poor, 0 no change, +1 good, +2 improvement) of the items coded into the video recording list (Fig. 7) of observed feelings, numerical zing the degree of effect. The calculation is to use the emotional points *2 + word points *2 + visual points *2 + action points *1 + other reaction points *2 + excited points *1 of the list. It will increase the weighting of emotional, verbal, visual, behavioural, and other engagement and excitement values.

UI/UX design of portable simulation pet KEDAMA Initial impression Questionnaire

Basic user information questionnaire

Name: __________ Date: __________

1. Your age: ○ Under 18 ○ 18-26 ○ 26-34 ○ 34-44 ○ Over 44
2. Your gender: ○ Male ○ Female
3. Have you ever had or are you raising pets? ○ Yes ○ No
4. What kind of pets have you kept? (Multiple choices)
 ○ Cats ○ dogs ○ Birds ○ Mice ○ Others
5. Do you miss being separated from your pet? ○ Yes ○ No
6. Have you heard about virtual pets? ○ Yes ○ No
7. Do you think you can ease your yearning for pets through simulation pets?
 ○ Very necessary ○ Necessary ○ unnecessary ○Whatever
8. Do you live alone? ○ Yes ○ No
9. What price can you accept for Portable Simulated Pet ?
 ○Less than 10,000 yen ○10,000 to 50,000 yen ○50,000 to 100,000 yen ○100,000 to 200,000 yen ○More than 200,000 yen
10. If there is an intelligent portable pet product with reasonable price that can be customized according to your preferences, would you like to buy it or try it? ○ Yes ○ No

Fig. 6. KEDAMA initial impression questionnaire.

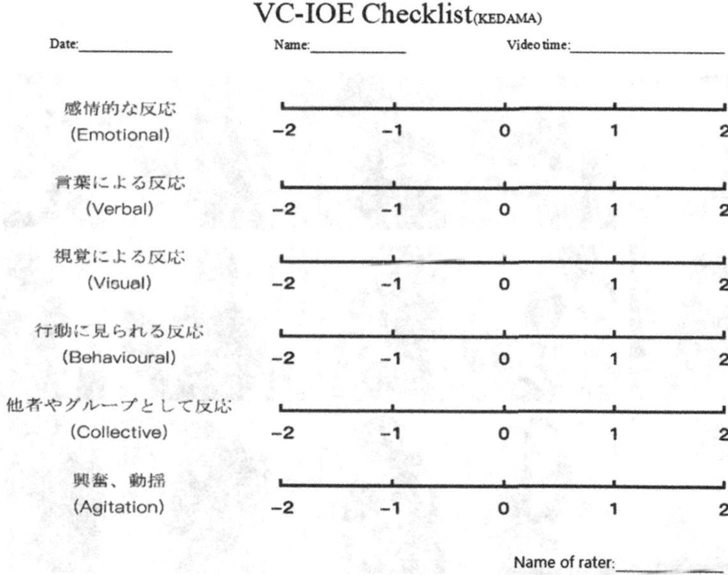

VC-IOE Checklist(KEDAMA)

Date:__________ Name:__________ Video time:__________

感情的な反応 (Emotional)	−2	−1	0	1	2
言葉による反応 (Verbal)	−2	−1	0	1	2
視覚による反応 (Visual)	−2	−1	0	1	2
行動に見られる反応 (Behavioural)	−2	−1	0	1	2
他者やグループとして反応 (Collective)	−2	−1	0	1	2
興奮、動揺 (Agitation)	−2	−1	0	1	2

Name of rater:__________

Fig. 7. VC-IOE checklist.

4 Results and Discussion

4.1 User Initial Impression Survey Results

Through the questionnaires filled in by the experiencers, we can learn about the basic situation of the experiencers and their desire to experiment with the KEDAMA experience. The results were as follows: among the 20 participants (Fig. 8), 8 were male and 12 were female, with an average age of 22.65 years. Of the 20 participants, 16 had experience with pets and 4 had never owned a pet. Among the pet owners, 5 had dogs, 8 had cats, 2 had both cats and dogs, and 1 had fish and dogs.

87.5% chose to miss their pets very much. Only two of the 20 participants hadn't heard of virtual pets, suggesting they didn't understand. But 85% of the 20 people who have experienced it said they believe that a simulated pet should ease people's desire for pets.

As for the price of virtual pets, most of the people who have experienced it think that the price is between 10 and 50,000 yen. No one thinks that more than 200,000 yen is acceptable, mainly because the experience users are all international students, and because of the epidemic, they can't afford to work, so the price is too high to afford. All experiencers have chosen to buy and try to first-hand experience together if there are reasonably priced smart portable pet products that can be customized according to the preferences.

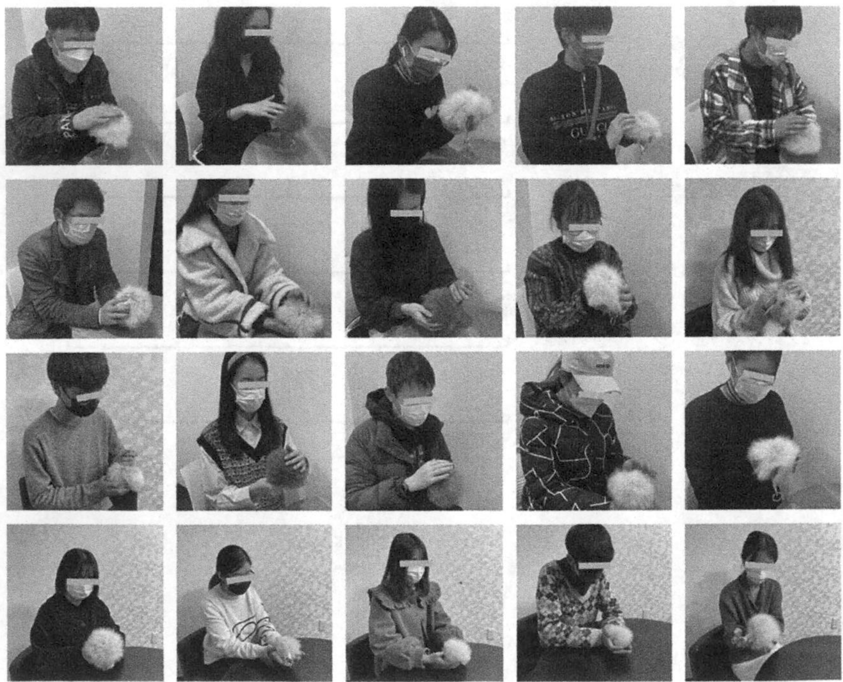

Fig. 8. Sceneries of 20 users evaluating the experiment.

Next, give each experimenter a KEDAMA, and record the experimenter's response to the first KEDAMA experience, and then use the checklist to evaluate according to the VC-IOE index. A total of three reviewers watched and scored: a psychotherapist, a teacher in charge of student mental health, and a product reviewer. Initial impressions of KEDAMA, data summarized in Fig. 9.

Score data was aggregated from the three reviewers' checklists, and an average was calculated based on the responses to the six dimensions of the VC-IOE index. The first impression survey of the experiencers' Emotional was 0.798, the Verbal was 0.856, the Visual action was 0.863, the Behavioral was 0.851, the Collective was 0.803, and the Agitation was 0.656. Each calculation result reflecting the average effect degree was greater than 0. It can be concluded that users' first impressions of KEDAMA were positive. KEDAMA had no bad feelings from the beginning. So users can continue to experience the experiment for the next three weeks.

4.2 Comparison Effect Before and After KEDAMA Experience

Over the next three weeks, users were videotaped for 10 min each week, then rated by reviewers based on their responses. In this experiment, 3 experiencers had special conditions: 1 experiencer returned to home country due to visa problems, 1 experiencer lost KEDAMA on the tram due to negligence and has not yet been found. The video of 1 experimenter was damaged by the machine. 1 experiencer damaged the video due to the machine of the video equipment, and the image was damaged and could not be evaluated.

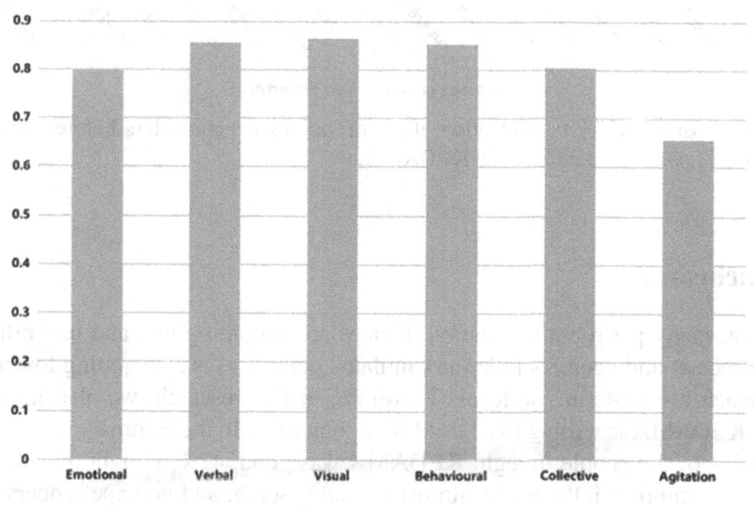

Fig. 9. Statistical chart of first impression evaluation of KEDAMA by experiencers.

Therefore, 17 (85%) of the 20 users in this experiment met the requirements. After the data is aggregated, calculations are performed, as shown in the Fig. 10. During the video observation, many participants expressed their love for KEDAMA's design and repeatedly praised touching KEDAMA like touching a real pet. Some of them are touching the KEDAMA from the beginning to the end of the video, touching the KEDAMA and keeping a smile on the face of the experiencer.

Positive responses to emotion ($p < 0.02$) and vision ($p < 0.005$) were specifically observed in the statistically calculated data. KEDAMA's experience is particularly evident in the emotional and visual realms. In addition, according to the summary data, comparing the effect of everyone, the user's response effect showed an upward trend around 3 weeks, and the calculated average validity of KEDAMA rose from 8.0 three weeks ago to 10.92 after three weeks of experience. (Paired T-test result $p = 0.00502174$), it can be concluded that the portable virtual pet KEDAMA has a positive effect on people. This reflects that users' experience with KEDAMA for three weeks has not leaded to aversion but instead resulted in positive improvements in all aspects.

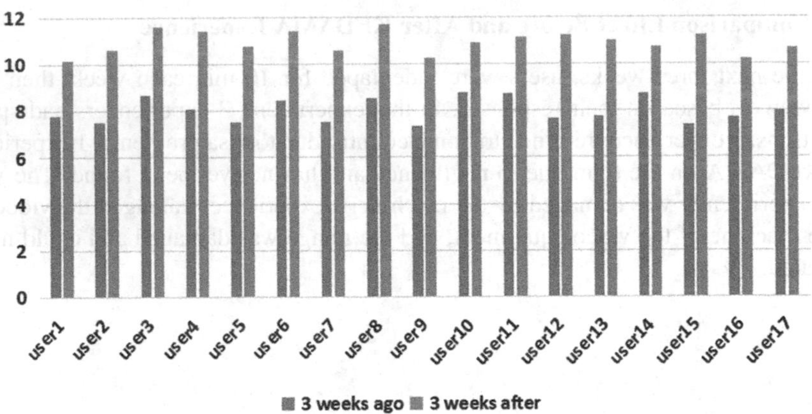

Fig. 10. Comparison chart of evaluation effect of various experimenters before and after the introduction of portable Simulated pet KEDAMA.

5 Conclusion

At present, many pet robot simulation devices are becoming less and less efficient in the use process, and people's love for simulated pet robots is also getting lower, which cannot reach a long-term use level. Therefore, in this research, we also investigated whether KEDAMA is willing to be used for a long time. In the summary survey of each item, 55.2% of the people thought KEDAMA was good, 42% thought that KEDAMA needed to be improved, there was almost no "bad" score, and no experiencers thought KEDAMA was bad. After this test, it is likely that KEDAMA can be used for a long time and would maintain its effects.

This also indicates that the longer the user uses KEDAMA, the emotional aspect would be effectively improved. These results also show that long-term use of KEDAMA does not affect users' experience results. We can try to put KEDAMA into people's lives for a long time, and further replace pets to improve the mental health of young people.

However, only 20 subjects were selected for this research, and because of the pandemic, the experience often only lasted 3 weeks. In future research, we hope to expand the experience to 50 users, increase the experience duration to 6 weeks, and expand the user selection to make the results more generalizable. To further explore whether the use of KEDAMA can improve the mental health of young people. In addition, when evaluating through VC-IOE, the reviewers still have some subjective feelings in the evaluation. Next, we will consider trying to make the experiencer wear biosensors to obtain more objective data for analysis. And in this research, since 1 experiencer lost the KEDAMA during the experience and has not yet found it, we also consider installing a detectable positioning sensor in the KEDAMA to make it easier for the user to find the location of the KEDAMA.

Acknowledgments. This research was partially supported by JSPS KAKENHI Grant Number JP20J10461. The authors would like to thank the JSPS Program for Leading Graduate School (Graduate Program in Gerontology, Global Leadership Initiative for an Age Friendly Society, The University of Tokyo) for providing financial support to Jiang Wu. Special thanks to Dr. Mio Nakamura for her help and comments on the evaluation of this system.

References

1. Usher, K., Durkin, J., Bhullar, N.: The COVID-19 pandemic and mental health impacts. Int. J. Ment. Health Nurs. **29**(3), 315 (2020)
2. WHO characterizes COVID-19 as a pandemic. https://www.paho.org/en/news/11-3-2020-who-characterizes-covid-19-pandemic. Accessed 11 Feb 2022
3. New Ministry of Health Guidelines. https://www.gov.il/BlobFolder/generalpage/virus_17032020/he/159409320.pdf?fbclid=IwAR3XcXLy4DgEQC7uruTQyuaZiJaBYRtP5vVyUAJ5TAP0jgJwtejhs8FInLE. Accessed 11 Feb 2022
4. Achdut, N., Refaeli, T.: Unemployment and psychological distress among young people during the COVID-19 pandemic: psychological resources and risk factors. Int. J. Environ. Res. Public Health **17**(19), 7163 (2020)
5. Ren, S.-Y., Gao, R.-D., Chen, Y.-L.: Fear can be more harmful than the severe acute respiratory syndrome coronavirus 2 in controlling the corona virus disease 2019 epidemic. World J. Clin. Cases **8**(4), 652 (2020)
6. Cheng, C., Cheung, M.W.L.: Psychological responses to outbreak of severe acute respiratory syndrome: a prospective, multiple time-point study. J. Pers. **73**(1), 261–285 (2005)
7. Panchal, N., et al.: The implications of COVID-19 for mental health and substance use. Kaiser family foundation, 21 (2020)
8. U.S. Census Bureau, Household Pulse Survey (2020). https://www.cdc.gov/nchs/covid19/pulse/mental-health.htm. Accessed 6 Jan 2022
9. Jennings, L.B.: Potential benefits of pet ownership in health promotion. J. Holist. Nurs. **15**(4), 358–372 (1997)
10. 2021–2022 APPA National Pet Owners Survey. https://americanpetproducts.org/Uploads/NPOS/21-22_BusinessandFinance.pdf. Accessed 6 Jan 2022
11. When pets are family, the benefits extend into society. https://theconversation.com/when-pets-are-family-the-benefits-extend-into-society-109179. Accessed 6 Jan 2022
12. China Enterprise Consulting Network. China Pet Food Market Analysis and Investment Analysis Report, 2021–2027. https://www.mordorintelligence.com/industry-reports/china-pet-food-market. Accessed 6 Jan 2022

13. Morgan, L., et al.: Human–dog relationships during the COVID-19 pandemic: Booming dog adoption during social isolation. Humanit. Soc. Sci. Commun. **7**(1), 1–11 (2020)
14. Jiang, W., Dai, Y., Li, J., Yuan, Y.: UI/UX design of portable simulation pet 'KEDAMA' hairball for relieving pressure. In: Stephanidis, C., Antona, M., Ntoa, S. (eds.) HCII 2021. CCIS, vol. 1499, pp. 215–223. Springer, Cham (2021). https://doi.org/10.1007/978-3-030-90179-0_28
15. Ma, M.Y., Yin, Z., Liu, W.L., Jing, Y.L., Jiang, Q.Q.: Study on the application of doll therapy in the care of patients with Alzheimer's disease. Chin. J. Pract. Neurol. Disord. **22**(04), 449–453 (2019)
16. Cooper, A.: The inmates are running the asylum. In: Proceedings of Software-Ergonomie 1999, p. 17. Vieweg+Teubner Verlag, Wiesbaden (1999)
17. Yanagisawa, K., et al.: A basic study on robot appearance evaluation using NIRS. Biomedical Engineering (2018). Abstract: S207-S207
18. Hayashi, R., et al.: Influence of physical embodiment on therapeutic effects during interaction with artificial pets. Trans. Jpn. Soc. Kansei Eng. **16**(1), 75–81 (2017)
19. Wu, J., Dai, Y., Yuan, Y., Li, J.: UI/UX design methodology of portable customizable simulated pet system considering human mental health. In: Proceedings of 2022 IEEE 4th Global Conference on Life Sciences and Technologies, pp. 488–492. IEEE (2022)
20. KEDAMA, Welfare equipment contest 2021. https://www.resja.or.jp/contest/data/2021/2021001.pdf. Accessed 6 Jan 2022
21. Jones, C., Sung, B., Moyle, W.: Assessing engagement in people with dementia: a new approach to assessment using video analysis. Arch. Psychiatr. Nurs. **29**(6), 377–382 (2015)
22. Cohen-Mansfield, J., et al.: An analysis of the relationships among engagement, agitated behavior, and affect in nursing home residents with dementia. Int. Psychogeriatr. **24**(5), 742–752 (2012)
23. Kolanowski, A., et al.: A randomized clinical trial of theory-based activities for the behavioral symptoms of dementia in nursing home residents. J. Am. Geriatr. Soc. **59**(6), 1032–1041 (2011)
24. Cohen-Mansfield, J., Dakheel-Ali, M., Marx, M.S.: Engagement in persons with dementia: the concept and its measurement. Am. J. Geriatr. Psychiatry **17**(4), 299–307 (2009)

Design of Somatosensory Interactive Balance Training Exergame for the Elderly Based on Tai Chi

Yahui Zhang, Ting Han(✉), Yi Ding, and Shuyu Zhao

School of Design, Shanghai Jiao Tong University, 800 Dongchuan Road, Minhang District, Shanghai 200240, China
hanting@sjtu.edu.cn

Abstract. Systematic research proves that long-term scientific balance training is beneficial to improve the balance ability of the elderly and reduce falls. However, due to the lack of professional teaching guidance, boring training process lacking feedback, lack of companions, laziness and other problems, it is difficult for the elderly to obtain scientific and systematic balance training to improve their balance ability. Based on the current pain points in the process of balance training for the elderly, this study designs an interactive balance training based on Tai Chi exercise for the elderly, called "Balance Challenge", in which the user will receive scientific and systematic guidance instruction to train the stability of static and dynamic posture control under low center of gravity and to improve the balance ability of the elderly. The elderly will be allowed to complete scientific training in a game-based way. A randomized controlled experiment was conducted among 18 elderly people (mean age 63 ± 2.9 years, 10 females) living in the community. The experimental group performed balance training using balance training at a prescribed exercise frequency, while the control group completed a physical exercise routine at the same time. During the 4-week study period, participants are advised to take 20-min unsupervised exercise at home at least three times a week. The outcome measures were gait speed, standing balance, five-time sit-to-stand, timed up and go performance, and neuropsychological function (attention: Letter–digit test and Stroop tests) evaluated at baseline, 2 weeks, and experiment end (4 weeks). 18 participants completed the experiment and reassessment, and the experimental group completed an average of 9.7 20-min sessions with no adverse events reported. Throughout the trial period, participants in the experimental group showed significant improvements in gait speed (25%), standing balance (6%), five-time sit-to-stand (21%) and timed up and go performance (12%) (all $P < 0.05$). Letter–digit test (13%) and Stroop test (12%) showed no significant improvement. Compared with the control group, the performance of the experimental group in gait speed, standing balance, five-time sit-to-stand, timed up and go performance was significantly improved (all $P < 0.05$), but the improvement of Letter–digit test (10%) and Stroop test (7%) was not obvious.This study found that Balance Training is scientific and feasible for the elderly, and leads to significant improvement in gait, standing balance, and acting ability, which can reduce the risk of a fall injury. The exercise compliance of the elderly is also better. It is hoped that the somatosensory interactive balance training exergame based on Tai Chi for the

Q. Gao and J. Zhou (Eds.): HCII 2022, LNCS 13331, pp. 305–319, 2022.
https://doi.org/10.1007/978-3-031-05654-3_21

elderly can be included in the exercise plan aimed at improving the balance ability of the elderly.

Keywords: Exergames · Balance training · Somatosensory interaction · Elderly

1 Background

Declining balance is a very common phenomenon among the elderly population, and population aging has become a common problem of global concern, and the balance ability of healthy aging elderly people starts to decline rapidly at the age of 60 [1], which has become the first cause of death from falls in people over 65 years old [2]. Systematic studies have proven that long-term scientific balance training is beneficial to enhance the balance ability of the elderly and reduce falls. In terms of balance enhancement, the feasibility and effectiveness of gamified design interactive products for motor training in muscle strengthening, balance movement, body control, and other motor functions have been demonstrated by several studies [3, 4]. Also studies using Tai Chi exercises have improved physical and cognitive functions and enhanced balance in older adults [5].

Although research has proven that exercise is an effective strategy for balance improvement in older adults, it is difficult for older adults to obtain scientific and systematic balance training to improve their balance ability due to the lack of professional teaching guidance, boring training process lacking feedback, lack of peers, and laziness. To improve the effectiveness of the training program, it is necessary to improve the user experience of the elderly group using it, develop a reasonable intrinsic motivation mechanism, and enhance both internal and external motivation of the elderly, and then positive feedback to improve the elderly exercise adherence [6]. In terms of improving adherence, several studies have shown that older adults can maintain a higher percentage of adherence with exercise interaction product interventions compared to regular exercise, based on training completion rates, attendance, and exercise frequency [7–10].

To date, most of the balance training products in this field are not specifically designed for older adults [11]. In terms of training programs, the five elements of warm-up, intensity, duration, frequency, exercise type and mode are not fully suitable for the physical condition of older adults. In terms of product design, the training rhythm and interface elements are not fully suitable for older adults. The exercise interaction products at home and abroad are compiled, which provides a reference for studying the principles of aging-appropriate design of products [12–22]: a. Age-appropriate products should consider the physical condition of the elderly and be better adapted; b. Add appropriate gestures and reduce smaller elements on the page; c. Provide timely movement records and positive feedback on health; d. Clear user interface; e. Encourage social interaction; f. Ensure the safety of the elderly, etc.

In summary, we developed a customized somatic interactive exergame for elderly people's balance based on Tai Chi exercises to provide a more user-friendly and effective way of balance training. It was designed with the elderly user in mind for the training program and the training product. The Tai Chi exercises in the product training have been shown to improve the balance ability of the elderly [5, 23, 24], and the balance training was designed in different training phases according to the exercise prescription guidelines for the elderly [25–27], allowing the user to complete the training in a gradual and safer manner.

The purpose of this pilot study was to evaluate the feasibility and effectiveness of balance training using the Balance Challenge in a targeted group of older adults, as well as to assess the efficacy of this intervention in improving physical and cognitive function in older adults and to analyze the associated factors.

2 Materials and Methods

2.1 Participants

Older adults living in the general community of Shanghai were invited to this study. The inclusion criteria for the study population were age 65 ± 5 years, stable health status, fluent in Chinese, not suffering or having suffered from a major illness affecting balance, able to live independently and walk independently (reinforced Romberg examination [28] $\geq$ 41), no cognitive impairment (Moca [29] score $\geq$ 26), vision and hearing at normal aging levels, and educational background of elementary school and above.

2.2 Exergame Content

This study aims to apply light gamification elements to traditional exercise workouts to form exercise interaction products that ensure the scientific validity of training while enhancing the user experience and helping users to generate intrinsic motivation and improve adherence. Exercise content and game elements together determine the quality of the game [12], and the gamification design of exercise therapy needs to be predicated on achieving the appropriate exercise efficacy [25].

Based on the current pain points in the process of balance training for the elderly, this study designs a Tai Chi-based somatic interactive balance training for the elderly called Balance Challenge by means of expert interviews and field research. Users will receive guided instruction in a scientific system when performing balance training and complete the scientific training in a game-based way [30].

Based on interviews with physicians and kinesiologists, we selected the simplified twenty-four Tai Chi as the prototype movements for training. This set of movements trains the stability of static and dynamic postural control of the elderly in a low center of gravity. The movements were classified into three levels: simple, medium, and difficult. Four training phases were designed in the order of easy, medium, difficult, and medium according to the exercise prescription guidelines for the elderly. Figure 1 shows the movement prototype diagram of each stage (see Fig. 1).

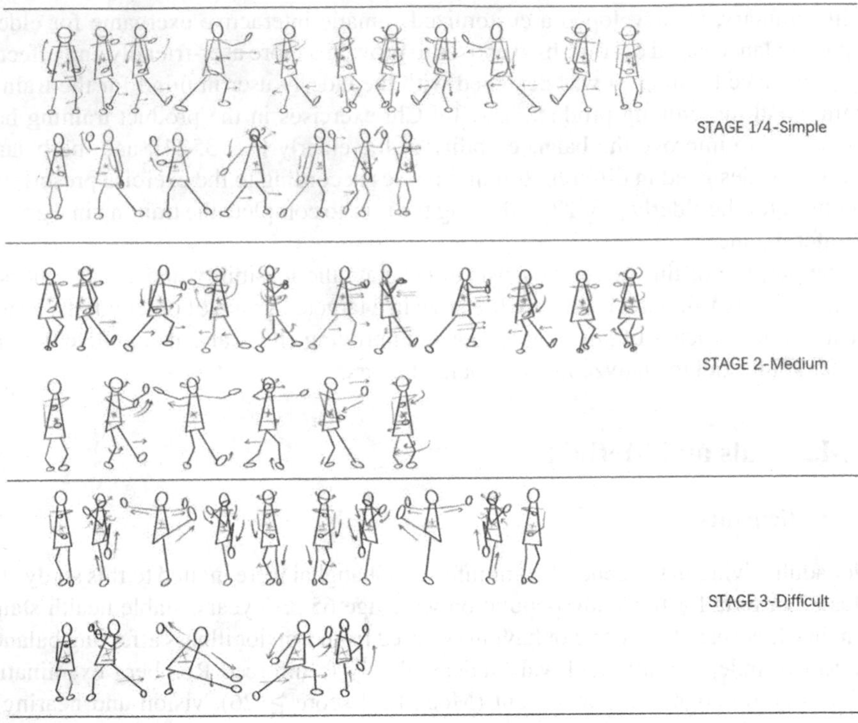

Fig. 1. Classification of action levels

In addition, the design of this balance training was completed based on the research on the elderly (see Fig. 2). In the design of training method design, different users have different familiarity with Tai Chi, so each training stage has corresponding nodal movements. In the Balance Challenge, there are two ways to start the training: "start training directly" and "learn node action", so that seniors can choose the learning method according to their own situation, and ensure that even seniors with zero foundation in Tai Chi can train without burden (see Fig. 3).

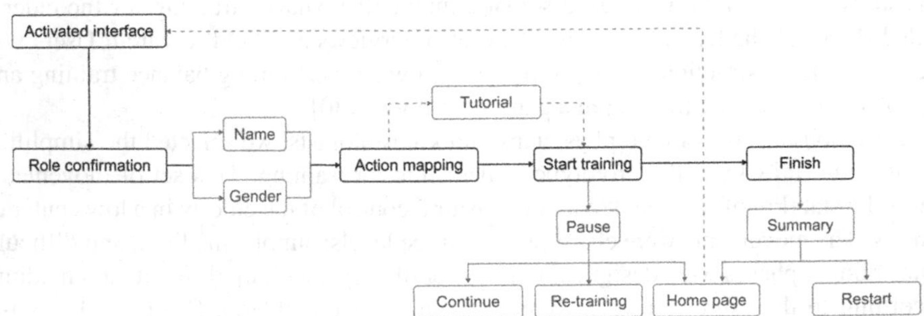

Fig. 2. Flow chart of training interaction

Fig. 3. Select node action interface

In the training process, the left interface is the teaching animation, the user can understand the current training progress according to the continuous movement animation above and the silhouette of the movement below. The user is required to perform the same movements as the teaching animation as much as possible. On the right side, the user's movements are mapped directly to the character model in the interface. The target floating object on the right side of the screen provides guidance to the user and guides the user through the standard movements. The user needs to complete the standard action to touch the target float. After touching the target float, the product will give positive feedback to the user in terms of voice and interface, and the points will be increased (see Fig. 4). When a training phase is completed, the amount of training completed during the training phase will be displayed on the screen (see Fig. 5). The interface will also display the user's last stage points and stage summary, so as to achieve the role of motivating users.

In addition, Balance Challenge uses character models in Tai Chi costumes and seasonal elements that fit with the game stages to give users a more enjoyable and relaxing user experience.

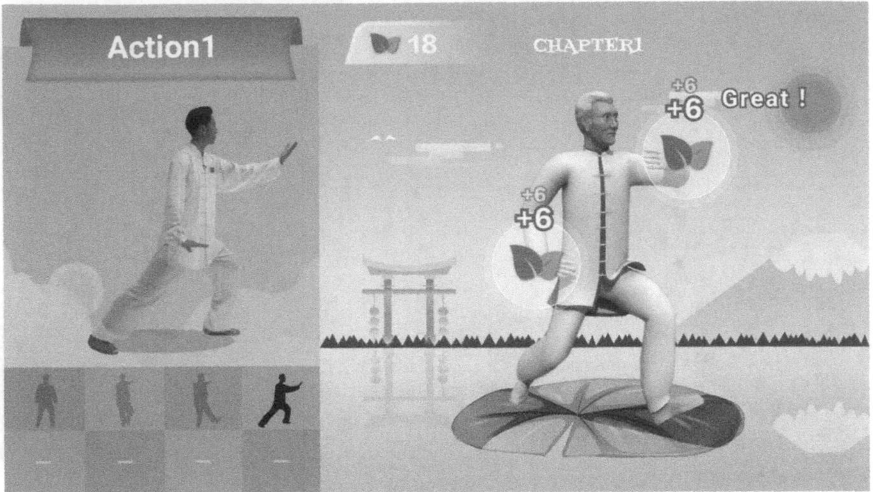

Fig. 4. Training process interface

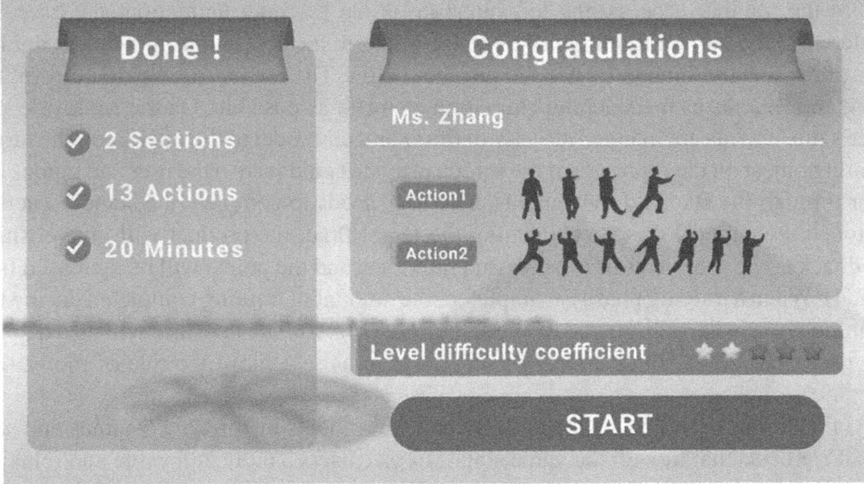

Fig. 5. Stage summary interface

3 Process

During the 4-week trial, we assessed changes in balance in older adults. We randomly and equally divided 18 older adults living in the community into an experimental and a control group. The experimental group performed balance training using balance training at the prescribed exercise frequency, while the control group completed one daily physical exercise session. Participants performed 20 min of exercise at home at least three times a week.

Gait speed [31], Standing balance [13], Five-time sit-to-stand [32], Timed up and go performance [33], and cognitive function (attention: Letter-digit test and [34], Stroop test [35, 36]) were assessed by certain metrics at week 0, week 2, and at the end of the experiment (week 4). The following Table 1 gives a summary of evaluation methodolody..

Table 1. Evaluation methodology

Type	Name	Content
Key metrics	Standing balance	Participants were asked to perform six poses of progressively increasing difficulty for a given period of time, holding each pose for 10 s while crossing their arms over their chest. The total time that the participant was able to maintain balance was recorded as 10 s over 10 s
	Five-time sit-to-stand	The test is used to assess the lower extremity strength and balance of older adults. Participants are asked to cross their arms over their chest, sit with their backs against a chair without armrests, and stand up and sit down five times quickly at the start of the clock to record the total time taken to complete the test
	Gait speed	This test is used to assess the change in gait speed of older adults during the experiment. Participants were required to walk a distance of 10 m, with 2 m provided at each end of the 10 m to provide the participant with normal acceleration and deceleration. The average time for participants to walk the 10 m at normal gait speed was collected three separate times
	Timed up and go performance (TUGT)	TUGT refers to the time it takes for a participant to sit in a chair, stand up on the command, walk forward in a straight line for 3 m, and then turn around and walk back to sit down in the chair. Patients were required to sit in the chair with their backs against the back of the chair and their hands on the armrests. The total time taken for the whole process of TUGT was recorded
Cognitive ability metrics	Letter–digit test	This test is used to test processing speed by providing participants with alphanumeric pairs and then providing them with a sequence of 30 letters appearing in random order, for each letter participants must quickly enter the corresponding number based on the known alphanumeric pair, recording the average response time of the participants

(*continued*)

Table 1. (*continued*)

Type	Name	Content
	Stroop test	The test is used to assess the participant's ability to perform and control. Participants are required to make a consistent choice under certain conditions. Each time one of the four colors and the corresponding Chinese character appear on the screen, the Chinese character is randomly displayed in one of the colors, and the participant has to respond to the consistency of the color and the content of the Chinese character. The average response time of the participants was recorded

User satisfaction with the Balance Challenge is also evaluated. We used a usability evaluation method [37] to assess the pleasure and safety of use of the product by older adults to make a more comprehensive analysis of Balance Challenge. In this study, attitudes and suggestions of elderly users towards the balance challenge were obtained from three dimensions: perceived ease of use (PEOU), enjoyment, and challenge [38].

Perceived Ease of Use (PEOU). Perceived ease of use is derived from the TAM model [39]. Design for the elderly should improve product ease of use and reduce the learning cost of product use for the elderly. PEOU is proportional to the experience of product use, and the higher the PEOU the better it is for the elderly to respond in an unconscious state.

Enjoyment (EN). Enjoyment is derived from the PACES scale. High pleasantness is an important factor in attracting users to physical exercise, and at the same time reduces users' anxiety and powerlessness to perform physical exercise, increasing their intrinsic motivation to use the product.

Challenge (CH). Challenge refers to the physical and cognitive level required to complete Balance Challenge. Maintaining an appropriate level of challenge can motivate older adults to consistently and actively engage in balance training. Too high or too low a level of difficulty can reduce the user experience of older adults.

We asked older adults about their experience using the Richter 5-point scale based on three dimensions and asked the following questions (Table 2).

Table 2. Questionnaire on three dimensions of user experience

Dimension	Number	Content
Perceived ease of use (PEOU)	Q1.1	I think I can easily understand the content of the Balance Challenge
	Q1.2	I can play the Balance Challenge alone without help from others
	Q1.3	I think it is easy to control the Balance Challenge game
	Q1.4	I don't need extra people or instructions to guide me in using the Balance Challenge
Enjoyment (EN)	Q2.1	I like to play Balance Challenge
	Q2.2	I think playing Balance Challenge can exercise my balance ability well
	Q2.3	I am very relaxed when I play the Balance Challenge
Challenge (CH)	Q3.1	I think it is difficult to complete all the training of balancing challenges
	Q3.2	I feel proud when I finish a stage of Balance Challenge
	Q3.3	I need a quick response to complete the Balance Challenge
	Q3.4	I want to get a higher score in the Balance Challenge

4 Results and Discussion

4.1 Participant Descriptions

A total of 30 older adults of appropriate age were invited to participate in the study. 18 older adults (10 females and 8 males) with a mean age of 63 ± 2.9 years (SD1.9) agreed to participate in the trial. All participants were able to walk independently, had normal vision and hearing in a normal state of aging, and had no cognitive impairment. Most reported good health (N = 15), one had a major medical condition that did not affect balance, and two had diabetes mellitus. The older adults who participated in the trial met the literacy criteria, all had an educational background of elementary school or higher, and were able to complete the Balance Challenge product content reading and cognitive assessment tests without difficulty.

During the assessment, all 18 experimenters completed the experiment and reassessment, with the experimental group completing an average of 9.7 20-min sessions with no adverse events reported and the control group performing a normal exercise routine. For the experimental group, the median total play time was 189 min (IQR = 179–233), with 4 participants (22%) completing the required 240 min of total exercise time. Based on the exercise records of the 9 participants in the experimental group, the exercise frequency of these experimental group participants averaged 2.7 exercises per week. Most participants could strictly follow the training phases designed within the product for exercise training.

4.2 Results

Table 3 shows the scores of participants in the experimental group on physical and cognitive function measures at weeks 0, 2, and 4. Throughout the trial period, participants in the experimental group showed significant improvements in gait speed, standing balance, sit-to-stand, and timed up and go performance scores, with statistical differences in three indicators. Gait speed and sit-to-stand showed statistical differences at both week 2 and week 4 compared to week 0. Two cognitive indicators showed a trend towards improvement during the trial, but no statistical difference, and the Letter-digit test (13%) and Stroop test (12%) showed no significant improvement.

Table 4 shows the experimental results of the experimental group compared to the control group, which showed significant improvements in gait speed, standing balance, sit-to-stand, and timed up and go performance (all $P < 0.05$), but not in the Letter-digit test (10%) and Stroop test (7%).

Table 3. Physical and cognitive function scores during the trial in the experimental group

	Week0	Week2	Week4	Percentage of change
Gait speed (m/s)	1.09 ± 0.12	1.22 ± 0.16*	1.36 ± 0.21**	25##
Standing balance (s)	54.86 ± 2.12	55.93 ± 1.76	58.41 ± 1.17*	6#
Sit-to-stand (s)	15.93 ± 5.33	13.72 ± 4.21*	12.54 ± 3.22*	−21##
Timed up and go performance (s)	7.18 ± 0.53	6.79 ± 0.68	6.21 ± 0.76**	−12#
Letter-digit test (ms)	2549.73 ± 513.22	2376.03 ± 200.27	2240.21 ± 316.42	−13
Stroop test (ms)	1210.97 ± 112.7	1156.34 ± 90.39	1067.52 ± 102.24*	−12

Friedman ANOVA change during the trial: $*P < 0.05$, $**P < 0.01$. Wilcoxon signed-rank test difference between retest time point and week0: $\#P < 0.05$, $\#\#P < 0.01$.

Table 5 shows the results of the user experience evaluation. During the usability evaluation after the experiment was completed, a total of 9 people completed the user experience evaluation. Overall, the results of the experience factors in all three dimensions were relatively positive. Most of the older users had positive feedback on the Balance Challenge for training and were willing to continue to try the exercise.

Table 4. Comparison of the difference between the experimental group and the control group before and after the experiment

	Group (mean ± standard deviation)		Percentage of change	P
	Experimental group	Control group		
Gait speed(m/s)	0.27 ± 0.24	0.19 ± 0.17	29	0.026*
Standing balance (s)	3.55 ± 2.66	3.31 ± 2.49	7	0.034*
Sit-to-stand (s)	3.39 ± 2.72	2.78 ± 2.28	18	0.029*
Timed up and go performance (s)	0.97 ± 0.58	0.66 ± 0.46	12	0.043*
Letter-digit test (ms)	309.52 ± 277.81	278.92 ± 227.62	10	0.067
Stroop test (ms)	143.45 ± 102.62	133.39 ± 107.76	7	0.324

Paired samples T-test: *P < 0.05, **P < 0.01.

Table 5. Results of the elderly user experience evaluation

Dimension	Number	Totally disagree		Disagree		Neutral		Agree		Totally agree	
		N	%	N	%	N	%	N	%	N	%
Perceived ease of use (PEOU)	Q1.1	0	0	0	0	1	11	7	78	1	11
	Q1.2	0	0	1	11	0	0	6	67	2	22
	Q1.3	0	0	0	0	0	0	5	56	4	44
	Q1.4	0	0	1	11	1	11	6	67	1	11
Enjoyment (EN)	Q2.1	0	0	0	0	0	0	8	89	1	11
	Q2.2	0	0	0	0	0	0	5	56	4	44
	Q2.3	0	0	0	0	0	0	0	0	9	100
Challenge (CH)	Q3.1	0	0	0	0	2	22	6	67	1	11
	Q3.2	0	0	0	0	1	11	7	78	1	11
	Q3.3	0	0	0	0	0	0	0	0	9	100
	Q3.4	0	0	0	0	0	0	0	0	9	100

4.3 Discussion

Balance Challenge is a Tai Chi-based balance training exergame customized for healthy aging older adults, designed for situations in which the elderly improve their balance on their own. The results of this study suggest that it is feasible, safe and effective for older adults without major medical conditions, balance dysfunction or cognitive impairment.

Feasibility and Safety of the Balance Challenge. The Balance Challenge had a guide page. Participants were able to use the product smoothly, select the appropriate training method and training phase according to their needs, and perform the training tasks to obtain training scores. The participants in the experimental group made positive comments about the health feedback of the Balance Challenge, and no adverse events related to the intervention were reported during the use. This suggests that balance training is a safe training modality for use by older adults to autonomously improve their balance.

Effectiveness of the Intervention. The 4-week intervention for older adults using the Balance Challenge game improved physical and cognitive functioning and balance-related indicators in older adults. Throughout the trial period in the experimental group, participants showed significant improvements (all $P < 0.05$) in gait speed (25%), standing balance (6%), sit-to-stand (21%), and timed walk performance (12%) in balance-related indicators. Also the experimental group showed statistically significant differences in all indicators related to balance ability compared to the control group for the intervention effect. The effect of the intervention may have been underestimated due to the ceiling effect of standing balance.

User Experience of the Balance Challenge. In terms of perceived ease of use, Balance Challenge's has a simple and easy-to-read guide page with simple start steps, so participants can enter the game quickly. Participants and the character models in the product can correspond in real time, which facilitates users to establish a direct connection with the game and allows seniors to interact more naturally. In terms of enjoyment, we used elements of Tai Chi and the four seasons to cater to the preferences of the elderly, and adopted a lighter color scheme to reduce the tension of the elderly in training; from the results of the user experience evaluation, most of the elderly found it more pleasurable to use the Balance Challenge. In terms of challenge, according to the evaluation results, users find it difficult to complete the whole training process, they need to concentrate on their responses when using the Balance Challenge, and they hope to get a high score, which indicates that the Balance Challenge is challenging for seniors and can keep them intrinsically motivated to continue training.

Limitations. The results obtained in this study are not broadly representative due to the relatively small sample size of the randomized controlled trial due to the specific study population. Regarding the indicators related to cognitive function, we were unable to assess the effective factors that really played a role. It was not possible to monitor the participants' behavior at all times during the controlled experiment, and it was not possible to rule out whether the improvement in the subjects' balance and cognitive function was due to factors other than the balance challenge intervention. The duration of the intervention in this experiment was only 4 weeks, which has some limitations in the trial period. Conducting a longer-term intervention could yield more valid and comprehensive findings.

Regarding the user experience, the upper limits of exercise frequency and intensity could be higher to accommodate a wider range of physical conditions in older adults. The interface could also be more simple to further reduce the threshold of product use.

5 Conclusion

This study found that Balance Challenge is scientific and feasible for the elderly, and leads to significant improvement in gait, standing balance, and acting ability, which can reduce the risk of a fall injury. The exercise compliance of the elderly is also better. It is hoped that the somatosensory interactive balance training exergame based on Tai Chi for the elderly can be included in the exercise plan aimed at improving the balance ability of the elderly.

Acknowledgement. The research is supported by National Social Science Fund (Grant No. 18BRK009).

References

1. Ageing-and-health. https://www.who.int/zh/news-room/fact-sheets/detail/ageing-and-health. Accessed 4 Oct 2021
2. Bureau of Disease Prevention and Control. http://www.gov.cn/gzdt/2011-09/06/content_1941745.htm. Accessed 6 Sept 2011
3. Nawaz, A., Skjret, N., Helbostad, J.L., Vereijken, B., Boulton, E.: Usability and acceptability of balance exergames in older adults: a scoping review. Health Inform. J. **22**(4), 911–931 (2016)
4. Abbas, R.L., Po, H., Al, M., Nayal, I.E., Khatib, A.E.: The effect of adding virtual reality training on traditional exercise program on balance and gait in unilateral traumatic lower limb amputee (2020)
5. Zhang, J.: Meta-analysis of the influence of Tai Chi on the static balance ability and lower limb proprioception of middle-aged and elderly people. J. Chaohu Univ. **19**(06), 66–71 (2017)
6. Ryan, R., Deci, E.: Self-determination theory and the facilitation of intrinsic motivation, social development, and well-being. Am. Psychol. **55**, 68–78 (2000)
7. Nagano, Y., Ishida, K., Tani, T., Kawasaki, M., Ikeuchi, M.: Short and long-term effects of exergaming for the elderly. Springerplus **5**(1), 793–793 (2016). https://doi.org/10.1186/s40064-016-2379-y
8. Pichierri, G., Murer, K., de Bruin, E.D.: A cognitive-motor intervention using a dance video game to enhance foot placement accuracy and gait under dual task conditions in older adults: a randomized controlled trial. BMC Geriatr. **12**, 74 (2012)
9. Corregidor-Sánchez, A.-I., Segura-Fragoso, A., Criado-Álvarez, J.-J., Rodríguez-Hernández, M., Mohedano-Moriano, A., Polonio-López, B.: Effectiveness of virtual reality systems to improve the activities of daily life in older people. Int. J. Environ. Res. Public Health **17**(17), 6283 (2020)
10. Valenzuela, T., Okubo, Y., Woodbury, A., Lord, S.R., Delbaere, K.: Adherence to technology-based exercise programs in older adults: a systematic review. J. Geriatr. Phys. Ther. **41**(1), 49–61 (2018)
11. Skjæret, N., et al.: Designing for movement quality in exergames: lessons learned from observing senior citizens playing stepping games. Gerontology **61**(2), 186–194 (2015)
12. Garcia, J.A., Schoene, D., Lord, S.R., Delbaere, K., Valenzuela, T., Navarro, K.F.: A bespoke kinect stepping exergame for improving physical and cognitive function in older people: a pilot study. Games Health J. **5**(6), 382–388 (2016)

13. Chen, M., Tang, Q., Xu, S., Leng, P., Pan, Z.: Design and evaluation of an augmented reality-based exergame system to reduce fall risk in the elderly. Int. J. Environ. Res. Public Health **17**(19), 7208 (2020)
14. Weber-Spickschen, T.S., Colcuc, C., Hanke, A., Clausen, J.D., James, P.A., Horstmann, H.: Fun during knee rehabilitation: feasibility and acceptability testing of a new Android-based training device. Open Med. Inform. J. **11**, 29–36 (2017)
15. Konstantinidis, E.I., Billis, A.S., Mouzakidis, C.A., Zilidou, V.I., Antoniou, P.E., Bamidis, P.D.: Design, implementation, and wide pilot deployment of FitForAll: an easy to use exergaming platform improving physical fitness and life quality of senior citizens. IEEE J. Biomed. Health Inform. **20**(1), 189–200 (2016)
16. Velazquez, A., Martínez-García, A.I., Favela, J., Hernandez, A., Ochoa, S.F.: Design of exergames with the collaborative participation of older adults. In: Proceedings of the 2013 IEEE 17th International Conference on Computer Supported Cooperative Work in Design (CSCWD), pp. 521–526 (2013)
17. Planinc, R., Nake, I., Kampel, M.: Exergame design guidelines for enhancing elderly's physical and social activities (2013)
18. Brox, E., Konstantinidis, S.T., Evertsen, G.: User-centered design of serious games for older adults following 3 years of experience with exergames for seniors: a study design. JMIR Serious Games **5**(1), e2 (2017)
19. Velazquez, A., Martínez-García, A.I., Favela, J., Ochoa, S.F.: Adaptive exergames to support active aging. Pervasive Mob. Comput. **34**(C), 60–78 (2017)
20. Kappen, D., Mirza-Babaei, P., Nacke, L.: Gamification of older adults' physical activity: an eight-week study (2018)
21. Muñoz, J.E., Gonçalves, A., Rúbio Gouveia, É., Cameirão, M.S., Bermúdez, I.B.S.: Lessons learned from gamifying functional fitness training through human-centered design methods in older adults. Games Health J. **8**(6), 387–406 (2019)
22. Jin, C., Zheng, Y.: Influence of Tai Ji Chuan exercise on static balance ability of middle-aged and elderly people. Bull. Sport Sci. Technol. **29**(001), 44–48 (2005)
23. Sun, W., Mao, D., Pang, F., Wang, L.: Influence of Tai Chi and brisk walking exercise on balance ability of elderly women. China Sport Sci. **48**(5), 75–80 (2012)
24. Chodzko-Zajko, W.J.: ACSM's exercise for older adults (2013)
25. Mazzeo, R.S., Tanaka, H.: Exercise prescription for the elderly: current recommendations. Sports Med. **31**(11), 809–818 (2001)
26. Armstrong, L., Balady, G., Berry, M., Williamswilkins, L.: ACSM's Guidelines For Exercise Testing and Prescription. Physical Therapy (2006)
27. Maki, B.E., Holliday, P.J., Fernie, G.R.: Aging and postural control. J. Am. Geriatr. Soc. **38**(1), 1–9 (1990)
28. Dalrymple-Alford, J.C., et al.: The MoCA well-suited screen for cognitive impairment in Parkinson disease. Neurology **75**(19), 1717 (2010)
29. Ambrosino, P., Fuschillo, S., Papa, A., Minno, M., Maniscalco, M.: Exergaming as a supportive tool for home-based rehabilitation in the COVID-19 pandemic era. Games Health J. **9**(5), 311–313 (2020)
30. Guralnik, J.M., et al.: lower extremity function and subsequent disability: consistency across studies, predictive models, and value of gait speed alone compared with the short physical performance battery. J. Gerontol. A Biol. Sci. Med. Sci. **55**(4), M221–M231 (2000)
31. Lord, S.R., Murray, S.M., Kirsten, C., Bridget, M., Anne, T.: Sit-to-stand performance depends on sensation, speed, balance, and psychological status in addition to strength in older people. J Gerontol. A Biol. Med. **57**(8), M539 (2002)
32. Timed Up and Go Test. Handbook of Disease Burdens and Quality of Life Measures (2010)

33. Wim, V., Boxtel, M.V., Breukelen, G.V., Jolles, J.: The Letter Digit Substitution Test: normative data for 1,858 healthy participants aged 24–81 from the Maastricht Aging Study (MAAS): influence of age, education, and sex. J. Clin. Exp. Neuropsychol. **28**(6), 998–1009 (2006)
34. Kane, M.J., Engle, R.W.: Working-memory capacity and the control of attention: the contributions of goal neglect, response competition, and task set to Stroop interference. J. Exp. Psychol. Gen. **132**(1), 47–70 (2003)
35. Zysset, S., Müller, K., Lohmann, G., Cramon, D.: Color-word matching stroop task: separating interference and response conflict. Neuroimage **13**(1), 29–36 (2001)
36. Branaghan, R.J., O'Brian, J.S., Hildebrand, E.A., Foster, L.B.: Usability evaluation. In: Branaghan, R.J., O'Brian, J.S., Hildebrand, E.A., Foster, L.B. (eds.) Humanizing Healthcare – Human Factors for Medical Device Design, pp. 69–96. Springer, Cham (2021). https://doi.org/10.1007/978-3-030-64433-8_4
37. Yu, R.W.L., Yuen, W.H., Peng, L., Chan, A.H.S.: Acceptance level of older Chinese people towards video shooting games. In: Gao, Q., Zhou, J. (eds.) HCII 2020. LNCS, vol. 12208, pp. 707–718. Springer, Cham (2020). https://doi.org/10.1007/978-3-030-50249-2_50
38. Davis, F.D.: Perceived usefulness, perceived ease of use, and user acceptance of information technology. MIS Q. **13**(3), 319–340 (1989)
39. Kendzierski, D., Decarlo, K.J.: Physical activity enjoyment scale: two validation studies. J. Sport Exerc. Psychol. **13**(1), 50–64 (1991)

Analysis on Influencing Factors of Medical Seeking Behavior of the Elderly Under COVID-19–Based on the DEMATEL Method

Shuyu Zhao, Ting Han(✉), Chunrong Liu, Yahui Zhang, and Yi Ding

School of Design, Shanghai Jiao Tong University, 800 Dongchuan Road, Minhang District, Shanghai 200240, China
hanting@sjtu.edu.cn

Abstract. The aim of this study is to investigate the factors that influence the choice of health care for the elderly population after Covid-19. Based on previous studies, the study innovatively adds the influence of the improvement of digital medical technology and the degree of aging-friendly of different hospitals on the choice of medical institutions for the elderly. The study used a combination of literature research, questionnaires, interviews and factor analysis to identify the main factors influencing the choice of healthcare for the elderly. The results of the study showed that the three most important factors influencing older people's choice of medical seeking behavior were their willingness of treatment, community evaluation and the aging-friendly improvements.

The data from this study will be used to analysis the pain points of the elderly in seeking medical treatment and to make recommendations to improve their medical experience. It is hoped that this study will provide some ideas for the development of a model of healthcare access for older people, and better guide them in their healthcare seeking behavior.

Keywords: Medical seeking behavior · Decision-Making Trial and Evaluation Laboratory · Elderly

1 Introduction

1.1 Background

According to the statistics of China Statistical Yearbook 2020 for the past five years, the number and proportion of elderly people aged over 65 in China have been increasing year by year, with some mega-cities experiencing a more pronounced ageing of the elderly. The ageing of the population has brought changes in various needs in terms of living, among which the changes in medical needs are more significant. The elderly have a greater need for medical services than young people due to the decline in their physical functions. However, medical services for the elderly presents a contradictory situation of high demand, low access [1]. Since the rapid global spread of Covid-19, the transmission characteristics of the virus has prompted hospitals to implement diverse

Q. Gao and J. Zhou (Eds.): HCII 2022, LNCS 13331, pp. 320–332, 2022.
https://doi.org/10.1007/978-3-031-05654-3_22

online healthcare services, including online appointment and online consultation, to avoid person-to-person contact. As a result of the Covid-19 pandemic, difference medical institutions also need access to big data of the health status of patients prior to consultation.

These online medical services have improved the efficiency of medical consultations to some extent, and also squeezed the space for offline hospital services. The barriers to living of the elderly gradually increase with aging, and many of them cannot enjoy the convenience of online services because they do not use or resist using electronic devices. How to get medical treatment quickly and easily comes to be the biggest issue for older people.

Each touch point throughout the elderly's medical journey has a different influence on their sensory experience [2]. Many hospitals have made aging-friendly improvements on different levels to address the aesthetics and needs of the elderly, so as to increase the satisfaction for them.

1.2 Literature Review

Medical seeking behavior, referred to as health-seeking pattern, is a patient's preference for the type and grade of medical institutions and different models of medical services. The Anderson theoretical model (Fig. 1) is the most classic international model for predicting medical services [3]. We apply it as an explanatory framework to examine the patterns and factors that influence the medical seeking behavior of the elderly in China. The model classifies the factors influencing the elderly's medical seeking behavior into predisposing characteristics, enabling resources and healthcare needs. The predisposing characteristics are divided into gender, age, region, urban residence, educational background, marital status, drinking habits and smoking habits. Enabling resources include income, health insurance, pensions and intergenerational support. Needs factors are self-rated health status, Chronic condition and functional limitations [4].

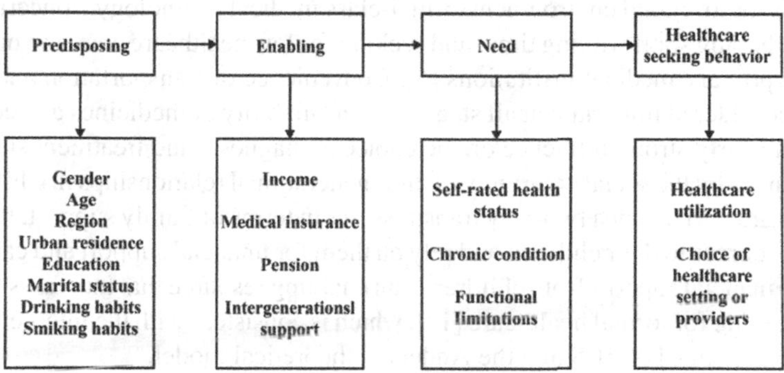

Fig. 1. The Anderson theoretical model

In a study of patient preferences in Shanghai, the authors found that patient access preference was influenced mainly by healthcare providers' characteristics, illness severity, and sociodemographic characteristics [5]. A revised questionnaire report based on preliminary findings of *Analysis Report of the National Health Services Survey in China, 2008 (NHSS)*, which was published by the National Health and Family Planning Commission of the People's Republic of China, assessed various basic characteristics including gender, occupation, age, monthly income, marital status and education level to examine the socio-demographic characteristics of participants [6].

The China Health and Retirement Longitudinal Study (CHARLS) also disaggregates the socio-demographic characteristics of participants. The socio-demographic characteristics include health insurance, gender, age, education background, income, marital status, residence, and health self-report. Zhonghua Wang et al. [7] assessed the impact of different types of social health insurance and other relevant factors on healthcare utilization among middle-aged and elderly Chinese, based on CHARLS statistics conducted in 2015.

In general, Chinese healthcare policies aim to provide a hierarchical healthcare system structure, while patients are free to choose the medical institutions [5]. However, the actual choice of different grades of medical institutions by the elderly does not match the roles and functions of them. A study conducted in China reported that elderly patients preferred the diagnostic and follow-up services offered by secondary and tertiary hospitals [8]. Thus despite the convenience of community health centers for the elderly, urban patients still tend to choose secondary and tertiary hospitals [9]. Rural patients, on the other hand, tend to choose primary medical institutions, as they are more concerned about cost and convenience [10].

The elderly often suffer from multiple illnesses due to declining physical functions [11]. Chronic diseases do not only place a heavy health and financial burden on the elderly, the families and the healthcare system, but also influence patients' decisions to medical seeking [12]. Some chronic diseases affect the convenience of the elderly's travel, and those people with poor self-rated health conditions and exhibiting impaired activities of daily living (ADLs) are more likely to choose outpatient and inpatient services. Wenya Yu also concludes that primary medical institutions are the most frequently chosen healthcare providers for mild diseases. Besides, patients with no personal preference, no favor to a good environment or first-class medical technology, concerned about distances, hoping short waiting time, and seeking for low healthcare costs are most likely to choose primary medical institutions [5]. Convenience of transportation and medical level are considered important at all stages. The availability of medicines and equipment has a particularly strong influence on the choice at diagnosis and treatment stages [10].

Influenced by the social environment, intergenerational relationships in Chinese families are characterized by a two-way transmission. In terms of family support, the elderly provide resources to their children and rely on them for financial support and care in their old [13]. Financial support from children is an enabling resource that increases the likelihood of seeking for formal healthcare [14], which is consistent with the intergenerational support factors in CHARLS and the Anderson theoretical model.

Patient preference for treatment, acquaintances, and media advocacy, also have a strong influence in their choices of medical institutions [15]. Most people tend to choose reputable doctors and medical institutions (especially top-tier tertiary hospitals) regardless of the type and severity of their disease. This phenomenon of medical preference gives rise to other problems, such as increasing workload of doctors in reputable tertiary hospitals, which directly leads to increased waiting time for patients and other problems.

In order to solve such problems, as well as to prevent and control the Covid-19 pandemic by avoiding person-to-person contact, online services have been opened up by different grades medical institutions to offer medical help. And the healthcare industry has accelerated research and use of healthcare technologies to improve quality of life for the elderly [16]. Age-friendly improvements have also been made by providers, considering different levels of acceptance by the old patients. Quesada, BC et al. [17] surveyed the use and perceptions of telemedicine tools among the population aged over 65 and found that the usage of these technologies was limited though rated very positively. Despite the fact that the surveyed participants were highly educated, living in large cities with their children or partners, they are still lack of confidence in using the internet for e-health, which resulted in the low level of telemedicine care technologies application.

1.3 Research Purpose

Based on the Anderson theoretical model and other theory, this paper analyses the realistic problems encountered by the elderly in the development of "Internet + Medicine" due to their own characteristics. This paper also identifies the influencing factors of medical seeking behavior of the elderly. According to data obtained from the DEMATEL method and the interview results, this paper also analyses the increasing demand for medical services of the elderly in the community, proposes optimization of the medical treatment process for the elderly, so as to further improve the community medical service system.

2 Analysis of Influencing Factors

2.1 Summary of Factors Influencing Older People's Medical Seeking Behaviour

Based on the literature search, a preliminary overview of 25 influencing factors of healthcare choice among the elderly in terms of predisposing characteristics, enabling resources and need factors are shown in Table 1 below.

Table 1. Preliminary summary of factors influencing medical seeking behavior of the elderly

Number	Influencing factors	Factors description
1	Gender	Gender of patient
2	Age	Age of patient
3	Urban residence	Permanent residence of patient
4	Educational background	Educational background of patient
5	Marital status	Unmarried/Married/Divorced
6	Drinking and smoking habits	Whether the patient has a habit of smoking or drinking alcohol

(continued)

Table 1. (*continued*)

Number	Influencing factors	Factors description
7	Income	Personal income of patient
8	Medical insurance	Whether the patient has commercial insurance or social insurance
9	Pension	Whether the patient has social pension benefits
10	Intergenerational support	Next generation care for patients' lives and financial aspects
11	Self-rated health status	Assessment of self-health status
12	Chronic condition	Whether the patient has a chronic disease
13	Functional limitations	Basic activities in daily life related to self-care activities such as dressing, eating, maintaining personal hygiene
14	Career	Differences of patient's career
15	Distance to medical treatment	Distance from the patient's residence to the hospital
16	Waiting time	Length of time to wait for medical treatment
17	Urgency of the disease	Urgency of medical treatment
18	Convenience of transportation	The type of transportation required to reach the hospital and the total time required
19	Medical skills	The skill of the practitioner
20	Accessibility of medicines and equipment	Availability of medicines and equipment in the medical facility
21	Medical facility environment	Cleanliness of the medical environment; Attitude of medical staff
22	Preference for treatments	Patients' personal preferences for treatment
23	Aging-friendly improvements	Convenience of self-service registration machines and other types of equipment for the elderly
24	Distribution of medical resources	Distribution ratio of online registration and offline registration, etc.
25	Media/Acquaintance advocacy	Media coverage of each hospital; evaluation of hospitals by close friends

2.2 Screening of Factors Influencing Medical Seeking Behavior of the Elderly

Due to the excessive number of influencing factors in the initial study, it led to serious homogeneity among the factors. Moreover, there are certain geo-graphical and age restrictions when conducting the questionnaire research in the later stage. Too many influencing factors also lead to problems such as low understanding of the questionnaire and poor completion of the questionnaire by the participants. This study used factor analysis to extract important factors from the above 25 influencing factors, and to filter and combine the homogenised factors.

Considering that the population who answered the questionnaire at the time of the authors' research was the elderly living in Shanghai and there was consistency in the results, the 25 preliminary influencing factors such as gender, age, region, educational background and marital status were listed separately as mandatory items in the questionnaire for specific completion. The influencing factors were divided into three main dimensions: patient personal factors, hospital factors and subjective influencing factors. The final summary of the 12 main influencing factors that have the greatest influence on the choice of medical care for the elderly is shown in Table 2.

Table 2. Major factors influencing medical seeking behavior of the elderly

Number	Dimension	Influencing factors	Factors description
1	Patient personal factors	Medical insurance	Whether the patient has commercial insurance or social insurance
2	Patient personal factors	Family support	Partner, children's care in terms of financial and life
3	Patient personal factors	Self-awareness of health status	Assessment of self-health status
4	Patient personal factors	Capabilities of daily activities	Basic activities in daily life related to self-care activities such as dressing, eating, maintaining personal hygiene
5	Patient personal factors	Purpose of treatment	Purpose of treatment
6	Patient personal factors	Diagnosis	Prognosis of possible follow-up treatment after the end of the diagnosis
7	Hospital factors	Convenience of transportation	The type of transportation required to reach the hospital and the total time required
8	Hospital factors	The comprehensive strength of hospitals	Hospital equipment, physician resources, environment and other conditions

(*continued*)

Table 2. (*continued*)

Number	Dimension	Influencing factors	Factors description
9	Hospital factors	Aging-friendly improvements	Convenience of self-service registration machines and other types of equipment for the elderly
10	Hospital factors	Distribution of medical resources	Distribution ratio of online registration and offline registration, etc.
11	Subjective influencing factor	Willingness of treatment	Attitudes of individuals going to medical appointments
12	Subjective influencing factor	Community evaluation	Media coverage of each hospital; evaluation of hospitals by close friends

3 DEMATEL Procedure

First developed by the Geneva Research Centre of the Battelle Memorial Institute, Decision-Making Trial and Evaluation Laboratory (DEMATEL) method visualizes the structure of complex causal relationships through matrices or directed graphs [18] and is considered to be an effective method for identifying the components of causal chains in complex systems. The method deals with the interrelationships between assessment factors and finds the key factors through a visual structural model [19].

The DEMATEL procedure in this study was carried out in the following steps: (1) Preliminary identification of factors influencing medical seeking behavior of the elderly; (2) Further screening of influencing factors according to the target population of the questionnaire; (3) Complete the mandatory questionnaire items and then use the DEMATEL questionnaire to estimate the interaction between the factors; (4) Calculate the mean value of the data and generate the direct relationship matrix Z; (5) Calculate the λ values, the normalized direct relationship matrix and the direct/indirect relationship matrix T; (6) Obtain the degree of influence (D), degree of being influenced (R), degree of centrality (D+R) and degree of cause (D−R) corresponding to each influencing factor based on the above calculations; (7) An influence relationship map (IRM) corresponding to the (D+R) and (D−R) values of each influencing factor was obtained.

3.1 Participants

The sample was collected in Shanghai, and users were selected to be over 60 years old, conscious and able to understand the questionnaire. The questionnaires were collected using both field interviews and in-home interviews. Considering that this is a study on medical seeking behavior of the elderly, the interview locations were chosen to be hospitals and communities with a large number of elderly people. The specific locations selected are the Shanghai Minhang District Central Hospital and the Hongqi Community in Minhang District, Shanghai. For the household interviews, households with elderly people were selected. The author was allowed to enter the household and interview the elderly with the help of their children or grandchildren and complete the questionnaire.

A total of 31 questionnaires were distributed in this study, of which 28 were valid. Some of the participants were unable to complete the questionnaire, making it invalid. The survey period was from May 2021 to November 2021. Individual interviews ranged from approximately 20 min to 40 min.

3.2 Tasks and Materials

In the DEMATEL questionnaire distributed, the 12 main influencing factors screened of medical seeking behavior of the elderly were arranged to form a 12 * 12 matrix of ranks. Define the degree of interaction between the relevant factors as four levels. 0 means "essentially no impact", 1 means "weak impact", 2 means "large impact" and 3 means "extreme impact". The questionnaire was used to estimate the direction of the interaction and the relative degree of influence of each factor listed in the first column on each of the factors listed in the first row. The degree of impact is judged according to the situation of the elderly, while filling in the questionnaire.

3.3 Procedure

Data analysis based on the valid questionnaires returned. The average direct relationship matrix Z calculated according to the equation is shown in the Table 3.

Table 3. Average direct relationship matrix Z

	1	2	3	4	5	6	7	8	9	10	11	12
1	0.000	0.429	0.000	0.143	0.000	0.000	0.000	0.571	0.429	0.000	0.000	0.000
2	1.000	0.000	0.857	1.286	0.857	0.286	0.571	0.143	1.143	1.000	0.286	0.000
3	0.143	1.000	0.000	1.571	0.143	0.429	0.000	1.143	0.429	0.000	0.429	0.000
4	0.143	1.000	0.857	0.000	0.143	0.286	0.000	0.143	0.000	0.000	0.143	0.000
5	0.714	0.000	1.286	1.000	0.000	0.000	0.143	0.429	0.143	0.143	0.286	0.143
6	0.000	0.000	0.429	0.571	1.286	0.000	0.000	0.429	0.143	0.000	0.000	0.000
7	0.000	1.000	0.000	0.286	0.143	0.143	0.000	0.571	0.857	0.286	0.571	0.286
8	0.429	0.000	0.143	0.000	0.143	0.000	0.143	0.000	0.571	0.429	0.429	0.286
9	0.429	0.000	0.000	0.000	0.286	0.143	0.429	1.143	0.000	1.000	0.429	0.857
10	0.714	0.000	0.000	0.000	0.000	0.143	0.429	1.286	1.714	0.000	0.429	1.000
11	1.286	1.571	1.286	1.714	1.429	1.143	1.857	2.571	2.000	1.429	0.000	2.571
12	0.000	0.000	0.000	0.000	0.000	0.429	0.571	2.857	2.571	2.286	1.571	0.000

Because of the excessive number of digits obtained, the average relationship matrix retains three decimal places. Then the matrix is calculated as follows equations.

$$\lambda = \frac{1}{max\left(\sum_{j=1}^{n} z_{ij}\right)}, ij = 1, 2, 3, \ldots, k \tag{1}$$

$$\chi = \lambda \cdot Z \tag{2}$$

The direct relationship matrix is obtained from the above equations. The direct/indirect relation matrix T is calculated based on the existing Eq. 3 proved by scholars and the derived Eq. 4.

$$\lim_{k=\infty} \left(1 + \chi + \chi^2 + \cdots + \chi^k\right) = \chi(1 - \chi)^{-1} \tag{3}$$

$$T = \lim_{k \to \infty} \left(1 + \chi + \chi^2 + \cdots + \chi^k\right) = \chi(1 - \chi)^{-1} \tag{4}$$

Table 4. The direct/indirect relation matrix T

	1	2	3	4	5	6	7	8	9	10	11	12
1	0.003	0.024	0.002	0.010	0.002	0.001	0.002	0.033	0.026	0.004	0.002	0.002
2	**0.063**	0.013	**0.056**	**0.080**	**0.052**	0.021	0.037	0.030	**0.077**	**0.063**	0.024	0.012
3	0.017	**0.062**	0.011	**0.093**	0.016	0.028	0.007	**0.072**	0.035	0.010	0.028	0.007
4	0.013	**0.058**	0.051	0.011	0.013	0.018	0.003	0.015	0.008	0.005	0.011	0.002
5	0.043	0.010	**0.074**	**0.063**	0.004	0.005	0.011	0.036	0.018	0.013	0.020	0.013
6	0.005	0.004	0.030	0.037	**0.070**	0.002	0.002	0.028	0.011	0.002	0.003	0.002
7	0.010	**0.059**	0.008	0.025	0.016	0.013	0.009	0.047	**0.062**	0.029	0.037	0.026
8	0.028	0.004	0.011	0.005	0.011	0.003	0.013	0.014	0.041	0.031	0.028	0.023
9	0.031	0.006	0.005	0.006	0.020	0.012	0.031	**0.082**	0.022	**0.066**	0.033	**0.056**
10	0.046	0.006	0.004	0.005	0.006	0.013	0.032	**0.094**	**0.111**	0.020	0.035	**0.066**
11	**0.094**	**0.106**	**0.090**	**0.119**	**0.095**	**0.075**	**0.119**	**0.201**	**0.166**	**0.119**	0.034	**0.160**
12	0.022	0.013	0.011	0.014	0.015	0.033	0.051	**0.195**	**0.175**	**0.148**	**0.100**	0.033

Take the upper quartile of all elements in the relation matrix T as Q1, i.e., 0.051. This value is the threshold value to measure the strength of the interaction between factors. If all values in the rows and columns corresponding to a factor in the direct/indirect relation matrix T are below the threshold, the factor and the corresponding rows and columns should be deleted. Since no such factors existed in the table, all factors were retained. Values above the threshold (Q1) are bolded in the Table 4.

Take the upper third between Q3 and the maximum value as Q2, i.e., 0.097. Values above Q2 are considered strong influences, while values between Q2 and Q1 are considered average influences.

3.4 Results

Each influence factor corresponds to the degree of influence (D), and the degree of being influenced (R). The D and R of each factor are obtained by summing up the values of the rows and columns corresponding to that factor in the matrix T. The following Eqs. (5–6) show the calculation process for the values D and R.

$$D_i = \sum_{j=1}^{k} t_{ij}, (i = 1, 2, 3, \ldots, k) \quad (5)$$

$$R_j = \sum_{i=1}^{k} t_{ij}, (j = 1, 2, 3, \ldots, k) \quad (6)$$

The degree of influence (D) and the degree of being influenced (R) are calculated to obtain the degree of centrality (D+R) and the degree of cause (D−R). The larger the degree of centrality value (D+R), the more important this factor is among the influencing factors. If the (D−R) value is positive, this factor directly influences other factors. If the (D−R) value is negative, this factor is influenced by other factors.

The results of the study show that the three most critical factors influencing medical seeking behavior of the elderly are willingness of treatment, community evaluation, and aging-friendly improvements. These three factors have a strong influence on other influencing factors. The partial (D+R) values and (D−R) values are shown in Table 5 and 6 below respectively.

Table 5. The top three and last three of (D+R)

The top three of (D+R)	The last three of (D+R)
Willingness of treatment	Purpose of treatment
Community evaluation	Medical insurance
Aging-friendly improvements	Diagnosis

Table 6. The top three and last three of (D−R)

The top three of (D−R)	The last three of (D−R)
Willingness of treatment	Medical insurance
Community evaluation	Aging-friendly improvements
Family support	The comprehensive strength of hospitals

The Influential Relation Diagram. Make the Influential Relation Diagram (IRD) with $(D_i + R_i)$ as the horizontal axis and $(D_i - R_i)$ as the vertical axis. Different dimensions are marked with different color labels. The orange label is patient personal factor, the green label is hospital factor and the blue label is subjective influencing factor. The strength of the relationship between the factors is determined by Q1 and Q2. The direction of the arrow indicates the influence of one factor on the other factor. The location of each factor and the relationship between the factors are shown in Fig. 2.

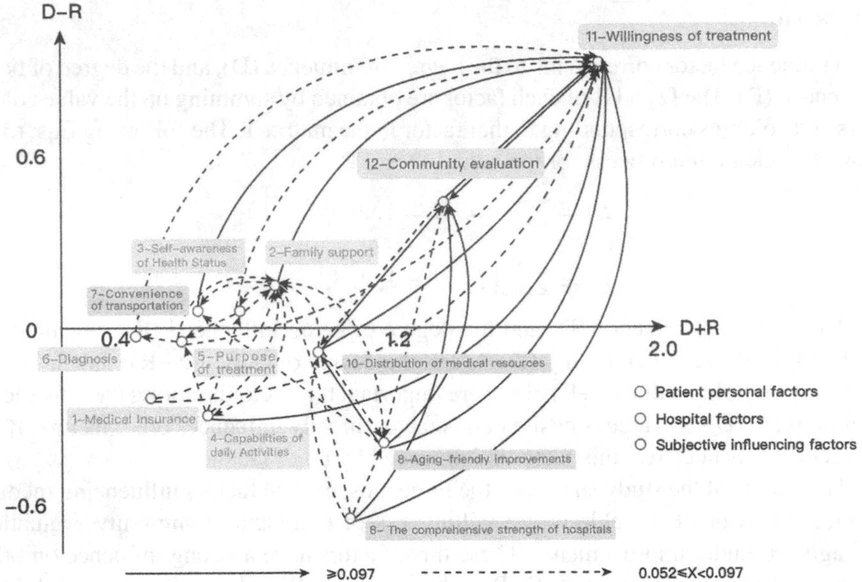

Fig. 2. The Influential Relation Diagram

The Influential Relation Diagram (IRD) shows that willingness of treatment and community evaluation have a significant influence on medical seeking behavior of the elderly. Willingness of treatment and community evaluation are also influenced by many other factors. Secondly, distribution of medical resources and age-friendly improvements are also two core factors that need high attention.

3.5 Discussion

Based on the Influence Relationship Diagram (IRD) and interview results, the following analysis and recommendations for improving the medical seeking satisfaction of the elderly are provided.

Balance the Ratio of Online and Offline Medical Resources. A large percentage of older adults do not know how to operate electronic devices. The expansion of online medical services has become a barrier to accessing treatment for people who are not equipped with smartphones. Some older adults in the research think they can use their smartphones and other devices for online medical services flexibility, but such people are still a minority. Some other older adults say they use old-fashioned phones. If offline medical services requires smart devices, they can only seek help from young people, not to mention online medical services. Considering the special characteristics of the elderly population, medical institutions should balance the ratio of online and offline medical resources to ensure that the elderly population can complete the medical process smoothly when they go to the hospital. The reservation of offline resources also reflects the society's humanistic care for the elderly.

Improve the Aging-Friendly Degree of Medical Institutions. Many respondents indicated that they have a stronge preference for highly age-friendly hospitals. There is a high degree of autonomy in many hospitals today. For the elderly, they are intimidated by all kinds of unfamiliar equipment. Volunteers or guidance staff can be regularly arranged in the hospital to guide the elderly in need. Guidance texts, patterns, and voice announcements in the hospital can be improved to suit the characteristics of the elderly population to some extent.

Use the Traditional Media and the Public to Advocate Reasonable Medical Seeking Behavior. Despite the continued acceleration of the digital society, older people still rely more on traditional media propaganda and evaluation of the surrounding people for their understanding of society. Therefore, these dissemination methods can be used to advocate the reasonable medical seeking behavior, such as seeking hierarchical treatment.

4 Conclusion

This study discusses the factors of medical seeking behavior of the elderly in the post-epidemic period. Three major dimensions are identified through literature review and user interviews: patient personal factors, hospital factors and subjective influencing factors. The authors used factor analysis to summarize 12 major factors. Relevant questionnaires were distributed to the elderly in hospitals and communities for Decision-Making Trial and Evaluation Laboratory method. The direction of influence and the degree of interaction between 12 influencing factors were assessed through a series of calculations and data visualization. Based on previous studies, the study innovatively adds the influence of the improvement of digital medical technology and the degree of aging-friendly of different medical institutions on medical seeking behavior of the elderly. Based on the results, recommendations are made to optimize the access process and improve the medical satisfaction for the elderly. It is hoped that this study will provide a new focus for building a model of medical seeking behavior for the elderly.

References

1. Chen, P., Wu, L., Zhu, L.: Analysis of medical service utilization among the elderly and its influencing factors–based on data from the China Health and Aging Tracking Survey. Chin. J. Soc. Med. **32**(2), 3 (2015). (in Chinese)
2. Yao, Y., Zhou, X., Zhu, T.: Research on service design of community medical facilities based on aging-appropriate and elderly-centered. In: IOP Conference Series: Materials Science and Engineering, vol. 573, no. 1, p. 012075 (2019)
3. Andersen, R.M.: Revisiting the behavioral model and access to medical care: does it matter? J. Health Soc. Behav. **36**(1), 1–10 (1995)
4. Zeng, Y., Wan, Y., Yuan, Z., Fang, Y.: Healthcare-seeking behavior among Chinese older adults: patterns and predictive factors. Int. J. Environ. Res. Public Health **18**(6), 2969 (2021)
5. Yu, W., Li, M., Ye, F., Xue, C., Zhang, L.: Patient preference and choice of healthcare providers in Shanghai, China: a cross-sectional study. BMJ Open **7**(10), e016418 (2017)

6. Sun, X.: China Health Service Survey Research. China Union Medical University Press (2009). (in Chinese)
7. Wang, Z., Li, X., Chen, M., Si, L.: Social health insurance, healthcare utilization, and costs in middle-aged and elderly community-dwelling adults in China. Int. J. Equity Health **17**(1), 17 (2018)
8. Wang, T.: Research on the choice of community medical treatment behavior of urban elderly with chronic diseases and its influencing factors. Master thesis, Sichuan Academy of Social Science, Sichuan (2017). (in Chinese)
9. Shi, J., et al.: Options for care of elderly inpatients with chronic diseases: analysis of distribution and factors influencing use of care in Shanghai, China. Front. Public Health **9**, 216 (2021)
10. Liu, Y., Zhong, L., Yuan, S., van de Klundert, J.: Why patients prefer high-level healthcare facilities: a qualitative study using focus groups in rural and urban China. BMJ Glob. Health **3**(5), e000854 (2018)
11. Marengoni, A., Winblad, B., Karp, A., Fratiglioni, L.: Prevalence of chronic diseases and multimorbidity among the elderly population in Sweden. Am. J. Public Health **98**(7), 1198–1200 (2008)
12. Yang, S., Wang, D., Li, W., Wang, C., Yang, X., Lo, K.: Decoupling of elderly healthcare demand and expenditure in China. Healthcare **9**(10), 1346 (2021)
13. Hu, A.: Providing more but receiving less: daughters in intergenerational exchange in mainland China. J. Marriage Fam. **79**(3), 739–757 (2017)
14. Zhu, B., Mao, Y.: Intergenerational support, social capital and medical service utilization—an empirical analysis using CHARSL data. Soc. Secur. Stud. **1**, 48–59 (2017)
15. Chen, R., Du, X.D., Yang, Z., Ning-Xiu, L.I.: Analysis of choice of healthcare services and the influencing factors among outpatients in Chengdu City. Mod. Prev. Med. **43**(22), 4217–4220 (2016)
16. Low, S.T.H., Sakhardande, P.G., Lai, Y.F., Long, A.D.S., Kaur-Gill, S.: Attitudes and perceptions toward healthcare technology adoption among older adults in singapore: a qualitative study. Front. Public Health **9**, 588590 (2021)
17. Criado Quesada, B., Zorrilla Muñoz, V., Agulló Tomás, M.S.: El uso de tecnologías de asistencia sanitaria digital por parte de la población mayor desde una perspectiva de género e intrageneracional. Teknokultura. Revista de Cultura Digital y Movimientos Sociales **18**(2), 103–113 (2021)
18. Gabus, A., Fontela, E.: World problems, an invitation to further thought within the framework of DEMATEL. (1972)
19. Si, S.-L., You, X.-Y., Liu, H.-C., Zhang, P.: DEMATEL technique: a systematic review of the state-of-the-art literature on methodologies and applications. Math. Probl. Eng. **2018**, 33 (2018). Article ID: 3696457

Aging, Communication and Social Interaction

Intergenerational Digitally Mediated Relationships: How Portuguese Young Adults Interact with Family Members Over 65+

Inês Amaral[1,2](✉), Ana Marta Flores[1,2], Eduardo Antunes[1], and Maria José Brites[3,4]

[1] Faculty of Arts and Humanities, University of Coimbra, Coimbra, Portugal
ines.amaral@uc.pt, {amflores,eduardo.antunes}@fl.uc.pt
[2] Communication and Society Research Centre of the University of Minho, Braga, Portugal
[3] NOVA Institute of Communication, Lisbon, Portugal
mariajosebrites@ulp.pt
[4] CICANT, Lusófona University, Porto, Portugal

Abstract. Considering the issue of population ageing, its differences and inequalities, also in a pandemic context, this paper aims to explore intergenerational digital mediation relations and practises in Portugal. Therefore, this research departs from the following questions: (RQ1): How do Portuguese young adults interact online with family members over 65+?; (RQ2): Do digital relationships across generations promote active citizenship participation? The survey has a representative sample (N = 1500) of the Portuguese population of young adults between 18 and 30 years old. Results show that the most frequent activities to interact with relatives over 65 years old are a) sending messages through mobile apps (48.67%); b) using social media (48.66%); c) making audio calls with them via mobile apps such as WhatsApp or Messenger (46.45%) and d) encouraging them to look for reliable information on the Internet (44%). The study's main conclusion is that the Portuguese context suggests intergenerational solidarity associated with technologies helps combat social isolation, promote autonomy, and prevent dependence within older generations.

Keywords: Intergenerational digital relationships · Digital practices · Active citizenship participation · Intergenerational solidarity

1 Introduction

The challenge of population ageing has been a reality for some decades. The European continent has been particularly affected by this demographic tendency. Following the European trend, in 2020, the older population in Portugal aged 65 or over will represent 22.3% [1]. According to data from PORDATA, in 2020, the longevity index was 48.7%, and the ageing index was 165.1, which means that there are 165.1 people aged over 65 for every young person in Portugal. Furthermore, the Covid-19 pandemic has increased the isolation and dependency of a population that is often homogenised in public policy and therefore more fragile in the face of lockdowns and restrictive measures.

Q. Gao and J. Zhou (Eds.): HCII 2022, LNCS 13331, pp. 335–348, 2022.
https://doi.org/10.1007/978-3-031-05654-3_23

During the pandemic, "the population most affected by the lockdown is also the population least helped by the digital tools aiming to mitigate the negative effects" [2]. Therefore, in Portugal, the authorities, voluntary movements and non-governmental organisations have sought to support the older population in everyday tasks. However, social isolation remained, and technologies were one of the ways for older people to keep in touch with their families and friends. As restrictive measures progressed, and at the time of writing this paper, the pandemic had arrived two years ago, and it became clear that the use of technology was essential to carry out everyday tasks once offline. For example, the population was summoned to the vaccination process through SMS, and many other services went online. In fact, the motto adopted by the Portuguese government was 'We are ON', ensuring the maximum number of services available digitally. This paper argues that intergenerational solidarity associated with technologies can combat social isolation, promote autonomy, and prevent dependency.

The integration of digital media is transforming audiences' practices into everyday life. Contemporary media systems are based on convergence, related to media hybridity [3], supporting the contention that audiences are intrinsically cross-media [4]. Media consumption tends to occur increasingly in a cross-media and multichannel perspective [5]. Therefore, the "ecological reconfiguration" produces new media consumption patterns [6, 7] and participation [8, 9]. As audiences become more active than ever, there is an intensification of public connection [10, 11], with several media serving as a resource for social interaction among generations within different contexts of participation [12]. Therefore, intergenerational interactions shape collective identities [13] and promote cross-generational digital participation. Furthermore, scientific research has shown that contemporary societies seek to overcome the digital divide and digital inequalities from the so-called notion of intergenerational solidarity [14–16].

There is no solid research on intergenerational digitally mediated relationships and practises in Portugal. Hence, this article aims to analyse digitally mediated relationships from young adults with family members over 65 years old. Therefore, this paper departs from the following research questions: RQ1: How do Portuguese young adults interact online with family members over 65+? RQ2: Do digital relationships across generations promote active citizenship participation?

The study is twofold as it endeavours to understand the role of technology mediation in intergenerational relationships and how the youngest communicate with and support older people (+65) in financial, political, civic and recreational activities. By drawing on a survey to a representative sample of the Portuguese population of young adults between 18 and 30 years old, the results shed light on how intergenerational family relationships have been mediated through the digital in times of pandemic. This empirical study is the first-ever in Portugal with a representative sample to consider the issues and relationships of intergenerationality in young adults' digital uses and practises.

1.1 Blurring the Homogenisation: The Diversity of the Ageing Process

As ageing is one of the most significant challenges of contemporary societies, the Covid-19 pandemic exacerbated problems that the older population already suffers. As a result, the discursive requalification of 'active' as productive [17] has receded, giving way again to the idea of 'healthy ageing' based on the United Nations Principles for Older Persons, which defined the concept of 'active ageing' as "the process of optimising opportunities for health, participation and security in order to enhance the quality of life as people age" [18].

Scientific research has highlighted the enormous inter-individual heterogeneity that distinguishes people as they age. New vocabulary or euphemistic expressions designate people at advanced ages [19]. Although using a word or expression to name a group always presupposes a homogenisation process, the scientific literature does not commonly use pluralised terminologies to account for the heterogeneity of old age. Moreover, this issue is problematic insofar as it is assumed that older people share the same trajectories when, in reality, life experiences are multiple [20]. As empirical evidence confirms that socio-cultural diversity and complexity interfere with how individuals age similarly to the economic variable, homogenising assumptions that portray the ageing process as one, categorising older people as an identical group, ends up blurring the heterogeneity that characterises ageing. The generalisations of this process are denounced in some critical studies that show that differences and inequalities are hidden, according to works by Paúl [21] and Cabral et al. [22]. The ageing process is plastic and diverse [23]. There are ethnic, age, gender and socioeconomic differences that contribute to the diversity of the ageing experience [24]. As mentioned by the World Health Organization, multiple factors contribute to the heterogeneity of the ageing process, being determinants and transversal such as culture and gender; issues related to the health and social care systems; behavioural factors; dynamics related to personal aspects; aspects associated with the physical environment; and, finally, elements related to the social environment and economic factors.

In Western societies undergoing digitisation and ageing, the number of older adults using digital is increasing. However, these societies are also confronted with the spectre of so-called digital divides, of which at least three have been distinguished. The first is between those with and those without access to the digital; a second digital divide is between those with the skills and those without the skills to make use of the digital [25, 26]; and a third digital divide is related to "gaps in individuals" ability to translate their access and use of the Internet into offline outcomes" [27]. Older adults are among those who may be affected by these digital divides, something we know to be a global phenomenon [28]. Lack of experience, rather than age, is an essential factor that plays a role in this reality [29, 30]. Therefore, in this paper, we argue that technology can be a central tool in the autonomy of older individuals from intergenerational relationships, contrary to a large part of the scientific literature that essentially assesses digital skills and practises or ignores that technology is a variable to consider when studying population ageing and the quality of life of individuals, in particular from the European continent.

1.2 From Generations to an Intergenerational Perspective

Colombo and Fortunati [31] argue that media experiences occur within cultural environments. Therefore, [32] postulated that media environments could be considered "generational contexts", promoting a "generational identity" [33, 34] that also occurs from generational digital practises. However, "from a life course perspective, age is also a dynamic of its own, with different stages that have their specific characteristics, and that influence media behaviour in conjunction with other social circumstances that make up phases of life" [35]. In fact, technology encourages a 'digital global generation' [35] from a cross-generational connection perspective [36, 37].

Digital media are changing the nature of media consumption and connecting generations' preferences [38]. Even though television is still a hegemonic media for news consumption cross-generations [39–41], digital media uses and practices are contributing to bringing closer generations [42].

Generational contexts started to blur as the concept of "we sense" postulated by Corsten [34] is amplified by major societal transformations such as the Covid-19 pandemic. Appropriations of media and digital media started to be shared by different generations within the sense of belonging to explain social experiences [34]. Despite different experiences anchored to age and different backgrounds, during the confinements because of the Covid-19 pandemic, several generations started using digital to communicate and inform themselves about what was going on in the outside world. Intergenerational solidarity on ICT usage [14–16] gained greater expression when families were separated to avoid contagion between different generations, seeking to protect the older ones.

As Comunello et al. [43] argue that "the rhetoric embedded in the concept of so-called digital natives (Prensky 2001) depicts ICT devices as tools inherently fitting for younger people, in a context in which youth has become a (positive) symbolic value" [43]. The authors state that "generational semantics are produced by senior citizens to interpret their own relationship with ICT deals with the perception of both personal abilities and socially expected performances and might be shaped by their own perception of age and ageing" [43]. However, older people have experienced many societal and technological changes [44], and adults have followed technology since they were young in living with technology [42]. In addition, young adults and older people share a cross-generational use of social media, which means that "the repertoires of the past are interwoven with current ones" [45].

Patterns of media consumption-based on everyday life contexts and options are in a changing time, crossing generational consumptions. Nevertheless, television remains a strong media that increasingly divide time with new media repertoires, indicating fragmentation of online news consumption [46, 47]. The ways society encounters citizen participation are complex in changing times, and digital media is a way to engage citizens. This 'mediated engagement' directly results from media practices that enhance civic involvement [48]. Media practises in the digital era have generalised informed audiences, massive media use, and user engagement, which is a fallacy that promotes divides across generations. Therefore, intergenerational solidarity is essential to bridge the digital divide and promote family well-being as "ICTs contribute to household meta-work, such as schedule management, availability, and communication, as well as serving intangible needs of families, ranging from entertainment and networking to a sense of security." [15].

1.3 Intergenerational Solidarity in ICT Usage

Several studies show that older people use technologies to communicate and deepen relations with their family and friends [49–51], which improves their self-esteem and creates positive intergenerational relationships [16]. However, the social integration of older people is often pointed out as depending on family intergenerationality [52], considering different dimensions. Bengtson and Roberts [53] created a model of intergenerational solidarity based on social cohesion as a form of empowerment. This model presents six types of solidarity: associational solidarity - interaction patterns that promote integration and combat isolation; affectual solidarity - feelings of understanding, respect and trust; normative solidarity - emphasising family obligations; consensual solidarity - consensus regarding the sharing of life values and beliefs; and finally, structural solidarity - existence and availability of a structure that ensures physical proximity and the necessary support in this respect.

Bengtson and Roberts' model can be thought of in the context of using digital media to improve well-being and quality of life by promoting autonomy and empowerment practices that ensure active civic participation in its multiple dimensions. Following Taipale proposal [54], we argue that ICTs are connected with associational and functional patterns of solidarity across generations, promoting social bonding through social platforms and enhancing autonomy through intergenerational learning with digital technologies [55], fighting social isolation [56].

The study presented in this article took place during the pandemic period after two states of emergency were declared by the Portuguese government, which resulted in two months of confinement, the isolation of the older population being one of the main concerns of health authorities. The results link social support to combat digital inequality and promote autonomy from an intergenerational solidarity perspective.

2 Method

The article explores how mobile applications feature in the lives of young adults in Portugal and how their uses are associated with older family members. With a quantitative-extensive methodological strategy, it was applied to an online questionnaire survey with thematic questions. The respondents were a representative sample of Portuguese young adults (N = 1500) aged from 18 to 30 years.

The sample selected users of mobile applications, with quotas by gender and region (mainland Portugal and islands) according to the population distribution. The final sample is composed of 49.8% of people aged 18 to 24 and 50.2% of people aged 25 to 30. With regard to education, 53.1% of the respondents had higher education (Table 1). Among the questions focusing on intergenerationality, more than 40% of respondents answered that they help grandparents or relatives over 65 to post photos online (47.3%), carry out operations in finance (44.9%), participate actively in political issues (44.2%) or carry out operations in home banking (40%).

The survey was conducted by an external contracted company between 8 and 17 October 2021. The sampling guarantees a margin of error of ± 2.53% at the 95% confidence level. The data were analysed using the IBM SPSS statistical analysis program and using descriptive and inferential (bivariate) statistical analysis.

Table 1. Sample distribution

Heading level	Count N	Count %
Age		
18–24	747	49,80%
25–30	753	50,20%
Gender identity		
Man	696	46,40%
Woman	796	53,07%
Non-binary	6	0,40%
Agender, genderqueer or genderfluid	5	0,33%
In question	3	0,20%
Rather not answer	1	0,07%
Marital status		
Single	1145	76,33%
Married or in non-marital partnership	349	23,27%
Divorced or Separated	6	0,40%
Widower	0	0,00%
Other	0	0,00%
Education		
Basic education	48	3,20%
High school	655	43,67%
Bachelor's degree	516	34,40%
Master's degree	260	17,33%
PhD	21	1,40%
Occupation		
Student	425	28,33%
Self-employed	130	8,67%
Employee	759	50,60%
Liberal worker (Freelancer)	36	2,40%
Unemployed	150	10,00%

Source: Authors

3 Results and Discussion

Among the 1500 respondents, 1444 (96,3%) answered they use the internet to communicate with family members, without any statistical significance to highlight when analysing the results according to the variables of gender, age group, educational level or main occupation.

However, only 450 out of those 1444 (31,16%) answered they use the internet to communicate intergenerationally with grandparents or other relatives over 65 years old. There are significant statistical differences regarding the respondents who use the internet to communicate intergenerationally, when it comes to differences of age group, educational level and main occupation, according to Table 2. The respondents between 18 and 24 years old show a significant statistical higher percentage of internet usage to communicate intergenerationally, among the three possibilities of family members: grandfather (22,97%), grandmother (28,57%) and other relatives over 65 years old (17,23%). In fact, in total, the younger age group shows a higher frequency of internet usage to communicate with the total of the family members who are over 65 years old (36,41% in comparison to 26,03% of the respondents aged between 25 and 30 years old). There is also to highlight the differences concerning education, with a tendency for smaller overall frequencies as the level of education, gets higher. Almost half of the respondents with basic education (45,45%) who use the internet to communicate with family members, answered they use it to communicate with family members over 65 years old, while the percentage of respondents with a high school education who do so is 32,86% and even lower is the frequency between respondents with higher education levels (28,96%).

Table 2. Frequency of respondents who use the internet to communicate intergenerationally by age and education

	Age		Education		
	18–24 (A)	25–30 (B)	Basic education (C)	High school (D)	Higher education (E)
Grandfather	22,97% B	12,60%	27,27%	20,48%	14,94%
Grandmother	28,57% B	17,67%	34,09%	25,56%	20,39%
Other relatives over 65 years old	17,23% B	13,15%	20,45%	16,35%	13,90%
Total: over 65 years old	**36,41%**	**26,03%**	**45,45%**	**32,86%**	**28,96%**

Source: Authors

If the analysis spans over the main occupation variable of the respondents, there are significant statistical differences to highlight, according to Table 3. Students and unemployed respondents reveal significant statistical frequencies in comparison with respondents who are employed, in terms of using the internet to communicate with their grandfathers (24,14% between students and 25,35% between unemployed respondents in comparison to 12,62% of employed respondents). There is also a statistically significant difference between students (29,06%) and employed respondents when it comes to using the internet to communicate with their grandmothers. Between the aggregators of relatives with more than 65 years old, self-employed (38,71%), unemployed (37,32%) and students (35,71%) show higher tendencies to use the internet to communicate intergenerationally than employed (26,59%) and freelancer respondents (25,00%).

Table 3. Frequency of respondents who use the internet to communicate intergenerationally by main occupation

	Main occupation				
	Student (A)	Self-employed (B)	Employed (C)	Freelancer (D)	Unemployed (E)
Grandfather	24,14% C	17,89%	12,62%	19,44%	25,35% C
Grandmother	29,06% C	26,83%	19,40%	11,11%	24,65%
Other relatives over 65 years old	18,23%	14,63%	13,43%	5,56%	18,31%
Total: over 65 years old	**35,71%**	**38,21%**	**26,59%**	**25,00%**	**37,32%**

Source: Authors

The applied survey also intends to understand the educational level of the family members over 65 years old who are communicated with by the 450 respondents who answered they use the internet to communicate intergenerationally, i.e., with their grandparents or other relatives with more than 65 years old (Table 4). The analysis crosses such answers with the educational level of the respondents themselves.

70,00% of the respondents' family members over 65 years old have basic education; 43,78% have a high school level and 35,11% have a higher education degree. Only 0,44% of such respondents' family members have levels of education that the respondents are unaware of. Between all educational levels of respondents, the family members over 65 years old tend to only have basic education (with 95,00% of basic education respondents' family members, 69,57% of high school ones and 68,16% of higher education ones).

The results seem to point to a linear correspondence. The level of education of those family members over 65 years old tends to be matched by the same level of education of the young adults' respondents. Among the family members over 65 years old who have basic education, their corresponding respondents have a bigger percentage of levels of basic education (95,00%). The same applies to the over 65 years old family members with a high school level of education, whose corresponding respondents' most significant level of education is also high school (48,31%). It also applies to family members with higher education, whose corresponding respondents' most significant level of education is, as well, higher education (39,46%).

Table 4. Educational level of the family members over 65 years old who are communicated with by the scholarly level of the respondents

Family members over 65 years old	Total	Education		
		Basic education (C)	High school (D)	Higher education (E)
Basic education	**70,00%**	95,00%	69,57%	68,16%
High school	**43,78%**	45,00%	48,31%	39,46%
Higher education	**35,11%**	15,00%	32,37%	39,46%
Does not know/does not answer	**0,44%**	0,00%	0,48%	0,45%

Source: Authors

The survey included a Likert scale question measuring the frequency that respondents do a range of different activities with their relatives over 65 years old, through ICTs. The results are presented in Table 5. According to it, the most frequent activities are using social media to relate with relatives over 65 years old; sending messages through mobile apps; encouraging them to look for reliable information on the Internet; making audio calls with them via mobile apps such as WhatsApp or Messenger. In fact, the activity "encouraging them to look for reliable information on the Internet" is the one answer to be more done everyday by the respondents (17,56%). In a similar sense, concerning a frequency of "several times a week", respondents predominantly affirm they do send messages through mobile apps (31,56%).

On the other hand, there are three activities that seem to be the least frequent according to the Portuguese young adults, gathering more than 30% of "Never" answers. Exchanging emails stand out (38,22%) as a highly unpopular activity performed with relatives over 65 years old; while helping such relatives with home banking operations (35,11%) is also highly unpopular, with it being the activity less affirmed to be performed everyday (7,11%). The other activity that gathers more than 30% of "Never" answers by the respondents is "support them to participate in petitions" (34,22%).

Table 5. Frequency of activities done by the respondents with their grandparents or other relatives over 65 years old

	Frequency				
	Everyday	Several times a week	Once a week	Rarely	Never
Exchanging emails	10,22%	14,00%	12,00%	25,56%	38,22%
Using social media to relate with	16,22%	32,44%	21,11%	21,11%	9,11%
Making video calls with	14,67%	27,11%	26,00%	25,33%	6,89%
Sending messages through m-apps	17,11%	31,56%	26,89%	16,89%	7,56%
Helping them with homebanking	7,11%	17,56%	15,33%	24,89%	35,11%
Encouraging them to look for reliable information on the Internet	17,56%	26,44%	17,78%	21,78%	16,44%
Supporting them to do leisure activities on the Internet like watching videos or listening to music	14,67%	26,89%	20,00%	23,33%	15,11%
Helping them carry out online Finance operations	11,78%	13,78%	19,33%	25,33%	29,78%
Helping them publish photos online	9,11%	21,11%	17,11%	26,67%	26,00%
Support them to have access to health information and/or schedule appointments/exams…	16,67%	23,56%	20,00%	24,67%	15,11%
Making audio calls with them via mobile apps such as WhatsApp or Messenger	15,78%	30,67%	26,22%	19,78%	7,56%
Help them to read the news online	14,44%	22,89%	18,22%	25,33%	19,11%
Support them to participate in petitions	9,33%	14,89%	15,11%	26,44%	34,22%
Help them to actively participate in political issues	10,00%	16,00%	18,22%	26,22%	29,56%

(*continued*)

Table 5. (*continued*)

	Frequency				
	Everyday	Several times a week	Once a week	Rarely	Never
Help them to have access to information from State services about where they live	14,67%	15,56%	23,11%	25,56%	21,11%

Source: Authors

4 Conclusions

Between the 1500 surveyed Portuguese young adults (aged from 18 to 30 years old), 1444 (96,3%) use the internet to communicate with their family members, with 450 of those 1444 (31,16%) answering they communicate intergenerationally, i.e., with grandparents or other relatives over 65 years old. In point of fact, the younger age group (from 18 to 24 years old) shows a tendency to more frequent internet usage to communicate intergenerationally (36,41%) than the older age group of the sample (26,03%). Respondents with lower levels of education reveal that they use the internet more frequently to communicate with such family members (45,45% of the inquired sample with basic education). Even though the majority (70%) of the young adults' family members over 65 years old have basic education, results reveal also a fairly linear correspondence. The level of education of the respondents' family members over 65 years tends to find a parallel with the same level of education of the young adults inquired.

Young adults revealed their most frequent intergenerational activities with the use of the internet. Encouraging them to look for reliable information on the Internet is the most frequently done on a daily basis (17,56%). However, there are other tendencies to register in terms of higher frequencies, like helping such intergenerational relatives send messages through mobile apps, encouraging them to look for reliable information on the Internet, and even making audio calls with such family members via mobile apps like Whatsapp or Messenger. The main conclusion of this empirical study is that intergenerational solidarity is based on digital practices as a form of empowerment of older adults, namely concerning leisure and information seeking, as well as political activities.

Future research should also address older people's perspectives on intergenerational solidarity concerning digitally mediated relationships with younger generations.

Acknowledgements. Financial support from Portuguese national funds through FCT (Fundação para a Ciência e a Tecnologia) in the framework of the project "Mediated young adults' practices: advancing gender justice in and across mobile apps" (PTDC/COM-CSS/5947/2020).

References

1. PORDATA Homepage. https://www.pordata.pt/Portugal/Popula%C3%A7%C3%A3o+residente+total+e+por+grandes+grupos+et%C3%A1rios-513. Accessed 07 Dec 2021

2. Van Jaarsveld, G.M.: The effects of COVID-19 among the elderly population: a case for closing the digital divide. Front. Psychiatry **11**, 577427 (2020)
3. Chadwick, A.: The Hybrid Media System: Politics and Power. University Press, Oxford (2017)
4. Schrøder, K.C.: Audiences are inherently cross-media: audience studies and the cross-media challenge. CM Komunikacija i mediji **6**(18), 5–27 (2011)
5. Amaral, I.: Redes Sociais: Sociabilidades Emergentes. Editora LabCom.IFP, Covilhã (2016)
6. Gurevitch, M., Coleman, S., Blumler, J.G.: Political communication: old and new media relationships. Ann. Am. Acad. Pol. Soc. Sci. **625**(1), 164–181 (2009)
7. Silva, M.T.D., et al.: Audiências e cross-media: estudo de padrões de consumo de notícias em Portugal. Estudos em Comunicação **25**, 177–199 (2017)
8. Boyd, D.: É Complicado. As Vidas Sociais dos Adolescentes em Rede. Relógio DÁgua, Lisboa (2015)
9. Brites, M.J.: Jovens e culturas cívicas: Por entre formas de consumo noticioso e de participação. Labcom, IFP, Covilhã (2015)
10. Couldry, N., Markham, T.: Public connection through media consumption: between over-socialization and de-socialization? annaçs Am. Acad. Polit. Soc. Sci. **608**(1), 251–269 (2006)
11. Couldry, N., Livingstone, S., Markham, T.: Media Consumption and Public Engagement: Beyond the Presumption of Attention. Palgrave Macmillan, Londres (2007)
12. Helles, R., Ørmen, J., Radil, C., Jensen, K.B.: Media audiences—the media landscapes of European audiences. Int. J. Commun. **9**(21), 299–320 (2015)
13. Aroldi, P., Colombo, F.: Questioning 'digital global generations' A critical approach. North. Lights: Film Media Stud. Yearb.ook **11**(1), 175–190 (2013)
14. Dolničar, V., Hrast, M. F., Vehovar, V., Petrovčič, A.: Digital inequality and intergenerational solidarity: the role of social support in proxy internet use. AoIR Selected Papers of Internet Research (2013)
15. Taipale, S., Petrovcic, A., Dolnicar, V.: Intergenerational solidarity and ICT usage: empirical insights from Finnish and Slovenian families. Routledge Key Themes in Health and Society (2018)
16. Azevedo, C., Ponte, C.: Intergenerational solidarity or intergenerational gap? How elderly people experience ICT within their family context. Observatorio (OBS*) **14**(3), 16–35 (2020)
17. Amaral, I., Daniel, F.: The use of social media among senior citizens in portugal: active ageing through an intergeneration approach. In: Zhou, J., Salvendy, G. (eds.) ITAP 2018. LNCS, vol. 10926, pp. 422–434. Springer, Cham (2018). https://doi.org/10.1007/978-3-319-92034-4_32
18. WHO: Active Ageing - A Policy Framework, Geneva, Switzerland (2002)
19. Daniel, F., Antunes, A., Amaral, I.: Representações sociais da velhice. Análise. Psicológica **33**(3), 291–301 (2015)
20. Daniel, F., Caetano, E., Monteiro, R., Amaral, I.: Representações sociais do envelhecimento ativo num olhar genderizado. Análise Psicol. **34**(4), 353–364 (2016)
21. Paúl, C. A.: construção de um modelo de envelhecimento humano. In Paúl, C., Fonseca, A. (Orgs.), Envelhecer em Portugal, psicologia saúde e prestação de cuidados. Climepsi, Lisboa (2005)
22. Cabral, M. V., Ferreira, P. M., Silva, P. A., Jerónimo, P., Marques, T.: Processos de envelhecimento em Portugal: Usos do tempo, redes sociais e condições de vida. Fundação Francisco Manuel dos Santos, Lisboa (2013)
23. Amaral, I., Daniel, F., Abreu, S.G.: Policies for gender equality in Portugal: contributions to a framework for older women. Revista Prisma Soc. **22**, 346–363 (2018)
24. Daniel, F., Simões, T., Monteiro, R.: Representações sociais do «envelhecer no masculino» e do «envelhecer no feminino». Ex aequo **26**, 13–26 (2012)
25. Attewell, P.: Comment: the first and second digital divides. Sociol. Educ. **74**(3), 252–259 (2001)

26. Hargittai, E.: Second-level digital divide: mapping differences in people's online skills. arXiv preprint cs/0109068 (2001)
27. Van Deursen, A.J., Helsper, E.J.: The third-level digital divide: who benefits most from being online? In: Communication and Information Technologies Annual. Emerald Group Publishing Limited (2015)
28. Norris, P.: Digital Divide: Civic Engagement, Information Poverty, and the Internet Worldwide. Cambridge University Press, Cambridge (2001)
29. Loos, E.: Generational use of new media and the (ir)relevance of age. In: Colombo, F., Fortunati, L. (eds.) Broadband Society and Generational Changes, pp. 259–273. Peter Lang, Berlin (2011)
30. Loos, E., Bergstrom, J. R.: Older adults. In: Eye Tracking in User Experience Design, pp. 313–329 (2014)
31. Colombo, F., Fortunati, L.: Broadband Society and Generational Changes. Peter Lang, Frankfurt (2011)
32. Mannheim, K.: The problem of generation. In: Mannheim, K. (ed.) Essays on the Sociology of Knowledge, pp. 276–320. Routledge Kegan Paul, London (1952)
33. Aroldi, P.: Generational belonging between media audiences and ICT users in broadband society and generational changes. In: Colombo, F., Fortunati, L. (eds.), pp. 51–68. Peter Lang, Frankfurt (2011)
34. Corsten, M.: The time of generations. Time Soc. **8**(2.3), 249–272 (1999)
35. Aroldi, P., Colombo, F.: Generational belonging and mediascape in Europe. JSSE-J. Soc. Sci. Educ. **6**(1), 34–44 (2007)
36. Bolin, G.: Media Generations: Experience, Identity and Mediatised Social Change. Routledge, Abingdon (2016)
37. Bolin, G., Skogerbø, E.: Age, generation and the media. North. Lights **11**, 3–14 (2013)
38. Kõuts-Klemm, R., Brites, M.J.: How digital converges cross-media news typologies across countries: a comparative study of news consumption in Estonia and Portugal. Participations **14**(2), 464–483 (2017)
39. Brites, M.J.: Jovens e culturas cívicas: Por entre formas de consumo noticioso e de participação. Editora LabCom.IFP, Covilhã (2015)
40. Burnay, C., Ribeiro, N.: As novas dinâmicas do consumo audiovisual em Portugal. ERC–Entidade Reguladora para a Comunicação Social. Portugal (2016)
41. Pacheco, L., Torres da Silva, M., Brites, M.J., Henriques, S., Damásio, M.J.: Patterns of European youngsters' daily use of media. Observatorio **11**(4), 1–18 (2017)
42. Amaral, I., Brites, M. J.: Trends on the digital uses and generations. In: Proceedings of INTED2019 Conference, Valencia (2019)
43. Comunello, F., Fernández Ardèvol, M., Mulargia, S., Belotti, F.: Women, youth and everything else: age-based and gendered stereotypes in relation to digital technology among elderly Italian mobile phone users. Media Cult. Soc. **39**(6), 798–815 (2017)
44. Hagberg, J.E.: Being the oldest old in a shifting technology landscape. In: Haddon, L., Mante-Meijer, E., Loos, E. (eds.) Generational Use of New Media, pp. 107–124. Routledge, London (2016)
45. Napoli, A.: Social media use and generational identity: issues and consequences on peer-topeer and cross-generational relationships - an empirical study. Particip. J. Audience Recept. Stud. **11**(2), 182–206 (2014)
46. Newman, N., Fletcher, R., Kalogeropoulos, A., Levy, D., Nielsen, R.K.: Reuters Institute digital news report 2017. Available at SSRN 3026082 (2017)
47. Nielsen, R.K., Newman, N., Fletcher, R., Kalogeropoulos, A.: Reuters institute digital news report 2019. Report of the Reuters Institute for the Study of Journalism (2019)
48. Amaral, I.: Citizens beyond Troika: media and anti-austerity protests in Portugal. Int. J. Commun. **14**(21), 3309–3329 (2020). 1932-8036/20200005

49. Roberto, M.S., Fidalgo, A., Buckingham, D.: De que falamos quando falamos de infoexclusão e literacia digital? Perspetivas dos nativos digitais. Observatorio (OBS*) **9**(1) (2015)
50. Sinclair, T.J., Grieve, R.: Facebook as a source of social connectedness in older adults. Comput. Hum. Behav. **66**, 363–369 (2017)
51. Quinn, K.: Cognitive effects of social media use: a case of older adults. Soc. Media Soc. **4**(3), 1–9 (2018)
52. Silverstein, M., Bengtson, V.L.: Do close parent-child relations reduce the mortality risk of older parents? J. Health Soc. Behav. **32**(4), 382–395 (2009)
53. Bengtson, V. L., Roberts, R. E.: Intergenerational solidarity in aging families: an example of formal theory construction. J. Marriage Family **53**, 856–870 (1991)
54. Taipale, S.: Intergenerational solidarity. In: Taipale, S. (ed.) Intergenerational Connections in Digital Families, pp 103–114 (2019). Springer, Cham. https://doi.org/10.1007/978-3-030-11947-8_8
55. Patrício, M. R., Osório, A.: Intergenerational learning with ICT: a case study (2016)
56. Lee, O.E.K., Kim, D.H.: Bridging the digital divide for older adults via intergenerational mentor-up. Res. Soc. Work. Pract. **29**(7), 786–795 (2019)

Cognitive Difference of Generations in the 1970s and 1990s Towards Ancestor Worship Culture

Chia-Ling Chang(✉)

Department of Education Industry and Digital Media, National Taitung University, Taitung, Taiwan, ROC

idit007@gmail.com

Abstract. Ancestor worship is an important Chinese culture and custom, and it symbolizes the inheritance of tradition and filial piety. However, with the development of the economy and technology, social demographic structure changes which influences the family structure. The spirit and form of the ancestor worship culture thus become different. Therefore, this study aimed to explore different values and cognition of the generations of the 1970s and 1990s towards ancestor worship culture. Through a questionnaire survey, this study analyzed the cognition of the generations of the 1970s and 1990s towards meaning, festival, place, items, rituals, and taboos of ancestor worship culture in different financial situations, environments of growth, and families. There were 153 valid questionnaires, including 89 subjects in the generation of 1970s and 64 subjects in the generation of the 1990s. It adopted the independent sample t-test analysis and explored the cognitive difference of two generations towards ancestor worship culture. According to research findings, the generation of the 1970s paid attention to the spirit and the meaning of ancestor worship culture, items of ancestor worship, worship places, and ancestors' tablets and they recognized the meanings of the objects. With the accessibility of online information, they were willing to obtain knowledge related to ancestor worship through online learning. Cognition of the generation of the 1990s towards ancestor worship culture was insignificant. They thought that ancestor worship was not the responsibility of the elderly and they showed low intention to learn the details of ancestor worship. They agreed that online ancestor worship can still show gratitude towards ancestors to replace traditional ancestor worship. The cognition analysis of the two generations towards ancestor worship culture can serve as the reference for digital ancestor worship culture in the future. It not only extends the development of Chinese ancestor worship culture but also meets the trend of the time.

Keywords: Ancestor worship culture · The 1970s and 1990s · Cultural cognition

1 Research Motives

Ancestor worship is an important Chinese culture and custom, and it has lasted for several thousand years. However, with the development of the economy and technology, it changes social demographic structure which influences family structure. Regarding

Q. Gao and J. Zhou (Eds.): HCII 2022, LNCS 13331, pp. 349–359, 2022.
https://doi.org/10.1007/978-3-031-05654-3_24

ancestor worship, young people of the 1990s mostly listen to the instruction of the parents of the 1970s and the elderly. They are, in fact, unfamiliar with the significance and process of traditional ancestor worship. In addition, values and environment of growth influence the cognition of two generations towards social culture. In terms of economy, the generation of the 1970s has experienced two times of oil crisis in the global depression. The generation of the 1990s encountered Asian Financial Crisis. Although they both experienced financial crises, the environments were different. In the environment of growth, those who were born in the 1970s were the first generation who grew in the time with multiple values. The generation of 1990s grew in the era of computer and internet and there were more methods to obtain information. They were familiar with foreign cultures and the pursuit of novelty.

This study aimed to explore two aspects: (1) Significance, process, and related rituals and customs of ancestor worship culture. (2) Effect of values and environments of growth of generations of the 1970s and 1990s on ancestor worship culture and cognition. Through literature, it approached the significance and related rituals and customs of Chinese ancestor worship culture and the values of life of the generations of the 1970s and 1990s. By questionnaire survey, it probed into the cognition of generations of the 1970s and 1990s towards ancestor worship culture.

2 Literature Review

2.1 Difference Between the 1970s and 1990s

The 1970s means 1971–1980 and those who were born in the time are called the generation of the 1970s. The 1990s means 1991–2000 and those who were born in the time are called the generation of the 1990s. Different generations show different backgrounds of growth and financial changes. With different environments of growth, different generations reveal different values, preferences, attitudes, and behaviors. The family structure thus changed [1–3]. Thus, this study explored the difference between two generations by the economy, environments of growth, and family pattern and structure.

In terms of the economy, between 1973 and 1975, the oil crisis broke out, and there was a global depression. Production costs in Taiwan increased, and exports were reduced. Taiwan withdrew from the UN, and it resulted in a low intention of investment. In the 1970s, although the global economy declined, in 1974, the government implemented Ten Major Construction Projects and Taiwan became Four Asian Tigers and created economic miracles [4]. In the 1990s, the global work division resulted in high environmental protection conditions and high public service expenditure, and Taiwan was no longer the paradise of export processing. As wages in China and the countries in Southeast Asia were low, factories were transferred to low-cost countries. At this time, Taiwan encountered the transition from the manufacturing industry to the service industry. The economic growth rate was low, and the unemployment rate was high [5].

In terms of environments of growth, after the 1970s, Taiwan had lifted martial law and the development of TV stations and newspapers was diverse. The children born in the time grew in the era with multiple values [6]. The reform of politics and economy had been accomplished in the previous generation. Authority declined successively. The generation of the 1990s experienced the stage when Taiwan declined from the economic miracle. SARS in 2003 and financial crisis in 2008 caused thc industrial recession, such as low wages and high unemployment rate [7, 8]. However, with the growth of the internet and the introduction of high-tech products and smartphones, the generation of the 1990s experienced the accessibility of information. There were various channels to obtain information in their lives.

In terms of family structure, in the 1970s, most of the parents lived with their married sons. At the time, the percentage of traditional extended families was less than that of three generations under one roof. In the 1970s, Taiwan was based on families with three generations under one roof (stem families) and three generations of lineal relatives included grandparents, parents, and unmarried children [9]. In the 1990s, with the change of economic structure, family structure was different. The percentage of extended families or three generations under one roof was lowered. Small families (nuclear families) consisting of parents and unmarried children became mainstream [10].

2.2 Study Related to Ancestor Worship Culture

Ancestor worship culture was originated from a primitive society, and it symbolized the extension of family culture. The fear and respect for ancestors became self-regulation and it showed filial piety. Humans' lives are associated with ancestors. In terms of traditional customs, ancestor worship rituals are practiced from birth to death, in annual ceremonies and the phases of growth, marriage, and birth giving [11–14].

The significance of traditional ancestor worship customs in Taiwan should be recognized and there are some aspects for further reflection to respond to the modern environment and trend. Folk ancestor worship includes four meanings: (1) life: in tradition, ancestor worship symbolizes the extension of ancestors' lives and connection with ancestors and it shows the inheritance. (2) Culture: ancestor worship is traditional Confucian filial piety. (3) Family: ancestor worship shows significant family ideology. It shows the family cohesion and unity of clan relatives. (4) Religion: ancestor worship significantly shows "worship to the spirit". People worry that their ancestors become hungry and lonely souls which influences the family situations and safety of members. Thus, it is necessary to worship ancestors.

Generally speaking, the Taiwanese people's worship includes the following: (1) bare-handed worship: they only worship with hands put together in front of the spirit without joss candles and gold and silver money. (2) Worship by burning spirit money: they worship the spirit by joss candles and gold and silver money. (3) Worship by flesh offering: worship with flesh offering is solemn and it is generally held in festivals, on gods' birthdays, or for god rewarding with regular rituals [15].

As to the festivals of ancestor worship, Chi (2019) [16] generalized common festivals of ancestor worship in modern Taiwan: Spring Festival, Thc Lantern Festival, Qingming Festival, Dragon Boat Festival, Ghost Festival, Moon Festival, Double Ninth Festival, Winter Solstice, and New Year's Eve. This study compared Chi (2019) [16] and Essence of Worship of Block Studio (2018) [17] and reorganized festivals, time, and worship offerings of traditional ancestor worship in Taiwan, as shown in Table 1:

Table 1. Festivals and offerings of traditional ancestor worship in Taiwan

Festivals	Time	Worship items and offering
Spring festival	The first day of the first lunar month	Three kinds of flesh offerings, a pair of fresh flowers, three cups of alcohol, a plate of candy, twelve bowls of dish, chopsticks, and incense sticks
The lantern festival	The fifteenth day of the first lunar month	Three kinds of flesh offerings, three kinds of fruit, three cups of alcohol, six bowls of dish, chopsticks, and incense sticks
Qingming festival	The fourth or fifth day of the fourth month in the solar calendar	Three kinds of flesh offerings, five kinds of fruit, three cups of alcohol, several cakes, a pair of fresh flowers, a pair of candles, a package of five colored paper, one sickle, several ducks' eggs, chopsticks, incense sticks, and a pair of firecrackers
Dragon boat festival	The fifth day of the fifth lunar month	Three kinds of flesh offerings, three kinds of fruit, three cups of alcohol, six bowls of dish, several rice dumplings, chopsticks, and incense sticks
Ghost festival	The fifteenth day of the seventh lunar month	Three kinds of flesh offerings, three kinds of fruit, three cups of alcohol, six bowls of dish, chopsticks, and incense sticks
Moon festival	The fifteenth day of the eighth lunar month	Three kinds of flesh offerings, three kinds of fruit, three cups of alcohol, six bowls of dish, chopsticks, and incense sticks
Double ninth festival	The ninth day of the ninth lunar month	Three kinds of flesh offerings, three kinds of fruit, three cups of alcohol, chopsticks, and incense sticks
Winter solstice	The twenty-first day of the twelfth month in the solar calendar	Three kinds of flesh offerings, three kinds of fruit, three cups of alcohol, six bowls of dish, a pot of rice, three bowls of stuffed dumpling, several steamed sponge cakes, chopsticks, and incense sticks
New year's eve	The thirtieth day of the twelfth lunar month	Three kinds of flesh offerings, three kinds of fruit, three cups of alcohol, six to twelve bowls of dishes, chopsticks, incense sticks

As to worship items and offering of sacrifice, Chi (2019) [16] and Lee (2015) [18] classified "items" into five colored paper, a pair of candles, incense sticks, cups, incense burner, golden vessels, spring flowers, towel, washbasin, and rice cups; "offerings" are eatable and they include three kinds of flesh offerings and alcohol, dishes, cooked rice, sweets, rice food, cookies, fruits, thin noodles, and fresh flowers.

As to "worship places", Cheng (2013) [12] argued that worship in Taiwan includes family worship, tomb worship, and shrine worship. With the change of time, worship places successively become the worship hall, Columbarium Pagoda, grave, and shrine of home. (1) The worship hall: family worship is a personal one. People place statues and ancestors' tablets in the main hall of the house to represent the gods and spirit. (2) Columbarium Pagoda: interment was common in early times. With the growth of population, lack of graveyards, and simplified process, cremation increases successively. Bone ash and corpses are placed in Columbarium Pagoda. (3) Grave: it means to worship ancestors on the grave and the subjects include close and distant ancestors [18]. (4) Shrine of home: it is an independent worship space.

Taiwanese people are careful about "worship taboos" which are derived from legends, long-term experience, and religion. Acceptable taboos can be followed continuously to preserve the culture. Outdated or suspicious taboos should be corrected [18–20]. Common taboos are shown below: (1) general worship taboos: according to folk saying, cleaning by the right hand is inappropriate. Thus, it is a taboo to put incense sticks by the right hand when worshipping ancestors. (2) Guava, tomato, strawberry, and wax apple are not allowed as offerings: guava, tomato, and strawberry, the fruits can be eaten with seeds are considered disrespectful for gods. In addition, "Lian" of wax apple refers to "connection" and the meaning of "Wu" refers to Yin. (3) Taboos of specific festivals (such as Ghost Festival): banana, pineapple, plum, and pear are not allowed. In Taiwanese, "Jiao" is the homophone of "invite", "Lee" is the homophone of "you", and "Lee" is the homophone of "come". It suggests the invitation of spirit.

Based on the above, it shows the different backgrounds of the generations of the 1970s and 1990s. As to the economy, the era of the 1970s, in comparison to the 1990s, was vigorous. However, the generation of the 1990s encountered economic declination. Industrial development turned from the manufacturing industry to the service industry. In terms of environments of growth, although the era of the 1970s was based on the society of information freedom and diversity of media, in comparison to the 1990s with the vigorous development of the internet, the prevalence of learning channels and convenience were different. As to family pattern and structure, the families of the 1970s were mostly three generations under the roof. For the generation of the 1990s, they were mostly small families. In Taiwan, folk religion was the most. Ancestor worship refers to an extension of tradition and filial piety. In different worship festivals, Taiwanese people show their respect and fear towards their ancestors.

3 Research Method and Procedures

This study intended to explore the cognition of the generations of the 1970s and 1990s towards ancestor worship culture and the related factors. By literature, it proposed related variables.

This study treated the generations of the 1970s and 1990s living in Taiwan as the population. The research tool was a questionnaire in Likert 5-point scale. In order to enhance the precision and propriety of wording in the questionnaire, it invited Chairman of Taitung County Religious Sacrifice and Etiquette Product Service Association, to provide suggestions on the ancestor worship content of the questionnaire. After the accomplishment of the draft, this study conducted a pretest questionnaire on respectively four subjects in the generations of 1970s and 1990s to recognize the wording. After revision, it developed the formal questionnaire, including three parts:

1. Personal backgrounds: There are eight dimensions, including gender, year of birth, area, religion, family pattern, ancestor worship habit, economy, and living environment. Religion and ancestor worship habits are based on the subjects' religion. Different generations show different family patterns, economies, and living environments. The subjects' families are divided into the extended family, three generations under the roof, and small families.
2. Cognition of ancestor worship culture: There are six dimensions, including the meaning of ancestor worship, worship festivals, worship places, worship items, worship rituals, and worship taboos, with 33 items.
3. Cognition of financial and living environments: There are two dimensions, including economy and living environment, with 12 items.

The test of a formal online Google questionnaire lasted from November 16 to December 1, 2020. At the beginning of the questionnaire, it explained the research purposes and instruction of responses and emphasized on the confidentiality of data. After the subjects finished responding to the questions, the questionnaires would be sent immediately for the screening. The encoded valid questionnaires were further included in data statistics and archives. By average analysis, it compared the difference between the two groups.

4 Research Results and Analysis

This study retrieved 163 questionnaires. After deleting invalid questionnaires, it obtained 153 valid ones, and the return rate was 93.8%. There were 89 subjects in the generation of the 1970s and 64 subjects in the generation of the 1990s. As to reliability, the Cronbach's α tested the reliability of the items of the questionnaire. All items met $0.908 >$ common reliability standard 0.7. Thus, the items of the questionnaire were reliable.

4.1 Analysis of Personal Backgrounds

The personal backgrounds asked in the questionnaire include the subjects' fear of birth, gender, area, family pattern, and ancestor worship habit. The overall subjects' personal backgrounds are listed in Table 2.

Table 2. Subjects' personal background

	Type	1970s' percentage	1990s' percentage
Gender	Male	37%	28%
	Female	63%	72%
Area	Northern	65%	47%
	Central	31%	33%
	East	2%	14%
	South	1%	6%
Family pattern	Extended family	6%	9%
	Three generations under one roof	20%	20%
	Small family	73%	70%
	Other	1%	0%
Ancestor worship place	Grave	17%	20%
	Columbarium Pagoda	25%	29%
	Ancestral hall	10%	6%
	House of gods	42%	36%
	Other	6%	4%
	None	0%	6%
*The total cost of ancestor worship[a]	Below 500	3%	9%
	501–1000	31%	50%
	1001–1500	29%	13%
	More than 1501	28%	20%
	None	8%	8%
Internet hours/day	0–4 h	29%	5%
	5–8 h	28%	34%
	9–12 h	22%	33%
	More than 12 h	10%	28%

[a]Unit: New Taiwan Dollar (NTD).

4.2 Analysis of Ancestor Worship Culture

This study explored the cognition of the generations of the 1970s and 1990s towards ancestor worship culture (including the meaning of ancestor worship, worship festivals, worship places, worship items, worship rituals, and worship taboos) and the cognitive difference towards the economy and living environment. It conducted an analysis by the independent sample t-test. According to the two-tailed significance of $P < 0.05$, two generations showed a significant difference in ancestor worship culture. Due to the limitation of space, the analytical results are summarized below.

1. The meaning of ancestor worship: In comparison to the generation of the 1990s, that of the 1970s recognized the meaning of ancestor worship which referred to the inheritance of family culture. It enhanced family cohesion and showed filial piety.
2. Worship festivals: In comparison to the generation of the 1990s, that of the 1970s was more familiar with the types of spirit money for related and different ancestor worship festivals. For instance, spirit money for Qingming Festival includes Jiu Jin (九金) (little Fu money), Jiu Yin (九銀) (little silver money), Jin Yi (巾衣), and Bei Qian (白錢); spirit money for Ghost Festival includes Jiu Yin (little silver money), Jin Yi, and Bei Qian.
3. Worship places: in comparison to the generation of the 1990s, that of the 1970s paid more attention to worship places for ancestors and they recognized the importance to place ancestors' tablets at home. However, the two generations did not show a significant difference on two items "cremation would cause the declination of ancestor worship culture" and "ancestor worship in front of the tombs is sincerer". Thus, their views were consistent.
4. Worship items: in comparison to the generation of the 1990s, that of the 1970s was more familiar with the items and offerings for ancestor worship. The items include candles, incense sticks, cups, incense burner, towel, and washbasin. The offerings include flesh offerings, dishes, cooked rice, sweets, rice, cookies, fruits, thin noodles, and fresh flowers. Besides, the generation of 1970s was familiar that the ritual of five colored paper and five flavor bowls mean the dishes eaten by the ancestors when they were alive and they recognized the usage of longevity peach pile and three kinds of flesh offerings and alcohol.
5. Worship rituals: in comparison to the generation of the 1990s, that of the 1970s significantly agreed that by ancestor worship rituals, they could approach ancestors and knew that three kinds of flesh offerings and alcohol are the offerings for worship. Five flavor bowls refer to sour, bitter, sweet, spicy, and salty. However, in the following items, two generations shared consistent views: "I know that worship by bare hands means to put hands together in front of the spirit", "I know that worship by burning spirit money means to bring joss candles and gold and silver money to worship the spirit", "ancestor worship rituals can be simplified" and "sincerity of ancestor worship is more important than rituals". It shows that two generations valued the original rituals of ancestor worship.
6. Worship taboos: in comparison to the generation of the 1990s, that of the 1970s knew the fruits which are not allowed in worship and the reasons. For instance, they knew that pineapples and bananas cannot be used in Qingming Festival and Ghost Festival and it is due to the homonyms of Taiwanese. However, two groups showed a consistent view on "we should follow worship taboos" and "in ancestor worship, we cannot put incense sticks by right hands".

4.3 Analysis of Financial and Living Environments

The generation of the 1970s experienced two times of oil crisis, meanwhile, that of the 1990s encountered Asian Financial Crisis. As to the study on the effect of the economy on the cognition towards ancestor worship, two generations did not show a significant difference on the items of the economy: (1) Different economic backgrounds result in differences of thoughts and cognition between the generations. (2) Financial situation would influence the frequency of ancestor worship. (3) I worship ancestors with less expenditure. (4) It is sincerer to prepare abundant dishes or offerings in ancestor worship.

As to the effect of living environment on cognition towards ancestor worship, the generation of 1970s mostly was based on the family structure of three generations under the roof. When they were born, martial law was lifted. TV stations and newspapers were developing. They were the first generation in the era of multiple values. The generation of the 1990s was mostly small families. They grew up at the developing phase of the internet and they successively obtained information online. According to statistical analysis, the generation of 1990s suggested that ancestor worship is not only the responsibility of the elderly. It is associated with them. Besides, they agreed that online ancestor worship can replace traditional ancestor worship. However, with the prevalence of the internet in modern times, the generation of the 1970s was willing to learn ancestor worship culture online.

5 Discussion

Ancestor worship culture is not simply worship. It refers to gratitude to the ancestors and family cohesion. It shows family cultural heritage. According to previous findings, the generations of the 1970s and 1990s showed consistent views towards general spirit and significance of worship. However, in terms of the details of ancestor worship, the group of 1970s, in comparison to the generation of 1990s, showed significant familiarity. For instance, they should prepare different items and offerings for different ancestor worship festivals. There was ancestor worship spirit money for related rituals and worship taboos. In other words, although the generation of 1990s valued ancestor worship culture, they were less familiar with the details of ancestor worship. The reason can be in that the generation of 1990s had worshipped the ancestors with their parents since childhood and the parents of 1970s were responsible for the items and offerings. Thus, they were not familiar and did not actively learn the knowledge of the details.

Nevertheless, the generation of 1990s agreed that they should be responsible for ancestor worship and they did not think that it was the responsibility of the elderly. In comparison to the generation of the 1970s, they agreed that online ancestor worship can replace traditional ancestor worship. The reason can be that the generation grew up in the era of the internet and their lives were associated with the network. Thus, in comparison to the generation of the 1970s, that of the 1990s significantly agreed that ancestor worship could be practiced online by clicking the mouse. They did not have to be familiar with the complicated process and preparation of offerings and they could still be grateful to their ancestors. In order to preserve Chinese ancestor worship culture, this study suggested reviewing and integrating reliable data of ancestor worship with the experts and updating and promoting knowledge of ancestor worship culture in Taiwan. Thus, they enhance the interaction and instruction of online ancestor worship and the operation can be different according to different ages. In preschools and elementary schools, they introduce digital methods to learn ancestor worship culture. For instance, they can introduce ancestor worship festivals through animation, games, and interaction to avoid the stereotype of ancestor worship culture. The interesting instruction not only enhances the students' image of ancestor worship culture but also triggers their curiosity and learning. This study suggested combining ancestor worship culture and entertainment and creating board games by stories and games. Through playing the games, students can recognize the knowledge and rituals of ancestor worship. By simple and repetitive songs, the children can obtain knowledge. Thus, they learn about ancestor worship culture since childhood to show their gratitude towards ancestor worship culture.

6 Conclusion and Suggestions

This study conducted a questionnaire survey on Chinese ancestor worship culture by the economy and living environment to explore the views and cognition of the generations of the 1970s and 1990s towards ancestor worship culture. It referred to modern university students and their parents. By literature review and analysis of 153 valid questionnaires, this study proposed the conclusion below:

1. Generally speaking, the generations of the 1970s and 1990s showed consistent views towards the general spirit and significance of worship. The generation of the 1990s agreed that they should be responsible for ancestor worship, and it is not simply the responsibility of the elderly.
2. As to the details of ancestor worship, the generation of the 1970s, in comparison to that of the 1990s, showed the familiarity, particularly the ancestor worship festivals, items, offerings, and the meanings of related worship taboos.
3. The generation of 1970s experienced two times of oil crisis, whereas that of 1990s encountered Asian Financial Crisis. As to the effect of the economy on ancestor worship, the two generations did not show a significant difference.
4. The generation of the 1990s grew up in the era of the internet. Although the young generation recognized the importance of ancestor worship culture, they were not familiar with the details of ancestor worship, and they were not motivated to learn and preserve it. They even agreed that online ancestor worship can replace traditional ancestor worship. With the convenience of the internet, the generation of the 1970s was willing to learn more knowledge of ancestor worship culture online.

This study adopted a questionnaire survey, and the subjects were from the generations of the 1970s and 1990s. The selection of the generations was based on the time of the researcher and the parents. It attempted to find if the cognition between parents and children towards ancestor worship culture showed a significant difference. It is suggested that future researchers can increase the interval of the subjects' generations, such as the 1950s and 1990s. They can enhance the questionnaire survey by in-depth interviews to approach the results of differences between the generations towards ancestor worship culture in order to strengthen the diversity of research findings.

The questionnaire survey of this study only explored the effect of different economies and living environments of the generations on ancestor worship and neglected the effect of education. It did not show the possible effect of the subjects' education on the cognition towards ancestor worship. Thus, future researchers can include education which can be divided into family and school to recognize more factors on the difference of the generations.

Acknowledgement. This study received partly financial support from the Ministry of Science and Technology, under Grant No. MOST 109-2813-C-143-028-H.

References

1. Kuo, H.P.: Effects of filial piety on living arrangement between baby boomer and X-generation. Chang Jung Christian University, Tainan (2010)
2. Chiang, M.C.: The Effect of Generational Differences on Monetary Attitude, Work Values, and Team Commitment - A Case Study of Practitioners. Lungh Wa University of Science and Technology, Taoyuan City (2018)
3. Tseng, Y.C.: On the problem of community care for the elderly from the influence of family structure and function changes. Commun. Dev. J. (Q.) **106**, 150–158 (2004)
4. Hsiung, C.C., Wu, W.H., Huang, Y.J.: The influence of the time on the choice of job- example of two generations. Wham Poa Interdisc. J. **72**, 15–25 (2017)
5. Lin, W.I.: The Wealth Gap and Social Security in Taiwan. Reflections and Dialogues of Intellectuals. Yu Chi-Chung Cultural and Educational Foundation, Taipei, pp. 238–259 (2008)
6. Hsu, T.H.: The Antecedents and Consequences of Work Values on Work Attitude for the Different Generations - A Study of High Technology Industries in Taiwan. Chung Yuan Christian University, Taoyuan City (2003)
7. Wu, K.S.: The Rise of Internet and concepts of war and security: changes and Continuities. Soochow University, Taipei (2012)
8. Ye, Y.J.: Open the history of 4 generations of Taiwanese workplaces. Cheers, Taipei, p. 153 (2013)
9. Chang, Y.H.: Household compositions and the attitude of support for parents in a changing society: the case of Taiwan. Natl. Taiwan Univ. J. Sociol. **23**, 1–34 (1994)
10. Lin, Y.C.: A preliminary study on parenting education under social changes. J. Internet Sociol. Commun. **52** (2006)
11. Peng, W.Y.: Fujian and Taiwan Family Society. Youth Cultural, Taipei (1998)
12. Jeng, C.R.: Research on Paper Money and Han Family Sacrifices. Fo Guang University, Yilan County (2013)
13. Fan Jiang, Q.Q.: Inheritance and Change of Hakka Culture: Using Ancestor Worship as an Example. National Central University, Taoyung (2017)
14. Yeh, W.F.: Research on the Folk Custom of Taiwanese Ancestry Worship – Based on the Population Whose Family Names are "Chen" and "Lin" in North Taiwan. National Taipei University, Taipei (2007)
15. Lin, W.Y.: On the first day of the Chinese new year, prepare flowers and fruits and pay homage to the Virgin Mary. https://blog.xuite.net/mm8888mmm/twblog/122518994, Accessed 5 Aug 2020
16. Chi, J.Y.: A Design of Taiwanese Familes' Religious Worship Culture Board Game. National Taichung University of Education, Taichung (2019)
17. Pài-Pài. https://paipai.blog/. Accessed 8 Aug 2020
18. Lee, H.O.: Illustration for Taiwan Folk Festival. Morning Star, Taichung (2015)
19. Chien, D.X.: On the Taboos of Etiquette and Customs in Taiwan and Penghu Areas—Taiwanese Taboos. Fu Wen Bools Co. Ltd., Kaohsiung (2005)
20. Lin, W.P.: The Comparison of Religious Beliefs and Folk Taboos between Taiwan and Japan. I-Shou University, Kaohsiung (2009)

Prototype Development of an Interpretative Game with Location-Based AR for Ecomuseum

Chun-Wen Chen(✉) and Ya Hsin Chen

Taipei National University of the Arts, No. 1 Hsueh-Yuan Rd., Peitou District, Taipei 11201, Taiwan
junbun@ahe.tnua.edu.tw

Abstract. To improve the visiting effect of ecomuseum, this research proposes to utilize augmented reality (AR) technology and to study how to integrate appropriate interaction design can help get better experience in such museums. Augmented reality is a technology attaching computer generated images and information on the real world. AR users can see the original real world, and also can see supporting information images or virtual objects, that help provide related information and interaction of the real world and objects.

With a perspective of interaction design, this research considers the form of an interpretative game with location-based AR to combine the benefits of field interpretation and game tasks. We took Beitou area in Taipei city as the sample of ecomuseum, to develop the contents of the game. Prototypes with location-based Web AR were made and tested. Field user tests were conducted to understand the issues and satisfaction of interaction design. Qualitative data were collected and analyzed.

Issues about learnability, satisfaction, storytelling, user interface, and technology are discussed. Then a more suitable design guideline could be concluded to improve the formal model of interpretative game for ecomuseum.

Keywords: Location-based augmented reality · Interaction design · Interpretive media · Game-based learning · Ecomuseum

1 Introduction

Ecomuseum is a kind of museum in concept. The concept is to utilize real sites or objects of culture, history or nature as subjects for visiting. Because the subjects are not located in indoor venues, it is an important issue about how to process an appropriate exhibit interpretation.

This research proposes to utilize augmented reality (AR) technology and to study how to integrate appropriate interaction design can help get better experience in such ecomuseums. Augmented reality is a technology attaching computer generated images and information on the real world. It is different from virtual reality (VR) for the fully immersion in the virtual world. AR users can see the original real world, and also can see supporting information images or virtual objects, that help provide related information and interaction of the real world and objects. With a perspective of interaction design,

Q. Gao and J. Zhou (Eds.): HCII 2022, LNCS 13331, pp. 360–370, 2022.
https://doi.org/10.1007/978-3-031-05654-3_25

this research considers the form of an interpretative game with location-based AR to combine the benefits of field interpretation and game tasks.

This research took Beitou area in Taipei city as the sample of ecomuseum, to develop the contents of the game. We developed a prototype of interpretative game for ecomuseums with location-based AR technology. We tested the prototypes on the real site with fewer participants. Guidelines are concluded to make the final model of the on-site interpretative game.

2 Literature Review

2.1 Interaction Design of Location-Based AR

Location-based service is a kind of information service systems combined with GPS and cellular communication technologies to provide digital map, navigation, location-based reminder, location-based personal AD, automatic weather forecast, etc. Location-based games are becoming a popular genre of mobile games with location-based service. For example, Pokémon GO is one of the most popular location-based game in recent years. Players could see virtual objects or roles near themselves on the game map by their real-world positions, and they could interact with such objects. In the stage of monster chasing, it is also possible to activate the AR effect to see the realistic scene with virtual monsters' appearance at a real place.

Augmented Reality (AR) is a kind of technology with computer-generated image attached to the real world. It is very different from Virtual Reality (VR) that is fully emerged in the virtual world. The most scenes or backgrounds that AR users see are parts of the real physical world. In an AR environment, they can also see informative images or virtual objects providing assistive information and interactive mechanism of the real environment and objects [8]. Azuma [1] proposed AR as systems with the three characteristics: (1) Combines real and virtual, (2) Interactive in real time, (3) Registered in 3-D, to avoid limiting AR to specific technologies, such as head-mounted displays or other devices. He thought AR is a specific example of what Brooks [4] calls Intelligence Amplification that is defined as using the computer as a tool to make a task easier for a human to perform.

By the classification of Milgram & Kishino [9], the possibility of spatial com-position from real environment to virtual environment is named as *Reality-Virtuality Continuum* (see Fig. 1). In the continuum, the left is fully real environment and the right is fully virtual environment. Between the two ends there are kinds of Mixed Reality (MR) with combinations of different ratios of real and virtual environments. Real environment with some virtual objects is named as Augmented Reality (AR), and virtual environment with some real objects is named as Augmented Virtuality (AV).

The AR combined with location-based service is Location-based AR. It uses the user location and geographic information system to attach the virtual objects and information to the real environment. The location of the user can be measured with GPS, accelerometer, compass or other sensors. Because the virtual objects can be attached to the locations of real sites, it is easy to connect the real world and its related information with visual means. For the assistive information provided in real time, AR is a suitable technology for site interpretation or vehicle navigation.

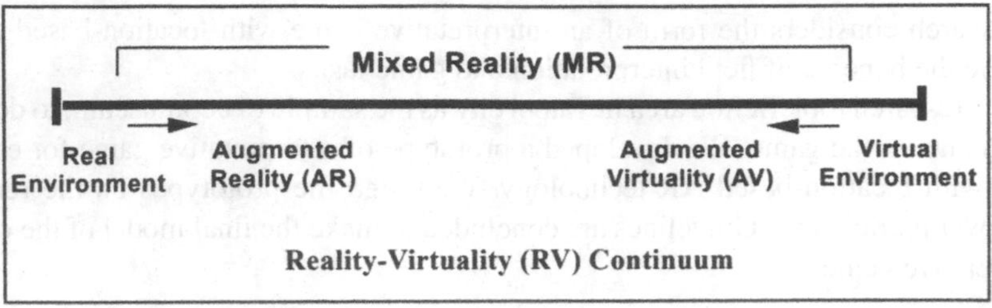

Fig. 1. Reality-virtuality (RV) continuum (Source: Milgram and Kishino 1994).

Haahr [5] compared several kinds of location-based games, and found that some games like Pokémon GO emphasized the *immersion* of the challenges. It is very different from the *presence* of traditional cultural interpretation. The players may focus on the challenges of the game, but not on the experience of cultural resources. Therefore, Haahr [5] suggested more connections to physical space and more interactions of virtual objects related to the site in such cultural location-based games.

The interaction in AR is most about to interact with virtual objects to acquire information or action instruction, and to have fun in interaction itself. Virtual objects mostly show in the space, and can be triggered to activate reactive methods and feedbacks. The interactive mode of virtual objects in AR matches the microinteraction defined by Shaffer [11]. The structure of design and analysis can be classified as four parts including trigger, rules, feedback, and loops & modes. Trigger initiates the interaction; rules decide how to react; feedback provides perceptible clues that users can confirm; and loops & modes guide how to end the interaction and return to initial status and mode. The triggers include manual trigger and system trigger. Manual trigger happens by users' intension. System trigger happens while a specific system event appears. Various system events can be used as system trigger, especially location-related ones, which are useful for this research.

2.2 Interpretation

Interpretation is multiple methods and media of demonstration and explanation for visitors to understand the themes and contents of exhibits. Tilden [14] provided a definition of *interpretation* as follows:

> *An educational activity which aims to reveal meanings and relationships through the use of original objects, by firsthand experience, and by illustrative media, rather than simply to communicate factual information* (p. 33).

Beck & Cable [2] took interpretation as a procedure of transmitting information and inspiration, to promote the understanding, appreciation, and protection to cultural and natural heritage.

Experiential learning (or experience-based learning) is a way of learning through experience, especially learning by reflection in operation. Kolb [7] proposed the experiential learning theory that defines experience learning as the process of knowledge generation through the conversion of experience. Kolb's experiential learning model (ELM) is divided into four stages, from individual concrete experience, reflective observation, abstract conceptualization, and finally to verification of the concept (active experimentation). Knowledge is obtained by summing up experience from actual situations, and promoted from verification and application.

Tilden [14] proposed the two concepts that the interpreter should think about. One is that the statement must go beyond the facts to inspire more important meanings behind the facts. The other is that the explanation must make full use of human curiosity to enrich and enhance human intelligence and mind. This means that interpretation can use people's instinct of curiosity for novelty, to provide multiple experiential environments to trigger learning motivation, and to open up potentially important meanings.

The interpretative media is the medium that carries the content of the message. Sharpe [13] divides the interpretative media into two categories: 1. staff interpretation: the use of personnel to explain directly to tourists. And 2. non-staff interpretation: using a variety of facilities to explain the subject matter.

2.3 Game-Based Learning

Game-based learning (GBL) is a learning method that uses games to achieve specific learning purposes. The game-based learning using digital media is called digital game-based learning (DGBL). There are researches on the effectiveness of digital game-based learning [3, 10, 15].

It is difficult to determine whether the museum visitors have learned something. Regardless of whether visitors pay attention to and understands the theme information, the entertainment effect can still be achieved. Screven [12] proposed two modes of museum participation: *passive participation* and *interactive participation*. Passive participation plays only the role of the exhibit initiator. The visitors can see the dynamic demonstration, but has no choice. Interactive participation is to encourage visitors to find the answer from the exhibit to achieve the best cognitive learning effect before making a decision. Interactive participation is a better way of participation in education and entertainment.

About digital games on real site, Hwang, Tsai and Yang [6] discussed the location-based mobile learning system on the topic of context-aware ubiquitous learning environment. They suggested the learning system should be environment-aware, that is, the state of the environment can be detected before the system can perform learning activities. And the learning system should provide personalized support at appropriate paths, locations, and times that based on the learner's personal, environmental factors and learning process.

3 Method

This research utilizes a qualitative method to collect and analyze data from the field test of the game prototype.

3.1 Prototype Design of Location-Based AR Game

From the history of Beitou area, we adapted the story of a Japanese, Hirada Gengo, the owner of the first hot spring hotel in Beitou. The setting is that four game players of a team play roles as brothers and sisters in the fiction story. They have to walk around to find clues in the Beitou hot spring area to re-construct the story of the friendship between their grandfather and Mr. Hirada Gengo. Nine sites were selected as game spots for them to visit. They can use their personal mobile phone to see and interact with AR virtual objects to get information of the sites and the tasks to do. Instructions will be given by the mobile phone to guide to complete their mission.

First, at the starting place they read a letter from their grandfather. In the letter, there are some important words missing like a puzzle and they are encourage to find clues in the Beitou hot spring area. A game map that show nine sites in the area is also attached in the letter. The team members play their roles as the Leader, the Navigator, the Recorder, and the Adventurer. Second, they go out to the hot spring area to visit the sites to find the clues. They can use their mobile phone to visit a web site that we provide at the starting place via QR code to search the virtual objects at the sites. The Navigator follows the guide in the web site to lead the players to assigned sites with the game map. When their approach a site, they will see two virtual objects appear. When the Adventurer interacts with the objects, information or a task will be showed. A task is a question that they must find the answer at the site or an action that has to be done at the site. After completing the task they can get a code. The Recorder have to input the result of the task to a LINE chatbot, and it will feed back the name of the following site to visit. Third, the players visits all nine sites to complete the tasks, and they will arrive at the ninth site, Tiangouan Historical site, the first hot spring hotel in Beitou. The players will find the final missing words to finish the mission, and the game ends here.

The interface of web AR included a cursor and two kinds of virtual objects. The cursor is set at the center of the screen. When a player moves his mobile phone, the object can be aimed and hovered with the cursor. One kind of virtual objects is for site information. Then the site information will be triggered to show a window that contain text and image about the site (see Fig. 2). One kind of virtual objects is for site task. Similarly, the site task will be triggered to show a window that contain text of a multiple-choice question or an action to perform (see Fig. 3).

3.2 Data Collection and Analysis

User Field Test. The participants forms a team to play the prototype of the game at real site, around the Beitou hot spring area. It's about one and half hours to complete the mission of the game.

Observation. During the game playing, the researchers observe the discussions and actions of the participants. Especially mistakes and doubts should be noted carefully.

Interview: After game ends, the participants of a team are interviewed together. Questions are focused on the most impressive parts, understanding of the design, fun to play, learning, satisfaction, problems and suggestions, and any opinion or idea.

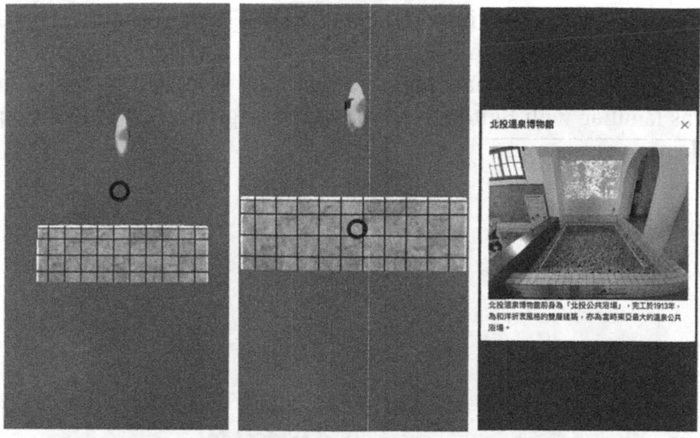

Fig. 2. An image virtual object as a trigger of site information

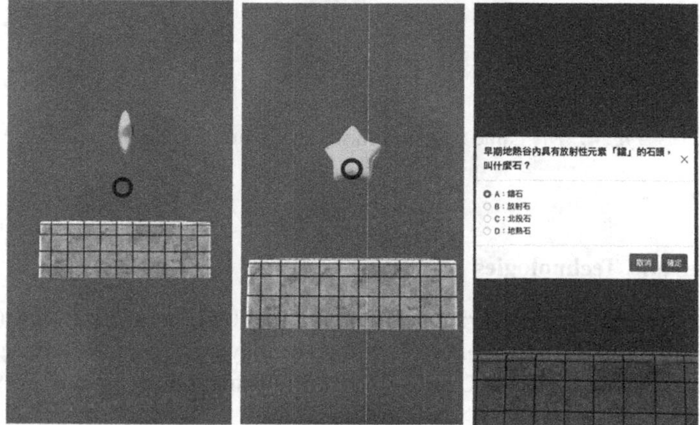

Fig. 3. A 3D star virtual object as a trigger of a site task

Questionnaire Test. Pre-test of SUS (System Usability Scale) and IMI (Intrinsic Motivation Inventory) for the game usability are conducted. Just for test of filling questionnaires in future product use, not for formal quantitative analysis in this research.

Qualitative Analysis. Qualitative data are collected and analyzed with a QDA (Qualitative Data Analysis) application. Coding and category are made to conclude the axial concepts and the structure of this research.

3.3 Test Site and Participants

This research takes Beitou area in northern Taiwan as the sample site of ecomuseum. In Beitou, many cultural and historic sites are very worth visiting. To develop the contents of the interpretative game, nine important sites near the hot spring area are selected to form an appropriate visiting path (see Fig. 4).

Four participants (three female and one male) were invited in this prototype test. Only one was familiar with Beitou, but not with hot spring area. All participants were college students.

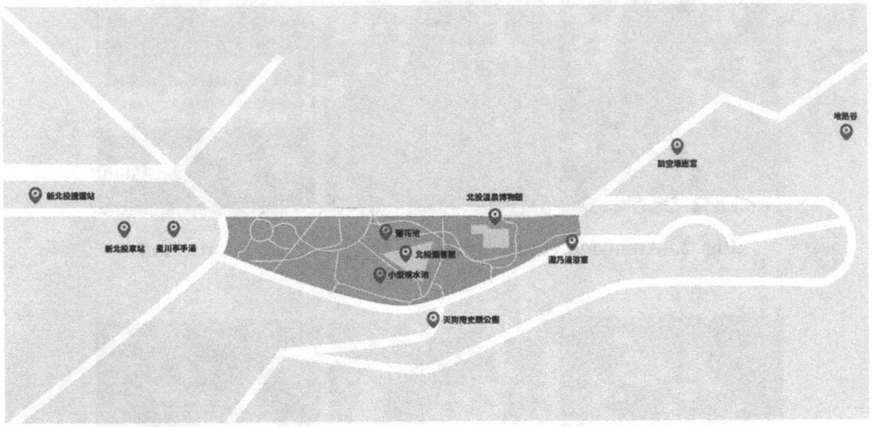

Fig. 4. The game map that shows the Beitou hot spring area

3.4 Devices and Technologies

Devices. (a) Notebook computer: for programming and user interface design, (b) Mobile phone with GPS and Internet connection: for game playing to get interactive guides and tasks in location-based AR, (c) Camera: for site information design and prototype test observation.

Technologies. (a) Virtual web host: a host service to provide interactive guides and tasks of the game, and web AR service platform, (b) Web AR: AR.js, a JavaScript framework for AR, integrated with Three.js, A-Frame.js, ARtoolkit tools, (c) Location-based Web AR: GeoAR.js, a JavaScript framework for Location-based Web AR, (d) LINE chatbot: a chatbot service operated by LINE. Much people in Taiwan own a LINE account, a text and media message service integrated with multi functions.

4 Results and Discussion

4.1 Results

Learnability. *Experience and Pleasure to Find the Correct Answer at the Site.* Players thought the experience is very impressive if they can find the correct answer from the clues at the site. For example, one question is "Why were the Tiger Windows of New Beitou Train Station added from three to four?" The players cannot answer the question from the appearance of the station. But when they entered the station to see the exhibition about the station history, they searched for related information in it and happily found the answer in a chart. They got a very delightful experience to know something through clue searching at the site.

How Tools Help Experience. It's possible that new tools attract players to use for fresh experience. Thus, players found they can get more fun and deeper experience from the interaction with tasks and the various sites themselves. They could walk through the path and touch the real sites and objects physically. The design of tools needs to emphasize on the smoothness of use, but not on how to attract too much attention.

More Clear Understanding of the Sites and Space. Players found it's easier to memorize the information of the sites naturally after playing the game. They could understand the spatial structure well among the sites. The Navigator (U2) learned the spatial knowledge with intense use of the map and continuous comparison between the map and the environment. It's possible that situated learning made the players to learn the spatial knowledge with more connections of multi experience.

Scale of Interaction. Some players liked to solve the puzzles with standard solutions. But also, some players (like U3) liked to answer open questions. Open questions could lead to more thinking and physical actions to form more creative answers or works. Most players liked to have chance to observe and interact with the environment by themselves.

Satisfaction and Pleasure. *Team Roles and Tasks.* The roles setting made the players more situated. They found they would like to focus on their parts in site tasks. They could help each other to complete the mission of the game. They had some responsibility to share information and thought without too much effort. The roles setting let them enjoy the pleasure of team cooperation.

Benefit for Learning Context. For casual visiting, a player (U3) thought the game maybe not so interesting or exciting for fun. But for learning context, like outdoor learning of school children, it could be very suitable to learn as in a museum.

Willing to Recommend Others to Play. After playing the game, the players had the willing to recommend others to play the game, especially for newcomers of Beitou area. With the help of the game playing, visitors should enjoy to understand the historical area much more.

Storytelling. *Connections among Tasks and the Place.* A good and clear story can help build the connections among tasks and the place. The players liked the story behind the game. It could help the players situated in the historical context. They enjoyed to play roles to complete the mission to visit an old friend, given by the ancestor in the story.

Playing and the Experience Acquired in the Story. The game told the story by the arrangement of site visiting. The players thought they got the experience of engagement in the story. The fun and experience came from the storytelling of the game.

Story as Context. Some players noticed that the story is good to understand and to play the roles, but it could run through the game even more. Perhaps the introduction session and the user interface could be re-design to utilize more elements of the story to form a nostalgia mood.

Order of Tasks. The order of the game was arranged by a path around the hot spring area. Some played thought it was not so close to the storyline. It is possible that the story was told according the order of the sites, but it was not so compatible with a good story structure. For better experience, the story might need modification to get a better story structure.

User Interface. *Clear Presentation of Tasks.* Some targets of the tasks were ambiguous. When the players go they t such tasks, they would use their imagination to guess how to process. Because such tasks had no standard answer, the players were not sure whether they had completed the tasks or not.

Need of Sites Information for Game Playing. The information provided from the virtual objects is some basic knowledge about the sites. It was not designed to play a necessary part in the tasks. Players found they can skip it to take the following new task more quickly. For the learning goal of ecomuseum interpretation, it is not an expected phenomenon. The information presentation could be designed to come up first when the objects are triggered. The information itself may also play a part in storytelling and task executions.

Gap Between Guide and Execution of Tasks. When the guides is not clear enough, the players continued to play it, but toward another direction the designers didn't expect. It is a gap between designers' and users' mental models. We might need a mechanism to correct the mistake and let players back to the designed path.

Technology. *Precision of Positioning.* Because of the poor GPS signal, the positioning of the location-based AR didn't work well. We cannot count on the function fully to see the virtual objects on the precise positions of the sites. The virtual objects were put at right coordinates, but the position of the mobile phone might be set to wrong position. So a virtual object on the mobile phone's screen could not been displayed well at the correct distance and direction. Our temporary solution was to expand the range of trigger to show the objects, although some objects still could not been shown correctly.

Power Consumption of Web AR. The web AR in our game worked well. But the web browser use the Internet and camera consumes much power. The battery would drain quickly. So the players were noticed not to use the web AR all the time. They could rely on the Navigator's guide to approach the sites and then take out the mobile phone playing web AR to get the information and tasks.

4.2 Discussion

Orientation of Tasks. The tasks design of the game could be a continuum between puzzle-based and experience-based. The original intension to introduce a game into ecomuseum interpretation is to get deeper experience by multi perception received in the tasks. But the tasks may not be interesting enough. Some players' expectation about a game is to solve a puzzle or conquer a enemy to get clues or enter the next level. In this research we try to find a balance in the continuum. A background story was created to form the path to walk through. The task design is focused on how to get personal experience from puzzle-solving to satisfy the both needs.

Randomness and Customization of Game. In this game prototype, we used only fixed sites, tasks and paths. It's possible to create more sites and related information and tasks.

We can try different combinations of the elements, or even thc background story. Thus, the game can be played by same played again and again.

Natural Conversation. Personality of chatbot. The dialogues of the chatbot were set as necessary information. One player suggested the dialogues could be more like human conversation. We think that even without advanced AI technology, the dialogues can be designed like ones spoken by a role in the story. Chatbot can perform better like a human.

Sole Player. One player suggested that we should think about the condition of sole player without team members. It means the map, web AR, and dialogue window of chatbot need to be integrated in one system or user interface. It's possible but due to the limitation of the screen size, the functions can only be displayed by different tab, mode, or overlay window.

5 Conclusion and Suggestions

5.1 Conclusions

Learnability. Experience and pleasure to find the correct answer at the site is the goal and key feature of the interpretative game. In the test of the game prototype, it helped the players get rich experience and pleasure.

Satisfaction. The roles setting made the players more situated and enjoy the pleasure of team cooperation. They had the willing to recommend others to play the game, especially for newcomers of Beitou area.

Storytelling. A good and clear story can help build the connections among tasks and the place. The players thought they got the experience of engagement in the story. The fun and experience came from the storytelling of the game.

User Interface. Is a clear presentation of tasks necessary or not for a game? We found some targets of the tasks were ambiguous. The players would use their imagination to guess how to process. It could result in unexpectable mistakes of site understanding.

Technology. In the game prototype test, the positioning of the location-based AR didn't work well for the GPS performance of the mobile phones. It cannot be guaranteed to see the virtual objects on the precise positions of the sites. Our temporary solution was to expand the range of trigger to show the objects.

5.2 Suggestions

One Object per Site. For the learning goal of ecomuseum interpretation, the virtual objects should show information first then the tasks. By combining the two buttons of information and task, we need only one virtual object per site. The information presentation can be re-designed to come up when the objects are triggered.

Demo Playing as Introduction. To prevent misunderstanding of the interface and tasks, a demo playing of operation and task execution would be necessary. It should be an important part of the game introduction.

Smaller Range for Better GPS Precision. Consider use a smaller range for better GPS precision of mobile phone, especially for new ones.

Acknowledgments. This research was partly sponsored by grants, MOST 109-2410-H-119-001, from the Ministry of Science and Technology, Taiwan.

References

1. Azuma, R.T.: A survey of augmented reality. Presence: Teleoperators Virtual Environ. **6**(4), 355–385 (1997)
2. Beck, L., Cable, T.: Interpretation for the 21st Century: Fifteen Guiding Principles for Interpreting Nature and Culture, 2nd edn. Sagamore, Urbana (2002)
3. Bedwell, W.L., Pavlas, D., Heyne, K., Lazzara, E.H., Salas, E.: Toward a taxonomy linking game attributes to learning: an empirical study. Simul. Gaming **43**(6), 729–760 (2012)
4. Brooks, F.P., Jr.: The computer scientist as toolsmith II. CACM **39**(3), 61–68 (1996)
5. Haahr, M.: Creating location-based augmented-reality games for cultural heritage. In: Alcañiz, M., Göbel, S., Ma, M., Fradinho Oliveira, M., Baalsrud Hauge, J., Marsh, T. (eds) Serious Games, JCSG 2017. LNCS, vol. 10622, pp. 313–318. Springer, Cham (2017). https://doi.org/10.1007/978-3-319-70111-0_29
6. Hwang, G.-J., Tsai, C.-C., Yang, S.J.: Criteria, strategies and research issues of context-aware ubiquitous learning. J. Educ. Technol. Soc. **11**(2), 81–91 (2008)
7. Kolb, D.: Experiential learning as the science of learning and development. Prentice Hall, Englewood Cliffs (1984)
8. Lee, K.: Augmented reality in education and training. TechTrends **56**(2), 13–21 (2012)
9. Milgram, P., Takemura, H., Utsumi, A., Kishino, F.: Augmented reality: A class of displays on the reality-virtuality continuum. In: Telemanipulator and Telepresence Technologies, vol. 2351, pp. 282–292 (1995)
10. Prensky, M.: Digital game-based learning. Comput. Entertain. **1**(1), 21 (2003)
11. Saffer, D.: Microinteractions: Designing with Details. O'Reilly Media, Sebastopol (2013)
12. Screven, C.G.: Information design in informal setting: Museum and other public spaces. In: Jacobson, R. (ed.) Information Design, pp. 131–192. MIT Press, Cambridge (1999)
13. Sharpe, G.W.: Interpreting the Environment, 2nd edn. Wiley, New York (1982)
14. Tilden, F.: Interpreting Our Heritage, 3rd edn. University of North Carolina Press, Chapel Hill (1997)
15. Van Eck, R.: Digital game-based learning: It's not just the digital natives who are restless. Educause Rev. **41**(2), 16–30 (2006)

Intergenerational Contacts During the COVID-19 Pandemic: Personal or Electronic?

Mihaela Hărăguş[(✉)]

Centre for Population Studies, Babeş-Bolyai University, 68 Avram Iancu Street, 400089 Cluj-Napoca, Romania
mihaela.haragus@ubbcluj.ro

Abstract. The paper investigates intergenerational associational solidarity in the specific context of COVID-19 pandemic and associated first lockdown in Europe. Adult children are often a source of support for older parents, especially in countries with a weak welfare state. On the other hand, older persons are the most vulnerable in front of the new virus and restrictions specifically addressed reducing personal contacts for older people. Our aim is to see how the recommendations for physical distancing combined with the need for different forms of support. More specifically, we investigate whether electronic contacts with non- coresident children could substitute personal contacts when there is need for support and care. Our investigation on data from SHARE Corona Survey from eight European countries show that a worsening health status or lack of opportunities for digital connections translate into face-to-face rather than electronic intergenerational contact and support. Results differ by country group, as an expression of different intergenerational relations regimes, with responsibilities for vulnerable older persons placed mainly on family or on the state.

Keywords: Associational intergenerational solidarity · COVID-19 pandemic · Europe

1 Introduction

Relations and support between parents and children continue throughout their lives, even after children have reached adulthood and established careers and families of their own, as the paradigm of intergenerational solidarity shows [6]. There are six dimensions of intergenerational solidarity: associational, affective, consensual, functional, normative and structural. Shared activities and interaction between family generations (associational solidarity) are important for maintaining family unity. Meeting in person is the closest form of contact, but with the development and increasing accessibility of information and communication technology (ICT), digital communication became a widespread efficient way of keeping a sense of belonging in families scattered across large geographical areas, even beyond the borders of a country. Digital families [19] or digital solidarity [15] are concepts that describe present realities of associational intergenerational solidarity.

Q. Gao and J. Zhou (Eds.): HCII 2022, LNCS 13331, pp. 371–382, 2022.
https://doi.org/10.1007/978-3-031-05654-3_26

COVID-19 pandemic and associated restrictions directly affected relations between parents and their adult children. On the one hand, adult children are often a source of support for older parents, especially in countries with a weak welfare state. On the other hand, older persons are the most vulnerable in front of the new virus and restrictions specifically addressed reducing personal contacts for older people. The role of ICT in this new context becomes evident and studies point out an increase in electronic contacts of older persons, as well as a beneficial effect on their mental wellbeing [2, 3]. However, there are situations when the use of ICT is restricted by the health condition, difficult access to digital technology or lack of digital literacy, and personal contacts with family members remain the norm. Or situations when the person needs hands-on care, with physical presence. Our research question addresses exactly these circumstances: how the recommendations for physical distancing combine with the need for different forms of support? More specifically, whether electronic contacts are enough to fulfil the needs of frail and vulnerable older persons.

We try to answer using the Survey of Health, Ageing and Retirement in Europe (SHARE) [8–10], the wave conducted during spring of 2020, adapted to the COVID-19 outbreak and the prolonged lockdowns, released under the name of SHARE – Corona Survey. We chose for our analysis 8 countries that were most recently included in the SHARE project: two Baltic countries (Lithuania and Latvia), three Central and Eastern European (Romania, Bulgaria and Slovakia), two Southern European (Malta and Cyprus), and one Northern country (Finland). This allows us to see whether the interplay between support needs and intergenerational contacts acts in similar ways across different welfare states and intergenerational relations regimes [17].

In the following sections, we present the intergenerational solidarity paradigm, then discuss the role of ICT and digital solidarity, followed by a discussion of associational intergenerational solidarity in the new pandemic context. Factors that may influence the frequency and intensity of associational intergenerational solidarity are discussed in a subsequent section. Presentation of data, indicators and analytic approach follows. Results are presented comparing four group of countries (Baltic, Eastern and Central, Southern and Northern European), capturing the role of structural contextual factors, too. Discussion on the prevalence of personal contacts in case of a worsened health status or lack of opportunities for digital connections in countries with familialist intergenerational relations regimes concludes the paper.

2 Intergenerational Solidarity Paradigm

The theoretical construct of intergenerational solidarity is used "as a means to characterize the behavioral and emotional dimensions of interaction, cohesion, sentiment and support between parents and children, grandparents and grandchildren, over the course of long-term relationships" [7, pp. 8]. In other words, it refers to bonds and interactions between family members of different generations [18].

The original model of intergenerational solidarity contains six dimensions, five of which refer to behavioral, affective and cognitive aspects of the parents–children relation: associational (common activities), affective (emotional closeness), consensual (similarity or agreement in beliefs and values), functional (exchange of support in various forms), and normative (perceptions of obligations and expectations in respect of intergenerational connections). The sixth dimension, structural solidarity, refers to opportunities for transfers between parents and children [6]. A recent adaptation of Bengtson's conceptualization was proposed by Szydlik [18], who considers that not only structural solidarity but also normative and consensual dimensions reflect the potential for intergenerational solidarity, while functional, affectual and associational dimensions reflect actual solidarity.

Functional solidarity comprises monetary transfers (financial assistance), assistance in the form of time, and co-residence (sharing the same household) [18]. Assistance in the form of time may take various forms, from offering advice and practical help around the household to providing personal care to the frail elderly. Affectual solidarity describes emotional bonds or emotional closeness of the relationship. Associational solidarity refers to shared activities and interaction, with meeting in person being the closest form of contact.

3 Digital Solidarity

With the expansion of information and communication technologies (ICT) use, contacts between generations in the family have diversified; gradually, older generations started to familiarize with the new digital media and communication technology. ICT serve not just for information seeking, but also for connecting with family members and significant others [19]. The concept of digital families [19] was introduced, referring to extended and geographically dispersed families who rely on ICT use for maintaining their sense of unity in the absence of regular face-to-face contact. However, this is a development characteristic to the economically more developed countries [19]. Other authors [15] talk about digital solidarity - ICT use between parents and their adult children - as a new dimension of associational solidarity, with implications for functional solidarity.

Digital families and digital solidarity enable the provision of both expressive and instrumental support [15, 19]. Communication through ICT implies less effort and coordination than face-to-face contacts and therefore can be more frequent and perceived as less intrusive [15]; it is more convenient even when geographical distance is not an issue [5]. Adopting the use of ICT would be beneficial for older persons in expanding their opportunities of intergenerational interactions, even when geographical distances between other family members are not necessarily big, as their face-to-face interactions may decline with decreasing mobility associated with older ages [15].

Most of ICT use by older adults involve communication with family members [5, 15], so the role of intergenerational support in digital literacy of older generations is important. The grandchildren's role in the transition of older persons from non internet users to proxy internet users has been emphasized [13]. Moreover, a new form of upward functional intergenerational solidarity appears in the form of assistance provided by grandchildren to their grandparents in technology usage [19]. Not only the spread of ICT has led to new forms of intergenerational solidarity, but authors point out that ICT use and digital families contribute to re-familialization in countries where previously the intergenerational responsibilities were shifted away from the family through welfare provisions, as in case of Finland [19].

In the same time, technological advancements have created a new form of inequality, which is digital inequality, which manifests at many points during the life course and builds up on the existing inequalities [16]. In this way, older, less educated and economically disadvantaged seniors lack the ability to use ICT to stay in touch with their caregivers [16], be they family members or not.

4 Associational Solidarity in a New Context – The COVID-19 Pandemic

Contacts between parents and their adult children represent associational dimension of intergenerational solidarity, but also the potential for exchange of support. The role of ICT use becomes preeminent in the pandemic context, when there were specific recommendations for older persons to refrain from direct contacts with others. COVID-19 pandemic and associated restrictions directly affected relations between parents and their adult children.

COVID-19 outbreak was accompanied by an outbreak of ageism, as many accounts in international media portrayed older people as helpless, frail, and unable to contribute to society [4]. However, physical distancing does not necessarily mean emotional distancing; strengthened intergenerational closeness at family level, through ICT use, may contribute to the reduction of negative effects of stereotyping and stigmatization of older persons in public discourse [4]. Studies show that electronic communication was essential for reducing negative mental health outcomes (depression) during the lockdown, and the effect was stronger in case of intergenerational than other contacts [2].

Other studies show that adults who respected the regulations of physical distancing, reduced their face-to-face contacts with children and non-kin, with increased loneliness as a consequence [11]. Authors [3] found a substantial increase in non-physical intergenerational contacts among parents who decreased the face-to-face contacts with children during the lockdown. However, respondents with difficult financial situation had a lower probability of increased frequency of electronic contacts. These results draw attention on the disparities of beneficial effects of electronic communication during the lockdown and on the role of resources (access to internet and technology, digital literacy) that shape the digital inequality.

Our study addresses intergenerational contacts in a new context that favors the new dimension of associational solidarity over the traditional one of face-to-face contacts. Above-mentioned studies highlighted its role in protecting older persons' mental well-being. However, we will further investigate whether electronic contacts were enough for frail and vulnerable older persons, who needed care, besides emotional support.

5 Factors that Influence Associational Intergenerational Solidarity

There are a considerable number of factors that are discussed in the literature as having an influence on the frequency and intensity of intergenerational exchanges and different classifications of these factors exist. Albertini and collaborators [1] distinguish between micro (individual and family) and macro (anything above) levels only, and for each level, between three broad categories of factors: structural, institutional and cultural [1]. Szydlik [18] discusses four conditional factors for solidarity: opportunity, needs, family and cultural-contextual structures. At the individual level, opportunity structures refer to the opportunities or resources for intergenerational solidarity, such as the residential proximity of family members, occupational status (availability of time to offer support) or economic status (availability of financial resources). The needs structure indicates the need for intergenerational solidarity, which can be a result of health, financial or emotional problems. At the familial level, the history of life events (such as divorce) may shape intergenerational solidarity, as well as family composition (the number of siblings) or family norms. Cultural-contextual structures refer to the societal conditions in which intergenerational relations take place, such as the economic and tax system, welfare state, and labor and housing market.

As we mentioned before, our research question is how the recommendations for social distancing combine with the need for different forms of support? More specifically, we ask ourselves whether electronic contacts are enough to fulfil the needs of frail and vulnerable older persons. Associational intergenerational solidarity, be it digital or traditional face-to-face, is influenced by the same categories of conditional factors as proposed above. Our research hypothesis is that when there is a need for support, personal contacts continue to be the main form of associational intergenerational solidarity. Studies have shown that parents' characteristics play a larger role in ICT use than those of children [15], so we focus mainly on the role of elderly's needs. However, we also consider their opportunity structure, family configuration, as well as structural factors.

Need for intergenerational support may be an expression of health problems, as well as an expression of social exclusion, in its multidimensional character. On the one hand, poor or declining health may be an obstacle in ICT use [15]; on the other hand, persons in bad health condition may need more hands-on care and support, and consequently face-to-face contact with own children. Hence, we hypothesize that frail older persons, especially those whose status has worsened during the lockdown, would rely mainly on personal contact with their children.

Material deprivation is related with the affordability of ordinary consumption goods, of health-related expenditures and the inability to cope with extraordinary expenses [14]. Social isolation is more complex, it includes being isolated (difficulties in getting around for basic services), living in an unclean or dangerous neighborhood, living in an overcrowded home, and having no local social activity [14]. Both material and social deprivation are found to be associated with limitations in performing daily activities and need for long term care [14] and may also be associated with a lack of access to electronic devices. Therefore, we expect deprived elderly to resort to face-to-face contact rather than to electronic one.

Our main focus is on older persons' needs, but we also take into account the opportunity structure. Higher education may mean a larger social network, not confined merely to own children [20] or a certain familiarity with ICT use, so we expect that better educated elderly would rely mainly on electronic, not on personal contact during the pandemic. The level of (computer) literacy is also expected to be associated with ICT use for intergenerational contacts. Regarding family configuration, having more children means more opportunities for intergenerational contacts. The presence of partner in the household during the lockdown may mean the existence of a support provider, so less need for intergenerational support and less in person contacts with others.

Age is important, since older age may mean increased support needs, as well as decreased ability to use ICT. Gender has been shown to be associated with the frequency of intergenerational contacts, with women more likely to ensure digital communication in the family [19].

Intergenerational responsibilities are divided between the state and the family, which, in connection with the typology of welfare regimes, leads to different regimes of intergenerational solidarity [17]. On the continuum of familialism - defamilialization, the proposed typology distinguishes between (1) familialism by default (where the care of the vulnerable persons is entirely the family's responsibility, with no financial support for family care or publicly provided alternatives); (2) supported familialism (where families are financially compensated for caring responsibilities); (3) defamilialization (that reduces family responsibilities and dependencies), and (4) optional familialism (an option between supported familialism and de-familialization) [17]. We investigate intergenerational associational solidarity in eight countries that distribute across the categories presented above. Except Finland, which is an example of defamilialization, other countries illustrate various degrees of familialism, rather closer to implicit than to supported familialism when it comes to responsibilities towards older persons. We expect that in countries with familialist intergenerational relations regime to find more involvement of children in providing support and care to their parents during the lockdown, so a stronger effect of elderly's needs on intergenerational face-to-face contacts.

6 Method

6.1 Data

We conduct our investigation using the Survey of Health, Ageing and Retirement in Europe (SHARE) [8–10], the wave conducted during spring of 2020, adapted to the COVID-19 outbreak and the prolonged lockdowns, released under the name of SHARE – Corona Survey. SHARE survey has a panel design, so we also use data from Wave 8, conducted in autumn 2019, for several characteristics that were not registered in the Corona Survey. We chose for our analysis 8 countries that were most recently included in the SHARE project: two Baltic countries (Lithuania and Latvia), three Central and Eastern European (Romania, Bulgaria and Slovakia), two Southern European (Malta and Cyprus), and one Northern country (Finland).

6.2 Indicators

For the construction of the dependent variable, we combine the frequency of personal contacts (face-to-face) and the frequency of electronic contacts (by phone, email or any other electronic means) with their children from outside their home. The constructed dependent variable is a dichotomic one, us being interested in the situation of personal contacts being more frequent than electronic contacts with non-coresident children.

Independent variables refer to older parents need for support, as well as opportunities for intergenerational contacts and family structure. As mentioned above, we take into account needs stemming from health problems, as well as from different forms of deprivation: material or social.

For needs linked with health problems, we have the health status before the pandemic, recoded as a dichotomic variable (good/bad), and a variable showing the change in health status since the outbreak of COVID-19 (worsened, remained the same, improved).

Material deprivation is a constructed dichotomic variable that refers to households that had answer positive to one of the following deprivations: food (they cannot afford meat three times per week), heating (they suffered cold in order to save heating costs) or unexpected expenses (they cannot afford unexpected expenses without borrowing). The social deprivation constructed variable considers not participating in social activities in the last year/not taking part in any organization in the last year (such as: done voluntary or charity work, attended an educational or training course, gone to a sport, social or other kind of club; taken part in a political or community-related organization etc.). These variables were measured prior to the lockdown (in wave 8).

We use two variables describing the opportunity structure of respondents: education level (low, medium and high) and a constructed variable describing the level of skills such as reading, writing, using computer or navigating the internet (an index from 0 to 100).

We also consider family configuration, through the number of non-coresident children and the existence of a partner in the household. Respondent's age (as a continuous variable) and gender are also controlled for.

6.3 Analytic Approach

There were 5,384 family respondents[1] in the eight countries we are interested in. After the merge with SHARE Wave 8 and the selection of respondents with at least one child and with valid information on all variables included in the analysis, our whole working sample consists of 3,771 persons aged 50 years and older. For testing our hypothesis, we employ a binary logistic regression model. The dependent variable is personal intergenerational contacts being more frequent than electronic ones. Independent variables refer to different support needs, opportunities for intergenerational contact and family configuration. Since the eight countries under the analysis differ in terms of intergenerational relations regime [17], we perform our analysis separately on four groups of countries.

7 Results

From Table 1 we see that the four groups of countries differ greatly in terms of the frequency of face-to face or electronic contacts, as well as on variables considering various needs. On the one hand, Eastern and Central European countries (Romania and Bulgaria) have a familialist by default intergenerational relations regime (with Slovakia also close to this group), with family bearing the main responsibility for elderly wellbeing. On the other hand, in countries with higher social inequality, such in countries of this group, intergenerational support shifts from financial to non-monetary assistance [12]. So, it is

[1] Family respondents answer questions about children and social support [8–10].

Table 1. Descriptive analysis of parents

	Baltic N = 1,107	Eastern & Central N = 1,494	Southern N = 583	Northern N = 587
Personal contacts more frequent than electronic contacts	7.1%	16.3%	3.3%	9.5%
Health status before the outbreak				
Good	42.6%	69.7%	62.8%	71.6%
Not good	57.4%	30.3%	37.2%	28.4%
Health status change during the lockdown				
Improved or remained the same	87.9%	92.2%	90.7%	89.9%
Worsened	12.1%	7.8%	9.3%	10.1%
Material deprivation				
No	50.9%	45.7%	61.4%	80.9%
Yes	49.1%	54.3%	38.6%	19.1%
Social deprivation				
No	77.8%	51.3%	61.6%	97.4%
Yes	22.2%	48.7%	38.4%	2.6%
Education level				
Low	18.6%	34.9%	52.7%	28.6%
Medium	46.1%	56.4%	38.8%	33.2%
High	35.3%	8.6%	8.4%	38.2%
Partner in the household				
Yes	45.8%	58.2%	65.4%	65.4%
No	54.2%	41.8%	34.6%	34.6%
Number of children				
Only one	23.0%	18.9%	11.1%	20.3%
More	77.0%	81.1%	88.9%	79.7%
Gender				
Men	23.9%	32.9%	37.9%	44.8%
Women	76.1%	67.1%	62.1%	55.2%
Age				
Mean	69.44	67.12	71.30	69.23
Std. deviation	10.032	8.976	9.268	9.152

no surprise that in these countries we find greater reliance on intergenerational hands-on care even during the lockdown.

For results of the multivariate analysis, we see that effects of independent variables are different across the country groups (Table 2).

Table 2. Results of logistic regression model for personal contacts more frequent than electronic contacts

	Baltic		Eastern & Central		Southern		Northern	
	Exp(B)	Sig.	Exp(B)	Sig.	Exp(B)	Sig.	Exp(B)	Sig.
Health status before - not good	0.793		0.863		*0.185*	**	1.226	
Health status worsened	0.880		*2.178*	***	*7.948*	***	*0.236*	*
Material deprivation	*1.875*	**	1.036		1.184		0.889	
Social deprivation	1.413		0.827		1.440		1.671	
Low education (ref. high)	*1.974*	*	*2.119*	*	0.745		1.958	
Medium education (ref. high)	1.375		*2.071*	*	2.147		1.466	
Skills	1.013		*0.984*	**	0.993		0.994	
Only 1 child	1.256		0.918		*4.771*	***	*0.348*	**
No partner in the household	0.881		1.169		0.660		1.189	
Men (ref. women)	*1.723*	**	0.905		1.092		*2.141*	**
Age	*1.029*	*	0.991		1.034		1.013	
Number of respondents	1,107		1,494		583		587	
Nagelkerke R square	0.044		0.046		0.163		0.098	

Note: *p ≤ 0.1, **p ≤ 0.05, ***p ≤ 0.01

An existing poor health status produce a cautious intergenerational behavior, with lower likelihood of prevailing personal contacts, only in the two Southern European countries. A worsened health condition, on the other hand, highly increase the likelihood of predominant personal contacts in Eastern and Central and Southern European countries, showing an urgency of hands-on care from one's children. In Finland the effect is opposite, a worsened health status highly reduces the odds of more frequent face-to-face than electronic contact. We connect this result with the state responsibility for vulnerable persons, especially when medical care is involved and decreased family responsibility.

Measures of deprivation show an effect only in Baltic countries, where material deprivation increases the likelihood of relying on intergenerational exchanges with physical co-presence. A lower level of education shows a similar effect, both in Baltic and Eastern and Central European countries. Low education may indicate low digital literacy, as well as reduced access to electronic devices and internet. The skills level, which includes also digital skills, appears to matter only in Eastern and Central European countries: the higher the skills level, the less likely to rely mainly on face-to-face contacts.

The effect of number of children emphasizes the differences in intergenerational relations regimes in Southern and Northern countries. Reliance mainly on family support and care in the former translates into highly increased odds to have more intense face-to-face contacts with the only child, while de-familialization and geographically dispersed families in Finland translate into reduced odds of prevalence of face-to-face contacts with the only child.

Men appear to be more involved in face-to-face than into electronic contacts with non-coresident children than women, similar with results referring to the pre-pandemic times [19]. More reliance on personal than electronic contacts with increasing age appears only in Baltic countries.

8 Discussion

Broadly, our hypothesis that when there is a need for support, personal contacts continue to prevail, has been confirmed. However, results differ by intergenerational relations regimes. In countries where the responsibilities of care of older persons falls almost exclusively on family, a worsened health status or lack of opportunities for digital connections (lower education, that may indicate low digital literacy or restricted access to digital communication devices) translate into face-to-face rather than electronic intergenerational contact and support. Conversely, in Finland, a country where the care of vulnerable persons falls into the state's responsibility, intergenerational contacts remain rather electronic than face-to-face, a situation that characterized the pre-pandemic times as well [19]. Intergenerational support there is mainly emotional and can be provided through digital communication. Digital families are a feature of Finish society and intensified intergenerational electronic communication may indicate a process of re-familialization [19], but not in case of hands-on care. In other countries, mainly in Southern and Eastern and Central ones, family steps in to provide hands-on care, even in times when intergenerational face-to-face contacts are discouraged.

Our study has a series of limitations, mainly in terms of indicators included in the analysis. Differentiating between medical conditions, considering the geographical distance between parents and children or including adult children's characteristics may have brought more light on how increased care needs influence intergenerational contacts. However, SHARE Corona Survey did not differentiate among non-resident children in questions about intergenerational contacts.

Despite its limitations, our study draws attention on frail and vulnerable older persons and the role of their needs in shaping the intergenerational contacts in the pandemic context, when recommendations for physical distancing specifically addressed older persons. Developing digital devices adapted to persons whose poor health prevent them from using existing technology, as suggested by Peng and collaborators [15], might allow family members to better monitor their parents' health condition and to assist them in providing better care. However, where family bears the main responsibility for the wellbeing of vulnerable older persons, direct care with physical copresence would not be replaced by digital care, from a distance.

Acknowledgements. This paper uses data from SHARE Wave 8 (DOIs: https://doi.org/10.6103/SHARE.w8.100, https://doi.org/10.6103/SHARE.w8ca.100), see Börsch-Supan et al. (2013) for methodological details.

The SHARE data collection has been funded by the European Commission, DG RTD through FP5 (QLK6-CT-2001–00360), FP6 (SHARE-I3: RII-CT-2006–062193, COMPARE: CIT5-CT-2005–028857, SHARELIFE: CIT4-CT-2006–028812), FP7 (SHARE-PREP: GA N°211909, SHARE-LEAP: GA N°227822, SHARE M4: GA N°261982, DASISH: GA N°283646) and Horizon 2020 (SHARE-DEV3: GA N°676536, SHARE-COHESION: GA N°870628, SERISS: GA N°654221, SSHOC: GA N°823782) and by DG Employment, Social Affairs & Inclusion through VS 2015/0195, VS 2016/0135, VS 2018/0285, VS 2019/0332, and VS 2020/0313. Additional funding from the German Ministry of Education and Research, the Max Planck Society for the Advancement of Science, the U.S. National Institute on Aging (U01_AG09740-13S2, P01_AG005842, P01_AG08291, P30_AG12815, R21_AG025169, Y1-AG-4553-01, IAG_BSR06-11, OGHA_04-064, HHSN271201300071C, RAG052527A) and from various national funding sources is gratefully acknowledged (see www.share-project.org).

References

1. Albertini, M., Kohli, M., Vogel, C.: Intergenerational transfers of time and money in European families: common patterns - different regimes? J. Eur. Soc. Policy **17**(4), 319–334 (2007)
2. Arpino, B., Pasqualini, M., Bordone, V., Solé-Auró, A.: Older people's non-physical contacts and depression during the COVID-19 lockdown. Gerontologist **61**(2), 176–186 (2020). https://doi.org/10.1093/geront/gnaa144
3. Arpino, B., Pasqualini, M., Bordone, V.: Physically distant but socially close? Changes in non-physical intergenerational contacts at the onset of the COVID-19 pandemic among older people in France, Italy and Spain. Eur. J. Ageing **18**, 185–194 (2021). https://doi.org/10.1007/s10433-021-00621-x
4. Ayalon, L., et al.: Aging in times of the COVID-19 pandemic: avoiding ageism and fostering intergenerational solidarity. J. Gerontol. Ser. B **76**(2), e49–e52 (2021). https://doi.org/10.1093/geronb/gbaa051
5. Azevedo, C., Ponte, C.: Intergenerational solidarity or intergenerational gap? How elderly people experience ICT within their family context. Observatorio **14**(3), 16–35 (2020). https://doi.org/10.15847/obsOBS14320201587
6. Bengtson, V.L., Roberts, R.E.L.: Intergenerational solidarity in aging families: An example of formal theory construction. J. Marriage Fam. **53**(4), 856–870 (1991)
7. Bengtson, V.L.: Beyond the nuclear family: the increasing importance of multigenerational bonds. J. Marriage Fam. **63**(1), 1–16 (2001)

8. Börsch-Supan, A., et al.: Data resource profile: the survey of health, ageing and retirement in Europe (SHARE). Int. J. Epidemiol. **42**(4), 992–1001 (2013). https://doi.org/10.1093/ije/dyt088
9. Börsch-Supan, A.: Survey of Health, Ageing and Retirement in Europe (SHARE) Wave 8. Release version: 1.0.0. SHARE-ERIC. Data set (2021). https://doi.org/10.6103/SHARE.w8.100
10. Börsch-Supan, A.: Survey of Health, Ageing and Retirement in Europe (SHARE) Wave 8. COVID-19 Survey 1. Release version: 1.0.0. SHARE-ERIC. Data set (2021). https://doi.org/10.6103/SHARE.w8ca.100
11. Cohn-Schwartz, E., Vitman-Schorr, A., Khalaila, R.: Physical distancing is related to fewer electronic and in-person contacts and to increased loneliness during the COVID-19 pandemic among older Europeans. Qual. Life Res. https://doi.org/10.1007/s11136-021-02949-4
12. Deindl, C., Brandt, M.: Social exclusion and support between generations. In: Börsch-Supan, A., Kneip, T., Litwin, H., Myck, M., Weber, G. (eds.) Ageing in Europe – Supporting Policies for an Inclusive Society, pp. 161–168. De Gruyter, Berlin (2015). https://doi.org/10.1515/9783110444414
13. Dolničar, V., Filipović Hrast, M., Vehovar, V., Petrovčič, A.: Digital inequality and intergenerational solidarity: the role of social support in proxy internet use. AoIR Selected Papers of Internet Research, 3 (2013). https://journals.uic.edu/ojs/index.php/spir/article/view/8543
14. Laferrere, A., Van den Bosch, K.: Unmet need for long-term care and social exclusion. In: Börsch-Supan, A., Kneip, T., Litwin, H., Myck, M., Weber, G. (eds.) Ageing in Europe – Supporting Policies for an Inclusive Society, pp. 331–342. De Gruyter, Berlin (2015). https://doi.org/10.1515/9783110444414
15. Peng, S., Silverstein, M., Suitor, J.J., Gilligan, M., Hwang, W., Nam, S., Routh, B.: Use of communication technology to maintain intergenerational contact: toward an understanding of 'digital solidarity'. In: Neves, B.B., Casimiro, C. (eds.) Connecting Families? Communication, Technologies, Generations, and the Life Course, pp. 159–180). Polity, Bristol (2018)
16. Robinson, L., et al.: Digital inequalities and why they matter. Inf. Commun. Soc. **18**(5), 569–582 (2015). https://doi.org/10.1080/1369118X.2015.1012532
17. Saraceno, C., Keck, W.: Can we identify intergenerational policy regimes in Europe? Eur. Soc. **12**(5), 675–696 (2010)
18. Szydlik, M.: Sharing Lives. Adult Children and Parents. Routledge, London/New York (2016)
19. Taipale, S.: Intergenerational Connections in Digital Families. Springer, Cham (2019). https://doi.org/10.1007/978-3-030-11947-8
20. Tomassini, C., et al.: Contacts between elderly parents and their children in four European countries: current patterns and future prospects. Eur. J. Ageing **1**(1), 54–63 (2004)

Virtual Museum Visits in a Pandemic: Older Adults Discuss Experiences of Art, Culture and Social Connection

Constance Lafontaine(✉) and Kim Sawchuk

Concordia University, Montreal, QC, Canada
constance.lafontaine@concordia.ca

Abstract. This paper focuses on a series of guided virtual museum visits designed for older adults over the COVID-19 pandemic. The visits were undertaken as part of a research project in collaboration with the Montreal Museum of Fine Arts (MMFA) and brought together small groups of older adults for weekly guided visits facilitated by trained guides. The visits were held for twelve weeks between March and May 2021. We conducted a qualitative study on the visits, which included weekly observations as well as interviews with the older tour participants, the guides and the research and museum staff to understand the experiences of the virtual guided museum tours from the perspective of older adults. We explore how virtual museum tours provide opportunities for engagement with art, technologies and people, especially during the pandemic when visits to the museum were limited by social distancing measures. We bring these findings into conversation with our previous work with on-site museum visits and reflect on questions related to accessibility of virtual museum visits as well as the challenges for socialization.

Keywords: Virtual museums · Older adults · Guided virtual museum tours · COVID-19 pandemic

1 Introduction

With the onset of the COVID-19 pandemic, there was an increased effort to engage older adults in virtual activities. This paper focuses on a series of guided virtual museum tours for older adults, which were held over three months over the course of the pandemic. These visits were organized as part of a larger project on art, health and well-being targeting older adults experiencing social isolation. In the context of this larger project, both in-person and virtual tours for older adults have been organized with the Montreal Museum of Fine Arts (MMFA) since 2019.[1]

[1] This qualitative study is part of a larger multi-methodological project designed to assess the potential effects of museum visits on the well-being, quality of life and health of socially isolated older adults. The project is led by Dr. Olivier Beauchet of the Université de Montréal and the operations of the project are coordinated by Kevin Galery, both of whom are affiliated with the *Centre de recherche de l'Institut universitaire de gériatrie de Montréal* (CRIUGM). This study is funded by the Fonds de Recherche du Québec - Société et Culture (FRQSC).

Q. Gao and J. Zhou (Eds.): HCII 2022, LNCS 13331, pp. 383–397, 2022.
https://doi.org/10.1007/978-3-031-05654-3_27

We seek to understand the experiences of older adults who followed these virtual guided visits in 2021, as well as the implications of the shift from an in-person, on-site format to a virtual format over the pandemic.

1. What were the experiences of older adults with the guided virtual museum tours?
2. How might virtual museum tours provide opportunities for engagement with art and people, and how do these experiences differ from on-site visits?

To answer these questions, we draw from group observations undertaken over twelve weeks of museum visits held in 2021, and interviews with the participants, guides, museum, and research staff. We bring this data, and the 2021 experience with guided virtual museum tours more broadly, in conversation with a previous series of on-site guided museum tours for older adults undertaken in 2019 *before* the pandemic hit Montreal. We conclude by providing some recommendations that may be conducive to improving the delivery of guided virtual museum tours, with an eye towards bolstering their potential for providing opportunities for social interaction among older adults.

2 Literature Review

Over the last two decades, museums have dedicated increasing attention to digitizing content and engaging the public virtually [1] and developing interactive or immersive content to enhance visitor experience [2]. The development of online content accelerated swiftly over the pandemic, as museums were faced with unprecedented closures [3] and strived to maintain connections to the public [4] under difficult circumstances. Several museums sought to connect to populations who were at increased risk of social isolation over the pandemic, such as older adults [5]. The pandemic put into focus the roles that museums hold in the lives of some older adults, including what Grácio refers to as their "caregiver" role [6]. Museums, they argue, care not only for art but people, as they have made deliberate efforts to engage with vulnerable populations like older adults to mitigate the harms of social isolation.

Online museum content, including virtual visits, are identified as a means to maintain access to cultural institutions in extraordinary episodes such as pandemics, but also in conditions of disability or reduced mobility [7], including those experienced by older adults [8]. Virtual museums, it is suggested, could be especially valuable for older adults living in care homes [8, 9]. According to Hilton et al., for example, virtual museums have "leveled the playing field for non-mobile older adults" by providing access to cultural institutions [8].

There is a limited amount of research exploring how to be attuned to the heterogeneity of later life in devising online arts-based content, building museum platforms, and creating related programming for older adults. As we suggest, this includes the importance of accounting for the diverse needs and motivations that older adults have when they engage with museums [10]. There is also a need to be cognizant of the differential digital [6, 11] and cognitive [11] capacities, which can impact older adults' abilities to participate in and access digital programming.

Kostoska's comparison of online museum platforms suggests that designs that are interaction-free are the easiest for older adults to use, especially for those who are new users of digital technologies [11]. Yet researchers have considered other more interactive formats for virtual visits, finding that the interactivity and engagement are conducive to positive experiences for online museum visits for older adults [8, 9]. The type of digital device used for accessing virtual tours is consequential. For instance, the small screen of tablets can mitigate the "presence" of an artwork [9] while larger, more immersive, displays may foster a stronger connection between the remote visitor and the artwork.

Museums and arts-based activities are often credited for bringing benefits to their visitors, including older museumgoers. This has been documented from the intersecting perspective of art therapy [12], mental and physical health [13] and social isolation [14, 15]. Largely absent in the literature, however, is a focus on the ways in which museum visits for older adults–whether they be virtual or on-site–can be a worthwhile avenue of pleasure or leisure [16].

3 Methodology and Analysis

This study employed a two-pronged methodology. We conducted observations of a group of participants weekly over the course of twelve weeks. During the observation of the visits, two members of our research team took notes and completed two analytic grids that were designed to describe and understand the participants' commitment to and engagement in the guided tours. Second, we undertook a series of semi-structured interviews with a total of sixteen actors involved in these museum visits. This included a member of the research team at the *Centre de recherche de l'Institut universitaire de gériatrie de Montréal* (CRIUGM) (one), the Head of Educational Programs and Volunteer Guides at the MMFA (one), the volunteer guides (four), as well as older adults who participated in virtual tours and who were recruited from all eight groups (eleven). These interviews took place in either French or English, according to the language preferred by the participants (throughout this paper, we indicate in a footnote when quotations have been translated by the authors). Due to the pandemic, all interviews were conducted using Zoom. Interviews were conducted by at least two members of the ACT team. We recorded and transcribed these interviews to support our analysis.

The analysis was conducted by coding emerging themes from the observations and interviews. The interviews and observations were analyzed by a minimum of two team members. We employed four analytical strategies. a) A set of themes emerged from our preliminary observations. These themes were identified by virtue of the frequency with which they were raised and the importance that these comments had in the data. b) We were attentive to moments in the interviews and observations where differing or even conflicting perspectives were highlighted. c) Even if some issues were mentioned only once, they were included if they raised a significant issue for the participant in question. Although some experiences may be unique within our sample, they are nonetheless significant to the participant. They are also likely to be repeated in future iterations of the project. We also considered that, in some cases, respondents would be unlikely to disclose these issues in other contexts.

4 Background: From In-Person in 2019 to Online in 2021

The pilot stage of this project began in 2019. A series of guided on-site museum visits for older adults were organized by the CRIUGM and the MMFA. This was done in partnership with local community organizations who supported the CRIUGM in the recruitment of older adults from French and Mandarin-speaking communities at risk of experiencing social isolation. In the aftermath of this visit, our team at the ACT Lab[2] undertook qualitative interviews with participants, guides, and other actors involved in the visit. The follow-up cycle of museum visits was originally designed as another round of on-site visits in 2020.

Faced with the COVID-19 pandemic and the inability to gather in groups and in public spaces, the decision was made to first postpone the visits. After realizing the pandemic was not subsiding, the project redesigned the visits to deliver them online *via* the teleconference software Zoom. The shift from on-site visits to an online format was born out of necessity, and it posed some important and unforeseen challenges in terms of recruitment. It was difficult for local community organizations, who serve older adults in positions of vulnerability and who faced multiple pressures during the pandemic, to participate in identifying and mobilizing older adults who not only had access to the Internet in their homes, but also had the appropriate device and sufficient digital skill to participate independently in weekly virtual museum visits.

Faced with this conundrum, many of the participants were recruited because of their existing affiliation with the MMFA or because of previous participation in research projects led by the team at the CRIUGM. This resulted in a pool of older adults who met the criteria for social isolation, but who were digitally proficient and could partake in virtual sessions with a relatively low level of one-on-one support or training. This contributed to assembling a cohort of individuals who were already avid museumgoers and thus largely well-versed in the arts. Yet, for most of these older adults, the online guided visits represented a first encounter with virtual museum tours and, more broadly, with organized group activities online.

The cycle of virtual visits that took place between March and May 2021 included eight groups and forty participants aged 65 and over. The eight groups were divided between four MMFA volunteer guides, who each took charge of two groups. The visits began at the same time and day each week for twelve consecutive weeks and lasted thirty minutes each. Six of the groups spoke French and two spoke English. Over the course of the thirty minutes, roughly three art pieces (most often paintings but also sculptures and video art) were presented *via* a PowerPoint presentation by a technical facilitator who shared their screen and navigated the slideshow. On occasion, short interpretive videos about the artworks were shown. For the last visit, an artist participated in a portion of the visit to talk about his work, and to answer questions from the group.

In order to maintain a balance of uniformity and spontaneity, the same art pieces were presented to each of the groups, but there were no scripts for the guides to use (although

[2] Aging + Communication + Technologies (ACT) is a lab based at Concordia University that is studying the experience of aging in a digital world. This study was conducted with research support by Marie-Ève Ducharme, Albane Gaudissart and Andrea Tremblay, as well as students from Dawson College in Montreal.

they pooled their research in advance of the visits). The pieces were all selected from the permanent collection of the MMFA by the guides and organizers before the visits began, and they were grouped thematically to follow a narrative structure and arc spanning from simpler to more complex approaches to art. The guides, drawing from the dialogic approach [17], would share information at the same time as they instigated conversations by asking participants questions about the artwork. This could include asking participants about the elements they observed in the artwork, their impressions of the artistic methods behind the work, the cultural and historical contexts, how the pieces made them feel and how the paintings might relate to their own life experiences.

5 Findings

5.1 Encountering Digital Technologies Through Museum Visits

The Need for "Warm Expertise" and Digital Support. Even if the group members owned digital devices, had connection to the Internet and had relatively advanced digital skills, a significant amount of work was devoted to making sure the visits would be accessible in advance. The coordinator of the project took on the role of a warm expert, who could mediate "between the technological universal and the concrete situation, needs and background of the novice user with whom he is in a close personal relationship" [18]. This support was crucial in the weeks and days leading up to the first session. As the coordinator stated:

> Half the people had zero problems. They knew about Zoom, they were using it already so it was super easy. And 25% needed a little bit of guidance to install the software, to get used to it, to use it. And for the remaining 25%, it was hands-on support, it was by phone, we told them where to click and what to fill in to install it for the first time.[3]

Some of the older adults we interviewed reported receiving support from friends and family to participate in the sessions. Despite this, two people stated that they would have benefited from a more in-depth knowledge of Zoom and its features before the tours began (*e.g.*, knowing how to access the gallery mode). The observations of the visits highlighted how limited prior knowledge of Zoom affected their experiences. These participants were not able to enlarge artworks easily, see the other participants in the gallery or even participate in the conversation because of intermittent issues with their microphones. Prior digital experience and skills affected the participants' ability to fully engage with the virtual activities developed by the museum guides, at least initially.

Learning to Use Zoom. Despite the challenges we observed, the large majority of older adults we interviewed (nine of eleven) stated that they did not have major difficulty becoming accustomed to the Zoom format during the visits. One participant noted, "I liked this format better than I thought [I would]." According to one participant, "it was very, very easy to participate" in the tours. Indeed, some participants learned how to

[3] Translated from French.

use Zoom for the first time through their participation in the tours and reported using it afterwards to connect with friends and family. Others improved their knowledge of the software, which they thought could have a positive impact on their ability to use the software to participate in other virtual activities after the virtual visits.

Digital Distractions. Several participants mentioned that noise from other participants or their late arrival to a session could be distracting. One participant noted that "the way participants wouldn't turn off their microphones, blabbering, was very distracting. They didn't have that sort of basic Zoom etiquette down" (it should be noted here that participants were instructed to leave their microphones on as much as they could, to foster their ability to quickly and frequently intervene in the conversations). We observed that the presentation of a particularly serene video artwork (Nadia Myre's *Portrait in Motion*) was particularly hindered by a participant's live microphone. A participant made noise without knowing that she could be heard by the other group members. This caused a significant disturbance that interfered with the group's experience of this piece.

5.2 Encountering Art Through a Screen

Affordances of Virtual Tours. We sought to understand how virtual tours, for this group of avid museum visitors, compared to their previous in-person encounters with art. Experiences were mixed on this front: approximately half of the participants interviewed found virtual tours to be a "very good" format for encountering artworks. Some features of the virtual tour format, in particular, were appreciated, as they allowed participants to interact with the art in a way that was unusual for them. For example, participants appreciated seeing video art or interpretive videos as they thought this enlivened their virtual experience. Even more memorable for the participants–and a feat that is likely easier to accomplish with virtual tours–was the presence of the artist Moridja Kitenge Banza, who joined the Zoom visits and answered questions about his work for each of the eight groups. The artist spoke briefly about his practice, live from his studio, and answered questions from the participants. Having an artist currently exhibiting at the MMFA attend a session to engage 'live' was a noted highlight for participants. As one explains: "it was uplifting actually, he gave another viewpoint on the whole situation. [… his presence] made it more alive." This feature puts into focus what could be uniquely accomplished *via* the virtual visit.

Other features of the virtual tours were noted. Three participants mentioned that taking part in the tours using a tablet allowed them to enlarge portions of the screen, with a gesture of their fingers, so that they could see the details of a work. For these participants, the virtual format allowed them to appreciate museum works in a new way and to discover visual details. Another participant noted that she was able to get closer to her screen and felt that, with her iPad, she was closer to the works than she would have been in the museum.

> I think I prefer the virtual visit both because it's easier to get to and parking at the museum is difficult, but also because I think you have closer access to the art. Not to the actual art obviously, but to see it blown up on a screen is very useful.

What is Diminished with the Virtual. While the virtual tours that used the Zoom platform convey some unique aspects of the artworks and provide a unique vantage for some, other aspects of encountering art were thought to have been evinced by the online experience. During the weekly observations, we noted that some individuals expressed that they had difficulty distinguishing colors on the screen. Others would ask the guide about the texture of the works and the dimensionality of the brushstrokes. Almost systematically, participants asked the guide the size of a work to better imagine the space it occupies in the MMFA. Despite the guide's efforts to provide context about the rooms in which the artworks were placed through explanations and photographs, there was an enduring lack of context, or sense of the overall atmosphere and grandeur of the MMFA. As Kaplan notes "we implicitly measure and assess the space and objects around us in relation to our bodies" [19], and in these terms the embodied experience of an on-site visit to the museum was notably absent.

There was a sense, conveyed by the participants and guides alike, that viewing art on a screen deprives it of an intangible quality, what Benjamin in his classic piece, *The Work of Art in the Age of Mechanical Reproduction*, refers to as its place in space and time, its authenticity [20]. One participant noted that, for her, there was a marked lack of "sensory" or "emotional" triggers when viewing work through a Zoom screen. A participant encapsulates her ambivalence about her experience with the virtual tours:

> You can see them [the artworks] closer, actually, [virtually] than if you are there. You can't get up that close to a painting [in person]. But it certainly isn't the same. I mean when you see live art, it is living and so, to me, it's like a human being. It's different when we're in person than [when] we're talking like this. You get the full impact of the spirituality in it, and perhaps the goal of the artist. It's an emotional experience for me.

Deepening and Broadening Connections to Art. Even if all participants did not find that virtual museum visits were an ideal way to engage with art, almost all of them appreciated the visits as a means to compensate for their inability to attend the museum in person, especially at a time when museums were closed due to the pandemic. The virtual tours allowed many participants to further their knowledge and interest in the arts. In fact, many participants specifically used the terms "deepen" and "broaden" to talk about the impact that virtual guided tours can have on their connection to the arts.

They appreciated all the work that went into selecting the pieces chosen, the coherence of the themes and the overall narrative approach of the guides who mediated their virtual visits. The structure of the tours, in which guides focused on a few specific works, allowed participants to consider them more thoughtfully, and in more detail. Mieke Bal refers to focalization as "[t]he relationship between the vision, the agent that sees, and that which is seen term" [21]. Along these lines, the virtual museum visits entailed a focalization that defined the interaction and relationship between the visitor and the artwork. As one participant noted: "you appreciate and observe certain things because you are focused on the work whereas in the museum you are walking around." Another participant appreciated that virtual visits brought more focus to the art-viewing experience: "each of the works was highlighted as opposed to when you go to the museum, it's overflowing everywhere." The hyper-curated format of the guided tours, where visitors could only see three predetermined artworks at a time, gave them a more intense encounter with individual pieces, and in a sense trained them in how to look closely.

The virtual tours also exposed them to art they otherwise would have not encountered in a typical museum visit. For some participants, the visits introduced them to Inuit or Indigenous art. One of the participants mentioned: "I liked the discovery of African art. I am now planning to visit this wing." Others said they had a better understanding of contemporary art, which they disliked before being exposed to it in this setting. Most of the participants stated that the visits allowed them to discover the museum's permanent collection. In fact, through the visits, they realized how little they had previously encountered the permanent collection despite years of living in Montreal and visiting the MMFA. When we asked the participants what they do at the MMFA when they frequent it, the vast majority stated they went to view special exhibits. Several participants expressed a desire to now see these works in person: "I plan to go see all of them in person for sure."

Virtual and On-Site Visits as Complementary. Most of the participants stated they would like to continue to participate in virtual museum tours, even in a post-pandemic context. But this would need to happen in a specific way. For instance, participants thought that the virtual option was "convenient" and required less effort and organization. They determined that this would be ideal for periods when they may experience specific mobility issues (be it because of health, weather, or confinement measures). Many participants volunteered that they would prefer hybrid in program delivery that would allow them to alternate between virtual visits and on-site tours so they could benefit from the distinct advantages of each format. It was clear that, for these participants, the virtual program of visits did *not* replace on-site visits. In some cases, it just made participants keener to go to the museum in person: "after the virtual visits I was just really eager to go to the museum in person. I can't wait to go." (see Footnote 3).

5.3 Virtual Visits to Bridge Inaccessibility

Montreal is plagued with cold, icy winters that often make commuting treacherous for older adults. Parking in the downtown area, where the MMFA is located, is difficult–even in summer–and expensive. Para-transport for those with reduced mobility can be unreliable or inflexible. During much of the pandemic, health measures in the province of Quebec forced the museum to close and restricted people's ability to gather in public spaces. The MMFA, with its large rooms, multiple buildings, and limited seating, can be difficult to navigate for people with reduced mobility. Although mobility aids are available to visitors, our interviews with older museum-visitors indicates that older adults who could benefit from these aids are hesitant to actively request them or even accept them when they are offered because of fears of being stigmatized.

For these reasons, the virtual guided tours may be an attractive alternative that mitigates some of the accessibility challenges posed by the MMFA or other museums. For one participant with a mobility impairment, the virtual format gave her a chance to access a museum she would not have visited and an activity in which she would not have participated in, otherwise. With a foot injury, she is unable to walk through a museum and standing in front of an artwork for several minutes is especially difficult. She told us that she had stopped going to the MMFA in recent years: "the museum has become a painful experience because of so much standing, Zoom makes it nicer for that." This difficulty of standing still in front of a work of art for several minutes was identified by many participants as a problem with on-site visits, and one of the benefits of virtual tours. According to another participant "lots and lots of elderly people are coming to the museum and having no place to sit, it's really hard." Another woman, reflecting on a recent museum experience, noted: "there were no benches to sit down. I had to miss out on the last two rooms [of the exhibit]." These participants welcomed the virtual alternative but still feared that the lack of accessibility of the museum would limit their ability to engage with art in their old age in the ways they favoured.

The virtual tours also allowed participants to access the museum's works during the pandemic, especially during a time when the museum was closed to visitors. The virtual tours were particularly appreciated by participants who were out of town when the tours took place. They felt privileged to be able to access the MMFA's works from the comfort of their own homes: "It's great for people who can't travel and live far from Montreal." (see Footnote 3).

5.4 Encountering Others Through Guided Virtual Museum Tours

Difficulty Building Social Connections Through Virtual Visits. As we mentioned, this study is inscribed in a larger project centred on the potential role of museum visits in improving health, well-being, and quality of life for older adults who find themselves in a situation of social isolation. Because of this, the potential for virtual museum visits to be a space for social interaction was front of mind for organizers. Yet, among the participants interviewed, only one person mentioned having created meaningful bonds or friendships with others: "We became quite good friends. We are all going to meet in July and have an outside tour and lunch. I did not expect that. I usually don't set too many expectations when I sign up [for activities like this one]."

This experience of connection to others as a result of participating in a virtual visit, however, was not the norm. For a participant belonging to a different group, the dynamic was much less conducive to a friendly outing: "Let's just say that at the beginning it was a little fixed, then it developed quietly, but not really fast. It remained rather fixed, rather formal." (see Footnote 3). The majority of participants felt that the virtual format posed challenges to socializing within the group. For one of the participants, the virtual mode directly and negatively impacted the quality of interpersonal exchanges: "It's not a social context like it would be in a personal encounter. So, the personal context is missing and always will be missing if it remains virtual. There's really something missing in the virtual encounters." Others told us that the structure and parameters of a short virtual session (it bears repeating that the visits were only thirty minutes) were not conducive to bonding between participants. As one participant explained, "It is hard to make permanent connections in small boxes, also it was too short." Another participant answered similarly: "it's very brief, everything is very small, so it didn't have a huge impact on me. You know, the connection with the people, even with the art, it's hard to really connect."

Engaging with Others as a Rewarding Experience. Even if most participants did not make lasting social connections *via* the tours, this does not mean that they did not appreciate the interpersonal dimension of the visits. All of the participants reported that they liked listening to the others' opinions about the works of art: "everyone has a different imagination. It opens our minds to have the comments of others." A guide echoed a comment she heard during a visit: "participants mentioned how much they appreciate talking to each other and seeing these paintings together."

In fact, the social aspect of engaging with art was appreciated to such an extent that nine of the eleven participants interviewed would have preferred that a greater portion of the visit be allocated to this type of exchange. One participant explained: "I would have liked more discussion to be encouraged. I wish there was less recap of the week before." Another participant agreed: "participants should talk more and the guide less." (see Footnote 3). For some participants interviewed, visits to the museum normally represent a solitary activity, and the cycle of virtual visits has made it possible to conceive of the museum as a social experience. A participant noted "I really appreciate another perspective on art, as I am used to going to the museum on my own." (see Footnote 3).

6 Discussion

The pandemic prompted organizers to hold the museum visits in videoconference mode using Zoom software. This unexpected change–and the need to recruit digitally-proficient older adults–excluded many of the participants who would originally have been targeted for the activity. During the 2019 visits, on the other hand, participation was not contingent on the use of digital technologies.

The juxtaposition of an on-site cohort with relatively low digital skill and low exposure to art and museums (2019) with an online cohort of relatively high digital skills and high exposure to art and museums (2021) helps us put our findings into context. It also generates new questions. The differential experiences of the older adults with guided museum tours generates added critical questions on the accessibility of the museum for older populations, particularly those who are experiencing social isolation, and the challenges to socializing with others online.

6.1 Enduring Digital Divides Thwart the Accessibility of Cultural Institutions

There is an increasing interest in digital activities to counter social isolation among older populations [22] and a desire to make online museum content accessible to older audiences through online programming. Yet, which socio-economic classes of older adults actually can access emerging opportunities for online engagement with art and culture and take advantage of the benefits often associated with museums [12–15]?

As we have argued above, our study confirms that the virtual mode provided opportunities for older adults with reduced mobility or other disabilities to continue to have or to regain access to the museum, as long as they were digitally connected in advance. We also found that older adults who enrolled in the virtual visits still wanted to maintain a physical and embodied access to museum spaces throughout later life. The 2019 and 2021 participants all agreed that on-site museum tours could be physically challenging due to differential capacities for mobility, hearing, and vision. The digital option remains important and valuable for these older adults, yet they also wanted access to the museum, which is an important cultural institution in the city, in person. In other words, the virtual visits do not diminish the responsibility that museums have for maintaining accessible physical spaces, a mission commensurate with their social role as public stewards of knowledge and culture.

Further, as we explore the potential of museums as space to socialize and engage with art and culture, the difficult recruitment process experienced by this project suggests activities like these are a non-starter for older adults already at the margins of digital society. Accessibility, in digital and socio-economic terms, also needs to be considered from the perspective of the digital. Access to the Internet is far from being just a question of age; it is linked to other socio-economic factors such as income, levels of education and literacy rates. In Quebec, 74% of seniors aged 65 and over are internet users. That number tumbles down to 43% for older adults who earn less than $20,000 a year [23]. Access to digital technologies for low-income adults is contingent on several intersecting social and structural factors [24]. In fact, many of the factors associated with social isolation in the city of Montreal [25] are also predictive of digital disconnection among older adults.

All of this means that an activity that has Internet access, use of a device and digital proficiency as requirements quite likely excludes those individuals who may gain the most from the opportunities for engagement with culture, art and individuals. As such, there is a risk of further entrenching the museum's traditional image as elitist institutions [26] that cater only to a narrow segment of the population.

6.2 The Challenges of Online Socialization

A crucial difference between the 2019 and 2021 tours was the degree to which people felt as though they had socialized with others. Many of the older adults who followed the 2019 visits had developed relationships with the other project participants. For some, this included occasional outings in parks or for coffee, or ongoing communication online. Further, a notable number of participants (five of twelve) had taken up language classes, art classes or new art practices in the aftermath of the visits and directly credited the on-site museum visits for motivating their decision to partake in these activities.

In our analysis of how online museum visits compare to on-site visits, we do not see corresponding impacts among the 2021 participants. Despite the success of the visits and the demonstrated potential for building virtual spaces to socialize through the experience of art, the online museum tours did not cultivate social engagement in the same way that the on-site activities did. Because the two groups were distinct, it is worth exploring some of the factors that may have contributed to these differences.

First, for the participants interviewed in 2021, an interest in art and the museum was at the forefront of their decision to enrol. The primary motivation for participating in virtual visits was to access art, not the desire to meet others or even the desire to find a fun or social activity during a pandemic. The primary purpose of the activity, for those we spoke to, was not to socialize and the majority was surprised when we asked if they had engaged in social interaction with other participants outside of the guided tours. One participant exclaimed, "I didn't know that was a possibility!". Meanwhile, most of the 2019 participants did not have an existing interest in art and had been drawn to the activity because of more varied motivations: from finding an enriching and fun activity, to passing the time, to learning about art, to connecting with others.

Second, on-site visits offer more opportunities for spontaneous connections between participants. In 2019, while the tours were taking place at the museum, many participants were chatting informally with the guides and other members of their group in the minutes before or after the guided tours. These discussions allowed people to identify a few others with whom they got along, build relationships from week to week, and eventually socialize outside of the tour context, whether online or in person. In a Zoom session with multiple participants, it is difficult, if not impossible, to start a conversation with just one other person without the entire group being involved in the conversation. The down times before and after the visits were also absent, as the Zoom room was opened promptly at the start of the visit and closed at the end. In other words, the platform's affordances do not readily make opportunities for informal conversation between participants possible.

Third, the majority of the social connections we saw in the previous cycle took place in a discussion group on the social network WeChat. This group brought together most of the Mandarin-speaking participants. This discussion group was designed to communicate with the participants in an effective way, but it fortuitously became a socializing structure that operated in parallel to the tour project. Through WeChat, older adults would share information about art, among other interests. As the pandemic struck in 2020, the WeChat group members have continued their exchanges online to this day.

Despite these differences, the 2021 group would have liked to have had an informal discussion at the beginning of the visits and would have appreciated to hear more of the opinions and perspectives of others on the works presented. There was a clear willingness to engage more with others, that may have been stifled by the rigidities of the online parameters. This provides opportunities to enhance the social aspect of future tour cycles and to build on the socialization potential of online museum visits.

7 Conclusions and Limitations

7.1 Limitations of Study

It is important to note a few limitations of this research. First, as we discussed in this article, the challenges linked to recruitment of participants to the museum visits meant that the group had a strong pre-existing interest in art and museums and a relatively high level of digital proficiency: this study should be understood within this context. As such, the experiences of our participants with online virtual tours likely were different than they would be for older adults with less of an established interest in art, and lower digital skills. Second, as we bring the 2021 online visits in conversation with the 2019 on-site visits in the discussion section, it is worth noting the distinct timelines of the data collection. We undertook the data collection for the 2019 group several months after the end of their visits. This gave us a desirable vantage into the long-term impact of the visits but also made our data suffer from diminished memories. Our 2021 data collection began mere days after the end of the visits, meaning that the older adults had a clearer recollection of their experience but not as fulsome an understanding of the longer-term impacts that the virtual visits might have brought to their daily lives.

7.2 How Museum Tours Provide Opportunities for Connections

We have presented the results of a study that documented the experiences of older adults who followed a series of twelve guided virtual museum tours over three months in 2021. We asked two research questions. First, we wondered "How might virtual museum tours provide opportunities for engagement with art and people, and how do these experiences differ from on-site visits?" In contrast with previous on-site visits, building social connections among group members tended to be more difficult and was less likely to lead to interpersonal connections outside the group. Likewise, the project and the recruitment challenges in the context of a pandemic puts into focus critical questions about the (in)accessibility of museums and emerging forms of virtual content designed for older adults. In answering this research question, we can briefly identify recommendations that may benefit future initiatives, especially as it pertains to improving the experience of older adults with museum visits, improving accessibility, and bolstering the role of virtual visits for mediating social encounters.

Improving Access for Digitally Disconnected Older Adults. Certainly, this matter is contingent on systemic factors that are outside of the purview of virtual tour organizers. Yet, some potential ways to mitigate exclusion could include strengthening the accompaniment of older adults who need additional support. Another strategy could include working in partnership with local digital literacy initiatives to provide new digital learners opportunities to hone their skills through virtual tours.

Improving the Quality of Social Encounters. Longer visits with a more relaxed pace can help older adults engage with each other. Consider increasing opportunities for spontaneous exchanges like asking questions, creating breakout rooms for discussion. This could also be done by providing time for informal discussions after the tour, which may be encouraged by providing questions related to art (*e.g.*, Do you practice art? Can you tell us about your most cherished museum experience?). Options for parallel engagement between tours could be considered (*e.g.*, email lists, Facebook groups or message boards). Reminding participants that the visits are not just about art but also about connecting with people can normalize conversation and social connections.

Improving the Overall Experience. Devising and communicating protocols for group members to participate (*e.g.*, you may speak up at any time), and repeating instructions frequently may help some group members feel more empowered to intervene. Questioning participants directly can also be a useful strategy to encourage more egalitarian participation.

7.3 Experiences of Older Adults

Our second research question was "What were the experiences of older adults with the guided virtual museum tours?" Our findings reveal our participants' diverse perspectives on matters such as engagement with technologies, art, and other individuals through the visits. Broadly, we found that the digital approach to guided museum visits provided for these digitally adept older adults an effective and simple means of participating in the offerings of a local cultural institution. Museum tours, which were facilitated by an experienced guide, allowed them to broaden and deepen existing interests in art. In particular, the participants valued partaking in museum visits as a collective rather than solitary experience: they welcomed the input and opinions of others, finding that it enriched their understanding of art. The digital's capacity for incorporating supplementary engaging elements (like interpretive videos or the presence of an artist) were appreciated, yet many participants still longed for an embodied museum experience. Especially notable for these participants was the convenience of the virtual format to maintain a connection to art and culture over the course of a pandemic, when there were options for in-person cultural activities. For most of our participants, the virtual tours were an initial–and highly positive–foray into online group activities upon which they could build.

References

1. Hogsden, C., Poulter, E.K.: The real other? Museum objects in digital contact networks. J. Media Cult. **17**(3), 265–286 (2012)
2. Stogner, M.B.: The immersive cultural museum experience–creating context and story with new media technology. Int. J. Incl. Mus. **3**(3), 117–130 (2011)
3. Presti, O.L.: Covid-19 and the cultural life of older people. Mus. Manag. Curatorship 1–11 (2021)
4. Markopoulos, E., Ye, C., Markopoulos, P., Luimula, M.: Digital museum transformation strategy against the Covid-19 pandemic crisis. In: Markopoulos, E., Goonetilleke, R.S., Ho, A.G., Luximon, Y. (eds.) AHFE 2021. Lecture Notes in Networks and Systems, vol. 276, pp 225–234. Springer, Cham (2021). https://doi.org/10.1007/978-3-030-80094-9_27
5. Tan, M.K.B., Tan, C.M.: Curating wellness during a pandemic in Singapore: COVID-19, museums, and digital imagination. Public Health **192**, 68–71 (2021)
6. Gracio, R.: Museums working with older people in times of pandemic. Work. with Older People **24**(4), 313–319 (2020)
7. McMillen, R.: Museum disability access: social inclusion opportunities through innovative new media practices. Pac. J. **10**, 95–107 (2015)
8. Hilton, D., Levine, A., Zanetis, J.: Don't lose the connection: virtual visits for older adults. J. Mus. Educ. **44**(3), 253–263 (2019)
9. Pisoni, G.: Mediating distance: new interfaces and interaction design techniques to follow and take part in remote museum visits. J. Syst. Inf. Technol. **22**(4), 329–350 (2020)
10. Hansen, A., Zipsane, H.: Older people as a developing market for cultural heritage sites. JACE **20**, 137–143 (2014)
11. Kostoska, G., Baez, M., Daniel, F., Casati, F.: Virtual, remote participation in museum visits by older adults: a feasibility study. In: CEUR Workshop Proceedings, vol. 1352 (2015)
12. Bennington, R., Backos, A., Harrison, J., Etherington Reader, A., Carolan, R.: Art therapy in art museums: promoting social connectedness and psychological well-being of older adults. Arts Psychother. **49**, 34–43 (2016)
13. Beauchet, O., Cooper-Brown, L., Hayashi, Y., Galery, K., Vilcocq, C., Bastien, T.: Effects of "Thursdays at the Museum" at the Montreal Museum of Fine Arts on the mental and physical health of older community dwellers: the art-health randomized clinical trial protocol. Trials **21**, 709 (2020)
14. Evans, S.C., Bray, J., Garabedian, C.: Supporting creative ageing through the arts: the impacts and implementation of a creative arts programme for older people. Work. with Older People. **26**(1), 22–30 (2022)

15. Todd, C., Camic, P.M., Lockyer, B., Thomson, L.J.M., Chatterjee, H.J.: Museum-based programs for socially isolated older adults: understanding what works. Health Place **48**, 47–55 (2017)
16. Smiraglia, C.: Targeted museum programs for older adults: a research and program review. Curator **59**, 39–54 (2016)
17. Styles, C.: Dialogic learning in museum space. Ethos **19**(3), 12–20 (2011)
18. Bakardjieva, M.: Internet Society: The Internet in Everyday Life. SAGE Publications, Thousand Oaks (2005)
19. Kaplan, D.: What does it matter where my body happens to be? A personal view of online art museum tours. J. Mus. Educ. **46**(4), 531–546 (2021)
20. Benjamin, W.: The Work of Art in the Age of Mechanical Reproduction. (J. A. Underwood, Trans.). Penguin Books, Harlow (2008)
21. Bal, M.: Narratology: Introduction to the Theory of Narrative, 3rd edn. University of Toronto Press, Toronto (2009)
22. World Health Organization: Socialization and loneliness among older people. Decade of healthy Ageing (2021)
23. van der Vlugt, E., Audet-Nadeau, V.: Bien vieillir au Québec: Portrait des inégalités entre générations et entre personnes aînées. Observatoire québécois des inégalités (2020)
24. Lafontaine, C., Sawchuk, K.: Accessing InterACTion: ageing with technologies and the place of access. In: Zhou, J., Salvendy, G. (eds.) ITAP 2015. LNCS, vol, 9193, pp 210–220. Springer, Cham (2015). https://doi.org/10.1007/978-3-319-20892-3_21
25. Gouvernement du Québec: Portrait des aînés de l'île de Montréal (2017)
26. Sandahl, J.: Addressing societal responsibilities through core museum functions and methods: the museum definition, prospects and potentials. Mus. Int. **71**(1–2), v–iv (2019)

Designing an Innovative Intergenerational Educational Program to Bridge the Digital Divide: The Cyber School for Grandparents Initiative

Elena Rolandi[1,2](✉), Emanuela Sala[3], Mauro Colombo[1], Roberta Vaccaro[1], and Antonio Guaita[1]

[1] Golgi Cenci Foundation, Corso San Martino 10, 20081 Abbiategrasso, MI, Italy
e.rolandi@golgicenci.it

[2] Department of Brain and Behavioral Sciences, University of Pavia, Piazza Botta 11, 27100 Pavia, Italy

[3] University of Milan-Bicocca, Piazza dell'Ateneo Nuovo 1, 20126 Milan, Italy

Abstract. The digitalisation of society may pose major challenges for active ageing promotion, representing a source of social exclusion for many older people lacking the basic digital skills. Older Italians are amongst the least digitally savvy in Europe. In this context, there is an urgent need for accessible and inclusive digital educational programs, targeting specifically the frailest group of the old age population. The Cyber School for Grandparents initiative is an innovative intergenerational educational program aimed at training secondary school students to become cyber tutors for their grandparents. The aim of this work is to present all the steps performed to design and implement the intervention in the school context and to perform a feasibility study on this educational experience, assessing pre-post changes on older adults' digital skills, use and attitudes as well as monitoring students' participation and learning outcomes. The study is ongoing and will provide useful information for the implementation of similar initiative in other contexts.

Keywords: Digital divide · Active ageing · Intergenerational intervention

1 Introduction

1.1 The Digitalisation of Society and the Challenges for Active Ageing Promotion

Europe has an ageing population and amongst the European Union, Italy is the country with the highest share of the population aged 65+ [1]. Indeed, in 2020, 23% of the Italian population was aged 65 or over, accounting to as many as 14 million people. Among those, 2 million people belong to the age group of the oldest old (aged 85 years or older) representing 4% of the total population. The proportion of the old age population is set to increase further over the next few decades. Besides having an ageing population, many western countries are also characterized by a process of increasing digitalisation.

Q. Gao and J. Zhou (Eds.): HCII 2022, LNCS 13331, pp. 398–412, 2022.
https://doi.org/10.1007/978-3-031-05654-3_28

Indeed, within a few weeks of the COVID-19 outbreak, the lockdown accelerated the adoption of digital solutions at an unprecedented pace, creating unforeseen opportunities for scaling up alternative approaches to social and economic life. In Italy, digitalisation is one of the three "strategic axes" of the National Recovery and Resilience Plan (NRRP) [2]. According to the NRRP, in the next few years, many public and private services, including the services provided by the health and social care sectors, will be digitalised.

The benefits of living in a digitalised society are widely recognised; however, the digitalisation of society may pose major challenges for active ageing promotion, representing a source of social exclusion for many older people lacking the digital skills to act and interact in such an unfamiliar social context. With this respect, older Italians are at risk of social exclusion, being amongst the least digitally savvy in Europe [3, 4]. To foster active ageing, the digitalisation of society should therefore be accompanied by innovative digital educational programs targeting specifically the frailest group of the old age population, e.g., the less educated, older people living in rural areas, older women. Indeed, the digital divide is likely to reflect a socio-cultural divide, rather than an effect of age per se, since Information and Communication Technology (ICT) use among older adults is associated with higher education, occupation and wealth [3, 4], leading to the paradox of having the people putatively most advantaged by the use of ICT as those most excluded. Adoption of technology by older adults is a complex issue and is affected by a wide range of factors, such as cognitive abilities, perceived self-efficacy and related anxiety [5]. However, direct experience on computer use reduces the negative attitudes toward it, regardless of age [6–8]. Quite surprisingly, despite the relevance of these topics, digital education in older age is not at the top of policy makers' agenda. Indeed, the Italian Digital Education Plan (https://ec.europa.eu/education/education-in-the-eu/digital-education-action-plan_it) does not include older people amongst its target population.

1.2 Intergenerational Connections to Bridge the Digital Divide

ICT use among older adults may be favoured by properly designed educational interventions, focused on their interests, needs and concerns about technology. The literature on ICT interventions for older adults is abundant and several reviews were published in recent years to draw conclusions on their effects. Recent systematic reviews show that ICT interventions had a positive impact on older adults' social and psychological well-being, specifically with regard to measures of social support and connectedness, social isolation, life satisfaction and depression [9–12]. The influence on loneliness were mixed: the majority of studies reported a positive effect, while some showed no or negative effects [9, 10, 12]. The interventions reported mainly deal with computer training, but most recent studies favour mobile devices coherently to the wide spread of these technologies among the aged population [9]. All the reviews conducted highlighted several methodological limitations of the studies in the field: lack of control group or randomization, small and convenience sample without power calculation, absence of follow-up to assess the long-term effects after intervention completion [9–12]. Moreover, the majority of the studies reported so far enrolled older adults from the community with some starting digital skills and/or a positive attitude toward technology learning.

The real challenge is to design digital educational programs able to reach those older adults without any basic digital skill or device. Thus, an important first step is to change the initial negative attitude of older adults ICT non-user, so that they take this first step and start using the technology.

In order to enhance the feasibility and the acceptability of an intervention, it is useful in the planning and design phase to synthesize previous qualitative studies of user experiences of similar intervention and/or target population and to identify key issues, needs and challenges reported [13]. Systematic reviews of qualitative studies on older adults ICT users highlighted that the principal drives for use were the desire to keep in touch with family and friends and to enter into intergenerational communication, whereas main obstacles are their distrust in terms of perceived utility, privacy concerns as well as technical difficulties [14, 15]. As regards the preferred learning context, old ICT users rely on their own social network to acquire digital competence and spontaneously refer to their younger family members (for instance children and grandchildren) that may act as "warm" experts [16–19].

Based on this knowledge, we search the literature for intergenerational programs aimed at improving the digital skills of older adults. There are few studies in which students (from secondary school or universities) act as mentors for seniors to improve their digital competences. Even these educational interventions generally involved older adults enrolled from the community on a voluntary basis, who therefore already have some initial digital skills and/or a positive attitude toward technology. These preliminary experiences showed encouraging results regarding the participation and satisfaction of both generations, mainly based on qualitative analysis performed on students' learning logs and from interviews or ad-hoc questionnaires for seniors [20–22].

Recently, a well-designed pre-post study on a group intergenerational intervention reported significant and positive changes on attitude toward technology, technophobia and perceived social isolation of older adults, with medium to large effect sizes [23]. On the other hand, qualitative analysis on students' narratives reveal positive learning outcomes in several dimensions: self-awareness, empathy, empowerment and new perspectives about ageism [24].

Altogether these initiatives show preliminary but encouraging insights on the feasibility of intergenerational intervention to bridge the digital divide, also highlighting the mutual benefit for both generations.

1.3 An Innovative Intergenerational Educational Program

Based on this background and on previous research experiences in the field, we develop the Cyber School for Grandparents initiative, an innovative intergenerational educational programme aimed to train secondary school students (aged 15–17 years) to become cyber tutors for their grandparents. The educational intervention was designed to give to the students both the theoretical knowledge and the soft skills to help seniors to learn, thus contributing to a social innovation process.

Compared to the previously reported intergenerational programs on ICT use described in the previous paragraph, the present initiative shows relevant innovative features: the educational lessons will be embedded in the students' school program instead of being offered on a volunteering basis, the students will independently plan and implement the cyber sessions for their grandparents outside the school as extracurricular activities and, whenever possible, the program involves familial dyads. This novel approach have the potential to reach older adults with very diverse sociocultural background and digital competences, thanks to the mediation of their own nephew as "warm expert" [17].

The project is ongoing. In the present work we describe all the steps performed to conceptualize, design and implement the Cyber School for Grandparents initiative. In the third section we briefly describe the design of the feasibility study aimed to develop the intervention in a specific school context and to provide preliminary evidence on the effect of this innovative educational intervention. We will provide evidence to answer to the following research questions:

1. Does training secondary school students to become cyber tutors for seniors, lead to measurable pre-post intervention changes in seniors' self-reported digital competence and attitudes toward Internet?
2. How do the students reflect on their learning throughout the experience?
3. Is there any measurable pre-post intervention change on psychosocial well-being of the participants?
4. Is there any measurable pre-post intervention change on students' aging stereotypes?

2 Conceptualization and Funding

The project is conceptualized and coordinated by the Golgi Cenci Foundation (GCF), a research centre devoted to interdisciplinary research on aging and dementia set in Abbiategrasso, a small city in the Milan metropolitan area (Italy). The initial idea arose from the shared visions, direct experiences, competencies and collaborations developed through previous projects in the field.

At first, the participation in the Aging in a Networked Society project with the University of Milan-Bicocca produced a number of useful findings on the value of bringing older adults closer to new technologies (https://aginginanetworkedsociety.wordpress.com/). Drawing on this research experience, we decided to implement an intergenerational educational intervention with the collaboration of the local Human Science High School (Bachelet Institute), which has been among the Dementia Friendly Community (DFC) stakeholders since 2016. The DFC is a nationwide social innovation project coordinated by Federazione Alzheimer Italia, the main Italian non-profit association for patients with dementia and their families, aimed at making of a community a place more welcoming to people with dementia. The Human Science High School is primarily aimed at the acquisition of specific skills in Psychology, Sociology, Pedagogy and Anthropology, making it an ideal context for this kind of initiatives. Relying on this long lasting and fruitful collaboration, we performed the "Digital Grandparents" online survey among Bachelet Institute students, to obtain preliminary information on the use of digital tools by students' grandparents.

Based on the data collected, the study proposal was built and then selected by the third Bicocca University of crowdfunding (BiUniCrowd) call, a yearly funding program that supports the research and ideas of young scientists, students and former students of the University of Milan-Bicocca through the direct contribution of people and society.

In the present section, we describe these experiences which contributed to the conceptualization of the Cyber School for Grandparents initiative, following their temporal sequence.

2.1 Previous Experience: The Aging in a Networked Society-Social Experiment Study (ANS-SE)

The project "Aging in a Networked Society. Older people, social networks, and wellbeing" (funded by Fondazione Cariplo, grant number: 2017-0946) was aimed at investigating the impact of offline and online social networks on older people's well-being.

The GCF was in charge of running a social experiment (ANS-SE) to assess the causal impact of Social Networking Sites (SNS) use on loneliness and social isolation, cognitive functions and physical health, whose methodology is reported elsewhere [25]. Briefly, the study was aimed to enrol 180 participants aged between 79 and 83 years and residing in Abbiategrasso without previous experience on SNS use to be randomly allocated to one of three conditions: the treatment (SNS training course), the active control group (lifestyle course) and a waiting list. The SNS course consisted of 5 group lessons on smartphone, Facebook and WhatsApp. When looking at the impact of the SNS training course on the measures of interest, we found mixed results. In the short term, we did not find any significant impact of the treatment on cognitive functions [26] and on social well-being (unpublished work). However, one year after intervention completion, older people trained for SNS use reported significantly higher usage of SNSs and reduced feelings of being left out [27]. These latter findings are of particular interest, since follow-up was performed through a phone survey during the COVID-19 Italian lockdown in May 2020, when any in-person contact was forbidden and digital technology became essential to maintain social contacts.

Along with quantitative research, we further performed qualitative interviews to understand the experience of new older users. The majority of the participants reported a positive experience on SNS use, because it simplified intergenerational communication (mainly within their own social network) and it was useful to find information, funny video or images [28]. As previously reported by the literature, the main reasons for seldom or not use were technical difficulties, risk of being scammed and low self-confidence in SNS use [28]. As regards the teaching approach, some participants would enjoy more training lessons to feel confident in it, while others reported the need to further refer to their own social network to consolidate and improve what has been learned [28]. From these previous data emerged important indication for planning a new teaching experience on ICT: the key role of assisted training, the importance of the relationship with the tutor, the need of multiple training sessions and self-paced learning.

These personal views and experiences give us precious insights to design an inclusive and personalized ICT intervention, able to meet the needs of all old individuals and to overcome eventual barriers.

2.2 Preliminary Data: The "Digital Grandparents" Online Survey

To obtain preliminary information on the potential beneficiaries of the intervention, we performed an online survey between 23/11/20 and 13/12/20 among the Bachelet Institute students. The students were asked to compile an online questionnaire interviewing their grandparents by phone (due to the COVID-19 restrictions in place) on their sociodemographic features, ICT access, online activities and interest on its. Three hundred twenty-three respondents provided 513 valid questionnaires on their grandparents aged between 60 and 97 years (63% women). Among the grandparents interviewed, a high portion (40%) had neither basic digital competence nor digital devices ($N = 206$). As previously reported, non-users were older (mean ± SD: 80.0 ± 5.8 vs 75.2 ± 5.6; $p < 0.001$ at Independent Sample t-test) and less educated (6.8 ± 3.4 vs 9.1 ± 3.7; $p < 0.001$ at Chi-squared test). The main reasons reported for non-use (more than 1 response possible) were: lack of interest (64%) and absence of digital competences (41%). Among ICT users, 90% had a smartphone and they reported a broad Internet use spanning 4 different activities on average. The Internet was mainly used for communication (72% video-calls, 85% instant messaging), searching and reading information (56%) and recreational activities (55%). The percentages were lower for social networking sites use (37%), home banking (29%), public services (23%) and online shopping (20%), thus showing the potential for further learning even in the old ICT users.

Altogether, these data give us more specific information on the ICT use profile and sociodemographic features of the potential beneficiaries of the intervention, confirming the presence of a wide digital divide even within the aged population itself. The overarching goal of the intervention was thus to meet the needs and interests of each student-senior dyad, regardless of their starting digital skills and attitudes toward technology.

When asked about their interest in learning new technology usage, non-users were significantly less interested (yes response: 24% vs 71%; $p < 0.001$ at Chi-squared test). This latter finding makes us aware of the challenge to involve older adults with this usage and motivational profile in ICT interventions.

Moreover, tablets specifically designed for older adults will be provided to "analogic grandparents", namely those without neither digital devices nor Internet access. This mobile tool may be suitable for many different everyday tasks and could provide optimal usability for seniors (e.g. in case of reduced hands dexterity or sight problems).

2.3 Funding: The Crowdfunding Campaign

The crowdfunding campaign lasted 2 months, between April, 29th 2021 and June, 29th 2021 with the aim of raising 10.000 euros. It was a reward-based campaign following the 'all-or-nothing' model, in which only projects reaching the collection goal are actually financed. The BiUniCrowd program provides support and workshops to train the project team in campaign preparation. Moreover, the press office of the University of Milan-Bicocca is actively involved in the communication.

The overarching goal of the Cyber School for Grandparents initiative is to generate a social impact on individuals and communities. Therefore, communication and dissemination activities are essential, to spread the messages and inspire similar initiatives in different contexts. Therefore, we found this microfinancing tool particularly attractive for the project.

The BiUniCrowd program was recently included among the best practices on the Knowledge Valorisation Practice platform of the European Commission (https://ec.europa.eu/research-and-innovation/en/research-area/industrial-research-and-innovation/eu-valorisation-policy/knowledge-valorisation-platform/repository/crowdfunding-university-born-projects-biunicrowd). The collecting goal was successfully reached, giving us the economic resources needed for the personnel devoted to the intervention and for the tablets supply.

3 Study Design and Implementation

We planned to start the training course during the 2021/2022 school year, involving two to four classes of the Human Science High School. Furthermore, we were interested in collecting relevant information on the effect of this innovative educational program. Thus, between July and August 2021 the research team drafted the study protocol of a mixed-method feasibility study aimed at assessing pre-post changes on older adults' digital skills, use and attitudes as well as monitoring students' participation and learning outcomes. The study was approved by the Ethic Committee of Milan Area 3 on September 29th (ASST Grande Ospedale Metropolitano Niguarda, approval number: 597-29092021) and pre-registered on ClinicalTrials.gov (NCT05135819).

The detailed description of the study design is beyond the scope of the present work. Therefore, in the present section we only describe the key features of the study design and provide information on the steps necessary to implement the initiative in the school context.

3.1 Study Design and Aims

The Cyber School for Grandparents intervention consists on a training course for secondary school students to become cyber tutors for their grandparents. The study take place at the Bachelet Institute in Abbiategrasso, a town of around 30.000 inhabitants in the Metropolitan City of Milan (Lombardy, northern Italy). The course is part of the curricular activities of the participating classes of the Human Science High School. Thus, each student is asked to involve at least one grandparent willing to participate in the initiative, so as to constitute a grandfather and grandson dyad. No specific inclusion criteria were set regarding age, ICT proficiency, socioeconomic, health or mobility status of the grandparents, since the program was expressly designed to be as inclusive and personalized as possible, in order to favour a wide participation. However, context information on these relevant aspects are collected [29], since they all are well-known factors affecting technology use among older adults. To assure the active participation of the entire classes, if some students are not able to involve any grandparents, community-dwelling older adults would be enrolled among those participating in other ongoing studies at the GCF. The primary aim of the study is to evaluate students' participation and learning throughout the training course and to measure grandparents' pre-post changes in mobile device actual use, self-reported digital proficiency and attitudes toward technology. Secondly, eventual pre-post changes on aging stereotypes and psychosocial well-being of the participants will be explored.

To this end, both students and grandparents are evaluated at different time-points to collect pre-post outcome measures and to monitor their participation through the course. Assessment is performed through online surveys shared within the web-based platform adopted by the school to perform remote lessons during the COVID-19 pandemic (Google Classroom). All the instruments selected are suitable for self-compiling by both young students and older adults. The students will help and supervise grandparents to manage possible technical and/or sensory difficulties with the online compiling procedure. Table 1 shows the GANTT chart of the study, including both intervention and assessments timing.

3.2 The Training Course

The training course for students is composed of 3 different parts: theory (1 lesson), research method (2 lessons) and practice (4 lessons). The theoretical lesson deals with the aging process and its effect on cognition and learning process, issues and peculiarities of older adults ICT use, andragogy and strategies to favour the learning process of new skills.

The methodological lessons provide information on the research lifecycle, with a specific focus on the importance of data collection for research purposes and on the specific assessment tools to be compiled by the participating seniors (see paragraph 3.4 for details). Indeed, each student will act both as the tutor and as the researcher in charge for data collection for their grandparents.

Finally, in the practical module, students are guided in the implementation of the one-to-one cyber sessions for their grandparents, which are then conducted independently during extracurricular hours and customized according to the needs and interests of each senior involved. Each class lesson for students deals with a broad use/function of digital technology, as follows: basic functions of mobile devices, communication and entertainment, information and health, utilities. At the end of each practical lesson, students will be guided to set goals to be achieved by their trainee and to plan potential strategies to facilitate their achievement, providing both tutoring in presence and remotely. This help to tailor the content and delivery modality of the one-to-one cyber session to the interests, needs and skills of each senior.

3.3 Participants Assessment

As shown in Table 1, students compile self-reported questionnaire investigating aging stereotype [30] and psychosocial wellbeing [31], before the first lesson scheduled and then one month after the end of the class lessons (secondary outcomes). To collect information on students' participation and learning (primary outcomes), students compile an online diary for each of the 4 practical modules, before the next group lesson scheduled, comprising both an activity and a learning log. The activity log consists of structured questions on the number, frequency, duration, content and modality (in-person

Table 1. GANTT chart of the study

	Months						
	1	2	3	4	5	6	7
Training course							
Theory (1 lesson)	x						
Research methods (2 lessons)		x					
Practice (4 lessons)			x	x	x	x	
Students' assessment							
Aging stereotype (aging semantic differential [30])	x						x
Psychosocial well-being (Italian Mental Health Continuum short form [31])	x						x
Learning diary				x	x	x	x
Satisfaction questionnaire							x
Grandparents' assessment							
Context information (Tilburg Frailty Indicator [29])		x					
Digital literacy (Mobile Device Proficiency questionnaire [32])		x					x
Attitudes toward Internet [7]		x					x
Device use (log data)			x	x	x	x	x
Satisfaction questionnaire							x

or remotely) of the cyber sessions performed with the senior mentee, (measures for student's participation). The learning log will comprise broad guiding questions to reflect on the learning process favoured by the activities and to record the student's observations. Qualitative analysis will be performed on students notes to derive the main themes reported.

As regards grandparents' assessment, they were asked to compile self-reported questionnaires before the beginning of the practical module and one month after the end of the training course. Specifically, we are interested to investigate pre-post changes in digital literacy [32] and attitudes toward Internet [7] as primary outcomes and psychosocial wellbeing [31] as secondary outcome. Moreover, to directly investigate the actual changes on mobile device use throughout the intervention, senior participants were asked to install an ad hoc app (RescueTime) which records log data, previously used for research purpose on older adults [33]. The app installation was not mandatory for study participation.

Finally, at the end of the initiative, both students and grandparents will compile a semi-structured questionnaire to rate their satisfaction and opinion on the experience.

3.4 Actual Implementation in the School Context

The implementation of the intervention in the school context requires minor adaptation to fit with the organization's needs, thanks to the proactive collaborations of 3 referent teachers, which already collaborated with the DFC social innovation program. This planning process comprised 2 in-person meetings at the beginning of the school year with the teachers and the team leader (ER), in order to define the numbers of class involved, the course duration and the delivery modalities. The team agreed upon the following aspects: an overall duration of the course of 14-h, 3 classes involved (2 in the third year, 1 in the second year) and an overall preliminary plan for the lessons' distribution across the year.

The project was then internally discussed and approved in two steps. First, a project plan was formally submitted for approval. Then it was discussed and approved within the council of each class, a periodic meeting involving all the class teachers and students and parents' representatives. The intervention started on October 2021 and involved 57 students attending the third and second school year and 63 seniors (38 grandparents, 6 students' relatives or acquaintances and 13 volunteers enrolled by the GCF). The last lesson is scheduled on March 2021 and post-intervention remote assessment will take place one month after intervention completion.

4 Conclusions, Limitations and Future Directions

The Cyber School for Grandparents is an ongoing intergenerational educational program aimed at promoting senior citizens ICT access and use by training secondary school students to become cyber tutors for their grandparents or, alternatively, for volunteers from the community.

The peculiarities and strengths of this innovative approach can be summarized by the following key concepts:

- Personalisation: due to the internal variability that characterizes the population of older people, personalization is necessary [18]. Our dyadic approach allows for a tailored sensitization of grandchildren, leveraging on major drivers (e.g.: perceived usefulness, perceived ease of use, social pressures) and overcoming possible hinders (e.g.: lack of self-efficacy, anxiety) that hamper ICT use by older adults [34].
- Inclusion: older people really benefit from using social technologies, through which the contact not only with family and friends, but also with other network members and society can be facilitated and strengthened [18]. Further, our dyadic approach is rooted in the real family world, with almost no exclusion criteria, being thus potentially able to reach older adults with a very diverse sociocultural background and starting digital skills. The crowdfunding campaign itself performed to obtain the economic resources for project implementation, contributed to spread knowledge on the digital exclusion of older adults.
- Innovation: training programs may be useful in enhancing mobile device competency and self-efficacy among older adults, but more work is required to understand how to effectively implement this type of interventions [35, 36]. At variance with previous experiences, we settled down our initiative within the high school curricular

educational path, and thereafter within family relationships. We aim at studying the effectiveness of our program on relevant dimensions for both components of the participating dyads, through a mixed method approach, paying attention also to the path followed by the dyad.

- Interdisciplinarity: our project harvests contributions from different agencies. Since its inception, and ongoing, intertwined contributions came from academy, a foundation for research on ageing, an high school. Hence, actors involved cover a wide range of professionalisms such as sociology, psychology, pedagogy, geriatrics. Moreover, in this participatory research, students and teachers were both beneficiaries and active actors contributing to the design and implementation of the project.
- Education: the intervention has been designed to be useful and informative both for young students and for seniors involved. New technologies have great potential for building and enhancing intergenerational connections and expanding educational pursuits, but there is nothing that is automatic or guaranteed with regard as to whether such benefits will be realized. The connectedness between different generations can be stimulated through mobile device technology [22]. When older people start or improve using technology the distance that is often felt between the older and younger generations may be reduced, because they share the same interest. The promotion of meaningful intergenerational relationships is the core of intergenerational programs. The informal interaction allows both parties of the dyads to develop positive attitudes towards each other, and it could break down the stereotypical feelings that they are very different [37]: we shall check that. Furthermore, students will pursuit an experience of social research, in keeping with their school orientation.
- Pandemic context: our teaching delivery modalities are conceived in a way that they can adapt to restrictions; the high school could arrange to go through the program even during last confinement situations. Even in a restricted context, maintaining and promoting grandparent – grandchild relationships contribute to the wellbeing of both parties. On the young side of the dyad, positive intergenerational relationships provide positive long-term psychological benefits, whereas, on the old side, social interaction even outweighs physical and mental health condition in influencing older people's successful aging [37].

The feasibility study will provide useful preliminary information on the effect of this innovative intergenerational programs on both generations, in order to inform future initiatives in the field.

Specifically, we will answer to the study research questions as follows:

1. Does training secondary school students to become cyber tutors for seniors, lead to measurable pre-post intervention changes in seniors' self-reported digital competence and attitudes toward Internet?
   To address this research question, we will compare the score of 2 self-reported questionnaire administered by the students to their senior mentee through the Google Classrom platform before the beginning of the one-to-one cyber sessions and one month after the educational intervention completion (see Table 1 for details). Moreover, as complimentary information, actual use of the mobile device will be tracked by Rescue Time app, for those participants who agreed to install it.

2. How do the students reflect on their learning throughout the experience?
   Thematic analysis will be performed on the students' responses to the open-ended questions of the learning log, a pedagogic instrument widely used to record students reflections about the learning process and also previously adopted by intergenerational programs aimed at increase the digital skills of older adults [22]. The questions will be focused on the experience of planning and implementing the one-to-one cyber sessions for the grandparents. Students will be asked to compile a learning diary for each of the 4 practical modules. This qualitative approach will provide nuanced and personalized perspectives on the learning experience from the point of view of the main beneficiaries of the initiative: the high school students.
3. Is there any measurable pre-post intervention change on psychosocial well-being of the participants?
   Previous studies on ICT interventions for older adults largely reported benefits on measures of psychological and social well-being [9–12]. In our study, we will rate pre-post intervention changes on psychosocial well-being of young and old participants as secondary outcome, in order to verify if this innovative educational approach leads to measurable benefit beyond ICT use, proficiency and attitude. We selected a self-report questionnaire validated on an Italian sample aged between 18 and 89 years which assess mental health across 3 dimensions: psychological, emotional and social wellbeing [31].
4. Is there any measurable pre-post intervention change on students' aging stereotypes?

Intergenerational programs were generally effective in changing aging stereotype and attitudes of both young and old participants [30, 38]. Moreover, a recent meta-analysis of interventions primarily designed to reduce ageism showed the higher benefit in programs combining both education and intergenerational contacts [39]. We thus expect that our intervention, providing educational content on aging during the class lessons and promoting direct contacts with seniors through the one-to-one cyber sessions, would have a positive impact on students' aging stereotype.

Some limitations of the study and potential issues for its implementation should be discussed. First of all, the research staff will only meet the students, who will act both as cyber tutors and as raters by supporting and/or mediating data collection. Thus, we can expect variable level of skills and motivation in performing these tasks, which may affect the reliability and completeness of the data collected. To overcome this issue, we will monitor students' participation through direct and indirect observations and we will actively promote study participation and involvement in person during class lessons and remotely through the web-based platform and personalized communications when necessary. All these aspects will be recorded and combined with the other quantitative and qualitative measures collected.

Secondly, the study has some methodological limitations. We did not include in this preliminary phase a comparison group, so we will not be able to draw firm conclusions on the efficacy of the Cyber School for Grandparents intervention on the measures of interest. Moreover, the small convenience sample reduce the power and the generalizability of the study. However, the study design is appropriate for the aim of developing a new educational intervention in a specific school context. We adopted a mixed-method approach, as recommended for non-randomized feasibility study aimed at intervention development [40]. The combination of quantitative and qualitative data will indeed help us to enrich our understanding of the intervention effects, even in case of non-significant or unexpected results.

Acknowledgements. The project was supported by the BiUniCrowd program and by Fondazione Comunitaria del Ticino-Olona. We are grateful to all of our donors, with special thanks to Lions Club Abbiategrasso and Manuela Magistrelli.

We thank the teachers of the Bachelet Institute for their valuable contribution to the project: Paola Cucchetti, Sara Mazzetto, Alexia Scimè, Laura Platti. We finally thank Elena Bitetto for her support during the crowdfunding campaign.

References

1. Eurostat: Statistics—Eurostat. https://ec.europa.eu/eurostat/databrowser/view/tps00028/default/table?lang=en. Accessed 23 Dec 2021
2. MEF: The National Recovery and Resilience Plan (NRRP) - Ministry of Economy and Finance. https://www.mef.gov.it/en/focus/The-National-Recovery-and-Resilience-Plan-NRRP/. Accessed 23 Dec 2021
3. Sala, E., Gaia, A.: Older People's Use of «Information and Communication Technology» in Europe. The Italian Case. Auton. locali e Serv. Soc. **XLII**, 163–183 (2019). https://doi.org/10.1447/95863
4. Gaia, A., Sala, E., Cerati, G.: Social networking sites use and life satisfaction. A quantitative study on older people living in Europe. Eur. Soc. **23**, 98–118 (2021). https://doi.org/10.1080/14616696.2020.1762910
5. Czaja, S.J., et al.: Factors predicting the use of technology: findings from the center for research and education on aging and technology enhancement (CREATE). Psychol. Aging. **21**, 333 (2006). https://doi.org/10.1037/0882-7974.21.2.333
6. Czaja, S.J., Sharit, J.: Age differences in attitudes toward computers. J. Gerontol. Ser. B. **53B**, P329–P340 (1998). https://doi.org/10.1093/GERONB/53B.5.P329
7. Jay, G.M., Willis, S.L.: Influence of direct computer experience on older adults' attitudes toward computers. J. Gerontol. **47**, 250–257 (1992). https://doi.org/10.1093/geronj/47.4.P250
8. González, A., Paz Ramírez, M., Viadel, V.: ICT learning by older adults and their attitudes toward computer use (2015).https://doi.org/10.1155/2015/849308
9. Ibarra, F., Baez, M., Cernuzzi, L., Casati, F.: A systematic review on technology-supported interventions to improve old-age social wellbeing: loneliness, social isolation, and connectedness. J. Healthc. Eng. 2020 (2020). https://doi.org/10.1155/2020/2036842
10. Chen, Y.R.R., Schulz, P.J.: The effect of information communication technology interventions on reducing social isolation in the elderly: a systematic review. J. Med. Internet Res. **18**, e18 (2016). https://doi.org/10.2196/jmir.4596
11. Forsman, A.K., Nordmyr, J., Matosevic, T., Park, A.L., Wahlbeck, K., McDaid, D.: Promoting mental wellbeing among older people: technology-based interventions. Health Promot. Int. **33**, 1042–1054 (2018). https://doi.org/10.1093/heapro/dax047
12. Casanova, G., Zaccaria, D., Rolandi, E., Guaita, A.: The effect of information and communication technology and social networking site use on older people⇔s well-being in relation to loneliness: Review of experimental studies (2021). https://doi.org/10.2196/23588https://www.jmir.org/2021/3/e23588
13. Yardley, L., Ainsworth, B., Arden-Close, E., Muller, I.: The person-based approach to enhancing the acceptability and feasibility of interventions. Pilot Feasibility Stud. **1**, 1–7 (2015). https://doi.org/10.1186/S40814-015-0033-Z

14. Nef, T., Ganea, R.L., Müri, R.M., Mosimann, U.P.: Social networking sites and older users - a systematic review (2013). https://doi.org/10.1017/S1041610213000355
15. Newman, L., Stoner, C., Spector, A.: Social networking sites and the experience of older adult users: a systematic review (2019). https://doi.org/10.1017/S0144686X19001144. https://www.cambridge.org/core/journals/ageing-and-society/article/abs/social-networking-sites-and-the-experience-of-older-adult-users-a-systematic-review/3A780F958A4F3007254F2BE8FC2EB3E0
16. Freeman, S., et al.: Intergenerational effects on the impacts of technology use in later life: insights from an international, multi-site study. Int. J. Environ. Res. Public Health. **17**, 1–14 (2020). https://doi.org/10.3390/ijerph17165711
17. Hänninen, R., Taipale, S., Luostari, R.: Exploring heterogeneous ICT use among older adults: the warm experts' perspective. New Media Soc. **23**, 1584–1601 (2021). https://doi.org/10.1177/1461444820917353
18. ten Bruggencate, T., Luijkx, K.G., Sturm, J.: How to fulfil social needs of older people: exploring design opportunities for technological interventions. Gerontechnology **18**, 156–167 (2019). https://doi.org/10.4017/gt.2019.18.3.003.00
19. Bakardjieva, M.: Internet Society: The Internet in Everyday Life, pp. 1–220 (2005). https://doi.org/10.4135/9781446215616
20. Széman, Z.: A new pattern in long-term care in Hungary: Skype and youth volunteers. Anthropol. Noteb. **20**, 105–117 (2014)
21. López Seguí, F., de San Pedro, M., Verges, E.A., Algado, S.S., Cuyàs, F.G.: An intergenerational information and communications technology learning project to improve digital skills: user satisfaction evaluation. JMIR Aging. **2**, e13939 (2019). https://doi.org/10.2196/13939
22. LoBuono, D.L., Leedahl, S.N., Maiocco, E.: Teaching technology to older adults (2020). https://doi.org/10.3928/00989134-20191118-02. https://pubmed.ncbi.nlm.nih.gov/31895957/
23. Lee, O.E.-K., Kim, D.-H.: Bridging the digital divide for older adults via intergenerational mentor-up **29**, 786–795 (2018). https://doi.org/10.1177/1049731518810798
24. Lee, O.E.K., Kim, D.H.: Intergenerational forum to enhance students' engagement and learning outcomes: a community-based participatory research study. J. Intergener. Relatsh. **15**, 241–257 (2017). https://doi.org/10.1080/15350770.2017.1330043
25. Zaccaria, D., et al.: Assessing the impact of social networking site use on older people's loneliness and social isolation. a randomized controlled trial: the aging in a networked society-social experiment study (ANS-SE). Contemp. Clin. Trials Commun. **19**, 100615 (2020). https://doi.org/10.1016/j.conctc.2020.100615
26. Vaccaro, R., et al.: Effect of a social networking site training on cognitive performance in healthy older people and role of personality traits. results from the randomized controlled trial ageing in a networked society-social experiment (ANS-SE) Study. Exp. Aging Res. (2021). https://doi.org/10.1080/0361073X.2021.1982351
27. Rolandi, E., et al.: Loneliness and social engagement in older adults based in Lombardy during the covid-19 lockdown: the long-term effects of a course on social networking sites use. Int. J. Environ. Res. Public Health. **17**, 1–12 (2020). https://doi.org/10.3390/ijerph17217912
28. Casanova, G., et al.: New older users' attitudes toward social networking sites and loneliness: the case of the oldest-old residents in a small Italian city. Soc. Media + Soc. **7**, 205630512110529 (2021). https://doi.org/10.1177/20563051211052905
29. Mulasso, A., Roppolo, M., Gobbens, R.J.J., Rabaglietti, E.: The Italian version of the tilburg frailty indicator: analysis of psychometric properties. Res. Aging. **38**, 842–863 (2016). https://doi.org/10.1177/0164027515606192
30. Gaggioli, A., et al.: Intergenerational group reminiscence: a potentially effective intervention to enhance elderly psychosocial wellbeing and to improve children's perception of aging. Educ. Gerontol. **40**, 486–498 (2014). https://doi.org/10.1080/03601277.2013.844042

31. Petrillo, G., Capone, V., Caso, D., Keyes, C.L.M.: The mental health continuum–short form (MHC–SF) as a measure of well-being in the Italian context. Soc. Indic. Res. **121**(1), 291–312 (2014). https://doi.org/10.1007/s11205-014-0629-3
32. Roque, N.A., Boot, W.R.: A new tool for assessing mobile device proficiency in older adults: the mobile device proficiency questionnaire. J. Appl. Gerontol. **37**, 131–156 (2018). https://doi.org/10.1177/0733464816642582
33. Caliandro, A., Garavaglia, E., Sturiale, V., Di Leva, A: Older people and smartphone practices in everyday life: an inquire on digital sociality of Italian older users **24**, 47–78 (2021). https://doi.org/10.1080/10714421.2021.1904771
34. Bixter, M.T., Blocker, K.A., Mitzner, T.L., Prakash, A., Rogers, W.A.: Understanding the use and non-use of social communication technologies by older adults: a qualitative test and extension of the UTAUT model. Gerontechnology **18**, 70 (2019). https://doi.org/10.4017/GT.2019.18.2.002.00
35. Aranha, M., James, K., Deasy, C., Heavin, C.: Exploring the barriers and facilitators which influence mHealth adoption among older adults: a literature review. Gerontechnology **20**, 1–16 (2021). https://doi.org/10.4017/GT.2021.20.2.424.06
36. Wister, A., O'Dea, E., Fyffe, I., Cosco, T.D.: Technological interventions to reduce loneliness and social isolation among community-living older adults: a scoping review. Gerontechnology **20**, 1–16 (2021). https://doi.org/10.4017/GT.2021.20.2.30-471.11
37. Zhang, F., Kaufman, D.: A review of intergenerational play for facilitating interactions and learning (2016). https://doi.org/10.4017/gt.2016.14.3.002.00
38. Martins, T., et al.: Intergenerational programs review: study design and characteristics of intervention, outcomes, and effectiveness: research. J. Intergener. Relatsh. **17**, 93–109 (2019). https://doi.org/10.1080/15350770.2018.1500333
39. Burnes, D., et al.: Interventions to reduce ageism against older adults: a systematic review and meta-analysis (2019). https://doi.org/10.2105/AJPH.2019.305123. https://ajph.aphapublications.org/doi/abs/10.2105/AJPH.2019.305123
40. Lancaster, G.A., Thabane, L.: Guidelines for reporting non-randomised pilot and feasibility studies. Pilot Feasibility Stud. **5**, 1–6 (2019). https://doi.org/10.1186/S40814-019-0499-1

Applying Asymmetrical VR Collaborative Games to the Enhancement of Peer Collaboration and Oral Communication in Children with Autism

Wan-Chen Yang and I.-Jui Lee(✉)

Department of Industrial Design, National Taipei University of Technology, Taipei, Taiwan
t109588013@ntut.org.tw, ericlee@mail.ntut.edu.tw

Abstract. Autism is a condition in which children are born with social impairments in social communication, imagination, and empathy, thus, they have difficulty interacting socially with peers or effectively interpreting each other's intentions to engage in different social content. As a result of these deficits, most children with autism are unable to play cooperatively or effectively interact socially with their peers, which makes them socially isolated and difficult to integrate into the community.

In view of this, this study conducted an asymmetric VR collaborative game for children with autism, where children with autism and Typical Development (TD) children participated in a collaborative game in pairs, and both children were required to play the game through peer cooperation and oral communication.

A total of 6 participants aged 7–9 years old, including 3 children with high-functioning autism and 3 TD children, were recruited for this study. During the game, social assessments and behavioral observations were conducted by the researcher and the therapist to understand whether the asymmetrical VR collaborative game has an impact on children with autism in building peer cooperation and oral communication skills, in order to achieve outcomes that enhance social communication and trans-personal thinking skills.

This study used an asymmetrical VR collaborative game to present the game situation with different viewpoints, which allowed children with autism and TD children to work together to solve the game tasks and levels in a peer-to-peer and oral communication manner. In this game, children with autism were required to interact socially with TD children through an asymmetrical play style, thus, triggering the application of peer cooperation and oral communication skills in children with autism.

In this game, the researcher used the micro-behaviors for video coding (MBV) to observe and assess five domains, (1) mutual attention; (2) meaningful conversation; (3) collaboration; (4) proximity; and (5) turn taking. According to the results of this study, children with autism exhibited behavioral orientations in the asymmetrical VR collaborative game that were more oriented toward strengthening trans-personal and empathic abilities than traditional solo play, especially in peer cooperation and oral communication. On this basis, the expectation of this study was that the application of asymmetrical VR collaborative games had different degrees of specificity and implementation advantages for children with autism in

Q. Gao and J. Zhou (Eds.): HCII 2022, LNCS 13331, pp. 413–426, 2022.
https://doi.org/10.1007/978-3-031-05654-3_29

terms of social communication, imagination, and empathy skills. Children with autism could learn to grasp the meaning of others' spoken communication, and thus, develop the concept of peer cooperation during the game, which in turn facilitated their mastery of social skills in all aspects of the theory of the mind.

Keywords: Autism · Asymmetrical VR collaborative game · Empathy · Peer cooperation and oral communication · Peer-mediated intervention strategies

1 Introduction

1.1 Autism Spectrum Disorders

Autism spectrum disorders arise from congenital deficits in the neurodevelopment of the brain, where the major core impairments include impairments in social interaction, oral and nonverbal expression, and lack of empathy and imagination [1]. Due to these congenital deficits, social communication and interaction with others and groups are greatly hindered; at the same time, the harm and pain of autistic children become more pronounced as they age and become more aware of their social deficits and low abilities. In addition, the interaction process reveals that children with autism are often unable to understand each other's behavioral intentions and others' oral expressions during social interaction due to their inherent deficits in empathy and weaknesses in oral expressions. These insufficiencies make it difficult for them to maintain social relationships or to communicate and share their views or feelings with others, either orally or non-verbally, which in turn affects children with autism in learning to interact with others and to cooperate with peers.

1.2 Promotion of Interaction in Games on Children's Behavior Development

Interactions during games are an important guide for children's behavioral development. Generally, children learn how to interact with peers through play, which allows them to acquire different social intentions and play representations, and they generally develop symbolic play around the age of 2 to 3. The different tasks and rules of game interaction will help children master the social behavioral representations behind the play, as well as the ability to cooperate and communicate with others in a peer-to-peer manner. Ideally, children can use their past experiences and imagination to understand the underlying social meanings and develop more complex social behaviors and play content [2].

Furthermore, game interaction has shown a strong correlation in children's emotional building and social development, and the development of such abilities is considered to be one of the important social foundations. However, this form of game is a rather difficult challenge for children with autism. In a related study, Baron-Cohen and Howlin revealed that children with autism have difficulties in understanding the ideas and mental states of others due to their lack of the Theory of Mind Ability (ToM Ability) when playing with others [3], which leads to obstacles in the behavior of pretend play with imagination and speculation ability [4].

2 Literature Review

2.1 Barriers to Peer Cooperative Games and Oral Communication in Children with Autism

At the same time, autistic children lack spontaneity and flexibility in peer cooperative games and oral communication [5], which makes it difficult for them to master social skills and actively integrate into various group cooperative games. In this case, they suffer from exclusion from the group, and thus, dislike and reject the cooperative play and oral communication of their peers.

Many approaches have been researched to improve intervention strategies for children with autism on this issue, and one of the strategies for collaborative group play is Peer-Mediated Interventions (PMI). This strategy, which usually takes peer as the mediation strategy, also invites other peers or friends with normal social skills to jointly shape and strengthen the social behavior of the treatment case [6, 7]. Through a collaborative group approach, this strategy is combined with play-based interventions and role-playing to achieve the goal of engaging the autistic child's attention and ultimately giving birth to cooperative tasks and social interactions.

2.2 Current Status on the Use of VR Technology as a Social Skills Training and Intervention Method for Children with Autism

There are many new interventions that can be applied to the training of social skills in children with autism, such as Virtual Reality (VR). By applying VR to training the social skills of autistic children, the simulation and immersive reality of social situations can be enhanced. In this way, children with autism can be helped to master the social state in different situations and try to interact with different virtual characters in VR situations. This can be done by allowing children with autism to conduct mock interviews in a VR environment or by providing virtual classrooms and living situations through VR environments for children with autism to speculate about the environment. This can help to further reduce the autistic child's sense of discomfort or increase their self-confidence and sense of accomplishment in integrating into the environment [8]. In this way, more realistic effects can be achieved and better visual stimulation can be brought than traditional role playing or video modeling [9]. In addition, it can maintain autistic children's willingness to participate and increase their learning motivation. Moreover, the VR system can make use of repeated operation speculation and training for some less accessible situational states.

2.3 Deviations and Drawbacks of the Over-Enhancement of VR Technology in the Context of Single Operation and Immersion Effect Intervention

However, despite the significant training benefits resulting from using VR technology with game interventions to improve the social skills of children with autism, players wearing head-mounted displays are still the focus of most VR games, and most are played in separate operations. Thus, children with autism are mostly in a solo situation during the training process. At the same time, as the therapist or other players can only assist the children with autism through verbal guidance or by simply playing the role of "spectator", it does not directly help the children with autism learn to interact with their peers or communicate verbally.

Therefore, the interactive strategy adopted in this study, i.e., an asymmetric VR collaborative game system combined with peer-mediated interventions [6], will be useful in solving the problems and complementing the shortcomings of traditional VR games in this area, especially in strengthening the construction of peer cooperation and oral communication skills. This would preserve the immersive and interactive nature of VR game interventions and strengthen the characteristics of peer cooperation and oral communication. The application of such a therapeutic approach will help children with autism to develop peer cooperation experiences and enhance their interpersonal interactions. In addition, in a sense, this approach has a positive effect on the ability of children with autism to grasp each other's intentions during play to enhance empathy and transpersonal thinking [7, 10]. This approach can address the current deficiencies in single VR training, enhance the motivation of children with autism to participate in the game and decrease their tension during peer interaction [11].

2.4 Application of Asymmetric VR Collaborative Games

Current VR games are mostly designed for interactive content operated by a single player and focus on the immersion and fun of the players themselves [11]. In contrast, asymmetrical collaborative VR games that reinforce two-player collaboration are uncommon, and even more so in the field of autism research, where they have rarely been developed or applied.

However, as discussed above, if VR games that reinforce single-player manipulation are applied to social skills training for children with autism, the effect is only reinforced by immersion or simple contextual mastery. For children with autism, such reinforcement focuses only on contextual memory or repetitive recitation of manipulative tasks, which has little impact on the basic social skills required by children with autism, especially peer cooperation and oral communication, and tends to result in rigid behavior [12].

The reason for this is that the enhanced single player VR games isolate the interaction mechanism between autistic children and their peers or other game partners, and there are few opportunities for peer cooperation and oral communication [13]. In the over immersed VR environment, the interaction between autistic children and other players will also be reduced. Such game mechanics are not favored by educational experts because the over-enhancement of an immersive and homogeneous training environment tends to cause repetitive rigid behaviors and negative emotions in children with autism.

Thus, it is expected that asymmetric collaborative VR games [14] may become a new generation of VR games and be applied to strengthen the empathy and trans-personal thinking skills of children with autism. Through such an asymmetric collaborative game structure, the immersion of VR is preserved, and peer cooperation and oral communication between players can be enhanced. Such competency needs also echo the foundation of social skills that children with autism urgently need to build and serve as a building block for further development of deeper social cognitive skills, such as empathy [15] and symbolic play.

2.5 Advantages of Using Asymmetrical VR Collaborative Games for Training Children with Autism

In view of the abovementioned factors, this study aims to strengthen the ability of children with autism to cooperate and communicate with their peers through the application of asymmetrical VR collaborative games, and such mechanisms are essential for the construction of these abilities. As the asymmetric VR collaborative game has the characteristics of interdependence, mutual assistance, and physical sensory on both sides of the game, the VR players must participate in the game through oral communication and guidance between peers to complete the task of each stage to pass the level.

In the game process, VR players must judge the game intention and contextual state of both sides of the game, including cooperation and competition, thus, different gameplays will be developed, and the benefits are listed, as follows: (1) The performance of both players in peer cooperation and oral communication can be facilitated, as both players must communicate and collaborate with each other to perform the game tasks. (2) The tacit understanding between players to practice peer cooperation and oral communication can be strengthened simultaneously. In addition, (3) since most of the play patterns of children with autism are self-stimulation and individual interaction, there are relatively few interactive and cooperative games; the asymmetric VR collaborative game model plays an important role in addressing the shortcomings of existing social training strategies; the interaction between multiple players not only increases fun and social interaction, it also enhances the overall game experience [11].

Therefore, asymmetrical gameplay will have the opportunity to enhance the oral expression and cooperation skills of children with autism, while simultaneously providing players with different roles to play and role play identities, which are important to help children with autism gradually master the concepts and skills of transpersonal thinking and role play, and their social willingness and desire to interact with others will be naturally enhanced. Therefore, this study used the concept of asymmetrical VR collaborative play and peer cooperation combined with the intervention strategy of peer intervention to conduct a phased approach to play, which aims to gradually build up peer cooperation and the oral communication skills of children with autism during the process of play.

2.6 Summary

Based on the above discussion, it can be concluded that gaming interventions are increasingly being applied to the treatment of children with autism [16]. The theoretical foundation of previous literature reveals the prospect that asymmetrical VR collaborative games will have the opportunity to improve the abilities and skills of children with autism during peer cooperation and oral communication; moreover, asymmetrical VR collaborative games will be more attractive than traditional single VR game interaction mechanisms.

Therefore, it is expected that peer cooperation and oral communication among peers in asymmetrical VR collaboration games can be used to gradually guide children with autism to develop empathy and peer collaboration skills. Moreover, due to the fun nature of the game and the reinforcing effect of two-player collaboration, the asymmetrical VR collaborative game can increase the willingness of children with autism to participate in the training [11, 17].

In addition, since the concept of asymmetrical VR collaborative games has rarely been applied to the training of children with autism, this study aims to apply asymmetrical VR collaborative games and peer-mediated intervention strategies to the social skills training of children with autism. Through this application, this study aims to allow them to learn communication skills, and thus, improve their social skills, while playing the game, and to gradually build their ability to cooperate with peers and communicate orally.

3 Methodology

3.1 Participants

This study recruited a total of six participants aged 7–9 years, including three high-functioning autistic children (FIQ > 80) and three TD children, to participate in an asymmetrical VR collaborative game, and they were randomly divided into three groups (two players in each group, one of whom was a TD child). The game was taught in stages and played in pairs. Prior to the game observation, the research team obtained signed consent forms from the guardians of the six children and introduced the game content and instructional strategies for the participants and parents to understand. During the game, a therapist was assigned to assist in instructing and observing the peer interaction and performance of the six tested children, and finally, to evaluate the feasibility of the asymmetrical group collaboration game.

3.2 Training Objectives of the Asymmetrical VR Collaborative Game

There are many different intervention strategies that can be applied to children with autism, and different play strategies have been combined to provide variety in training. At this stage, many researchers have applied the concept of play interventions in conjunction with peer-mediated intervention strategies in social interventions for children with autism, which are intended to help children with autism gain interactive experiences and social skills through play.

This study conducted an intervention to observe children with autism in peer cooperation and oral communication through an asymmetrical VR collaborative game approach. The game indirectly reinforced autistic children's cooperative play and oral communication practice with peers, which had a positive effect on their ability to play and communicate with others in a peer-to-peer manner.

The abilities gained in such games will help children with autism to develop the higher level social cognitive aspects of the theory of the mind, such as trans-personal thinking and empathy, which can implicitly influence the social reciprocity skills of children with autism towards others.

3.3 Field Design and Equipment Configuration of Asymmetric VR Collaborative Game

During the game, participants are mainly divided into (1) players and (2) co-players (Table 1), in which the players wear HTC VIVE head-mounted displays for immersive VR game operation, and the co-players will cooperate and interact with the players through a flat screen for peer-to-peer gameplay. While both parties will see different virtual character perspectives through different displays (head-mounted display and flat screen) and have different screen perspectives during the process, they are both in the same virtual world for the game task (Fig. 1). In this way, an asymmetrical game structure can be created to promote fun and cooperative support mechanisms.

Table 1. Two-player game architecture and operation equipment configuration of the asymmetric VR collaborative game

	Role played	Target participants	Equipment used
1	Player	Children with autism	VR + head-mounted display
2	Co-player	TD children	Tablet computer

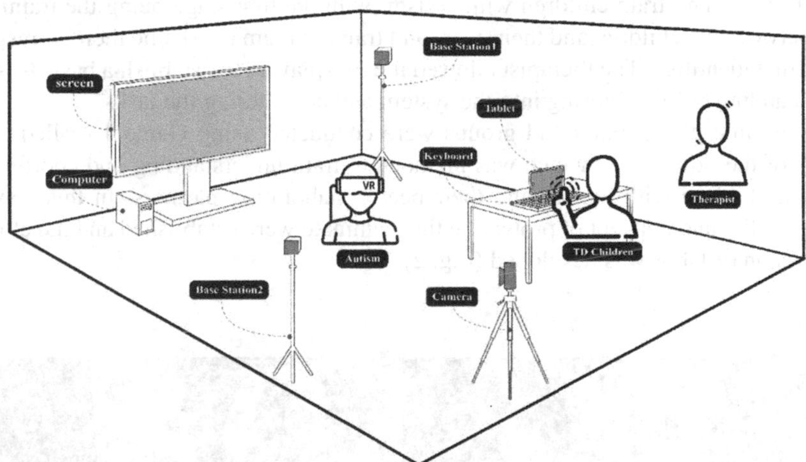

Fig. 1. Field design and equipment architecture of asymmetric VR collaborative game

3.4 Implementation of Instruction and Implementation of Games

Since a large space is needed for VR games, this study was conducted in the studio space of a school. The instruction was divided into two phases, with the Acron Attack of the Squirr¬els! system of Game 1 and the VR Giants system of Game 2 being used for the phased play content in pairs (children with autism were randomly paired with TD children in groups). The entire process was videotaped and accompanied by the therapist and instruction team (Table 2).

The two phases of the game took a total of 50 min, with each phase lasting 25 min, during which the therapist used the Micro-behaviors for video coding (MBV) approach with five dimensions, including (1) mutual attention; (2) meaningful conversation; (3) collaboration; (4) proximity; and (5) turn taking, in order to observe the interaction and social skills between autistic cases and general children and to give an assessment index from 1 to 7. One of the steps conducted prior to asymmetrical play was a systematic use assessment by the therapist to ensure that the children with autism did not feel uncomfortable or uneasy when operating the equipment.

Table 2. Instructional implementation of the two-stage asymmetrical VR collaborative game

	Phases	Name of the game	Duration
1	Phase 1	Game 1: Acron Attack of the Squirrels! system	25 min
2	Phase 2	Game 2: VR Giants system	25 min

Phase 1: To Help Children with Autism Adapt to the Virtual Roles in the Game and the Correspondence Between Partners. This study used a two-stage game program to teach and train children with autism, with the first stage being the training of trust between the children and their peers and training them to assume their corresponding virtual identities. The therapist allowed the two players to establish a basic trust and understanding before entering into the system and deciphering the tasks.

In the first phase, pairs and groups were conducted using Game 1 (called Acron Attack of the Squirrels!), which was intended to train understanding and coordination between children with autism and their peer collaboration partners. In this way, the responsibility and concept of protecting the teammate were established and the effect of the division of labor was developed (Fig. 2).

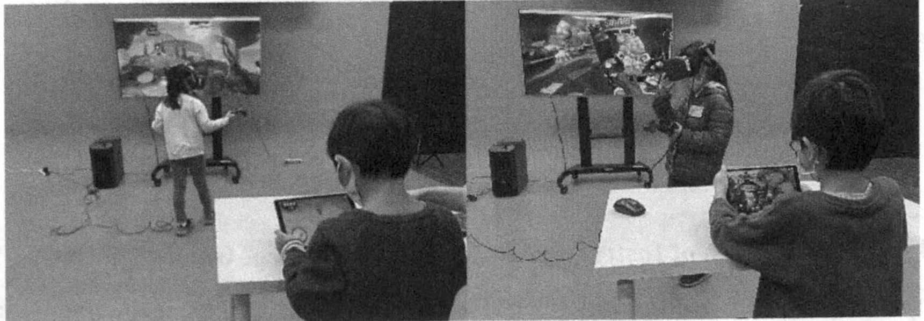

Fig. 2. Operation screen and use of the Acron Attack of the Squirrels! System of Game 1 (Children with autism need to be paired with TD children to play together)

Phase 2: To Conduct Practical System Operation Using the Asymmetric VR Collaborative Game with Peer Intervention Strategies. In the second phase, the dyadic group used Game 2 (called VR Giants) for peer collaboration and oral communication. Before the game, the autistic child and the TD child had to choose to play one of the parties (facilitator and challenger) in the game (Table 3), in which the HMD wearer was the facilitator (the giant), whose task was to protect the challenger (the little boy), who was controlled by the desktop computer operator. The facilitator (the giant) can help the challenger (the little boy) move to a higher position, and the range of movement was limited.

While the challenger (the little boy) could wander around the plane at will, the jumping range was limited. Given the different ability conditions and the asymmetrical viewing range, both players had to cooperate with each other and communicate verbally to play the game; while simultaneously being encouraged to individually break the limits of their roles to obtain more coins, which will open the door to the next level (Fig. 3).

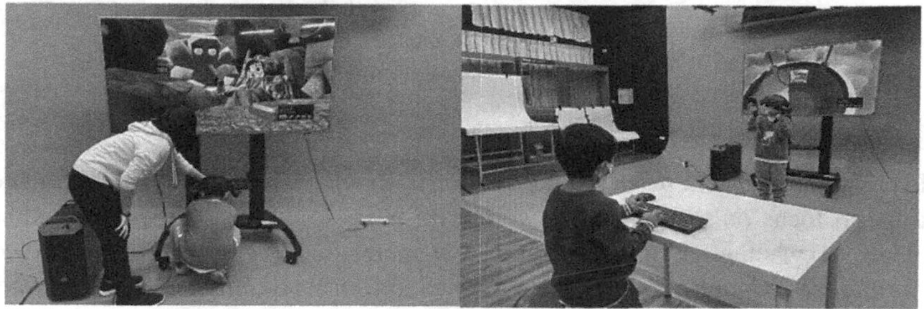

Fig. 3. The operation screen and usage of VR Giants system of Game 2

3.5 Evaluation

In this experiment, three groups of participants (one child with autism and one child with TD) were each given one session of cooperative play training. Each group participated only once, the session consisted of two phases of play, and the duration was approximately 50 min. A researcher and a therapist were assigned to assist the children with autism to discuss the cooperative strategies and ways to solve the levels in the game with their peers. At the same time, the participation of each child with autism and the average child was recorded by a camera, and the performance during the game was observed by Micro-behaviors for video coding (MBV).

During the three groups of individual game training, the researcher extracted five behavioral indicators from the MBV index as a way to observe whether the children with autism had strengthened their abilities during asymmetrical VR collaborative play, including (1) mutual attention; (2) meaningful conversation; (3) collaboration; (4) proximity; and (5) turn taking. Based on these five indicators, researchers were able to initially assess the play status and performance of children with autism with their peers.

The researcher focused on the following aspects of asymmetrical VR collaborative play through these five dimensions: (1) whether children with autism could seek assistance from peers or researchers when they encountered difficulties and whether they

Table 3. Role tasks and collaboration content assigned to different game parties

	Target audience	Role definition	Game tasks	Equipment used
1	Children with autism	Facilitator (the giant)	The task is to protect the challenger (the little boy), who is controlled by the general children, and help him to break through the level	VR + head-mounted display
2	TD children	Challenger (the little boy)	The task is that the challenger (the little boy), who can roam around the plane at will, has a limited jumping range, thus, they need to work with the facilitator (the giant) to break through the level	Keyboard + computer

could communicate with peers to find solutions, (2) whether children with autism could continue to focus on the game and work with peers to address difficulties and solve problems, (3) whether children with autism were able to engage in emotions and cooperate with peers through non-verbal communication during training sessions, (4) whether children with autism were able to cooperate and solve tasks with peers in asymmetrical equipment and perspectives during training, and (5) whether children with autism were able to role play and engage in emotions during play. By applying all of the above aspects, this study evaluated whether asymmetrical VR collaborative games can stimulate and increase the use of peer cooperation and oral communication in children with autism, and thereby, enhance their ability to think differently and empathize.

4 Results

In this study, the researcher and therapist conducted game interactions and behavioral observations with three children with autism and three TD children and recorded the entire training process. The aim was to determine whether the asymmetrical VR collaborative game could strengthen the autistic children's abilities in five areas: (1) mutual attention; (2) meaningful conversation; (3) collaboration; (4) proximity; and (5) turn taking.

In addition, this study evaluated the participation of three groups of participants during gameplay and attempted to understand the reinforcement of the game mechanics for children with autism in this area. A Likert type scale of 1–7 was used to evaluate whether the asymmetrical VR collaborative game could strengthen the ability of children with autism to concentrate on peer cooperation and oral communication to interact with their peers, where 1 indicates no such advantage and 7 indicates full compliance with this advantage.

Based on the short-term play experiments and observations of the three groups of participants, the performance of children with autism participating in asymmetrical VR collaborative play was discussed with therapists. It is worth noting that the score did not focus on whether the autistic children had improved ability changes after the game, but rather on whether the autistic children had triggered the application, as well as the application status, of their five abilities through the game mechanism. Thus, the data presented below do not focus on how well the ability was or whether it helped children with autism to improve their own abilities, but rather on whether asymmetrical VR collaborative play can effectively initiate the use and performance of the ability.

Based on the game observations of the three groups of participating cases, the therapists assigned the following performance scores for child reinforcement of asymmetrical VR collaborative games:

(1) A score of 5.1 denotes that the Asymmetrical VR Collaborative game mechanism will have the opportunity to strengthen the mutual attention of children with autism (1 denotes being unable to strengthen the mutual attention and 7 denotes being able to strengthen the mutual attention).
(2) A score of 6.2 denotes that the Asymmetrical VR Collaborative game mechanism will have the opportunity to reinforce meaning conversation for children with autism (1 denotes not reinforcing meaning conversation with peers and 7 denotes actively reinforcing meaning conversation with peers).
(3) A score of 5.8 denotes that the Asymmetrical VR Collaborative game mechanism will have the opportunity to strengthen the performance of children with autism in collaborative training (1 denotes not strengthening collaborative play with peers and 7 denotes strengthening collaborative play with peers during the game).
(4) A score of 5.9 denotes that the Asymmetrical VR Collaborative game mechanism will have the opportunity to reinforce proximity for children with autism. (1 denotes being unable to reinforce proximity and 7 denotes being able to reinforce proximity)
(5) A score of 5.2 denotes that the Asymmetrical VR Collaborative game mechanism will have the opportunity to reinforce children with autism's turn taking when role-playing with virtual peers (1 denotes not being able to reinforce understanding of the intentions conveyed by peers in role-playing, 7 denotes being able to reinforce the intention of turn taking conveyed by peers in role-playing).

The results of this study reveal that children with autism would have the opportunity to strengthen the abovementioned social orientations during the intervention using asymmetrical VR collaborative play, as well as increasing the frequency and motivation to engage in cooperative play and oral communication with peers; in addition, the training process showed that children with autism were perceived as joyful when engaging with their peers.

5 Discussion and Conclusion

Taken together, the use of asymmetrical VR collaborative games has been found to be positive in enhancing the activation of peer cooperation and oral communication in children with autism. As this study is a preliminary study, the learning effectiveness and the magnitude of improvement are yet to be verified in further experiments. However, we can still see from the three groups' play activities that the children with autism did increase their learning in (1) mutual attention; (2) meaningful conversation; (3) collaboration; (4) proximity; and (5) turn taking, as a result of using the asymmetrical VR collaborative game. These same orientations are the basis for enabling the development of oral communication and social reciprocity behaviors, we, therefore, attribute such performance and advantages to the following.

5.1 Asymmetrical VR Collaborative Games Are Useful for Increasing Opportunities for Cooperative Play and Oral Communication Between Children with Autism and Their Peers

The biggest advantage of asymmetric VR collaborative games lies in that it provides a world between the virtual world and the physical realm for children with autism and TD children. Through the asymmetrical visual conditions and functional limitations of the game setting, both players are prompted to cooperate and communicate verbally through different images and perspectives, in order to complete cooperative tasks to achieve gameplay.

Based on performance during the game, when children with autism interact with TD children in the game, they could see the operation status of both sides of the game through the screen, and communicate and cooperate with each other through oral communication to perform the task of breaking through the level, which includes the ability to judge intentions and cooperate and coordinate. Although the game was not always smooth, it was found that when children with autism encountered difficulties, they began to seek the assistance of their peers to interact with the game; at the same time, both sides of the game gradually established a tacit understanding of cooperation and became more fluid in the subsequent game through the assistance of the therapist.

5.2 Virtual Characters in Asymmetrical Games Help Children with Autism to Engage in Pretend Play

As the games were based on virtual characters as avatars, the role choices of autistic children and TD children could enable both parties to understand that the tasks and scope of action required to be performed by different characters were different, and then, they recognized the situational tasks and storylines set under the disguised game. In this way, they could establish game mechanisms and rules, and this process constitutes an opportunity for children to learn social communication and interaction. It was evident that such asymmetrical VR collaborative games can help children with autism to master and integrate different game roles, and to use virtual doubles to think and role play.

This phenomenon was evident in the participation of children with autism in the asymmetrical VR collaborative game. The developmental progression of the autistic participants in this study started from their lesser ability to communicate with peers and directly perform tasks, to slowly mastering peer collaboration and oral communication with peers after several play-guided sessions and therapist guidance, as well as imitating the tone of voice when asked by peers and practicing their oral expression skills.

For example, the researchers found that children with autism understood the limitations of the facilitator (the giant) through the differences in the identities of the surrogate characters during play, and were able to effectively help the challenger (the little boy) move on the stationary iron sheet, thus, the participants worked with each other to obtain gold coins to pass the level. This result ensured that they could successfully engage in trans-personal thinking and role playing through virtual characters, and clearly shows that the asymmetrical VR collaborative game allows children with autism to maintain their attention and interest in the game itself, and stimulates the participants' ability to initiate mutual support and trans-personal thinking.

In addition, since the three TD children played the role of co-players in the game to guide the autistic children to complete the tasks through peer cooperation, and the training strategy of the asymmetrical VR collaborative game was carried out in the form of oral communication to achieve the training objectives, such game mechanism has positive implications for helping autistic children to talk to others more easily during future socialization.

5.3 Future Work

This study focused on whether the application of an asymmetrical VR collaboration game has the opportunity to trigger the interaction mechanism of peer collaboration and meaningful conversation in children with autism. It also constructed the concept of collaboration between children with autism and their peers through the manipulation of virtual doubles in the game, in order to understand the role transformation and task performance of children with autism.

These play mechanisms and asymmetrical play strategies will deepen and strengthen higher level cognitive skills, such as empathy and trans-personal thinking, starting from the most basic social skills.

As a preliminary experimental exploration, this study was designed to determine whether the use of this asymmetrical VR collaborative game by children with autism and TD children was effective in activating the intrinsic social cognitive mechanisms of children with autism. However, the time constraints of this study allowed only three groups to be recruited and each group only received a single phase game intervention, which made it difficult to definitively determine whether children with autism had enhanced behavioral and social cognition. Therefore, future studies should adopt further experimental and game designs to obtain more evidence-based findings and data.

Acknowledgments. We are grateful to the Executive Yuan and Ministry of Science and Technology for funding under project No. MOST 109-2221-E-027-069-MY2.

References

1. Hooper, S.R., Poon, K.K., Marcus, L., Fine, C.: Neuropsychological characteristics of school-age children with high-functioning autism: performance on the NEPSY. Child Neuropsychol. **12**(4–5), 299–305 (2006)
2. González-Sala, F., Gómez-Marí, I., Tárraga-Mínguez, R., Vicente-Carvajal, A., Pastor-Cerezuela, G.: Symbolic play among children with autism spectrum disorder: a scoping review. Children **8**(9), 801 (2021)
3. Baron-Cohen, S., Leslie, A.M., Frith, U.: Does the autistic child have a "theory of mind"? Cognition **21**(1), 37–46 (1985)
4. Honey, E., Leekam, S., Turner, M., McConachie, H.: Repetitive behaviour and play in typically developing children and children with autism spectrum disorders. J. Autism Dev. Disord. **37**(6), 1107–1115 (2007)
5. Wu, J., Chen, K., Ma, Y., Vomočilová, J.: Early intervention for children with intellectual and developmental disability using drama therapy techniques. Child Youth Serv. Rev. **109**, 104689 (2020)
6. DiSalvo, C.A., Oswald, D.P.: Peer-mediated interventions to increase the social interaction of children with autism: Consideration of peer expectancies. Focus on autism and other developmental disabilities **17**(4), 198–207 (2002)
7. Xiaoyi, H., Lee, G.T., Watkins, L., Jiang, Y.: Combining preferred activities with peer support to increase social interactions between preschoolers with ASD and typically developing peers. J. Positive Behav. Interventions **23**(4), 272–287 (2021)
8. Gresham, F.M.: Conceptual and definitional issues in the assessment of children's social skills: implications for classifications and training. J. Clin. Child Psychol. **15**(1), 3–15 (1986)
9. Wright, J.C., Knight, V.F., Barton, E.E.: A review of video modeling to teach STEM to students with autism and intellectual disability. Res. Autism Spectr. Disord. **70**, 101476 (2020)
10. Humphrey, N., Symes, W.: Peer interaction patterns among adolescents with autistic spectrum disorders (ASDs) in mainstream school settings. Autism **15**(4), 397–419 (2011)
11. Gugenheimer, J., Stemasov, E., Frommel, J., Rukzio, E.: ShareVR: enabling co-located experiences for virtual reality between HMD and non-HMD users. In: Proceedings of the 2017 CHI Conference on Human Factors in Computing Systems, pp. 4021–4033, May 2017
12. Li, M., Li, X., Xie, L., Liu, J., Wang, F., Wang, Z.: Assisted therapeutic system based on reinforcement learning for children with autism. Comput. Assist. Surg. **24**(sup2), 94–104 (2019)
13. Zhao, M., Chen, S.: The effects of structured physical activity program on social interaction and communication for children with autism. BioMed Research International (2018)
14. Gugenheimer, J., Stemasov, E., Sareen, H., Rukzio, E.: Facedisplay: towards asymmetric multi-user interaction for nomadic virtual reality. In: Proceedings of the 2018 CHI Conference on Human Factors in Computing Systems, pp. 1–13, April 2018
15. Harmsen, I.E.: Empathy in autism spectrum disorder. J. Autism Dev. Disord. **49**(10), 3939–3955 (2019)
16. Macoun, S.J., Schneider, I., Bedir, B., Sheehan, J., Sung, A.: Pilot study of an attention and executive function cognitive intervention in children with autism spectrum disorders. J. Autism Dev. Disord. **51**(8), 2600–2610 (2021)
17. Jansen, P., Fischbach, F., Gugenheimer, J., Stemasov, E., Frommel, J., Rukzio, E.: ShARe: enabling co-located asymmetric multi-user interaction for augmented reality head-mounted displays. In: Proceedings of the 33rd Annual ACM Symposium on User Interface Software and Technology, pp. 459–471, October 2020

Older Women Images and Technologies to Increase Gender Peace in Crisis and COVID-19 Times

Vanessa Zorrilla-Muñoz[1,2(✉)], María Silveria Agulló-Tomás[1,3], Mônica Donio Bellegarde[2], Maria João Forjaz[4], Eduardo Fernandez[5], Carmen Rodriguez-Blazquez[6], Alba Ayala[7], and Gloria Fernandez-Mayoralas[8]

[1] University Institute on Gender Studies, University Carlos III of Madrid, Getafe, Spain
vzorrill@ing.uc3m.es

[2] Fundacion Pilares para la Autonomía Personal, Madrid, Spain
investigacion@fundacionpilares.org

[3] Department of Social Analysis, University Carlos III of Madrid, Getafe, Spain
msat@polsoc.uc3m.es

[4] National Center of Epidemiology, Institute of Health Carlos III and REDISSEC, Madrid, Spain
jforjaz@isciii.es

[5] Bioengineering Institute, Miguel Hernández University of Elche and CIBER BBN, Elche, Spain
e.fernandez@umh.es

[6] National Center of Epidemiology and CIBERNED, Institute of Health Carlos III, Madrid, Spain
crodb@isciii.es

[7] Department of Statistics, University Carlos III de Madrid, Getafe, Spain
aayala@est-econ.uc3m.es

[8] Institute of Economics, Geography and Demography (IEGD), Research Group on Ageing (GIE-CSIC), Spanish National Research Council (CSIC), Madrid, Spain
gloria.fernandezmayoralas@cchs.csic.es

Abstract. The violence - without the apparent "Gender Peace", if data and households are examined - occurs against adult and older women, is beginning to become apparent, but there is only information from recent years. The objective is demonstrate that social isolation can be a key factor in gender peace in the case of adult and older women, even more so in the case of disability or dependency situation. This work focuses on what we call older women gender peace based on qualitative techniques. Moreover, women in this vital stage continue to be vulnerable, defenseless, have more fear and risk, despite their plausible gender peace – expression that we contribute - which connects with the current post-health crisis scenario, armed violence and wars. This chapter also contributes to the consideration of technologies addressed to adults and older women to increase gender peace.

Keywords: Technologies · COVID-19 and another crisis · Social image · Peace and gender violence · Disabilities · Adult and Older women

Q. Gao and J. Zhou (Eds.): HCII 2022, LNCS 13331, pp. 427–440, 2022.
https://doi.org/10.1007/978-3-031-05654-3_30

1 Introduction

On March 11, 2020, the WHO [1] confirmed the current pandemic situation due to the incessant increase in cases related to Coronavirus-2 of the severe acute respiratory syndrome COVID-19 (previously SARS-CoV-2 or 2019-nCoV). This forced the most affected countries with a greater number of seriously ill people and high mortality to develop social isolation measures to prevent the transmission of infections and deal with the health crisis due to lack of resources in hospitals. In this stage, many countries made the decision that millions of people isolate themselves in their homes, thus limiting the freedom of movement. In addition, there was an increase in global gender and family violence, as recent research has indicated (see, for example [2–4]), even more so, from quarantine situations [5] in the current pandemic.

In this sense, it should also be remembered that all homes are not safe for women and girls according to the UN [6]. In 2017, of the more than 87,000 women murdered, intimate femicide occurred in about 35%[1] and, in total, 58% were at the hands of their partners or family members. In Spain, the data show alarming figures: In 2019, a total of 55 intimate femicides were recorded, reaching a figure of 1,051 women murdered at the hands of their partners or ex-partners between 2003 and April 2019 [8].

Some of the recent studies focus on various indicators of Gender-based violence (GBV) related to the sociodemographic profile of the victim: For Boira et al. [9] and other authors, the family is an analysis variable. More specifically, the presence of children increases the perpetuation of the risk of GBV [10]. For Vyas and Watts [11] and other authors, GBV is associated with the economic empowerment (or lack thereof; dependency at various levels) of women. Other studies have included variables such as socioeconomic level [12, 13], that is, educational level, low personal income [14] or housing instability (both to obtain and maintain housing when living in a situation of GBV) [15], among other investigations. Taken together, these authors offer important information on the different sociodemographic variables related to GBV, in particular, to GBV (see, for example, [16]). Although there is also a lack of studies in the exploration of various categories (for example, age) related to the social isolation of women over 65 years in relation to GBV. This is precisely part of the Spanish socio-sanitary crisis due to COVID-19, armed violence and wars. Therefore, it could be a key aspect of GBV. In other words, the need for indicators and explanations from a psychosocial

[1] Stoutdefines it as "the murder of women by intimate male partners" 7. Stout, K.D. Intimate femicide: A national demographic overview. *Journal of Interpersonal Violence* **1991**, *6*, 476–485, 10.1177/088626091006004006. In the same vein, it is defined by the WHO (2013:1) as "Femicide committed by a current or former husband or lover is known as intimate femicide or murder by the partner".

(sociological and psychological) approach and apparent Gender Peace (hereinafter GP) is clear[2], especially in older women [19].

In addition to social isolation as a global predictor of GBV, fear, anxiety and anger towards the aggressor are considered excellent indicators of the victim's own perception, regardless of their sociodemographic profile or other social characteristics, and also in the case of older women. In Spain, the victim's fear of the aggressor is also the main reason why victims postpone verbalizing, denouncing or informing about their situation, requesting help from third parties or socio-psychosocial support or services. Similarly, the fear experienced by the victims during the situation of violence is a factor that cannot be easily evaluated in less severe or ambiguous situations of GBV [20] which include other levels of emotions of learned helplessness, resignation, ostracism and similar psychosocial effects.

This work aims to demonstrate that in the case of the confinement measure (and post-social-health crisis) due to the pandemic (COVID-19) in Spain, there has been greater social isolation on the part of victims of GBV, and even more so in the case of vulnerable populations, such as older women, even more so in the case of disability or dependency situation. In this context of crisis, there are underlying difficulties in detecting the situation of violence, which could also lead to the emergence of new cases of GBV and increase the existing one, especially in the event that the woman is in a situation of dependence. In this line, it should be noted before the pandemic. It was estimated that the world population would be severely affected by neurodegenerative diseases, which mostly affects women and, as indicated by Weber and Clyne [21] differently according to sex. By 2040, Parkinson's [22] and Alzheimer's [23]. Thus, other similar neurodegenerative disorders will surpass cancer as the second most common cause of death worldwide. In fact, the World Health Organization, among other entities and authors, have recognized that these chronic diseases are one of the main causes of the deterioration of public health in the world, causing an unstoppable increase in social and health costs and care [24–27] being in turn one of the main conditions that cause irreversible disability.

The pandemic has also caused a worsening of neurocognitive diseases from a disorder of thoughts and/or behavior (for example, depression, suicidal thoughts, alcoholism, anxiety and impulsivity) [28]. The socio-spatial pandemic patterns have also acted as an additive factor to comorbidity, increasing musculoskeletal diseases and disorders due to reduced mobility and physical activity and, suffering from the disease or secondary

[2] For Rye 17. Centeno, R. La paz y la igualdad entre los géneros: una relación indisoluble. *espacio abierto* **2014**, *23*, 7–21. "Peace and gender equality must be understood as a continuous process of seeking social justice." From another perspective, the UN 18. UN. Peacebuilding. https://www.un.org/peacebuilding/policy-issues-and-partnerships/policy/women. **2021**. urges governments and the international community to invest in the political and economic participation of women, as they are part of the consolidation of peace and are essential partners in underpinning the three pillars of lasting peace: economic recovery, social cohesion and political legitimacy. In this article, we also refer to this continuum and to the improvement of the processes, but seen from the perspective of the women themselves to guarantee their own inner well-being with themselves. Even more, living from a biopsychosocial and sustainable positivism and freed from internal and external images and prejudices.

effects of COVID-19 and negative perception of health in groups with high mortality/vulnerability rate [29]. The worsening in people in a situation of treatment prior to the pandemic, due to the interruption of specialized rehabilitation care, has also been pointed out as another very negative effect [30]. All this highlights the need to make special mention of adult and older women with disabilities or dependency, understanding the vulnerability to GBV from these situations.

In this article, we start from the need to understand fear as an expression of anxiety, stress or, in general, any emotion, as a result of learned helplessness, of the victims towards their aggressor in order to define whether there may be a relationship between fear and social isolation. Following this context, it is also analyzed whether in those cases of social isolation (in particular, when the aggressor tries to prevent the woman from relating to her family or relatives), the victim can lose her fear of her aggressor ("plant them face", rebel or attack), continuing in this way also with the spiral of violence and even increasing the risk, compared to those who continue with fear and react early to the situation. By summarizing, this article aims to expand the concept of GBV and PG in adults and older women to show their vulnerability and invisibility, which would contrast with the scenario of confinement in the socio-health crisis and, in contexts of armed violence and wars.

2 Methods

A qualitative exploratory method was used through the discourses of different programs and projects previous to the COVID-19 and the current crisis (ENCAGE-CM, ENVACES and ENCAGEn-CM[3]), extracted 118 documents (testimonies of previous speeches of the LEDYEVA project were also exploited[4]) and 124 codes (generated from the previous scripts) and the following subcodes: "Gender violence" (714 discourses), "Loneliness" (178 discourses), "Abuse" (57 discourses), "Image" (182 discourses). Based on these codes/variables, the relationship or co-occurrences were assessed, and the citations/verbatims where codes/topics appeared more frequently were compared. The interviews were completely transcribed and anonymized, before carrying out a content analysis using the ATLAS.ti program (v8).

3 Results

It is confirmed from the discourses of/about older women that there is more vulnerability compared to younger women and, even more so, in the case of disability on her part or situations of dependency on the part of the aggressor, which makes them even more invisible when it comes to GBV. It is observed that the situation is different than in younger populations. There are also discourses that highlight that the treatment in the profile cases of older women should be very different from that of young women and, in part, it is due to the fact that gender differences and dependence (both economic and psychosocial and relational) towards their partner is higher in adult and older women, as can be seen from the discourse analysis of the different projects.

[3] See https://encage-cm.es/.

[4] See http://cuidadoresdemayores.blogspot.com/.

[...] And of course! They are very vulnerable women, the older ones and they have violence and such. And it is very complicated... [...] We also realized that this type of violence has to do with, is linked to, that you are older, is linked to dependency, getting older has to do with being more dependent, even in some or many cases there may be a disability that can be mild, moderate or severe. [...] Interview with CSO expert, EP_OSC_170504_JPC_V2.

[...] "...And I say to him, 'why are you turning off the TV? let's see, why do you turn off the TV for me?', 'because yes, because what do you see there?'. And then I got up again and turned it on, so he started with me... to hit me and well... [...] .. and nothing, well, and I said: 'what do you want? the closed window, well "it will close". And you don't want to watch the TV, should I turn it off? Well, "turn it off"'. And then he says 'throw yourself out there', that he's going to throw me out the window, that is, I'm going to leave him because... I'm going to get a divorce... [...] GD1: 37, Andalusia.

It is also observed that expressions of fear (and related emotions: Anxiety, anger, among others) appear when the abuse occurs and, in some way, tend to be more frequent when there is more family isolation (and social isolation in general, from the neighborhood and other close people).

[...] Well, she was a mistreated lady. With complaint from her husband. A lady who lived under a bed because she closed herself out of fear. She had to withdraw her complaint because of threats from her husband. I mean, I mean, supposedly they had given him one.... one of removal, but she removed it in the face of his threats, but they had to live in the same house. So she only went out to eat [...] Expert interview, EP_INS_170405_TB2_V2.

[...] the social worker gets in touch, she starts talking to her, she starts talking to her husband, we have annulled it, we already put the police device within her reach... hey, it seems that this fear is already and that beating or that fear he had that he was going to hit him, that has already dissipated and the man, as they told me yesterday, has become afraid and the woman threatens him, says "if you do something to me, I'll go and tell the center for older people", and it seems that he has taken fear. [...] Interview with institutional expert, EP_INS_170404_HS1_V2.

Another aspect linked to the phenomenon of isolation in older women seems to be related to aging depending on the socio-spatial environment (rural or urban environment) where it occurs. However, some discourses comment that there are hardly any differences, that isolation and "feeling like a prisoner" (that is, helpless or trapped) in one's own home can occur in any environment. In this sense, getting out of the situation of violence can become more difficult both in cities and in rural areas: in cities due to greater isolation and less contact with the neighborhood and social due to the greater population or demographic density. that makes social relations difficult, in some cases and, in rural settings, due to the lack of proximity of services to report.

[...] I think that perhaps aging in the towns is different, and then here in the city there is a lot of isolation of older people [...] we touch on the issue of violence

without saying that it is violence than in the towns You don't know either that it's very difficult to deal with this issue [...] because in rural areas the problem is terrible [...] Interview with a CSO expert, EP_OSC_170512_NA_V2.

[...] the rural environment that is most needed, you know, is an environment that is always smaller, always more masculinized, I don't know if it is more sexist than the urban one, which we still have here as well, but well, it is more closed and everyone knows each other with which everything is always more complicated. Everything is more complicated, from going to report a case of violence, everything is more difficult, right? [...] In-depth interview with an expert, EP_OSC_170512_NA_V2.

From another perspective and, coinciding with the questionnaire, older women are exposed to any type of violence, including those forms that are more invisible in the case of older women, such as sexual violence. In any case, any situation of violence produces, at all levels, a high psycho-emotional wear and tear to which women become accustomed and show their apparent GP. In addition, some discourses show that the aggressor, on occasions, is not only the partner, but also the one exercised by children, caregivers at home or in residences and transversally, from the dependent person to the female caregiver. For example, it is worth mentioning in the current pandemic situation,

[...] although it seems that the issue of sexual violence in these ages does not exist, it continues to exist. Even in the field of institutions there have been cases, people who were in the care and charge of these people and have sexually assaulted them [...] Rape of women as at any other age. Sight. Gender violence of course. Hey. [Long pause] sexual violence, psychological violence, economic violence and, furthermore, this violence was carried out by different, let's say, people. In the case of gender violence, of course by the couple, but also, there is domestic violence... Which is exercised by the sons or daughters. Mainly by the male child [...] Interview with OSC expert, EP_OSC_170504_JPC_V2.

[...] Yes, and they have phases, according to age, according to personality... [...] And depending on the day he cries, he gets angry [...] Some men become violent. [...] Look, what I can say about this is that it is not easy at all. No, it's not easy at all. This is horrible. The only thing that happens is that you have gotten used to it but you have to go through it. It is not easy under any circumstances. [...] GD5:12, Valencian Community.

Finally, it should be noted that there is currently a technological development potential both for the care of people in situations of vulnerability, disability and dependency, as well as for the treatment of the possible disease or chronicity, which can be used as a double path in the joint design of solutions to maintain GP in adult and older women.

4 Discussion

This article mainly confirms that social isolation can be a key factor in GBV and GP previous, the socio-sanitary crisis of COVID-19 in the case of adult and older women, even more so in the case of a situation of disability or dependency. This coincides with the fact that, in Spain, the data that has been known since the COVID-19 quarantine of thousands of families has meant, in itself, a slight increase in calls from women to the emergency number and also, an increase in cases not reported by victims due to the over control of the aggressors over their victims during the days of confinement, which has also produced multiple difficulties in the intervention [31–33]. Following this context, and although they do not focus on adult and older women only, it is worth mentioning Farris and Fenaughty [34] who examined the association between social isolation, domestic violence, and drug and substance dependence among users. Their study shows that there is a representative association of probability of having been physically abused by their most recent sexual partners in those women who reported being in a situation of social isolation. Also noteworthy is the study by Lanier and Maume [35] who analyzed social isolation in rural and urban spaces, where it stands out that rural women with support from family and/or friends may be less exposed to the risks of gender-based violence than those who do not have social support. In the same way, it is shown in this article that there are situations of violence (although there is an apparent image of peace) in socio-spatial environments with few resources and support beyond the family, from the public, associative, neighborhood or from CSOs, civil society organizations or the third sector) in the older women. Inversely, the availability of aid resources can empower older women to help them get out of the situation of violence. At the other extreme, they find older women leaders, who would be the ideal, the paradigm and social image of greater peace and gender equality at these ages. This was discussed and proposed to expand and make more visible these profiles of female leadership treated in other studies (see for example [36–38]).

In the same sense and more recently, it is worth mentioning Rivas Rivero et al.[39], who emphasize that social support is an effective measure to break the cycle of gender violence or Benavides et al. (2019) who found that women from Lima with greater contacts or social ties in their neighborhood were also less exposed to gender-based violence. In Spain, researches with this same perspective also stand out, although they also do so without the generational approach and without specifying the situation of adult and older women. For example, the Cruz Roja Española [40] conducted a study on gender violence in order to improve Atenpro's service. The report highlights isolation as a key factor in GBV and, according to the data reported in the document, the 80.5% of the victims treated during 2016, could not relate to their family. In short, the fact that the aggressor takes her away from her relatives can be decisive and negatively affect GBV, even more so when he is linked to highly vulnerable groups, as in the case of women with disabilities [41] or older women [42] which coincides with some testimonies presented in this article. This article is limited to a certain number of analyzes of women obtained from secondary data. In a future analysis, it could be useful to use our own questionnaire based on the database of this article and carry out an analysis by age groups, which could be of interest in future research.

On the other hand, this article also confirms that adult and older women continue to be a vulnerable, forgotten and stereotyped population group [43], which also affects and increases the situations of GBV [44]. Aging is a process where women are more subject to stereotypes and social image pressures [45], which leads to the violence chronicity [46], even more so in situations of disability [47, 48]) or dependency. Moreover, GBV is assimilated by the victims, which triggers the normalization of the situation of violence or, on the contrary, the increase in fear of the aggressor. Also, especially in the majors, the increase or fall in "learned helplessness" (in terms of Seligman and later authors), or resignation (admitting and normalizing once again the process of violence for not being able to get out of it, to protect other family members who are threatened by the aggressor, the fear of further reprisals and other consequences or, of being killed) and, in short, an apparent GP that hides different types of violence, not only by gender. For all this, social isolation is also increasing gender-based violence in older women and, in extreme cases, loneliness at these ages (living alone, women especially) has caused them to die unaccompanied not only in hospitals from COVID-19, but also there are and have been deaths in their homes during confinement, which is a topic that could be addressed in future research and on a gender perspective from the opportunities of technologies. In this way, it is also interesting to mention the double effect that can be considered in the use of technology in adult and older women in a situation of disability or dependency what are they coming integrating since the pandemic.

For example, it is worth mentioning the use of technologies connected to the Internet, such as video calls, online healthcare or online shopping [49], just like him the possible use of social robots [50, 51] and used for the affective human-robot interaction [52], new generation robots based on cyber-physical systems[5] [53], eHealth medical devices for home monitoring [54], including telerehabilitation exoskeletons [55], support devices such as EGARA [56], the neural interface for the rehabilitation of sensory and motor functions in people affected by stroke and spinal cord injury [57], the neuroprosthesis for stimulation in the case of suffering from certain neurodegenerative diseases [58], but also for blindness [59, 60], and cortical microelectrode arrays [61] that could serve as support in cases of disability and dependency for care [62], treatment, social and health control, but also for the maintenance of the GP in the women what they already have the same.

From another sense, Parlalis et al. [63] mention that the fear of the reaction of the perpetrator/aggressor is one of the common causes for not informing or denouncing the episode of violence, which constitutes the first limitation of this article, since the fear of the reaction of the aggressor has not been proven, but "the perception of fear" by women. Another of the limitations is related to the fact that only three forms (physical, sexual and psycho-emotional) of the multiple forms of GBV are considered. Even so, a second questionnaire could be used that uses more forms of violence, and even subtypes related to what is not related to "good treatment of older women" in order to expand and further detail the classification and understanding of violence into the different forms of GBV.

It is worth mentioning that in all the models a response of fear is observed in the face of the different forms of physical and psycho-emotional violence, while sexual violence hardly suggests a correlation with the perception of fear in women, although it is mentioned in some of the discourses of the analysis qualitative - which confirms that qualitative techniques are usually more suitable for more personal and intimate problems to emerge -. Sexual violence can also be interpreted in relation to previous

[5] Cyber-physical systems are based on devices controlled and/or monitored by algorithms and integrated with the Internet.

studies, which point to vulnerability and re-victimization in sexual assaults. From the older women, DeLorey and Wolf [64] suggested the difficulty in clinical identification and the need to include measures such as the promotion of safer environments and advice on potential vulnerability to prevent sexual violence, which is also collected more recently by Nobels et al. [65] declaring that the fact of getting older does not exonerate them from exposure to the risk of sexual violence and they should, therefore, also be considered as women with specific vulnerabilities and risks of sexual victimization. This also explains the justification and minimization of the incident by the victim [66]. From another perspective, the importance of the absence of significant results in the case of the sexual violence variables coincides with the arguments of the GBV normalization process of the reactivity itself (and less sensitivity) of the quantitative techniques, and even more, in the case of older women. In relation to this, older women are questioned, they cannot be raped, they are not considered attractive and the disgusting rejection of expressions such as "no longer having sexual attractiveness or to be raped" that is observed in some "sexist jokes and ageist" who reinforce the negative stereotype of asexuals. Following Gerger et al. [67] and Megías et al. [68], acceptance of the rape myth could act as a fear or anxiety buffer to reduce vulnerability to sexual assault. Also, research related to the study of emotions could facilitate the understanding of these situations and propose programs for change, greater awareness and detection of emotions to rationalize and denounce them, and not only aimed at young people but also at older people, at all stages of life. life and the resocialization process [44] in GBV for greater peace and real gender equality, not only apparent or for certain generations and life stages.

Although the perception of risk and fear in GBV are not the same concepts, they are connected [69] through the different forms of violence that can produce a panic situation in the victim. Resilient GBV survivors develop an anticipatory sense of constant fear that increases perception of injury risk [70]. Previous studies have identified a line of gradations of severity in the maximum risk, where the basic forms of violence (physical and sexual violence) are considered the main elements of analysis (see for example, [71, 72]), although they are not, generally, the first violence perceived, since the most basic are the psychological ones (social, or economic, which we have already alluded to), although the psychological ones remain in an invisible and less detectable spectrum and in which various emotions they flow in an unregulated way, that is, without emotional awareness. For Bliton et al. [73], emotional regulation deficits also suggest perpetration of GBV. All this, together with the desire for a social image that does not show the problems before society (not appearing to be a failure as a couple or family, depending on their husband, resisting for their children and the shame of "what they will say", among other arguments).In the case of the older ones, it is perceived too late to change, which means that the situation of violence is kept hidden for a longer time or a situation of isolation is produced in the victim, even more so if it is a question of violence in adults and older women - in supposed "peace" and gender equality -.

Indeed, older women are largely forgotten and invisible in GBV, and are also susceptible to a lack of social support ([74], among others) and also to social isolation as confirmed in this article and therefore, the proposal to refer to the apparent GP at these ages. The socio-sanitary crisis is offering very problematic social situations in this country (i.e. nursing homes) that contrast with other images that are observed (or do not even appear) of older women: in silence, in peace (without violence, apparently), helping in the domestic and family space, where care appears in the first stage, where older women are active but defenseless. With this, the current context of the pandemic and, despite the scarcity of current results, presupposes an increase in cases of GBV, which will probably be invisible to society in the case of older women. As has been confirmed, the severity could be more impressive in the case of women in a situation of dependency or disability, for example, in the case of neurodegenerative diseases.

In short, this article confirms adult and older women - who are usually the most dependent due to their socialization in the naturalization of violence and, in particular, those who have fewer support resources - are defenseless. Moreover, they are more afraid and there is an imminent risk. Their situation is only an apparent GP - there are fewer complaints and the victims live in silence - because the violence in its different faces persists, although this social image or data on women in these stages is not available vital. For this reason, they continue to be in need of support and socio-political and psychosocial attention. Furthermore, the development or technologies and systems could contribute to reducing this key problem. In this sense, a technological approach with a gender perspective would be one of help and reference to achieve the GP of adult and older women, especially in disability, dependency, violence and crisis situations.

Fundings and Grants. This work is part of: ENCAGEn-CM R&D Activities Program (Active Ageing, Quality of Life and Gender. Promoting a positive image of old age and aging combating ageism) (Ref. H2019/HUM-5698) (Funded by Programs of R&D in Community of Madrid Social Sciences and Humanities, co-financed with the European Social Fund. PR: G. Fernandez-Mayoralas, C Rodriguez-Blázquez, MS Agulló-Tomás, MD Zamarrón, and MA Molina).

We appreciate the support of the QASP (Quality of life, Aging in Sweden, Spain, and Portugal) research project, funded by the Institute of Health Carlos III, Intramural Strategical Action in Health AESI 2018, Ref: PI18CIII/00046, PR: MR Forjaz).

Moreover, this contribution takes parts of the grant PROMETEO/2019/119 from the Generalitat Valenciana and the Bidons Egara Research Chair of the University Miguel Hernández to Eduardo Fernández. The fieldwork for the qualitative analysis was financed by the ENVACES R&D+i project (MINECO-FEDER, ref. CSO2015-64115-R. PR: F. Rojo-Perez) and the ENCAGE-CM R&D Activities Program (Community of Madrid-FSE, ref. S2015/HUM-3367. PR: G. Fernandez-Mayoralas).

References

1. WHO: WHO Director-General's opening remarks at the media briefing on COVID-19 - 11 March 2020 (2020). https://www.who.int/dg/speeches/detail/who-director-general-s-opening-remarks-at-the-media-briefing-on-covid-19---11-march-2020
2. Usher, K., Bhullar, N., Durkin, J., Gyamfi, N., Jackson, D.: Family violence and COVID-19: increased vulnerability and reduced options for support. Int. J. Ment. Health Nurs. **29**, 549–552 (2020). https://doi.org/10.1111/inm.12735
3. Bradbury-Jones, C., Isham, L.: The pandemic paradox: the consequences of COVID-19 on domestic violence. J. Clin. Nurs. **29**, 2047–2049 (2020). https://doi.org/10.1111/jocn.15296

4. Campbell, A.M.: An increasing risk of family violence during the Covid-19 pandemic: strengthening community collaborations to save lives. Forensic Sci. Int.: Rep. **2**, 100089 (2020). https://doi.org/10.1016/j.fsir.2020.100089
5. Mazza, M., Marano, G., Lai, C., Janiri, L., Sani, G.: Danger in danger: interpersonal violence during COVID-19 quarantine. Psychiatry Res. **289**, 113046 (2020). https://doi.org/10.1016/j.psychres.2020.113046
6. UN: Gender-related killing of women and girls. Division for Policy Analysis and Public Affairs. United Nations Office on Drugs and Crime, Viena (2019)
7. Stout, K.D.: Intimate femicide: a national demographic overview. J. Interpers. Violence **6**, 476–485 (1991). https://doi.org/10.1177/088626091006004006
8. Secretaría de Estado de Igualdad. Mujeres víctimas mortales por violencia de género en España a manos de sus parejas o exparejas (2020). http://www.violenciagenero.igualdad.gob.es/violenciaEnCifras/victimasMortales/fichaMujeres/home.htm
9. Boira, S., Carbajosa, P., Méndez, R.: Miedo, conformidad y silencio: la violencia en las relaciones de pareja en áreas rurales de Ecuador. Psychosoc. Interv. **25**, 9–17 (2016). https://doi.org/10.1016/j.psi.2015.07.008
10. Hilton, N.Z., Eke, A.W.: Assessing risk of intimate partner violence. In: Campbell, J.C., Messing, J.T. (ed.) Assessing Dangerousness: Domestic Violence Offenders and Child Abusers. Springer Publishing Company, New York (2017). https://doi.org/10.1891/9780826133274.0006
11. Vyas, S., Watts, C.: How does economic empowerment affect women's risk of intimate partner violence in low and middle income countries? A systematic review of published evidence. J. Int. Dev. **21**, 577–602 (2009). https://doi.org/10.1002/jid.1500
12. Zorrilla, B., et al.: Intimate partner violence: last year prevalence and association with socio-economic factors among women in Madrid Spain. Eur. J. Public Health **20**, 169–175 (2010). https://doi.org/10.1093/eurpub/ckp143
13. Kothari, C.L., et al.: Intimate partner violence associated with postpartum depression, regardless of socioeconomic status. Matern. Child Health J. **20**(6), 1237–1246 (2016). https://doi.org/10.1007/s10995-016-1925-0
14. Barrett, B.J., Pierre, M.S.: Variations in women's help seeking in response to intimate partner violence: findings from a Canadian population-based study. Violence Against Women **17**, 47–70 (2011). https://doi.org/10.1177/1077801210394273
15. Pavao, J., Alvarez, J., Baumrind, N., Induni, M., Kimerling, R.: Intimate partner violence and housing instability. Am. J. Prev. Med. **32**, 143–146 (2007). https://doi.org/10.1016/j.amepre.2006.10.008
16. Ministerio de Igualdad. Mujeres mayores de 65 años víctimas de violencia de género (2019). https://violenciagenero.igualdad.gob.es/violenciaEnCifras/estudios/investigaciones/2019/estudio/Estudio_VG_Mayores_65.htm
17. Centeno, R.: La paz y la igualdad entre los géneros: una relación indisoluble. espacio abierto **23**, 7–21 (2014)
18. UN. Peacebuilding (2021). https://www.un.org/peacebuilding/policy-issues-and-partnerships/policy/women
19. Agulló-Tomás, M.S., Zorrilla-Muñoz, V.: La aparente paz de género en las mujeres mayores: datos, emociones y discursos sobre las violencias. In: Avances de Investigación en Salud a lo largo del Ciclo Vital. Nuevas realidades, Dykinson, pp. 75–86 (2020). ISBN: 978-84-1377-223-3
20. Russell, B., Kraus, S.W., Chapleau, K.M., Oswald, D.: Perceptions of blame in intimate partner violence: the role of the perpetrator's ability to arouse fear of injury in the victim. J. Interpers. Violence **34**, 1089–1097 (2019). https://doi.org/10.1177/0886260516646999
21. Weber, C.M., Clyne, A.M.: Sex differences in the blood–brain barrier and neurodegenerative diseases. APL Bioeng. **5**, 011509 (2021). https://doi.org/10.1063/5.0035610

22. Dorsey, E.R., Sherer, T., Okun, M.S., Bloem, B.R.: The emerging evidence of the Parkinson pandemic. J. Parkinsons Dis. **8**, S3–S8 (2018). https://doi.org/10.3233/JPD-181474
23. WHO. Dementia (2021)
24. WHO. Global status report on the public health response to dementia (2021)
25. Kaji, R.: Global burden of neurological diseases highlights stroke. Nat. Rev. Neurol. **15**, 371–372 (2019). https://doi.org/10.1038/s41582-019-0208-y
26. Carroll, W.M.: The global burden of neurological disorders. Lancet Neurol. **18**, 418–419 (2019). https://doi.org/10.1016/S1474-4422(19)30029-8
27. Deuschl, G., et al.: The burden of neurological diseases in Europe: an analysis for the Global Burden of Disease Study 2017. Lancet Public Health **5**, e551–e567 (2020). https://doi.org/10.1016/S2468-2667(20)30190-0
28. Simard, J., Volicer, L.: Loneliness and isolation in long-term care and the COVID-19 pandemic. J. Am. Med. Dir. Assoc. **21**, 966 (2020). https://doi.org/10.1016/j.jamda.2020.05.006
29. Zorrilla-Muñoz, V., et al: Ageing perception as a key predictor of self-rated health by rural older people - a study with gender and inclusive perspectives. Land. **11**(3), 323 (2022). https://doi.org/10.3390/land11030323
30. Spielmanns, M., et al.: Covid-19 outbreak during inpatient rehabilitation: impact on settings and clinical course of neuromusculoskeletal rehabilitation patients. Am. J. Phys. Med. Rehabil. **100**, 203–208 (2021). https://doi.org/10.1097/PHM.0000000000001686
31. Lorente-Acosta, M.: Violencia de género en tiempos de pandemia y confinamiento. Revista Española de Medicina Legal **46**, 139–145 (2020). https://doi.org/10.1016/j.reml.2020.05.005
32. Agámez Llanos, V.d.l.Á.; Rodríguez Díaz, M.: Violencia contra la mujer: la otra cara de la pandemia. Psicología desde el Caribe 37, 1–3 (2020). https://doi.org/10.14482/psdc.37.1.305.48
33. Ruiz-Pérez, I., Pastor-Moreno, G.: Medidas de contención de la violencia de género durante la pandemia de COVID-19. Gac. Sanit. **35**, 389–394 (2021). https://doi.org/10.1016/j.gaceta.2020.04.005
34. Farris, C.A., Fenaughty, A.M.: Social isolation and domestic violence among female drug users. Am. J. Drug Alcohol Abuse **28**, 339–351 (2002). https://doi.org/10.1081/ada-120002977
35. Lanier, C., Maume, M.O.: Intimate partner violence and social isolation across the rural/urban divide. Violence Against Women **15**, 1311–1330 (2009). https://doi.org/10.1177/1077801209346711
36. Agulló-Tomás, M.S., Zorrilla-Muñoz, V., García, M.V.G., Criado-Quesada, B.: Liderazgo, envejecimiento y género. In: Alonso, A., Paz, T.L.d., (eds.) The Time Is Now. Feminist Leadership for a New Era. Red Global Cátedras UNESCO en género, Paris, pp. 112–122 (2019)
37. Ballesteros Pena, A., Franco Alonso, S., Donayre Pinedo, M., Serrano Garijo, P.: La evaluación del Proyecto Lideresas del Ayuntamiento de Madrid: Una experiencia de evaluación desde la teoría del programa sensible al género y los derechos humanos. Revista Prisma Social **21**, 356–390 (2018)
38. Zorrilla-Muñoz, V., Blanco-Ruiz, M., Criado-Quesada, B., Fernandez-Sanchez, M., Merchan-Molina, R., Agulló-Tomás, M.S.: Género y envejecimiento desde el prisma de las organizaciones que trabajan con mayores. Revista Prisma Social **21**, 500–510 (2018)
39. Rivas Rivero, E., Panadero Herrero, S., Bonilla Algovia, E., Vásquez Carrasco, R., Vázquez Cabrera, J.J.: Influencia del apoyo social en el mantenimiento de la convivencia con el agresor en víctimas de violencia de género de León (Nicaragua). Informes psicológicos **18**, 145–165 (2018). https://doi.org/10.18566/infpsic.v18n1a08
40. Española, C.R.: El aislamiento social, una de las claves de la violencia de género. Boletín sobre vulnerabilidad social **130** (2017)

41. Hernández Mancha, I., Rodríguez García, M.I., Llopis Giménez, C.: A propósito de un caso de violencia de género, ciberacoso y sexting en una pareja con discapacidad. Revista Española de Medicina Legal **45**, 29–31 (2019). https://doi.org/10.1016/j.reml.2018.01.006
42. Pathak, N., Dhairyawan, R., Tariq, S.: The experience of intimate partner violence among older women: a narrative review. Maturitas **121**, 63–75 (2019). https://doi.org/10.1016/j.maturitas.2018.12.011
43. Agulló-Tomás, M.S. En tercer plano. Estereotipos, cine y mujeres mayores. In: Muñoz, B., (ed.) Medios de comunicación, mujeres y cambio cultural, pp. 245–276. Dirección General de la Mujer de la Comunidad de Madrid, Madrid (2001). ISBN: 84-451-2010-7
44. Zorrilla-Muñoz, V., Agulló-Tomás, M.S.: Emociones y violencia desde una perspectiva de género e intergeneracional. Proceedings of the Paper presented at the XXVI Congreso Internacional De Psicología Y Educación. INFAD (Infancia, Adolescencia, Mayores Y Discapacidad) (2019)
45. Delgado Álvarez, C., Gutiérrez García, A.: Percepción de la violencia de género en personas mayores. Int. J. Dev. Educ. Psychol. **2**, 329–338 (2013)
46. Gracia Ibáñez, J.: Una Mirada Interseccional sobre la Violencia de Género contra las Mujeres Mayores (An Intersectional Perspective on Gender-based Violence against Older Women). Oñati Socio-legal Series **5**, 547–569 (2015)
47. Stern, E., van der Heijden, I., Dunkle, K.: How people with disabilities experience programs to prevent intimate partner violence across four countries. Eval. Program Plann. **79**, 101770 (2020). https://doi.org/10.1016/j.evalprogplan.2019.101770
48. Ballan, M.: Intimate partner violence and women with disabilities: the public health crisis. Family Intim. Partn. Violence Q. **10**, 65–69 (2017)
49. Criado-Quesada, B., Zorrilla-Muñoz, V., Agulló-Tomás, M.S.: El uso de tecnologías de asistencia sanitaria digital por parte de la población mayor desde una perspectiva de género e intrageneracional. Teknokultura **18**, 103–113 (2021)
50. Abou Allaban, A., Wang, M., Padır, T.: A systematic review of robotics research in support of in-home care for older adults. Information **11**, 75 (2020). https://doi.org/10.3390/info11020075
51. Jecker, N.S.: You've got a friend in me: sociable robots for older adults in an age of global pandemics. Ethics Inf. Technol. **23**(1), 35–43 (2020). https://doi.org/10.1007/s10676-020-09546-y
52. Val-Calvo, M., Álvarez-Sánchez, J.R., Ferrández-Vicente, J.M., Fernández, E.: Affective robot story-telling human-robot interaction: exploratory real-time emotion estimation analysis using facial expressions and physiological signals. IEEE Access **8**, 134051–134066 (2020). https://doi.org/10.1109/access.2020.3007109
53. Yang, G., et al.: Homecare robotic systems for healthcare 4.0: visions and enabling technologies. IEEE J. Biomed. Health Inform. **24**, 2535–2549 (2020). https://doi.org/10.1109/JBHI.2020.2990529
54. Nakshbandi, G., Moor, C., Wijsenbeek, M.: Home monitoring for patients with ILD and the COVID-19 pandemic. Lancet Respir. Med. **8**, 1172–1174 (2020). https://doi.org/10.1016/S2213-2600(20)30452-5
55. Bertomeu-Motos, A., et al.: User activity recognition system to improve the performance of environmental control interfaces: a pilot study with patients. J. Neuroeng. Rehabil. **16**, 1–9 (2019). https://doi.org/10.1186/s12984-018-0477-5
56. Zorrilla-Muñoz, V., et al.: Technology, gender and COVID-19. Analysis of perceived health in adults and older people. In: Gao, Q., Zhou, J. (ed.) HCII 2021. Lecture Notes in Computer Science, vol. 12787, pp. 363–379. Springer, Cham (2021). https://doi.org/10.1007/978-3-030-78111-8_25
57. Fernandez, E.: Selective induction of fingertip sensations for better neuroprosthetic control. Neurology **98**, 261–262 (2021). https://doi.org/10.1212/WNL.0000000000013177

58. Milekovic, T.: A brain-spine interface complements deep-brain stimulation. In: Guger, C., Allison, B.Z., Gunduz, A. (eds.) Brain-Computer Interface Research, pp. 87–93. Springer, Cham (2021). https://doi.org/10.1007/978-3-030-79287-9_9
59. Brandtstädter, J., Baltes-Götz, B.: Personal control over development and quality of life perspectives in adulthood. In: Baltes, M.M., Baltes, P.B. (eds.) Successful Aging: Perspectives from the Behavioral Sciences, pp. 197–224. European Network on Longitudinal Studies on Individual Development; Cambridge University Press, Cambridge (1990)
60. Chen, X., Wang, F., Fernandez, E., Roelfsema, P.R.: Shape perception via a high-channel-count neuroprosthesis in monkey visual cortex. Science **370**, 1191–1196 (2020). https://doi.org/10.1126/science.abd7435
61. Fernández, E., et al.: Visual percepts evoked with an intracortical 96-channel microelectrode array inserted in human occipital cortex. J. Clin. Investig. **131** (2021). https://doi.org/10.1172/JCI151331
62. Agulló-Tomás, M.S., Zorrilla-Muñoz, V.: Technologies and images of older women. In: Gao, Q., Zhou, J. (eds.) HCII 2020. LNCS, vol. 12209, pp. 163–175. Springer, Cham (2020). https://doi.org/10.1007/978-3-030-50232-4_12
63. Parlalis, S.K.: Women aged 45–64 and IPV in Cyprus. J. Adult Prot. **8**, 184–194 (2016). https://doi.org/10.1108/JAP-11-2015-0033
64. DeLorey, C., Wolf, K.A.: Sexual violence and older women. AWHONNS Clin. Issues Perinat. Womens Health Nurs. **4**, 173–179 (1993)
65. Nobels, A., Vandeviver, C., Beaulieu, M., Lemmens, G.M., Keygnaert, I.: Are older women forgotten in the fight against sexual violence? Lancet Glob. Health **6**, e370 (2018). https://doi.org/10.1016/S2214-109X(18)30074-3
66. Hlavka, H.R.: Normalizing sexual violence: young women account for harassment and abuse. Gend. Soc. **28**, 337–358 (2014). https://doi.org/10.1177/0891243214526468
67. Gerger, H., Kley, H., Bohner, G., Siebler, F.: The acceptance of modern myths about sexual aggression scale: development and validation in German and English. Aggress Behav. **33**, 422–440 (2007). https://doi.org/10.1002/ab.20195
68. Megías, J.L., Romero-Sánchez, M., Durán, M., Moya, M., Bohner, G.: Spanish validation of the acceptance of modern myths about sexual aggression scale (AMMSA). Span. J. Psychol. **14**, 912–925 (2011). https://doi.org/10.5209/rev_SJOP.2011.v14.n2.37
69. Sweet, E.L., Ortiz Escalante, S.: Bringing bodies into planning: visceral methods, fear and gender violence. Urban Stud. **52**, 1826–1845 (2014). https://doi.org/10.1177/0042098014541157
70. Salcioglu, E., Urhan, S., Pirinccioglu, T., Aydin, S.: Anticipatory fear and helplessness predict PTSD and depression in domestic violence survivors. Psychol. Trauma **9**, 117–125 (2017). https://doi.org/10.1037/tra000020
71. Ali, T.S., Asad, N., Mogren, I., Krantz, G.: Intimate partner violence in urban Pakistan: prevalence, frequency, and risk factors. Int. J. Womens Health **3**, 105–115 (2011). https://doi.org/10.2147/ijwh.s17016
72. Amor, P.J., Echeburúa, E., de Corral, P., Zubizarreta, I., Sarasua, B.: Repercusiones psicopatológicas de la violencia doméstica en la mujer en función de las circunstancias del maltrato. Int. J. Clin. Health Psychol. **2**, 227–246 (2002)
73. Bliton, C.F., et al.: Emotion dysregulation, gender, and intimate partner violence perpetration: an exploratory study in college students. J. Family Violence **31**(3), 371–377 (2015). https://doi.org/10.1007/s10896-015-9772-0
74. McGarry, J., Ali, P.: The invisibility of older women as survivors of intimate partner violence. In: Bows, H. (ed.) Violence Against Older Women, Volume I: Nature and Extent Palgrave Studies in Victims and Victimology PSVV, pp. 41 55. Springer, Cham (2019). https://doi.org/10.1007/978-3-030-16601-4_3

Author Index

Abushanab, Nariman II-3
Adapa, Karthik II-210
Agulló-Tomás, María Silveria II-427
Akiyama, Hiroko I-541, II-134
Alayed, Asmaa S. I-139
Amaral, Inês I-3, II-335
Antunes, Eduardo II-335
Ayala, Alba II-427

Barbosa de Oliveira Camargo, Mayckel I-151
Blum, Rainer II-107
Bomsdorf, Birgit II-107
Brites, Maria José I-3, I-335, II-335
Brown, Julie A. I-12
Buscicchio, Giulia I-451
Bustamante, Felipe I-584

Cao, Cong I-276
Carlo, Simone I-451
Castro, Teresa Sofia I-3
Cerqueira, Carla I-265
Chan, Alan H. S. I-641
Chang, Chia-Ling II-349
Chang, Ya-Ting I-127
Chaparro, Alex II-71
Chaparro, Barbara II-71
Chen, Chun-Wen II-360
Chen, Jiangjie I-93
Chen, Sinan II-52, II-197
Chen, Xiatong II-183
Chen, Ya Hsin II-360
Chen, Xin I-160
Cheng, Xi II-170
Choy, Elaine II-71
Chu, Junjie I-500
Chu, Ku-Hsi I-27
Cole, Amy II-210
Colombo, Mauro II-398

da Cruz Landim, Paula I-151
Dai, Yihang II-290
de Araújo Barbosa, Maria Lilian I-40
Ding, Xinyi I-276
Ding, Yi II-229, II-305, II-320
Dinh, An T. I-12
Donio Bellegarde, Mônica II-427
Dumitru, Elena-Alexandra I-291

Edström, Maria I-311
Eftimova, Andreana I-381
Elbaz, Sasha I-346

Feng, Linlin I-321
Fernandez, Eduardo II-427
Fernández-Ardèvol, Mireia I-212
Fernandez-Mayoralas, Gloria II-427
Feuer, Shelley I-555
Flores, Ana Marta II-335
Forjaz, Maria João II-427
Fournier, Helene I-485
Fujisaki-Sueda-Sakai, Mahiro I-541, II-134
Fulbright, Ron II-3

Ghosh, Ritam I-201, II-14
Gliozzi, Rachel I-555
Goonetilleke, Ravindra S. I-224
Gu, Chao I-93
Guaita, Antonio II-398
Guerra, Josefa I-584

Han, Ting II-229, II-305, II-320
Hărăguş, Mihaela II-371
Hebblethwaite, Shannon I-346
Helal, Sumi I-466
Heponiemi, Tarja I-596
Homma, Keiko II-243

Ifukube, Tohru I-541, II-134
Ito, Kenichiro I-541, II-134
Ivan, Loredana I-291, I-365

Jakob, Dietmar I-175
Jia, Liang-Ming II-255
Jiang, Qianling I-93
Jin, Quanxin I-625
Johnson, Andrew I-201
Jokinen, Kristiina II-122

Kaihlanen, Anu-Marja I-596
Kainiemi, Emma I-596
Kang, SooIn II-134
Kanižaj, Igor I-335
Kehusmaa, Sari I-596
Keohane, Susann I-466
Khalili-Mahani, Najmeh I-346
Khan, Nibraas I-201, II-14
Khasawneh, Amro II-210
Ko, T. H. I-641
Kogami, Hiroki II-134
Kondratova, Irina I-485
Koponen, Päivikki I-596
Koskinen, Seppo I-596

Lafontaine, Constance I-411, II-383
Latshaw, Emily II-14
Lawton, Paige II-71
Lee, Brian Y. H. I-658
Lee, Chang-Franw I-27
Lee, I.-Jui II-277, II-413
Li, Dan I-276
Li, Shuyuan I-160
Li, Wen-Yi II-268
Li, Xinyue I-521
Li, Xueai I-500
Liu, Bingjian II-154
Liu, Chunrong II-229, II-320
Liu, Na II-170
Liu, Ruisi I-500
Liu, Tianchang I-521
Liu, Yi I-248
Loos, Eugène I-212, I-291
Lovell, Jade II-71
Luo, Jing I-321
Luximon, Ameersing I-224
Luximon, Yan I-224, I-658

Magnenat Thalmann, Nadia II-29
Mandache, Luminiţa-Anda I-365
Matsumoto, Hiroshige II-134
Matsumoto, Yoshio II-243
Mazur, Lukasz II-210
Melis, Giulia I-53
Metanova, Lora I-381
Migovich, Miroslava I-201, II-14
Mion, Lorraine C. II-14
Mishra, Nidhi II-29
Miura, Takahiro I-541, II-134

Nakamura, Masahide II-52, II-197
Nakano, Koki II-134
Nichols, Elizabeth I-555
Nihei, Misato II-134

Oh, Chorong I-12
Oinas, Tomi I-614
Oliveira, Ana Filipa I-3
Olmsted-Hawala, Erica I-555
Ortet, Cláudia I-69, I-80
Ozono, Hayato II-52, II-197

Pálsdóttir, Ágústa I-567
Pang, Marco Y. C. I-658
Patel, Shivani II-71
Peine, Alexander I-212

Raycheva, Lilia I-381
Regalado, Francisco I-398
Ribeiro Okimoto, Maria Lucia Leite I-40
Richardson, Daniel R. II-210
Rodriguez-Blazquez, Carmen II-427
Rolandi, Elena II-398
Rosales, Andrea I-212
Rosell, Javiera I-584

Sainio, Päivi I-596
Sakurai, Yuriki II-134
Sala, Emanuela I-53, II-398
Saplacan, Diana II-88
Sarkar, Medha I-201
Sarkar, Nilanjan I-201, II-14
Saukkonen, Petra I-596
Sawchuk, Kim I-346, I-411, II-383
Schak, Monika II-107
Schroder, Matt I-201
Seifert, Alexander I-237
Sementille, Antônio Carlos I-151
Sugawara, Ikuko I-541, II-134
Sullivan, Elizabeth II-3
Sun, Jie I-93
Sun, Xu II-154
Swarbrick, Caroline I-466

Taborda Silva, Célia I-265
Taipale, Sakari I-614
Tang, Liu I-109
Tate, Judith A. II-14
Taylor, Curtis I-201
Timm-Bottos, Janis I-346

Tørresen, Jim II-88
Tsai, Cheng-Min I-127
Tsai, Jen-Yu II-268
Tsai, Wang-Chin I-127, II-268
Tu, Jui-Che I-27
Tulsulkar, Gauri II-29
Tung, Fang-Wu II-255

Vaccaro, Roberta II-398
Vale Costa, Liliana I-69, I-80
Valério Rino, Marcelo I-151
Velinova, Neli I-381
Veloso, Ana Isabel I-69, I-80, I-398
Virtanen, Lotta I-596
Vizcarra, Julio II-122
Vongpanya, Tyler I-201

Wang, Hailiang I-658
Wang, Li-Lan II-277
Wang, Xindi I-432
Wang, Xinwei II-154
Wang, Yueran I-625
Wei, Wei I-93
Wilson, Devon II-14
Witherow, Austin I-201
Wu, Jiang II-154
Wu, Jiang II-290

Xiao, Yuxuan I-248

Yabu, Ken-ichiro I-541, II-134
Yang, Chun I-93
Yang, Hao I-625
Yang, Jieng-Sheng II-268
Yang, Wan-Chen II-413
Ye, Yanghao I-248
Yoshida, Ryoko I-541
Yoshioka, Daisuke II-134
Yoshizaki, Reina II-134
Yu, Rita W. L. I-641
Yuan, Yuan II-290

Zaccaria, Daniele I-53
Zeng, Jingchun II-154
Zhang, Jiaxin I-658
Zhang, Shengtai II-170
Zhang, Xinrui I-625
Zhang, Yahui II-229, II-305, II-320
Zhang, Zhang II-183
Zhang, Zhaorui II-170
Zhao, Shuyu II-229, II-305, II-320
Zhao, Ying I-625
Zhao, Yuxiang Chris I-432
Zhou, Jia I-109
Zorrilla-Muñoz, Vanessa II-427
Zuo, Yanling I-109

Printed in the United States
by Baker & Taylor Publisher Services